marillion/separated o

the complete history 1979

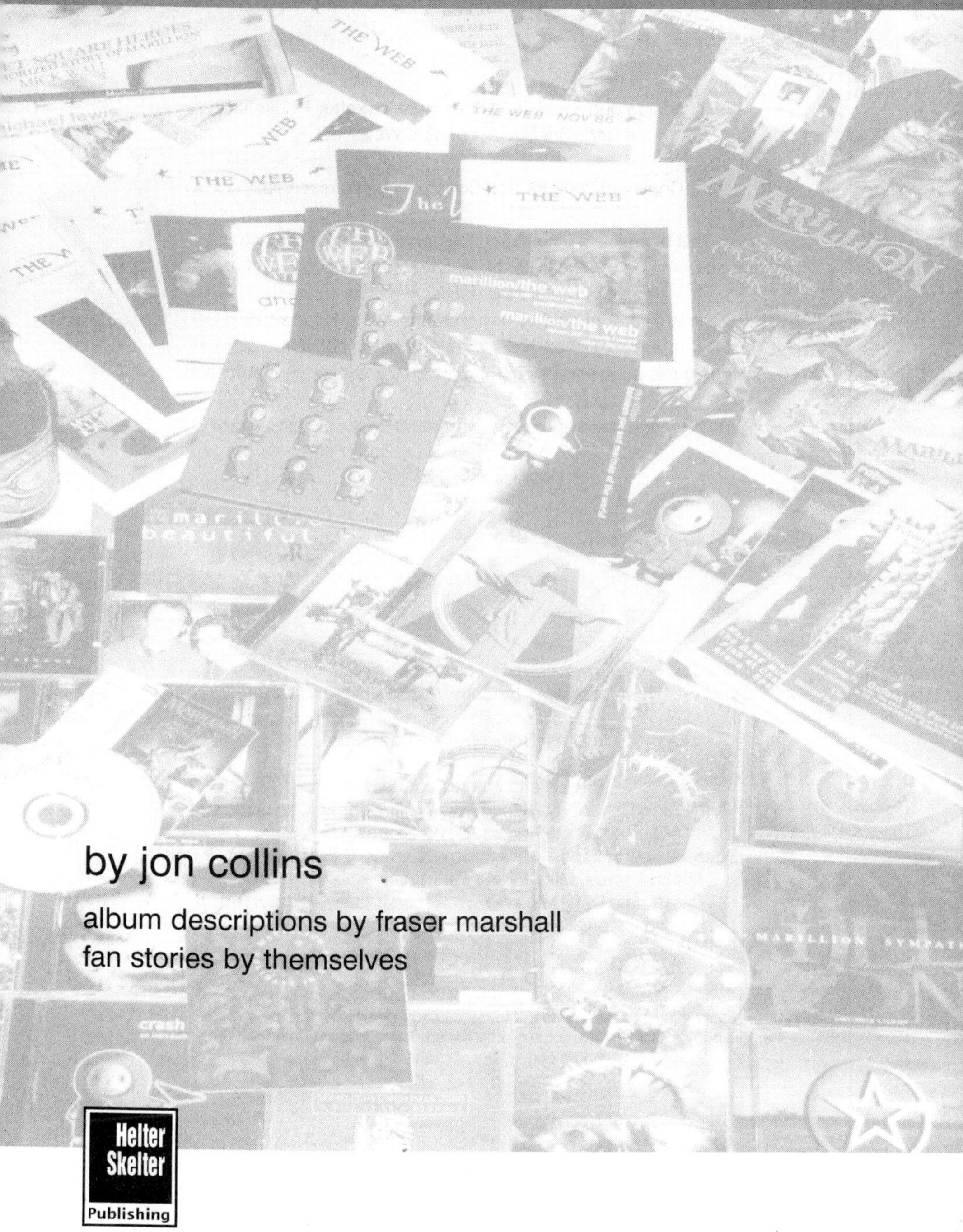

by jon collins

album descriptions by fraser marshall
fan stories by themselves

Helter Skelter Publishing

First edition published in 2003 by **Helter Skelter Publishing**
4 Denmark Street, London, WC2H 8LL.

A CIP record for this book is available from the British Library.

ISBN 1-900924-49-8

Cover designed by Darren Newitt.
Inner workings by Chris Wilson @ CWDGA.

Printed in Great Britain by The Bath Press, Bath.

Photos and images courtesy of:
Andy McIntosh, Andy Rotherham, Angie Cooper, Carl Glover, Dave Rogers, David Stopps, Dean Pedley, Jeff Pelletier, Jon Collins, Karin Breiter, Mark Kelly, Martin Thorpe, Mike Eldon, Paul Lewis, Rob Crossland, Ronald Den Dekker (www.wacon-images.com), Simon Clarke, Steve Rothery, Stuart James, Studio M.

For Liz, Ben and Sophie.

For Paul Spenceley, who will always be
out of this world.

And for Marillion fans everywhere.

contents

preface/foreword/introduction

preface

Shortly after this book was started, the earth was rocked by the terrorist attacks on the US targets of World Trade Center and on the Pentagon. The community of Marillion fans worldwide stopped discussing music and tour dates, and turned their attentions to each other - checking on New Yorkers and government workers in Washington, expressing and sharing the horror, and supporting fellow fans and their families through the tragedy.

I would like to dedicate this book to those who lost their lives, the heroes who survived, their families and friends and all those who were affected by the tragic events.

Jon Collins 17th September 2002

foreword

In 1987 Mick Wall wrote a biography called 'Market Square Heroes', an up-beat account of the rise to international stardom of the rock band Marillion. The final chapter told of how Marillion were set to conquer the USA with the release of their 4th album. A few months later Fish left the band. How could Mick have got things so wrong? Didn't he tell the whole truth? There have been a number of attempts to write the story of Marillion over the years. Depending on who you talk to, that story has many versions. In researching and writing this book Jon Collins has spent many months talking to everyone who has ever had anything to do with the Marillion story, including the five of us. If you want to read the true 'warts and all' account, this is it.

After 21 years of Marillion my memories of events sometimes get a bit vague. This book will prove very useful when I sit my grandchildren down to tell them what it was like.

Thanks Jon.

Mark Kelly November 2002

introduction

"You are the music while the music lasts."
T. S. Eliot

Look on the bright side...

There is no grey with Marillion. For many, here is a band that saw short-lived success in the Eighties before its deserved demise. Castigated by the press, reluctantly accepted by the mainstream, it was with some relief that the ship that was Marillion sank slowly beneath the dark surface.

But it didn't. For hundreds of thousands of people worldwide, Marillion is alive and kicking, continuing to push its artistic boundaries, refusing to compromise or accept the adopted wisdom. Marillion has turned its back on the fashions of the time, the expectations of the mass market, and the adopted practices of the industry. Who else has financed its own album through sales advances negotiated directly with its fans; who else then had the audacity to pick up a major label signing for the album distribution.

To outsiders, Marillion does not (or probably should not) exist. To its fans, Marillion is up there with the best of modern music: Each release is waited for with anticipation, listened to with delight and supported unequivocally. Gigs inspire the spectrum of emotions from quiet reverence to the rapture that can only be achieved by singing along at the top of one's voice. There are few bands that have managed to command such a level of support from their fans. This level cannot be measured in terms of album sales, or revenue generated: clearly Marillion are not the most listened to band in the world, nor do the band's images adorn the most walls. However they do enjoy a unique relationship with their fans, one which many other bands small and large would love to replicate.

This relationship started in the usual, humble way, in pubs and school halls - even then there were those who started to latch onto Marillion as something special. It survived the dual onslaughts of the huge success of 'Kayleigh' in 1985, and the seeming collapse of the band in 1989. Over the past decade the relationship between band and fans has firmed up and grown, catalysed by the Internet. The past five years have seen event following event that bears witness to the band's enduring success, from the US tour fund to the pre-order campaign for *'Anoraknophobia'*, not to mention Simon Mayo's learning experience or the song that inspired the search for (and discovery of) the Bluebird.

But that's telling you the plot.

Acknowledgements

It was all Hugh's fault. When, having discovered the world of work, he came into school that Monday morning, waving a cassette recorded from Tommy Vance's 'Friday Rock Show', little did he know what he was getting me into. "You've got to listen to this," he said and so we did: we knew we had stumbled upon something unique, we felt the magic and took it from there. When I drifted away from the pack in the mid-Eighties, it was co-worker Gordon Gillies who re-introduced me and who provided the bridge between the two eras. Thanks, guys.

Twenty years later the magic is still with me. It's a different magic: at the outset it involved the music and lyrics, now they're blended with the live performances and the community. Having long dragged reluctant friends and colleagues to performances, it was only in late 2000 that I discovered that community, when I was lucky enough to get tickets to an intimate performance at the Bass Museum. I'd always assumed that bands (at least famous ones) were generally found "up there", on the stage and apart from the audience: in the two hours that followed, I had those preconceptions quashed. That was it - I was hooked. I started writing Separated Out in early summer 2001, both to justify my own position as a fan and to sate my desire to understand the full story. Before a gig in Wolverhampton, I happened upon Mark Kelly in a bar and approached him about the idea of a book. "Great idea, go for it," he said, so I did, little realising that numerous fans had no-doubt asked much the same question in the past. Ignorance really is bliss.

Thanking people is a dangerous game, because I am bound to forget someone really important. If it's you, you could try to think yourself honoured as only the really important people get forgotten! My biggest debt is to Liz my wife, who has stuck with this project ever since she first rolled her eyes at my suggestion. I didn't know what I was getting myself into; she did. Thanks also to Sean Body at Helter Skelter, who put his faith in me way before he should have done. Then there are the fans who made this possible: firstly, Max Rael, Dave Rogers, and Angie and Gary Cooper, that I met at the Bass Museum and who welcomed me in from the cold like an old friend. Second, the book might not exist without the urging of two people who had faith in the project from the start. There was Lynn Wells of the Web UK, whose remark "I can't wait to read it!" really got the ball rolling. Then Karin Breiter, a US fan who told me to "shut up and write" when I was faffing around and who has been amazingly helpful in assuring the credibility of the project. Other fans who have gone out on a limb include Fraser Marshall who has been an inspiration, Georgina Wistow who has been a trouper way beyond the call of duty, Darren for his superb cover and Dave Cooper, Simon Clarke and Andy McIntosh for their close scrutiny of the facts. I'd like to give special mention to Andy Rotherham who donated several interviews and in the process closed the door on his own book project, as well as Claus Nygaard, Robin Lauren, Tim Glasswell, John Epstein, Mike Eldon, and Michael Huang, who allowed me to quote from their own web sites and interviews. There are so, so many others who have helped and supported the project throughout the past year – Alan Hewitt, Nicola Yates, Mark and Tracey Donald, Jeff and Michelle Woods, Gary Grady, Monica Diaz, Mark Blamey, Vicki Harding, Martin Thorpe, Jeff Pelletier, all the Marillion Mondays crowd, Ave, Dean, Mark and Badger to name a few (and to get into trouble with the others), John Boye, Andy Saks, Jonathan Mock, Bruno Galli, James Fishwick, John Deveraux, Gina Achord, Chrischa Van de Voorde, Mike Palmer, Anne Bond, Paul Rael, Tony Turrell, Rich Harding, Jeroen Schipper, Brandon O'Connell, Andy Westmoreland, Steve and Tony Wood, Dave Woodward, Linda Southern, Krys and Geoff Boswell, Ade Holmes, Mark Nelson, Judith Mitchell, Andreas Dahl, Rob Crossland, Dan Sherman, Chris Brockwell, Heidi Huff, Mike Palmer, JJ, Bubba, Nathan Vines, Kim Waring, Jolijne Viergever, Stuart Mitchell, Ronald Den Dekker, Andy McIntosh and He Who Should Not Be Named. All the subscribers to the Opium Den and Freaks mailing lists, you know who you are. Oh boy am I in trouble now, who did I miss? There are over two hundred names quoted in the text: I thank you all.

As for the band's collaborators, the list reads like a roll call of Marillion's history. Special mention should be given to Steven Wilson of Porcupine Tree, who (unbeknown to himself) was the first person to respond to my call for information, thus keeping the fires alight. Paul Lewis has been superlatively helpful, as well as John Arnison, Mike Hunter, Carl Glover, Mark Wilkinson, Dave Stopps. Peter Gee, Mark Daghorn and Marc Mitchell, both Bill Smiths!, Dave Meegan, Aziz Ibrahim, Nick Davies, John Mitchell, Danny Flynn, all at Studio M, Chris Kimsey and Chris Neil, Paul and Jayce, Peter Gee, Phil Beaumont, Chris "Privet" Hedge, Jingles, Rex Hossi, Rich Wilson, Thomas Stiehler, Tim Bricusse, John Price, John Jones, Avril Mackintosh, Mike Portnoy, Dave Gregory, John Helmer, Mark

Wilkinson, Simon Hanhart, Steve Davis, Jo Mirowski, Guy Hewison and Sylvain Gouvenaire.

A final thank you goes to the band that inspired this book. It wasn't just the music, though clearly that helped: what twigged it was the way that Marillion manage to be so good at what they do, at the same time as so utterly approachable and grounded. When I suggested the project, Mark was immediately positive, and he has consistently gone out of his way to ensure its success. Pete, Ian, Steve and Steve gave up many hours of their time to answer many of the same old questions, sometimes more than once as I lost track of what I had asked. I admit to having wondered what I would find if I ever met the band close up. I have discovered that they are as honest, friendly and above all human as a world class act could possibly be. A big thank you goes also to past members of the band and its precursors, not least Fish, who also went out on a limb to help ensure the completeness of this narrative. Jonathan, Mick, Diz, Brian, Martin, and Andy, thanks for your time and trouble. Huge and heartfelt thanks also to Colin, Lucy and Erik at the Racket Club, and a warm welcome to Rod. After Pontins, Stewart Every moved on and is now working for a corporate events company. Good luck, Stewart!

When all that is said, there does remain the music. Pete Trewavas told me, "We like to write songs that make people cry." Well you do, and I have; I've also felt the laughter and joy, the anger and the heart-rending loss, the spectrum of emotions that are woven like silk throughout the past twelve albums and beyond. As one fan wrote, Marillion has provided "a soundtrack to my life" and I can only agree with that.

Author's Note

Just for the record, I have tried to use the past tense for quotes I have referenced from elsewhere, and the present tense for my own interviews. I originally had each quote together with its source, but it made for a bit of a dull read! Each source is referenced at least once, or at least it should be!

I should comment on names. To work for Marillion, it appears you have to have a name that is impossible to spell or impossible to pronounce (Mark Kelly is the exception that proves the rule). I have tried to be as accurate with names as possible, for example I am pretty sure it is Jelleyman rather than Jelliman, Irving rather than Irvine, Marter rather than Martyr. I have quite deliberately said H rather than h for Steve Hogarth, simply because it stands out better in the text.

When researching the book, I endeavoured to contact as many people involved in Marillion's history as I could. Some have not been possible: for example, Doug Irving has remained true to his word of leaving the band behind him, to the extent that when Steve Rothery bumped into him in a car park in Aylesbury a few years ago, Doug wasn't interested in saying hello. There are others that I couldn't find, or didn't manage to reach in time. Sorry guys!

The preparation of this book has leaned heavily on resources already on the Web - go to www.separatedout.com for links.

May all your roses open slowly.

Jon Collins 17 September 2002

chapter one reciting the script/1979-1984

"There's a basic rule which runs through all kinds of music, kind of an unwritten rule. I don't know what it is. But I've got it."

Ron Wood

Where did it all start? Marillion's history can be traced back to 1977, the year of punk. Anarchy was in the UK. As punk moved from subversive to mainstream, the disenfranchised adolescent masses (and the press) were given something to sneer about, while other musical styles were gradually pushed out of the limelight. Driven underground they gave birth to the New Wave of British Heavy Metal, a rebellion against the rebels, a return to rock and roll, a musical backlash against the perceived melodic mediocrity of punk.

That wasn't entirely true, of course. 1977 was also the year of Disco, of Abba, David Soul and Leo Sayer, Stevie Wonder and the Jacksons. Star Wars and Saturday Night Fever were released, each sparking their own revolutions. Elsewhere, the big band sound of progressive rock was refusing to roll over and play dead, with the likes of Pink Floyd, Genesis, Rush and Yes continuing to draw strong support wherever they went. Meanwhile, oblivious to the press frenzy or the musical obsessions of the few, the masses continued to get up, brush their teeth and go to work. Against this mundane background some were choosing to play the kind of music they wanted to hear. To these people, the traditional heroes had either vanished or had sold out to the mainstream, so they formed their own bands to uphold the traditions. One such band was Electric Gypsy.

pre-history

The 1977 line-up of Electric Gypsy included Alan King on vocals, guitarist Andy Glass, Doug Irving (who founded the band) on bass and a drummer whose name has long since been forgotten. Sparking a tradition that would be upheld for a good five years, the drummer did not last long. Fortuitously, the drummer's fiancée heard someone practicing in a shed next door to her parents' house on Brae Road, in the village of Brill in Buckinghamshire. That "someone" was Mick Pointer.

An Unexpected Party

The timing was perfect for Mick, then in a band called Stockade, formed some eighteen months before with an old classmate, Martin Butler. With Stockade going nowhere, Mick agreed to an audition with the Gypsies. He got the gig, left Stockade and his mate Martin on amicable terms and joined Alan, Andy and Doug. "We played rock, along the lines of Hawkwind," says Andy Glass.

Mick's optimism was short-lived. "They spent less time doing music, and a lot more time talking crap and smoking dope all day!" says Mick. The Gypsies did play a few times, "Our big gig was at Stone Free Festival near Aylesbury," says Andy. "Magic!" By early 1978, Mick and Doug decided to leave the Gypsies and form an instrumental ensemble.[1] From Mick's home base at Station Road, Long Marston, near Aylesbury, they recruited local lads Neil Cockle[2] on keyboards and Martin Jenner on guitar. "The place was a complete mess. The only food on offer was the dead mice brought in from the fields by the cats," Mick recalls. It was here that the four-piece sought inspiration for a name. "We went through hundreds of names, I saw the Silmarillion book on the shelf and said, 'Hey, how about that?' The name stuck."

The fledgling band had high aspirations for its musical style. Explains Martin Jenner, "The music was inspired by a blend of Camel and Genesis: Neil had a string synthesizer (popular in early Camel music) and played this to good effect on

Silmarillion

A book by J. R. R. Tolkien, 'The Silmarillion' is the story of the creation of Middle Earth, which would be the setting for his subsequent works such as 'The Hobbit' and 'The Lord of The Rings'. It describes how three magic jewels, known as the Silmarils, were recaptured from the Dark Lord by the elves.

some of the slower segments and also to give that nice filling sound behind some of the stronger riffs. The Genesis influence came with things like song construction and most notably off beat timings." The band then added its own stylistic preferences - Martin describes himself as: "A die-hard rock guitarist who likes to play Gary Moore-style solos," while Mick sought to emulate his drumming hero, Neil Peart of Rush. Eager to take their message to the world, the Sils used a studio in Amersham to write and rehearse an hour-long, largely instrumental set with Doug adding the occasional vocal.

Finally, on April 22 1978, at the Hanborough Tavern in Southall, London, the band was ready to play. The gig was in support of punk band Robert and The Remoulds: Neil, Martin and the Remoulds' drummer all worked for the same company[3] at the time. "We had no vocalist so we played instrumentals only, all band compositions," recalls Martin Jenner. "We had no strong vocalist in the band and had not yet auditioned a lead vocalist." Despite a successful gig it was not the best of starts - not only was it the last that the four played together, but the next day signalled the start of the 1978 Southall riots, made notorious with the death of protester Blair Peach, following a baton charge by the police.

Neil and Martin were both to leave not long after the Hanborough gig, with Martin the first to go. "We started auditioning soon after the gig and tried some (I thought) very good vocalists," says Martin, "Doug and Mick were not happy with them, seemingly knowing exactly what they wanted. It was this slow forward motion to accept a vocalist and get out playing regularly, that helped me decide to leave the band." Following his departure, Mick and Doug placed an ad in Melody Maker for a guitarist. Despite numerous auditions with a good twenty hopefuls, nobody really fitted the bill until a young player arrived one Sunday morning in August. "I had called but they'd forgotten," explains Steve Rothery. "I'd got up at six in the morning to drive down in my Renault 5, and when I got there they were still in bed!" After the 250-mile journey from Whitby, Steve was raring to go, but as sure as Sunday morning follows a heavy Saturday night, he didn't receive the warmest of welcomes when he turned up with a mate at Station Road. Reluctantly, Doug and Mick agreed to listen to Steve's demo tape, but that didn't help matters. "It wasn't especially good," says Steve, "I'd made it when I was playing with a chap called Edwin Hart; he was a huge Beatles fan. They weren't too impressed!"

Despite the sleep deprivation and the dubious start, Mick and Doug felt enough sympathy to let Steve come in and have a jam. "He set up his gear in the living room while we all sat there, bleary-eyed," recalls Mick. It worked: "He was very impressive. We sat there and watched, he played to us and we gave him the job there and then." Steve drove back up North to consider his options, before long deciding to accept the invitation a couple of days later, on 19 August 1979. "It was obvious I was in a similar area of music to them," comments Steve, "Pink Floyd, Genesis, Camel - but not Rush! I got the gig and just moved down. I kind of gave everything up for a bass player and a drummer." Steve must have been convinced, considering the accommodation that was on offer. "The cottage didn't have any hot water and had mould growing on the walls," Steve recollects. "I had to share a sofa with two cats!"

Steve's arrival coincided with the departure of Neil Cockle, for whom the final straw had been the rest of the band helping itself to equipment out of his car. "We turned up for a rehearsal (the second time I'd been down from Whitby) to find Neil's car, full of Doug's keyboards unlocked and with nobody around," recalls Steve. "After a blazing row between Neil, Doug and Mick we were a three piece!"[4]

Help was at hand: a friend of Doug's, Brian Jelleyman, had expressed an interest in taking part. Brian was no mean pianist, as pointed out by schoolmate and future band member, Pete Trewavas. "He had classical lessons and I think he was grade 8, he was good!" A few weeks later, following another audition in the front room of the cottage, the newly formed line-up went about developing and rehearsing a set. "The style we had already begun had started to take shape," notes Mick. Concerned about copyright, and besides, it was "too Tolkien," according to Steve, they also decided to drop the 'Sil' from the band's name. "Doug had Silmarillion painted on his guitar case - all he had to do was paint out the Sil," explains Steve.

Following a few rehearsals at an old music shop in Hemel Hempstead and in The Queen's Head pub a few doors down (also "the main venue for band meetings," according to Brian), in February 1980 the band tramped off to The Enid's studio in Hertford. "We were big fans, we knew they had a studio and did their own recording," says Mick. They recorded a two-track demo tape for their own use. Remarks Steve, "It was quite exciting, my first experience of recording!" The session included 'Lady Fantasy' and 'Alice', the latter would go on to become part of 'Forgotten Sons'. Also present was Chris "Privet" Hedge, a resident of Long Marston who was invited to the rehearsals during a party at Station Road.

Heartened by the results of the studio session the freshmen pushed forward, playing their first gig as an ensemble at the Berkhamstead Civic Centre on 1 March 1980. It was not the most comfortable of settings, remembers Brian, "I know it was cold, as the fog from the dry-ice machine didn't stay on the ground where it was supposed to be!" The material included 'Close', 'The Tower' and a couple of long-forgotten tracks, 'Herne The Hunter' and 'The Haunting of Gill House'. The latter was accompanied by explosions provided by Privet. "One of the flashes didn't go off, so he scraped the contents into another one," recalls Steve. "When he let that one off there was a huge sheet of flame up my back that nearly blew me off the stage! That was quite a first gig!" Privet, who was "up in this little booth upstairs doing the lights," remained oblivious to the goings on below. "I'm not sure if I blew Steve Rothery up there, but I'm inclined to think not," he says, dubiously.

job steady

Besides working at Shaw's, Rothers worked his way through a number of jobs including driving a bakers van for a day ("I found I had to get up at 5 every morning!"), a caravan factory ("A lady had a finger sliced off, I thought this is no place for a guitarist!") and giving some guitar lessons. One job he didn't get was at the National Film Archive in Aston Clinton. "Fortunately I didn't get it," it could have proved to be something I'd find hard to give up!"

Of the performance itself, perceptions vary. Mick remembers little other than the reaction. "Some guy came up and said, 'you guys are really excellent, you should be playing in London!' I thought, if he says that on the first gig... well!" Rothers' rosy memories include no fewer than six encores. "Mind you," he says, "That could have been because they were all stoned out of their heads!" whereas early fan, Mike Eldon, remembers the audience (which included an 11-year-old Steven Wilson, later of Porcupine Tree) as being less than receptive. Mind you, that could have been because the audience were all stoned out of their heads... At least a major milestone was out of the way. After Berkhamstead, 14 dates were played between March and November 1980, including a Battle Of The Bands at the Horn Of Plenty in St Albans, and the Students Union in High Wycombe where Doug's girlfriend was President. Very early on, the band was keen to build a rapport with the people attending the gigs. Already there were t-shirts, and before the performance the band handed out flyers saying, "We hope that you enjoy the gig and will come and see us again." A phone number was included, so that budding fans could call to find out where the band were was playing next. Not the actions of a typical pub band. "From very early on, we made the point of going out to the front, signing autographs and so on," says Mick. "You've got to have that contact."

Most band members had day jobs - Brian worked at the local benefits office, Doug was a photocopier engineer and Mick was a joiner and kitchen fitter. Steve worked at

he nose, you know

It's true that in the early days Marillion would play anywhere - including a mental home in St Albans and a street trader's fair in Watford supporting, amongst others, a magician with a flair for sticking six-inch nails up his nostrils.

Shaw's Pet Products, situated ten doors down on Weston Road. "I was working in the warehouse and driving a van," he says. Things were all going so well that by the autumn, they looked like they could carry on that way forever. However, by November the time seemed right to capture the compositions that were working so well live. A session was booked at Leyland Farm recording studio, in Gawcott near Buckingham. Leyland Farm was owned by Wild Willy Barrett, a frequent partner of John Otway (a regular at Friars, of which, more later). The studio was not ideal, recalls Brian, "It was the lower part of a converted stable, with the mixing desk in the room above." This had the unfortunate knock-on of not being able to see the person you were recording. Recalls Diz, who would later experience the joys of Leyland Farm during his own tenure in the band, "There was no direct connection with whoever was doing the mixing. You couldn't see them. I think we got free studio time there because Mick worked a deal where they used his microphones in exchange."

Nonetheless, it was a serviceable studio and the first session there was deemed a success. It was when the band were planning to record 'Close' there, that with unfortunate timing Doug Irving announced his resignation from the band. "He had always said that if the band hadn't made it by the time he was 25 he would leave," explains Mick. So he did, for the relative simplicity of his nine-to-five day job as a photocopier engineer, taking the only Silmarillion demo tape with him and leaving Mick, Brian and Steve to pick up the pieces. "At that point, we were even more determined to continue," says Mick. The band fell back to the local pub and regrouped; the Leyland Studio recording session took place soon after, during which the instrumental 'Close' was laid down to tape with Steve playing the bass line.

On 6 December 1980, another advert was placed, this time in the weekly paper Musicians Only.[5] It read, "Competent bassist/vocalist required for established Progressive Rock group with own material in Aylesbury." To a couple of unemployed, would-be musicians living in Scotland, it couldn't have been better timed.

Civic Duties by Steven Wilson

Berkhamstead Civic Centre is local to where I was brought up in Hemel Hempstead. I went along with my friend and his big brother to see a local punk band, the Chiltern Volcanoes. We heard that they were supporting another local band called "Marilyn" (sic). When we got there Marillion were handing out some flyers[6] and among other things mentioned some Marillion T-shirts for sale and the fact that Geddy Lee from Rush had one. When Marillion came on most of the punks departed, which left about 25 people. Consequently my friends and me had a pretty good view of the show. I don't know what we were expecting but it certainly wasn't what we got.

Being a 'normal', rebellious 11 year old, I was listening to Heavy Metal like Iron Maiden at the time, but also starting to discover more sophisticated rock music, so I was pretty amazed to be seeing something that wasn't in the standard punk/metal anyone-can-play-guitar fare in a local venue. The line up was Steve Rothery, Mick Pointer, Doug Irving and Brian Jelleyman. I recall that in one song Mick Pointer came to the front of the stage and played some flute. As for repertoire, I'm pretty sure, they played 'The Tower' but of course it was all unfamiliar to me.

Although it made a pretty big impression on me, I don't think I really expected to hear the name again, the music was just too out of place in Britain circa-1980. Two years later I was amazed to hear the first Tommy Vance Radio 1 session and started to follow the band from that point on.

Vocalist/Bassist Required

By Christmas 1980, Mick and Steve had moved out of Long Marston. Mick moved to Waddesdon[7] and Steve was sharing a cottage in Aston Clinton with Privet on Weston Road. It was all very quaint. Diz later described it as "a tiny little Rothschild cottage," with three rooms downstairs and two above. Despite having no heating, it was still "a big improvement," according to Steve. Equally, it was no palace - Priv called it "the bear pit" and Brian simply referred to it as, "a filthy disgusting dive." Oh, how idyllic country life can be! Also in residence was Guy Hewison, sharing a bedroom with Priv as Steve had negotiated a room of his own (he was the original tenant). Guy had met the band through his sister Claire, who used to drink at the Queen's Head in Long Marston, one of Steve's favoured haunts. "I got involved 'cos I was over 21, so I was the only one who could drive a transit!" remarks Guy, referring to the unreliable, green Commer van, Margaret. Guy also mucked in as crew and booking agent and, remembers Steve Rothery, "He fancied himself as our manager." As Guy rented the house by this time, nobody was about to complain.

central perk

One thing Fish and Diz unloaded was a paraffin heater, which despite the fact that "it stunk the place out," provided a welcome respite from the cold. Mark Kelly, who would later join the residents at Number 64, recalls how "We used to put it in the middle of the room and called it central heating!!!"

A few hundred miles north, things were close to very hard indeed for two young fellows called Derek William Dick and William Roberts Minnitt, known to their friends as Fish and Diz (short for Dizzy, and as in, "Come here diz minitt!"). Money and time were running out for the would-be musicians: explains Fish, "I'd had a bit of savings from my time in the Forestry Commission and we were getting a little bit of money from my parents but it was very tough. We were nicking turnips out of fields and stuff!" It was looking dangerously like they'd have to find alternative gainful employment, when the pair saw the small-ad in Musicians Only. The requirement was for one fellow, not two, so a bit of fancy talking was required. Remembers Mick, "Diz phoned me and said, 'I'm a bass player, but I don't sing. I know a guy who does. How about I send you something with his voice on?' The tape must have gone down well, because Fish and Diz were sent the Leyland Farm demo of 'Close' in the return post, not to mention an invitation to audition.

The journey that took place on 1 January 1981 was a little more fraught than planned, as (according to Diz) the pair got rather lost along the way. Eventually they arrived at Aston Clinton, then Weston Road. "We turned up outside and they all came out, thinking that we'd come for an audition," remembers Diz. "We said, bugger the audition, we're here and that's that!" The residents were not so sure. Mick remembers thinking, "a big, loud, tall, arrogant Scotsman, just what we needed." The band allowed the van to be unloaded before everyone headed for the Rothschilds Arms, a pub a few doors down, to exchange

some milk with that?

"One morning after we had been up all night taking various things and drinking black tea we heard the milkman. Imagine being confronted by five guys totally off their faces at that time in the morning. Then we realised how bizarre it must look so we cracked up and ran back inside!"

Diz Minnitt

rounds and pleasantries and leave the harder decisions for the days that followed. The next few days were spent back at Leyland Farm, where Fish performed a couple of songs by Genesis ('I Know What I Like') and Yes by way of audition. Showing off his ability to mimic both Jon Anderson and Peter Gabriel, he quickly impressed the rest of the band. Despite some reservations about Diz's bass playing, the two were recruited on the spot. "I was self-taught and I'd only been playing for a couple of years, it was because Fish said we came as a package that was why I was there," says Diz.

On the same day, Fish took the opportunity to record his lyrics over the top of the 'Close' demo tape. Everyone was delighted by the close fit between Fish's voice and the feel of the music. "We could see the potential in Fish; he had a really interesting voice," recalls Steve. The final seal on the contract was made between Fish and Priv, who went out on the razz that evening. "We got blatted and fell into a ditch," laughs Priv. "We walked back with no trousers on. It was all a bit weird and crazy." All in all, it was a near-perfect start.

The weeks that followed saw the newly completed line-up spending the days reviewing, re-vamping and refreshing the old material, either at Leyland Farm or Anthony Hall. The first rehearsal with Fish and Diz at Anthony Hall, gave the incumbents their first experience of Fish's wrath - triggered by problems with the PA. "We hadn't used it for ages, so it took a while to get it working," says Priv, "And Fish started throwing his toys out of the pram. A roaring hangover from the night before didn't help!" The addition of a proper vocalist enabled new possibilities, real songs, not just meandering instrumentals, could be put together. Commented Mick Pointer at the time, in an interview with Hugh Fielder of Sounds, "Before they joined, we were a lot more laid back although the style was similar... it was more pretentious too. We would drag out an idea for about five minutes when it was really only worth about 30 seconds. When Fish and the others joined, it added that bit of punch."

Out of this fervour came a much-required creative injection, which later yielded tracks such as 'Garden Party', 'He Knows, You Know' and 'Charting The Single'. But Fish's ambitions went way beyond the music, not to mention beyond the previous aspirations of the band. "Up to Fish's arrival we were drifting, but we immediately became a lot more professional," explains Steve, "Fish was so ambitious, ruthlessly so - all his qualities that made him difficult to work with also gave him his drive." Guy concurs: "Without Fish's pushiness, the band wouldn't have had the measure of success it had. It probably wouldn't have amounted to anything." After all, most of the band had started with day jobs - adds Fish, "Apart from Steve, we were the only ones who had given up a lot to come down. Steve really came through, but in the rest of the band there was still this weekend gig atmosphere." With Fish and Guy manning the phones, it was only a matter of time before the new line-up was ready to go out and play.

skeeeen-'eads!

Marillion's triumphant return to the Students Union, High Wycombe was slightly marred by a crowd of skinheads who decided to trash the place. The implacable Fish was not having any of it - remembers Privet, "Fish went after them with a mic stand. He was rock-hard and scared the crap out of them. I'm surprised they didn't come back though - he looked ridiculous in a cape!"

After "three months of rehearsals," according to Guy, the first gig was on 14 March 1981, in the back room of the Red Lion, Bicester.[8] "It was a bit of a squaddies' pub," remembers Mick, "I remember walking round these streets wearing these bloody ridiculous costumes trying to drum up support!" It didn't work. According to most sources, and despite Guy's additional fly-posting efforts around the town, about fifteen people turned up. Amongst the audience were members of a local band called Toad The Wet

party on

The popping of corks at the beginning of Marillion's first demo of 'Garden Party' was in celebration of Stef's birthday, which coincided with the recording sessions. "We had all this Asti Spumanti!" smiles Diz. "It's no wonder the recordings went so smoothly."

Sprocket,[9] named after a Monty Python sketch. Remembers Diz, "They came over to give us fatherly advice. Bastards!"

Despite the poor turn-out, Marillion deemed the evening to be a success. The five were savvy enough to realise that success would not come easily with the style of music they'd chosen to play: a definite, deliberate and distinctly unfashionable throwback to the progressive rock styles of ten years previous. Instead, recalls early fan Mike Eldon, came the active decision "to swamp every possible venue within a fifty-mile radius with demands to book them." Bicester was one of the last appearances that Guy would book, as Fish took over and started to manage the gig bookings.

Several dates were played at The Britannia Pub, Aylesbury, including one attended by future bandmate Pete Trewavas. The set list included 'Madcap's Embrace'[10] which was 'graced' by a flute solo from Mick. "I bet everybody likes to forget that," says Pete. "Mick had his flute moment 'cos I think at that stage Fish hadn't been in particularly long, and it was still very much Mick's band." Not that Fish wasn't making an impression. Continues Pete, "The ceiling was very low so he had to stoop. He had blood capsules and all that kind of stuff and they put on a good show considering it was a pub. I could see they needed a bit of work on them, but I thought they had something. Fish certainly had a presence, you couldn't stop watching." The band also became a regular draw at The Wheatsheaf in Dunstable, a pub which happened to be fan Mike Eldon's local. "It was a typical 2-room pub," recalls Mike. "By the time they got their equipment in I was standing about two feet from Fish! That was quite an experience!" Not that Mike was too daunted. "They were absolutely excellent," continues Mike, "It was music I was into from people of my own age!"

Soon the pattern of phone calls, bookings and live gigs attracted the attention of David Stopps, manager of Aylesbury's Friars Club. "Fish was a larger than life character," recalls David. "His presence was felt in the town as soon as he moved down!" On 29 May 1981 David had booked Marillion to play the Aston Hall, a small hall just off the bar of Aylesbury's Civic Centre, in support of John Cooper Clarke during Aylesbury's annual arts week. Incidentally, John Cooper Clarke's manager was the well-connected, London-based John Arnison.

About six months after Fish joined, Brian found him a job at Aylesbury's faceless, depressing benefits office. "He was very popular with everyone, but not really a civil servant!" laughs Brian. Being of a generous disposition, he also invited Fish to share the flat at Winchester House in Aylesbury, with himself and his girlfriend Fran who paid the rent. Fran was a nurse at Stoke Mandeville Hospital, and it wasn't long before the rest of the lads were patronising the nurses' accommodation. "We used to sneak there for parties," says Priv. It was back to Fran and Brian's flat that Fish first brought a girl called Kay Atkinson, who was also a nurse. Kay only stayed a few months before moving to Earls Court in London, the scene for a number of spats that would lead to her immortalisation in a song.

It was at the benefits office that Fish, coming down from an acid trip, penned the lyrics to 'He Knows, You Know'. Recounts Diz, writing a song wasn't the only thing that the trip inspired. "Some bloke came to sign on while Fish was completely off his face, and instead of getting him to do this, he made him do four circles and six signatures on this piece of

out of hell

"Some Hells' Angels were there making a lot of noise at one gig, so Fish gave them some verbal. While the band were playing one of them rode his motorbike through the front door. It started getting a bit dodgy. Then the next thing I saw was Fish having a drink with them. They became fans after that."

Priv

paper. The guy went home thinking that he had signed for his benefit. At one point Fish wouldn't come out of the toilet because he was convinced there was an enormous spider, about six-foot across, sitting on the ceiling. Straight after this he wrote the song!"

By July, Marillion had counted its pennies and saved enough money to hire a studio, ostensibly to record a demo tape to send to gig promoters, club managers and record labels. Fish had been introduced (by David Stopps) to Les Payne, an established local performer who was also training as an engineer at Roxon Studio in Watlington, near Oxford. Fish proposed that Les produced the session, so one Saturday morning he took the band to Roxon. "It was a grey industrial kind of building with no sign of it vaguely looking anything like a studio on the outside," remembers Diz. "It reminded me of my father's piggery!"

Once inside it was straight down to business. Unforeseen circumstances (the planned engineer had been up all night and was falling asleep at the desk) led to Les engineering the session, which included 'Garden Party', 'He Knows, You Know' and

1981: IN THE proverbial Market Square, Aylesbury. Standing: Brian Jelliman (keyboards, left) and Fish (who?). Sitting (from left): Mick Pointer (drums), Steve Rothery (guitar) and Diz Minnit (bass). Pop stars in the making? Hahaha . . .

'Charting The Single'. Everything went smoothly (despite this being Les's first attempt), and the final mixes were laid to tape on the Monday night. "It was surprising to hear the finished result," comments Rothers. "It sounded pretty good!"

Unfortunately the tape did not cut any ice with the record companies, despite being sent to every major label in London. It was almost inevitable (and strangely prophetic, given events twenty years later) that the band turned to developing its already sizeable live following instead. "We were defiant, we knew we'd get somewhere with it," says Mick. "When you're young, you can't believe you could possibly fail!" Fish concurs: "We thought, fuck it, it's going to happen! It was absolute, total youthful arrogance!" As he noted in a 1983 interview with Jay Williams of Sounds, "Every record company was saying, 'We don't want a band like you, we want singles' and the only way we could sit opposite them and not be dictated to, was to build up a big live following."

So they did. Promotion of the band continued relentlessly. Clubs were sent copies of the demo tape, along with a clutch of posters bearing a design by Diz. "I wanted to use an eye as part of the Marillion logo for a long time," Fish wrote later. "We played around with Egyptian designs, Diz drew the eye crying into the palm of the hand and feeding the

David Stopps and The Friar's Club

David Stopps first opened the doors of Friars Club in June 1969, in Aylesbury's New Friarage Hall. Says David, "I'd tried managing bands, and I changed to being a promoter as I thought it was easier to buy bands than sell them!" Within a year the venue had hosted bands as diverse as Free, King Crimson, Mott the Hoople and Blodwyn Pig, not to mention Genesis who were paid the princely sum of ten pounds for their first gig at Friars. Throughout the seventies and early eighties, Friars Club ranked alongside such venues as The Moles Club in Bath and Nottingham Boat Club as one of the places to play outside London. By the eighties, Friars had taken up residence at the Aylesbury Civic Centre. The big bands were still attracted - U2 (who were still small fry back then!), The Cure, Squeeze and the Police among them - but David was keen to introduce good local bands to his stage, not least Marillion. "I wanted to create a band out of Aylesbury that would take on the world!" he remarks.

Following his stint with Marillion, David had decided that managing acts was not the thing for him when another local artist - Howard Jones from High Wycombe - approached him to be his manager. "Howard persevered with me," recalls David. He bit the bullet and took Howard under his wing in September 1982. This time things happened a little more smoothly - the signing, the hit single (which slowly but surely overtook 'Garden Party' in the charts - "I remember it distinctly!" smiles David), the next hit single, the string of hit albums, breaking America and a long-lasting professional relationship that lasts to this day. Looking back, David says he would have steered Marillion's career in a very different way had he remained their manager. "I would have gone for the US market from the outset rather than focus on Europe," he remarks.

Unfortunately Friars, like all good things, had to come to an end. A number of reasons including the increasing pressure of managing Howard Jones' rapidly developing career and the venue's limited capacity, led to the demise of the club. "We had 87,000 members at the end," David grins. "Only the AA and the RAC were bigger!"

The final Friars gig took place on 22 December 1984. It was a Marillion gig.

root of the stem from which the eye grew, indicating a sort of self-sufficiency or symbiotic relationship." The design, known as the Saliva Tear, was the mainstay of the band's image right up to its signing with EMI.

Frying Tonight

As summer came, the band started to attend to its fan base with increasing vigour. The band was playing at least weekly, and when they weren't out gigging the various members were calling venues, developing new songs and trying to hold down jobs. When Fish packed in his job at the benefits office, he trudged the streets with Diz, putting up posters and looking for new places to play. Rehearsals continued at Leyland Farm and Anthony Hall[11] before resorting to the tin-roofed Scout Hut in Aston Clinton. Remembers Diz, "The acoustics were appalling, but it was very cheap. I think we did a skeletal version of 'Three Boats Down From The Candy'."

New tracks were added to the set such as the 19-minute 'Grendel', with lyrics based on an adaptation of 'Beowulf' by John Gardner which examined the legend from the perspective of the monster. With its origins in 'The Tower', the song had evolved into a form structurally similar to Genesis' 'Supper's Ready', a worry to some. "We were concerned," Fish agreed, "But it all flowed and the fans loved it!" Another crowd-swayer was the irreverent 'Margaret', which had started life before Fish joined the band. Brian happened to play 'Scotland The Brave' in the studio, and Steve and Mick started jamming around it. It was originally tagged 'Scotch Porridge', then 'Margaret Gets Her Oats'. On stage, Fish continued to develop his visuals, starting with painting his face in ever-more dramatic styles. On the band's third ever gig, he sported his first 'full facial' - a Union Jack mask. "I thought the Union Jack looked really good!" comments Steve. "Some of the others looked a bit naff, though!"

Marillion had a number of objectives before it could start to tackle finding a label or getting airplay. One was to headline at the Friars Club, considered by all as the most important venue in the region. Fortunately, having seen them in action during Aylesbury Arts Week in May, David Stopps was quick to book them again, offering the band their first "proper" gig at Friars in support of US band Spirit. The date was set as 1 August, with the stage once again being the Aston Hall. The now-familiar Les Payne, suggested they should all wear costumes of some sort, so off Fish went to the Hammer House Of Horror TV studios at Hampden Woods. "The studios were closing down and Fish went up there and bought loads of stuff in the sale. The outcome was that the stage was crammed with the stuff," remembers Les. Indeed it was - a full graveyard setting, complete with gravestones and dry ice. The performance started with the tolling of a bell, the band surprising even its hardcore fans by walking up to the stage from the back, through the audience.

Everything went as smoothly as a 'Spinal Tap' outtake. According to Steve, "We went on in these long monk-style gowns without trousers on. We had some floor level lighting shining up. During the gig I turned around to see Diz. As I did, the lights came on and the material became transparent. So, there he was stood in his undies. I thought, well if I can see him... I couldn't help but feel a bit exposed after that!" The stalwart players played on, undaunted, and all in all it was a great show. Fish reeled out some of his favourite party tricks, such as the ketchup-filled cucumber for 'Garden Party' and the blood capsules for 'Forgotten Sons' (during which he wielded the microphone stand as a rifle). By the end, recounts Diz, "We had about four hundred people crammed into this tiny hall. You couldn't physically move!"

Everyone that attended Marillion's Friars debut recognised they had witnessed something special. "It was a bloody amazing gig," remarks Priv. "One of those things where you didn't realise how important it was until afterwards. More people came to see us than to see the gig in the main hall!" It doesn't need a rocket scientist to work out why Marillion was invited back. Before long the band had moved up the rankings, playing support to a number of acts (including virtuoso blues guitarist Rory Gallagher) before becoming a regular headliner at the venue. Not only did this lead to even bigger gigs elsewhere, but the media was starting to pay attention to the band's steady progress. There was the occasional disaster: such as the 101 Club in Clapham, on 12 November 1981, where four people turned up and the band ended up having to pay for the PA, and eight days later at the reggae-based, Caribbean Club, also in Oxford. Explains Mick, "We were the only white faces there. They asked us to stop. It was the kindest thing to do." But in general, the now-well-trodden live circuit and the mood of the travellers, was heading upwards.

Genesis was undoubtedly an influence on the band, or at least their approach to music. Laughs Steve, "We were showing our influences maybe a little too clearly - it was clumsily done, but it was sincere, it wasn't done to be pompous! Something set us apart though; I don't know what it was. Somehow we had more of an edge." Adds Mark, "I can see why people said it - look at Grendel and the face paint - but the music was more aggressive."

Comments David Stopps, whose club had been an integral part of Genesis's own story, "Fish felt there was room for another band of that ilk. With the advent of punk in the late seventies, bands like Genesis had become uncool at street level, but there was a huge audience just waiting to come out of the shadows." Despite a clear lean to the progressive, Marillion were never exclusive about either their influences or their audiences - all were welcome. "I've got pictures where there are about 40 or 50 Mohicans down the front pogoing away!" Fish recalled later. As Bicester was an army town, some crowds were inevitably military. Comments Mick, "We used to play to a lot of drunken, crew cut squaddies. God knows what they made of it!" Unfortunately this diversity was not to last, as media attention led to increasing pigeonholing of the band. Commented Fish, "As soon as the Genesis tag came in, the Yes/Floyd audience came to see us along with a lot of metal and heavy rock aficionados and it shut out a lot of the fans I'd liked to have seen at the gigs."

Long-time fan Steve Woods was one such aficionado - he recalls, "I started noticing mention of a Genesis/Prog-influenced band called Marillion. Being a devout Genesis follower it caught my attention. Genesis was public property, meanwhile here was a band we could call our own."

By now it was felt that some form of fan club was necessary, and so The Web was founded. Fan Tim Hollings, who had met the band for the first time in September of the previous year and was now a mate, kicked things off with the first clutch of Web magazines. 400 more copies of the Roxon tape were made and advertised in the small ads and other fanzines, one of which was picked up by fan Anne Bond's older sister. "Jan saw an advert in the Genesis magazine for some demo tapes of a band who sounded like early Genesis," remembers Anne. "She sent off for them but they were very poor quality." In any case, it was enough to hook Jan and another few hundred followers.

The second prong of Marillion's promotional attack was to ensure its message reached the higher echelons of Soho. PR agent Keith Goodwin was employed by Fish to ensure a wide coverage as possible. According to fan Claus Nygaard, "The term 'employed' is quite right according to Keith, as Fish just stormed into his office in London one day and almost forced him to be Marillion's PR agent!" It would have been rude not to accept!

Backstage at Friars by Darren Newitt

As a 13-year-old schoolboy coming into his musical awakening, Marillion were more to me than just a successful 'Heavy Metal Band' from Aylesbury (as described by The Sun newspaper at the time). It was a time everyone in Aylesbury either knew, or knew someone who knew, or knew somebody who knew somebody who knew, a member of Marillion! All had a story to tell about the band, from the semi-believable, to the completely ludicrous (supposedly Fish painted his entire house in harlequins!) Quite simply, the band was contagious. They generated excitement.

I'll never forget the time I first saw Marillion perform at Friars. This was more than just the infamous venue of past giants, this was THE hometown gig. Utterly amazed and astounded by the performance and the audience's response, my belief in, and appreciation of Marillion was infinitely reinforced. It was then that a cheeky 'young' scamp decided to try and get back-stage to meet his favourite band.

So, armed with a shovel, torch, sewer maps, compass, and rifle(!)... hmmm... I managed to casually sneak past the security guards into the after-show party, And yes, my dream came true... I got to meet and talk to Marillion. What struck me the most about Marillion back then (and which in retrospect would not seem so surprising) is how 'normal' and down to earth they were. For a young naive schoolboy meeting his musical idols, this was quite unexpected. I had elevated Marillion to... well how can explain it... I know it sounds cheesy, but 'musical gods' (well, what else would you think a teenager would think of their fave band?!). Marillion were all happy to talk and joke with me. There were no Prima Donnas here. Marillion made me feel very appreciated and special. I think I smiled for at least a week!

going to London

London is generally understood to be the starting place for any aspiring southern UK band, not just because of the potentially larger audiences, but also because most record companies are based in the West End. Reps from the major labels already have their work cut out sifting through the many bands that have taken the trouble to move to the capital, so there is little chance of being spotted outside the M25. And so it was that, like many bands before (and after) them, Marillion followed the Watling Way[12] and headed for the lights.

The boys were not travelling alone. Already the structures were in place to support the band's ventures - not least the newly implemented telephone hotline linking fans with the band's movements. By the end of the summer in 1981, Marillion's relentless self-promotion (supported by Keith, who got the band its first listings in Sounds and Melody Maker) was having a ripple effect that reached the heart of the city - so much so that by October, they were playing their first gig at the Marquee. As this was happening however, there were some minor administrative details to settle. Not everyone in the band was as fully committed, devoted, even as obsessive, as the other members. It was time to unsheathe the long knives.

Kelly The Hero

Marillion's debut gig at the Marquee on 20 October 1981 was a riot. "The place had a real vibe, but it was disgusting - you'd stick to the floor!" recalls Steve. Supporting US glam-rock outfit Girl,[13] the band had left nothing to chance and in now-habitual style, had booked a coach from Aylesbury for its growing entourage. The result, according to a gig review in Sounds, was to "give the Aerosmith rip-off merchants a bit of a scare - it's not often a support act gets an encore at the Marquee." Fortunately, as Fish was later to say, "Girl had a good attitude about it, they gave us congratulations afterwards." The Sounds review also gives us an insight into the more devoted elements of the early fan base, which it described as "rather a large contingent of ageing hippy 'eadbangers. No denim and leather here mate, more like kaftans and

Marillion fans go about their business, November 1981

loonpants." Hmm...

The beginning of November saw Marillion embark on their most extensive tour plan yet, christened the Saliva Tears tour after Diz's posters. It was not quite as glamorous as the name would suggest, "We used to chuck everything in the back of the van and go off somewhere and play," recalls Mick. The first 'official' date (Marillion had already played 15 times in October) was at the Red Lion in Gravesend on 1 November, and 20 further dates were played. However Brian Jelleyman would not survive to the end of the tour.

Although handy with the keys, to the others, it was apparent that Brian's heart and soul were not into the band. Explains Guy Hewison, "Brian didn't feel that he could give up his job." "I never really put the practice in," says Brian, "I can understand the frustration Fish and the others felt at the time. I knew my attitude wasn't right. I knew the band was destined for success but I couldn't become what was needed. Everyone needed to be as totally dedicated to the band as Fish was, and I wasn't." Brian carried on, hoping things would sort themselves out, while (largely encouraged by Fish), the other members of the band agreed to keep their eyes open for a potential replacement. The moment came on 11 November, when Marillion supported Chemical Alice at Chadwell Heath. On keyboards was Mark Kelly, a competent player who (as luck had it) had been bored with his own band for some time. "The guitarist was into all this cosmic stuff from groups like Hawkwind," remembers Mark. "All he wanted me to do were silly synth noises." Even before the support band approached him, Mark was sold. "I watched their set and decided that I really wanted to play with them, so when they asked me to join them at the end of the night, I said yes." And the deal was done - well, nearly.

dyb, dyb, dyb

Early recordings took place in a variety of places. Notably, after Mark joined the band, a Scout Hut in Aston Clinton was used to record a cover of the Genesis song 'I Know What I Like' - some pirate copies (wrongly) present this as Fish's first recording with the band.

Brian Jelleyman's last gig: Elgiva Hall, November 1981, Steve R, Brian, Doug Irving

Brian Jellyman, Steve Rothery

Without telling Brian (though "it didn't come as a total surprise," says Brian), Mark was invited to attend Marillion's 69th gig at Chesham's Elgiva Hall, a performance held in aid of Amnesty International. Brian played that night, but Mark went back to Aston Clinton with Fish. The pair stayed up all night talking (Mark on adrenaline, Fish on acid), then the following morning Mick and Diz joined them. "They all went round to Brian's house to sack him," says Mark. Brian comments, "I was a bit upset at first, but we parted company as friends. Once it was over it was quite a relief! Mark had been waiting in the wings and to be fair, did a much better job." Mark joined the band a week later on 27 November, the day after which, Marillion played Aston Village Hall as a 4-piece without the new, as-yet-unrehearsed player. There was to be no easy ride for Mark, Steve went to pick him up on 28 November in Romford, following which he spent a few days at Leyland Farm in intensive rehearsals, before playing his first gig at the Great Northern in Cambridge on 1 December. "I didn't know any of the songs. 'Grendel' was the main one. I had to write all the chords down to jog my memory!" Mark was even playing for two bands at once for a while! In an interview with fan Claus Nygaard, he recalled, "There was a bit of a cross-over period. I said to the guys in Chemical Alice that I was leaving, but I'd play the gigs they already had booked. So there was one week where Marillion were playing in Chadwell Heath and then Chemical Alice were playing in Chadwell Heath. That was a bit strange."

Mark's welcome included the lack of warmth offered by the cottage in Aston Clinton with Fish and Guy: Steve, Diz and Privet had already left for better accommodation at Ingram Avenue in Aylesbury. "The shampoo used to freeze in the bottle," says Mark. His residence didn't last long; two months later he had moved out to Victoria Street, Aylesbury,[14] a house rented by Diz's girlfriend Helen Main (now Mrs Minnit!) "We had to move out 'cos Guy wasn't paying the rent!" recalls Mark. "We were paying him though -

Doug Irving,
Fish,
Mick Pointer
(behind there somewhere!)

when we found out, we already were six months in arrears with no way of paying it again!" With Mark on board it was back to business as usual - gig, write, rehearse, promote, work a bit to cover the bills. Well, nearly - one thing had changed. "Mark's arrival made everyone aware of the limitations of the others," remarks Fish. But there was no time to worry about such things, not yet.

By this stage much of the promotional activity was being handled by Fish, who could "talk anybody into anything," according to Mark. "Nobody wanted to book us - if you didn't play dance music, punk, or new wave, forget it; you couldn't get a gig anywhere. But Fish would spend all day on the phone, ringing up different clubs. Eventually we were doing three or four gigs a week, which was pretty good for a band that nobody wanted to book." Mick Pointer concurs - "Fish had a much more clued idea of publicity and marketing. He was a massive asset in the start."

The first song that Mark was involved in was 'Three Boats Down From The Candy': he wrote the music for the second half of the song in the front room at Weston Road. 'Market Square Heroes' was written shortly after, the first melodies being composed in the garage at Victoria Street and with lyrics penned by Fish at St Mary's Church, Aylesbury as he was coming down from yet another acid trip.

Christmas Eve 1981 was the band's 75th performance, at the Starting Gate, Milton Keynes, "a notable gig" according to Tim's Web magazine. It was the first time out for 'Three Boats' and for 'Institution Waltz'; Marillion also performed a cover of the Genesis songs 'I Know What I Like' and part of 'The Lamb Lies Down On Broadway'. In the Friars Club annual poll ("We were accused of being a monopoly, so we tried to be a bit democratic!" laughs David Stopps), Marillion were voted best local band and best support band, not to mention a very honourable 18th as best band of all time (Genesis came 5th!). Little did anyone know that Marillion would be voted best new UK band by the readers of Sounds magazine less than a year later.

All made up, Fish struts his stuff, Elgiva Hall

Tommy's Tape

Marillion's first date of 1982 was back at the Marquee, supporting a band called Spider. This had two impacts, not least the fact that Nigel Hutchings, the manager of the Marquee[15] (as well as Ginny Arnison's cousin's husband) was so impressed that he offered Marillion a headline on the 25th of the same month. "Word spread quite quickly, before long we were packing it out," says Mick. More exciting still was the presence, unbeknown to the band, of Tony Wilson who was producer of the BBC's Radio 1 'Friday Rock Show' at the time. In the 1980s, Radio 1 had a reputation for discovering and showcasing new music, particularly on the late night shows of DJs John Peel and Tommy Vance. Whilst John Peel tended to focus on the indie and punk scene, Vance's 'Friday Rock Show' played music from rock bands old and new. According to Mark, "Spider's manager was a girl called Maggie Farren, Tony Wilson's girlfriend." A fortunate coincidence indeed, leading directly to the offer of a slot on the show.

The day after Marillion's first Marquee headline, the band was invited to the BBC Studios at Delaware Road, London to record a session for Tommy Vance's show. The recording took place with Tony Wilson at the production helm, to capture old favourite The Web, as well as two newer tracks - 'Three Boats Down From The Candy' and 'Forgotten Sons'. The broadcast was made a month later on 26 February, a significant event in that Marillion's trademark sound had, for the first time, left the Thames Valley and reached the furthest points of the United Kingdom. It also proved to be Diz's last recording, though he didn't know it at the time. Regular listener Steve Wood heard the session and found plenty to whet his interest. He admits, "I was slightly disappointed with the music, but there was something there that made me continue to follow them. I also knew they wouldn't stay unsigned for long."

In February 1982 the first issue of Marillion's official fanzine, The Web, was released. Written by Tim Hollings,[16] its first words were, "Hi, this newsletter is designed as a means of expression for both the band and you, the people who have supported Marillion in the past and we hope, the future."

Little did anyone know at this stage that this "means of expression" would still be published 20 years later! The Web proved its value very early on, as a request in an early edition encouraged fans to request the FRS session again. "Write to the Beeb and ask them to play the track again SOON; it's the thing to do!" wrote Tim. It was indeed, setting the scene for two decades of fan power. The BBC were inundated with requests, leading to a repeat of the session in May "by popular demand." As the band's popularity continued to grow, Mick's girlfriend Stef Jeffries was brought in to help Tim write the fanzine.

On 7 March, six weeks after their first headline, Marillion made a "triumphant return" to the Marquee. The band was supported by Solstice, which included no less than former Electric Gypsy Andy Glass on guitar! "We were formed in 1980 as a result of meeting fiddler Marc Elton," says Andy.[17]

This was the beginning of a 13-gig marathon at the Marquee, some of the later dates being used to preview the title track of the planned new album.

Did someone mention an album?

By March 1982 it was time for a second twist of the knife: it was Fish's long-time friend, Diz who would meet the sharp end. "We couldn't have a band with passengers," explains Fish. "The band had come to me and said he wasn't good enough. I couldn't argue my corner, I don't think the band would have happened like it did with Diz still in it. That was a tough for me, he was one of my best friends."

Meanwhile, not so much passenger but driver, Guy was realising that his own time with the band had reached the end of the road. "With the number of gigs I was finding it more and more difficult to get time off," explains Guy. "Besides, once the band had found an agent (and then a manager), I was becoming more and more sidelined." And that was that for Guy, well almost: he went on to perform a similar role for Andy Glass's band, Solstice.

Fish had heard about a 'pop' band called the Metros who were on their last legs, but who also had a pretty good bassist. He turned up at a Metros gig at The Kings Head in Aylesbury, in fact a leaving party for the bar staff before the place shut down for refurbishment. To quote then-bassist for the Metros Pete Trewavas, "There was quite a big occasion being made of it, we did a whole evening of rock and roll which seemed to go down quite well!" The stout Scot chatted to the diminutive bassist about Marillion's predicament. Fish played his cards quite close to his chest, explains Pete, "He told me that they'd held some auditions but he wasn't sure how it was going to go. They had a tour coming up and he was asking me if I knew of anyone." Pete, who had already seen Marillion play, quite fancied the job for himself. "I'd been into pop and new wave as that's where the work was, but Marillion were very different!" Despite being unsure if he would be taken seriously (or if Marillion would be taken seriously, as he remarks, "I wasn't sure there was room for it in this day and age!"), Pete asked for an audition. "I felt they were going places, just purely because of the way they acted and put themselves across," says Pete.

Whilst Diz holidayed with Helen, Pete was secretly auditioned in the garage at the back of Victoria Street. The audition was a bit uncomfortable - remembers Pete, "I had very short, slightly red hair at the time and I was wearing white trainers which was a bit of a no-no! They asked me what music I was into, I told them that I'd been listening to Haircut 100 and their eyes got wider and wider! If I'd said that I had a load of Caravan, Pink Floyd and

Marillion with the first, uncomfortable tour bus

Genesis in my collection, maybe they would have taken me a bit more seriously..." Pete pressed on regardless, plugged in (he recalls being told, "You can use Diz's amp, he won't mind") and started tuning up. "We were so impressed by his tuning up, that we gave him the gig there and then!" remembers Mark. Nearly true - the boys had one more person to see, but Pete was pretty much in. The decision was made in a well-concealed pub at the end of an alley off Market Square, known as The Dark Lantern. "We decided to go to a pub we'd never been to before so we wouldn't meet anyone we knew," recalls Mark. Ironically, it was here that he bumped into Suzy Coleman, who would become his future (ex-) wife - "She came over 'cos she recognised Fish," says Mark.

The axe fell at what was reputed to be the band's 100th gig; 26 March 1982 at the Starting Gate, Milton Keynes. Unbeknown to Diz, the band had invited another bassist,[18] along to the gig so he could check them out. Diz got wind of things and asked Steve Rothery what was going on - before long it had all come out. Fish broke it relatively gently, but Diz did not take the news well. "Fish said, 'you can hit me if you like,'" says Diz. "I was devastated, but having been involved in Brian's departure I couldn't say I had no blood on my hands. As an observer I can see why they did it, my standard of musicianship and my style did not fit with the others, but I'd poured all my energy into it, emotionally and physically." Asking the others to ensure his equipment was returned (it was already on stage), Diz went home before the performance. The remaining four managed to cover for the missing bass line, coping admirably for a one-off. However, with a North of the Border tour already planned, Pete had to be up and running, sharpish. Nonetheless, the mood was up: with the addition of Pete, Marillion had a band that could face the world. Fan Paul Gates notes, "I have several recordings from 1981 and it's pretty obvious when Pete replaced Diz and Mark replaced Brian, the quality and complexity of the music leaped forward!"

Back home, other loose ends had to be tied up, including the fact that Fish, Mark and Privet shared with Diz and Helen at the time. Priv stayed on, "I was still there even after 1983 when we went to America for the first time!" he laughs, but before long Mark and Fish moved out to Rothers' place at Ingram Avenue, Aylesbury. Steve describes it as, "A semi-detached house on quite a nice estate. The locals saw it as some sort of hippie commune. Someone threw a brick through the window once! The drug squad raided it, but luckily I was on tour at the time!" Privet, who moved in later, recalls trying out the PA on the front lawn. "Someone said, 'Let's put *'The Wall'* on.' I said, OK, you get the ice-creams and I'll get the PA! That didn't make us any friends! The landlord was always trying to kick us out. We kept paying the rent so I think it proved to be more trouble than it was worth for him!"

The worst was yet to come for Diz, when he found himself written out of history, 1984-style. He never claimed to be the artistic key player of the band, but when he found that his contribution was to be annulled (not to mention his take on any rewards for it), it was more than he could bear. "Fish told me they'd rewritten the bass tracks with Pete and I wasn't going to get anything. Having known I did contribute to various tracks, I felt totally abused, my trust was violated completely. That was the bit I found by far the hardest." It would be four years before an out-of-court settlement later recognised both Diz and Brian's input. "The driving force was never financial, it was to get a co-writing credit," says Diz, "They said I was there as a passenger, that always galled me!"

Pride Of Passion

Following his unexpected departure, Diz Minnitt joined a band called World Service in Northampton. "They were a bunch of misfits," says Diz, "The singer was like Boris Karloff!" As Diz's confidence grew, he went and joined a band called Benzene, that featured a guitarist called Nigel. "There was an instant affinity, we clicked as musicians," says Diz, who invited Brian to join as keyboard player. Benzene re-formed as Pride of Passion, inviting Debbie Hopper to join as singer. "Debbie was a really good singer," says Brian, who before long bowed out gracefully. "Me and Steve Rothery were a lot more in tune with each other, with Nigel things were far too Tony Banks," comments Brian.

Pride of Passion went though its own revolving drummer phase, with one participant being Grant Gilmour of The Enid; towards the end of its existence, it included an 18-year-old keyboard player by the name of Steven Wilson, who would go on to form Porcupine Tree in 1987. The circumstances of Pride's demise are shrouded in mystery, as the band was packing out the Marquee at the time. "Nigel was convinced we were jinxed, because suddenly we couldn't get booked," says Diz, "The whole thing imploded!" Small consolation that Diz had just settled with Marillion at about the same time.

On The Scene by Claus Nygaard

Who was on the scene in 1982? Who was there besides Marillion that one could pick out and identify oneself with? Ideals in music were indeed hard to find. The old school was falling apart, as brilliantly demonstrated by bands like Pink Floyd, Genesis, Supertramp and Jethro Tull, and the new was divided between pure anarchistic punk, pure techno or pure pop. In between came Marillion, urgently needed, quickly highly praised and broadly taken to the heart! They were not the only outfit going about in the sphere of music we could label as Progressive Rock or Art Rock, because bands like Pallas, Solstice, Pendragon, Twelfth Night and Guizerjal were there too; but Marillion were the ones to draw the longest straw. They had a storyline; they demonstrated rare musical talent with their unique compositions; they played with craftmanship rather than machines; and they allowed the listener more than 12 straight bars. Here, finally, was a band to sit down to, to listen to, to drink to, to think to, to cry to. Simply a band to experience and grow with. These were combinations that made Marillion a true success. A new, up and coming band even in the early days of 1982!

I think a lot of us die-hard fans experienced Marillion in our early teens and grew up with them, so in a way they hit a part of a generation right on the spot, and these youngsters would follow the band over the years to come. With 1982 lurking right around the corner, they were ready to prove for sure that the punk waves were only temporary and that they were more than a bunch of discarded hippies themselves - even if they did wear weird costumes and had a barefooted, longhaired, face-painted frontman crooning well thought out and meaningful end-of-the-bar style lyrics in a falsetto voice. Call it psychedelic, experimental or progressive rock revival. What meant something for Marillion was the fact that they composed and performed from their hearts and not with the charts in mind.

Saliva Tears

The concept of a Scottish tour had been long in the planning, based on the desire to find new and ingenious ways of reaching out to potential fans. Scotland was chosen for a multitude of reasons, from there being few (if any) examples of English bands touring Scotland, plus the fact that Fish was a Scot, to the sublimely illogical 'hell, why not?' factor. Neither was this some lip service to the North - rather than nip up to Edinburgh and Glasgow and say 'that's done then' the band had a total of 29 dates planned. As Mark Kelly confirms, "We thought it was better to get everywhere and really do a proper tour." Not that all of the dates were Scottish: a significant proportion of the tour did not actually take place in Scotland, as the band toured their way to and from the border. Things were not always set in concrete before the tour started, there were some empty dates, or partial arrangements, so the gig guide in Issue 2 of The Web made the request to "check all venues before travelling!"

Due to the prior arrangement of the tour, the new bassist received the same baptism of fire that Mark had experienced. "It must have been weird for him joining us lot fresh from a pop band, and me and Mick were both a bit mouthy I expect," say Priv. Adds Mick, "I'm a piss taking bastard! Harmless, but I do love banter." Pete wasn't so sure about the 'harmless' bit. "He used to go on about wearing white shoes or whatever which used to get me a little bit upset at times," says Pete. "Priv did as well, but it wasn't as *meant*." Pete got on immediately with Steve Rothery, he wasn't so sure of Mark ("It felt like him and Fish were best mates") and as for Fish, well. "I didn't trust him an inch, I thought anyone who can sack his best mate could sell his grandmother!" he says. The band departed for the North almost immediately following Pete's arrival, with a bare two weeks for rehearsals and writing sessions. "It was quite hard work, I definitely put the hours in," says Pete. Fortunately, Pete's previous experience with Orthi (the prog band he had joined previously with Robin Boult) helped him through. "The music had a definite structure that reminded me of Orthi," Pete recalls. "It was snappy and hooky, I could just jam along." With Pete on board, the rehearsals had yielded a completed Chelsea Monday, which was first played live only 3 weeks before he joined.

On April 2 Marillion played the General Wolfe in Coventry, Pete's first live date. It was also Priv's first performance, as he recited the prayer in 'Forgotten Sons' while Fish 'mixed'. "He sat by the mixing desk drinking beer," says Priv. "I was utter crap, the reviews were scathing!" A week later it was Mark's 21st birthday, and seven days after

professional signings

"Everyone (apart from Mick) decided to go professional when I joined, so that meant giving up jobs. Actually turning professional meant signing on! We had to sign off when we went to Scotland, we were away for five weeks. There was no way they were going to let us claim without signing for that long without realising we were working!"

Mark Kelly

that, the band had already played Bathgate, Bannockburn and Edinburgh. On 22 April, at the Inverness Ice Rink, Marillion met a young fan called Avril Mackintosh. "I'd won a competition on the Tony Ferry show on Radio Scotland," says Avril. "The boys were really friendly, but Fish was a bit funny." Avril took the opportunity to seek some advice from Mr Hedge (who was on no mean learning curve of his own). "I went to Priv and asked, how do I become a sound engineer?" recounts Avril. Whatever he said, it triggered the first step of the journey that led to Advision Studios, six years later, where Avril assisted the mixing of *'Clutching At Straws'*. It's a funny old world.

As the band toured, it drew the attention of both local and national press. Not all reviews were favourable, for example the Mayfair in Glasgow (reputed to be the best night of the tour) was reviewed by Andrea Miller in Melody Maker, June 26 1982. "The band sound like early Genesis without the wit... going on and on, they do about five numbers but make them last an hour."

Fish looking very girly in 1982

Clearly not a fan in the making. Phil Bell of Sounds was kinder. "Mark my words," he said, "Critics may choke and chuckle *en* bleeding *masse*, but when action's sizzling at grass roots level, to ignore it would be tantermount (sic) to dodging our duty."

Other reviews, though positive, demonstrated early signs of the potential for rifts within the band. Fiona Dempster wrote in Scottish newspaper Gaudia that Marillion's support of Pallas at The Venue was "A shining performance - it would be difficult to say who was better." Fiona went on to note how "The rest of the band took a back seat to Fish's eccentric appearance. This is not to say that the others are not accomplished musicians - they just lack the charisma of Fish."

For now there was no time to worry about such trivia. By May the band were heading south again, playing Glasgow before crossing the border to play Penrith on the 8th. There was a detour through Wales, notably Bangor University attended by local lad (and later, Jump front man) John Jones. "They were dynamic in the extreme, and Fish was compelling in the extreme!" remembers John. "I walked up the road with my then-drummer and said, they'll be famous!" His opinion was despite Priv making another, final attempt at stagecraft at Bangor, this time with a harmonica. The intensive tour achieved all of its major objectives, sowing the seeds of a huge following. "The enthusiastic anorak fan thing started on the Scotland tour," remembers Priv. "There were some lads from Luton who just kept showing up and the Scottish fans increased by the gig. It was a great vibe with just our little team." Wrote Mick in the Web fanzine. "Everywhere we went the people were so friendly and responsive, we all had an amazing time!"

The tour left a warm glow that the band could quite reasonably bask in. What was more, it had firmly positioned Marillion as a touring outfit. "After Scotland, I felt that we weren't playing at rock bands any more, it was a profession," continues Priv. "Except for the getting paid bit! It was about that time that I knew that the band were going to 'make it'. A truly golden time."

Finding a Manager

With the lands of the North receding fast in the band's collective memory, Marillion got back on with developing its fan base and profile closer to home. It was also time to fall back, regroup and prepare for what would hopefully be The Big Time. Housing arrangements were reshuffled once again, as Steve, Pete, Mark and his now-girlfriend Suzy moved into Grafton Road, Aylesbury. Not that it lasted - 6 months later, Mark and Suzy moved to Willow Road following the birth of Freya (an event he missed - "We were playing Bournemouth that night, I must have been mad!" says Mark), and Pete moved to Mount Pleasant, having finally enough credit to get a mortgage.

Articles of a most positive nature continued to appear in the mainstream music press: Dave Dickson wrote in Kerrang!, "When did you last get really excited about a band? When was the last time you saw a band and realised you were seeing the birth-pangs of something potentially devastating?" If that wasn't effusive enough, he went on: "Marillion generate a real passion. The chemistry is there waiting to be unleashed: the effect could be explosive. Catch them while they are still in their infancy." Such strong reports went straight to the heads of the band members - the cool calculating bits that is. A record deal was so close it could be smelled (according to fan Mike Eldon, "It became quite usual for representatives of various record companies to appear at gigs"), and a good manager was being sought as a matter of urgency.

synth on a rope

"The Mellotron I had was quite old, it was always chewing up tapes. I used to take it apart before every gig to clean the heads. I would clean the whole frame, in fact, by swinging it into the shower and washing it down with soap and water!"

Mark Kelly

Peter's friend

Incidentally, Peter Mensch had taken Fish to one side and proposed a solo career for him. "I was totally against it, I was fighting for the unit, I've always been a unit player," says Fish. "Besides, I thought, we've just fought for two years, it would have been totally mercenary for me to do it."

First to try on the shoes of manager was long-time friend and ally of the band David Stopps. Clearly experienced in running clubs such as Friars, David had frequently been approached by Fish to take on the role of Marillion's band manager. "He was the big fish in a small pond," remarks Fish. "I was very reluctant, but I could see they had potential, it was quite an honour to be asked," adds David. "The band were quite organised, this was a train that was already moving, I was impressed with how the band (and in particular Fish) were getting things together. They had a loyal following and it was obvious it was growing!" By the end of May 1982, David finally gave in and immediately got to work. He contacted 15 recording companies and sent them copies of the demo recording, posted out numerous press kits, fixed meetings with agencies and generally put his back into the thing. He also offered to put in some money to buy a PA, rental of which was a major expense for the band.

Unsurprisingly, success wasn't handed on a plate. Most of the labels returned the requisite rejection letters, but one did not: EMI (in the shape of Ashleigh Goodall,[19] who had seen the band play at the Marquee at the beginning of July) agreed to let the band record a demo or two. Rumour has it that two A&R men at EMI drew lots for for the privilege: recounts Pete, "Ashleigh had just changed jobs, leaving Dave Ambrose and Hugh Stanley-Clarke. They tossed a coin and Hugh lost!" The demos were recorded at the end of July, in the basement of EMI's Manchester Square studios[20] - the selected songs were 'Market Square Heroes', 'He Knows You Know' and 'Chelsea Monday'. "They were quite happy with the results though they would have liked more time," Tim reported in The Web. Not quite true - according to Pete, "They weren't very good!"

It was a very busy time for David, who was also seeing Friars grow from strength to strength. "I think Fish expected me to drop everything but I couldn't," he comments.

With events like a 3,000 ticket gig at Stoke Mandeville stadium with the Clash, and a string of dates at Friars including gigs by The Police and Joe Jackson already in the pipeline, David could not give Marillion 100% of his time. "We had a lot going on. It was a very busy, magical time," continues David. "My intention was to cut back on Friars and make a slow transition." Maybe so; meanwhile there was an impetuous band gagging to take on the world and it didn't want to hang around. Comments Fish, "We became concerned that we'd put on an anchor rather than wings." Concurs Mark, "We panicked, we thought he was being too relaxed and we were getting nervous!"

Just five weeks after his recruitment, with plenty of regret on both sides, David was asked to give back his horsewhip. The spokesperson was, of course, Fish. "He came and saw me, he said he'd talked to the other guys and Marillion didn't want me to be manager any more." Following a heated debate (after all, David certainly hadn't been idle during his tenure and, according to his notes, "A manager has to be able to manage, and not be a tea boy"), the relationship was over. "I was really annoyed that I'd been fired, as I knew I could do really well for them," says David. "David was very upset," recalls Mark. "He went on to manage Howard Jones. We thought it was to prove to us that he had the ability to break an act!" Not only had the band lost a good mate, but also a supportive promoter - it wasn't until March of the following year that the band would play Friars again.

In stepped John Arnison, a young manager who had previously worked for Quarry Management, the company representing Status Quo and Rory Gallagher. Quarry was based on Wardour Street, directly opposite the Marquee and John was a regular in the Marquee bar. "There was nothing quite like it, it was where all the agents and music company people used to hang out," recalls John. A few months before, he had gone to the Marquee to meet with Sony about a signing for John Cooper Clarke, when a new band happened to be taking the roof off the place. What most surprised him was the following - "These weren't old Genesis fans, this was a new band with a new audience!" John stopped for a chat with Marillion's press officer Keith Goodwin. Recalls John, "I said, listen, you know my numbers, any help or advice, give me a call." And that was that, until a few weeks later. "There was a phone call from Fish, out of the blue. He said, 'I understand you'd be interested in managing us, do you want to meet?'"

John met the band at the Prince Of Tech pub, on Earls Court Road in London. Laughs John, "They all got up and went to the loo together, but came back without having made a decision. I don't know who wasn't sure!" Assuming that the band would go with Peter Mensch, a more established manager who had bands such as AC/DC under his belt,[21] and who also had Marillion in his sights, John went home with low expectations. To the band, however, John was a no-brainer.

Strat

Tony Stratton Smith also included Van Der Graaf Generator, Rare Bird and the Bonzo Dog Doo-Dah Band on his books, all of which would have a part to play in the Marillion story. Tony died of stomach cancer in March 1987, and *'Clutching At Straws'* was dedicated to his memory. He was and is missed by many in the industry, as someone who according to 'Legs' Larry Smith of the Bonzo's, "had vision, compassion and he bloody well cared."

Having already determined that they weren't going to be a mainstream act, to be represented by the manager of off-the-wall performers such as Pauline Murray and The Invisible Girls (ex-singer of punk band Penetration) and John Cooper Clarke, as well as more regular acts like Rage (previously known as Nutz), seemed ideal. "I've never been an out-and-out pop manager!" laughs John. In addition, having followed the band himself for some months, he had a good idea of where they could go and how he could get them there. "I liked the music first and foremost," comments John. In addition he could bring to bear his many contacts with the Soho elite. The next day the call came through from Fish - "Congratulations, you're Marillion's manager - if you want to be of course!"

John's impact was, according to Fish, "dramatic." He was quick to pursue the relationship with EMI, first proposing new demos, so the band went to a house in Hayes, Middlesex, for another try. The second batch was still pretty mediocre - according to John, "They were made in a shed in the back garden, the band played live and nobody was producing them so it's no wonder they weren't very good!" An alternative plan was agreed with Hugh Stanley Clarke - to pack out the Marquee and invite the senior executives to attend. "They'd already spent money on us so they came along," remarks Pete. "They saw us at a packed venue and decided they'd be mad not to sign us."

According to John Arnison, "Everything moved unbelievably fast from that point on." The first gig John participated on was at the Liverpool Warehouse, which happened to coincide with the stag night of his friend and tour manager, Paul Lewis. Present was John's other signing, Rage. The relationship between the two bands was initially cool. "There was a bone of contention between us and Rage in particular," recalls Pete. "We

Reading, August 1983

thought John was giving them too much attention, and they thought the same back." Everyone got on OK in the end - "We used to go drinking together and they supported us on a few shows!"

Within the band the excitement was building to unprecedented levels: Fish got his picture in the July 1982 issue of Kerrang! (Tim wrote in The Web "He has been hell to live with ever since!"). Fortunately, the inevitable swelling of heads was kept in check by continued live appearances, which added a certain unpredictability - for example, somebody forgot to turn the telly off when Marillion played its first Manchester gig, at a venue called The Gallery. A fan called Simon wrote in The Web that Mark appeared "hesitant and nervous" - unsurprising as Clint Eastwood's 'High Plains Drifter' was showing above his head. "It was something of a triumph that the band got the enthusiastic response they thoroughly deserved," commented Simon. Fan Dave Rogers concurs - "It was so refreshing to see guys actually playing - after all, this was the pop-driven early-eighties, where pre-programmed 'product' was very much the flavour. Yet here was a band with a distinctive sound - each musician displaying a style that was individual and skilful."

EMI were not the only label to show an interest in Marillion: Charisma Records, represented by Tony Stratton Smith, was also very keen. Time was not, in this case, the great healer: Tony went on holiday, leaving a subordinate to negotiate a deal. Recalls Mark, "He came along and offered us a two-single deal but we weren't going to sign that!" EMI then offered the band a five-album deal... well, which one would you have picked? As Tony came back from holidays he thought the band would be signing to Charisma, and nobody was around to put him right. The train was rolling on - on Wednesday 25 August 1982, a deal was agreed with EMI; in the afternoon, John drove up to Liverpool to attend Paul Lewis' wedding; on the Thursday, the band played at The Warehouse in Liverpool. By the weekend it was festival time and the first rencontre with still-hopeful Tony Stratton Smith.

The success that Marillion had been nurturing over the many months of hard graft, arrived as a double whammy. Not only did the boys finally pick up a contract with EMI, but days later they played an exultant performance to their biggest audience to date.

Reading

The Reading Festival was renowned as the live outdoor stage for Marquee bands, and on Sunday 29 August it was Marillion's turn, alongside giants of the day Michael Schenker Group and Dave Edmunds.[22] "We were really low on the bill," recalls Mark. Hearing of the Theakston Music Festival being held at Nostell Priory in Wakefield the day before, Fish proposed to play there as well, in support of Jethro Tull and Lindisfarne. Headliners Jethro Tull thought it was a good idea, so off they went. It was not Marillion's best ever gig remembers Mark, "It was a nightmare! Ian Anderson was standing at the side of the stage watching us, and half the gear wasn't working!" Despite everything, the gig was enthusiastically received. "Nostell Priory was a fantastic summer's day... and one act just grabbed me," says fan Dave Rogers, "They rose to the task of playing a much larger audience superbly: resplendent in stage costume and make up, Fish had the audience captivated." For the band, at least it provided an opportunity to try out the festival thing before climbing onto the Reading stage.

Show time came the next day, 29 August at the Thameside Arena in Reading. At the start of the set, Fish announced the new contract with EMI, triggering jubilant applause from the 35,000-strong crowd that barely ceased before the end of the performance. However, this was not only premature (the ink was still firmly in the pens, and would not reach the paperwork for a good few weeks), but also big news to Tony Stratton Smith, who had booked a marquee at the festival in anticipation of the signing. "He was horrified!" remarks John Arnison. Thinking on his feet, Tony asked whether a deal had been signed for the publishing. Continues John, "He immediately wrote out a cheque for five thousand pounds, he said, "Whatever you get offered from anybody, I'll pay that plus five thousand!" Through guilt as much as good business sense, Strat won the publishing deal.

Marillion's festival performance was genuinely well accepted: as Kerrang! reported, "Marillion provided a marked contrast with what everyone had secretly desired for the whole weekend - a dose of keyboard rock." Or, Tim wrote more bluntly, "Marillion's set was a breath of fresh air on what was a dire diet of Heavy Metal." Among the wider audience was fan Mike Palmer whose soft-edged memories (largely due to the alcohol haze, a staple of Reading) were rendered crystal clear by Steve's fretwork. "This glorious, soaring guitar solo kicked in, and that was it - I stood up and couldn't believe this guy's guitar playing."

For some fans, the sounds of Reading were enough to reel them in. Remembers a US fan known as Bubba, "Back in 1983 I was stationed in West Germany, I made friends with the German heavy metal people, one was called Eddie. I was looking through Eddie's record collection - he had a live double LP called *'Reading Fest'*, featuring bands that I had never heard of like Budgie, Twisted Sister, and Marillion. We played the record and 'Three Boats Down From The Candy' came on. I fell in love with Marillion's music and had Eddie play the song over and over. He ended up giving me the LP. I still have it to this day!"

Kerrang!'s final word on the gig is a fair indication of what was going on - the key turning smoothly in the lock and the door swinging open to reveal a brave new world of rock stardom. Not so much a compliment but a fact - "The piéce de résistance, 'Forgotten Sons', resulted in one of the loudest ovations of the weekend." To hear this observation when standing alongside MSG and Dave Edmunds, the members of Marillion knew that they had arrived.

market square heroes

The official signing with EMI, a month or so after Reading, was a mundane affair - well, if you ignore the alcohol and the fact that Steve Rothery fell asleep during Hugh Stanley-Clarke's inaugural speech! According to Pete, "After the signing, we went around the corner to a burger bar. Since seeing the Beatles play at Shea Stadium on television at the age of 7, that's what I wanted to do, but it was weird. I felt no different - there was a real anticlimax about it." The occasion was graced by a cheque for £20,000 which certainly helped the chips slip down more easily!

Signing to EMI

Not every Marillion follower was comfortable with its major label status. "People wanted us to be their little secret," explains Steve. Mark agrees: "We did get some stick from the hardcore; people like to have a band nobody's heard of!" So was the plan to attract a following to be dropped the moment the band achieved chart success? At the time, some said so. "It was disappointing," says fan Mike Eldon. "We'd got into local bands rather than watch the stadium players go through their paces, but things were going full circle for Marillion." The next five years were to be a roller coaster. "It started off we cared about the fans," agrees Pete. "But once we had signed with EMI, there wasn't time to care about our families, never mind the fans." However, the band came good in the long run. Long-time Marillion fans have the benefit of twenty years of experience and hindsight to prove so.

Before long, the rewards of working for a major label started to come through. The band picked up new equipment, and Priv was officially named as the guys' sound engineer. "We got budget: proper lights and real PA systems," says Priv. "Oh,

rust in peace

Also in October 1982, the trusty van Margaret died. An obituary was placed in the Bucks Herald on Thursday 14 October, entitled 'Sad Times'.
"In loving memory of our hard working friend and companion.
May she rust in peace."

three boats

"We awoke under the boat at the beach at Brighton on March 18th '81.
I said, wouldn't it be romantic if the boat had a name to remember the night by.
The boat had a number and the nearest with a name was the Candy. I looked on that as being a symbol of how far away I was from a genuine fulfilling relationship and my attitude to sex at that time."

Fish, August 1991

and catering. And wages!" A chap called Gary Townsend was brought in as production manager, to the dismay of the other two members of the entourage, who were more than the deal could afford. Gary didn't stick around for ever, according to Priv: "Last count he was selling cars to big companies, he got sick of touring in the end. It happens a lot." Then it was show time. Marillion went back to EMI's studios once again, only this time the recordings were for real.

Charting The Single

Given the head of steam that had built up behind Marillion's live act before the signing, it was no wonder that they were keen to get into the studios at the earliest opportunity. It was agreed that the first release would be a 12-inch, extended play single - as Fish was later to conclude, "To satisfy the album demand that had generated over nearly 18 months of touring."

The single included a bank of tried-and-trusted live material, not least its title track, 'Market Square Heroes'. "It seemed to be an obvious choice. It had a message and a chorus," remarks Pete. The song started out as a commentary on the band's own performances. "I'd get images of the 1937 Nuremberg rallies," Fish commented to Sounds of his live experiences. "It used to be that after I'd sung the line, 'Are you following me?' They'd go, "YEAH!" It doesn't happen now; it's finally sunk in that they're not, in fact, sheep." The two other tracks on the EP were 'Three Boats Down' and the now-infamous 'Grendel'.

Recording started following yet another headline at the Marquee on the 25 September 1982, a thank-you-to-the-fans gig entitled the 'Garden Party For Forgotten Sons'. "It was packed and the atmosphere electric, an amazing night indeed!" Tim wrote. Peter Gee of Pendragon, who played support, remembers the atmosphere as being "Very exciting, very powerful. Much of that was due to the charisma of Fish, and the atmosphere of the Club packed with 700 or 800 people, when the capacity was meant to be something like 500!"

The recordings took place at Park Gate Studios near Battle, Hastings. Available as

Mark Wilkinson

Mark had long wanted some involvement with music but it was clear that his forte lay in art rather than music. Fresh out of Art College, he sought work with Jo Mirowski's company Torchlight. "I got my first job with them by doggedly not accepting my fate and knocking on doors continually until art directors would see me," he recalls. "Within a week I appeared to have fended off the competition and won a contract to paint three single sleeves and one album sleeve for this new signing at EMI."

Mark produced the covers for the entire Marillion catalogue between 1982 and 1988, including numerous designs for posters, tickets, badges and other merchandise. He went on to work with Fish solo, producing all of the cover art apart from *'Songs From The Mirror'* - at the time, Mark and Fish decided that a break from each other was long overdue.

In 2001 Mark and Fish released a book entitled 'Masque', covering Mark's many collaborations with the band and the solo artist.

producer was David Hitchcock, who had produced the Genesis album *'Foxtrot'* some ten years before. This was a double-edged sword: although Marillion acknowledged its roots in the pre-punk, glory days of progressive rock, it they wanted to promote its their own, unique sound and musical style and exist in its own right, not as a 'Genesis covers band'. To employ David could be interpreted as a regressive, rather than a (small-p) progressive step; however he did his best to convince the band that he was not stuck in the seventies. "David said he would do anything to avoid getting a sound like Genesis or Camel," Fish recollected. "He had got really cheesed off, he wanted to get a band of the '80s with the David Hitchcock sound."

In the end, time (or lack thereof) made the decision academic. As Mick explains, "We had to do the EP by the end of October and because we hadn't any experience in a proper studio, we had to find someone we could get on with." No problems there - David was an affable chap, and (as well as Genesis) he had also produced the band Van Der Graaf Generator who had been a big influence for Marillion.

Despite a total running time of 27 minutes, the EP had to be recorded and mixed in ten days. In the middle of everything, Mark Kelly got married to Suzy on 4 October. The inordinate pressure was taking its toll: Fish had suggested to John Arnison that the marriage was a bad idea ("That was a bit of a blow to our friendship," says Mark) and on the night the EP was completed, David Hitchcock crashed his car on his way home. "He fractured his neck, bust his legs, he was a hell of a mess and we were told he was out for 3 months," Fish recalled at the time. "Dave was physically ill at the end. I feel incredibly bad because the reason he had the smash was because he was exhausted."

EMI brought in Jo Mirowski's company, Torchlight, to produce the artwork for the new single. "EMI wanted a similar formula to the Iron Maiden logo and character," explains Jo, whose first job was to design a logo. This took some months according to Jo, "as each time EMI accepted a design they were happy with, the band were not keen." Eventually he was able to circumvent the record label, and things happened a bit faster. "I remember Fish calling me from a gig in Brighton, he asked me to give a softer feel to one of the proposed designs, a little bit of Yes logo in feel," continues Jo. "The next attempt everything finally fell into place." Not for everyone, however: "I hated it!" says Mick. "It looked like the designer had been eating a bar of Old Jamaican chocolate and thought, I know, I'll do that!" Adds Pete, "It was only years later that we realised it was exactly the same as Barclay James Harvest's logo." You can guess who designed that one!

With the logo complete, Jo then visited the band with an A2 folder packed with ideas from different artists. The Marillos selected an artist that they thought would be appropriate, but Jo thought better. "Upon reflection and with a better understanding of the band's direction, I phoned EMI and convinced them that Mark Wilkinson would be by far more suited," says Jo. "'Market Square Heroes' was done by proxy through Jo, it was not until the second single that I met the band," comments Mark. "Jo was very workmanlike," comments Pete. He didn't want us to speak to Mark at all: he was the conduit." There may have been a reason for that... Mr Wilkinson's artwork was accepted without criticism, and it only became apparent to the band years later that he had not, in fact, been the artist that the band had selected initially.

The single was dedicated to David Stopps and Friars - both in recognition of his help and through "a sense of guilt," according to Mark. "We liked him and he really helped us, and we repaid him by a sacking!" It was released on 25 October to audiences old and new. Recalls fan Peter Gifford, "I'd been intrigued by articles I read in Sounds and Kerrang! and after speaking to a bloke in the local post office, I bought the single. I remember him commenting on a gig t-shirt I was wearing and asking if I'd heard of Marillion. I told him what I'd read and he suggested I check out the single, he particularly liked this 20 minute track on the B-side!" That would be 'Grendel', then. "Funnily enough, I actually preferred 'Grendel' to 'Market Square Heroes'," laughs fan Rich Dowson. He wasn't be the only one, - as notes Steve Wood, "The 12-inch version gave me my first listen to 'Grendel', a track I had been reading about for months, and which gives me goose-bumps to this day!"

'Market Square Heroes' achieved the No.60 slot in the UK charts - a very respectable start, prompting an appearance on the teenybopper show, 'Top of the Pops'. A subtle change was made to the lyrics, "I am your Antichrist" being replaced by "I am your Battle Priest." Antichrists were so seventies after all! John Arnison postponed his honeymoon to the long-suffering Ginny in order to attend this first TV appearance. "In hindsight, I must have been mad! But I wanted to be on that rollercoaster, everything was moving so fast!"

All was well that ended well for everyone apart from David Hitchcock, who became a casualty in more ways than one. The intention was to use David again for the album, with The Web's Tim requesting, "Please get better by December!" He did indeed get better by December, but he returned to be told his services were surplus to requirements. Fish commented at the time, "A lot of people think we ditched Dave. It looks that way, it looks very like that way." With reason - it was that way. According to the movers and shakers, the Hitchcock experiment had not succeeded, and a more modern producer was sought. "We've never spoken to him since," Fish noted a few years later, a little glumly.

Warming Up by Dave Cross

I became the social secretary at City University in summer 1982. One of the things I found in my new office has a large box of demo tapes that the previous social secretary had discarded. I found the Marillion tape in that box. I wouldn't have bothered listening to it, but I'd read a couple of reviews of Marillion gigs in NME or Sounds and everyone said they sounded like early Genesis. I loved early Genesis, so I thought I'd listen to the tape.

I remember thinking that they didn't sound very much like Genesis, but I thought that the tape was really good. I decided that I'd like to book them, but thought that as they were getting so much press attention they'd be too big to play a small student union bar, so I thought no more about it.

I'm not entirely sure about the next sequence of events, but at some point in September or October I was speaking to an agent about some other bands and one of us mentioned Marillion in passing. It turned out that he was either their agent or a colleague of their agent and knew that they were looking for somewhere to play a low-key warm up gig just before their first major tour. This was to coincide with the release of their first single 'Market Square Heroes'. He asked if I'd be interesting in that booking and I leapt at the chance. The date was Tue 26 October 1982. I know that I already had another band booked that night that I had to cancel. As the contracts had been signed, I had to pay them off too.

Normally on the day of a gig I'd let the roadies in and let them get on with the set-up, but on this occasion I hung around in the venue for as long as I could. I chatted a bit to the band and they all seemed like a really friendly group of people. Unfortunately, Marillion's music was apparently not what City students wanted to listen to at that time and the turnout was pretty small. There were maybe twenty people in the audience. I do remember that a number of other London college social secretaries came along (on my guest list) to see what the fuss was all about.

To be honest, I can't remember what they played that night - I didn't know very many of their songs. I know I'd been sent a copy of the 12" of the single by the agency, so I recognised all of those tracks, plus 'Garden Party' from the demo tape. I also remember that the few people who came all had a great time.

A few weeks later their agent rang me again, to tell me that they were playing an extra gig at the Venue at the end of this short tour and to ask if I would like to be on the guest list. It was lucky that I said yes as that gig was a huge sell out. It was great to see them again - and this time with a massive and appreciative audience.

Rehearsal of The Script

In November it was back to business again. The band members moved into an EMI-rented flat in Fulham, ready to record an album at the Marquee studios on Wardour Street, Soho, London.

The first practicality resulted from David's ill-concealed sacking as producer. "We thought shit!" remarked Fish at the time. "We had to start looking for producers again to do the album in December!" Finally the band settled on Nick Tauber - once again a rushed decision. Nick had previously produced *'Anthem'* by Toyah Wilcox, as well as albums by Thin Lizzy and Girl. The boys hit it off immediately. "He was cynical and sarcastic enough to be another member of the band!" commented Fish at the time.

Nick had a methodical approach to recording, capturing the drums first and layering the other instruments and vocals on top. "I'd spent a fair amount of time in studios, but I'd never given this much attention to detail," comments Pete in the sleeve notes to the remaster. Having said this, it was not an unpleasant experience, since all were keen to make a good impression. "It was immensely pleasurable and uplifting," remarks Mark, "It was an amazing experience," adds Steve, "Being in London, working in Soho, going next door to watch bands at the Marquee Club, there was never a dull moment!" Simon Hanhart, who was brought in as sound engineer, had the time of his life. "I was in a similar band when I was a teenager," says Simon. "I'd only been engineering for eight months, it was a big break for me!"

Some of the best material had already been used on the album-sized single which had just been released, so the band found themselves a bit short in the sessions. By the time the band arrived at the recording studios, the title track still lacked several sections, a particular problem because it was intended to set the scene for the whole album, linking what had been a number of pieces developed over many years into a coherent whole. A couple of the sections were written relatively quickly, while the band was in the studio. "It's amazing what a bit of pressure can do for the creative juices," Mark Kelly commented on the sleeve notes to the remaster. The opening section was written on the last day of recording, with a to-the-wire thought process that had the added benefit of keeping the final result simple. "If I'd had a bit more time to play with it I probably would have made it more complicated and ruined the atmosphere," said Mark. It was this song that became the title track to the album, trialled at some of the band's 13 dates at the Marquee, in late '82.

At the end of recording and mixing, both band and management knew that it had all been worthwhile. For Mick,

too early to say I'm sorry

During the recording of *'Script'*, Fish wanted to put a personal message to his girlfriend Kay on the album. Producer Nick Tauber reluctantly agreed but endeavoured to hide it in the mix. Its still there, playing backwards, as the whispers before the line "a scream that's borne from sorrow" in the title track. Of course, the big apology came two albums later!

it was the culmination of "Five years work, finally realised with the release of an album." Recalls Fish on the sleeve notes to the remaster, "One EMI executive was actually in tears at the end of the playback." So much for cool, calculating record execs!

'Script For A Jester's Tear'

Ambitious, varied, moody, dramatic, lyrical, accomplished...

People weren't meant to be making debut albums like 'Script' *at the time it was released. Later described by Fish as an album of bed-sit thoughts, it recounted a series of stories "relating to a character in a particular situation, and reflecting the different moods that the character will go through."*

Though never mentioned explicitly, the character was the jester, representing the hedonistic alter-ego of Derek Dick, or, as we would come to know it, "Fish". The conceptual costume was one the big man had grown accustomed to pulling on, originally to protect against the taunts of the schoolyard and latterly to enable a stage presence that Derek could not sustain by himself.

"So here I am once more..." a whispered, attention-grabbing vocal line, trailed by a solitary piano, and slowly we're drawn into the depths of the song. Introspection gives way to anger, and frustration boils over as the band soar into a showpiece of Marillion musicianship... Of the meaning behind the title track, Fish confessed, "Only one person has ever truly understood."

Its origins lie in the first song that he ever wrote, 'The Crying Jester'. "It was a total rip-off of a Jon Anderson song. It was written on the night that Keith Moon died; he was a jester, the crying jester." Consider the line: "Yet another emotional suicide, overdosed on sentiment and pride." There were other influences; "'The Script' referred not only to the album itself, but also harked back to the album *'Over'* by Peter Hammill - the song 'Lost and Found' appears to inspire many of the lyrics. Additional emotional input was Fish's break-up with Kay - It is no wonder that he remarked, "When I was doing the vocal I actually cried in the studio, it hit me that bad. It's probably the heaviest song we've ever done."

The second track would offer little respite. 'He Knows, You Know' was, "about someone who went from nervous exhaustion, through depression then full-scale drug abuse," explained Fish, who witnessed the experience through his own excesses and through a friend of his. "He ends up in a hospital bed and someone comes up to him and says, 'I told you so.' which helps him damn all."

One of Marillion's oldest performance pieces, the maudlin, and brooding 'The Web', started life as an instrumental, way before most of the line-up had even heard of Marillion. Fish's tale of ambition vs. creature comforts, took some of its lyrical inspiration from the tale of Penelope, wife of Odysseus. Claiming she would choose a new husband once she had finished making a death shroud for Odysseus, she would unpick her work at night, allowing her more time to procrastinate. Fish's take on the song sees him assume the role of the jester once more. Mark Kelly would also offer some considerable assistance in the arrangement of the song. The mid-section of the song is worthy of comment, contrasting as it does Pete Trewavas's underpinning of the song with fluid bass work, compared with the drumming limitations of the hapless Mick Pointer.

Side Two opened with the upbeat 'Garden Party', a spiritual kin of 'Market

Square Heroes'. With biting, satirical lyrics originating from Fish and Diz's Cambridge days in the winter of 1980, 'Garden Party' upset many of the people it was written about - after all, it's an attack on the class system of hereditary privilege, encapsulated in a Cambridge University Garden Party. "It's our most Genesis-y song!" Fish was later to comment.

Nevertheless, this Kelly-led rocker was a huge live favourite for many years. Unlike the delicately sung version on the LP, crowds delighted in screaming 'I'm fucking!' at the tops of their voices.

'Chelsea Monday' was a product of the bohemian days spent at the flat in Fulham. "Early morning walkabouts gave me examples of so many wannabes and could-be's and I wrapped them all up in a female character drowning in romanticism, unable to cope with reality."

Not only about the dreams of the band, it concerned "the fear of failure I went through," remarks Fish. The fear was manifested through a girl performing an outrageous and deadly act in order to achieve some recognition. It asks, "How far would you go to achieve fame?" How far, indeed? As Fish screams the words 'Chelsea Monday', Steve Rothery launches into a long guitar interlude, and as he does so, seals his reputation as a top guitarist.

To close the debut, 'Forgotten Sons' was a masterpiece, a grand finale that transcended its subject matter. "It's about government manipulation," remarked Fish. Set in Northern Ireland, it was based on Fish's experiences of how his cousin was injured in a riot. "I realised no one really cared," he commented in the sleeve notes for the remaster. "News of his plight was difficult to extract from the Army, and the Irish situation had lowered in the agenda of the media." With its fierce reworking of the Lord's Prayer for the middle section, and Mark Kelly evoking church choirs during the coda, the song is almost a religious experience. Fish summed up the album saying, "We would never sound so innocent again..."

Mark Wilkinson's work on 'Market Square Heroes' was more than enough to ensure he was brought in for the cover of the album, although it was still not certain he would have a long-term relationship with the band. The portents were good however - as Fish would write, "Mark's style paralleled our musical and lyrical vision."

As with the lyrical and conceptual content, it was agreed early on that there would be a central character whose story would also be told on the sleeves. This would be Fish's crying jester, his childhood alter ego, and a powerful symbol of love and loss. This was to be no one-shot wonder - indications of themes and concepts, such as the chameleon and the Punch on the TV set, were introduced, to be developed on later albums..

Oh Please Do Come

Before the release of *'Script For A Jester's Tear'*, EMI planned a second single as a taster, this time to be taken from the album. The single was 'He Knows, You Know', with the initial idea for the cover coming primarily from Mark Kelly. Mark Wilkinson was brought back to do the artwork, getting a chance to meet with the band for the first time. He recalls, "I'd heard the first single by then, it sounded tinny on the radio and the vocals were trebly and light, so I assumed the singer was a small guy!" Little did he know, as his first meeting with Fish illustrated, "Wearing a leather tasselled jacket, boots with strides tucked in, clanking silverware, studiously positioned kerchiefs hanging every-which-way, every inch the perfect model of the perfect Scottish rock star. He was huge in every way, exuded bonhomie and grabbed my hand to shake the bejeezus out of me!"

With significant support from EMI, as anyone who can remember the massive posters will testify, 'He Knows, You Know' entered the UK charts at No.35 and was also released in the US, the first time that Marillion's sound left the UK. It achieved instant recognition and a transatlantic fan base. "I was hooked on Marillion when I first heard 'He Knows, You Know' on KSHE-95," remarks US fan John Chudy. "This was, at the time, the premier rock station in St Louis." Oh, the advantages of major label backing! Not everyone liked it - of 'He Knows, You Know', Edwin Pouncey in Sounds declared, "The pomposity on this record is astounding! Marillion think the Peter Gabriel incarnation of Genesis was shit hot, so much so that they feel compelled to hobble into a recording studio to transfer their necromantic urges to record." Careful now, Edwin... you never know what might be around the corner!

Pete in his Jester costume, for the 'He Knows, You Know' video shoot

'Script' was released on 14 March 1983. Its chart position exceeded all expectations, as the album climbed to No.7 in the first week of release. It received many excellent reviews, especially from Phil Bell of Sounds who gave the album five stars, a genuine accolade as this was the first time he had ever given such a seal of approval. The press were not unanimous in their praise - another Sounds reviewer declared the album to be "a clichéd load of humbug."

Much of the negative press reaction was down to Marillion being perceived as unfashionable (which they were) and unoriginal (which they weren't). Comments Peter Gee of Pendragon, which suffered similar criticisms, "Not many of the press took them seriously. There was this big Gabriel/facepaint/voice rip-off thing levelled at Fish most of the time. Many journalists' attitude was, we buried all that Genesis stuff in the '70s, the last thing we want is for it to come back. There was the anti-long song lobby, and the fact that Marillion were themselves and not trying to be overly commercial."

Fans far and wide were delighted with the debut. "In those days you'd see people walking around at school with an album under their arm, *'Script'* was one of those," says fan Simon Clarke. "It created a bit of a buzz!" Recalls Dan Sherman, "I checked out *'Script For A Jesters Tear'* because I was intrigued by the artwork and loved it immediately. I was a big Rush and Jethro Tull fan at the time and thought it had elements of both, punchy rhythms, skilful keyboard and guitars, and interesting lyrics."

Where were we? Ah, yes. Poor Edwin was forced to eat his own words on February 19 1983, when Sound's readers voted Marillion the Best New Act. In an interview in the same mag, Edwin assented to interview Fish and Mick, understandably hesitant as his previous reviews had been far from generous. In a later piece Edwin admitted he didn't have a clue what Gabriel-era Genesis sounded like. Sounds was not the only rag to recant on its opinions, as Fish remarked, "I can see we're going to start getting hip now, the NME want to do us now! They're

proud dad

The video for 'He Knows, You Know' included new dad Mark Kelly's daughter Freya, when she was only 3 weeks old. "It was a spur of the moment, cool thing," says Mark. "I'm really glad she was in it!"

apologising practically for ignoring us, it's hysterically funny: we're going to make this unfashionable music become so sickeningly fashionable no one will believe it!"

The Genesis comparisons may have filled column inches, but they didn't fool anyone who had actually listened to the band. To admit influences was in no way unique to Marillion, besides which there was already a sound that was distinctly their own and a vocal and lyrical angst that was unmistakably Fish. As fan Tony Wood recalls, "I loved all of it - Fish was without doubt the most passionate vocalist that I'd heard, the guitar tone was great and the music was intelligently put together. It tugged at the heart strings ('Script', 'The Web'), it made you laugh ('Garden Party'), and it made you angry ('Forgotten Sons')." Some fans saw very little association between the two bands. "I liked Peter Gabriel's voice but didn't like Genesis," says fan Jonathan Mock. "Enter Marillion. The singer sounded similar to Gabriel, but the music was more modern and just so different to everything else out there. I was hooked in an instant. Script was a revelation to me and I still maintain it's one of the best albums ever recorded by anyone."

porcelain tears

Fish had the idea of a spoken soliloquy to open the album. Though dropped at the last minute (due to Nick Tauber's fears of "commercial suicide") nothing was ever wasted - it became the opening verse to 'Incubus' on the second album!

With money rolling in, Fish purchased a house in Albert Street,[23] just round the corner from Victoria Street. The purchase took place with a little pressure from other members of the band. "We were trying to get him to settle down 'cos he'd come off tour and carry on touring," says Pete. "Before he bought the house he didn't have anywhere to live, so he'd try and crash round at various peoples houses and drive them mad!" After Fish had split up with Kay he stayed in Blackheath with John and Ginny Arnison, who had just got married. Fish didn't think much of Ginny and the feeling was mutual. "They used to argue all the time," remembers John. "One day, she accused him of lifting his words from various books, while he was saying it was there he found his inspiration." Fish later vented his spleen in a number of lyrics on *'Fugazi'*; the walls of the cell were indeed enticingly thin, as Fish slept in the living room of The Arnisons' one-bedroom flat. "John was Fish's playmate, he was never really forgiven for getting married," comments Mark. Indeed - Fish had even suggested to Ginny that John had been having an affair, before they were wed and before the first album had been recorded! "Fish liked to have a drinking partner, someone as debauched as he was," explains Steve. "There were lots of tensions in the early days; Fish didn't like to lose his drinking partners, and he did some despicable things in the process."

In early 1983 the band returned to what it was best at, and went on tour. In place as tour manager was Paul Lewis, a colleague of John's who used to do the sound for Nutz and who had just returned from a two year stint with Van Halen; production manager was the aforementioned Gary Townsend; and Mick's drum roadie was Andy Field, who would later become production manager. On the mixing desk was the unstoppable Priv. "Gary and Andy taught us young lads so much," he says. "Patient, charming gentlemen. I was more than happy to take any advice offered, particularly by Gary, who was a fine sound engineer himself." Touring started as it was to go on - with barely a pause for breath after the release of the album. "I felt we had to keep working to increase the fan base, after *'Script'* came out," explains John. Indeed - the band's devotion to live duty ensured a constant stream of new fans, not to

fly off the handle

Deciding to include the 'He Knows, You Know' and 'Garden Party' artwork on the *'Script'* gatefold sleeve, Jo Mirowski went to put up posters on Wigmore Street in London, to photograph them with perspective. "One of Terry The Pill's fly poster boys turned up and immediately assumed we were encroaching on his territory!" says Jo. Having resolved that situation, a certain John Arnison happened to be walking past on his way to EMI and saw the now-happy gang fly posting what were redundant posters as the singles had already been released. Continues Jo, "When he arrived at EMI all hell let loose! It all ended in an explanation and a laugh!"

mention starting a pattern that continued, virtually unbroken, for the next four years. It also ensured a certain constancy of adrenalin, fatigue, distance from loved ones, alcohol and various other things... but that's getting ahead of ourselves...

One occasion indicated all too clearly a weakness in the line-up. On 16 March 1983 at the Reading Top Rank, the band launched into 'Charting The Single', but somehow it didn't seem quite right: it transpired that Mick was playing the beats the wrong way round. "Nobody changed, Fish couldn't work out what was wrong but got increasingly frustrated as he couldn't work out where to come in!" recalls Mark. An honest mistake maybe, but Mick's days were numbered from that point on. By the Scottish dates a month later, things came to a head: "Fish and I had our first blazing row in a hotel in Glasgow," recalls John. "He told me the band thought Mick had to go, but I felt he still needed a chance to grow; I was worried as Mick had formed the band, and because his wife, Stef was running the fan club." Despite such hiccups the larger gigs didn't cause the band too many problems, particularly Fish who was riding a wave of adrenalin. One attendee was fan Kim Waring, who went along to see Marillion play at Bristol's Colston Hall on 28 March 1983. "My boyfriend dragged me along," says Kim. "It was very loud, and there was an awful lot of strange people! At first it was quite daunting. At the end I was overwhelmed, by the show, the sound, the atmosphere... I went to as many concerts as I could after that!" A couple of weeks later, fan Chris Lewington (who had just relocated to Aberdeen) had his first opportunity to see the band. "I was staying in a hotel called the Treetops. I was looking for something to do when what was obviously a band checked into the hotel. I asked at reception who they were, and was told they were playing at the Capitol Theatre on Union Street that night. I called the venue and they had a few tickets so off I went. They were Marillion and they were bloody brilliant!" As Chris was staying in the same hotel, he found himself in the same bar as the after-show party. "I remember a couple of the roadies taking bets on whether the barmaid was wearing stockings or not, and a serious cocktail drinking competition when one of the band took on a bet that he couldn't drink 10 blue bombers. I gather he was sick down the corridor later on that night! John Arnison was obviously in a good mood as he was buying Champagne and Guinness for everyone." What an introduction! Four days later, on 15 April 1983 it was fan Peter Gifford's turn. He recalls, "My first gig was at Manchester Apollo. I was absolutely blown away. Fish made his entrance through the crowd, which I thought was fantastic. I've got a tape of the show somewhere; the highlight is hearing myself shout for 'Grendel' only to be shot down by Fish!"

The tour closed at the end of April with a number of sold-out dates at the Hammersmith Odeon.[24] It came as a surprise to some journalists, how the band managed to fill such a theatre after only one single: Fish patiently reminded them of the 200 gigs that had gone previously. "I took a gamble," remembers John. "I wanted to get out of clubs and into theatres as soon as possible." The gamble paid off - Marillion remains one of the few bands that has sold out the Odeon before releasing an album. Despite the potential to lose sight of the fans, Fish was in no doubt of their importance and would make frequent forays into the audience. He explained in an interview that, "to communicate with the audience on an eye-to-eye level, you have to be prepared to go out on a limb now and again, just to see what happens."

As the tour came to an end, so did an era as band and management decided to part with its remaining founder member. While Fish cheerfully admits his role as knife-wielder-in-chief, the decision was not his alone. "The person I went to for 100% confirmation was Steve Rothery," says John Arnison. "He told me, sorry, he's going to have to go." This was not only following the incident at Reading: while the others had all improved substantially over the months since, in their eyes Mick had not. Comments Pete, "Fingers were pointing at the rhythm section, but Diz had been a better bassist than Mick was a drummer, and Diz had already been sacked so it was only a matter of time." It was all a bit messy - Mick wasn't the lie-down-and-accept type, and Fish did not let him down gently. "Mick thought Fish had joined his band as a singer," remarks Steve. "Fish vented his anger, he ripped into him!" recalls John. "It was just unnecessary, he didn't want to sack him, he wanted to destroy him!" comments Steve. The situation was difficult for all members of the band: Mark had been rooming with Mick on tour so Mick thought Mark was conspiring against him; meanwhile, Steve, who had been closer to Mick than Fish, felt betrayed. "It ended up a fait accompli that Mick was being sacked, I was very angry at the time as it had all happened behind my back. In a band, you have a camaraderie, a family feeling, but there were too many things happening for me to call Fish a friend," remarks Steve. "I could never really relax with him after all that." Mick's feelings were of shock and disbelief. "I was playing Hammersmith Odeon one night and two weeks later I was standing in the dole queue," says Mick. "It took me an incredibly long time to realise how much of an effect it had on me. I had my dream taken away from me, then I watched them go on and achieve more."

And so, Marillion entered its revolving drummer phase.

First Impressions by Mo Warden

My boyfriend (Andrew) had bought an album that he couldn't stop talking about. He kept forgetting to bring it with him to play for me - in retrospect, I think he probably knew that he'd end up giving it to me. We were living in the West Midlands and when this "mystery band" announced a gig at the Birmingham Odeon, right at our door, Andrew talked everyone into getting tickets. It wasn't difficult, as we all shared fairly common tastes and generally enjoyed the gigs we went to on recommendation of the others in our little group. 'Fairly common' encompassed a lot of genres, from rock to punk, to glam, to folk and more. But it was usually the 'fringe' bands we saw, - the ones who didn't quite fit into the category that the press bestowed onto upon them. I was a single parent at the time. The guys used to buy my tickets and pay my petrol-share, and my neighbour sat with my two kids. Bless them all.

Anyway, there we were, in the queue at the Brum Odeon. What an unusual bunch of people waited with us, some face-painted and costumed, some in painted black leathers, some in corduroy and 'Cornish pastie' shoes - a wide mix. I remember this huge, painted demon at the front of the stage. He acted like a natural, kicked high and involved the crowd to the point of dragging one poor voluntary soul onto the stage to rip into lyrical shreds. I was near the front and - I'm not sure if it was this night or another soon - watched him on one knee at the edge of the stage, leaning forward to sing, six inches from one girl's rapt face. With one light finger under her upturned chin, greasepaint sweat dripping from him, he sang into her eyes. I also remember clearly, the impression that the guitarist and the keyboard player had on me. I came away thinking 'this is one amazing band'. The rest of the gig is a blur - goddamn my failing memory, - but within a week Andrew had bought *'Script For A Jester's Tear'* for me and within a month I'd joined the Web fan club.

'Fugazi'

Pete gets behind the drums and Rothers rehearses (below) at Monmouth

A second album is never a straightforward affair, particularly if the first is a success. In Marillion's case there was pressure from EMI to build on the reputation of *'Script'*, and demonstrate that this band was no one-disc wonder. This was exacerbated by the reasonably fundamental lack of a band member, and to cap it all Marillion had used up most of their material on the debut album, singles and B-sides and now they had to develop something new. Following some time off at the end of the tour, the band locked themselves away at Mountain rehearsal studios in Monmouth, Wales - "Not a professional recording studio, more a hippie commune!" laughs Mark. Attempts to generate some new material were not, initially, a pleasant experience. "I thought the game was up," recalls Mark on the *'Fugazi'* remaster sleeve notes.

"We only really had one song written!" Fortunately, as Mark and the others were to discover, some sort of hiatus would always be necessary before the ideas started to flow.

Meanwhile, the band had to find a new drummer.

More Drummers Than Spinal Tap

Mick's sacking was a break with tradition, in that no replacement had been found prior to his departure. Following adverts and a number of dead-end trial runs,[25] the first to sit on the vacated stool was ex-Camel stickman, Andy Ward. It was clear from the outset he was a good fit with the rest of the band, and as such was virtually given the job without interview. "Andy was one of my favourite drummers, when we bumped into him it was like manna from heaven!" Andy joined in May 1983 and joined the others in Wales to help develop the ideas for the next album.

Andy's first contribution to Marillion history was on 29 May, with the video for 'Garden Party' in which "the band members dress up as 1950s schoolboys and play some hilarious pranks on unsuspecting garden party revellers." Released in June, it reached No.16 and stayed in the Top 40 for four weeks. The UK music journos did not want to be caught out again, as illustrated by top write-ups in a number of rags (including Sounds referring to 'Garden Party' as "the classic single").

This time it was the TV stations' turn to resolve the paradox. Here was a band that were was clearly popular, yet so totally out of synch with what fashion was dictating should be popular. Commented Fish, "We're supposed to be Genesis clones, yet we've had three hits, How come? People get annoyed..." The result was that Marillion's appearances were begrudged rather than welcomed. The band were introduced with a sneer on 'The Old Grey Whistle Test', and cold-shouldered by other 'pop' acts on 'Top of The Pops'. "The thing is, we don't change our style or our image to accommodate those programmes," Fish remarked. "We look the same on 'TOTP' as we do the next night at Bradford City Hall, or at Glastonbury." At least the audiences appreciated the band - fan Judith Mitchell, for example. "I was into the Police and ELO at the time when I saw Marillion play 'Garden Party' on 'TOTP'," recalls Judith. "They kept getting chart hits after that, so I started to follow them."

I'm miming

On one occasion when Marillion were performing 'Garden Party' on 'Top of The Pops', as Fish had lost his voice, he did the show with the lyrics scribbled on a large pad. As the song progressed, he peeled off each page in time to the music.

TV and radio appearances were happening outside the UK as well. Recalls fan Rod Taylor, "I can remember watching 'The New Music', at the time Canada's one-and-only music program, and hearing 'This is the first video from a new UK band called Marillion, and the song is called 'Garden Party'." And the rest, as they say..." Dutch fan Jolijne Viergever remembers the first time she heard the band. "I heard some tracks - 'Market Square Heroes', 'Garden Party' and part of 'Script' - on a radio programme, and it just gave me the shivers!" she recalls. "They were introduced as a very promising band that had released a single last year."

Meanwhile, back with Mr Ward, all was going well as Marillion departed on its first foray across the channel, with a series of festivals in Germany, Denmark and Holland, as well as a few dates in the UK, including on 17 June 1983, the CND festival at Glastonbury. "We were hip for an instant!" chuckled Fish on the *'Fugazi'* sleeve notes.

As the band travelled together, it started to become apparent that Andy liked his drink a bit more than was strictly appropriate. This issue seemed to be exacerbated by the demanding life on the road, but he was likeable and a good drummer... and besides, who didn't like a drink? So he stayed.

First 'Assassing', Last 'Grendel' by Adrian Holmes

Having just finished the final exam of my HND, myself and a few friends piled into my aging Transit van to head for the CND Festival at Glastonbury. The festival in those days was a long way from the huge, smoothly run affair that it has come to be (and a fraction of the cost - at £12!). The bill was diverse to say the least! Everything from UB40 to King Sunny Ade, and lurking somewhere well down the bill, Marillion. Myself and Neil (the other fan in our group) were unsure of what to expect from the band's performance. Mick Pointer had left and ex-Camel drummer Andy Ward was now occupying the stool.

Having arrived at the site on Thursday night, we parked the van (in sight of the stage!), pitched our tents and got rather drunk watching 'The Blues Brothers' in the film tent. We spent most of Friday chilling out in the scorching sunshine (and getting sunburnt) and letting the music wash over us. Around lunchtime, we spotted a large, long-haired individual wandering through the crowd - Mr. D. Dick himself! We wandered over and chatted with Fish for quite a few minutes and learned that we would get to hear a brand new song called 'Assassin' (sic) in the set later on. From Fish's description of the Eastern influences included in the track, it sounded very intriguing.

When Marillion took to the pyramid stage, it was in front of a crowd who for the most part hadn't got a clue who they were. However, despite a far from perfect sound mix, the band soon started to win over the audience. Andy Ward was playing well and the 'new' track 'Assassin', with its long build up and rocky main section, boded well for the second album. The highlight of the set had to be the closing 'Forgotten Sons', which after Fish's introduction outlining the subject matter of the lyrics, went down a storm with the Glastonbury crowd. I think the band made quite a few new friends that day.

A few months on and we headed off to the second main festival of the summer: Reading. Once again we didn't know what to expect from Marillion; having played a few festivals in Europe, the band had just returned from their first trip to The States and there were rumours of another change of drummer!

The band had been elevated up the bill from Glastonbury and were due to play late Saturday afternoon. Having picked up our American versions of the Script tour shirts from one of the merchandise stalls, we fought our way forward through the crowd to try and get a reasonable view of the right hand stage, where the band were due to play. When at last the billowing white curtains opened, the stage was covered in smoke... and two sets of drums ?!?!? We found out later that although John Marter was now occupying the drum stool, Andy Ward had specifically asked to play this gig as he was really looking forward to it. As a result, we heard the only outing of the band with both a drummer and a percussionist.

The opening notes coming over the PA were not what we expected to hear... 'Grendel'? Sure enough, the whole of Marillion's first epic was to be the opening song of the set. It was my first experience of hearing and seeing this track live and although it's not one of my favourites, it was still great to witness it being performed. As the band had had a reasonably big hit single during the summer with 'Garden Party', the crowd were more aware of the band than the Glastonbury audience. However, there were quite a few puzzled faces during 'Grendel' (especially when Fish donned the mask for the closing section).

As the set progressed with more well-known tracks from *'Script'*, the crowd soon warmed to the band. The new track, now subtly retitled 'Assassing', was aired again, sounding stronger than ever. 'Garden Party' really got the crowd going and once more the band triumphed over a potentially hostile festival audience.

Following the release of the 'Garden Party' single on 6 June, the band set off to the US for a flit down the East Coast starting at Youngstown, Ohio on 14 July. It wasn't a great success. For most of the band, the US club circuit was a sobering experience; for Andy it was very stressful and anything but sobering. Andy was not a happy man. Unbeknown to Marillion before he joined, the reason he had left Camel the year before was that his playing had been limited following an attempt to slash his wrists. He frequently argued with other members of the band (though sometimes deservedly; Fish was probably incorrect to say "We shouldn't be supporting this shit," in reference to Todd Rundgren, though perhaps he had reason) and was uncomfortable to be associated with such upstarts. To quote Andy, "they had a ridiculous opinion of themselves!" Recalls Pete, "Some nights he was fine and some nights he wasn't so fine, which was a shame. I think he was going through a bit of a depressing patch." "Andy was a great drummer and a good friend," remarks Rothers. "It was very sad what happened with him."

Sad indeed, and ironic given that his drink problem was no worse than those several others in the band would experience before the decade was out. "He was a man before his time," comments Mark. It became inevitable that the band would be looking for another drummer before long, leaving the band more disappointed than anything as Andy really had seemed to fit the bill. The incidents started to pile up - the can of coke Andy would nurse and sip from all morning. Explains Steve, "I'd brought a half bottle of whisky with me, he had nicked it and was topping up his cans!" Other incidences included driving through Harlem throwing empty beer bottles out of the window with the rest of the band saying 'please, don't do that!' Things came to a head at the Holiday Inn in New York, the day before the performance at Pier 84 on 9 March. The band and Paul Lewis were attempting to check in (according to Paul, the rooms weren't ready), when Andy went off to get some fags. "All of them came out of the machine at once!" remembers Mark. "He started giving them out, asking around who wanted some..." This didn't go down well with the hotel staff, who told the band they couldn't stay. This proved too much for the hapless Andy. "We asked him, 'What do you want to do?'" recalls Mark. "He wanted to go home, so we started planning to cancel the tour." Remembers Paul, "I booked Andy's flight ticket home that afternoon." Nobody plucked up the courage to tell him before the gig, however!

not a hand out

During a take in the middle of the recording for *'Fugazi'*, Mark stopped playing due to there being a hand reaching through from behind his keyboards. He assumed it was Steve but on looking up he saw him 5 yards away... and nobody else was anywhere within reach! His protestations didn't stop the merciless laughter of the rest of the band!

The night of the Pier gig was the last straw, if one had been needed: following the aforementioned row, triggered when Fish received a rotten peach to the chest by an overzealous Todd Rundgren fan. "Fish turned on the person in the audience," remembers John. "The audience turned on the band from that point." After the gig Andy was informed that his flight had been booked, and Paul drove him to the airport for 6am the next morning. "I checked him in and waited until he went airside to try and be sure he got the flight," explains Paul. And then there were four again.[26]

As the remaining four followed Andy home, they were faced with the daunting task of another Reading festival looming before them. The band were not too downhearted - explains Steve, "It was the most fun we'd had in the US, it was all so new to us!"

Time was short, so John Arnison proposed session drummer John Marter (who had previously played with Mr Big - the UK version who'd had a hit with 'Romeo' - and ex-Whitesnaker Bernie Marsden's SOS) to fill the gap. Explains Rothers, "John was never really in the band, he was always just a stand-in." Following a hasty warm-up two days before at the Royal Court Theatre in Liverpool, he was up and running in time for Reading Festival on 27 August. Marillion played second on the bill, just before a recently reformed Black Sabbath (with Ian Gillan). Recalls Mark, "We were on one stage and Black Sabbath were on the other stage following us. They had these enormous plastic stones, like Stonehenge. While we were playing their stage caught fire!" Black Sabbath were, if you'll pardon the pun, paranoid about being upstaged - as demonstrated by Reading Council's U-turn on permission for Marillion to use lasers in their show. Explains Mark, "We found out that the council had already agreed, but Don Arden (Sabbath's manager) knobbled the council people so they refused the application!"

In the crowd on that day was fan Andy Rotherham, seeing Marillion for the first time as he attended in support of his then-favourite band, The Stranglers. Marillion opened with 'Grendel', and what an opening. Recalls Andy, who was next to a remotely placed speaker stack at the time, "They literally blew up the PA speakers, I spent the rest of the gig listening to the distorted sound of Marillion through the remnants of the stack!" Even through the distortion it was enough. "I just took it from there!"

The encore saw Andy Ward replacing John on drums. According to Pete, "Andy just turned up, bless him. We got him to play the gong and a bit of percussion towards the end of the show, just to sort of say thank you, really." By the time Marillion left, the crowd was so exhausted it could only manage a lukewarm response to the main attraction.

With batteries recharged, the Marillos returned back to the studio to lay down new versions of 'Market Square Heroes' and 'Three Boats Down From The Candy'. "They were originally to try John Marter out in the studio with Nick Tauber," says Pete. Nothing was wasted however, as the songs were later included on the 12-inch release of 'Punch And Judy'. Then it was time for a second bash at those West Atlantic shores, playing five nights at New York's illustrious Radio City Hall in support of Rush. It all sounded wonderful: "The stage was enormous - we had to take a lift to get to it!" recalls Mark. However, if the last tour attempt had been a crisis, this was an abject disaster. The band were restricted to ten-minute sound checks and limitless rules and regulations about what they could and could not do, but before the gig there would invariably be a Peter Gabriel or a Genesis track playing. And when they actually walked out on the stage, the fans treated them[27] like unwashed peasants. It was awful, terrible, humbling. "The audience hated us, I remember one guy standing on a seat in the front row with his trousers down!" remembers Mark. "It was a nightmare!" By the end of the stint, the guys used to travel up in the lift saying, "It's Christians and Lions time - off we go!" After the five days were up, the boys went home, despondent.

In the end John Marter was not to be - he was a fine drummer (according to Mark, "Steady but not enormous flair") but, once again, he was not considered up to the band's ever-increasing demands. Comments Pete, "He was solid, but not as musical as Andy or Ian. He was also a little over-eager for the incumbents. Laughs Mark, "He talked himself out of the gig!" And then there were four, again!

One good thing came out of New York, or so it seemed, a young, talented drummer called Jonathan Mover. Ironically Jonathan, who had picked up copies of *'Script'* and 'Grendel' when he was in the UK playing with Toyah Wilcox, had not been enamoured with Marillion on his first listen. "I was so not into it, merely for the fact that too much was blatantly stolen from Genesis," he says. "I think I played it once or twice and shelved it for good." As these things happen in the music industry, Nick Tauber made a comment to Phil Spalding (Toyah's bassist) which was passed on to Jonathan. By the time the band came to New York the loop had been closed. "I got the call to meet them if I was interested in auditioning for the gig," recalls Jonathan. "Of course I said I was interested, figuring maybe the newer material would/could have some potential or it would at least be a stepping stone to more." Unfortunately, his first live experience was to watch Marillion's ill-fated support act at Radio City Hall. "I felt terrible for Fish, all made up with his grease paint and believing in himself, but the audience just laughed and booed. Meeting the band though, I liked everyone very much and wanted to get back to London for music reasons, so I accepted the offer to audition."

Auditions happened over a two-day period a couple of weeks later, with Jonathan being one of the last people to play. Everything went well - with only a twenty-minute try-out, he got the gig and was even offered a place on Fish's floor. "We were inseparable," says Jonathan. In what was fast becoming a tradition, on 1 October 1983 Jonathan was rushed off to Baunatal in Germany to play a gig that was broadcast live on the radio. Then it was back to the Old Mill House studio in Monmouth, Wales, to continue the writing sessions where the others had left off. Things started out fine, but before long Fish started to have misgivings about the new drummer. "It was all very exciting to be doing things now on a 'professional' level, or so I thought," recalls Jonathan. "It didn't last very long... just enough time for me to co-write and record the demos for 'Punch And Judy', 'Incubus' and 'Jigsaw'." As the uncompromising Fish remarked on the *'Fugazi'* remaster sleeve notes, "I didn't like him or his technical abilities which I thought were out of line with our quintessentially British style."

The level of comments became increasingly barbed, until one night they reached a level that was beyond the pale. What started as an open discussion about whether *'Fugazi'* could be a concept album, ended with Fish saying some things he probably shouldn't have done. "That was the straw that broke my back - whether or not he is anti-Semitic[28] or was just using that to get to me, his remarks were tasteless and completely uncalled for," says Jonathan, who gave back as good as he got. "I firmly told Fish where to go and woke up the next morning to find out that he told the band it was him or me... obviously it wasn't going to be him." So that was that.

picking up the pieces

By now the boys were getting distinctly worried. It was agreed that another session player would come in on a purely a temporary basis, so that recording could start in earnest. John had someone in mind, a chap called Ian Mosley, who had already applied for the post shortly after Marillion had accepted Jonathan Mover. The band's initial reaction, according to John Arnison, had been that Ian was "too old!" but John rang him and suggested he join the band up in Monmouth. He arrived at about tea time and joined Fish in the canteen. "As soon as I walked in, I saw the glint in his eye and I knew we would get on well," remarks Ian. "I asked Fish what had happened with Jonathan Mover, he said, 'He's American.' So I said, you'll get on well with my (American) wife then - Fish just put his head in his hands..." The next thing Ian knew, the door to the canteen had been knocked off its hinges by the arrival of another. "That was Mark, he hasn't changed much!" laughs Ian. Incidentally, all ended quite well for quick-thinking Jonathan who went on to work for Steve Hackett on his supergroup project GTR. As he explains, "Ian's name was on Marillion's audition list from a few months before, so when I heard that Ian got the call after I split, I called Steve Hackett to see if he was looking to fill that spot. He had just finished auditioning quite a few drummers and had chosen one. I convinced him to hear one more..."

Back in Monmouth, Ian's cool personality and obvious experience worked their collective magic. "My first reaction was that I was enjoying the playing, I wasn't thinking of the long term but I knew we were getting on well, says Ian. "They rang two days later and said he was the one!" smiles John.

On 14 November, a stabilised Marillion went to record the album at the Manor studios, at Shipton-On-Cherwell near Oxford. The 15th century building was then owned by Richard Branson, and such names as Mike Oldfield (with *'Tubular Bells'*) and The Sex Pistols had previously passed though its hallowed halls. Once again, Nick Tauber was tapped for producer, and Simon Hanhart as sound engineer. "We went into the studio unprepared, to say the least. We hadn't even finished the writing," remarks Pete. Plenty went wrong, including the attempts to record on dodgy equipment, two 24-track analogue decks that suffered continuously from synchronisation problems, resulting in minutes of

support slots

The crew hired a girl in bondage gear to come on stage after Fish with a big whip. We were on stage with Marillion jamming 'Margaret' for their last encore when she came on. Unfortunately she didn't just go after Fish, but anyone else. Fish and Pete and Steve all had wireless systems and ran off, that left us Pendragon guys who were plugged in with leads. Fortunately we got off safely in the end.

Peter Gee, Pendragon

delay every time a playback was attempted. According to Pete, "It was just a nightmare!" Eventually things got too much for Nick, with the pressure of the recordings (and certain habitual behaviours) taking their toll. "Nick had a bit of a domestic problem," explains Ian. "He wanted to work on Christmas Day - that's always a bit of a giveaway." The band started to take action as Nick's attention to detail went beyond the call of duty. "He was making me change my drum heads every day," remarks Ian. "Once, he asked me to change them when they'd only been used for half an hour, I left them, went away for a bit and came back and said how's that? Nick agreed it was much better!" With incidents like this, the band decided to keep Nick out of the loop, with the plan to co-produce with Simon. Recalls Pete, "We'd just managed to talk Nick out of finishing the project when a chap came down from EMI, who wasn't privy to all of this, and he persuaded Nick to carry on." So much for that.

Things got so fraught that John Arnison decided to insert a tour at the end of the year, to give everyone a breather and to allow the engineering works to catch up.. "I put in a tour to keep going despite Nick Tauber," explains John. "How about rehearsing?" asked Ian at the time. Nobody seemed that bothered apart from Pete, who helped Ian learn the two albums' worth of material in two weeks flat. After all, Pete had been there before, and besides, thought Pete, Ian had raised the bar. "Ian was such a good drummer, I spent a couple of tours wondering if I was good enough!" he recalls.

To Ian, the live dates were, "magical." As he explains, "When we walked out on stage I felt something special, I can't put my finger on it, I can't pin it down." This was no starry-eyed remark from a young fan. "Before Marillion, I'd played with some top musicians - you can get four or five fantastic musicians together and they won't always get that same magic." The rest of the band was similarly fired up - leading to Ian being offered a permanent position on the drummers stool halfway through the tour. "John came up to me on the tour bus, he said, you're an official member of the band now, if you want to be!" And he did, following a brief negotiation about pay. "I said to John, I can't live on seventy five quid a week! So we all got a wage rise to 150 quid, I was really popular after that!" This was still a pay cut for Ian, but that was of far less concern than the coup of taking a full time position in a band on the up, playing the music that he loved.

On their return there was an album to finish, and the time slot at the Manor had run out. Thus began a frantic chase around various London studios, still with Simon Hanhart as engineer. It didn't help Pete's situation that his Mum had a heart attack half way through the process, leaving Pete rushing back and forth to Aylesbury in between sessions. The studios included Odyssey and Wessex, as well as Maison Rouge and Sarm, where the assistant engineer happened to be a certain Dave Meegan. "We asked if we could take him with us, 'cos he was so good!" recalls Mark. As Marillion darted around London to complete the recording, Dave ended up working with the band at a number of studios. It became his job to ensure all the equipment was set up correctly each day, quite a challenge when there was a change of studio involved. Recalls Dave, "We'd finish one night, I'd have to pack up and have it all set up in the new studio the next morning!" This included the intricate job of lining up tape machines, which would take an hour by itself!

Deadlines continued to be missed and schedules were

Geezabun!

Fish had (and still has) a habit of telling stories and jokes between songs. A regular was: how does an elephant tell you it's hungry? It says Geezabun! This works if said in a Scots accent while impersonating an elephant. According to Jeroen Schipper, "It became standard procedure at gigs and members of the audience would bombard the stage with buns at the appropriate moment."

Marillion: 'Foxtrot'

Marillion are a completely different sound. New and original, the band defies pigeon-holing. Their unique blend of early GENESIS and late GENESIS, puts them at the forefront of modern rock bands who sound like GENESIS. According to the sleeve notes, Marillion's musical roots derive from "jazz, soul, funk, rock, blues and not GENESIS, no siree." Strange then that this album should start with 'Watcher Of The Pies' which sounds remarkably like the famous GENESIS track 'Watcher Of The Skies' with the letters 'sk' replaced by 'p' throughout. "This makes me really furious," said lead singer Fish in a recent TV interview. "It's like saying our concept track 'Supper's Nearly Ready' is like the GENESIS concept track 'Supper's Ready'." And it must be annoying for them, because it's plainly untrue. As for the album - I thought it was brilliant. There's only one comparison for a band this good - the Seventies supergroup, GENESIS."

'Spitting Image' Annual 1985

overrun. On one occasion, a man threatened to break into the studio wielding a machete. Fair play, he did have most of an orchestra waiting! Exhaustion was the order of the day. "I remember one occasion when I was falling asleep at the desk, and Simon Hanhart was falling asleep in the room behind!" smiles Dave. Adds Simon, "We'd all roll up at lunchtime and then sit there staring at each other, we were so tired! Nobody thought of stopping and taking a week off to consolidate, then blitzing it." Eventually Tony Platt, producer of a number of albums for Iron Maiden, stepped in to help with the remixing at Abbey Road. According to Mark, "He mixed 'Incubus' and 'Fugazi' at the same time as the rest of the tracks were being mixed by Simon, to speed things up."

Finally it was finished. While Dave also checked in for a few days' hospital leave at the end of the process, diagnosed with "extreme exhaustion," (says Dave, "It's stuck in my memory - enjoyable but painful!") the band could only hope that the birth would be less painful than the gestation.

'Fugazi'

"Where 'Script' *was bedsit thoughts,* 'Fugazi' *was hotel thoughts," said Fish. Furthermore, where* 'Script' *was wistful and grief-stricken,* 'Fugazi' *was barbed and cynical - "Anger at its finest," as one fan wrote. The album takes its name from a British Army slang term, meaning "Fucked Up, Got Ambushed, Zipped In." It was popularized by US Servicemen during the Vietnam conflict, and Fish picked up the term in a book called 'Nam' by Mark Baker.*

The album was heavy - probably the reason for the band's misplaced reputation as a heavy metal band - and, with Ian Mosley taking over on drums, noticeably tighter and more rhythmically interesting. According to fan Michael Huang, "The music represented a large leap forward from 'Script'. Shedding many of their Genesis influences, they began to forge a sound of their own."

'Assassing' was originally written about Diz Minnitt, but extended to include Mick Pointer. "We basically sacked them, it's about how hard it is," Fish recalled. The Islamic flavour to the track was inspired by an album Fish was loaned by one of his heroes - Peter Hammill, formerly of Van Der Graaf generator, and a support act on the Script tour. The track shows considerable musical development by the band, fusing far more contemporary sounds with their existing palate.

'Punch And Judy' is a cynical mediation on marriage. It concerns a husband who, according to Fish, "takes out his frustrations on his wife, using her as a [...] punch bag for his inadequacies." He further explained the notion powering the lyric for this and the next two songs of "How couples in the '60s would go to Hops, then maybe get married via the idea of perfection that the music gave them. Then of course they'd get divorced, the music would let them down." The odd 5/8 syncopated verse rhythm, inspired by temporary drummer Jonathan Mover, certainly makes for an odd choice of single!

'Jigsaw', described by Fish as "About the relationship that splits up and forever comes together again [getting] worse each time."

Although he still feels the lyric makes sense, he has also described it as "particularly wordy!" The music on the first two verses seems almost nursery-rhyme like: guitar and keyboards chiming like a child's xylophone, underlying the sense of conciliation in Fish's words. The chorus could not be more different, as Ian Mosley batters his skins into submission, and Pete Trewavas's bass thuds like punches. As it gives way to the solo, Steve Rothery creates one of those soaring, melancholic guitar lines for which he is justifiably lauded.

'Emerald Lies', describes an accusation of infidelity; the sense of power before the accusation is made, and the realization that, though proven false, the accusation has destroyed the relationship. Perhaps the most straight-forward song on the album, it nevertheless showcases some superb percussion work by Mr Mosley - imagine Mick Pointer handling it! It would prove not to be a band favourite - by the Misplaced tour only the opening bars remained as an intro to 'Script'.

'She Chameleon' describes the whole groupie phenomena, which the band had begun to experience on the Script tour. "Who was using who?" Fish asked. Perhaps the most obviously retro-track, the song betrays its 1983 roots.

Another Islamic-influenced track, 'Incubus', is a slow-burning track about a porn director whose former lover and lead actress has just opened as the lead in a legit West End play. Spying her spurned former paramour in the audience, she freezes, not knowing whether he'll reveal her secret to the press. Much of the track is built on a groove until, the director's hurt building to a dangerous level, the band take us into a waltz. The director's Machiavellian manoeuvres are like a dance - Rothery unleashes wave upon wave of heart rending passion from his spiralling guitar lines - then the bile's really unleashed! The actress, mute on the stage, writes her own death notices, and he's watching it all, a glint of pure evil in his eye...

The closing, title track details Fish in mid panic attack on the underground en route to the Marquee in Wardour Street. On a come-down from LSD, Fish said "Viewing the other occupants of the carriage, it summed up the album and my views on life at the time, 'Fugazi' we were."

The song has several movements - akin to 'Script' in this regard. Initially based purely on the observations of the other travellers, Mark Kelly's piano gives way to steadily more edgy synth lines. From here, we move outside the carriage to consider unhappy relationships, racial unrest, prostitution and our treatment of war veterans. Then, as the whole world dissolves into a fearful smear of guitar string scrapes, screams and doom-laden keyboards, Pete and Ian paint a quasi-militaristic regime of cold war nuclear paranoia.

Finally, as Fish desperately asks to be shown inspiration for a way out of this terrible mess, the band become the pipers of the apocalypse and Fish is swept along with the crowd, as it marches blindly on its way to its doom.

We would have to wait until the next album for some optimism.

Mark Wilkinson described his cover brief as "illustrating the Faustian 'payback' after the trappings of success had kicked in."

The jester lies, sheathed within the halo of distortion, whilst around him, his material gains litter his hotel room. Successful, but no more content than he was in his bedsit, the jester has merely exchanged one hell for another. Along with the returning chameleon - 'She Chameleon' was a reworked *'Script'*-era track - we see our first magpie. One for sorrow, no less.

With one of the weirdest perspectives ever seen, Mark has described the finished cover as "overworked", whereas Fish declared it "a clean acid trip".

Unleashed Melody

Following the same format as *'Script'*, EMI released 'Punch And Judy' as an advance party on 30 January 1984. "The song suggested a single," recalled Fish. At least, it did to him - he had informed EMI that it would be the next single when only the lyrics (and not the music) had been written! Things worked out fine - writing in Sounds, Jay Williams commented that, "The most common criticism levelled at Marillion is that they are irrelevant, but this is simply the direct result of preconceptions. When you come up against something so brilliantly sharp and at the same time so bittersweet as 'Punch and Judy', it's very hard to see why." All the same the single did not fare too well, only reaching 29th position despite considerable publicity.

The album itself was released on March 12, a month after the tour had commenced. The expectant audience was a mix of both old-timer fans and new recruits who had joined up on hearing *'Script'*. "I remember queueing for hours at HMV in Middlesbrough to buy *'Fugazi'*," laughs Rich Dowson. "It was release day and the boys were there doing a signing session. For some reason I was too terrified to speak when I got to Fish. Still, I was only 15 at the time!" For Lee Clark it was a revelation - "I fell in love with *'Fugazi'* and have followed the band ever since." US fan Ray Achord was attracted to Marillion through their appearance: "Every other week I would grab a Kerrang! magazine from the counter of the record store at my local mall. One particular issue had a full page picture of Fish in make-up, the headline, "*'Fugazi'*... what a scorcher. The image was shocking and strange, and I had to find out what it was all about. The same store also got in the British Marillion imports, so I bought *'Fugazi'* and though it seemed extremely strange to me at first, I listened to it many times, and fell in love with it!"

Not all the fans liked *'Fugazi'*. While some found that the despair of *'Fugazi'* matched their own angst, others saw it as indulgent, the lyrics a little too complex, the melodies self-serving. Comments fan Geoff Boswell, "Fish swallowed a thesaurus." Fish agrees with the sentiment. In one interview he remarked, "The danger is that you can become so involved with words that it ends up like masturbation. *'Fugazi'* became too wordy from an ego point of view." For Fish, *'Fugazi'* was very personal: it was his own anger that was being explored in public. Perhaps anger was not a subject to be shouted about? It is for this reason that current Marillion vocalist Steve Hogarth has always resisted performing any of the songs on *'Fugazi'*, believing them too personal to Fish.

'Fugazi' sold well and as a second album it established Marillion as more than a one-album wonder. However it sold less than its predecessor. In April, 'Assassing' was released as a single, and made it to No.22 in the charts.

The Fugazi tour was extensive and highly successful. One fan to pick up on events was Chris Brockwell: "I'd seen the band at the Zero-6 in Southend, it was a half-full, midweek crowd, a good reaction, in all honesty I don't recall it that well, but liked it enough to catch them again. The next time was at the Cliffs Pavilion. There was a very psychedelic light show, Fish burst thro' the stage backdrop, he took the piss big time by getting the idiots there to bleat like sheep! There was loads of heckling, Fish loved it, he slaughtered any wisecrack or jibe, the man was larger then life, I was caught hook line and sinker!" It also included a few nights, 9-11 March, at the Hammersmith Odeon with Pendragon as support. Recalls Peter Gee, "It was also a dream come true for us - the Hammersmith Odeon was the venue we most wanted to play in the UK!" Off-stage, spirits were as high as ever, with nights being packed with the kind of party fun that would need a whole book in itself. In June the band also managed to get across to the US and Canada again. One member of the audience was Dave Meegan, who was over staying with a friend in New York when he saw they were playing. "I called John Arnison up and asked if there was any chance I could come along!" recalls Dave.

Moving On

Following *'Fugazi'*, the band found itself on a plateau of its own creation. Having sated both label and fans, Marillion had 'made it' and was guaranteed a living for a few years at least. It would be folly in the extreme to rock this status quo. However, not everything was perfect - as fan Michael Huang noted, "Both *'Script'* and *'Fugazi'* were inaccessible to a certain degree (the latter more so) and while they enjoyed fairly widespread popularity throughout the UK, they felt they could do something different." In addition, the old complaint continued to surface.

Genesis. Bloody Genesis. Every interview, every review mentioned the G-word, even though many of the journos had little knowledge of what they were comparing to. It was starting to grate with the boys. "Christ, I only saw Genesis once!" remarked Fish. "One and a half hours isn't enough to build a career on!" "I was never even a Genesis fan," laughs Mark, but he wasn't laughing at the time - he commented in an interview, "We're actually throwing out ideas, good ideas at that, because we are scared people will think they sound too much like Genesis."

Meanwhile, external pressures continued to build on the band. Not least in that a number of people, including Peter Hammill and Peter Mensch, had taken Fish to one side and suggested he should go solo. They cut no ice, at least not at the time, "Fish wanted the band to succeed, not a solo career," recalls Mark. Besides, with John Arnison ensuring that the next tour was always just around the corner, there was barely time to sit down, never mind plan a sabbatical. At the end of the tour it was time to go home for Christmas, fall back, regroup and do something radical.

Marillion and Me by Mark Wilkinson

I've only been obsessive about one band - Pink Floyd was really where it started and ended with me. I was a musical snob when first I encountered Marillion, so my early impressions were rather perjurious I'm afraid.

I was given a coupla tickets for a show one evening and went along for my first glimpse of the band live. I was astonished that it could exist...post punk...post (ahem) prog rock... post just about every damn thing that had come along for the past 10 years. The bastard child of Genesis and Beowulf was not my idea of a fun

night out! But I was in a minority of one that night. Some time later I went to see them at the Hammy Odeon with Jo Mirowski. Jo leaned over halfway through, when the crowd had reached the 7th plane of Nirvana and said "They're gonna be huge!" I wasn't so sure. Although I loved doing the surreal imagery I was asked to produce for the album and single sleeves, the music left me stone cold. I couldn't see that they had a shelf life beyond an album or two.

What I hadn't got about Marillion became clear, once I had witnessed a glimpse behind the curtain in Oz. They believed in what they were doing musically and progressed (in the true meaning of that word) album to album, very quickly. Fish wrote his home thoughts, borne of experience, dressed them up in costumes and concocted an original idea. The band shifted their influences and developed a voice of their own, which they wanted to communicate to their fans. When I saw them a year later at the Reading Festival, everything was exponentially better than before. Fish had stopped arsing about with a rubber plant on stage, taken to editing out his more florid prose and worked the audience like a seasoned pro. They were a different band. If not quite the road to Damascus for me, it was a revelatory experience. I spent the next few years trying to tell my other pals that "actually, despite what you might think, Marillion are fucking great... forget what you read in Q magazine and listen to them." They didn't of course. I dare say if I hadn't worked for them I would not have given them a cat's chance in hell either.

It means a lot to follow a band for so long and to feel that no sell-out was involved in their longevity. That's a rare thing. I gave up on Pink Floyd after *'The Wall'*... too much whingeing. I'll listen to most things now without prejudice... perhaps that's the legacy that Marillion and Fish have left behind for me. I've worked for this band and then Fish for almost as long as I've been a professional artist/designer. It's been a rich, varied canvas to work on.

For that alone I owe them a huge debt of thanks.

NOTES: 1 Andy Glass went on to play for Solstice, a band that would support Marillion frequently at the Marquee and elsewhere. **2** Neil Cockle now deals in kitchens. In a bizarre twist, he supplied Running Frog studios in Windsor, while Mick Pointer's band Arena were rehearsing! **3** Coopers Payern Ltd, Slough. **4** Neil went on to join Robert and The Remoulds, no less. **5** This was free of charge to advertise, later taken over by Melody Maker. **6** These were written by one Darrell Kirsop. **7** 53 Quainton Road. **8** By 1994 this was called Leo's. **9** This was not the reasonably famous, US band of the same name. **10** The set list also included 'The Web', 'Skyline Drifter', 'Herne The Hunter', 'The Haunting Of Gill House', 'Time For Sale' and 'Garden Party'. **11** 'Institution Waltz' was also written at Anthony Hall. **12** A Roman road running from Buckinghamshire to London. **13** 'Girl' featured future Def Leppard guitarist Phil Collen. **14** This house also became the first home of the fan club. **15** John, Nigel and Jack Barry (the owner, who used to run a fish and chip shop in King's Lynn) used to hang around in the bar together. **16** Gained a reputation as the band's first bootlegger. It is confirmed that he asked Diz for copies of tapes that later appeared as bootlegs. And it wasn't Diz! **17** According to Andy, "Marillion kindly gave us Marquee supports which led to headlines and the relationship only ended when Solstice split in '85." **18** According to Diz, from a Saxon-like band in Northampton. **19** Ashleigh Goodall's brother, Howard Goodall, wrote the 'Blackadder' theme tune! **20** July 26 and 27 at EMI studios. **21** And later, Def Leppard, Queensryche and Metallica! **22** Not to mention Bernie Marsden's SOS band, with John Marter on drums. **23** Fish wrote 'Going Under' here. **24** These dates were immortalized in the video *'Recital Of The Script'*. **25** Including an audition for the drummer from Not Quite Red Fox, according to Diz. **26** After his departure, the papers were rife with rumours that Andy Ward was to join Kajagoogoo. It was not to be. **27** Among the audience was Mike Portnoy, later of Dream Theater and Transatlantic. **28** The lyrics to 'White Russian' four years later would suggest not.

chapter two childhood's end/1985-1988

"The life of a rock & roll band
will last as long as you
can look down into the audience
and see yourself"

Bruce Springsteen

For bands that experience the level of success that Marillion had discovered, there are three options. First, take the money and run. Second, milk the cow until the cash runs out, repeating the same formula ad infinitum. Third, reinvent itself as a pop band, denying its history (typical of the era) and throwing its principles on the pyre of commerciality.

Marillion created option four. Build from scratch, ignoring the past, ignoring the fans, ignoring the pressures imposed by the record company, by the recording industry, by the pundits with their fingers on the supposed pulses of the listeners. Wipe the slate clean and carve upon it something beautiful, original, stunning. Leave behind, once and for all, any criticisms about being throwbacks, irrelevant niche players, copycat artists.

As the formulation began to take shape, everyone in the band reached the same conclusion about the paradox they were heading towards. The next album would be a concept album, an idea inextricably linked with the progressive rock label that had so constrained the popularity of the band. And yet, it would be mainstream, accessible, popular. Furthermore time would prove it to be hugely successful. The last laugh would be with Marillion, as it played the fashion game by being resolutely unfashionable, and won. But in winning, it would pay the price.

'Misplaced Childhood'

Following the end of the Fugazi tour, nobody in the band knew what form the future would take. Considerable touring had left little time to think about what would come next; what was more, it had been physically and emotionally draining for the band, who were paying the price for their commitment. Their primary goal was to return to Aylesbury for a well-earned rest.

The Answers To The Questions

Time slowed to a near standstill as Marillion recovered lost energies. Some musical ideas were being developed at home, with the occasional phone call or meeting to enable cross-fertilisation. According to Fish in the sleeve notes to the remaster of the coming album, the lyrical and musical structures received an unexpected boost following a "white knuckle ride roller coaster of a night" after an unusually powerful acid trip!

Soon, all agreed the time was right to collect together the ideas and start the writing process proper. John Arnison had arranged a six-week stint across October and November of 1984, at Barwell Court near Chessington, a huge old Victorian house hired out as a residential rehearsal studio. Writing proceeded at a steady, relaxed pace, immediately obvious to the five was the lack of pressure to be creative. Pete noted, "There was none of the mayhem compared to *'Fugazi'*." After the commercial pressures imposed on the last recording, everyone felt truly let off the hook. "We were fed up with the whole idea of chasing a hit single and were preparing to turn our backs on commercial success." comments Mark. Pete continues, "The whole process was so much easier than *'Fugazi'*, when we were still working out the writing partnerships. We'd got comfortable with the things we liked playing on, and which of each other's ideas would work together."

The first track to be trialled was based on a new riff from Steve and a set of lyrics from Fish. The riff came about as Steve tried to demonstrate to his then-fiancée Jo how he came up with ideas. "I wonder if we would have written it if she'd asked me if there was anything good on the telly instead!" Steve laughs. "I remember thinking, this is very catchy!" says Pete. While the band were happy with the sentiment of the lyrics, they squirmed a bit about the subject, a girl called Kay (middle name Leigh, who had been

Fish's girlfriend until *'Script'*); four of the five knew her well. Despite the doubts, the title stuck. The music for the 'Misplaced Rendezvous' section of 'Bitter Suite' was also written by Steve for his wife-to-be. "Funny that it became part of our most successful album," he smiles. Steve's coming marriage also meant he would no longer be a drinking partner to Fish. "Until *'Fugazi'*, we did all those things you do when you're young, free and single," explains Steve.

As the musical and lyrical ideas took shape, they started to look a bit too like a complete story than individual songs. The decision to make a concept album was not

Waiting to play - getting dressed for the Milton Keynes Garden Party

conscious, it was happening by default. "It's just the way those songs turned out," Mark remembers. "We were so useless at coming up with starts and finishes to songs!" Before long each member concluded that it was the only way to go. Despite the obvious comparisons drawn with the 'proggist' '70s, the band was unrepentant. "We just wanted to do what excited us," Mark continues. Not everyone was comfortable with this laissez-faire attitude, according to Fish in the sleeve notes to the remaster. "Outside our creative circle there was a nervous but respectful air that questioned our decision to pursue such an obviously uncommercial venture." Seeking to reassure the wider public, the boys were very keen to express how positive they felt, remarking in interviews that the release would be "our most successful yet." This was not as prophetic as it sounds: "He said that about every album," laughs Mark Kelly.

In the end, whatever pressures were coming from outside the band, from within they felt unassailable. As Fish commented, "With this one we've gone in and said fuck it; if you want us, you take us, if not screw you!" The attitude paid off, creativity flowed, and the first side of the album was virtually written in the first two weeks of the band's residence at Barwell Court.

The budget-priced *'Real To Reel'* live album was released Monday 5 November 1984. The material was recorded by Simon Hanhart at a number of dates, including Montreal, Ontario and New York. "I had ten days away, it was great!" says Simon, who then had the task of mixing the album at Rick Parfitt's home studio in Surrey. This was the band's first

keep it clean

"At the time of Marillion playing several nights at Hammersmith Odeon and minutes before the band were due to be on stage to 3,500 people, we were huddled in the dressing room discussing the merits of different dishwashers. Rock'n'Roll!"

Paul Lewis

introduction to overdubs (in which live tracks are replaced by re-recordings of instruments or vocals). "Practically everything was replaced apart from the drums!" admits Mark. Explains Simon, "A lot was reworked. Mark's keyboards had been recorded as a stereo pair and not as the full sound, some of the guitar sounds weren't quite doing it either. Fish came down and cut the vocals again to give me the choice, they were a bit of a mix and match!"

Looking to capitalise on its release, John Arnison was having the same 'attitude problem' as the rest of the band. He decided to ignore touring the US and get the band out to Europe, where their following was growing the quickest. He also recognised that the best option was not to throw money around. Starting in Liverpool on 3 November, expensive hotels were foregone in place of sleeping in the tour bus, enabling the band to travel further and play to more people than they could otherwise have done.

As well as growing the fan base in previously unplayed halls, the tour offered the band an opportunity to trial some of the new material from the writing sessions at Barwell Court, notably what became the first side of the coming album. In mid-December, the band played three nights in a row at the 3,800 capacity Hammersmith Odeon. While the songs were musically close to their final form, the lyrics were still in an embryonic state, sometimes changing from night to night.

As Marillion toured, the feeling grew that some hard-core fans were holding on to the past a little too tightly. As the concert halls grew to arena proportions, the band was already distancing itself from some of its earlier glories. The cries for old stalwarts like 'Grendel' (which Ian has proudly never learned) grew louder.

So Very Far Away

The writing sessions nearing completion, it fell to the band to find a producer. Few wanted to touch it, particularly when they got wind it was going to be a concept album, few wanted to take what appeared to be a regressive step, such albums were surely ten years out of date. Fish commented at the time, "A whole lot of producers said no because they thought they couldn't make money out of it. They were looking at the American market." Unknown to Marillion, was EMI's desire to record the next album on the cheap. *'Fugazi'* had sold less than *'Script'*, and worse, EMI were considering dropping them! "John Arnison didn't think it was a good idea to tell us," elaborates Mark. Fortunately, as *'Real To Reel'* and its associated tour had started to break the band in continental Europe, EMI were content, but didn't want to expend any more than necessary.

At the beginning of 1985, the band trooped off to Bray Film Studios, owned by Gerry Anderson (creator of 'Thunderbirds'), for six weeks, to make a demo. Recalls Pete, "Gerry came into the studio when we happened to be playing the 'Thunderbirds' theme, I think he was tickled pink!" At Bray the boys met with Chris Kimsey, a producer with a number of Rolling Stones albums under his belt. Chris listened to the demo and offered constructive criticism, there was no "Where's the hit single," they were so used to hearing. "I loved the idea. It hadn't been done for a while and Marillion were that kind of band," says Chris. The band liked him, however as a tax exile, Chris spent a lot of time abroad, so he proposed the album be recorded at Hansa Studios, next to the Berlin Wall. Fortuitous as it would cost EMI much less than to record it in the UK! Not everyone in the band was convinced by the idea of spending three months out of the country, but they all agreed eventually.

By March, nearly the whole album had been written to

last nail in the coffin

Soon after they met, Chris Kimsey spent an evening with Fish, deliberately weaning him away from the band that was refusing to stop being an influence. "I never liked Genesis," says Chris, "He was playing *'The Lamb Lies Down'* and I was deliberately pulling the songs to bits! I just wanted to get Genesis out of his mind, to get him away from any idea of emulation!"

demo level. EMI was not convinced there was a single, but Chris Kimsey came to the rescue. "Chris put his foot down, he said, I'm the producer, this is what works, let me work on it," explains Pete. The recording entourage included Andy Field, who had been newly promoted to production manager. While he was there, he started to get pains in his legs, "It was diagnosed as sciatica," says Mark. Nobody realised it was something more sinister.

Arriving at the Hansa Studios in Berlin, the band met up with Chris and Thomas Stiehler, engineer and general madman, who remembers their arrival well. "They looked a little bit like a school band, so young and untouched!" Not an opinion with any longevity given their antics, but the signs were there. "Mark looked like a crazy guy!" says Thomas. Rehearsals started in the main hall of the studios, as band and producer developed a rapport. Chris remembers Ian worrying about the way the playback was sounding. "I was recording everything in-your-face and dry," says Chris. "Ian said to me, it didn't sound expensive enough!" Agrees Ian, "He went away, fiddled with the EQs and added some reverb and said how's that then?" It was fine.

Before long the six were working as a unit. Unlike Nick Tauber's divide-and-conquer approach, Chris Kimsey concentrated far more on the way the band members worked together, to capture the essence of the band in every song. "I wanted it as accessible as possible, both sonically and in terms of production," says Chris, "everything was recorded as it could be played live." At times, the concept album concept was a source of inspiration, at others (according to Pete in the remaster sleeve notes) it was "a bit tenuous." Recalls Thomas, "Chris took real care with each little detail, he was the guy who put it together, maybe I'm wrong but that's how I remember it!" Ian is not so sure. "We could play it from beginning to end before Chris was involved," he says. "The only track that wasn't written was 'White Feather'." Aided by Chris, the band shuffled lyrics and music back and forth, to make the whole thing work. "We had a huge chart up on the wall to see how it all segued together!" says Chris. Back in Blighty, EMI was getting more and more nervous about the commercial nature of the album. "They wanted us to come back, reorganise and regroup," says Chris. "We were recording the album in sequence, so soon afterwards we sent them 'Kayleigh' and they were alright after that!"

in the mix

The Hansa mixing desk was dysfunctional due to Geordie (Kenneth Walker) the guitarist from Killing Joke, the last band to record there before Marillion, having let off a fire extinguisher in the control room. "It was a strange situation," explains Thomas. "Chris and I had a day off, but the band had come in to rehearse. For some reason, the assistant was persuaded to unlock the control room, and there was too much alcohol; Geordie's not normally like that!"

In between takes, and remembering the proximity of the studios to the (then-still-standing) Berlin Wall, Thomas's sense of humour outdid even Mark's for its audacity. In 1981, Thomas had escaped from the East by hiding under a vehicle. "People were thinking for you, it was like living in school or kindergarten, I thought, I don't want to live in this fucking shoebox!" says Thomas. He'd left a girlfriend behind on the other side of the wall, "We used to wave to her from the studio windows," says Ian. "After four years she was allowed to come," adds Thomas, "Four years just on the telephone, it was crazy!" Crazy indeed, remembers Mark, "He had this megaphone, once there was a solitary old lady walking across the wasteland below, he opened the window of the studio and shouted HALT!" Thomas had also bought a car, "It was a fucked-up old Volvo I'd bought just to drive around, we used to do car racing around the streets of Berlin, once I hit a traffic sign and smashed up the front, another time Mark and Fish jumped on the roof, but I didn't care!" The megaphone also came in handy, says Thomas, "I pulled the window down and said to the other cars, Turn right! Stop! Police! And they did!"

With Thomas as the chaperone, it was clear early on that the boys were going to have too much fun. The most depressing feature was the Hervis Hotel. "The beds were like Ryvitas with a fig roll at the end," says Ian. As a consequence the band didn't spend much time there, with nights largely occupied by a wide variety of extra-curricular activities. "It was an exhilarating place, it had a great vibe," continues Ian. Many of the stories remain locked inside the heads of our merry men and their crew, but it doesn't take a huge leap of the imagination. There was alcohol on tap, drugs a-plenty and women and song were only a stone's throw away. But then, so were the landmines, a surreal situation which (coupled with the distance from family life and recording label executives) served to catalyse the creative juices still further.

Against this background, emotions were running high as one incident would illustrate. "Fish came into the control room with a whisky glass in his hand, he threw it into the wall, acoustic material came flying off," says Thomas. "The argument was about money, I thought, why do they do it, they're making a really good sound, why argue about money?" It wouldn't be the last time. Later, the ground floor café was the scene for a major falling out between Fish and Rothers. "Fish and I had been talking to Hugh Stanley Clarke about solo projects," recalls Steve. "Fish wanted mainstream success, he had this idea about a ghost rider who commits suicide while listening to his music, and Fish would sing cover versions of the songs the rider held dear.[1] I had the idea of doing something more rock-based and less keyboards. Hugh really liked my idea and didn't like Fish's." Steve continues, "The next thing I know, Fish grabs me and holds me up against the wall, screaming that I'm holding back the best songs for my solo album! I thought, that's marvellous, I'd just written the majority of the music for the new album and here's a 6-foot-6 Scot hurling abuse at me! Any friendship that was left in me for Fish went away at that moment. It was like a switch flicked off."

internal exil

Exil was an old Austrian restaurant reputed to have been frequented by Hitler and popular with yuppies and lawyers. We were sitting at a long table, talking, drinking and joking, I noticed Mark and Fish were making a bet about something. The next thing I noticed, Fish had nothing on but his belt! The whole thing ended with half of us leaving the restaurant naked, we had a good laugh! One day later, Chris and I decided to go out without the band, for a quiet evening. We said we couldn't go back to Exil but nowhere else was open, we expected to go in there and be told to get out, but when we went in, the staff all stood in a row and welcomed us, that was really nice, it was very funny for us!

Thomas Stiehler

Bands argue, that's creative folk for you, and the cocoon was bound to result in the members getting on top of each other. The team took a few days off at Easter, then returned to the creative hotpot and madness of Berlin. "Fish used to take the U-Bahn [subway] and go to East Berlin, I wonder why he wasn't caught by the border police," says Thomas. "I think we all aged at least three years during our time there," admits Steve on the sleeve notes. Fish also met his future wife Tamara Nowy there, where she worked in an exclusive bar. Within two weeks, she had appeared in the 'Kayleigh' video.

With Chris taking tapes back to his hotel and playing them on his portable cassette recorder to ensure the sound was accessible, it all came together. The lyrical ending of the album was furnished at the last minute by Mark Wilkinson, who loaned Fish a copy of 'Damian' by Herman Hesse. There had been three attempts in the UK to get the mastering right, Chris says, "The masters came back sounding nothing like the original mix, they were just awful!" Eventually Chris took matters into his own hands and had the album mastered at vinyl mastering specialists Teldec, in Berlin. According to Thomas, "Teldec had developed Direct Metal Mastering, where they cut sound directly into the metal rather than using lacquer."

'Misplaced Childhood' was the cheapest album the band had made. At £74,000 it

was 6K under budget and cost half as much as *'Fugazi'*. Fish wrote in the sleeve notes that *'Misplaced Childhood'* was "the turning point of all our lives." Little did anyone know just how much of a turning point it would be.

'Misplaced Childhood'

The base concept for the new album had been established as part of the trilogy that saw a lovelorn jester go from grief, to anger and now to reflection, acceptance and hope. According to Fish, "This album is the analysis, trying to come out of the problems by saying, 'yes, that is a limitation; yes, that is a negative aspect of personality.'"

At the same time as being part of a pattern, 'Misplaced Childhood' *breaks the mould - it is more accessible than its predecessors, and less fixated on the past (both in musical style and influence). Noted fan Michael Huang, "It was a backlash against the brooding nature of previous albums, a self-rebellion." A suitably peculiar result for an album whose lyrical impetus came from a nightmare acid trip!*

From the opening notes of 'Pseudo Silk Kimono', it is clear this is not going to be a selection of jingles. Short and none too sweet, it glides smoothly into the opening notes of a love song, a story of a girl, of many girls, of break-ups and breakdown: the enormo-hit 'Kayleigh'. Second single 'Lavender', introduces the child to the tale; the boy in the man. As Fish wrote, "The guy's looking back on childhood all the time. He looks on his childhood as being the ideal world, the simplicity of then. He can't figure out at what point he stopped being a kid and became an adult and he's wrong because you never stop being a kid while you're still prepared to learn."

With 'Bitter Suite', there is no more childhood. The band lead us through several sections, memory snapshots of loves lost, climaxing with the return to the haunting themes of 'Lavender' in 'Blue Angel'. This emotive sub-section of 'Bitter Suite' sees Fish seeking solace in the arms of a lady of the night, although he has since admitted "[she] wasn't a prostitute. That was a compounding of events made under poetic license."

'Misplaced Rendezvous' and 'Windswept Thumb' sees the band drag us back into the present, Fish in the middle of writing his acid-fuelled memoirs, and then drops us under the spotlight in centre stage, for the first part of 'Heart Of Lothian'. The gloriously overblown first section has the rock star in full flow, singing his heart out to his fans, whilst recalling his Scottish roots. The introspection of 'Curtain Call', reveals the star desperate to go and live up to his hedonistic image, but hamstrung by the business side of being a musician, the photo-calls and listening back to the show.

Escape he does, in 'Waterhole (Expresso Bongo)'. The band evoke the rush and head-fuck of hedonism. And Fish? He's out of it; the girls, the booze, the powders, whilst at the back of his head, there's an incessant ticking that something isn't quite right.

'Lords Of The Backstage' offers up Fish looking back at his relationship with 'Kayleigh', and realising his desire for success outweighed his need for her.

Steve Rothery string-bends to perfection as 'Vocal Under A Bloodlight', revisits the fragmentation of a relationship and Fish realizes the emotions of the love song 'Kayleigh' are nothing but "twinkling lies" that "sparkle with the wet ink on the paper."

The death of band friend John Mylett, drummer with Rage, who was killed in a car crash in Greece in June 1984, is recalled in 'Mylo'. "He was the first of our own," wrote Fish. Chris Lewington, long-time friend and near-roadie for Rage comments, "Mylo was one of the nicest blokes I'd ever met." The music and lyrics see Fish cracking up under the strain of maintaining both sides of his personality; Fish and Derek William Dick. In mourning and sick of his rootlessness, he endures another press interview; his only way of coping is retreating from real life even further. Immersed in the drug cocoon of Pete Trewavas's ominous bass rumbles and Ian Mosely's heartbeat drums, he has a sudden recollection of a time when life was less complicated, a time of innocence. Threshold sees him dancing on the razor's edge of insanity, as the cruelty of modern life - loneliness, war, homelessness, emotionally damaged children - assault him. How the hell is he supposed to deal with this horror?

Then the payoff! As the drug fades into comedown and the sun comes up, the singer suddenly finds himself able to cope, he sees a future before him. The band create a bubbling, optimistic ode, tinged with Mark Kelly's poignant keyboards of regret. Steve Rothery's guitar squeals out with a heart-rush of excitement. Fish can see past his worries and we segue into the hopeful resolution of this dark trip.

Recalling the "Where are the prophets, where are the visionaries?" coda to *'Fugazi'*, Fish puts his faith in humanity. Together, he says, we can make it through, and to back him up, the music fizzes with thrilling elation. As the last notes fade out, the nightmare ends.

The cover sees the Jester, the symbol of heartache and disillusionment, disappearing through a window. Taking pride of place is the spirit of childhood, in the form of Mark Wilkinson's next door neighbour Robert Mead. Although there are storm clouds behind him, a rainbow gives us hope, and the magpie transmutates into a dove, the bird of peace. Simpler and more powerful than the previous covers, the image is the perfect metaphor for the music.

Upward Curve

On 7 April 1985, 'Kayleigh' was released as a single. On the B-side was 'Lady Nina', a thrown-together track, based around a drum loop of Ian's. The band had managed to keep 'Lady Nina' at arms length from the album (despite the US record company's desires otherwise[2]). To everybody's surprise, 'Kayleigh' was hugely successful. HUGELY successful, it spent 11 weeks in the UK charts, missing out on the No.1 slot due to the charity record released in support of the victims of the Bradford City fire disaster. Chris Kimsey recalls the success, "I was ecstatic, chuffed to bits!" "It was as much to do with timing as anything, a bit of a happy accident," comments Pete, modestly. "EMI was right behind it, it was marketed well and distributed well!" Ian remembers Rothers saying, "That's a doddle, writing that sort of stuff!" However, a series of bizarre happenings resulted in low airplay in the US. "The Head of Capitol, our record label in the States, was photographed handing brown paper bags of cash to underworld bosses,"[3] recalls Pete. "There was an airplay embargo on any singles from Capitol from that point." Despite Capitol's woes, airplay became global, even the commercially focused MTV found room for the video. This was US fan Jeff Pelletier's first experience of Marillion, but as he would

about a boy

Robert Mead, a neighbour of Mark Wilkinson, became the unsuspecting hero of the single and the album cover. "I had to stand and look serious in Mark's living room," he recalled on the sleeve notes to the remaster. It would not end there, with video shoots and PR events following.
He only ever received one piece of fan mail.

find out later, there was even more to 'Kayleigh' than a world-class single. "I remember liking its unique sound and nostalgic and introspective 'lost love' theme. Yet, the song seemed to end somewhat abruptly…"

In May and June 1985, prior to the release of the album, the band toured Germany, Switzerland and Spain, to begin with playing only the first half of the album. It was off with the old, not only squeezing the older mainstays such as 'Forgotten Sons' and 'He Knows, You Know' out of the set, but also, Fish's face paint was no longer obligatory, he had established himself and the mask had become redundant. For the first few shows, Fish unmasked himself half way through the gig, but before long he walked on stage with his face as nature intended.

With radio and TV appearances too numerous to mention, the tour, and 'Kayleigh' being played in rotation on radio stations around the globe, it appeared inevitable the album would do well.

It did better. The band had already been told there was a fair chance of *'Misplaced Childhood'* [4] reaching the No.1 spot, based on the number of albums that had been pre-ordered. This didn't prevent the shock when, on its release on 17 June, it raced to the top of the UK charts. "It was an incredible feeling, a dream I had when I was a kid!" says Fish. It was almost inevitable that this was not comfortable for the old fans, however new fans proved as devoted as any who had come before. Mike Portnoy of Dream Theater, for example, had been heavily recommended to give *'Misplaced Childhood'* a try. Explains Mike, "As a big fan of Progressive music and concept albums, I was immediately blown away by this album and it became one of my favourites of all time. It still is!" This experience was echoed by fan Angie Cooper. "I really only got into the band with *'Misplaced Childhood'*," remarks Angie. "I was aware of them before, but to tell the truth I did not reckon much to them!!" Over in Mexico, Bruno Galli also saw the light. "It was *'Misplaced Childhood'* that made me a believer!" Inevitably, those who had followed the band before 1985, scorned the arrivistes. "Many were those who felt the album was too commercial and uninspiring," notes fan Marc Roy. Fan Anne Bond's stalwart sisters Jan and Sue felt the same. "They didn't like the commercial exposure and felt Marillion were selling out," says Anne. But disillusioned fans were pushed quickly into the minority, as the album's reach grew from thousands to millions.

'Misplaced Childhood' sold 1.4 million copies in its first year, turning platinum several times over in the process. Thomas Stiehler remembers a gig he attended at the Deutschlandhalle in Berlin. "They gave me a platinum record and said, 'Hey, Thomas, just for you!'"

In the US, Capitol continued to refuse to play ball. "We had this terrible period where *'Misplaced Childhood'* was hugely successful over here and not over there," says Chris. Back in the home territory, there were no such problems, 'Lavender' (with 'Freaks' on the reverse) was released as a single in the UK on 27 August 1985, reaching No.5 in the charts and hanging in there for seven weeks.

Too Late To Say I'm Sorry by Georgina Wistow

"My older brother St John was quite into Marillion, I never really took that much notice. Then the summer 'Kayleigh' came out, we went on a family holiday.

St John inevitably snogged one of the waitresses one night (he was 15) and having phoned his girlfriend back home every day until then, he stopped ringing her cos he felt guilty (not guilty enough to stop snogging the waitress obviously). Anyway the girlfriend smelled a rat (which if she'd have been better at she would never have been going out with him in the first place!) and when we came home wouldn't speak to him. But 'Kayleigh' was in the charts and he was inspired.

St John bought and sent her a copy, saying he wanted to say he was sorry but he was "too scared to pick up the phone." Obviously a move that smooth was rewarded and he got his girlfriend back. Unfortunately for him, 'Kayleigh' stuck around for a long time, which gave us all time to torture him by singing along to the "I just want to say I'm sorry..." line really loudly every time we heard it. St John is no longer with us, but whenever I hear 'Kayleigh' it makes me smile because I think of him and this story."

Lords Of The Stage

The next decision John Arnison made was possibly the single most important decision in the early history of the band. Of the (correct) opinion that Marillion were first and foremost a live act, he capitalised by continuing touring, rather than rushing to the studios to produce a follow-up. "The band hardly got any air play until 'Kayleigh', so the only way forward was to play live," says John. "When 'Kayleigh' was a worldwide hit, it opened countries for the band to play that we had not been able to get into." Fish no longer felt it was the best plan, however. "It was understandable in 1982, 1983, 1984, but by the time it got to 1986, it was becoming a bit of a joke!" says Fish. All was forgiven at the time, as the tour happened to be a massive global success. "We went into hyperspace," says Fish. And they stayed there until the summer of 1986, cementing the relationship with a worldwide fan base, which both Marillion and Fish retain to this day. Later, John would be accused of sending the band on tour because it was most profitable to him. Comments Pete, "I don't think John set out to rip us off, but touring was a way for him to make money…" What is true is that he had little incentive to stop the band touring. On 17 August 1985, Marillion played the Monsters Of Rock festival at Castle Donnington, alongside headliners ZZ Top. Like Black Sabbath at Reading, the band was a hard act to follow. One attendee was Simon Clarke, seeing Marillion for the first time. "I thought they were really good," says Simon. "They did some of *'Misplaced Childhood'*, not all of it and in kind of a weird order. It was a scorching hot day, a good first gig!" He was one of the lucky ones. The Misplaced Childhood tour proper, was planned to start on 4 September with two nights in Dublin, followed by Belfast, then returning to London for a fan club show, before four nights at the Hammersmith Odeon. All of which (not to mention the other eleven dates) sold out. Ten days before it started, Fish went with John Arnison to Japan, spending ten days in an intensive round of interviews and promotional work. Coupled with the alcohol-soaked stresses and strains that had hit the band since their return from Berlin, what happened next was as inevitable as it was depressing.

When disaster struck, it chose its target well, the one instrument that couldn't be replaced. Fish lost his voice halfway through the first night in Dublin, struggling bravely on until, by Belfast on the third night, it went completely. It didn't help that

rumours of a split

One of Fish's more embarassing live moments came 11 November 1985, when his trousers split in front of 12,000 people at the Hans-Martin-Schleyer-Halle in Stuttgart, Germany. He later commented, "I had to shout at Steve to extend his guitar solo whilst I 'crab-walked' off stage..."

Fish's nights out had been as fast as the days. "Fish never looked after himself while he was touring," remarks John. According to Mark, Fish didn't go to bed for three days running! "We couldn't believe it, we all said, he's finally done it!" Explained Fish at the time, "I went out razzing, something had to give. I ended up paying for my sins by losing the use of my voice for a month!" Following visits to various doctors, the cancelled dates were rescheduled for the following year by a fleet-footed Mr Arnison. However the decision to reschedule came too late for the fan club show booked at the Marquee on 10 September, four days after Belfast. Ian decided to lead a drum clinic, Pete chose to join him for a jam, Mark and Steve threw in their hats and Fish mucked in as 'Maître D'.

live forever

Marillion were approached to write the soundtrack for a film called 'Highlander'. Unfortunately, the band was on tour at the time with *'Misplaced Childhood'*, so they didn't have time. Instead, the soundtrack was given to Queen.

By the end of September, with Fish's voice rested, it was time to hit the road again. Only one date of the UK leg of the tour had been kept, the de Montfort Hall in Leicester, on 29 September. Following a successful night, the band hit the furthest reaches of Europe, Israel and Japan. "We were riding on the crest of a wave and feeling unstoppable!" noted Fish. In West Germany, where both the single and the album had found major success, Marillion were named the biggest selling touring act in Germany, 1985. Fish was quick to hire a bodyguard in Germany, as some of the crowds proved a little too fanatical, even for a man of his stature.

Marillion play Japan, Dec 1985, with Robbo, Smick, Priv, Chops, Mark and John

Under record company pressure, 'Heart Of Lothian' was released as the third single on 18 November, as the band finished in Germany and headed for Japan. It reached a gentlemanly, but unimpressive, No.29 in the UK chart, and was gone in a fortnight. On 10 December, the band returned to the UK to film for 'The Old Grey Whistle Test' at the Marquee, during which *'Misplaced Childhood'* was played for the first time live in its entirety. As it continued, the tour went from strength to strength. 19 December saw Marillion play its first headline at the NEC, to an 11,000 crowd. Following a two-week break at Christmas, there was no respite, the first of eight sold-out dates at the Hammersmith Odeon was played on 8 January 1986. The last of these came a month later, on 6 February, a gala performance, the proceeds going to charity. It was to be a roll-call of collaborators. Peter Hammill, John Otway, Robin Boult, all faces from the past, were joined by Mike Oldfield, Roger Chapman and Mickey Simmons (Oldfield's keyboard player) before Steve Hackett was welcomed to the stage. The big band played a triumphant 'I Know What I Like (In Your Wardrobe)', the same song Fish had sung at his audition five years, a month and four days before.

In March of the following year, the band finally reached the west coast of the USA. It had taken *'Misplaced Childhood'*, along with its 25,000 US album sales, to convince Capitol Records that a full US tour would be viable. Even then, 12 of the 23 dates were supporting Rush's stadium crowds on its Power Windows tour. This was a brave move

considering the band's last attempts to support Rush, however, this time the band had achieved success in their own right, were no strangers to 20,000 audiences, and had received Rush's assurances that there would be no repeat. "This time, they asked us back," recalls Mark. "When we arrived, they'd left a bottle of champagne in the dressing room!" Indeed, this time the crowds were more receptive. Rush's legacy proved strong, "Our audiences have always been strongest in places where we toured with Rush," comments Mark. Remembers fan Miles Macmillan, "Marillion came to Toronto for the Misplaced Childhood tour and six of us piled into my friends VW Rabbit (one guy had to sit in the hatch) and took the three hour trip down there, then met up with two other carloads of friends who also took the trip. That was one of the best times ever for all of us and we still talk about what a great show it was!" Following the return, Marillion played a number of festivals across Europe, with four performing second on the bill to Queen. Unlike Black Sabbath and ZZ Top, both of whom had played before audiences sapped of their energies by the Marillos, with Queen the band finally met its match. "Freddie was very sharp," comments John Arnison. "After Queen went on, their tour manager came round the back and said, "Freddie wants Fish on stage with him." Of course, when he went on stage, the crowds went absolutely wild!" Fish departed after sharing a song, leaving the throng firmly back in the palm of Freddie's hand.

A late highlight of touring was June 28 1986, the Garden Party at the Milton Keynes Bowl, to which Marillion invited Magnum, Mama's Boys, Gary Moore and Jethro Tull, along with 35,000 people. "We were just trying to find a bunch of compatible bands, who would draw some people!" explains Mark. Bizarrely, Gary Moore and Jethro Tull had a disagreement over who should be top of the bill, resolved in the end by paying Gary Moore (whose name appeared second as a result) several thousand pounds less than Jethro Tull. Reports of the concert were unanimous in their praise. One reporter enthused, "Fish sang with an intensity you could feel came from the heart. 'Garden Party' had thousands singing along." "It was a buzz for us," recalls Pete. "Having a band like Jethro Tull support us was great!" Paul Lewis, tour manager, found it particularly special. "The band have played other stadiums but that was a home gig," Adds Peter Gee of Pendragon, "A band has really arrived if they can play at the Milton Keynes Bowl. It was a great show, and another coming of age for the band. They really should have continued to grow in popularity and been a long term band at that kind of level."

Rush unplugged

Marillion and Rush went out for a meal one evening. Halfway through the meal, Fish whispered to his own band, "I think Alex Lifeson has had a plug job! Hang on, I'll ask him... Excuse me Alex, have you had a plug job?" Indeed he had benefited from a hair transplant, and he very kindly discussed it with Mark and Fish, both of whom were becoming a little thin up top!

The writing was already on the wall, however. Long months away were taking their toll, not just separation from loved ones, the fatigue of incessant live dates and

Sleepy boys crossing Japan on a bullet train, Dec 1985 (don't mention Priv's trousers...)

press calls, but the life of plenty and constant partying, becoming a way of life for the band and its manager. "I thought we were just having a good time," remember both Mark and Ian. But the drink, drugs and decadence were taking over. Fish blames John Arnison for, "living a lifestyle that was reliant on the band being out on tour." But John was following the only path he knew, the band was still on the up and, given its credentials as an anti-musical-establishment band, it appeared to John that touring was the best option. Fish concludes, "Take any seven people, and put them into a situation like the one we were in and see what happens... We never had the time to grow up, the partying was a symptom of people crying out for help." Of the band and management, only Steve and Ian were relatively immune, at least from the drink and the drugs. Ian had never been a heavy drinker, and Rothers earned the moniker "St Stephen of Whitby" for his ability to stay on the straight and narrow. Says Steve, "I like to have a drink or several, as much as most people, but my life didn't revolve around getting fucked up every night."

Despite Fish's misgivings, the band was content to get on with what it did best, "We were so focused on the music, we handed John our complete and utter trust," says Steve. "John was very good with people, very good at going to EMI and doing a deal, but that put us in a situation where we were always slightly in debt."

Fish was also looking for other channels for his art. He had taken on a theatrical

John Arnison

John started in the business through serendipitous circumstances, when training to be a solicitor. Joining Quarry on his year out ("I thought I'd do something a bit different!"), he was given Liverpool-based Nutz (who subsequently became Rage) to manage. He became Marillion's manager some months after.

Marillion fitted John's desire for a challenge. He says, "In the 1980s it was us against the world!" He was renowned for his timing, according to Pete in a fan club interview, "He was always in advance, while the band was still playing the Marquee, he would be saying, 'I think we'll do a Hammersmith!' When the band was playing Hammersmith, he was saying 'I think we'll do Milton Keynes!' And so it would be." "Management is about taking opportunities," comments John. "Certain times you have to wait until the market forces are ready."

"If someone had a problem, then I always thought it should be aired," remarks John. Pete concurs, "We called him torn-pocket-Arnison, because he'd just come out with a thing and you'd think, "I wish I hadn't told him that!"

On joining Hit And Run, John ran the London office, taking on Aswad and MN8. When he parted company with the band in 1997, he was invited by Tony Smith, senior executive at Hit And Run, to become general manager of the group and run its sports division. Six months later Tony closed down the entire company. "What might have happened if I'd stuck with Marillion?" he wonders. More recently, John has also managed Gabrielle. Things didn't work out too bad then!

agent and, feeling lyrically stale, was considering writing a novel. "Fish had written some fantastic words, particularly in the early days," says Steve, "but he'd peaked with the early stuff." It was clear he was becoming frustrated, but all the same he didn't see a solo career as a viable option. A solo album was discussed, but there was never time to fit it in, "I had no time to, that was the problem. The band was continually forced out on this tour-album-tour-album cycle..." Even Fish's acting plans were held back by the release of *'Misplaced Childhood'*, as he recounted at the time, "I was offered a part in 'Highlander', but the timing was wrong." Fish's frustrations surfaced in various ways, his hot temper has been widely documented, and he would not baulk at taking it out on the others. "Paul Lewis was in the firing line quite a few times, as was John Arnison." says Mark. "John was prepared to put up with a lot, he shielded the rest of the band."

On Friday 1 August Steve married Jo, at Aspull in Lancashire, with Pete as best man. The party afterwards, at nearby Haigh Hall, included a performance by Dave Lloyd's band, Sliced Bread, following which Steve and Jo headed off for their honeymoon to to St Lucia. Two days later, the band played at a 'private' Roland exhibition in London, with Robin Boult standing in on guitar. Of course, several hundred fans turned up. It was the last time the band played together for five months and, for Marillion, the honeymoon was over. Nobody could say exactly when the line was crossed, but most would mark it at some time during the Misplaced Childhood tour.

'Clutching At Straws'

After the phenomenal success of *'Misplaced Childhood'* and 'Kayleigh', things were difficult for Marillion. Second album syndrome which the band had already experienced and coped with, was nothing compared to the second globally successful album syndrome, that now beset the band.

The strains within the band were becoming more and more visible, not only due to the incessant touring (and partying). The press considered the band and Fish as one and the same, and the man himself was starting to feel a discrepancy between his cut of the takings, and his role both as front man and lyricist. Against this background a fourth album, particularly one that would be of similarly high quality to its predecessors, seemed unlikely at the outset.

Just For The Record

Writing began at Steve Rothery's house in a series of reasonably productive sessions, spawning what would become 'Hotel Hobbies' and 'Warm Wet Circles'. In the late summer of 1986, thirteen months after Marillion had last been inside a studio, they returned to once familiar haunts, Barwell Court, Nomis[5] and Bray Studios, to begin the writing process anew. This time the album would be anything other than a concept album, but it was most certainly themed, with drinking a central element. By autumn, the band moved to Stanbridge Farm studio, on the road to Brighton. The initial good start was grinding to a halt, as Marillion found itself treading a paradox: to do something different to, but as successful as, the last album. EMI (in the shape of Hugh Stanley Clarke) heard the first demos of the new material, but thought they all sounded too similar to *'Misplaced Childhood'*, so they were binned and the writing process was started again.

one boat down

The Marillion was a hydroplane driven by Robert 'Chops' Flury, the band's lighting designer, competing in the European Hydroplane Championships in Nottingham on 2 August 1986. Unfortunately, due to Steve's wedding the previous day, the hangovers made it impossible for anyone from the band to attend.

The Zelda Club

Gerry Anderson's studios at Bray provided some unusual inspiration. On the *'Clutching'* tour, 'Thunderbirds' characters were used as tour passes and pseudonyms. Fish was Scott Tracy. Furthermore, the Zelda Club was formed based on the excesses that had to take place to reach looking like an old hag...

The effort to be creative proved a huge strain, and the sessions became increasingly fraught as a result. Mark recalls, "Chris Kimsey heard the beginning of the album, 'Warm Wet Circles' and 'At That Time Of The Night'. He made encouraging noises but then went back to John Arnison and told him that Fish was lyrically losing the plot." To be frank, the original music was not great either. John Arnison recalls being called to the studio, "Chris asked me to listen to what had been produced, I did so and said, its not that good, is it? Everyone heaved a huge sigh of relief, it's what they all wanted me to say, but nobody would stand up to Fish!" 'Warm Wet Circles' remains one of Marillion's oddest songs, lyrically poignant, but undoubtedly strange. The continued arguments took their toll, Fish remarks in the sleeve notes, "This was the first time I seriously considered leaving the band." The creative strains were not the only reason. Fish had already been to see John about the money. "Fish said he wanted a bigger cut," recalls John. "I told him he was being unreasonable, Once I had told Fish that, I knew I was in the firing line. That pressure certainly led to me hitting the booze harder than usual."

All this was beyond the ken of the fans, who were keen to know how Marillion would follow their platinum-selling album. At the end of 1986, Marillion conducted a five-date fan club tour, the first gigs for five months. The opening night, on the 27 December in Aylesbury, was a charity gig, Fish wore face paint for the first time in many years to the delight of many fans. "It was completely wrong! I decided to do it for a laugh, it was like trying to squeeze into your school uniform!" says Fish. The Web gigs provided a welcome opportunity to preview some of the new material, 'White Russian', 'Warm Wet Circles' and 'Incommunicado'. "Oh, let it be a single!" wrote fan Judith Mitchell of the latter. Of Liverpool, another fan Clive Aspinall remembers it was "one of the best gigs I have ever seen!" In early 1987, the team entered Westside Studios near White City in London to start recording, Chris Kimsey once again heading the production team... "We were in London because there was more money available. After Berlin, working in London was a real downer. I said at the time it was a mistake." Chris was accompanied by Westside's house engineer, Nick Davis. "It was one of my first big engineering gigs," says Nick. Westside provided the musical catalyst but, while the music was coming together, the band relationships were falling apart. Substances of various kinds were impacting the process, heightening not creativity but obsession and paranoia within the musicians and the production team. Ian recalls how David Munns (head of A&R at EMI) came down to see how the writing was getting on. "Everyone was completely out of it. We played him 'Delilah', John Arnison was crashing around in the vocal booth! David drove back with me, he was so worried he filled his car up with diesel!"

Paul Lewis, working from his hotel room

On Mark's birthday on 9 April 1987, things started well. Mark recalls Chris arrived at the studio with a woman, "Everyone filed out, next thing I knew she was naked..." The festivities turned nasty when an argument blew up between Steve and Fish, ostensibly (again) about Steve holding back material for solo projects. "This was nonsense, I'd written most of the music on the album," frowns Steve. Continues Mark, "The next thing I knew, Fish had Steve up against a wall and was threatening to punch his head in!" Steve was beyond talking to, he stormed out and caught the train home. He explains, "I'd had enough of the egos and temper tantrums, I decided then that the thing I'd wanted to do more than anything else in my life, had become something I hated, as far as I was concerned that was it, I'd left the band." Ian called Steve at home and calmed things down. According to Steve, "If there's a person who can sort things out in the band, it's Ian." Steve returned to the studio long enough to get the recording finished but, he explains, "Fish hadn't realised how much he'd upset me, I'd made the decision that he'd never get to me in that way again." Things got harder as the album reached completion. "I was doing a lot of the work as Chris and Fish were partying," recalls Nick. Finally it was done, and the team celebrated the fact with a meal at Julie's Restaurant. Nick remembers, "I tried to keep up with Fish drinking, I got incredibly ill and was sick in the restaurant, it was very embarrassing!"

a cut above

In November 1986, Fish and Tony Banks released a single, 'Shortcut To Somewhere'. "He had the music written and I supplied the words," says Fish. The song appeared on Tony's *'Soundtracks'* album, as well as in the film 'Quicksilver'.

Fish backstage at a Queen concert, June 1987

The remaining overdubs and mixing were done by David Jacobs ("a funny little guy with a squint," according to Chris Kimsey) at Advision Studios, just off Oxford Street. The band were met by Avril Mackintosh, who had first met them some six years before, and who was now assistant engineer. "When I heard they were coming in I said, I have to work on that!" To Avril's surprise Fish, who had been standoffish in Inverness and unconcerned when she met him again a few years later, was the first to come over and said hello. "He said, I know you, I met you in Inverness," says Avril. At Advision things moved forward, but the undercurrents were shifting from black to worse. By all accounts, David Jacobs wasn't much help. "He didn't fit in, which didn't make the situation any easier," says Avril. "He just didn't have the right vibe." Despite the party atmosphere of evenings at Braganza's, a Soho restaurant, daytimes were a morose affair. What started as a complaint by Rothers about David Jacobs (explains Steve, "I thought that his mixes came across as boring and sterile sounding, compared to some of the monitor mixes we'd done with Nick Davis), was taken as a personal slight on Chris Kimsey, who then began to criticise Steve's guitar playing. "He said I wasn't playing as well as on the last album," says Steve, whose reaction was to re-record the 'Sugar Mice' solo there and then. Recalls Avril, "He played this blinding solo! That shut everyone up!" When it was over, the rest of the gang went back to Braganza's. "We had a really good night!" says Avril, who didn't think that much of the incident. "In bands, tempers flare, but they're usually smoothed over!"

Fish was thinking otherwise. Pete had driven home from Braganza's a bit the worse for wear and crashed his Porsche, a fact which emerged the next day at a band meeting at Fish's house at Gerrard's Cross.[6] "Ian and I stared at each other over a coffee and a smoke, firmly believing that the band was over," Fish wrote in the sleeve notes to the remaster. But it wasn't, not quite, there was enough momentum to carry everyone forward to the release of the album, and the tour from hell.

'Clutching At Straws'

'Clutching At Straws' *is mostly about the excesses of classic addiction, whether of alcohol, sex or power. Following much time on the road, the album was written in bars, about the people who drink in them. Indeed, specific bars are credited on the sleeve as the birthplace of individual lyrics, from Milwaukee to North Berwick.*

The album is notionally based around the character of Torch - "The pivotal figure, a guardian angel at the end of a bar," as Mark Wilkinson wrote, a drunken, coke-addled train wreck of a human being, attempting to conquer his demons to creating a new work. The lyrics are a barely disguised trawl through the singer's growing sense of frustration with the constant album-tour-album way of life, and the viewpoint frequently appears autobiographical rather than character-led.

Bubbling eddies of keyboards introduce us to 'Hotel Hobbies' and brings the curtain up on Torch, trapped by indecision, addiction and self-loathing, in his hotel room. As he sits at his desk, desperately writing and knowing it's worthless, the dawn, effortlessly conjured by the band, peeks through the cracks in the curtains, heralding another day.

The beautiful, emotive 'Warm Wet Circles' follows Torch, searching for inspiration and ending up in his old local. According to Fish, it's "about small, hometown stuff; the dangers of getting trapped in the 9-to-5 syndrome and then going down to the pub and talking about things you'll never really do. The local hero's the best darts player and you marry the girl you met in the pub at 16. Torch goes back to his old haunts and sees how he used to be and it scares him." As Torch recalls losing his virginity, Steve Rothery breaks into an aching solo, full of pathos and longing, and the band execute one of the finest wrought moments of their career. Ian Mosley's snare cracks and we feel the first bullet smashing into John Lennon on the steps of the Dakota building.

The band return us to Torch, sitting alone at the end of the bar, drinking once more, terrified by the thought he's perilously close to being one of the hometown guys, wistfully tracing the circles of liquid on the bar. 'That Time Of The Night' leads into a glorious outro, the band create the perfect sense of tension to underline how close to breaking point Torch really is. "[It] still reads like a resignation statement," Fish commented in the sleeve notes. Added Ian Mosley, "The album reflects genuine camaraderie, yet exposed the decaying tethers that held us together."

'Going Under', a lyric written on the spur of the moment over a Rothery guitar motif, sees Torch languishing in the depths of his depression, close to giving up and taking the final way out. It was, as Mark commented "very much a snapshot of what was going on at the time."

Just as it all gets too dark, 'Just For The Record's jaunty keyboard intro brings a note of hope to the album, albeit tinged with a note of self-deception.

Recalling past tracks such as 'Market Square Heroes' and 'Garden Party', the keyboard-led track has Torch cheer himself up with the thought that he could give it all up any time he wanted, the traditional excuse of the addict. Fish considers this to be a "non-song", one without heart or substance. The dark thoughts are never far away, Torch convinces himself he is a better writer when he's out of it.

The off-kilter rhythms of 'White Russian', bring to mind wartime dance halls, but as ever on this album, there's a Kelly-painted black cloud about to come down, as Torch observes the rise of Neo-Nazism in Austria. Knowing he should make a stand and say something, Torch fails and runs away, geographically and mentally, he searches for a dealer with something for the pain.

'Incommunicado', written as a jam, is a necessary mood-lifter after the tense and skull-crushingly dark 'White Russian', and reveals Torch imagining himself as a "winner in the fame game". The bouncy, up-tempo number was only included on the album at the behest of producer Chris Kimsey, most of the band thinking it too much of a Who sound-a-like.

'Torch Song', and its segue 'Slainte Mhath', document Torch's growing realisation that he's killing himself, and the notion he doesn't care, because it takes him away from the misery of real life. In arguably one of his best lyrics, Fish contrasts the wasted lives of World War I in the trenches, with the Scottish shipbuilders seeing their livelihoods destroyed by Thatcherism, and the band pull out all the stops to conjure Torch's helplessness. Pete Trewavas's bass lines scream poignancy.

'Sugar Mice', "born in a hotel room after a bad phone call home to a very upset girlfriend," sees Fish ruminate on the break up of a relationship. Commercial, yet impassioned, Steve Rothery launches into one of the purest guitar solos ever committed to tape.

Final track, 'The Short Straw', brings us back to Torch in his room. Hard at work, keys clattering against the paper, he muses on what he has seen, creating his masterpiece on the human condition. It's too late and the damage is done, the band turn savage and atavistic, building to a desperate climax as Torch realises it's too late to change and his addictions have beaten him. For him, it's the only way to survive, even though he knows it's killing him. In case we're in any doubt, Fish's mocking laughter tells us there will be no happy ending.

Shot in Colchester's Bakers Arms, the brooding cover depicted "The Great Bar In The Sky", populated with various artists, writers and poets who had a reputation of liking a wee dram! Great theory, but "it looked crap," Fish commented, Mark Wilkinson's timescale being considerably reduced to coincide with a hastily-arranged tour. "Some extra summer festivals slotted into the tour itinerary, produced a tighter deadline than I had originally been given," he remembers. "It was torture, but somehow I did it!"

Burn A Little Brighter

With no little relief and surprise, the band realised they had created a great album. Fish explains, "We were in a transitional period, there was so much conflict and friction, but no-one had their own way!" To the delight of fans, 'Incommunicado' was released 11 May 1987, entering the charts at No.6 in its first week, it peaked at No.5. In a belated tip of the hat to the people who had put them there, both the cover and the video involved members of The Web, together with an angel sporting a bear suit, ironically Fish's least favourite

John Arnison and Andy Field, June 1987

costume.[7] Fan Linda Southern recalls, "I became an accidental Marillion fan in the summer of 1987 when I turned on Radio 2 (2FM as it's now called, the Irish version of BBC Radio 1!) and heard this thumping loud rock song. I really liked it, the DJ said it was by a band called Marillion and the song was 'Incommunicado'. A month or so later, we made our annual trip to Bournemouth, and while there I bought the album *'Clutching At Straws'*. I was hooked, it was three days before I changed the tape out of my Walkman!" Fan Paul Hughes writes, "I first heard 'Incommunicado' on Tommy Vance's show in the middle of 1987. Its high entry status did not surprise me at the time, the mid-1980s were dominated by soft rock groups employing the latest in synthesiser technology. There was something intriguing in the song's construction, in its Who-inspired maniacal dash for the finish line, that convinced me to buy the album on the day it came out."

'Clutching At Straws' was released 22 June 1987, reaching No.2 in the UK album charts. Fan Jeff Pelletier, "As soon as I heard the 'Warm Wet Circles' trilogy for the very first time I was captivated, enthralled, mesmerized and left in a state of bewildered awe. This was literally unlike anything I'd ever heard. Such poetic phrasings and visceral images woven into musically complex tapestries, in a way that was completely accessible to anyone with a sense of adventure and open enough to appreciate it." For fan Max Rael it was an escape. "I got into Marillion in 1987 after the school bully 'persuaded' me to purchase a copy of *'Clutching At Straws'*, which he'd nicked from a record store! It was on a school trip to Weymouth and in the dark on the coach I put the tape into my Walkman. From the opening chords of 'Hotel Hobbies' I was transported away from my adolescent hell into a new world!"

Steve Rothery, waking up in his own time

Another fan Martin Thorpe recounts, "I was into Big Country, Simple Minds and U2 at the time. Previously, Adam and The Ants was THE band for me and then I just went off music. With *'Clutching At Straws'*, Marillion were the band that re-ignited the flame." Not all fans thought as much, "When *'Clutching At Straws'* came out I remember my hardcore fan friend thought it a bit of a let-down," recalls fan Paul Rael. "I thought it was a bit ropey too although I loved 'Warm Wet Circles'."

'Sugar Mice' and (a remixed) 'Warm Wet Circles'. followed as singles in July and October respectively, each reaching No.22 in the UK charts. To the outside world, the ship was holding steady.

Making the 'Incommunicado' Cover by Iain Watkins

The mid '80s were an exciting time for me, having just left home as a 17 year old and set out for a new life in Edinburgh as a college student. Music was a very important part of my life at that time, with nothing more important than grasping every opportunity to see Marillion live in concert and collecting every possible release, including bootleg recordings. It was quite common for me to travel the length and breadth of the country any time Marillion were touring in order to maximise my exposure to them, such was my obsession. I remember one time in particular, watching them on a Christmas tour at Friars, Aylesbury, one night and having to hitch it all the way home to Castle Douglas in the south-west of Scotland, in order to leave straight away and go up to Glasgow to see them play the following evening.

I didn't need a second invite when I heard they were looking for a handful of fans to attend the Marquee for a photo shoot. It was a young lady called Angie running the fan club who invited me down for the photo shoot. I had got to know her through another Marillion obsessive, Clive Aspinall (who also features on the cover). As soon as the letter came through, I was off to the bus station in Edinburgh, to work out how best to get myself down to London the following weekend. Being a student (in name only, most of the time I spent following the band) I was pretty hard up, so I had to dig deep to find the fare down to London. I worked out that I would save a few pounds by going on the overnight service from Edinburgh, getting me into London just in time to make a mad dash via tube to Wardour street in time for the shoot. The journey there was a nightmare from hell. I had a really bad toothache so I spent most of the journey crunching aspirins and swigging on a half bottle of whisky, to try and numb the pain. By the time I arrived in London, the combination of adrenalin and whisky had killed the pain and probably rotted away the nerve causing all the pain in the process. I arrived at the Marquee, met up with a lot of familiar faces and spent the next half hour swapping Marillion stories and catching up. Shortly after, Fish turned up with Mark Wilkinson. Before the actual photo-shoot began, Fish pointed out that there was something missing, cans of beer! I went to a local mini-market with a couple of other fans, to purchase a load of cans, courtesy of Fish. Even though it was about 7am and just getting light, we had to make it look realistic by drinking cans of beer for the camera, not too much of a hardship for the average Marillion fan in those days!

The photo shoot itself lasted about half an hour, Mark Wilkinson taking umpteen photos in various poses. My heart missed a beat or two when Fish picked me out from the crowd of about 20 and asked me to stand against one of the lampposts and look up towards the Marquee sign. How I prayed for that pose to be the final choice for the cover, but alas it wasn't to be. I was slightly disappointed with the final choice, as most of my body was blackened out to make it look like it was night time. Still, at least there was no mistaking my face, what little there was of it, a massive thrill! I'm not sure the counter assistant in HMV Edinburgh shared my enthusiasm when I rushed in there first thing in the morning on the day of the single's release, what a strange look he gave me when I pointed out that that was ME on the cover of the new Marillion single!

As soon as the photo session was over, we spent about half an hour chatting with Fish and getting various bits and pieces signed. Then it was off to McDonalds around the corner for breakfast, where I managed to get Mark Wilkinson to sign my entire collection of Marillion 12" singles and had a brief chat with him - brilliant!

I had made an 800-mile round trip for the sake of a couple of hours in the company of my teenage hero and to get my photo taken. Some would say mad, but these are the things that you do when you are a hardcore Marillion fan.

Off I set on my return journey to Edinburgh, with a handful of wonderful memories to recollect on the way home.

The Last Tour

Following a video shoot for 'Incommunicado' on 14 April 1987 at the Marquee, (according to Avril Mackintosh, "It was the most boring, tedious afternoon you could ever have!"), touring started for real in Poland on 22 June. After the studio debacles, the band hit the road with some relief. It was to be another globetrotting, high-living tour, however this time really was the last straw. Even at the start, Fish knew the end was in sight. "Fish came to see me at the beginning of the tour and said he was definitely leaving at the end of it," recalls John. "I kept quiet with the others, but asked him not to leave, I said it's been a rollercoaster for five years, go and do a solo album." The possibility of a solo project was always there, at least in theory. In practice, touring and promotion were everything, even more than the personal lives of the bands. "Solo project? When was that supposed to happen?" asks Fish. Says Ian, "If John had been stronger at the time then Fish could have done his solo project." The high living that had been so much fun was turning sour for everyone, including the manager. On one occasion (reputed to be a production rehearsal in Aberdeen), John surpassed himself by throwing up all over the brand new stage set. "John didn't do himself any favours," continues Ian, but nor did anyone else, as the majority of the band continued to believe they were just having fun.

full circle

The appearance of fans on the 'Incommunicado' cover was decided at a meeting with EMI, Fish and Mark Wilkinson. "The song mentioned the Marquee, we wanted to put the Angel on the cover, it was a nice tie-in!" says Fish. "A lot of the fans were those that had been to see us since 1982."

June 1987, playing with Queen in Germany

A month into the tour, two weeks after the release of 'Sugar Mice' and following a festival gig at Lorelei[8] in Germany, everyone (including John Arnison and his heavily pregnant wife Ginny) headed back to Haddington in Scotland for Fish's wedding to Tamara. One invitee to the events of 25 July 1987 was Avril Mackintosh. "What do you get someone like that!" she laughs. "I got him a whole Scottish salmon; I thought he'd like that!" Ian and Privet were Fish's 'best men'. Says Fish, "I'd always got on really well with Ian; we'd stayed at his house, me and Tammi, she was around when Michael was born. Ian had already done a lot of stuff and ticked it off, he was very grounded and very solid. He was a lot more mature than I was, I was drawn to him for that reason." For Fish, family was the one thing that everyone had and he did not. "A lot had a family situation waiting for them, Mark would go back to Suzy and his kids, Steve to Jo, Ian to Wanda. I didn't have a relationship to go back to, it was strange!" says Fish. Immediately he got his chance to be 'normal', it was whipped away from him. Fish and Tammi, spent their 'honeymoon' in the US, having 'volunteered' to do promotional duties prior to the planned tour. Rod Smallwood, Iron Maiden's (and later Marillion's) representation in the US, offered use of his house and car to make up for the honeymoon. As the single didn't do as well as hoped, the tour was postponed but nobody told Fish. "We were just sat there for two weeks. John Arnison never had the balls to tell me that the tour had been put back." he says. Counters John, whose attention was on soon-to-deliver Ginny at the time, "As I'd gone into partnership with Rod, I felt he was in good hands and that Rod would keep him up to date." Fish and Tammi returned home, then a few weeks later, in September, Marillion left to tour the US and Canada for real, leaving John Arnison behind. "I missed the start of the US Tour," says John, "then four days after the birth I travelled to Denver to meet up with the band."

Birth or no birth, by the time John arrived in the US, Fish was livid. Through an ironic twist, it was also time for John's contract to be renewed. Fish's view was that the contract should be annulled. However, the rest of the band felt entirely in Fish's shadow. "We saw John as a buffer between ourselves and Fish," says Mark. Agrees Fish, "They were terrified that I would bring someone else in and turn it into the Fish band! I just wanted strong management!" Things were getting far too much for John, who turned up at venues drunk (or worse). Fish was understandably cross, but given John's valid complaints about his off-stage antics, he was not in a position to preach. Comments Mark, "We knew John was out of order, he couldn't function." But Fish's suggested alternative, Andy Field, was not much of a better role model. "Fish suggested we replaced John with Andy, but all three were out of order!"

An additional bone of contention was the way John was paid, as he took his percentage before many of the bills had been cleared. If there were plenty of bills, the result could be that John took his percentage, and the band could be left with nothing. "If we toured for a year and didn't make any money, he did," remembers Mark. "But that's what he knew, he was a touring manager, he was good at organising tours. There were

clutching at gold

Ian's reputation as a sober individual took a battering the night after Lorelei, when he was found, unconscious, in a hotel corridor with coins lying all around him, clutching a gold album to his chest. He claims it was the brandy in the chocolate milk!

tours we did where he didn't take a commission or he took a reduced commission, but if we let him get away with it, he would!" John remembers it slightly differently: "It was quite simple, if the band did not make money, neither did I," he says. Perhaps the real issue was that the band had absolutely no idea of where and how the money was being spent. "We were a running joke at the air freight company - when we came back from Japan, everything was air freighted, it would have cost less to buy it all new!" says Fish. Unconscious of cost, the boys would choose to sleep in a hotel for the night, rather than on the tour bus. So would the crew! The band required two articulated trucks to carry all their equipment, laughs Mark, "When we arrived at The Coach House in San Juan Capistrano, the owner couldn't believe it, two huge trucks for his tiny club!" "We only unpacked one of them," comments Pete, "The other [a triangle set, used for the bigger venues] was used for the two big shows in Canada."

smooth mover

On 22 December at the NEC in Birmingham, Mark Kelly tried strapping a portable keyboard around his neck so he could move around. He recalls, "The strap was too short and the mains lead pulled out and it wouldn't work. I got a bit annoyed and slung it on the ground, it seemed the best thing to do at the time!"

In the end the majority of the band decided to stick with the management status quo. "Steve Rothery was my saviour," says John. "He came to me and basically said, 'John, you are a great manager but your drinking is starting to worry us. You need to sort yourself out.' So at the end of the tour with a nudge from Ginny I did." From Fish's perspective the replace-John-with-Andy campaign had been more of an stipulation than a suggestion, when it wasn't to be, his isolation was complete. "I was alienated from the band by their decision and my cards were marked by the manager, who now knew of my intentions and realised it was him or me," Fish confirms in the sleeve notes to the *'Clutching At Straws'* remaster. John quickly ordered a shake-up in the crew, to ensure dissent was minimised. He sacked Fish's mates, even Andy Field was nearly out. "John was ruthless with the crew," says Mark.

Thus started the most successful tour of Marillion's twenty-year career with any vestiges of team spirit gone. According to Ian, "[Fish] used to disappear into his hotel room and not come out for several days." Fish's black mood became blacker still. "It was tough," he says. "We were playing shit gigs with shit PAs, we went though monitor engineers like jelly babies!" In Canada at the beginning of October, Fish lost his voice again. To the relief of the others, he agreed to confine himself to quarters. Says Rothers, "When we went to find him two days later, he was completely out of it!"

Marillion returned for the second European leg of the tour on 3 November, starting with three nights in a row at a sold-out Wembley Arena. "That was big time!" says Ian, but it was also the last time. "It all started to come apart," recalls Mark. "We were partying pretty hard, we went nuts in Berlin!" It was becoming increasingly clear that Marillion was no longer a unit. Continues Mark, "We started to avoid Fish, he just didn't know when to stop. We used to make Paul room with him as nobody else wanted to!" "I hated the tour," remarks Pete. "I could see the end coming, the shows were too big, the audiences didn't care, the band didn't play as well as they could, there was rowing all the time, and we were kept in a bubble, we couldn't communicate with anyone." Date after date, in front of the largest crowds ever, each night Fish's demons were the same as the last. Steve elaborates, "The realization of the success he'd craved had left Fish feeling trapped and exploited." Fish concurs, "I knew I was isolated, I was suffering, I was gone. I needed a break, I had girlfriend problems, my whole relationship was falling apart." Says Ian, "That tour was our most successful, but our most unhappy. We could tell he was frustrated. I've never taken anything for granted, I remember walking out on stage in the soundchecks, there were

Fish in touch with his audience, Birmingham NEC, Dec 1987

thousands of lights above my head, three artics [articulated lorries] in front of me, about 60 people all working for us, it was amazing, but Fish took it all for granted." Hindsight suggests this would have been a good moment to can the tour, but the damage was already done.

After a couple of weeks off for Christmas, the band went back on tour. Feeling alienated, Fish found solace in the bar. "He overindulged his naturally excessive tendencies and became harder and harder to work with," recalls Steve. "He seemed to be on a mission to self-destruct, something was going to give." On 12 February 1988, Fish lost his voice again in Modena, Italy, resulting in a number of cancelled dates as the seams finally unravelled. "I sang one whole gig a tone down, the hotel walls were really thin, I could hear the band talking about how they were going to replace me," says Fish. "It was obvious to all of us that things couldn't continue like that," remarks Ian. Remembers John, "The boys asked me if I thought they could carry on without Fish. I said 'Yes'" Unfortunately, the bus driver was in earshot, and reported what he had heard. "You can imagine what Fish's reaction was," continues John. The band was united in its opinions, and was unanimous against the front man. Fish had too many reasons not to go with the flow, and the band had too many reasons not to listen.

At the end of the tour in February 1988, John Arnison checked into a clinic in Chelsea for six weeks, prompted by his wife Ginny who had had enough. "Ginny kicked me out, she accused me of being an alcoholic, so I checked in to find out." It turned out drink was largely the symptom, and extreme stress was the main cause of John's ailment. Various band members went to see John during his stay, "I remember saying hello to Frank Bough on the way in!" laughs Ian. According to Mark, "At the clinic John told the story of what we had been up to, they recommended that he should get the band in as well!" The sojourn in the clinic was proof to Fish of John's inability to manage them. "The band told me we had to give him another chance," says Fish. Dwayne Welch stepped in as interim manager, but with John absent, the man who was best at keeping the band together was out of the frame for just long enough for it to matter.

The gigs resumed 10 days later in Cornwall for what was the very last leg of Marillion's Fish-fronted touring history. Only eleven more dates would be played with Fish in the line-up. The tour ended in Bourges in France, on the 4 April. Three weeks later the band played the Marquee Club, following which Fish and Tammi had their honeymoon in the Caribbean, "It was the first break in a long, long time," says Fish. Too little, too late.

Runaway Boy by Dan Henderson

In the summer of 1987 the 'Marquee Choral Society', as we were known, jumped on a concert trip to Lorelei, for a fantastic trip to see the boys' *'Clutching At Straws'* tour, which wouldn't be coming to the UK until November.

About twelve coaches made the journey from Waterloo to Frankfurt and there was plenty of clowning about as you can imagine. They were strange days. Nobody could quite work out what was going on with the backing singer, Cori I think her name was. Temperamental by all accounts, floods of tears and "I'm not going on!" being quite frequent occurrences. The Cult were originally due to be supporting along with Magnum, but had double-booked themselves playing gigs in the States with Billy Idol. It Bites, who had the previous year been in the charts with 'Calling All The Heroes', were drafted in at short notice to fill in. They were great, but not really much compensation for the sixty or so Cult fans who had little interest in anyone else on the bill.

I worked that summer doing all manner of brainless jobs to get as much cash as I could to get out to America to see the shows there. Patsy Smith ('Angie' from the Web) gave me details of the tour itinerary so I could plan my jaunt. I only got to three shows while I was there and I know the band didn't really enjoy the tour, but for me they were great. The first show was in NYC at the Ritz and I was surprised at the following they had built up, having heard the tales of woe from the Script tour with Rush.

Later that week I went to Albany to catch another show, I think it was at the State Theatre. The exchange rate at the time was about £1 to $1.07 so my £450.00 wasn't going to last me too long and as I needed to be a bit more economic than the extravagance of the YMCA in New York, I went down to the Salvation Army! They didn't have anywhere for me, but gave me the address of a runaway shelter who they thought might put me up! I went to the address and they welcomed me in. There were about 15 people staying there, from young lads and girls of about 8 to about 19 and they were very welcoming, if a little strange. They got about $30.00 each a week to spend and I managed to get them all to spend most of that on tickets to go see a band none of them had ever heard! It was a weird show. Only about 200 people in a theatre about the size of the Edinburgh Playhouse! We were all down the front and loving it!

The other show I got to was in Rochester, New York. This one was really odd. I'm sure it was in the crypt of a church with no stage and after the second song, 'Assassing', Fish got everyone to sit down which the 500 or so people duly did. Cross-legged for about 2 hours, very rock'n'roll!

going under

To outsiders, all seemed well as Marillion headed to Glenshee in Scotland to record the next album. The fans still had the upper hand. When *'B'Sides Themselves'* was released (initially on CD only) on 4 January 1988, EMI caved under pressure from the fan base to release the album on other formats in June. "Again, fan power has succeeded!" the Web magazine announced. Despite such external positivity, cliché followed cliché from this point on. The end was in sight, starting with the gig too far, Fife Aid.

Castles In The Sand

The summer of 1988 was the charity season and everyone was feeling generous. Few who were at the Wellhead Inn in Wendover on 27 May 1988, on the occasion of Trevor Dorking's (who later became Mark's keyboard tech) wedding to Mark's then-wife Suzy's sister, knew it would be the last time Marillion would play in the Aylesbury area with Fish at the helm. "It was just a party," recalls Mark. "Some of us got up and played a few songs." Two weeks later, on 11 June 1988, Mark and Fish appeared as part of Midge Ure's All-Star band at the Nelson Mandela concert, Wembley Stadium. They performed 'Kayleigh' with Phil Collins on drums and Midge on guitar. According to a Web fanzine, "Steve was in the audience watching, he gave a nod of approval" to Midge's attempt at the guitar solo!

On 18 June the band played a festival gig at the Weissensee Radrenbahn in East Berlin. Paul Lewis wrote in The Web fanzine, "With an audience of 95,000 people it was the largest headline the band had ever done. It was one and three quarter hours, and three

Still having fun at the Wellhead Inn, Wendover, 27 May 1987

encores long and it was wonderful!" "It was an amazing atmosphere, it was just before the wall came down," remembers Ian. "We played a blinding gig, and couldn't help being on a high, but as we came off Fish said, 'I didn't really enjoy that.'" I thought, we're in trouble here!" Mark, Pete, Ian and Steve all went to bed early that night, leaving Fish to hit the town by himself. "This was a common occurrence by then," explains Mark, "We avoided Fish as much as possible; no one could keep up with his partying!"

23 July saw the band play the second Fife Aid festival at Craigtoun Country Park in St Andrews, Scotland. According to Mark, Fish had manoeuvred the others with typical aplomb. "He told John Arnison that we were into it, then told us that John was into it, we fell for it that time!" There was still little outside indication that the band was on its last legs. Fan Paul Hughes, who met the band, remembers, "picking up very little in the way of bad vibes concerning the band's future. Their professionalism did them credit!"

As the band returned from the North, Ian's long-time drum roadie, crew boss and true gent, Andy Field, was diagnosed with Hodgkinson's Disease. Remembers Ian, "He went through all the chemo, and came back all clear." Marillion returned to

Buckinghamshire in their red van, spending time writing and testing out ideas at Hayden Hill Farmhouse, Aylesbury, Pete's house... "The band used to rehearse in Nomis Studio in London, but it got very expensive." Pete explains. Priv and Andy Field sound-proofed Pete's double garage with Rockwool and hardboard, providing a perfectly acceptable rehearsal room. The sound quality, "wasn't too bad" according to Rothers, who had experienced far worse. Meanwhile, the band relations were steadily worsening; it was becoming clear Fish's attitude was hardening. "He was forcing an awful lot of himself on what we had all worked on, and in a way lessening our input, our work was becoming a bit too much of a musical backdrop," remarks Pete, "It seemed that we would spend months working on stuff, then he'd come in with a lyric he'd just written down the pub and just sing that, so we thought, why do we bother?"

Finally some demos[9] were produced at Tone Deaf studios, in Wallingford, near Oxford. Bob Ezrin[10] came over as a potential producer. Ironically he had previously been brought in to co-produce *'The Wall'* for Pink Floyd, at a time it was having its own internal conflicts. Bob surmised the material was nowhere near recording standard. "I had huge respect for Bob Ezrin until I met him," says Pete, "he didn't really like what we had done, he said it was stuff we could knock out in our sleep. But when he sat at the piano and showed us what he might do, it was much too Andrew Lloyd Webber!" Ironically, despite his isolation Fish recalls a better Ezrin experience than the others. "We got on brilliantly!" says Fish. "He asked me to produce a drinking song, I came back with 'The Company', he loved it!"

A Victorian folly at Dalnaglar in Scotland, was proposed by Fish (through a Scottish Nationalist friend, Robbie the Pict) as a location that could keep out the world and let the five attempt to be creative. So the band and Andy Field trudged to the Highlands with the weight of the world on their shoulders. The tenuous progress wasn't helped when Mark Wilkinson sent an ill-timed proposal for the cover of a book about album artwork to the rest of the band. The covers had already caused conflict. "Fish was trying to put his stamp on everything, some ideas were his, but some weren't! We thought Fish was going behind our backs," explains Pete. The vast majority of the concepts on the album covers were the fruits of Fish's imagination, but principle was taking over. Says Pete, "Fish appeared

Dinner with Fish and Ian Mosley, Dalnaglar Castle, July-August 1988

to want the rest of the world to think that Marillion was him, and that was unacceptable to the rest of us."

Some writing did take place at Dalnaglar, notably the lyrics for a song entitled 'Internal Exile', rejected by the rest of the band due to their rather nationalist content. Fish was not unaware of the difficulties his nationalism would cause, "I think I used it to drive a wedge between me and the band," he

remarked later. Visitor Paul Lewis, noticed things were abnormal. "I had gone up on my motorcycle and, after dinner, Fish and I went to the local pub for a beer but none of the rest of the band would come out to play, which I thought was a bit weird." According to Mark, "we'd just had enough!"

An Expected Departure

The walls of Dalnaglar were not high enough. Marillion was pursuing a seven- figure publishing deal with Charisma that would have made each member very well off. "It was a five-album deal, and they really believed in the band, they were prepared to pay a sizeable chunk up front," remarks John Arnison. "We agreed as a band, including Fish, that we couldn't really sign the deal," says Ian. "It would have taken another three years to sort out the litigation!" Fish's position was untenable for the rest of the band, and vice versa. "We set up two separate creative camps," commented Fish, who spent time at neighbour Mickey Simmonds' place, ostensibly to give him someone to work with. "Fish would turn up very occasionally; he just wasn't interested," remarks Ian. Adds Mark, "He used to stay long enough to tell us the music we were working on was 'shite' and then leave. To be fair, we were as complimentary about the lyrics he showed us." One was the lyrical beginnings of *'Vigil In The Wilderness Of Mirrors'*. Remembers Fish, "I sang the whole start of *'Vigil'*, and at the end of it, they just said, nah."

Pete looking content, and Rothers practising at Dalnaglar

Bizarrely the final nail was nothing to do with music, money or management. It related to the back-catalogue of artwork, which was in store at Mark Kelly's, as John Arnison was moving office. "I said I'd take them home," recalls Mark. "Fish said he wanted them all so I suggested he picked the ones he wanted. He said he wanted them all." Incensed, Mark took the hugely valuable, carefully crafted originals of Marillion's album and single covers, and dumped then on Fish's doorstep. Matters came rapidly to a head. On Thursday 15 September, Fish wrote a three-page letter saying he couldn't believe the vitriol Mark was showing, and by the way he wanted 50% of the income. According to Ian, "We called each other up and everyone's response was the same, well, he can just fuck off!" Fish was returned a half-page note with words to the same effect, signed by Mark, Pete, Ian and Steve. A final meeting at Ian's house between John

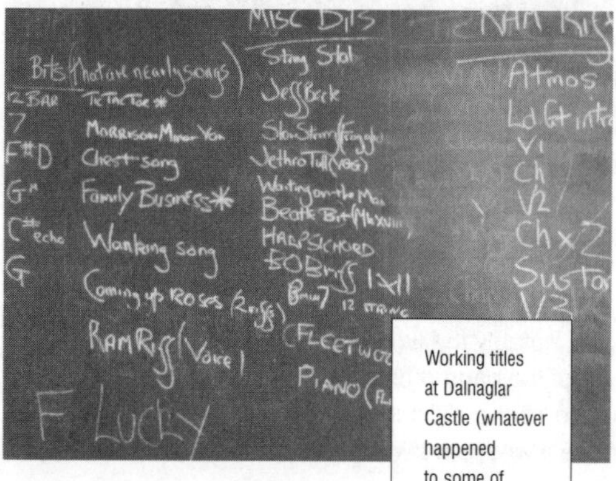

Working titles at Dalnaglar Castle (whatever happened to some of those...!)

and the band failed to resolve matters, and the following day Fish announced to the world that he had resigned from Marillion. His official resignation letter said, "I've had a brilliant seven years with Marillion; however, recently the musical directions of the band have diversified to such an extent I realised the time had come to embark on a solo career." Unofficially, Fish's reaction was, "Fuck it, I'm off, there's no point in hanging around." Marillion composed a letter to the fanclub: "During the process of writing the new album it became apparent that differences, both musically and lyrically, between Fish and the rest of the band were irreconcilable." For some fans, Fish's departure was unbearable. "I just about cried when Fish left," says fan Lee Clark. Judith Mitchell concurs, "I was really depressed, I didn't talk to anyone for about two weeks!" Paul Hughes remembers, "I was the only fan at my school, and well known for it. Many took great pleasure in announcing the news to me like they'd just caught a messenger pigeon carrying the details."

As far back as 1984, Fish had remarked that his stay in the band might have a sell-by date. It is difficult to say whether things could have ended any differently. Comments Paul Lewis, "He was in one of the most successful bands of the day, drinking lots and not happy with his life, something had to change. Perhaps a year off might have helped them all recover, but the band were hot and that would have slowed down their career a great deal." Concurs Mark, "We needed six months off! If we'd had that, we probably wouldn't have broken up!" Once Fish had decided to go, there was no changing his mind, nor did anyone particularly want him to. "I felt, what a bloody shame!" remembers Steve. "I was pissed off!" remarks Paul. "That year would have been a big earner for all the band, myself included!" Adds Priv, "It also split up what was one of the greatest crews I have ever worked on. That for me was at least as great a hardship."

As a goodbye and thank you to the fans, 'Freaks' was released as a last single on 21 November 1988, and eight days later a live album, *'La Gazza Ladra'*, was also sent to the shops. "It gave us all a bit of breathing space," explains Pete. Overdubs had been recorded at Westside with Nick Davis, the last time that Fish would collaborate with the others in the band on a recording. "He insisted none of us were there!" says Mark. The album took its name from Rossini's original music in 'The Clockwork Orange'. "The music accompanies every scene of violence or rape," explains Fish, poignantly.

ashes to ashes

The vinyl version of *'The Thieving Magpie'* had the inscription "and out of the ashes..." engraved in the inner spiral of side two of the second disc.

And, with that, it really was history.

NOTES: 1 This was to be called Gheisterfahrer. **2** 'Lady Nina' eventually was released as a single in the US, briefly reaching the Billboard Top 100. **3** The Head of Capitol at the time was Walter Lee. According to Fish this was linked to Payola, documented in the book 'Hit Men' by Frederic Dannen. **4** Notably, the first digitally mastered album in the UK. **5** Where the band stored its equipment. **6** Fish's house was just round the corner from Ian's, making either place the logical choice for meetings according to Ian. **7** Fish's favourite costume was Torch's flame suit, also used on the Clutching At Straws tour. **8** Recorded for *'Live at Lorelei, St Goar - Freilichtbuhne Lorelei'*. The gig was supported by Magnum, whose production manager at the time was Kelvin George Boys-Yates, better known as Yatta. **9** Later to appear on the *'Clutching At Straws'* bonus disc. **10** Although at odds with Mark's memories on the *'Clutching At Straws'* sleeve notes, these timings are correct.

The four-piece band, Utrecht, airport Nov 1988

chapter three new seasons/1989-1994

"If I told you what our music is really about we'd probably all get arrested."

Bob Dylan

Fish's departure had lost Marillion a lyricist, a singer and a rock star with crowd-pulling charisma. Despite such calamitous circumstances, there remained a few steady rays of hope. The band had completed a good proportion of the music for the planned album; the remaining members were as close as they had ever been; finally, the contract with EMI was still in place, providing some guarantee of support, coupled with the backing of re-invigorated management in the shape of John Arnison.

The next few months, not to mention years, would test Marillion's mettle and determination as it came to terms with its past and set about deciding its future. They would also offer new freedom and opportunity, in the way only a crisis can. Quite early on it was agreed that to quit was not an option - each member had invested too much of himself to give up now.

The only way was forward.

keeping the momentum

To many outsiders, Fish's resignation spelled the end of Marillion. To the band however, crisis there may have been, but no drama. "The biggest feeling I experienced was relief," recalled Steve Rothery at the time. "It was like a huge weight being lifted off my

Pete sings his heart out at the Utrecht fan gig

shoulders." Neither had the resignation been a total surprise, as Mark Kelly remarked, "Things were not going well, we sort of expected it so we weren't as devastated as people might have thought." There remained always the music - the torch was still burning, though its bearer might have thrown it down. "The music's powerful pull and unique sound is self-sustaining," Ian commented, "But its components would undergo a dreaded yet inevitable transition."

One conclusion was obvious: Marillion was not seeking another Fish. Not that anyone denied the gaping holes that he had left. "We knew we were going to spend ages looking for a singer," remarks Pete. "We knew we didn't want to be 'the best Marillion covers band around.' But we didn't really know what we did want!" Rather than trying to find one person possessing all the facets of the now-solo vocalist, the remaining members set about filling the gaps, one by one.

We Wake Up Without You

When it took stock, the band found itself with plenty of musical ideas. "'King Of Sunset Town', 'Seasons End' and 'Berlin' were pretty much all finished," remembers Steve Rothery. Parts of 'The Space' and 'Uninvited Guest' also had shape, written in at Dalnaglar in Scotland. Rehearsals continued in Pete's garage. There was, however, a shortage of words. "Fish was a brilliant lyricist," comments Pete. "None of us really felt we could write a good lyric." First priority, then, was to fill the lyrical void. A number of songwriters were considered, including Viv Stanshall of the Bonzo Dog Doo Dah Band. "He showed myself and Ian a bunch of lyrics that he'd already written but, although we thought they were good, we didn't think they had enough depth for Marillion," says Mark. Adds Rothers, "Charming chap, though - and a complete nutter!" Finally EMI came to the band's aid by recommending Brighton-based John Helmer. John had been involved in a number of bands, notably The Piranhas. His only knowledge of Marillion had been the occasional TV experience and the tenuous connection of a girlfriend having worked on a Marillion video with Fish. All the same, he was interested. "Marillion came at the right time for me," he comments. "I was making house records and doing some remixing, I'd just got married and I felt there were more things to do than being in a band." John was sent some sheets of Fish lyrics, which were instantly daunting: "They included lines like 'a hand held over a candle in angst-filled bravado'. Whatever followed had to be equally distinctive - I couldn't get away with 'Fish lite'!"

And then there were four - Tivoli Theatre, Utrecht, November 1988

While commercial gigs were cancelled, a couple of fan club shows had been booked, and the show just had to go on. The first, at the Tivoli Theatre in Utrecht, was without a singer at all, explains Jeroen Schipper who had certainly chosen his moment to get into the band. "The first Marillion concert I had tickets for was cancelled. However I did become a member of the fan club and went to my first Marillion fan club meeting in Utrecht. To my surprise the remaining four Marillion members were there and they played a few songs. The audience was responsible for the vocals (together with Pete) which was truly amazing!" At Liverpool's Royal Court the job was handed to Dave Lloyd of Rage, John Arnison's other signing and a good mate with the band. "Dave was a good choice, he could be front man and keep the troops going," comments Pete. Adds Mark, "It went down surprisingly well, especially considering that Dave didn't know any of the songs!"

In early winter 1988, John Helmer met with Rothers at a Hammersmith pub round the corner from the Odeon, to get a handle on Marillion's lyrical requirements. First on the agenda was a piece of music inspired by the three months the band spent in Berlin in 1985. Fortunately, John had his own reservoir of thinking man's rock experience. "I was into bands such as King Crimson as a teenager; to me it was like revisiting roots!" So he got out his pen and wrote a first cut of what would become 'Berlin', before heading up to Aylesbury to meet with the other members of the band. Comments John, "I'd never been to Berlin, so I referenced literary sources like Tasker and TS Eliott to see if anyone would notice! Whatever it was that John drew upon, it worked. "John was the one lyricist who stood out to me," recalled Rothers. "It was so different to the stuff Fish was doing - good, strong, colourful imagery, but emotionally very direct."

The Marillos felt comfortable enough to let John get going on some other ideas. Each time, Mark and Steve ran

freshly squeezed

"They'd got all this gear set up in Pete's garage.
It was just ridiculous, like all the gear in the world crammed into an outside toilet. Mark's setup had walls of keyboards in those days. It was a bit like cramming into the back room of a music shop!"

Steve Hogarth

through what they had in mind without playing him the music, not the easiest starting point for a lyricist but somehow, John came up trumps. "My lyrics struck the right chord, something that really amazed me because they were born out of a completely different style of music, but it worked," remarked John at the time. One brief concerned the environment - "Before it got trendy!" laughed Rothers in a web interview. "John went away over Christmas and wrote 'Seasons End' exactly as it is on the album."

Now I'm Here

With Pete Trewavas filling in vocally during the songwriting sessions, in November an advert was placed in the back pages of popular music mags such as Melody Maker. The response was significant - hundreds of tapes were received, and a shortlist of potential singers was auditioned at Westside and Nomis Studios, including Stuart Nicholson of Galahad and Nigel Voyle of Cyan. "We had some hilarious rehearsals," laughs Pete. "People would dance around - one guy even acted out 'Fugazi' word for word!" However, nobody ever quite fitted the bill.

Six months after the fatal day in September, the band had "an unexpected piece of good luck" in the shape of a tape, which came in the post from Rondor, the music publishing house. Ironically, Rondor had been contacted in the search for lyricists, not singers! "I used to pick up bags of cassettes from the office and play them in the car on the way to Pete's where we were rehearsing," recalls Ian. "I put on the tape that Rondor had sent us and straight away I thought, this fellow's got a great voice, it's going to be too much to ask!" The rest of the band was bowled over as well. "I was very excited by what I heard," comments Pete. Even John Arnison, who usually kept out of the musical side of things, was impressed. "I listened to the tape and thought, that's the voice," he recalls.

Following a not insignificant number of pleas from interim manager Duane Welsh ("I kept fobbing him off!"), Mr Steve Hogarth went for an audition at Pete's house, the same

John Helmer

John Helmer was born and raised in Essex, moving to Brighton "the minute I was old enough," at 18. He went to University, got married and decided he wanted to be a writer, "But first I needed some experience." He joined "reggae-influenced" punk band The Piranhas as vocalist/guitarist, first performing on Jubilee day 1977 at an anti-Jubilee gig ("Even the hand stamp said 'Fuck The Jubilee'"). As well as some Helmer-penned songs "laced with a dry, sardonic wit," the band included a couple of covers in the set including a punked-up 'Let's Spend The Night Together'. The band was later to turn to Ska with the inclusion of a saxophonist, Zoot Alors.

According to Suzy Horne of the Piranhas fan club, "Their live act was one of the best around!" Unfortunately, success led to the band's downfall as it earned a silver disk for its Stock/Aitken/Waterman-produced cover of 'Tom Hark'. The Piranhas spilt soon after. "We had a choice - take the money and run, or do something more interesting," recalls John. This took the shape of "mad busking band" Pookiesnackenburger, which John formed with Nick Dwyer, Luke Cresswell and Steve McNicholas - three out of the four would go on to form Stomp, near-famous for a 1986 advert for Heineken lager. John continued with his lyrical leanings, leading him to the four-piece Marillion in 1988.

Since this time there are few Marillion albums that John has not played a part on: the only exceptions are *'Radiation'* and *'Anoraknophobia'*. Lyrics are written on-spec - if the songs make money, John takes his share of the royalties. John found time to write his first novel 'Mother Tongue' in 1998, a book that "simmers with a crisp and disturbing malevolence." He's currently working in marketing for one of the few surviving dot-com companies, at the same time as writing his second book. "I've always done what I wanted - to other people this may have seemed to be wrong-headed at times, but I've always had a sense of 'you only live once.'"

venue that had hosted the final attempts for reconciliation between Fish and the band. Things did not happen exactly as planned - Steve arrived a day late because his car had been stolen, and when he finally turned up, on a Sunday afternoon, the initial meeting had to be held on Pete's patio as Steve was "violently allergic" to Pete's two cats! Despite the chilly circumstances, the conversations were a revelation to Steve H. In an interview he commented, "When I asked them what they were looking for, I expected them to say, 'we're this big progressive rock band and we sell this many copies. It's a good living, and do you think you can sing like this?' I would have gone, well no, and cheers, and that would have been the end of it." But that wasn't the end of it. "They said, 'we've heard you singing and we've heard some songs you've written and we really like what you do,'" continued Steve. "'We just want you to do what you do and we'll do what we do and we'll see what that produces.'" Pete, Steve and Ian were a friendly bunch, and a far cry from the rockers he expected to meet. Only Mark Kelly was a little brusque - not surprising given the difficulties they had had enticing Steve for the interview.

Mark through a fish-eye lens in Pete's garage, Dec 1988

Clearly it was worth a try-out, so they spent the afternoon jamming in Pete's garage. "We ran through some of the musical ideas that we had, asking him to do some singing on them," remembers Pete. Steve had a voice, to be sure, and it was uniquely his own. "All the things we saw were positive," remarks Pete. "None of the people we had auditioned were quite real enough, but Steve was a real artist, his own kind of singer. He was more interested in his music than other people's projects." Steve H wasn't so sure at the time - "I thought I was out of tune and horrible!" Progress was rapid - as Steve H tried adding John Helmer's 'King Of Sunset Town' lyrics to one piece of music, Rothers recalled, "By 20 minutes of us playing together, it sort of existed as a song! It was evident immediately that we'd work together, creativity was effortless."

The boys and Dave Lloyd at Liverpool Royal Court, December 10 1988

In scenes reminiscent of Fish's arrival seven years before, the participants found more than the missing vocalist they had been looking for. "Everything just clicked," recalls Steve Rothery. "The minute Steve started singing it was like our whole creativity became supercharged again." Steve Hogarth was a catalyst, able to release the others from their post-Fish doldrum, not to mention the creative blocks that had pent up since the end of *'Clutching At Straws'*. "We felt that same magic that we'd had in the early days with Fish," remembered Rothery. "It was obvious to us all, right from the word go, that this was the guy for the job." Neither were they concerned that Hogarth's musical background was too mainstream - as with John Helmer that was seen as an advantage, freeing the others from the shackles of the past.

In February, following a couple of background checks, a.k.a. calling up mates - Pete telephoned Robin Boult (who knew Steve through John Otway), while Ian checked with old band-mate Darryl Way (who happened to be Steve's drinking buddy) - Marillion proposed to take Steve on for a trial period. What was more, the band wanted to bring Steve in on the same financial terms as themselves. "It all seemed very, very fair, especially considering that they were already famous selling bucket loads of records and I wasn't!" laughed Steve at the time. "The band didn't want a salaried player any more than they wanted a dictator," remarks John Arnison.

True to form, the man to be known as H didn't rush the decision but asked for a week to think it over. Recalls Steve Rothery, "We felt strongly he was the person for the job but he didn't immediately say yes, he upped and went and thought about it which we found very surprising!" It wasn't his only offer, however, as he recalls, "I was lined up to tour with Matt Johnson (of The The) in the summer. Matt was about the hippest artist in England and Marillion were about the least hip artists." Meanwhile, the band were calling up everyone they knew who knew him, particularly the aforementioned Darryl Way. "Darryl and I met over a drink and I explained what had been happening," explains Steve H. "He said, "You should go and meet them, they're really nice blokes!!" This (and other gentle nudges) were more than serendipitous, according to Mark Kelly, "We said, listen, bend his ear a bit, 'cos we really want him to join!"

a load of hot air

Most recreation time was taken up trying to make ever-more-complex hot-air balloons. "We started with a single laundry bag and a strip of balsa," remembers Nick Davis, "and we ended with ten to fifteen survival bags attached to a Calor gas burner!" The lads would drive around the Oxfordshire countryside following the balloon until the Calor ran out. "Apart from one occasion when one went so high that we lost it completely! We saw a headline that there had been a fire at a stately home..."

It's Gonna Be Alright

The grinding down process worked. To Steve Hogarth's surprise he accepted the post, joining the others at The Music Farm rehearsal studio, a former mushroom farm near Brighton, for a couple of weeks to see how things went. They went very well indeed: the fit between Steve and the other members of the band was uncannily close, for example, his and Pete's voices complimented each other perfectly. But there was more in Steve's armoury than a good pair of lungs - he possessed keyboard skills, lyrical capabilities and more. "That was such a creative time. The adrenalin was really going, it was incredible!" remembers Rothers. "We all got on really well with Steve," adds Mark Kelly. "Everything was going well and we were all very excited!" Remarks Steve Hogarth in the sleeve notes to *'Seasons End'*, "Joining Marillion was like coming in out of the cold. It was all new, decadent, a bit surreal and, for me, incredible fun!"

Also present was Nick Davis, engineer from the previous album, who had been invited in as co-producer and sound engineer. "There were enough factors changing what our sound was going to be, so we wanted to keep control," explains Pete. "Nick was ideal: he'd worked with us before, we liked his sound, it was the right combination!" Jamming was the order of the day, as the band discovered Steve Hogarth's capabilities and, more importantly, what they could accomplish as an ensemble. Some song structures were laid down, revised or adapted from previous materials, and a few songs, such as 'Hooks In You', were written from scratch with demos being prepared on Steve Rothery's Akai 12-track. "It was a monster Portastudio thing, it used these big cassette tapes like Betamax," says Steve. In the timeouts and evenings the boys did as boys do - drinking, going out, playing pool and developing the rapport still further.

Steve Hogarth had arrived with a red bucket full of cassette tapes, ideas that had

Ta-dahhh!
Mark with
'balloon'

never quite made it to disk in his previous projects. Remembers Steve, "If we ran out of ideas the boys would say, have you got anything in the bucket? and I'd take out a cassette and say, what do you think?" One significant 'bucket moment' was when he played 'Easter' to the other members of the band.[1] It had been written the year before, when Steve had been in Northern Ireland for a How We Live gig, but had never been released. As Steve played the song and the band added their own interpretation of the music (including a trademark solo by Rothers), the relationship between singer and band was cemented. Says Priv, "You got the immediate impression that he wasn't joining them, they were joining each other."

John Helmer was also invited to the love-in. Explains Mark Kelly, "Their styles not only complemented each other, but where they had to, they merged quite nicely too." In the end the newcomer composed all the vocal melodies, not to mention a substantial part of the lyrics including 'Easter' and 'Holloway Girl' in their entirety. Only 'Seasons End' and 'Uninvited Guest' escaped. "The whole thing with Steve and John worked out extremely well," noted Mark with relief. "It was almost too easy!" There was one area in which writing styles differed, and that was between H and the band: Marillion were accustomed to spending months in the studios "noodling" with the latest opus, an approach that felt too indulgent and long-winded for the pop-steady Hogarth. Laughs Mark, "When H joined the band he said, 'I can't believe how vague you are, what's going on?'"

On 28 April the band went to Outside Studios at Hook End Manor, Stoke Row, Oxfordshire to record the album for real. According to Pete, "Hook End itself is a lovely place, a very old country manor house that used to belong to Dave Gilmour." The studios at Hook End Manor were residential, with each room being decorated in its own, distinctive style. H chose the oriental room and christened it The Opium Den.[2] "It was just like being on holiday," says Ian, "We just played tennis every day and built hot air balloons!" Progress was smooth and painless, apart from one day when a policeman turned up with a lawyer to serve an injunction from Fish. Explains Mark, "The injunction was to impound our equipment because technically, Fish still owned one fifth of it." As both camps were intent on releasing an album before the other, the band was not going to be slowed down. They stopped recording, for a little while anyway, then itwas back to business.

Darryl Way
and Steve H
at Hook
End Manor

On May 14 Steve H celebrated his birthday there, putting paid to his reputation as a lightweight. "I spent most of it upside down, I was doing handstands on the table because I was so drunk!"

With confidence high the boys could get on and complete what was to be Steve H's first album with Marillion. He later remarked that the recording was like, "Getting in bed with someone for the first time, some really special moments but there was some awkwardness for me." The mixing and completion of the album took place at London's Westside studios in early summer. Marillion were justly proud, particularly considering the ashes from which they rose. Rothers commented to journalist and fan Rich Wilson that, "Considering some people had written us off following Fish leaving, it was a very strong statement that the band still had a lot going for it. And what we found was something equally exciting and original as we had found with Fish." The final word goes to new boy Steve Hogarth who said to journalist Mick Wall at the time, "I don't know about the rest of the guys but this is definitely the best piece of work I've ever had a hand in."

'Seasons End'

Marillion's first album with a new singer had to work. Although the press interviews of the time suggested the band weren't worried about finding someone to replace Fish, there must have been considerable tension as the album was released. So, how does Hogarth compare? The honest truth is that Hogarth doesn't compare. Hogarth contrasts. Where Fish would have been bitter and twisted, Hogarth is optimistic - compare the two eras' comments on the Irish Troubles; Fish with the barbed anguish of 'Forgotten Sons', Hogarth with the plaintive lament, 'Easter'. In general terms, Fish is Lennon using horizontal tones - dissonant and harmonic, keeping close to the cadences of speech, to Hogarth's McCartney with vertical tones - consonant and melodic - the clearly musical mind always creating ways for his words to swoop and soar.

Lyrically, the album has a broad agenda of issues - climate change, wrongful imprisonment, the Irish Troubles, the Iron Curtain, but "It's more of a humanitarian thing, than a political thing," argued Pete to the Melody Maker.

The album opener, 'The King of Sunset Town' begins with a whisper of bubbling keyboards, punctuated by smoky clouds of atmosphere. Pete's bass gives us glimpses of something approaching through the mist, as Ian starts raising the tension with some nifty cymbal work. Just as it gets all too much, Steve Rothery cuts loose with an exuberant, uplifting solo, and Ian beats his drums to shiny pieces, before coming back to earth for the entrance of Steve Hogarth. After a soulful verse, Hogarth launches into his first chorus, and by God, the man reaches the outer stratosphere! An oblique dissection of the Tiananmen Square massacre, the song perhaps shows its dual lyrical authorship - outside writer John Helmer provided the original lyric, inspired by G.K. Chesterton. Musically not a million miles from traditional Marillion territory, the listener is under no illusions as to the power of the newcomer's talents, and there's a palpable sense that we can rest easy as it draws to a close. It's done its work - it's still the band we loved, and the new boy sure can cut it!

courting disaster

Both sides of the divide agree the only people to make money out of the split were the lawyers. Representing Marillion was John Ireland at Lee & Thompson, who had represented Roger Waters following his departure from Pink Floyd; representing Fish was Mr Reuben at Sheridans, who had worked for Dave Gilmour and Co. "Ireland was still smarting from having lost to Gilmour and Co. so he was spoiling for a fight!" says Mark. Eventually, an (even more expensive) QC advised Marillion to settle; Fish was advised similarly by his counsel. "Fish was right, we should have all been more mature then," remarks Ian, who used to take a chess clock along to meetings to keep the expense down.

'Easter' starts out like a distant cover of the 'Skye Boat Song', folky, gentle and whimsical, yet melancholy. Steve Hogarth paints pastoral vignettes of life in Ireland, interspersed with images of the fortitude of the people in carrying on in the face of the violence that, although unwanted by most, pervades their society. The chorus is a plaintive, though perhaps simplistic plea for peace. Steve Rothery delivers a heartbreakingly beautiful and haunting solo before the song changes direction, and gives an agenda. Based on W. B. Yeats' 'Easter 1916', Hogarth argues passionately against the violence, telling us it only harms one's own, and it's time to find a different way.

After such a song, 'The Uninvited Guest', both musically and lyrically seems like a welcome break, being a cod-gothic tale of the consequences of selfish behaviour. In fact, Helmer's lyric, far from being Hammer Horror, is a cautionary tale about living with the HIV virus, not that you'd probably guess without being told. Musically, it was designed as a sing-along rocker for the audience, and as such, works perfectly.

The title track tells of the destruction of the ozone layer, reflectively discussing the implications of our arrogance in poisoning our planet - this lyrically kicked off when John Helmer's wife mentioned the morning's headlines - "It will never snow again in England. Never Ever." This gave John the link he needed between writing a lyric about the ozone layer and making it relevant. "I thought about the year before, when I went for a sleigh ride with some mates, and I thought that will never be repeated." The band play with a desperate restraint that seems to plead for common sense, as Hogarth imagines looking out over a barren planet and apologising to his children. The song puts on the brakes for a moment, then we hear signs of something stirring and building. Is it the emergence of a common conscience?

The young Nick Davis at Hook End Manor

'Holloway Girl' is a discussion of the treatment of the mentally ill caught in the prison system. Specifically, it addresses the case of Judith Ward, imprisoned as an IRA bomber, despite overwhelming evidence to the contrary, largely to placate a hysterical public. Never blind to what it is discussing, the song is nevertheless one of hope that such injustices will be overturned.

'Berlin', on the other hand, sees the band at their most savage, as they watch a man machine-gunned to death in the no man's land between East and West at the Berlin Wall. In his hand, the man clutches a symbol of his desire to reach the west, a picture of a girl. As the blank-faced soldiers swing their guns around to cut him down, the band whip up a maelstrom of vicious anger. Unable to fathom how this death can be worth anything, Rothery's guitar rips nastily against the military brutality of Mosley's pounding drums and Trewavas' unstoppable throbbing bass. In the coda we learn that the girl that made a man risk and lose his life is a prostitute, living a life of deprivation of her own. No lessons here, no answers, just senseless brutality.

'After Me' is a simple paean to love, Steve Hogarth's dedication to a wife who understands his urgent, impatient and insatiable need to do his music. In it, he tells us that anything he manages to create is a reflection of the love she has given him in the first place. The playout shimmers with amazement and glorification, in recognition of this fact.

First single, 'Hooks in You' is an atypical rocker, musically and lyrically simple. It split the fans upon its release, but the fact that it is so different is perhaps what made it so enticing to release it in the first place - 'You're not getting Fish; we're different.' Lyrically, it's a song about a girl who ensnares and captivates men, and the effects that has upon them.

The closing track, 'The Space', is dominated by Mark Kelly's Nyman-esque keyboard. Beginning with a series of disparate images from Hogarth's life, we see how people alternate between aggressor and victim. The image of the tram crashing into the car was one that Hogarth had seen for real in Amsterdam, and he mused: "I have occasionally been the tram. And I have often been the car." In a heartfelt plea, the end section reminds us of the simple reality that all of us feel the same urges and desires and that we're all so very fragile.

The cover is a bridge between the past and the future. Although Wilkinson's expressive airbrushing no longer graced the covers, there are elements of his work - a feather, a chameleon, the belled cap and the clown from *'Fugazi'*. All have been re-contextualised over panels featuring the Aristotolean elements - Fire, Earth, Water and Wind. The old logo remains too. In the background, a grey sea rages, and icons depicting the movement of celestial bodies and snowflakes further reinforce the idea of nature. Finally, the apostrophe-free title reminds us that seasons do indeed come to an end. Perhaps we're left to work out for ourselves that they're followed by another one..?

Everybody's Got To Know

All that remained was to package and release the album. Marillion had been assigned to product manager Steve Davis at EMI, not through his own choice. "I wasn't the biggest fan of Marillion at the time," says Steve. The 6-year relationship with Mark Wilkinson had been forced to a close, with Mark taking up the offer of the cover for Fish's solo album, *'Vigil In A Wilderness of Mirrors'* (which had been planned before Fish left Marillion). Fortunately that fitted in with the band's desire to release itself from its past. "Mark tried to persuade us that he could continue to work with both Fish and Marillion without problems, but we decided we didn't want to work with him," says Mark Kelly. "We all felt it was a good time to change," adds Pete. "Besides, graphic artists are so much quicker than proper artists!" Through Steve Davis, the band approached Bill Smith Studios, famed for working with the likes of The Jam, Kate Bush and Mike Oldfield. "I met most of the band and showed them my portfolio," recalls Bill Smith. "We all got on pretty well, I really liked Steve Hogarth! We agreed not to alienate the existing fan base, go for a photographic approach but bring in idents from the previous, illustrated covers." Graphic artist Carl Glover developed a photomontage for *'Seasons End'*, keeping the key symbols alive (though barely) from Mark Wilkinson's designs. Along with the logo, it was the last time these images featured on a Marillion cover. The decision to use photography rather than airbrushing was also deliberate - recalls Carl, "Fish had Mark, so we needed to define another identity." Not everyone agreed, notably Jo Mirowski who had designed the original logo. Complains Jo, "They were successfully following the oldest formula in the book - the logo, the jester character, the artwork. From a graphic point of view they lost an identity!" This reaction was also felt by many fans, and is an issue that is debated to this day.

There was one, final complication. As Steve H had been pulling tapes out of his red bucket, he hadn't always checked the provenance. As he explains, "The end section of 'The Space' was nicked from a Europeans song called 'Wrap Me In The Flag'. I forgot to make sure that the credits were included, so when we put the record out there was no mention of the Europeans! When we pressed the second run there's about seventeen names on there!" Tricky, this provenance thing - if only the end section had been the end of the matter. Unfortunately, Colin Woore (who was still a bit miffed at the loss of his partner - "I'd done my damnedest to make that project work, it hadn't so those songs were never going to see the light of day!" says Steve) chose to go to town on the rest of the song, which was derived from a demo called 'So Far Away'. "I put my words and melody onto some chords that Mark had already written, but Colin said the chords were his chords, and they were too precious to him to be released." Ouch! Still, it was small potatoes compared to the legal harvest that was going on between his band mates and their old singer. The end result (an out-of-court settlement) was the same!

The intentionally bold first single, 'Hooks in You', was released on 25 August 1989. "It was a definite statement," says Steve Davis. A month later, *'Seasons End'* reached its hungry audience on 25 September 1989. One review considered the album to be: "A very solid effort with no sub-par songs." Kerrang! loved it, declaring it: "A legacy of some of the best and most beautiful music that can't be rubbed out with bad blood." In the same issue, Mick Wall wrote, "Musically, it's pretty much business as usual." As for the new boy, Mick noted "Hogarth's certainly got a voice, smooth as glass and emotive as hell. When you listen to it on tracks like 'Easter', 'Seasons End' or 'After Me', you can almost forget the band ever had another singer." Agrees Steve Davis, "I was very pleasantly surprised!"

Not all reviews were positive. Underground magazine Spiral Scratch wrote about the "obvious reservations about the ability of the new outfit to justify the name Marillion. Add this to the fact that the new material sounds a little tired and lack-lustre, and you are left with a fairly monumental hill to climb." No sour grapes there, then. A valid criticism was the perceived move towards the commercial, as Steve Hogarth was delighted to confirm, "I smashed the progressive approach apart." But he had not been alone in wielding the sledgehammer - the others had also taken plenty of swings, driven not by a desire to ignore the past, but to get on with the future.

The fan base had not been idle during the interregnum, far from it. Many, like Simon Clarke, had been hunting down everything they could find about the new singer and the new album. First impressions were not always positive. "There was a picture in Sounds of the band and the new singer, he had this foppish, Phil Oakey style haircut," says Simon, "I thought, you're fucking joking, how can he replace Fish, it's a New Romantic!" He wasn't the only one to be nervous. When *'Seasons End'* finally emerged, a good proportion of the fans found themselves relieved and delighted. Fan Geoff Boswell, who had gone off the band after *'Fugazi'*, happened to catch a German interview on cable TV. "I turned up the volume, gasped at the new songs and became a born again Marillion fan!" he laughs. Anne Bond, whose sisters had been such staunch followers in the early days, was discovering Marillion for herself. "I was interested to find out what they were like with their new singer," recalls Anne. "Well I loved it so much, especially Steve's voice, that I still really rate *'Seasons End'* as one of my favourite albums." As for Simon, the first single put him right. "I bought 'Hooks In You' as a CD single, I thought it was quite a good tune... then I heard 'After Me' and I thought, we're all right now!"

The band saw their fan base cut considerably, particularly in terms of album sales. Ironically, it was the places where the band were biggest, that they took the greatest hit. "We lost the heavy metal side of the fans," remarks John Arnison. "'Kayleigh' wasn't No.1 in Holland or South America, but we were OK there. We never really got as big again in the UK or Germany." This was an obvious disappointment to the band. Some fans, like Angie Cooper, gave the new album a chance nonetheless and were won over: "When Fish left Marillion I thought that the band was finished. At first I never gave H a chance and it was three months before I bought *'Seasons End'*. How wrong I was!" Others, like John Chudy, had their suspicions confirmed: "I followed them avidly until the day I bought *'Seasons End'* and found a new singer. My fan-hood lapsed then and there." Marc Roy notes, "I can personally attest that I, along with at least five friends, had a very unpleasant reaction to the 'Hooks in You' single. Then *'Seasons End'* was released and we all were won over except for one fella who decided to call it quits. Simply that. Bye-bye, and thanks for the music." Paul Rael took a similar path - "I remember watching the video for 'Hooks In You' and thinking, Jesus, what have they done! These guys used to be good!" The new singer was seen as having an unduly strong influence on proceedings. "Naturally they blamed him," writes fan Michael Huang. "He seemed to be subverting Marillion's progressive edge." This proved unacceptable to many fans - "I didn't bother with *'Seasons End'* for a least six months after it came out, I just didn't think it would be worth it!" notes Lee Clark, "How wrong I was!" Adds Dan Sherman, "Upon hearing *'Seasons End'*, I was devastated and actually didn't listen to it for weeks. When I reluctantly went to the concert at Park West on that tour, I was astounded at the new songs and wondered what I was missing!"

There was no going back however, particularly not for the new singer: Marillion considered Steve Hogarth's arrival as a launch pad not just for the vocalist but the whole band. First off was a number of prime TV appearances, including 'Rock Steady', 'TV AM' and 'Top Of The Pops'. One viewer was fan-to-be Vicki Harding, who thought, "Bloody hell, he's a vast improvement on Fish!" You can't displease everyone!

In hindsight, these events proved relatively gentle compared with the meet-the-parents moment of Steve Hogarth's first live experience. "Nothing really prepared me for singing with Marillion," he recalled at the time. "Steve wasn't aware of the sort of audience we had," remarked Mark Kelly in a later interview. "He had never seen the band, he had only heard the albums." But having decided to pick up the mantle, he had to carry it with pride. He explained to interviewer Mick Wall, "When I joined I wrote a letter in the fan club magazine announcing myself and telling everybody that I wasn't here to impersonate Fish, I was here to be myself," he explained. "I also said I would be giving 100 per cent to help make this version of Marillion happen for them." It was never going to be plain sailing for Steve. In a diary entry dated 11 July 1995, he recalled carrying Ian's cymbals through an airport terminal when a man asked him who the band was. "He naturally assumed I was the drummer and when I said Marillion, he asked me what I thought of the new singer. I said, he is not as good as

uninvited Cooper Clarke

'Uninvited Guest' was released as a single on 27 November. The initial plan was to ask John Cooper Clarke to narrate the lyrics on the 12 inch version, but there wasn't enough time!

guest performance

'Uninvited Guest' included a none-too-subtle reference to the previous singer. "It was originally eighteen-stone first footer," says Mark, "but Steve Rothery said he thought it was a bit much!" Ironically, the one song that looked clearly to be written about someone was a complete accident. "'Berlin' looks like it's written about Fish's wife Tammi, but John Helmer wrote those lyrics, it's a total coincidence!" says Mark.

the old one. 'No, I don't think so either,' he said. No pressure."

On the positive side, Hogarth was clearly nothing like Fish. "I was so completely different in every sense, nationally, physically, where my head was at," he remarked. A point neither fan nor foe would disagree with!

a ragged man came shuffling through

It was show time, after a fashion. The first live performance of the new line-up was 8 June 1989, at The Crooked Billet, Stoke Row, under the cover name of the Low Fat Yoghurts - a name coined by Nick Davis over breakfast one day. As Pete recalls, "The Crooked Billet was a tiny little pub we used to frequent while we were recording *'Seasons End'*. We were talked into it by a charming Australian barmaid, and good sense didn't prevail!" Everyone in the band and entourage remembers the Australian girl, particularly as she used to sunbathe topless by the pool outside the studio windows at Hook End Manor... where were we? On the day of the gig, Steve H was bricking it, not least because of the venue. "It was definitely the toughest gig, as I really had no idea what to expect," says H. "When we were sound checking at lunchtime, I was dismayed to find there was no stage, that the equipment took up half the room, and there was absolutely nothing between me and the fans. If someone was to take a dislike to me, there would be nothing to stop them just reaching out! Given my size, it was going to be more nose-to-nipple than nose to nose!"

Rehearsing for the Crooked Billet show

By late afternoon people had started to turn up, and before long it was obvious that there would be a larger audience than the pub could take. "Coachloads of people turned up - it was amazing!" laughs Nick Davis. It did the job - the crowds went wild. "It was a great place to play," comments Rothers. "And such an amazing vote of confidence to have that sort of buzz happening at that time." Agrees Pete, "It turned out to be quite a legendary experience, and quite a nice way of introducing Steve Hogarth to the mad Marillion fans!" Leaving was a bit of an issue however: Paul Lewis remembers how, "After the show the band was unable to get through the crowd to leave the stage so they climbed out of the very small window at the back of the room!" laughs Mark, "Climbing back in was a problem 'cos it was three feet high on the inside and about six feet high on the outside!" Steve H's reaction was: "An immense feeling of relief! Having come through that, it was all downhill from there!"

The second outing was seven weeks later at the Brixton Academy, for the video shoot for the 'Hooks In You' single. 600 fans paid six quid each for the privilege of participating in a mock-up gig, no less traumatic for Steve H. "I was up in the gods, looking at the kids coming into the hall," says Steve. "I thought, I wonder what they're gonna make of me? I knew that if I dwelt on it, it would get worse, so I didn't think about it. To be honest,

The White Gloves

Rather than a TV-friendly gimmick, the gloves started life as a problem to be solved: how to play keyboards while standing at the front of the stage.. "I had a dilemma when I joined the band," explains Steve Hogarth. "I knew I ought to be the front man, but at the same time I'd never really imagined myself as a singer, always as a piano player." Finding inspiration in John Otway's thigh-slapping body drums, which he had helped to make, Steve was introduced to John Kenton Price at Kenton Electronics through a mutual friend. Initial discussions were of a jacket - "but this proved impractical because everything's so soft," says Steve. Eventually the pair came up with a combination of two gloves on each hand, according to John: "An inner glove with the switches and wiring attached, and an outer glove to cover everything up." After a few months' development, John produced the gloves in the summer of 1989 at a cost of "considerably under £1000."

The issues to be overcome ranged from the practical - the gloves themselves had to be kept as small and light as possible - to the complexities of transmitting a MIDI signal. "There weren't any wireless midi systems available in those days," remarks Steve. Adds John, "We were using a standard guitar-type radio transmitter with an audio bandwidth, trying to send a digital signal with twice that bandwidth. We didn't want note hangs, so the digital signal sent between the units is not actually MIDI but my own version, compressed and made pretty well bomb proof to avoid glitches." First tests were a revelation. Says Steve, "I went to John's house. He had a synth on the floor hooked up to the new invention. We could play it with the gloves! We wondered over what distance the radio link would work so he called his home phone up on his mobile and left it off the hook as we went down the street. We were playing walls and lamp posts, listening to the synth still playing on the mobile phone. We were saying bloody hell, this is fantastic!"

Steve tried out several types of gloves before settling on a simple cotton pair of the kind used by waiters. "I think they came from a kitchenware and catering supplier on Old Compton Street in Soho," says Steve. The gloves required a regular refit, due to the effects of Steve's sweat which rotted the gloves, wiring and switches. Explains Steve, "They worked well until I sweated, which of course I did during a show because it used to get awfully hot in two pairs of gloves on stage."

Eventually the gloves (and the gimmick) came to the end of their natural life, and the switches and mechanism were transferred to the cricket bat that is a staple of Marillion shows to this day. John Price has subsequently worked on a number of one-off projects, including for 'Tomorrow's World', Genesis and the Body Zone of the Millennium Dome.

I felt pressure more from the video cameras than the crowd - I was under pressure to get it right. To this day I don't know if I did!" The fans' reactions spoke for themselves. Said Mark at the time, "The fans really took to him. I think they are quite a sensitive bunch, they didn't tear us apart." True enough. "As the shoot went on I realised there was the potential to have fun with the crowd," continues Steve. "My grin was genuine, I did have a good time!" So it was all alright. "He was a cracker, mental but a cracker!" laughs Paul Lewis.

Once the shoot was over it was time to plan for the real tour. While all agreed that the new line-up would only cover songs that the vocalist "could feel," H remembers how, the band felt obliged, "to play the songs the fans wanted to hear from the old days." This proved to be quite a few, including 'Kayleigh', 'Lavender', 'Incommunicado', 'Warm Wet Circles' and 'That Time Of The Night'. Others, such as 'Script For A Jester's Tear', were more testing. 'Heart Of Lothian' was also an option, but as Steve admitted to Mick Wall, "Maybe we should ask the Scottish fans what they think. I am Scottish on my grandfather's side though!" Some songs were out completely, such as 'Fugazi' ("Only Fish can sing that one properly and make it work. Well, one or two of them they'll have to see Fish for!").

The tour started properly on 5 October, when the band played to a 10,000 strong crowd at the Palais des Sports, Besancon in France. When Steve Hogarth thanked the fans half way through the gig, the roar of the crowd was sufficient to convince both fans and

Steve Rothery and Paul Lewis in the limo

band that it was all going to be alright. Four days later, when the band played the Rolling Stone in Milan, it was Steve H's unexpected pleasure to bump into his chum Dave Gregory from XTC. Dave was working with a singer named Alicé (as had been ex-Japan keyboard player and soundsmith Richard Barbieri). Recalls Dave, "I'd just checked into my hotel room when there was a knock on the door - who should be standing there with a grin from ear to ear but the esteemed Mr. H, now a fully-fledged member of Marillion!"

The tour rolled on like a wave, with Steve winning them over as he went. "I was conscious that the fans didn't want me to ruin their favourite band, but I never had to face an ugly or malevolent crowd, ever! They were all rooting for me!" Each show opened with the band already in position, and the new singer would arrive from the back of the stage just in time to deliver the first line of opening number, 'A Ragged Man Came Shuffling Through'. "That was deliberate," explained Steve H, "to let the band say hello momentarily, to be welcomed back by their audience before I showed up." Not that H was inanimate - he climbed speaker stacks and balanced precariously on top, and could do karate kicks with the best of 'em. "I did that stuff to generate a vibe," chuckles Steve. "The tour managers used to get cross - it always used to look more precarious than it was. Having said that, looking back I don't know how I didn't fall off!" Recalls Paul Lewis, "It was fraught as H used to feed off adrenaline: off stage there was Steve, a nice polite chap, and on stage he was an absolute maniac with no regard for personal safety." "It was great to find out he's a great front man onstage," commented Mark.

The tour bus went round continental Europe before a lightning tour of the USA: two dates, one on each coast. So, what did the fans think? Lucy Jordache, who attended the London Astoria gig on 5 November,[3] remembers well the palpable tension. "I stood on the balcony watching, with my arms crossed, thinking come on, then... the notes started for 'Script For A Jester's Tear', and by half way through the whole audience was on his side.

Carl Glover

Carl was born in 1961 in Hoo, Kent, UK. His Dad was an artist, "He described himself as a bohemian," laughs Carl. "He encouraged me and my three sisters to draw." Despite this influence, when he was young it was the army that beckoned. "I wanted to drive tanks!" Fortunately, his art teacher convinced him that his path lay elsewhere.

In 1979 Carl joined the first of many punk bands as singer. They had names like Churchill's Shoe, Poxy Music, The Spinning Pygmies, Total Big Bingo and Muscle Horse. He gave this up in 1998, then instrumental in setting up a recording studio. Carl left Bill Smith Studios in 2000, as times were getting hard and Carl's work wasn't generating enough revenue. "I started to look for another job," he remarks.

Working as a designer by day, Carl still finds the time for his photography, book and album cover art for bands including Porcupine Tree, No-Man and The Unconscious Collective. "A lot of my work is happy accidents - I work in the evenings, deliberately overexposing and underexposing shots, and see what comes out."

Carl is justly proud of his role in Marillion's progress the past 15 years. "I feel I've done my bit to change their image!" he laughs. "To see your work on fans' t-shirts, you get that 'I-did-that' feeling, its pretty cool!"

For me it was two for the price of one - I was still following Fish, and I had Marillion with H as well!" The gig at the Barrowlands in Glasgow was attended by old-timer Paul Hughes. "From the moment H came on stage the crowd was behind him, and there was a real magical feeling of rebirth in the room. I went home with my confidence renewed." H even had the confidence to "perform a snippet of 'Margaret' during 'Market Square Heroes'," noted Shaun Ryan. "The Scottish contingent went crazy! In between songs the crowd chanted 'Geezabun!' and 'Stevie, Stevie!' It was one big party!"

The reception was equally good across the pond. "I was impressed that Steve had the guts to tackle old songs, especially 'Script'," says US fan Dan Sherman. "I thought people would throw stuff at him but he sang it with such love and admiration that I believe he earned great respect." Many new fans were picked up along the way, including Karin Breiter. "I had broken up with my boyfriend who was in a band that covered a few Marillion songs. I wanted him back so I bought us tickets to see Marillion," explains Karin. "He ended up not going, but I dragged along a friend who had never heard of them, and I myself was only a marginal fan at the time. I met the band after the show and thought they were a great bunch of guys so I went to see them the following weekend and two weeks later drove to Canada to see them again!" Like with other new fans, the departure of Fish was irrelevant. "I didn't have anything to compare H's stage performance to so I thought he was very energetic and fun."

my round

"I'd agreed to meet Steve and the Marillos for an after-hours bevvy in the bar of the hotel in Milan. In a rare and rash moment of generosity, I stood the whole band a round of drinks, only to find that I didn't have enough spondulicks to pay for the round. The bar staff refused to charge it to my room, and it became obvious they were on the take. I mean, thirty quid for six drinks, in 1989! I emptied my pockets, and the band made up the rest; I was so ashamed."

Dave Gregory

The Barrowlands gig was nearly attended by ol' Geezabun himself. "I was interested to see the new band playing the old numbers, and watching Marillion from the audience perspective," Fish wrote. Fish arranged with the crew to sneak in "after the lights went down" at the show, but Paul Lewis got wind of events and called Fish to suggest non-attendance. Comments Paul, "This was not because of the bad feeling between the band and Fish but the fact that his presence would have disrupted the performance, don't forget he is 6ft, 6ins and cannot stand to one side and not be noticed!" Despite feeling a little peeved, Fish decided not to turn up after all.

wild ponies

With typical impromptu vigour, about this time Mark decided to lose his pony tail. "I went down the pub and said to the barman, pass me those scissors please, and - snip! - it was gone." The next day he turned up two hours late for rehearsals. "I was at the hairdressers," he explained, "I had to get it cut, it looked such a mess..."

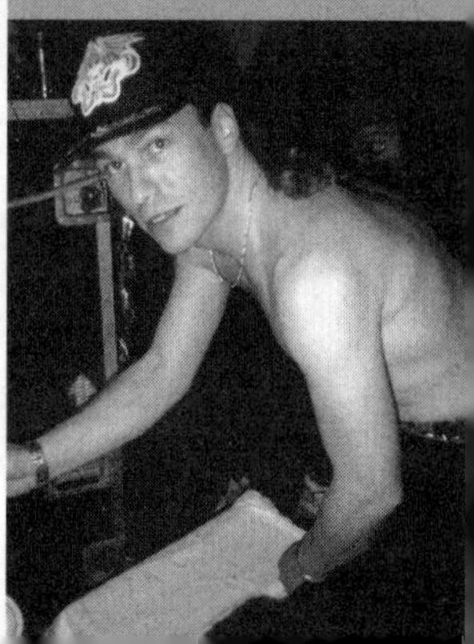

The tour broke for Christmas at the Hammersmith Odeon on 18 December, the band's 21st time at the venue (for which each band member received a plaque) and H's first (he was given a plaque as well!). After a short break Marillion headed back across the Atlantic. It was in Rio on 27 January 1990 that Marillion would play to an 80,000 crowd at the Hollywood Rock Festival at the Sambadromo, Steve H's biggest ever performance. "They weren't just there for us, we headlined with Bon Jovi, but it was still quite something!" he commented. Indeed - Steve joined the crowds at the Sambadromo the night before to watch Tears For Fears, but didn't expect to be recognised himself. In an interview, he explained what happened. "There was a flash of light and someone was

a new aura

This book wouldn't be complete without mentioning that women find H, um, a bit of a horn. "He's incredibly good looking, he has the voice of an angel, he lyrically touches a chord, he's very spiritual, it's the whole package," says an anonymous fan. "He just has this presence, it touches something deep inside." That explains that then. Ahem. Moving on...

pointing a microphone at me asking, 'What do you think of Brazil?' And I said, well, it's great. And they asked, 'What do you think of the women?' And I said, well, they're gorgeous. To die for. The following day I was on the six o'clock news, dancing around and telling this guy how beautiful the women are. They made me incredibly famous in three days flat!"

Steve made the front pages of the papers as well, including a half-page full colour cover shot of national daily, O Globo - arms stretched out Christ-like with Copacabana beach behind him. No wallflower, our Steve.

Marillion went back to the Americas in June: indeed, they spent the best part of a year touring. Recalls Mark, "We played 110 shows around the world, and not once did we get a bad reception from anybody." With H's arrival, the dynamics of the band also changed. Comments Peter Gee, "The appearance of the band on stage changed from being Fish up front with a band behind him, to being five equal guys on stage, all working on presentation together." Management was impacted as well: "I had to change my whole style of management," comments John Arnison. "While Pete and Ian stepped back, Mark, Steve and H all played a part." The tales were told as a video, entitled *'From Stoke Row To Ipanema'*: it wasn't the best produced (Kerrang! called it "worthy but stodgy"), nor was it of the highest quality, but it quickly sold out.

Support was provided by the aptly named Cry No More, an irreverent duo that served as much as a warm-up show as a support act[5]. "We were fed up of having dodgy progressive rock bands and dodgy pub bands," says Pete, "They were totally different!" Supporting the band in Europe was Sylvain Gouvenaire's band, Arrakeen. "It was very exciting for us, Marillion was one of our main influences at the time," says Sylvain. "In Lille, Steve Rothery came on stage for one of our songs 'Folle Marie', and played the final guitar solo with me. That was a great moment of the tour!"

Pete finds Jesus in Rio

On one of the last nights of the tour, on 20 December 1990 at the Junction Ten in Walsall, an overzealous fan handed Steve Hogarth his wife's brassiere. "I didn't quite know what to do with that," said Steve at the time! But there could be no doubt that he had been accepted into the fold. Steve was no longer the new boy, from now on Marillion were a complete band again.

Steve H Entertains the fans in Rio

Oh Come, Emmanuel by Alan Hewitt

Having heard that Fish had departed the band for pastures new in the spring of 1988, I did not hold high hopes of the band really carrying on. I had already been through this kind of drama before with Genesis and I suppose I should have known better than to give up hope on Marillion.

As usual I was proven wrong, but unlike previously with Genesis, I had to take the bull by the horns myself, purchase the band's new album and listen to hitherto unheard singer Steve Hogarth's first effort with them. By the time I reached 'Easter' I was hooked; and as soon as the UK tour was announced, tickets were duly booked for shows at Liverpool and Wolverhampton.

The 13 December 1989 duly arrived and I set off for the Royal Court Theatre in Liverpool, scene of so many other memorable Marillion evenings. Unusually for me, I opted to take a seat up in the balcony and settled in to see whether my initial reservations would be proven right or not. Even by Liverpool Marillion crowd standards; the crowd this evening were definitely feisty and new boy H's reception was ecstatic. His performance of several of the established classics from the band's repertoire blew away any doubts that might have been lingering in my mind that he was the man for the job.

What really sticks in my mind was one of those magical moments that sadly don't happen often at gigs these days. Steve came to the front of the stage and proceeded to sing the traditional Christmas carol: 'Oh Come, Oh Come Emanuel', totally unaccompanied until the now familiar strains of 'Season's End' began. The hairs stood up on my neck and I was absolutely awestruck! The rest of the gig passed in a blur for me but one thing was for sure my membership of the Marillion family was guaranteed! What was all the fuss about? Well, ask anyone who was at that gig and I am sure they will tell you.

'Holidays In Eden'

Thrilled by their success, the band started planning the next album as soon as the Seasons End tour was over. They returned to Brighton, the town that had been the context for so much inspiration - this time to Stanbridge Farm, another residential rehearsal studio.[6] Once there, the band came down to earth with a bump. The fivesome had to start working together from scratch, something they had never done before, and the honeymoon period was long since over.

Meanwhile, John Arnison had been putting his own house in order, signing up with Tony Smith's management company, Hit And Run. "I had to persuade the band!" he remarks. Indeed he did, and Tony Smith came to Stanbridge in his Aston Martin to assist, hinting he would get Marillion's next album onto the Atlantic label if they joined Hit And Run, not to mention dangling the potential for touring with Hit And Run's flagship, Genesis. Neither happened, and the band lost the major attentions of the man they had worked with for nigh ten years. "No longer were our destinies intertwined, we kind of lost him as a manager from then, he was given other things to manage." This was going to be no holiday.

cross the water

In 1990 Marillion recorded 'Sailing', a charity record with Steve Hackett, a cover of the Sutherland Brothers' song made famous by Rod Stewart.
The song appeared on *'Rock Against Repatriation'*, it's the only time that Steve Hogarth and Fish have sung on the same recording - although neither knew the other was there!

The Eden Project

Things had been going so well. After all, when H had joined the merry throng, it already had a good proportion of the music and a critical mass of lyrics. This time the band was starting as a unit, and people were to discover that success would not always be as smooth as it was for *'Seasons End'*. "*'Seasons End'* was easy as we had a huge stockpile of material," remarks Rothers. Starting from scratch, the writing for *'Holidays In Eden'* took eight months - "The sun was shining when we got there and when we left it was snowing," says Steve H.

Canada, Feb 1990

For a start, EMI were coming down hard for a follow-up. "We were under a lot of pressure from EMI for singles," says Ian. The stress was exacerbated by the open-to-anything attitudes becoming a thing of the past. "It was a bit like *'Fugazi'* all over again, we had to work out how to work together," says Pete. Mark puts it more bluntly, "We'd gone from being, 'Oh no - we'll do it your way,' to being, 'Oh fucking hell - can't we do it my way?'" It wasn't a straightforward process, explains Pete, "Although we didn't want Fish, we would have been quite happy to write the same kind of music and we didn't really want Steve H to mess with it. We'd got into the habit of working as a four-piece, so he probably felt some of the same frustrations that Fish had felt."

What was more, the band had their suspicions confirmed - that Marillion's

green screens

Stanbridge Farm was H's first computer experience. "The owner had a little word processor with a green screen, really primitive!" says Steve. "When I wrote words in print, I found them easier to judge." Meanwhile, Mark used to amuse himself by playing online Multi-User Dungeons (MUD), under the pseudonym Hrothgar, a character from 'Grendel'. Anyone for anagrams? OK, there's only one R...

approach to writing did not sit well with the new singer. Whereas most of the band was happy to capture an idea and shelve it, in case it proved useful later, the goal-driven 3-minute boy grew bored with the long jamming sessions. "I think they were worried that if I was left to my own devices we'd make the wrong kind of record," comments H. Eventually the stress became too much, and the unfortunate Steve H had to take some time out. "I got ill with it," he explains, "I went to bed for a week!" In fact Steve took two weeks out, leaving the band to stew. "I thought, there's a bit of a problem here," says Pete, "I just hoped we could work it out. He was frustrated at the speed we worked, but he was right to be!" In an ironic turnaround, when Steve H emerged, it was with the completed lyrics, piano and voice melodies for the most un-poppy 'The Party'. "I kind of had it during the writing of *'Seasons End'*, but I didn't have the confidence to give it to them," explains H. Meanwhile, the rest of the band had written the deeply mainstream *'Holidays In Eden'* title track!

Towards the end of the time at the farm, Marillion formulated a new writing approach. Explained Steve Hogarth, "There are elements of me doing what I do and them doing what they do on the new album. It took us the whole of the time recording the album to come to that conclusion." John Helmer was also to contribute, but not as much as on *'Seasons End'*. "It worked out that I wasn't available at the time the band could have used some help," recalled John. By January 1991 the quintet emerged, united once more and clutching what they felt was a good 30 hours of song material. From a business perspective, the band recognised that their album sales had taken a battering with the departure of Fish. As the writing sessions had yielded a couple of songs that had the feel of potential singles, the boys were after a hit and looked to Chris Kimsey, producer of both *'Misplaced Childhood'* and *'Clutching At Straws'*. Chris was keen but the album wasn't sufficiently ready for Chris in his window of opportunity in January. "I said to them, you haven't got enough songs," says Chris, suggesting another slot following the production of the live Rolling Stones album *'Flash Point'*.

Hook End, with Chris Neil (seated) and Rob Eaton

Hook End, Steve H and Mark about to be attacked by giant blob

Soon the band was ready for recording, but this time Chris was not. "He said he'd be a couple of weeks," commented Mark in an interview with Mick Wall. "Then Mick Jagger

making waves

The video for 'Easter' was recorded at The Giant's Causeway on the coast of Northern Ireland, which had been an inspiration for the song. It featured band members balancing precariously on the rocks - recalls Paul Lewis, "Several times a large wave would be seen bearing down and the entire crew would run for cover!"

got married and Ron Wood ["who had to do some guitar fixes," according to Chris] got run over or something. Eventually, Steve said, 'Ring him up and tell him to either shit or get off the pot.' So I phoned him up and came back to the rest of them and said, 'Well he got off the pot!'" He did indeed: shortly after he went to Scotland to help Fish with his own second album.

Wanting to increase the chart-friendliness of Marillion's sound, EMI in the shape of Nick Gatfield, head of A&R, proposed Chris Neil for the project. Chris, who had achieved chart success for characters such as Mike Rutherford (with Mike and The Mechanics) and Sheena Easton, had first experienced Marillion in Paris back in 1983. "I was in Paris with Sheena to record a load of B-sides," says Chris, "We went out one evening to this weird club. Fish came up and pointed at me, he said, 'I know you!'" Chris had already been suggested for *'Seasons End'*, but the band had decided against him at the time. Commented Steve Hogarth to Mick Wall, "What with me just joining the band, wheeling someone like Chris in at that stage might be too much."

Following some practice sessions at Nomis Studios, the band went on to Hook End Manor to record the new album. The studios were not nearly as much fun as before. Recalls Steve Rothery, "There was a different studio manager, funnily enough the guy who recorded the demos for *'Clutching At Straws'* at Bray Studios. The studio was a bit like Stalag 17, a shame really." "There was a different vibe than with *'Seasons End'*," says Ian, "Well, it was snowing this time!" Chris was under no illusion of why he had been selected, but was also conscious of the sensitivities of the band. "EMI brought me in to ensure a single and to help Marillion produce more contemporary sounds," says Chris. "They'd seen how Mike Rutherford brought Genesis into the mainstream, so they came to me." Chris promised not to lighten up the sound and turn us into Mike and The Mechanics," recalls H on the sleeve notes to the remaster. Mark: "When we first met him he said, "I know your music better than you lot do! I wouldn't mess it up because my son [who was a Marillion fan] would hate me!"

As Chris got to work, he set about introducing the band to such alien concepts as how to write a song. Says Steve H, "Chris Neil was good at generating a light-hearted atmosphere and he's got a pop instinct that homes in on the 'hooks' like a laser beam. No wonder he's successful - he's got a great talent for knowing what will move the masses." Agrees Pete, "We learned lots about song construction from Chris. In the past we'd spend a lot of time overdubbing but he didn't, he'd say, I want to hear the vocal, and let's have a hook - that guitar!" Chris also introduced more technology into the picture. "I brought electronics in tentatively, I didn't want things to go too synthetic," says Chris. It was the early days of sequencing, which Mark put to good effect on 'Splintering Heart'; Ian was also acquainted with the joys of electronic drum pads. Things went as well as could be expected: the band's occasional fears (such as the speed of recording - it took an unprecedented ten weeks from Chris's arrival to get to the mix) were countered by the prospects of commercial success.

Later, when chart success did not materialise, the band members took an unspoken vow about their artistic integrity. Chris Neil's involvement was in part due to external pressure from EMI to create a more commercial album. As the next album would prove, no record label would ever again exert such a hold over the band, artistic or otherwise.

'Holidays In Eden'

Whereas 'Seasons End' *was a bridge between Marillion's old and new styles,* 'Holidays In Eden' *seemed to hint at a departure from traditions. A significant part of the fan base was unable to deal with the notion that* 'Holidays' *might be the start of a journey into poppier waters. That said, it's fair to say that Steve Hogarth's comment, "If 'Splintering Heart' and 'The Party' are pop songs, I'll eat my pink telecaster," is more than true.*

A throbbing mechanised rhythm opens 'Splintering Heart', and Hogarth starts weaving his magic. A cold heart beats in the chest of a girl, and this unfamiliar sensation is causing her all sorts of anguish but... 'not as much as this..!' The snare cracks, snapping your spine straight, sending your head back as your heart explodes through your ribcage, like the alien viscerally bursting from John Hurt's chest. It's as though you've been shot, as the band pour every ounce of pain into a tormented scream and every little hurt you've ever suffered comes back to haunt you and the only way to cope is to harden up, and bury your emotions so deep nothing can touch them.

'Cover My Eyes (Pain And Heaven)' ruminates on 'that woman'. The one that every man has seen, the one who blows you away so absolutely utterly, she could crush you with a glance. Dangerous isn't the half of it. Steve Hogarth commented that the various images were "Stolen from movies, art, literature and pop videos. See if you can spot David Niven." An anthemic crowd-sing-along *par excellence*, 'Cover My Eyes' was the lead single from the album.

Mad Jack McKelly

Mark earned the nickname 'Mad Jack' during the *'Holidays In Eden'* sessions. It was based on two attributes - his reputation (of "being absolutely off his head") and the 'Blackadder' series - quote "He's madder than Mad Jack MacMad, winner of last year's Mr Mad contest."

'The Party' is an affecting tale of innocence lost, conjured with a sense of expectation by the band, as a young girl goes nervously to her first party. Beguiled by the new things she sees and experiences - drink, drugs and the coupling up - she allows herself to be seduced in what seems to be a magical garden. Steve Rothery's unusually-phrased solo conjures the sense of wonder and strangeness as her first toke on a joint takes hold. The images from the garden were written after H's first magic mushroom experience during the writing sessions for the album, where he watched the moonlight 'dripping in the trees like the juice of some unearthly tropical fruit.' And in the morning, the comedown. Was losing her virginity love? No... It was just a party.

'No One Can' sees the band in their most commercial mode, with Steve H narrating a tale about the difficulties of being separated from the people you love, commenting, 'It's okay, you're here with me' - that the distance doesn't matter. The band always considered it a travesty that it wasn't a hit. Much of the fan base considered it a travesty that it was on the album in the first place!

The title track starts with birdsong, followed by the roar of a jet overhead and the band whisk us off to foreign shores where we reinvent ourselves. John Helmer's lyric reflects on the fact that one day you have to return, and your new persona won't impress your old friends. In the sleeve notes to the remaster, Steve Hogarth comments, "We could have made it a lot wilder musically to reflect the primitive connotations in the lyric."

'Dry Land' first appeared on an album by How We Live - one of Steve Hogarth's pre-Marillion bands. Producer Chris Neil suggested the band try it out, and against their instincts they did. It's a song about trying to get past someone's defences and finding they've built them too high. The song is basically the same as the How We Live version, but is more dynamic, and most fans agree that Steve Rothery's solo is superior to the original.

'Waiting To Happen' seems to start in a similarly reflective mood to 'Dry Land', but all this is just a prelude, building tension through the middle eight to the bursting exuberance of the chorus. A paean to the glorious magic found in love and which transcends the greyness of ordinary life, the song contains one of Hogarth's most enduring and touching images; that of memorising your partner's face, and it becoming 'A jigsaw of an angel I can do when I feel low.'

'This Town', the first instalment in a cinematic suite, describing the corruption of a young couple moving to the big city to chase their dreams, and losing not only each other, but even their humanity in the process. Steve Rothery's chugging guitar conjures the confusion and excitement of someone caught in the crowds and lights of the city. In a similar manner to the girl in 'Holidays In Eden', one half of the partnership embraces the new surroundings. The other however, shrinks.

'The Rake's Progress' is a bridging piece, which asks 'What do you do when your roots have dissolved and broken down?' It answers by providing us with a tension-filled passage of tom rolls, bass pulses and shimmering, dreamlike, echoing keyboards. It charts the transition of the man as he becomes bitter, cynical and broken. Terrifyingly, as he emerges, as if from a cocoon, the music lifts... and we realise he's finding this experience liberating...

In the final section, '100 Nights', our anti-hero

logo therapy

There was no wastage from the ideas proposed for the band's new logo. "We had loads of ideas!" recalls Carl, "Many of which ended up on other Racket Records discs." There was a sphere, used for the *'Live At The Borderline'* release, and a shot of trees (from JRR Tolkien's garden, no less) ended up on the *'Barrowlands'* disc.

walks out as master of his world, able to bend anyone or anything to his will. We realise that his satisfaction is gained through manipulation and destruction of anything of beauty - he glories in destroying a marriage. The coda, a reprise of the chorus from 'This Town' was conceived by Steve Hogarth as a Greek chorus, "All the people on the escalators at Waterloo Station, mumbling the mantra together."

Sarah Ball's cover art portrays Eden as a study in blue. "I wanted to go back to illustration," explains Bill Smith. "I can't remember why but we went for cave-like drawings, with simplistic shapes and colours." The animals, seen flocking to the Tree of Knowledge, are reminiscent of the cave art found in Lascaux in France. With its highly impressionistic feel, the cover represents the H-era band's first album cover wholly divorced from the work of Mark Wilkinson, as well as being the last to be developed without the aid of computers.

Steve and Mark at a fan convention

Waiting To Happen

Having decided to go commercial, the band wanted to see the rewards. As many as six potential singles were hoped for: 'Cover My Eyes', 'No One Can', 'Dry Land', 'Waiting To Happen' and 'Holidays In Eden'. Laughed Steve H to Mick Wall, "It's like *'Thriller'* or something!" After some debate, 'Cover My Eyes' was planned as the first single. This was released on 28 May and reached No.34 during its fortnight stay in the UK charts.

When the album was released on 24 June 1991, there was no dispute about what it was trying to achieve. "Unashamedly commercial, it is still better than anything you'll hear on the radio," said one review. Not everybody was so polite: the conservative sections of the fan community found their suspicions confirmed. Writes fan Michael Huang, "Some prog fans assumed that Marillion had gone the way of Phil Collins led-Genesis and sold out to pop." A fan letter from W. Cox summed up the feelings of many. "You got big by writing those early songs, now you're forgetting those who made you famous. What about a full Marillion album next time?" Comments fan Jeff Pelletier, "The US version opened with two quite poppy songs in 'Cover My Eyes' and 'No One Can'. My initial negative reaction to these songs kept me from appreciating a majestic track like 'Splintering Heart' until years later." Max Rael adds, "I attended quite a few dates on the tour, but after the tour was over I found I didn't ever play the album, so that was that!"

Another letter to the Web disputed such findings. "It is now my considered belief that you are writing the finest music of your careers," wrote Stuart Wright. "Keep up the good work!" Another fan, Matthew Hammond responded in the next issue, "*'Holidays In Eden'* is a 100% Marillion album - 101% even!" So it wasn't all that bad. Neither was it the commercial success that had been hoped for, however. 'No One Can' was

Cheggers plays rock

Much to the surprise and embarrassment of the band, while they were mixing the album at Westside studios Marillion were 'gate crashed' by Janice Long, Michaela Strachan and Keith Chegwin who were recording an edition of TV show 'Go Getters', in which the presenters have to perform three tasks in a 24-hour period, one being to perform in a recording session.

meant to be

On 15 April 1992 the tour reached San Jose, California, and Steve Hogarth fell in love with a guitar for the first time.
"I saw a Rickenbacker 12 string Tom Petty limited edition beautiful sunburst guitar on a wall," says Steve. "Something about it said, "Buy Me Now."
It was $1000 and I couldn't help it. When I got it home, I found a certificate in the bottom of the case which said it was manufactured (I guess that means finished) on May 14th. This is my birthday. Spooky, eh?"

released on 22 July, which like its single predecessor managed to get into the top forty for a few weeks before dropping off the radar again. Unfortunately for Marillion, EMI were losing faith and had decided to promote Vanilla Ice (with 'Rollin' In My 5.0', which didn't fare much better) instead. "We were losing the confidence of EMI," remarks Steve R. And as confidence waned, so did the chances of success. 'Dry Land' was released on 23 September: unfortunately, though EMI may have tried, *'Thriller'* this album was not.

Touring In Eden

On July 13 and as a precursor to the tour, Marillion headlined at the Cumbria Rock Festival. The 'real' tour did not start until September, as the band had kept August free for Ian. "His wife [Wanda] was having a baby and we didn't want to travel too far afield," recalls Mark. Lindsay was born at Wexham Park Hospital on 18 July.

It was an eventful tour, as some tour dates bore the brunt of fans' disappointment. Recalls the Dutch Progressive Rock Pages, "During a concert in Ahoy in Holland a substantial part of the audience booed when Steve Hogarth announced they would be playing quite a lot from the new album." The tour also provided Fish with his first occasion to see the new line up, on 22 September 1991 at the Edinburgh Playhouse. Fish (and his minder, he'd had one since the Clutching tour) met Steve in the dressing room after the gig, just as Steve was coming out of the shower. H recounts, "So, I turned around and there was just me and him and his minder, so I was severely outnumbered physically, and I was half-naked. You never feel at your most confident when you're not dressed. But it was alright and we had a chat!"

Steve with his red guitar: "Is this how I hold it?"

This time the band was far less comfortable with the idea of a US tour. Despite nearly deciding not to cross the pond, the band eventually assented and conducted an extensive tour of the US, starting on 16 March 1992 at Allentown, Philadelphia. Support in the US was provided by John Wesley, who had started out as the band's guitar tech. "US immigration was being tricky about bringing crew, so we started to use local crew," explains Mark. One evening, Wes and the band went out for a meal at a place where live music was playing. After a few beers, he got up on stage (as you do) for a jam, and launched into a Led Zep-style solo. When he returned the boys said to him, "You're not really a guitar tech are you!?" Three days into the tour, the band agreed with the production manager that it was worth giving Wes a shot at the support slot. "And that was it for seven tours!" laughs Wes. Explains Mark Kelly, "He was someone we liked, the changeover

John Wesley

"It was music that decided on me, not the other way round," laughs Wes (as he is known). "I didn't know in my teens that I could make a career of it, I just knew it was what I wanted to do!" Having played in a number of bands since his youth, Wes was feeling fatigued when the opportunity arose to do something a bit different. "I got a call from a friend who was working with Hit And Run as a drum tech [called Andy - in fact, Wally Version at Hit And Run managed Dada, who had a hit with Dizz Knee Land], he told me they needed a guitar tech for some band coming from England. We rented a truck, picked up the band's gear and met up with them in Quebec for two days of rehearsals." The band was, of course, Marillion, who before long had offered Wes a support slot.

Things never came easily to Wes. The one time he had the chance of playing in front of his record company, at La Cigale in Paris, he was so ill he had to have a cortisone shot. "So did Steve Hogarth," remembers Wes. "I tried to look cool, but I fell over Pete's bass pedal bar. My record company thought I was drunk, they never really supported me after that." Despite such mishaps, Wes's time with Marillion was a great opportunity. "I was constantly learning - their calibre was much higher that what I was used to. There's a huge difference between being a good guitar player and a great musician, I tried to elevate to their standard!" His tenure came to an end in 1995, with the signing with Castle. "The band had been more than kind - they'd get me over to Europe, but there are plenty of techs and support acts out there and costs were an issue."

There remains one ambition: "To sell records on a truly international level." Good luck to you John, a man who will go down in history as one of the nicest guys in rock.

was convenient and he was guitar tech as well." In other words, he was perfect!

Wes's arrival enabled a number of other changes - Tim Bricusse,[7] who had been Steve Rothery's guitar tech when in Europe, moved more firmly into Paul Lewis's shoes as tour manager, enabling Paul to spend more time with his family (literally). Paul took over running Parr Street Studios in Liverpool, another asset in the Hit And Run portfolio.

Despite vehement denials at the time, the band admits to ending up with a poppier sound than they were comfortable with. Comments Rothers, "I don't particularly like *'Holidays In Eden'*. Chris took all the rough edges off the album, that would be OK for a single but it blanded it out too much for my liking." Noted Mark on the sleeve notes to the remaster, "Though not in any way bad, the end result was that for certain songs, Chris maybe wasn't the best choice." In particular, it is unlikely that 'Cover My Eyes', 'Dry Land' and 'Waiting To Happen' would have made it onto the release. "I think we were his acid test," says Steve H. "It was a test that cost a lot of money and, in so much as we never had a hit, it failed. 'No One Can' is a hit. Even now, you can just tell by listening to it. If EMI had made a little more effort marketing that one song, I'm certain the course of our career would have changed and EMI would have made a whole lot of money."

Chris agrees that it was perhaps a mistake to give Marillion a pop edge. "In hindsight, Marillion was not a pop band. Mike's writing and Phil Collins' voice helped Genesis make the transition, but Marillion did not have the same pop sensibilities." Unfortunately, the band had expected much more. "They had been convinced that it was going to be huge and that

no shrinking violets

On 21 October 1991 in Brussels, the last night before a ten-day break in touring, the lead guitar in support band The Violet Hour was a bit the worse for wear at the after-show party. Laughs Steve H, "They gaffer-taped him to a chair, then they carried him to a lift and down twelve floors, out of the hotel and over to the middle of a dual carriageway!"

ear we go

In July 1992 Ian had an ear infection and so was replaced by Mark Sugden for a date in Russia. Originally intended as a mime on TV, this became a live performance much to Mark's surprise! "Its not always like this," Steve H remarked!

the old guard would flock back in droves, but it didn't work!" comments the ever-sanguine John Arnison. "But just think - if they'd had a hit with *'Holidays In Eden'*, they wouldn't have made *'Brave'*!"

brave, brave world

As far as EMI was concerned, commercialism rocked and the next album was planned as no exception: it had been agreed as, "A rough and ready, garage-y album, fresh-sounding and edgy." While the record company were rubbing their hands in this knowledge, many fans were wringing their hands in despair at how their icons were forsaking their art for mammon.

Two years passed before the release of *'Brave'*, an album that would turn these opinions on their heads. Inside information was limited to the band and their close entourage. Driven forward by the disappointment of *'Holidays In Eden'*, only they had any idea of where the music was going.

'Sympathy' video shoot in Mexico

While hindsight would show *'Brave'* fitting the pattern of each album being a reaction to the one before, this was not obvious at the time. In early 1992, to appease the fans and celebrate the band's tenth anniversary with EMI, the compilation album *'A Singles Collection'* was released. It included six tracks from the Fish era and six from the Hogarth era (hence its UK title *'Six Of One, Half A Dozen Of The Other'* - according to Mark, "The US company said people wouldn't get it!"), and it also included two bonus tracks - a cover of 'Sympathy'[8] and a new track called 'I Will Walk On Water'. It achieved an entry in Kerrang!'s 20 best albums of 1992 - not bad for a compilation!

'Sympathy' was released as a single following the US leg of the tour, and after a sold-out concert on 5 September at Wembley Arena, again to celebrate Marillion's decade with EMI. "I wanted to make an event of it," explains John Arnison. "It was also trying to get the old fans back. We sold seven thousand, two hundred tickets - the maximum capacity is eleven thousand, but it can be arranged to hold six or seven and a half thousand." It was a memorable occasion, particularly for Steve H who fell off the front of the stage. "I had to go round security to get back on stage, still singing!" laughs Steve. As for the single, 'Sympathy' fared reasonably well - it reached No.17, the first time the band had been inside the top 20 since 'Incommunicado'. Still, it was not the great relaunch: almost as a litmus test, 'No One Can' was reissued as a single in July. At No.26, it fared better than the last time around but it was no giant killer.

1992 was also the tenth anniversary of The Web, so that had to be celebrated too. A party was held at The Borderline Club in London on Friday 1 May, attended by The Low Fat Yoghurts. An auction of Marillion memorabilia also took place, including items such as guitars from Steve R and Pete, Fish's trousers and a number of other items of clothing from Steve H, Mark and Ian, raising a total of £1,560 for Andy Field's family. "The auctioneer and MC of 'humorous but sarcastic banter' was Mark, a role he seemed made for. One fan wrote, "Did Mark Kelly start out as a stand-up comedian by any chance?"

Tenth Anniversary with EMI

The Writing

In November 1992 the writing sessions began for what would become *'Brave'*, at the band's new-found haunt, rehearsal and recording studio - The Racket Club. Where in the past Marillion had travelled abroad to gain release from the opinions of the outside world, now they had a place of their own; ironically, Ian had just moved to Florida due to his wife's asthma. "I was commuting," he explains, "It was only an eight-hour flight to Orlando, the boys seemed to think I could come over and work in blocks!" Ian would come over for a few weeks at a time and stay at his place in Aylesbury (Ian nicknamed it "cellblock" because it was so small), before going back for a few weeks - at least, that was the plan before *'Brave'*.

Some musical ideas and arrangements (such as Steve Rothery's riff for 'Hard As Love') already existed and John Helmer had come up with some lyrical ideas about a girl in crisis. A few weeks into the writing, Steve Hogarth suggested that these ideas be married to a police announcement he had heard a few years previously on GWR Radio in Bristol. As he notes on the sleeve notes, "The police had picked up a young woman wandering on the Severn Bridge who refused or was unable to speak to them." Steve's suggestion that the album be linked "to a series of snapshots about her life" was welcomed by the rest of the band. As notes Rothers, "It seemed to lend a meaning to the half-finished ideas we had and made planning the album in some ways easier." The downside was that the band was once again considering a concept album - nearly ten years had elapsed since *'Misplaced Childhood'*, and such an idea was even more unfashionable than it had been then. Given the fashion-consciousness (and subsequent disappointment) of

falling up

Wembley Arena wasn't Steve H's first trip off stage. Marillion played The Saga in Copenhagen on 11 October 1991, which happens to have a castellated stage. Half way through the show, H fell headfirst into a hole! "I climbed back up, then launched myself straight off the other side to make it look on purpose!" he grins.

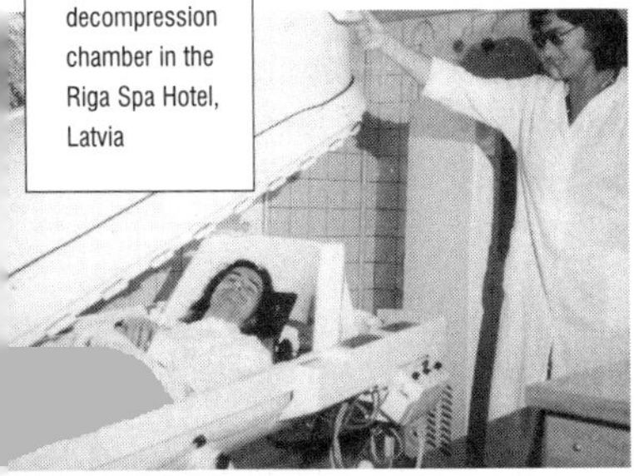

Steve H experiences the decompression chamber in the Riga Spa Hotel, Latvia

'Holidays In Eden', this factor captured the mood of the band. "Suited us just fine!" laughs H. This mood extended to some of the songs, such as the out-and-out rocker of 'Hard As Love'. "We felt we could do anything we liked!" agrees Rothers.

In January 1993, EMI (in the form of A&R man Nick Mander) proposed Dave Meegan as producer, a familiar face due to his involvement in *'Fugazi'*. "My wife was working for EMI at the time, so she knew Nick," remarks Dave. "He wanted to break with traditional, indie guitar bands, he wasn't aware that I'd worked on *'Fugazi'* but was pleased, it made it easier to convince the band!" The suggestion was willingly accepted. "We loved the vitality in a lot of Dave's work and felt he could really bring a different dimension to the band," recalled Rothers. For his part, Dave initially felt he was a strange choice for the project. "Up to then my productions were almost exclusively indie style," explains Dave in the liner notes. That was exactly what EMI had in mind, taking the band on a stage further from its progressive roots. Dave had received strict instructions from Nick, to carry out the recording sessions is a short a time as possible. Heh! Not likely!

When the writing sessions reached the rough demo stage, Marillion played Dave what they had done so far and he found that it was good. As Dave recalls, "I listened to a series of early, early sketches, roughly patched together lyrically. The band was trying to

Dave Meegan

Born Dublin in 1963, Dave knew his mind from an early age. "I saw a band rehearsing, I knew it was what I wanted to do," he recalls. At the age of sixteen Dave used a Short Wave radio transmitter ("the top frequencies overlapped with Medium Wave") to set up a pirate radio station. "I used to stack up my record collection in the morning and listen to them during the day!" At eighteen, Dave "begged, bought and borrowed" enough equipment to create a recording studio in his Dad's garage, which was used to create demos of local bands, some of which were picked up by Dave Fanning (Dublin's John Peel!). Before long the UK beckoned, and Dave got a job as a tape operator at Sarm East Studios in London. He worked with bands as diverse as Yes, Rush, The Psychedelic Furs and Killing Joke, not to mention Marillion with *'Fugazi'*. "When I left Sarm, I was their longest serving employee!" laughs Dave.

In 1987 Dave was seconded back to Dublin for what would be his big break - U2's *'Joshua Tree'*. With this experience and profile under his belt, it seemed the right time to try his luck in the US. Over in California, Shep Pettibone (with whom Dave worked on the Pet Shop Boys *'Actually'*) was producing some work for US singer/songwriter Baxter Robertson, and offered him a post. Baxter later ditched Shep and kept going with Dave and the other engineer (Spike Drake, who had also worked with the PSB). After working with Baxter, Dave stayed in LA and hunted local, unsigned bands for demo recording opportunities before a combination of an earthquake and a bad car crash suggested that it was time to come home.

Back in the UK, Dave started working for a producer called Stephen Hague. "He helped me to get producing," comments Dave. Indeed - when working on an album for the House Of Love, Dave started as engineer and ended up as producer. Thanks Stephen! Before long, Dave and Marillion's paths would cross again.

Dave has been referred to as the sixth member of Marillion, the band's George Martin. "I love the way I get the respect and trust that they give, it's a lovely feeling but it doesn't want to be overstated. I see their magic and try to focus it!"

Dave is still in touch with his roots, developing new acts. Dave's diverse experience has led to a love of "anything that's song-based." Two projects in particular are White Buffalo (who supported Marillion on the *'Anoraknophobia'* tour) and Pave. "It's all down to home production, luck and hard work!"

tie it together so they could record it and play it live." The lyrical work demonstrated how closely aligned Helmer and Hogarth had become. "The right hand really knew what the left hand was doing," remarked John. Apart from a couple of meetings early on, communication was by fax and telephone: John didn't feel the need to join the band for the recording sessions.

Sorted. Now it was time to find a studio.

The band came in from the cold in February 1993, when Miles Copeland offered the use of his château - the Château Marouatte - in the French Dordogne. The opportunity had come during the Holidays tour of the US, when a chap from IRS had mentioned the place. "I mentioned it to John, who gave Miles Copeland a call," explains Steve R. Dave was delighted - "I love working on location!" It was an imposing place on the top of a hill, with house and grounds jammed full of "gothic statues, pillars and other artefacts," according to Rothers. "After a few weeks I started to feel like I was in a Steven King novel!"

Steve H relaxing in the Château Marouatte gardens

Dave Meegan and Ian plan things out while Privet, Tony and Pete try to find out where they are

The band arrived at the château with a truck full of hardware. "I didn't quite realise how much gear we had," H's diary commented. Dave and Privet set about wiring up the place, installing microphones all over the place to tape the atmospheric sounds. It took two days to completely wire the château inside and out: locations included empty staircases ('to pick up any passing ghosts') and a water-filled cave, used for the splash that completed 'Paper Lies'. "There were even a couple of mics in the fireplace to pick up the crackle of the fire," laughed H in the sleeve notes. The main banqueting room was set up as the studio, and the mixing desk and other devices were positioned in the master bedroom. Cluedo-style, amps were situated in various other rooms including the wine cellar, the study and the chapel, with the lot linked together with an array of wires running up and down stairwells and according to Pete, "draped like washing lines between neighbouring wings." As the cabling and equipment transformed the château, the band moved inside their artistic cocoon. The environment provided a creative hotbed to

droning on

Steve Hogarth spent the first few days at the château locked in a room "with a keyboard full of drone sounds." Experimenting with the different possibilities, Steve was eventually to come up with the first few bars of 'Brave'. But not before disconcerted glances at such strange behaviour were shared outside the room!

complete the writing sessions and start recording overdubs - the sounds and rhythms that provide the backdrop for the music. "It just seemed to fall into place so easily," remarked Dave. The combination of the château and its technology performed their collective magic, as Steve H discovered while he listened to Pete recording the bass for 'Living With The Big Lie'. "From where I'm sitting it sounds like God's own bass sound," Steve remarked at the time.

Steve H spent happy hours with the guitar he had bought on the previous tour. "I had to learn to play the guitar really," says H, "Rothers showed me a few basic chord shapes and I spent my spare time at Marouatte fiddling around with it." Meanwhile, there was nothing else to do but relax. "We used to go into town a bit, or we'd drive around and look at the scenery," says Pete. Not quite the same as Berlin in 1985, then! Meals were cooked in what used to be the servants quarters at the château, ironically by an English couple. Rest assured that the wine did flow!

Time was short - the band had the château for two months, by which time the bulk of the recording was expected to be complete. It was not to be, however - unsurprising, as every take was being recorded and logged, each being carefully sifted in the evenings by Dave as a potential source of material for the album. Notes Pete in the sleeve notes, "He had a complete notebook of everything on tape from the very start of the project - literally weeks of listening time." As H remarked, "Dave was dedicated to capturing our most inspired moments!" And capture them he did, but though the writing was complete only one third of the overdubs had been captured to tape by the time the French castle had to be vacated.

Unfortunately for Ian, whose contribution was complete, time slowed to a standstill. "I spent four months at home in Florida, waiting for things to finish," explains Ian. "After a month, I was starting to think there's only so much of sitting by the swimming pool and driving speed boats that I could take so I gave the lads a call and asked how it was going. They said they hadn't even finished the bass - I was going potty!" Indeed, Ian got so bored he bought another house and did it up just for something to do! Meanwhile, with a little relief (it was a lonely experience, as H commented, "That's the trouble with a castle in the sky."), the guys went back to Blighty. Following a "week off" during which the band, Dave and Privet spent time recording sounds such as London tubes and coins being thrown

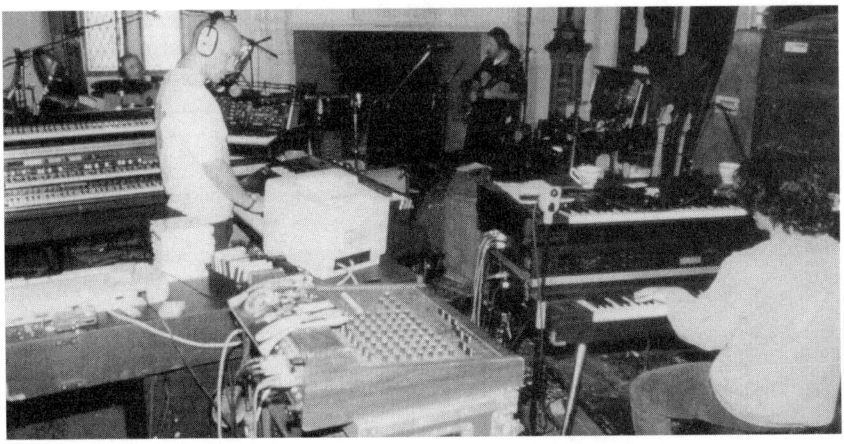

onto pavements, the seven made their way to Paul Lewis's Parr Street studios in Liverpool, on 19 April 1993, where they stayed for a further four months. Parr Street was expedient as it was owned by Hit And Run, "We got good rates there!" laughs Dave, who was assisted by local lad Mike Hunter. "Brave was such a logistical thing, my main job was to make sure all the gear was in the right places," says Mike. "I don't know if we did seven days per week, but Dave can be a bit of a monster worker when he gets going!" Despite everyone's best efforts, Steve R recalls how, after eight weeks with nothing to show, "Nick Mander was starting to have a fit. The band and Dave had decided however that we were in the middle of making a very special album and that it would be ready when it was ready. Fortunately Nick had little choice but to let events run their course." Not that anybody was having an easy ride - working evenings and weekends became the norm. "Technology was not on our side," remarks Dave. "This was hard editing with razor blades and sticky tape!" One of the obstacles was making the material flow - not only did it have to be in the right order, but key and tempo changes needed to be smooth, often requiring additional pieces of music to tie different song elements together. Band and producer had to always consider the complete album, "A bit like playing a game of chess," remarked Dave at the time. Everything[9] was up for grabs: new sounds were added all the time, including the voice of Cathy, the Japanese receptionist at Parr. H 'found' an Uillean pipes player called Tony Halligan busking in a doorway in Liverpool, so he went on as well.

There was no doubt in anybody's minds that something entirely new had been produced, but something that was most definitely Marillion. In a Web interview, Dave recalled "I deliberately tried pointing backwards in the direction of *'Fugazi'*, and it worked." But did it? The label and the world had yet to discover and, more importantly, to judge.

On Parr by Judith Mitchell

I got a phone call, guess who's recording at Parr Street? Someone who knew a friend of a friend who was rehearsing there had recognised the band. Suffice to say, I knew they were there the day after they arrived. At the time I was writing for the Flaming Shroud fanzine so my brother Andrew and I, plus Editor Alex, managed to arrange an interview at the studio. I was very nervous despite meeting the band several times before, but not really in this context.

All three of us ventured to the studio and were told to wait in the bar area. Mark finally arrived - but only after we'd said hello to Pete and Steve H which really shattered my nerves! Mark took us to the actual recording booth and we were asked to sit behind the mixing desk, he showed us how the controls worked and put in a tape. He said 'listen to this then we'll do the interview!

The tape was the near-final version of the album - all of it. We listened, sat in the console chairs with the album blasting out over the PA system. Mind-blowing! Imagine trying to take in all of *'Brave'* in one listen! Mark returned with a big grin, we were a bit short of words! The interview finally got going with all of us chipping in questions.

Once the interview was over we thanked Mark for his time and we wandered out into the Liverpool sunshine, it was about 8pm and the Friday night cabaret of the boys and girls going out to the pubs and clubs had just started. We managed to find a taxi home and the driver had *'Dark Side Of The Moon'* on - surreal. We wound down best we could listening to Genesis and talking about what we had heard. It was 2am before we felt tired - the adrenaline took that long to wear off. This remains a very fond memory, I still find it hard to believe that it happened at all.

Holding Breath

By May 1993 the suspense was killing many fans, particularly as the album had originally been touted as being completed by then, with a September release date. It was not to be - September would become the completion date, pushing the release back to January the following year. "They (the labels) have peaks during several months of the year for releasing an album," explained Steve in a Web interview. "If they miss one they pick another one and that's usually several months later." To downhearted fans the message was clear - it would be worth the wait. "It's all enormously exciting and it sounds sensational, I can promise you. It's the most sparkling thing we've ever made!" wrote the guitarist. Paul Craddick and Doug Ott of Enchant, who were recording at Parr Street at the time, had the opportunity to preview the album. What struck them the most was how buoyed up the band was about its creation. "Being long-time Marillion fans we've seen them, well, almost 'depressed' but its great to see them so pleased with this one!" Keith Andrews was mixing Enchant at the time, so was also able to sneak a preview. "I was absolutely knocked out by the sheer power, the detail, the expression and the absolute glory of the sound! It's fantastic!"

Things were looking good.

August saw final touches added to the album at Sarm West studios before it was moved to Abbey Road studios for assembly. Finally, the end of a hugely draining, yet productive period of thirteen months was reached, with the total cost amounting to £375,000. As far as the band was concerned, the result justified the time and money spent. Dave's creative involvement and hard work had been of primary importance. "He did a really great job," recalls Mark. Dave was equally complimentary - "It was such a pleasure to sit back and listen to the band create something from nothing, developing purely using that special gift they had of 'inter-band telepathy'."

Despite the feeling of pride, the players were just a little nervous about what they had produced. Noted Steve Rothery at the time, "The idea of a concept album is something of a cringe. But we wanted to make something like The Who's *'Quadrophenia'*. It's a concept album in that it's a story set to music." He was later to laugh off the criticism that the band wrote one long song because they couldn't think of 10 short ones. "It's the most natural, extensive and complete album we have ever made," he remarked. Progressive the album might have been, in the sense that it pushed against its musical boundaries, but in sonic structure and musical style it was a far cry from the fantasy landscapes of '70s prog bands such as Yes and Camel, even if they did provide the fertile ground from whence Marillion did spring. "What I call progressive is not anything I've ever worked on!" frowns Dave Meegan.

'Brave'

Based on the true story of a girl found wandering on the notorious suicide spot of the Severn Road Bridge, the band confound the expectations they might have built with 'Holidays In Eden' *to conjure an altogether different experience. Laced with depression and melancholy, the band takes us deep into the young woman's psyche. Deeper and deeper we go into her most private memories. The album has an intimacy that is almost claustrophobic, making us feel uncomfortable at being party to such things. This is an album built around the smoke and mirrors that camouflage the truth of the girl's desperate torment, and as such, the album is largely one of atmospheres. All of the band contribute to the cinematic feel: Mark painting water-coloured low hanging skies; Pete building expectations; Steve Rothery searing nerve endings with aching poignancy, Ian punctuating proceedings with deliberate foreboding tom rolls, and Steve H's voice never more emotive. Simply, it is one of the most moving albums ever created.*

From the opening, mournful foghorn guitar, to Mark Kelly's haunting keyboard intro to 'Bridge', it's clear that *'Brave'* isn't taking the easy route. It gives way to a plaintive Steve Hogarth setting the scene of the girl, stopped in the very act of throwing herself to her doom, to her first tentative recollections of what has brought her to this point. It's all here: family, love, drugs, homelessness, the chaos of modern life... All the themes that will build to an inevitable conclusion over the next seventy one minutes - linked by the ironic refrain of 'I got used to it!'

'Runaway' takes us out, scared and alone, onto the uncaring streets of London. The girl is found and taken home once more, but her family believe that a bit of sympathy is all that's needed to make it okay again, too fearful to investigate the terrible, hinted at, truth of what might have made her do it. And so the pain festers...

'Goodbye To All That' showcases Pete Trewavas's incredible bass skills as it takes us back on the bridge, preparing to let go and to embrace the dark comfort of the waters... and when we hear the maelstrom of what's coming next, is it any wonder she feels the way she does? We are flung, like a bottle caught in a rip-tide, through the pressure to conform, being institutionalised and into the welcoming oblivion of heroin and the friendships and relationships that accompany it, always using, always taking, always false, but better than what waits back in the real world. When the pain runs this deep, an air of concern earns nothing but contempt.

'Hard As Love' is the first respite, musically at least, from the descent into ever darker waters. Replete with Mark Kelly's Purple-esque keyboard flourishes, and with Steve Rothery throwing out cutting heavy riffs. The track investigates the difficulty of opening up to love, which is almost impossible once you recognise how it leaves you vulnerable to emotional destitution. In terms of the story, it seems that the girl is being implored to let someone through her defences to help her. Although she wants to, needs to, it's too little, too late... In the song's middle eight, Steve Hogarth spills out the dangers of allowing someone to love you. Ian Mosley's toms thunder down as Hogarth sums it up;

'Nothing's ever been as hard.'

'The Hollow Man' shows the other side of not opening up. This restrained ballad is inspired by T.S. Eliot's 'The Hollow Men', and the spacious, tasteful track reveals the emptiness caused by denying oneself love. 'We're tin hard and we rattle when we're shaken' indeed.

'Alone Again In The Lap Of Luxury' takes us back in time once more. Into a middle-class family house that shows all the signs of being entirely conventional. We scratch the patina of respectability to discover a far more distressing reality; a father that commits the ultimate transgression of his responsibilities and a wife who buries her head in the sand and prays the evidence before her doesn't really add up to what it seems. Does she have the strength to run away?

'Paper Lies' is the track that least obviously fits into the story. On the surface, it is a wryly witty dissection of the British press and their manipulative, Machiavellian ways of bending the truth to their own ends. Though the song is not featured in it, Richard Stanley's film of the album illustrates this theme more clearly. The papers get hold of the story of the mad girl who attempts suicide and twist, corrupt and pervert it, until reading her story, the girl barely recognises her own tale.

For the title track, the band conjures a smoky Celtic spirit, somewhat reminiscent of the traditional song 'She Moved Through the Fair'. The song appears to be from the perspective of the man who tried to throw her a life line. He reflects on the remarkable strength of character shown by the girl in coping with her many tragedies, despite the fact that her despair won out in the end. He carries her memory inside himself, 'She's inside you, and she's crying.' There follows the 'age section' in which each voice is older than the last, starting with the chattering of an infant (Steve Rothery's daughter Jenny, who also provides the crying at the start of the album) and finishing with an old woman saying, 'What a brave, brave girl.'

'The Great Escape' sees us heading for the bridge, the inevitable beckoning. Rather than seeing suicide as a terrible thing, the lyrics make it clear that it is in this act that she gains her redemption: 'heading for the dignified walk away.' The music, as always on this album, is perfectly attuned to the words; just listen to Mark Kelly's music hall piano flourish after the words, 'Quiet applause will do,' the music builds until Steve Hogarth's agonizing cry, 'You're holding on,' and both meanings are transparently obvious.

'The Last Of You' seems to concern the girl's father once more; perhaps his memory becomes flesh as she stands on the wrong side of the stanchions above the water. For the first time, rather than running away, hiding from what it going on, she is at last able to accuse her tormentor, 'Why did you hurt the very one, that you should have protected?' Musically, the 'Last Of You' is a reprise of the 'alone in the city' section of 'Big Lie', helping to bring the whole thing full circle. It is the same music with a very different feel.

The anger gives way once more as we segue into the gorgeous, emotive 'Fallin' From The Moon'. Along side the deep melancholy, there's an enormous sense of the pain, neglect and abuse lifting as they cease to matter anymore. It's as though a sense of wonder pervades the

team spirit

A few months after the release of *'Brave'*, H was in the offices of EMI International chatting to a staffer called Carol who remarked, "Those Radiohead boys were in here yesterday, and they all took a copy of your *'Brave'* album away." H took a copy of *'The Bends'* and has been listening to it ever since! Incidentally, Carol now works for Radiohead.

music, almost as though we were seeing a birth, rather than a death. As the girl ruminates, "a mountain isn't far to fall, when you've fallen from the moon," Steve Rothery launches into one of his finest solos, each note perfectly pure and astonishingly evocative. As the girl's body sinks into the water, as her last thoughts slip away, we're left with the sound of the gentle waves lapping on the shore.

'Made Again' was something of an afterthought to the album, and it shows. This is not to say it isn't a beautiful and affecting number, but that its optimism is at odds with the preceding 65 minutes of music. The opening bars were written by Steve Rothery for the birth of his daughter, which goes some way to explaining its sense of hope. It is perhaps a necessary addition, since it changes perspective from musing on someone for whom death is a merciful release, to a sense of glowing optimism. I like to think it is for the real girl who inspired such a powerful album, the band saying, "I hope you're doing okay."

Bill Smith Studios' cover artwork for *'Brave'* is the simplest and yet possibly most effective of all the H-era covers. Featuring a heavily shadowed girl's face taken from a photographer's card of a model, her eyes seem to stare out at us, and we immediately make a connection to her. There's something guarded about her; pretty though she is, there's a sense of much going on under the surface. The band's name and album title are small, as if to say, "It's the music you should be paying attention to."

The Release

With the masterpiece complete, the band had to go before EMI and explain why they hadn't produced a pop album. Writes Steve Hogarth, "I'm very proud of the fact that it was quite a dangerous commercial decision we took to make *'Brave'*. I'm proud of the fact we took the guts to do it - I wonder if it damaged our career; I think it damaged our relationship with EMI." Despite this, the label did accept a number of additional 'features', including a specially-cut fourth side of the vinyl album. It had two grooves, each with a different ending. This was Mark Kelly's idea, to solve the issue that the single version of 'The Great Escape' ended differently to the intended album version. "I stole it!" grins Mark. "There was a Monty Python album called *'Matching Tie And Handkerchief'*[10], I thought, that's a good idea. Side Four of *'Brave'* was only twelve minutes long so it fitted quite nicely!" For the listener it was random chance that determined whether the girl jumped from the bridge or was 'Made Again'.

There was also a cover to produce, but fortunately Bill Smith Studios found the album accessible enough to work with. "*'Brave'* is my favourite Marillion album cover, and in the top ten of all the album covers I have ever produced," confides Bill Smith. "Out of all the Marillion covers, it was the one that came closest to fulfilling the idea of words, music and images as a complete entity." "We had a story for *'Brave'*," adds Carl Glover. "It was like developing a book cover really." The initial idea for the cover was of a female form taking the shape of a cross: explains Bill, "EMI and the band were worried so we went off and looked for a facial representation." Despite being produced on a computer for the first time, an obvious boon, the cover had to be stored as nine separate images to achieve a better resolution than could be

fish 4 calls

"When *'Brave'* was released over here, the record company put a sticker on the plastic with our phone number on it, and you wouldn't believe how many people called trying to impersonate Fish's voice! Then one day Fish himself called for an interview and I didn't believe it was really him until a minute into the conversation..."

Dan Sherman, Web USA

fitted on the hard disk! Finally, a no-logo decision had to be made. "We wanted to put the name about without it getting in the way of the artwork," comments Carl. The handwriting on the cover was, in fact, a fragment of Anne Frank's original diary, written (according to the Dutch Progressive Rock Pages) about July 15th 1944. "I didn't want it to be obvious what it was saying, but I liked its form," explains Bill Smith. This was initially unknown to the band, and following its discovery the link was agreed to be played down for fear of misassociation between the experiences of the album's heroine and Anne Frank herself.

At least in the UK there were people at EMI who understood the album, whereas the US label IRS couldn't get a handle on it at all. Explained Steve H to Jon Epstein, "IRS admitted at a very early stage that they didn't 'get' it. They had a lot of trouble doing anything with it, especially on radio."

Before the release, the band went their separate ways for a while. "Everyone needed a bit of a release," remarks Pete. Rothers stayed at the studios to produce a US band called Enchant, the drummer for whom was Paul Craddick; meanwhile Mark produced the album *'Under The Red And White Sky'* for John Wesley in Florida. "I'd already told Wes I'd like to produce him, we'd stayed in touch, Ian was living in Florida at the time so I went out for a month!" explains Mark. "When I got out there, I found out that Wes had told the studio owner's brother, Jim Morris, that he would produce the album! Wes then persuaded Jim to co-produce, the first few days were a bit of a battle!" Mark eased his way into the situation, gently demonstrating that his production ideas did actually work. He also ended up playing most of the keyboards![11]

dearth of a name

John Wesley's full name is J. W. Dearth. "Nobody could ever spell it! I got fed up with having to tell people how to pronounce it, so eventually John Arnison suggested John Wesley and it stuck!"

On 5 January 1994, all bar Ian went to Holland to record acoustic treatments of 'Runaway', 'Made Again', 'The Hollow Man' and 'Lap Of Luxury' for live broadcast in the Netherlands. 'Easter' and an H-solo performance of 'Cover My Eyes' were also performed. Then the release cycle began again. 'The Great Escape' was released on 10 January 1994 as a taster, followed by *'Brave'* a month later on 7 February. When the record hit, it was given an immediate (and overwhelmingly positive) thumbs-up by the press. One magazine reported that "*'Brave'* is the first great concept album of the decade." It was awarded a 5-star review by Kerrang!, and is also listed in the Rough Guide To Rock as the best ever prog rock album - that's ever, folks! Paul Elliott wrote in Q magazine, "*'Brave'* is a tale of ordinary madness set to clever, spliff-assisted rock, and when it peaks on 'Fallin' From The Moon', it's beautiful."

Fan Simon Clarke remembers the very day. "I went out and bought it in all three formats, I had to go to three different record stores," he recalls. "That night we did what it said on the cover, we listened to it loud with the lights off." As they did, they were caught in the same wave of passion that crashed onto the heads of many. A letter from Ellie Purtill to The Web commented, "What can you say about *'Brave'* that wouldn't be hopelessly inadequate? I've questioned my whole existence since I heard that album. It's a drug." Fan Alan Hewitt notes how it is "difficult to assess *'Brave'* and be objective. I love that album so much," a view echoed by Wayne Kensett, at the time running the Web UK. "How do you remain objective when confronted by 70 minutes of something that must surely rank as one of the most complete pieces of music ever written?" Paul Hughes comments, "With *'Brave'*, Marillion moved up from a band I liked a lot, to by far my favourite band in the world. To this day, this piece of music utterly stuns me." This really was music beyond the call of duty, as explains US fan Mike Osborn, who was on vacation in Las Vegas when he bought his copy. "I will always remember that moment in time, racing through the lights of the Vegas strip, music surrounding me, tears wetting my cheeks as I felt the moment of epiphany when the melody, the arrangement, the lyrics all met in a swirl," remembers Mike. "In the words of Lenny Bruce (describing an injection of an opiate), it was like kissing God." Well, really. As Dave Meegan comments, "*'Brave'* re-affirmed Marillion's relationship with its fans. People who were into it, or who were in that situation took it surprisingly seriously, it took a lot of people a long time otherwise." Dave remembers the letters from fans: "Many talked about turning points. I like it when it upsets a bit!"

custard with that, Sir?

John Wesley found himself the butt of practical jokes on the Brave tour (though he gave as good as he got), including regular heckle checks (as opposed to sound checks). He was pelted with grapes by the stage hands throughout his last performance in Copenhagen. Thinking it was over, he was then covered in custard!

'The Hollow Man' was released as the second single on 14 March 1994, reaching a disappointing No.30 in the UK charts. The band members had been encouraging each other to write solo material, out of which came Rother's 'Winter Trees' B-side for 'The Hollow Man'. "In the end it looks like I was the only one actually doing it," laughs Steve. Mostly the B-sides came from live tracks. "The whole process of making the album took up so much time, it seemed the easiest thing to do," recalled Dave in a Web interview. Finally, 'Alone Again' was released on 25 April.

Following in the footsteps of musical opuses such as *'Quadrophenia'* and *'Tommy'*, the band decided to make a film of the album. EMI had allocated £100,000 for promo videos, but Marillion proposed to use the lot on a single, full-length movie. "We collectively felt it was pointless to make three pop videos for this album (EMI's normal expectation for an album at the time) and thought it might be better spending all the budget at once on a very low budget film," explains Steve H. Adds John Arnison, "The promo videos weren't being shown that much anyway!" Due to financial realism and time constraints, the band settled for a feature-length film. The band commissioned Richard Stanley, director of art-house films as well as music videos, as producer. Says cult movie fan Rothers (who had seen 'Hardware' and parts of 'Dust Devil', both by Stanley), "We auditioned scripts and it was Richard's that really caught our eye. He seemed to concentrate on the darker side of the story."

The band were involved in two days of filming, according to Steve H. "We had very little to do with the ideas contained in it, apart from having inspired them in Richard," he says. "Our only involvement in the film was as 'actors/ performers.' "Missing out 'Mad', 'Paper Lies' and 'Made Again' for budgetary reasons, the film was first shown on German TV/satellite channel RTL+, then edited to get past the UK censors for the video release. It failed the first time round - to quote Mark, "Richard Stanley wasn't really known for making children's TV." Some scenes were deemed "likely to have far too powerful and dangerous an impact on

depressed, potentially suicidal young people." It was finally released on video on 6 February 1995, a year after it was first shown.

Despite its popularity *'Brave'* didn't do well commercially. In a chat session, Rothers noted, "*'Brave'* was a difficult album to listen to for a lot of people." Maybe - but it still stands for many as the pinnacle of everything the fans have come to hope for. All the same it posed a problem for the bean counters in EMI, who were disappointed with the return on their investment: the label became more and more difficult to work with from this point on.

The Tour

Following a whole year without touring, the band was gagging to get back on the road, and equally wanted to give *'Brave'* the attention it deserved. "We'd started talking about the tour during the recording process," explains John. Adds Mark, "We agreed to a longer tour, to see if we could increase sales." The initial plan was to play smaller venues, as explained Steve in a Web interview, "We want something really special, they enable better interaction between the band and the crowd." He went on to say, "There is a chance we may play *'Brave'* in its entirety!" And so, they did. The whole-album-in-its-entirety thing was not a guaranteed success: as Rothers admitted, "It will be a bit of a learning process, to put it mildly! But everyone we've played the album to has been really enthusiastic." Agrees John, "It was a bit of a crazy thing to do."

Following fan club warm-up gigs in Germany, Italy and Liverpool, the tour proper started in Cardiff on 22 February. John Wesley was back in the support slot, once again performing an acoustic set. Following Wes, the ambient 'River' music was played while overhead, screens showed slides to accompany the *'Brave'* story. 'River' had been created by Mike Hunter at Parr Street using samples and off-cuts from the two previous Marillion albums. "It was Steve Hogarth's idea," says Mike, "*'Brave'* starts very quietly so he didn't want the usual live thing where the sound engineer is playing AC/DC before the gig. He asked me if I fancied doing it and I said, yeah!" Rather than hunting through the miles of discarded tape on the studio floor, Mike raided Mark Kelly's bank of pre-loaded samples. "I messed them about, reversed them, twisted them up and layered them onto tape. Any extra instruments, like drums, I played myself!" And that was 'River'.

wrong colour red

The Brave gigs also saw H's first live use of a guitar. "Before the tour it was decided (not by me!) that it would be handy if I played a few power chords during the live show," says H. He needed a six-string for the power chords, so tour manager Tim Bricusse sold him a red Fender Stratocaster. Explains Tim, "I'd bought it for Duran Duran's Andy Taylor, but he told me it was the wrong colour red so he let me keep it..."

'Brave' was the main performance, centrepiece and piéce de résistance, seventy-four minutes of music with only the quickest of breaks before 'Hollow Man', for H to say hello to the crowd. The show provided a forum for H to really perform, with bunches of tulips, black eyeliner and orange lipstick, pigtails, men in balaclavas dragging him off stage, candles in candelabras, incense and a variety of costumes. The audience was held spellbound, night after night after night after night, some fans turning up at every gig they could get tickets for, to get another fix of a musical feast that could not possibly last forever. After the triumphant finale came an entire Marillion set including songs from both eras, though with two albums to draw on there were only a couple of pre-1988 songs.

For many disgruntled old timers the Brave tour was a one-way ticket back to fandom. Mike Palmer recalls, "A work colleague of mine saw them on the previous tour and said that I must go and see the new guy, I went on the Brave tour and that's where it started again!" Newly re-ignited Paul Rael also saw the band perform *'Brave'* live. "I caught a gig at Cambridge and it was just phenomenal, I was staggered at how good Hogarth was and how brilliant his vocals were on stage. Steve Rothery's solos were heavenly. When they encored with six or seven tracks from the two albums I'd ignored, I instantly realised how much I'd missed out!" Liverpool-based Alan Hewitt remarks, "Having missed Genesis' *'Lamb Lies Down'* tour, I think seeing *'Brave'* performed was probably the closest I will ever get to that. Seeing it for the first time and in my own hometown and on my birthday is something I will never forget!" Wes himself rarely missed the opportunity to be with the audience. "Brave was one of the most intense shows I have ever seen," says Wes. "It was a consistently moving experience - I went out every night and watched; I must have seen it sixty times!"

"With *'Brave'*, Marillion became the best band on the planet," says fan Simon Clarke, who at the time was evangelising his new girlfriend, Vicki Harding. "Simon had made me a tape, one side was filled up with stuff including Marillion. I'm well into vocals and I really liked the voice." Simon booked tickets to the Brave gig on 28 February, on the understanding that this chap was nothing like Fish. "Vicki asked me whether he dressed up or wore greasepaint, I said, Nah!" Not that Vicki was the only member of the audience who stood, incredulous, when H reached for the lipstick! Nonetheless, both Simon and Vicki knew they had to see it again. The next time came in May, at the Royal Concert Hall in Nottingham, and the pair were standing a bit closer to the front than was healthy - they would be firm followers from that point on. Says Simon, "The intensity of the performance was amazing, we could feel the heat of the lights, H was just fucking scary! The bug sort of bit!"

All the same, *'Brave'* didn't rock everybody's boat. Recalls fan Andy Rotherham, "It is very easy to see *'Brave'* through rose-tinted specs, to say that it was all brilliant for everyone, but that wasn't true - I can remember people walking out of gigs, complaining that they just didn't get it." Simon Hoban concurs - "I'm convinced the release of *'Brave'* started a downward spiral which the band have never recovered from. I know it's much lauded over by fans and band alike, but it can't be denied among the general populace *'Brave'* went down like a lead balloon."

With such a long set, it is unsurprising that H followed in his forebear's footsteps and lost his voice, on Tuesday 22 March 1994 in Hamburg. Monitor engineer Geoff Hooper came to the rescue, advising H to eat, "fresh pineapple soaked in honey [12]," according to H's diary. He wasn't the only band member to have problems with *'Brave'* - the number of samples in the set was a nightmare for Mark. "We got various bits of equipment updated in the latter parts of the tour," he recalls. For Mike Hunter, not only was it his first crew job for anyone other than a pub band, but he was also dropped in at the deep end as Mark's keyboard tech. "Mark's a boffin, he didn't really need anyone to set his keyboards up!" says Mike. All the same, he continues, "The first couple of months were blind panic!"

After a brief sojourn to New York for Steve, during which he discovered that the music industry was child's play compared to the theatre (read on, MacDuff), the Brave tour came to an official end on 2 September at the 12,000 capacity Auditorio Nacional, Mexico City [13]. "It's a fantastic venue made for rock gigs," says Mark. John Wesley remembers it to be a "magical gig - just the number of people!" Amongst the thousands was fan Bruno Galli, who recalls, "When they finished playing *'Brave'* I thought I had been in Heaven, but ha! I was just standing at Heaven's gates. The encore was around 12 songs! What a treat! I have been to a lot of shows, including Marillion and Fish, but none has had the same impact as that one." Unfortunately there was not to be a video of the Brave tour. This was not through lack of trying - EMI didn't want the bother, but wouldn't give permission to other labels (for example UK label Castle, which was keen to film the Rotterdam show); also the few TV recordings (in Poland and Argentina, not to mention the recording of the Auditorio Nacional show by MVS, a copy of which was blagged by a certain fan in Mexico) were not considered to be of sufficient quality to make 'proper' releases. What a waste of eyes.

The First Of Many by Rob Crossland

I had a fleeting acquaintance with Marillion's music at the time of *'Fugazi'*, when I was interested enough to record a live gig from the Beeb. I still have it on Betamax! Something about the band must have caught my attention, but I think I was much more into other stuff at that time. I'd really like to check back when I have time to see exactly who I was into at that time - but it wasn't really Marillion at all. So, a lovely guy called Neil Stokes joined my new company in 1987, I think. He was still a student and asked me to help mentor his audio-visual Degree project. I didn't have to give any input at all as it was a great piece and featured 'He Knows, You Know'. I was knocked out by the feel and edge of this track, and went to my local record shop to pick up Marillion's 'latest' album. They sold me *'The Thieving Magpie'* and *'Seasons End'*, the second of which I thought was one of the most brilliant things I'd ever heard. Forget the fact that they'd missed out an album or two in between and ignored *'Holidays In Eden'*! I played *'Seasons End'* to my children on the daily run into school and they too approved. You can't force kids to like music, but they really loved it.

At that time, after several years of non-gigging (young family, etc, etc) I subscribed to Q magazine. Whatever negativity they have shown as an institution against the band, they did carry an advert for the Brave tour. I only spotted it the day of the Cambridge gig, and so, totally awestruck by *'Seasons End'*, off my wife Alexis and I went to see what these guys were like. I was annoyed with myself that we had missed the first night, which had been in their hometown of Aylesbury - as close to us as Cambridge. *'Brave'* was completely unknown to us. It was as much a play as a rock gig, and I was mesmerised not only by Steve Rothery's guitar playing (I love a guitar virtuoso) but also by Steve Hogarth's presence, his fabulous voice and the total passion of all the boys. We were fresh to the band, let alone the plot, and it was hair-raising. A real shock and a surprise. We were hooked. I really felt part of it straight away and as a visual communications person it started me thinking creatively about the slide show and lighting they used to such great effect...

We fell in love with Marillion that night, and the rest, as they say, is history... I think that there were 2 gigs in London following Cambridge. I think we missed the first, but managed to get tickets for the second from a tout in the pub next to the old Town and Country. Most touts were in France for an England game, so we were lucky and paid only 2 quid each over the odds. Within a year we were buying a dozen tickets for gigs there and dragging all our friends along to share what we had found. Mad? I guess so. Oxford followed soon after - in fact, I don't think Alexis and I between us missed a single UK gig from that day until the university tour of 2001.

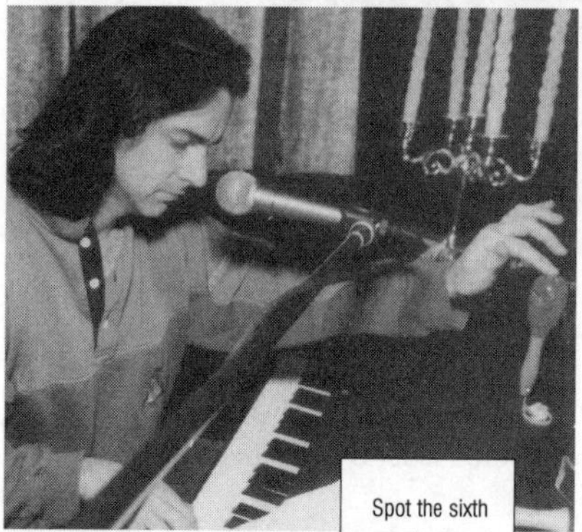

Spot the sixth member - Marillion in 1994

'Afraid Of Sunlight'

After *'Brave'*, Marillion returned to the real world. The entire band was emotionally and artistically exhausted, resulting in their first real creative blocks since before Fish had left. At the same time, EMI were hungry for the album that Marillion had promised before *'Brave'*. Indeed, the label was even once again considering dropping the band. "There was a major question mark over whether EMI would carry on with Marillion," comments John

Arnison. "Fortunately for us, when Jean-François Cecillon who now headed EMI was a junior product manager, *'Misplaced Childhood'* was his first gold album so he agreed to give it one more shot." Sentimentality aside, EMI would not let the band get away with another eight months in the studio. "We had a fairly strict deadline," remarks Steve R. Fortunately, with so much musical material and ideas accumulated before and during the previous album, the blocks were quick to pass. In the end writing took about five months and recording a further three, all done in the Racket Club.

'Afraid Of Sunlight' returned the band to a song-based format. "Every album we make is a reaction to the one before it. As a result this one is a good deal lighter," commented H to Jon Epstein. All the same it still managed to tell a story. It was musically solid and, somehow, Helmer and Hogarth managed to dredge yet more emotions and put them into the lyrics.

Knocking It Out

To kick off the writing sessions the Racket Club was moved to a bigger location. John Helmer had already written some lyrics, which served to catalyse the rest of the process. He'd just finished writing his book, 'Mother Tongue', resulting in "a heavy emphasis on narrative," according to John in a Web interview. Dave Meegan's sixth-member status was confirmed when he was brought in very early in the writing - "I was quite surprised - I thought they'd never want to see me again!" he laughs. His presence ensured continuity, not least in the inclusion of Pink Floyd-esque atmospherics and sampled effects. Dave's capacity to make each member of the band push out of his creative envelope had a particular impact on Steve Rothery's guitar. "I'd always try and do something over the top, to freak Dave out," laughs Rothers. Whatever he did, Dave was always positive, pushing Steve still further towards new sounds and shapes. "You can perceive yourself with certain strengths - doing something outside of that, you need external reassurance!" What was more, the presence of a third party 'mediator' took the pressure off each individual, in that production decisions could be made with less risk of offending each other. "He doesn't have the baggage that comes with being in the band," explains Rothers.

Finally, the gang got into their stride. All the material was fresh in the end - "The boys were so full of ideas that once they started writing new bits there was enough to choose from," recalls Dave. With Mike Hunter at his right hand, Dave once again logged everything that was captured. Steve Rothery came up with musical ideas that the band tried to tie into the lyrical outputs of the two H's, in particular Steve Hogarth who had a lot to get off his chest. "I'd reached critical mass on the Brave tour," he explains. "After a while I was starting to lose myself, I was taking on a new self. It became hard to reconcile the person I'd become with the person I was at home. On tour there was the constant waving goodbye to people on a daily basis, it started to get to me." Steve started to put more of himself into the lyrics - directly, rather than the thinly veiled drawings from his life that had made it to *'Brave'*. Explains Steve, "The pain in *'Brave'* was partly fictional - I was projecting myself into somebody else, who I made up, but the pain in *'Afraid Of Sunlight'* was one hundred percent personal. I'm a feeling person, sensitive to the feelings of others to the point that I'd given more than I should."

In addition, Hogarth and Helmer were playing their now-usual lyrical tennis, with 'Afraid Of Sunlight' and 'Afraid Of Sunrise' (both of which started with Helmer and were developed by Hogarth) being joined at the hip lyrically, but quite different musically. Rothers, who was not against a bit of acoustic guitar now and then, started to pick up the instrument a little more on the album. "I was going to see Crowded House a lot at the time," explains Steve. "Acoustic is a different mindset, its more dependent on the rest of the band for the arrangements, it can easily sound samey so its harder to make acoustic songs sound different!"

Dave's involvement was not without its problems. "I think we made the mistake of asking him to get involved too early," considers Mark. "He was there in the writing process and we started relying on him to make decisions that we should be making, like which tunes to work on, which ideas. He did a really good job as a producer. I just think we put too much work his way that we should have been sorting out for ourselves." It probably didn't help that Mark was living with Dave (and Mike Hunter) at the time, having just split up with Suzy his wife.

The recordings were completed in March 1995 at The Racket Club, and mixing took place once again at Parr Street Studios. Dave Meegan mixed everything apart from 'Beautiful' and 'Cannibal Surf Babe', as they were destined for singles. 'Beautiful' was mixed in New York by Michael Brauer[14], and the latter was taken on by Nick Davis. "It was such fun to mix," says Nick, "I mixed it differently to how it was sent, I thought they'll love this or hate it. Fortunately, they all liked it!"

'Afraid Of Sunlight'

Featuring the legend "This album was knocked out," the album muses on the destructiveness of fame. Despite this, there is a lightness of touch to much of the music, considered missing from the previous album. One track, 'Cannibal Surf Babe' is dripping with musical in-jokes. Although not truly conceptual, it would be fair to describe the record as thematic, given its musings on the effects of fame and the many fallen idols that crop up over the course of the album.

An American boxing MC introduces Jake La Motta's championship heavyweight bout, John Lennon describes what appears to be a drug trip and a voice says something about a house being surrounded by helicopters. Starting with a jaunty rhythm, the lyrics to 'Gazpacho' are somewhat at odds with the music, discussing a boxer who breaks down under the pressures of fame, most noticeably in his violent abuse of his wife. As she mops up the blood from her face, his main concern is convincing the press he's still in control. As the song comes to an end, we hear a radio report of the OJ Simpson car chase and we realise whose house was surrounded.

'Cannibal Surf Babe' comes in with a Beach Boys harmony then kicks in with a gonzoid bassline that reminds us of surf guitarist Dick Dale. Steve H leads the band along a supremely silly and fun romp through a tale of a sex-crazed surfer chick, replete with a brilliantly-observed Kelly-led Beach Boys' chorus. Unfairly derided by many for not being 'typical' Marillion, the song deserves kudos for precisely that reason.

A reading of a passage from 'Cannibal' in French segues into 'Beautiful', a ballad that speaks up for those among us who are made to feel worthless because they dare to believe in beauty. It implores us not to let the sniggering and the name calling cause us to give up those beliefs. In short, it's an anti-cynicism song. The song perhaps suffers from a slightly glossy production, making it seem a little saccharine sweet, something the rawer live versions overcome with ease. It remains a favourite for many fans.

'Afraid Of Sunrise' is the first part of a diptych of songs, again centred on the cost of fame. 'Sunrise' is the introspective side of the coin. Its gentle rhythms and melodies are evocative of a car journey through the American deserts. Special mention must be made of Pete Trewavas's fluid and supple basswork here. A widescreen slow-burner, the song's power is derived from its very simplicity. There's no Rothery solo as such, just simple and tasteful lines. Ian Mosley sticks mostly to brushwork on the drums, and you can hear the white lines passing incessantly under the wheels of the car. Lovely.

'Out Of This World' concerns the British speed king, Donald Campbell, and his attempt to break the water speed record. We start at the end, the band conjuring a waterscape full of hidden tensions, as Campbell starts his run across the waters of Lake Coniston. Listen as we reach that heart-stopping moment where H sings 'at such speeds, things fly...' and Rothery's guitar becomes the nosecone of the boat, lifting... lifting... too high... until the physics take over, and the machine flips under its own momentum. For anyone who has seen the black and white footage of the disaster, it's an impossibly evocative moment. The remainder of the song is a dissection of the motivations that made Campbell take that fateful ride, a force so overpowering that even love couldn't overcome it.

'Afraid Of Sunlight', with its impassioned chorus sees us back in the car, driving through the night desert. This time though, the calm has been replaced with the knowledge that, come morning, the newspapers will be full of career destroying stories; 'I'm already dead, it's a matter of time.' The build up of desperation, brought on by the encroaching fear of exposure, starting 'all your spirit rack abuses' and ending in Kelly and Rothery's searing solos is enough to make the tears prick behind your eyes.

'Beyond You' is a song that apes the famous "Wall Of Sound" production of the legendary Phil Spector. The lyric is immediately recognisable to anyone who has been left by someone they love, replete with the hopelessness of knowing their own actions are to blame. Ian's tampered-with drum sound, replaced with timpani and tubular bells give the song a timeless quality, as effective now as it was the first time you heard it. The lyric is said to be so personal to H that he will never perform it live again.

Although on tour it has been dedicated to the Spice Girls and Bill Clinton (amongst others), 'King' directly concerns the spiral of inevitability that led to the suicide of Nirvana main man Kurt Cobain. Musically, the band have only reached such savagery once before, in the middle section of *'Seasons End'*'s 'Berlin'. Here, as H describes the effects of sudden fame as 'the ensuing, all consuming mess," the band change pace and summon the whipping, whirling confusion in Cobain's head to great effect. Brought back to earth once more, H brings to live the constant in-your-face pressure of being on the fast track to fame; the faces, the praise, the outpouring of emotion, the blunt trauma of the road, the lies, the bullshit... and now it's gone too far, there's no turning back as the band thrash out the frenzied, fear-filled 'Kingasm' and the sudden realisation that the silence at the end of the song is because the pressure you just heard building and building, getting just too intense, ended in a shotgun blast... It's all too much.

Bill Smith Studios' cover for *'Afraid Of Sunlight'* features a grubby child (who happens to be Bill Smith's son) with angel's wings, surrounded by a halo of fire. It remains the least pleasing cover of the Hogarth era, something that is especially galling given that the other images produced for the CD booklet are extremely evocative and effective photomontages of elements from the lyrics - Elvis's suit, La Motta, the tail fin of a classic US Ford Thunderbird, the poppy (symbolising heroin) and the dayglo-ized Brazilian statue of Christ.

Driving On

By the time *'Afraid Of Sunlight'* was complete EMI was becoming decidedly awkward, and the band jumpy, as illustrated by the convoluted process to put a cover together. H had been working with Bill Smith Studios to agree the cover concept, and finally it was presented to EMI[15] at a meeting at Parr Street. "I thought it was wonderful," says H. Bad start - the rest of the band did not. For some reason the picture of the Rio statue of Jesus Christ on the cover was seen to have religious connotations. "Steve H and I were pushing for it, but the band and EMI said no," says Bill Smith. The sticking point was the religion aspect - laughable to Steve H, and missing the point to Bill. As the safety valves started to pop out, Bill came to the rescue. "I had a quick idea, why don't we keep the religious theme but use a figure of an angel on the cover, an Icarus-type, innocent figure?" Continues Carl, "Everyone liked that one so the front became the back!" Following a hastily arranged photo session the cover was completed, but the damage was done. Bill Smith Studios were virtually dropped by EMI, "The covers people have to trust you," says Bill. "It broke Bill and Carl's heart," says Steve H. "I felt ashamed, they had something inspired, a committee had thrown it out and the best reason given was that people might think we were a Christian band."

Ian on the Tour Bus with Simon Hanhart

'Beautiful' was released as a single on 29 May 1995, with backing vocals by Hannah Stobart.[16] It reached No.29 in the UK charts; it also topped the charts in Brazil, mainly due to the fact that it was used as the theme tune in a Brazilian soap series![17] It was through Freaks that Mark Kelly found out how the song was being used. "I phoned our manager, he contacted the label and 'Beautiful' was put out as a single over there." The video for 'Beautiful' was made by Russell Young and was, according to Steve Rothery, "Six hours of hanging around for five minutes of work." Hogarth adds, "I had to climb a ladder to get on top of this building at eight o'clock in the morning. I was half naked and it was freezing cold. At two o'clock the following morning I was still climbing ladders. The things we do for fame!"

'Beautiful' was the last time to the present day that Marillion would see chart success: despite 'Cannibal Surf Babe' being readied as a single, it was never released. "EMI had lost faith," comments fan Simon Clarke. Marillion would be an album band from this point on.

Mark and Wes, after the infamous Poughkeepsie NY gig, August 1995

With the tour underway the week before, *'Afraid Of Sunlight'* was released on June 24 to critical acclaim. Even the oft-cynical Q Magazine was to list it in its fifty best albums of 1995. Noted Dave Henderson of Q, "Sad to say that if *'Afraid Of Sunlight'* had been by a new, no-baggage of the past combo, it would be greeted with open arms, hailed as virtual genius." "I heard the press hated us," remarked Steve Hogarth. "So when that happened we went on medication! I almost got the feeling that it was a grudging nod, in the direction of well, we don't like them yet, but we'd better soften the ground for maybe we'll like them in a couple of years' time!"

The fans were in two minds. Many thought it was the best album the band had ever done, while others disliked it even more than *'Holidays In Eden'*. Some, like Paul Rael, were still on a high from *'Brave'*, and *'Afraid Of Sunlight'* cemented the relationship. "The music, lyrics and vocals blew me away, I was hooked now and 'Beautiful' just did it for me. I caught several gigs on the tour and on each occasion I was more and more impressed." Paul Hughes concurs: "*'Afraid Of Sunlight'*, is possibly even better than its predecessor!" For lapsed fan John Chudy, *'Afraid Of Sunlight'* would be his welcome home. "I found a copy of *'Afraid Of Sunlight'* and thought, these guys are still around? I'd better listen! *'Afraid Of Sunlight'* blew me away and I became a fan again!" Others, like Alan Hewitt, were less convinced. "At the time, *'Afraid Of Sunlight'* did not much feel like a complete album; merely a collection of demos, rushed together to get away from EMI." Paradoxically, it wasn't, but what was agreed as the band's best album for years by most who heard it.

It was apparently EMI in a rush to wash their hands, not Marillion.

The Horny Rhino Tour by Pete and Lynne Wells

Our journey started at Wolverhampton station for the train to Euston, we then took the tube to Victoria to meet the coach. Arriving early we had a bite to eat at McDonalds, little did we know that this would become very familiar over the next few days! We walked around the corner to find the coach was like a tour bus, with two levels, toilets and drinks facilities. At midnight we were off.

The journey started quietly. Once into France we slept most of the way through Belgium and Germany arriving at the Euro Park Hotel in Bonn. A shower and short nap later, we were off again to hunt for the Bonn Biskuithalle, the venue for the night's gig. After a very eventful journey under low bridges and getting lost we pulled up on an industrial estate! Surely this wasn't it? It was - as the name suggests it was a former biscuit factory and very dreary from the outside.

We had arrived very early for the gig, so about six of us ended up in a café eating steak and chips with a few beers to follow, now it felt like a holiday! Then it was back to the venue to join the queue. Once inside it was not half bad, we stood about half way back for Wes to open the show and as always he went down a storm. When Marillion hit the stage the place went mad! Those Germans really know how to enjoy themselves. 'Incommunicado' opened, followed by 'Hooks In You' and my favourite 'Gazpacho'. Lots of singing and shouting - the crowd was really up for this. 'White Russian' followed and then a bit of a James Brown 'I Feel Good' jam into 'No One Can' and then another jam containing bits of 'Walk On The Wild Side', 'Imagine', 'The Space' and 'All You Need Is Love'. The set ended with 'The Great Escape', 'Uninvited Guest' and 'Garden Party' and again the crowd went nuts. The other thing that sticks in my mind from that night is a very large German waiter holding a very large tray of beers above his head while walking through the crowd selling them. Oh, and the beer was really good as well! Again we got lost on the way back to the hotel before crashing out, what a day and night!

Day two started with a little breakfast, but still feeling the effects of the previous day we had a quick nap before boarding the coach for a four hour journey to Hanover. We parked up and had a group photo taken before wondering over to the venue to see the band's tour bus arrive. The band looked a little startled at all these Englanders watching them get off a bus and going into the hall! Most of us then wondered off in different directions except for a couple of fans (Julie and Bill), who had won a raffle on the coach to go into the sound check. Having found a McDonalds (again), we were sat eating when Wayne (Kensett, of the Web UK) rushed in to tell us that we were all invited, so we all dashed across the road and were ushered in. This was our very first time in a soundcheck and what a very interesting hour or so we had finished off by Ian signing drumsticks and giving one to everyone.

Back outside in the queue, we decided we could not stand up all night so we went up to the balcony with coach mate Gary Uzzell, where we found there were two bars! The set was much as the previous night, the highlight was H deciding to climb up the speaker stacks during 'Garden Party', about forty feet above the stage - the rest of the band just shook their heads! We slowly made our way back to the coach for the non-stop journey back to Calais. We managed to sleep most of the way until we stopped at a wine and beer supermarket just before the ferry port. On-board breakfast was a sight to behold as we were all starving. The coach left us at Victoria and from knowing no one we said a lot of goodbyes. Many of the people we met on that first trip are now good friends that we still meet up with at Marillion Gigs. It was a great trip.

NOTES: 1 Also in the bucket was an early version of 'Nothing To Declare', which later saw the light on H's solo album *'Ice Cream Genius'*. **2** Later a song title on *'Brave'*. **3** Before which H penned 'Eighty Days'. **4** 'The Ultimate Gift' which became 'This Town', and 'Eric', a showcase for the keyboard gloves and a demo for 'Splintering Heart'. **5** Pendragon also played one Seasons End gig. **6** Incidentally, the ex-mushroom farm used for *'Seasons End'* was no longer available, as it had burned down. **7** Helped by Nick Belshaw in the Americas, now David Bowie's production manager. **8** Originally by Rare Bird, 'Sympathy' was on the jukebox at the King and Queen Pub in Brighton during the writing of *'Holidays In Eden'*. **9** The working titles for *'Brave'* were *'Seven'*, *'Throwing A Seven'* and *'The Great Escape'*. **10** Incidentally Chris Blair, who cut the original Monty Python album in 1973, also cut the two-grooved *'Brave'*. He works at Abbey Road. **11** Ian and Steve Rothery also guested on a number of tracks. **12** Something he had observed whilst working with Sting who apparently swears by the remedy. **13** The last date of the tour was a wind-down club gig the night after, at La Diabla, Mexico City. **14** Having worked with artists from Michael Jackson to Oasis, Michael Brauer was later to mix Coldplay's debut album, *'Parachutes'*. **15** In the shape of Steve Davis and Jean-François Cecillon. **16** Who would collaborate on Steve Rothery's Wishing Tree project. **17** Later shown in Portugal.

chapter four the engine room/1995-1999

"The music business is uglier than most things. Perceived as some kind of cruel, shallow money trench through the heart of journalism, a long plastic hallway where thieves and pimps run free and good men die like dogs. There's also a negative side."

Anon. (attributed to Hunter S. Thompson)

The year was 1995, the month October. An extensive tour was coming to an end and with it an entire chapter in the history of the band. Over the four years to come Marillion would turn its back on the majors and re-enter the fray on an independent label. It would cast adrift from its management team and launch into cyberspace, gambling the future on its creative abilities and its self-belief. At the same time the Marillion fan base would prove itself to be more resilient, resourceful, proactive and downright responsive than the band could ever have imagined.

Cynics might say that Marillion had reached a point where the future was predetermined, that the termination of its contract with EMI signified the beginning of the end. From here, said the Greek chorus, the record sales would shrink tenfold, venues would contract from halls to clubs, reality would be replaced with alcohol-tinged nostalgia and thus the cycle that is rock and roll would be complete. Time would show that things don't always turn out as expected. At the end of this period in the independent wilderness, the band felt confident enough to trust its fan base completely, the results of which would take the music world by storm.

First, however, there were bills to pay and a hungry fan base to satisfy. Independent or not, Marillion had to make and sell a record.

'This Strange Engine'

Following the last dates of the Afraid Of Sunlight tour, the five players returned from the manic, chaotic life on the road to the mundane, regular pace of autumnal Buckinghamshire. The time up to December 1995 was spent catching breath, collating thoughts and meeting on occasion to plan the direction for the next album. However, the band was principally steeling itself for the rocky times ahead.

Leaving The Nest

The most recent tour proved as successful as Brave in the end, but its initially slow ticket sales left an uneasy feeling that was hard to shake off. Promotion of both *'Brave'* and *'Afraid Of Sunlight'* had been less than adequate; there was little airplay for 'Beautiful' on Radio 1 or Virgin, at the time the main target stations in the UK, though a good few local radio stations[1] were playing it quite regularly.

Coupled with this, album sales had been diminishing ever since Fish had left. Mark recalls, "I drew a graph of sales, to explain it to the rest of the band." It showed 1.4 million sales for *'Misplaced Childhood'*, then 900 thousand for *'Clutching'*, 600 thousand for *'Seasons End'*, 450 thousand for *'Holidays In Eden'* and 300 thousand for *'Brave'*. In the same period, the band had continued to take advances from EMI rather than negotiating better royalty deals. "We were always in debt - it was obvious that we were heading towards a crash," comments Mark. At the same time, Marillion were becoming more confident in both the material they were producing and the strength of their fan base. Something had to change - but how?

Meanwhile, a chain of events starting back on the Brave tour had left the band with time on their hands. Back in 1994, H had been in discussions with Marillion's German promoter Peter Rieger about a part in the stage version of 'Tommy'. "Peter decided to buy the rights to 'Tommy'," explains H. "He was going to buy a theatre, deck it out, put on the show and make some money." Peter asked H to play the lead, and flew him to New York to see the Broadway production. Steve's impressions were inevitably biased by the raw emotion that he had been injecting into *'Brave'*. "It was good, but not rock'n'roll - there was no feeling of restrained power there. I thought the lead wasn't 'it' and I could be 'it' but

I didn't know if I wanted to do it!" Having left Steve in no doubt that the role was his for the taking, Peter went ahead and bought the rights to the show, flying Steve to New York from Mexico to see the show again and to meet with the show's producer. "I liked it a lot more, but" - and this is a big but - "when I went out for dinner with the producer, he didn't have a clue who I was! It was a bit embarrassing!" It turned out that, unfortunately for Peter, the small print of his contract gave him absolutely no artistic control over the show. 'Tommy' was eventually staged in Germany in 1995, but with the lead from the Broadway production. "I think they wanted him out of New York!" remarks Steve H. At the time things got a little stressy - it was one of the few times that H fell out with John Arnison. "He complained because I had to go three times to Japan with Aswad," remembers John. "He thought I should have been back with him rather than out there with them." But Steve's discomfort was nothing compared to Peter Reiger's suffering. Relates Steve, "the next time I saw him, he'd had a heart attack and a nervous breakdown. He lost his shirt on that one."

John had already allocated a six-month hiatus for H and his stagecraft, so when it failed to materialise the band were left at a loose end. "We were thinking of other ways to fill our days," remarks Pete. To break the monotony, Rothers and Pete participated in a charity gig at Buckingham Town Hall, organised by ex-Whitesnake guitarist Bernie Marsden. "We knew him from the EMI days, he's a really nice guy!" says Rothers. Steve Rothery noted in The Web how, "we murdered 'Kayleigh' and Pete sang 'Sugar Mice', so it was... interesting. We did a good version of 'I Saw Her Standing There' though!" On December 12 the Marillos were (mostly) reunited at the Herringthorpe Leisure Centre in Rotherham, on the occasion of the Classic Rock Society awards. The event proved just a little incestuous - Pete had already been asked to present the awards, but one went to Steve Hogarth (who didn't attend) as Best Male Vocalist and another to Marillion for Best Gig of the Year. With Arena headlining, the awards ceremony was also "Mick Pointer's come-back gig," according to Martin Hudson, CRS Editorial Manager. Steve Rothery joined Mick for a rendition of 'Crying For Help IV', a track from *'Songs From The Lion's Cage'*, on which Steve had participated. The ensemble also played 'He Knows, You Know' and part of 'Grendel', which hadn't been played since Mick left the band some 12 years before. "All came back to my house for a party afterwards and I can remember one person saying that he had his favourite three drummers in my kitchen, Ian Mosley, Mick Pointer and Fudge Smith (of Pendragon)!" recollects Martin. With a four-month gap in the schedules after Christmas, the opportunity was ideal for the band members to try projects of their own. "It felt weird - it was the longest time the band had been apart since the earliest days," notes Mark Kelly. Not only was the break a welcome respite, a long-awaited escape from the album-tour-album cycle that had so dogged the band in the past, but it also proved an opportunity to clear a backlog of artistic ideas that had not been seen as suitable material for Marillion as a whole. Given the ever-widening range of influences that the band was already taking on, this could have been just in the nick of time! Indeed, the liberating experience of solo projects could be seen as a last nail in the coffin of 'that Marillion sound' as the following album was to demonstrate.

It was during the solo months that John Arnison and the boys decided to throw in the towel with EMI. All were frustrated by the falling support and increasing meddling from the label to whom they had signed some 14 years before. "We felt frustrated, we thought things could only get better," comments Steve R. This was no idle whim - especially considering that the band owed EMI several hundred thousand pounds due to the overruns in *'Brave'*. "The record company put a fixed amount of money up front for the recording so when we went over it started coming out of our own pockets," explains John. Everyone had hoped the sum would be recouped with *'Afraid Of Sunlight'*, but it wasn't; all the same, the lack of publicity for *'Brave'*, the pressured production of *'Afraid Of Sunlight'*, the tightening of the corporate manacles on artistic freedom, also added up.

Marillion hunted for another deal with a major label but it was not to be, prompting a departure from the mainstream labels altogether. "We hadn't been able to sustain the sort of interest on a business level with the record labels to get the message across," commented Steve Hogarth at the time.

The band's independent status was confirmed with a signing to UK-based Castle Records, an established name that included rockers such as Black Sabbath and Uriah Heep. Castle's traditional market was as a catalogue label - it would buy copyrights then release 'Best Of" albums at budget prices - but now it was trying to broaden its portfolio with more current acts. "They wanted to become more credible," remarks Pete. Remembrs Steve H, "A guy named Douggie Dudgeon at Castle was very knowledgeable about music, he was into the band and wanted to sign us." Things were a little unstable from the start - just before the signing, the owner Terry Shand sold his interests to a US company, amid promises of autonomy and freedom of control. The trouble was that no sooner had they bought them, the US company sold its interests on to Red Ant, which cared diddly squat about previous agreements, verbal or otherwise. Terry left and set up Eagle Rock in the UK, taking managing director John Knowles with him. The three-album deal went ahead regardless, with Joe Cokell brought in as Castle's managing director. "Little did we know," says Rothers with the pleasure of hindsight, "that a huge label like EMI, even when doing badly, would still do better than a small independent label like Castle!"

The first album to be released through Castle, on Intact, was the live double CD *'Made Again'*. The Intact label was Marillion's own creation, explains Pete, "Intact was our label name to be used through Castle, so we didn't end up with a heavy metal label name." A live album had been planned for a while, and live material was being collated to this end but the departure from EMI proved an opportune moment to make the release. Not only did it release Marillion from its obligations with EMI (as the fifth album in a five album deal), as well as paying off the debts without creating new ones, it marked a certain symmetry with the first seven years of the band. Mark noted, "Our first four studio albums were followed by a double live album that signalled the end of that chapter. Now, after another four studio albums, followed by a live album, we move from EMI." Featuring *'Brave'* in its entirety, the two-disc *'Made Again'* was released on 25 March as the final EMI-era Marillion release[2] in the UK, with Castle handling the release in Europe and the US: this was negotiated between John Arnison and EMI, to give the band the best start possible with the new label.

The release was followed by a brief tour at the end of April, ostensibly to promote the live album but also giving the band an opportunity to gel again before a return to the studios. Four dates were played, all in Marillion's traditional strongholds in the Netherlands, Germany, France and England. For fans Simon Clarke and Vicki Harding, the best night of the four was the first, at the Muziekcentrum Vredenburg in Utrecht on 22 April 1996. "It was amazing!" says Simon, "the best venue in Europe, the best crowd in Europe, it was just awesome!" Whatever the band did from this point on, they knew they had the fans behind them.

Moving To The Other Side by Angie Cooper

In August 2000 we went on holiday to the Greek island of Zante. I was unsure about going as my Mum was in hospital. She had been unwell for a few months with a suspected stomach ulcer. Her Doctor assured me that things would be fine and not to cancel the holiday, so off we went: myself, Gary my husband and our daughter Linzi. We had a fantastic two weeks. Argassi in Zante was such a beautiful town. It was just the best holiday ever... we made some really good friends, it was a non-stop party. I rang home everyday to be told not to worry, but my Mum was always in my thoughts.

Coming home was a day of highs and lows. We left our hotel at around 3.00am on a Friday morning. Not being the best of flyers, I was a little stressed and tired. Being honest, I had a very bad feeling about going home. We arrived at the airport at around 3.45am. Zante Airport is very small so we had to stand outside queuing for the check in desk.

My thoughts were on home so I was not really aware of things around me. I heard Gary say "Hi, Steve!" "Who are you talking to?" I snapped at Gary. "Steve Hogarth," he replied. It was not the first time Gary had wound me up in this way - where H is concerned I am a bit of a girly... sad but very true - he is a rock god. I was just about to say "Don't talk crap" when Linzi told me that it actually was H.

PANIC!! What should I do? After all, he was on holiday with his family, so I did not want to make a nuisance of myself. I had met H before but always after gigs. This was different... more personal. Gary and Linzi told me to go and say hi, or I would always regret it. So off I went... and we had a fantastic chat about all sorts of things.....the new album, his recent H band gigs and foreign travel. He also told me that his ideal holiday would be a private jet to Sri Lanka. It was a lovely moment and one that I will never forget.

I got home to really bad news. My Mum's condition had deteriorated and I was told to expect the worst. It turned out that she had cancer... the one word I was dreading to hear.

That night, my best friend Gina Andree rang from Michigan, USA to say that she was coming over to meet me for the first time in October. Gina was on the alt.marillion newsgroup, saw one of my postings and replied to me back in March of 2000. Thank God for the Internet - where have we heard that before? I told her about the day's events, the highs and lows.

I did not know, but that night Gina e-mailed the Marillion office in the hope that H might read it. She wanted to tell him about the bad news that I had got home to. The following day I received an e-mail from H, who suggested that if the worst should happen then I might gain some comfort by listening to 'Estonia'.

Sadly my Mum died a few days later. It hit me really hard.

Up until this happened, 'Estonia' was just another great Marillion song. I listened to the lyrics and I saw what H was trying to say. "No one dies, they just move to the other side." It is comforting to know my Mum is still watching over me. 'Estonia' says to me: "Don't be sad at my passing. I will be with you always."

In January 2002 I saw the H band live in Paris. They played 'Estonia'. I just sobbed and I was not alone. 'Estonia' must touch other people in the same way.

The Producers

Without their own solo projects, Mark and Pete had started sifting through previously unused material to assess its potential for the new album. This included near-complete songs such as 'Accidental Man'; other elements were still in a very raw form, such as the music that became the first section of the title track. Following a couple of months research and development (much spent round Ian's house, according to Ian, "It was hard work, there was me, Mark and Pete round my house trying to write, out of the months of work we did, we used about a minute! Steve H only got off on about one minute of it… probably because it wasn't that good!")

In May 1996 the band reunited at The Racket Club. The break had done everyone a lot of good, all agreed; what was more, the influences that had been picked up in the solo months were to prove just as liberating. As Steve Rothery commented, "I think the solo projects revitalised the band. When we got together not only did we appreciate the chemistry, but our enthusiasm had increased and we had new ideas as a result of our solo experiences." Adds Pete, "What was nice about it was coming back to Marillion. It felt very right and very real." Helped by a number of musical ideas that had not made it onto *'Afraid Of Sunlight'*, "we had a flood of inspiration," recalls Steve Rothery. Maybe so, but hard cash was tight. The separation with EMI freed them of any artistic shackles, real or imagined. However, without the backing of the major label, there was no longer direct access to producers, designers, promoters and distributors. Each decision had to be cost-justified by both John Arnison and the band against an all-too-tangible bottom line. This tightening of belts meant the loss of that major creative catalyst - Dave Meegan as a producer (besides, as he was making Phil Campbell's *'Fresh New Life'* at the time, he wasn't available). Instead, the band decided on the compromise of producing themselves, involving Dave at the mixing stages. To a large extent the mindset was similar to *'Season's End'*, where the band had been going through enough changes and wanted to retain control over the sound. The decision was also an expedient, given the undercurrent that Dave had come in too early in the previous album. "We wanted to have more control musically, this way we could record what we wanted," says Pete. But oh, did they miss him! "It's like going into town without your Mum, you know what to do but…" remarked Pete at the time. Sound Engineer Stewart Every also picked up the producer's baton on occasion. "I made suggestions of which about 80% were ignored and 20% were laughed at!" laughs Stewart.

cloud of wasps

"I was attacked by an entire nest of wasps whilst still a baby. I was stung in the face - particularly my nose which has been super-sensitive ever since. Wasps didn't sound so good in the lyric so I made them bees."

Steve Hogarth

As Marillion's first solo venture, this was a huge opportunity to practice what the band had always preached: to work outside the musical box. Not that Marillion had ever sat down to decide the kinds of music they wanted to create. "It's not something that we have meetings about or would discuss in the sense of where are we going next, what should Marillion sound like on the next album?" noted Mark in an interview. This time, more than ever, the band followed its mantra of never making the same album twice. No ideas were rejected; a wide array of styles and concepts were thrown into the pot. There were real trumpets and synthesised hunting horns, real dulcimers and string samples, with tracks drawing on influences from Salsa to Slavic Folk.

The album was to have a lighter, more acoustic feel, largely due to Steve Rothery's recent solo experiences. "With the *'Wishing Tree'* album, I was playing the acoustic guitar more often," recalls Steve, meaning that when the band recorded songs such as 'Eighty Days' and 'Man Of A Thousand Faces', acoustic guitar seemed perfectly natural. Meanwhile, band members were handing tracks back and forth. As Steve H wrote, "I took 'Memory Of Water' away and then arranged it, and then Mark took it away, and then he rearranged it, and then he gave it back to me, and I rearranged it again, so we just kept passing it back and to, so it was a fifty-fifty thing!"

Nothing was considered out of bounds - to the extent that, with the title track, Steve Hogarth rubber-stamped one of the most proggy tracks the band had done for many years.

strange night

H was having a sleepless night in the summer of 1995, when some words started buzzing like flies in his head at about 4 o'clock in the morning. In the end he had no choice but to get up and write them down. "It was over the space of about 20 minutes," remembered Steve in an interview. "This poem came flooding out."

"Oddly enough, I was the one who started it," conceded H in an interview. "I'm now at the stage where I think it's nice to do something retro-progressive." Steve Rothery felt the album to be both forward and backward looking. In a chat session, he commented, "Although this album probably represents another step forward in time for the band, there are some moments that take me right back to the beginning, particularly the synthesizer solo in the third section of 'This Strange Engine', when it goes back to the tom-toms it takes me back to 'Market Square Heroes' and all of that…" Liberation works both ways, then.

The effects of this process were not lost on the fans. "The aim of the album was to project a strong feeling of optimism; of hope for the future," notes fan Robin Lauren. "*'This Strange Engine'* was definitely a turning point," adds Alan Hewitt. "The band branched out into areas which they had barely (if ever) touched on before. As an album it was definitely a challenge to the perceptions of both the fans and the critics... a challenge which some people are still coming to terms with."

In an ironic twist, this time it was Steve H who slowed the process down, leaving the rest of the band frustrated. "Steve likes to spend a lot of time on the mixing and I haven't got the patience!" says Pete. "It was a difficult birth," remarked H, "but we came through it without even a minor fistfight!" It turned out the band didn't need the mediating touch after all. Of the final product Pete wrote, "we're as proud as punch!"

'This Strange Engine'

Goodbye to EMI (for a while) and in with Castle. Marillion's first album with a new label was, like its predecessor, thematic. According to the press release, the album was about, "human memory. Personal as well as biological [memory] is explored and a strong feeling of optimism and hope for the future permeates the music." The other key factor at work was Steve Rothery's usage of acoustic guitars. Inspired by his work on his solo 'Wishing Tree' *album, there is an acoustic feel to much of the album, making it feel rootsy and organic - very appropriate for an album about memory.*

The album sees the band continuing to develop the scope of their influences, with Crowded House, Russian and Caribbean folk influences nuzzling in amongst more traditional Marillion territory. Although Marillion friend Dave Meegan was on hand to mix the album, 'This Strange Engine' *marks another departure. It's the first to be produced by the band themselves.*

The album begins with a simple (but effective) acoustic guitar motif from Steve Rothery. H begins to weave a tale inspired by folklorist Joseph Campbell's 'The Hero Of A Thousand Faces', a book which postulates that one can trace common archetypes throughout history and different cultures. According to Steve Hogarth, "The song links Freud and his thoughts and Jung and his philosophies with tribalism and rights of passage. It takes in the Masons, secret societies, all the way from the Holy Grail and the Knights Templar to some of the conspiracy theories that still go around in the modern age." Mark Kelly breaks into an almost honky tonk piano break as we are taken from Adam and Eve to humanity's first forays into space; via ancient Greece, to the age of the machine, the dawn of the media age and rock and roll. Just as the song seems to be coming to an end, H begins to reiterate the themes over a pedal-toned outro that builds and builds, until you can almost hear the entire world singing the same song. It's a tribute to this astonishing band that a children's choir, rather than sounding trite or saccharine sounds inspiring and emotive, and just listen to Pete and Ian punctuating and directing the end into something truly powerful!

As the end of 'Thousand Faces' fades away, Steve Rothery breaks into a bluesy intro that gives way to a reflective chiming guitar line. 'One Fine Day' is a John Helmer lyric that deals with passivity - specifically the idea that it's all too easy to wish away your life waiting for that magical moment, rather than building towards it, and making it happen for yourself. It's a good enough song in its own right, but frankly, when you're talking Marillion, you need to be so much better than merely good, and it's one that perhaps doesn't do full justice to their powers.

'Eighty Days' is a song H wrote for the fans, written before his first Marillion gig at the London Astoria as he watched the fans file into the venue from a window above. It is a tribute to you and me, the people who pay our money to stand outside in the rain and cold because of our devotion to the unique beast that is Marillion. It's also a song about being on the road and the drudgery that can accompany those off-stage moments. It marries these two notions in the idea that it's on stage where it all becomes worthwhile, where the fans love of the music wipe out the tedium of hours of travelling in tour buses. Laughs H, "I really did lie in that bunk in the tunnel under the Alps all the way from Zurich to Milan, thinking of Iceland and Japan!"

H has said he would like 'Estonia' played at his funeral. The song was written after he found himself sitting on an aeroplane with film maker Paul Barney, the only British survivor of the Estonian Ferry disaster, in which over 900 people lost their lives. Coupled with the fact that a friend of his had recently lost his father, H attempts to find some solace, if not reason in such loss. Listening to the interplay between Rothery's guitar, chiming out almost like a sonar call, and Mark Kelly's echo-drenched keys, you can imagine the sight of the ferry disappearing under the waves with its terrible cargo. And then the chorus - so much choked emotion... 'No one leaves you when they live in your heart and mind.' With guest musician Tim Perkins on balalaika, it's close to overwhelming.

'Memory Of Water' is a sparsely orchestrated dirge (and I mean that in the dictionary sense, rather than it being dreary) about memory, and indeed life itself having come from water. Almost funereal, the music carries a measure of solemnity which we're somewhat unused to with the band. But, then again, as the recent live versions have proved, you should always expect the unexpected with this band. The Big Beat version of the song is an exercise in contrariness - frenetically lively and exuberant!

'An Accidental Man' sees Rothery unleash a deceptively-simple groove, over which Pete Trewavas pops wonderful bass harmonics. Cue Ian, four to the floor and Mark on Hammond organ and... we're in. Concerned with how breeding, social and racial culture imprints itself upon us, the song specifically addresses a tale of a man who realises that his whole identity has been formed by forces outside of his control, and realises, to his regret, he doesn't know how to break this programming.

'Hope For The Future' opens with a taut-strummed guitar full of tension that we just know has to break. It's just that... well... we weren't expecting this! 'Hope' is a gorgeous lilting pop romp through the hidden mysteries down the ages, and laced with a liberal dose of Caribbean rum! Rosicrucians, Egyptian astronauts, the limbic brain (the part which links emotions to specific memories)... If it confused some of the fan base then perhaps it's no surprise, but this is the sound of a band cutting loose and having some unrestrained fun.

The glorious title track is a tribute by H to his father, who sacrificed his life at sea for a job in a coal mine so that he could be close to his family. From its opening scene of the young H feeding swans, to Hogarth senior on the deck of his ship seeing the mysteries of the world, 'This Strange Engine' is one of the most expansive songs the band have ever attempted, mood after mood, scene after scene brought vividly to life. Just listen to the confusion of adolescence in the 'I never felt that I belonged section'. Or the evocation of the childhood thrill of riding on your dad's motorbike. You don't have to have done it to recognise the truth in these lyrics. As H's dad watches the sun dip beneath the water-kissed horizon, Steve Rothery slips into one of his best solos, full of regret, longing and most of all, the sense that this is a sight he'll remember all his life. We slip into the final section with H realising the magnitude of what his father has given up - something he himself is unable to do, even for his own family - and the understanding of the love involved in tearing himself away from his privileged existence to a life in a dreary northern town. There's simply too much great music here to comment on in detail, but a couple of standout moments come to mind. Listen to the loose, jazzy-swing[3] of the bees section; doesn't that just conjure the confusion of the air as they whirl above the young H's head perfectly? Or listen, in the final section, as H sings 'this love' and the purest guitar note rises and drops back again. Haven't you felt your heart do that when you're on the point of becoming overcome with emotion? Sheer genius. No wonder the band look shattered when they play it live!

The cover design for this album was again a break with tradition, will the Bill Smith Studio making way for Castle's in-house design team. *'This Strange Engine'* features a copper steam engine, in which a heart fuels the flames that burn. Strange that an album concerned with memory should feature a heart. Or maybe not. Maybe it's completely right. Maybe we're back at the old limbic brain again, with emotions being intertwined with memories.

The Release of 'This Strange Engine'

The album was completed in November 1996, pretty fast for a Marillion album. Dave Meegan took care of the mixing at Parr Studios in Liverpool. He could pick up where he left off - "When I came to mix the title track I knew the mood from the start," explains Dave. "I knew that a lot of the album came from the same mother as *'Afraid Of Sunlight'*, so the two albums were like Side 1 and Side 2 for me." Another Christmas passed, following which the new album gained its "classy" (according to Steve Rothery) packaging.[4] There was no Bill Smith Studio on this album. Castle had it's own art department headed by designer, Hugh Gilmour. He had designed the *'Made Again'* sleeve - the band having parted company with Bill Smith after the 'design by committee' compromise of the controversial *'Afraid Of Sunlight'* sleeve. Hugh Gilmour designed and assembled the *'TSE'* cover, using a copper steam engine built by his neighbour Andrew Gent. "The engine is made of 'every-day-items' such as a drain pipe, stop-cock and plastic pipe, but no sign of any sticky-back plastic!" explains James Fishwick of the Web UK team, who was later tasked with restoring the engine.

At the end of January 1997 the ever-generous Mark Kelly wrote an email to Freaks offering a number of pre-release CDs to UK fans. This was the first attempt to build a fan database, explains Mark, "We wanted their names and addresses!" Of course, Racket Records was swamped by email requests, not to mention complaints by disgruntled fans from overseas. It got worse - the CDs were never even sent. "Castle said they would send out the CDs, I compiled a list and sent it to Castle but they never were sent out!" says Mark. "We got a lot of grief for that!" This was not Mark's only revelation of fan power at the time, as he was already in discussions about the economic issues of touring the United States. Of this, more later.

Meanwhile, for the band's major label swan song in February 1997 EMI released *'Best Of Both Worlds'*, a double CD containing tracks from both eras of Marillion. Much of the effort had been co-ordinated by one Lucy Jordache, who was then working in EMI's catalogue marketing department. "I saw on the call sheet for the year that there was to be a Marillion best-of," explains Lucy. "I called up, said I was a huge fan and asked if I could help." Yes she could, but not as her day job - "I was taking stuff home in the evenings!" Despite there being little new for the hardcore, the album was instrumental in paving the way for the future. For a start, by its nature it had to involve both sides of the divide. "I'd met Marillion but not Fish, and I had to fly up to Edinburgh to meet him," explains Lucy. "By the time I arrived I was a blithering wreck!" Everything went as well as could be hoped - "We got on really well - Fish called me Henry Kissinger!" laughs Lucy. Together with Nigel Reeve who was co-ordinating the project, Lucy agreed to have two separate discs, one for each era. "We wanted two covers, with Mark Wilkinson designing the Fish-era cover and Carl Glover designing the H-era." Not only did the album bring the two sides together, it also brought record label and fan together in an unprecedented fashion. "Mark Kelly sent an email to the Freaks list, saying that fans should email me at EMI to say what they wanted to see on the album," explains Lucy. "Suddenly I was receiving all these emails out of the blue!" Lucy took the plunge and joined the list herself shortly afterwards - and it was a revelation. "there were all these fans out there, that were talking on the Internet." Whatever was happening out there in cyberspace, it was looking very interesting indeed.

'This Strange Engine' found its way to the shops on 21 April 1997, nearly two years after the release of *'Afraid Of Sunlight'*. The accompanying press release stated "Marillion's style of melodic rock is brilliantly played and sung and, although it is often soaring and majestic, the band never give way to musical excess or over-indulgence." Well, not too much anyway. In Kerrang!, Liam Sheils awarded 4 K's out of 5 and noted how "the commercial realities of running their own affairs have given Marillion a right old boot up the arse creatively," after the "bleakly impenetrable" *'Brave'* and the "downright weird" *'Afraid Of Sunlight'*. Q Magazine's Rob Beattie also applauded the album, "If occasionally they're still vulnerable to the charge of overindulgence, the deft pop melodies and substantial musicianship demonstrate that everyone recognises where the edge is these days. Mind you," Rob went on to say, "Anything that can survive all the sleeve note[5] guff about Jungian collective thought has to be a good record." Across the Atlantic, Joe del Tufo wrote in New York's Good Times magazine, "*'This Strange Engine'*... is a magnificent collection of eight tracks that balances the band's strengths with their propensity to seek new directions."

Some fans were won over immediately to the new look of their favourite band. "My first impressions of *'This Strange Engine'* were: what a fantastic album!" remarks Mark Donald. "I hadn't been to see Marillion live for four years, but when I heard this I thought I'd been out of the picture too long and nothing was going to stop me this tour." Despite its length, there was general agreement among the fans that the title track was one of the strongest songs on the album. "This was just brilliant!" remarks Paul Rael. "This is now one of my top three Marillion tracks - an absolute masterpiece!" Adds Paul Hughes, "three words: acoustic, well-produced (that'll have to count as one!) and emotional!" US fan Mike Richichi wrote, "This album doesn't disappoint, the feel of the music just carries you in and the songs are snippets of life, with some of Steve Hogarth's best lyrics and singing. Perhaps the newest album isn't quite as good as *'Afraid Of Sunlight'*, but it's very close..."

Not all of the new musical directions went down brilliantly with the stalwart followers. Some tracks, like 'Memory Of Water', were conceded to be "tricky"; others were considered "lacklustre." Steve Rothery's folksy-bluesy guitar left some listeners concerned that they had heard the last of his soaring trademark solos. Fan Rick Collins writes: "I was really keen to love this album, but I can safely say its my least favourite with H." "The weakest of all H-era releases, saved only by 'This Strange Engine'," agrees fan Martin Thorpe. Canadian fan Marc Roy concurs: "I felt there was a little something missing to most songs to take them right up there." Max Rael is more blunt: "I hated *'This Strange Engine'*, and to this day I don't like it much. I keep waiting for the moment when it all clicks into place, but so far, it ain't happened!" You can't please everybody.

the last laugh

'This Strange Engine' clocks in at 17 minutes, but shows 30 minutes on the display. After 13 minutes of silence, the unsuspecting listener is brought up cold to the sound of Mr Hogarth giggling uncontrollably, recorded on his return to the recording studio after a night on the town.

Two singles were released from *'This Strange Engine'*. 'Man Of A Thousand Faces' was released on 16 May, with a video directed by the charmingly named Golden Shower. The reality of this dabble into the brave new world of computer graphics didn't quite meet the hype. "Not enough money was spent on it to make it look good enough," comments Pete, "The end result wasn't that satisfactory!" Fan tribute 'Eighty Days' was released as a follow-up on 13 October.

By June 1998, *'This Strange Engine'* had sold over 300,000 copies: while sufficient to pay the bills, this did not amount to a lottery win. The problems were not over yet.

'This Strange Engine' by Nathan Vines

I can remember being picked up from my house one week-end, on a cold crisp Saturday morning back in 1996, by some new-found older friends. We all had a common goal that was restoring our very own 'Strange Engine'. These early morning weekend journeys would become commonplace and, along with the customary cooked breakfast en route, the music was always to my liking. At first I didn't know who was responsible for bringing me to my senses at such unearthly hours. The music had all the elements that I craved: a blinding voice, mesmerising guitar and melodic keyboards played to such a wide range of beats. Everyone in the car was of the same opinion that the music was of the highest order. This was always evident when at some stage of the journey someone was playing air guitar, drums in the back seat, keyboards on the dashboard, bass on the steering wheel or just humming along! I loved every minute of it and after finding out who was responsible I bought, borrowed and stole (OK I didn't steal anything!) Marillion.

I had no real pre-conceptions of the band, I knew of the name and had 'Hooks In You' on a compilation album, but that was about it. I only wish that more people had the same blank page to start with and an open mind banishing any false perceptions. I had just found my favourite band to date and wanted to tell the world how great they are! At the time I was in sixth form and most of my peers were into Britpop and dance music, generally everything that I despised.

Marillion are different; they have soul in their music, as well as passion and meaning - qualities lacking in many new acts. Musically, the band moves on with the times and has not stagnated like a lot of bands of their so-called 'era', churning out the same old stuff. The band have kept producing albums that are relevant to the times yet, still have that bit about them that says 'Marillion'. From 'Easter' to 'Enlightened', 'Garden Party' to 'The Great Escape', 'Berlin' to 'Between You And Me' and 'Sugar Mice' to 'Separated Out', there is something magic present, a chemistry that is so special to many. Live Marillion performances are something to savour in many ways not just musically but the interaction between the band's hardcore of loyal fans.

Over time, I have found an addiction that has simply grown each year since the day I first listened to the band's music. I was so excited to go to my first Marillion gig, yet I still feel that same excitement now when doing the UK legs of the tour. From being informed, to being the informer of my friends, I have grown up listening to Marillion.

It's hard to put down in words why I love Marillion so much, but I do know it's because they make such uplifting music that simply sounds fantastic in the house, car, live or anywhere for that matter. 'This band has turned me into what I have become'.

For any real hardcore anoraks, the Strange Engine is 50049.

This Strange Tour

The Strange Engine tour was started on 30 April 1997 at the Garage in Glasgow, to date the most recent occasion that Marillion have played Scotland. It was already planned to be worldwide, with the exception of the US and Mexico due to cost constraints. One of the best nights was, according to fan Paul Rael, 2 May at the Cambridge Corn Exchange. "It was magical and Steve's voice was like being hosed down by cool champagne after a month in the desert. *'This Strange Engine'* was almost a religious experience, there was a moment when the music stopped dead for a few seconds and the whole place was silent... you really could have heard a pin drop." The tour was a huge success, however there was truth in Martin Thorpe's recognition that this was "the last tour that the Marillos played the Corn Exchange - it would be smaller venues (and shorter tours) from here on in." Concurs Simon Clarke, "It was the last mega-tour they did!"

Following a two-week breather at the beginning of June, it was off to South America for another two weeks, playing Brazil, Argentina and Chile. A couple of festivals followed, notably Rock In Madrid on 5 July and, on 27 July, the Kingdom Festival at Bellinzona, Switzerland. On 4 October it was back to Germany, France, Luxembourg and Holland for the final dates of the tour, which terminated on October 27 at the Paradiso in Amsterdam.

The creation and release of *'This Strange Engine'* marked a watershed. Not only was Marillion moving with more confidence into new musical areas, risking offence to their fan-based life support system in the process. The band members saw themselves as having little choice. No longer signed with a major label, 1997 was both the end of an era and a whole new start. The only direction was forwards, so forward they went, hoping to take the fans along with them. 'Eighty Days' was on the album through choice, but it served as a stark reminder of what was at stake.

At the same time, the gilt on the edges of Castle's contract was starting to tarnish. Despite a better deal on paper, the impression was clear: the label wanted a minimum of fuss and a maximum of album output. "It was like a treadmill," comments Mark. "They just wanted to milk the fan base." Over the months that followed, and despite the disappointing reception for *'This Strange Engine'* relative to its predecessor, Marillion were to discover just how strong that fan base was.

The Tour Fund

The band members of Marillion had always known about the power of their relationship with the fans, but none could have predicted the events of early 1997. Already, Mark Kelly was no stranger to the Internet. "I surf the net and check out what people are saying about us," he remarked in one interview, adding with irony, "It's quite informative as well to see what's being said about the band in countries we're not visiting soon."

With the band in between projects in January 1997, Mark Kelly was paying more attention than usual to the Freaks mailing list and on occasion he felt moved to enter into the ongoing debates. And why not - email is such an innocuous activity.

Mark with Tour Fund instigator, Jeff Pelletier

An Idea is Born

It had always been Marillion's intention to play the US again, but economics were not acting in the band's favour. "We'd just left EMI and we reckoned we'd lose quite a lot of money if we did an American club tour," said Mark at the time. Explains Pete, "There is still a club circuit in the US that even the bigger bands still follow, it's a strange thing for European bands to come to terms with." Trouble was (and still is), the overheads of crossing the Atlantic, paying for visas and transporting equipment left little chance for profitability. "Over the years, we'd spent so much money and time and we weren't really getting anywhere," says Pete. The previous US tour had lost 30,000 pounds and, in addition, it only included dates on the East Coast and in the Mid-West, leaving West Coast fans out in the cold. On the lists, US criticism was running high. Finally, on 27 January 1997 Mark Kelly wrote:

> Hello to all the best Freaks....
>
> We love touring.
>
> It is just too expensive to tour some places! I'm not saying it's impossible to tour everywhere, but it is expensive to put on a Marillion tour... we are not prepared to put on half a show with second rate equipment and a crap sound system, just so we can get to the west coast and not lose our shirts!

Mark's post generated some radical responses, including a suggestion from fan Jeff Pelletier. Maybe Jeff did not know what he had stumbled across when he proffered:

> What if all the US freaks donated to a "Marillion Tour The USA" fund. I'd gladly throw $50 in the hat if that guaranteed a chance to see them in several US locations... What do you think? There's several hundred US Marillion fanatics on this list alone, right? I know it wouldn't cover all the costs but it might help...

This response, from Kevin La Rue, was typical: "Count me in for much more than $50 and a whole lot of time." Another Jeff, this time a Mr Woods, thought it was a fabulous idea. His email, directed at Mr Kelly, asked: "Shall we talk, or is this idea just another sugar mouse?" Mark was quick to reply, "I think you're all crazy! It would make a great story if it came off."

Jeff Woods' response was to act, not talk. He recalls, "Given a large number of Freaks knew who I was due to my proposal to Michelle the year before,[6] it was one of those 'hell, why not?' moments!" Setting up a shell company and a trust fund, Jeff posted to Freaks, "All I need is a go from a Marillo... and I'll kick the fund off with $200." Before long the 'go' was received, and the fund became a reality. "We'd met Jeff before, and he seemed like an upstanding guy," says Mark. The band put its seal of approval on the initiative by proposing a one-off CD to be given to contributors. The CD proved quite an incentive, according to UK fan Tony Wood: "If I'm honest it was the 'We'll give a CD free to anyone that gives more than $x' - can't remember the figure. I admit it - I can be a mercenary b***ard!"

Nothing else was offered to the fans who contributed. There were no free tickets, no venue decisions, no special concessions. The donors wanted nothing but to help their favourite band tour. Even Mark Kelly donated - he was the fourteenth person on the list, "to give the whole project a certain legitimacy," according to Jeff Woods. Donations came from all over the world - not just the USA, but from other countries including the UK, Germany, Netherlands, France, New Zealand, Thailand and Mexico. Most donations were between

$25 and $50, with a UK fan in the Bath area proffering $1,500! "The further it went, the more I was in awe of people's generosity!" remarks Jeff Woods.

"Once it got past the $25,000 mark, we started making plans for the tour," commented Mark. And from that point on the US tour became inevitable. Well, nearly - the fun wasn't over yet!

The Tour Fund by Jeff Pelletier

In hindsight, it doesn't seem like that radical a concept, does it? Yet at the time, it had never been done before.

It was a long two years since the Afraid Of Sunlight tour, but *'This Strange Engine'* was awaiting release in 1997 and I could not wait for this tour. I was ready to travel this time and see more than just the one local show. Just tell us where and when and we'll be there. But it was not in the plans. Mark Kelly posted to the Freaks list with the bad news. They had signed a record deal with another small independent label (Red Ant) in the U.S., but sadly a tour in support of *'This Strange Engine'* in 1997 was not going to happen.

I was frustrated, disappointed, and when it comes right down to it - in denial. This couldn't be. There had to be something that could be done.

Marillion charged less than $20 a ticket on the Afraid Of Sunlight tour - of course they lost money. The club was packed, but that's still not a lot of income when you take out the middlemen and the expenses of an international tour. I had just paid $160 for a pair of Eagles tickets - surely Marillion could charge more than $40 a pair, couldn't they? The answer was No. A band without name recognition could not get the clubs to charge higher ticket prices for fear of keeping out the casual fans.

[*Sidenote: Is there such a thing as a casual Marillion fan?*]

I said to myself - We can make this happen. Every North American on the Freaks list would be willing to pay more if that was the only way to make a tour happen. That's why they call us Freaks. At that point, I said to myself "let's just take everyone else out of the equation". There are over 1,500 people on the Freaks list alone. If 500 of them could put $50 into a hat, that would make $25,000. Why not do that and give it directly to the band in exchange for a tour?

I wrote the infamous post to the list. Did I think it would really happen? No... but it could. Part of it was just venting my frustration at the obstacles in the music industry that keep musicians from doing what they want and music lovers from getting what they want. But things were going to change.

The day after I sent in that post, I was busy at work. I hadn't had a chance to read the Freaks lists waiting in my Inbox. Julie called me up and said, "You're a genius!"

I said, "Huh..? What are you talking about?"

"You haven't read Freaks yet? Read it! Everyone responded to your Tour Fund idea and Mark Kelly said they'd do it!"

Needless to say, I set work aside and read it for myself. Pledges had poured in, dozens and dozens of them, and not just from North America. This wonderful little community wanted this idea to succeed so much, that people were pledging from all around the world. People that wouldn't even get to see the tour were promising their money. I couldn't believe it.... but then again, actually I could.

All in all, the Tour Fund raised over $60,000. For the first time in history, the fans of a band promoted an entire international tour without a cent from the music industry.

I have now been lucky enough to get to know the members of my favourite band. When I go to concerts here and abroad, there are people to this day who recognize me. I usually don't bring it up anymore when I meet new fans, because I don't want to seem like I'm expecting a certain reaction, but it's still nice when I meet someone new at a Marillion or Porcupine Tree or Transatlantic concert and they recognize my name and thank me. Funny how one small action can change your life.

Getting The Tour Moving

By April, time was getting short, and the Freaks' pockets were bottoming out. Dan Sherman of the Web North America provided a thousand mail addresses, almost doubling the subscriptions to $40,000, but it was still not enough. MC Jeff Woods wrote: "We are short $13,281 as of Monday evening and we are running out of time. I can't really say why, but we've pretty much got a deadline of this week to meet the Tour Fund Goal - some basic decisions regarding a US Tour are likely to be made THIS WEEK." At the time, John Arnison was meeting with the record companies in New York and needed to make an impression. "We wanted a big dollar amount there," noted Jeff.

Back in the UK, John Arnison was trying to organise the tour in the best way possible. "I was amazed," comments John. "Again it was something instigated by Mark, I put a tour budget together and said it needed 50K. They raised it. It was incredible!" Jeff Woods visited London on May 12, meeting with Mark and John Arnison to make arrangements, based on Mark's idea, "to keep the shows that Red Ant wanted to front, separate from Tour Fund shows." Jeff was sent back with a mission to identify places away from those already planned by the promoters, but near enough to big cities to ensure attendance figures could be met. "We'd raised so much money, we could stretch it out a bit!" laughs Jeff Woods. "Mark had sent a schedule; there was a huge gap after California so I suggested a convention at Rochester. The band were quite happy to do that!" Jeff's growing involvement included everything from bookings, selling the tickets and provisioning the tour rider at what turned out to be three dates: Pittsburgh, Poughkeepsie and Rochester itself.

More complications came in the form of the record companies and the management. Tensions had already surfaced in May with Red Ant, who did not want to accept the money at all, "They thought it made Red Ant look bad," said Jeff W at the time. "Mark feared something like this might happen from the outset." By June tempers were fraying, and matters came to a head with Wally Version at Hit And Run USA who appeared (to Jeff Woods) to be anti-fund. Matters were quickly resolved, as a post by Jeff confirmed:

> ......The tour will happen. It will be extensive.
> ......On shows that the fund sponsors, Hit And Run will manage them, the fund will receive the gate receipts and the fund will pay the expenses.
> ......The fund will pay for the transportation from the UK to the first show.
> ......The CDs will happen, exactly 1000 of them.
> ......The fund has succeeded and will continue to succeed.
> ......The fund is in good hands with Hit And Run.

The tour organisers - band, management, record companies and fans - were not out of the woods (sorry) yet. Throughout the period coming up to and during the US tour, the band was dogged with record company and management problems. In July Red Ant's mother company, Alliance Entertainment, filed for bankruptcy. Suddenly it was all hands to the pumps again, to raise another $15,000 to replace money the record company had planned to put in. Meanwhile, the band turned to their old colleagues from Castle UK, in particular ex-CEO, Terry Shand and ex-MD John Knowles who had formed a new company, Eagle Rock, which was allied with US label VelVel. Are you following this? Well, nor did anyone else!

According to Hogarth at the time, "we've had the kind of year where I no longer believe anything that they tell me - management or record label." Fortunately, Velvel were being more proactive. "They seem really committed to the band and they're having a lot of ideas. So we're more optimistic about the future than we otherwise would have been at the moment." The positive aura did nothing to speed up the release of *'This Strange Engine'* in the US, which now looked like it would be delayed until after the tour. Steve H was sanguine - "The timing wasn't nearly as useful as it could have been, but we had already committed to this tour and we weren't going to try to move it back." Besides, by the start of the tour many of the fans had already obtained the album on import!

Finally the band came over and toured the USA, Canada and Mexico. It was a riotous success, starting back at old haunt The Coach House in San Juan Capistrano on 24 August, and managing to squeeze in 25 dates before it wrapped up on 27 September in Mexico City.

Jeff's fan club show was held on 30 August, at the Graffiti Showcase in Pittsburgh. There was an unexpected surprise for fans that arrived during the afternoon, as there was nobody on security to prevent them from entering the sound check. It had been the intention to play a wide

The Remasters Project

Back at EMI long-time Marillion fan Lucy Jordache was busy managing the remasters of the Marillion albums up to *'Afraid Of Sunlight'*. "We were given the green light after the success of *'Best Of Both Worlds'*," explains Lucy. "I wanted to make it really special because I knew fans would already have everything - I wanted a bonus disc, I asked the band for access to their archive material, the band really came through for me!"

The plan was to release the remasters two at a time, each pair comprising a Fish-era and a Hogarth-era album. Each release consisted of two CDs, one including previously unreleased archive material and 28-page booklets including interviews with band members past and present. The band stumped up copies of archive material from their own collections, much of which were to be found in biscuit tins and in the backs of cupboards! Both Mark Wilkinson and Bill Smith had also dredged through the archives for the original ideas to be used on the covers. Mark Kelly had already contacted the freaks mailing list asking for suggestions for the remasters. Where there were potential conflicts, Lucy was quick to get back in touch. This email is typical: "A lot of you have mentioned the original versions of 'Market Square Heroes'. There seem to be two versions floating about, and I'm not sure which is the one that everyone is really after. Please email me as soon as possible with your views."

The albums were mastered at Abbey Road studios by Peter Mew, who had previously worked on projects for Pink Floyd and The Beatles. The first remasters - *'Script For A Jester's Tear'* and *'Season's End'* - were released on 29 September 1997, and the final two - *'Clutching At Straws'* and *'Afraid Of Sunlight'* - were released on 22 July 1999.

spectrum of songs on the tour, so early arrivals witnessed Steve Hogarth grappling with the lyrics to a couple of Fish-era songs - 'White Russian' and 'Warm Wet Circles'. "It is harder to remember what you're supposed to be doing when there's a few hundred people in front of you all cheering!" recalled Steve at the time. "In the end, I gave the microphone to one of the kids in the crowd[7] and he sang 'White Russian' while the band played!"[8]

On 31 August, all bar Steve Rothery (ironically - he was at the dentists) played an acoustic set, including 'Made Again' with Pete on guitar, at the House of Guitars in Rochester, New York State; meanwhile Jeff was discovering the kinds of things that can go wrong on a tour. "There were no towels at the venue!" recalls Jeff. "I had to find 20 towels, for the band to wipe off the sweat during the show. Eventually I had to run back to the hotel and beg the desk clerk to borrow the towels, then race back to the venue!" The gig that evening was, in fan John Stevens' opinion, "the best I've ever seen the boys play." It was recorded and mixed by Stewart Every, to be released as a special limited edition CD for all contributors to the tour fund.

Abraham, Martin, John and Diana by Jodi Tack

So, yes, I am completely insane and I did travel thousands of miles and spend hundreds of dollars just to see a band a few more times on their North

American tour. After seeing the first two dates in San Juan Capistrano and Hollywood, I figured I could go home to my mom's, spend my birthday with my family and catch the shows in the Massachusetts area. I noticed that Marillion was also playing in Montreal the Saturday night I arrived home, the day before my birthday. I mentioned it to Ed, my then-ex-boyfriend, and he said he'd like to go and would even drive.

On Friday September 5 1997, I took the red-eye flight home from California. I was so excited about the upcoming events that I couldn't sleep at all. In fact, it would be Sunday morning - more than 48 hours of being awake, before I would sleep again. As I arrived at the terminal I heard the tune of 'Candle In The Wind'. Elton John was singing at Princess Diana's funeral and it was being televised live for the entire world to witness. It was such a senseless loss of such an incredible human being.

I finally got home and called Ed who came to pick me up in his very beat up van. When he pulled into the driveway, I just said, "We're going to Montreal in that?!" He swore that it was all going to be fine and we set out on our way. He was right - we got to Montreal around 7.00 pm and found Le Spectrum. As we waited for the doors to open, I learned that Canada is a hell of a lot colder than California! But I toughed it out... and boy was it worth it!

The show was incredible - it turned out to be the longest show Marillion has ever played: almost three hours with four encores! When they came back after 'This Strange Engine' and played 'Brave', I'd managed to weasel my way up closer to the stage and I just let H's voice overtake me. I literally had tears in my eyes, it was so powerful.

And then there was 'Abraham, Martin & John'. After playing 'Made Again' and saying goodnight, the crowd screamed for close to five minutes and then H came back out and sat in front of the keyboard. He started playing this song; I recognized it but didn't know the name. I knew it was an old song about great political figures who'd been assassinated (Abraham Lincoln, Martin Luther King, Jr. and John F. Kennedy). In place of the last verse, H sang, "Have you seen my friend Diana..." Again, the tears welled up in my eyes and by the end of the verse, one had actually spilled out. Then, on the last line - "I just turned around...and she was gone" - H's voice cracked with emotion, he turned sideways on the bench, put his head down in his lap and I could see him wiping his eyes. I lost it. I just started weeping. As the crowd clapped and cheered respectfully, H approached the front of the stage. His eyes were a little red and you could still see the tears threatening to spill over yet again. It was, without a doubt, the most moving, emotional experience I have ever had at a concert and I'll never forget it.

When they left the stage for the last time, I couldn't even be sad that it was over. I had just seen the best concert ever, I was in a foreign country for the first time in my life and it was well into my 23rd birthday. It was the best present I could have ever imagined. It was about 2.30 am and I had officially been awake for over

40 hours with seven more to go...and I wasn't even tired! I would have loved to have stayed and tried to secure a birthday kiss from H, but we had a long drive ahead of us, so we headed home.

Look Back in Surprise

'This Strange Engine' was finally released in the US, on 7 October 1997. Much of the delay was due to the three different pressings, required to correct poor mastering production by the new label. A number of lessons were being learned, not just that labels really were becoming a nuisance! The tour fund was a first, not just for Marillion but for the whole world of contemporary music. Ever since it happened, other fan-rich bands, from Dream Theater to Alphaville and the Foo Fighters, have considered using a tour fund to get to otherwise off-limits places. None have succeeded to the same extent as Marillion's own tour fund, or rather that of its fans. It was no easy ride - there were several points along the way where the fund could have been canned, the money misdirected, the fan support withdrawn. Yet somehow, despite all the record company shenanigans and other complications, it all came together in the end.

So - why did the fans do it? "We did have one theory," laughs Steve Hogarth, "that maybe they were going to burgle our homes while we were away!" Steve Rothery adds, "I don't know many groups that have such a supportive and passionate fan base, to the extent that they would be willing to invest so much time and money!" Of course, it could not have happened without the Internet. "What a leveller the Internet is turning out to be," remarked Hogarth at the time. "It gives ordinary people the freedom to talk to each other, to publicize something and to bring together international small communities of enthusiasts for whatever it happens to be."

Perhaps most importantly in the band's first year on an independent label, the fans gave Marillion something they needed more than tour money - the assurance that whatever the band did, there would be a solid fanbase to support them. "The tour fund gave us much more flexibility and freedom," recalls Rothery. "There's a refreshing honesty in that."

Eventually the transatlantic fun came to an end, the band returned and completed the last dates on its European leg of the tour. Marillion fans such as Jeff Woods could return to their normal, more mundane lives. "In hindsight I didn't know what I had got myself into - booking three shows, selling tickets and so on! I have nothing but respect for the tour managers - Paul Lewis and Tim Bricusse!" Jeff's final words on Freaks were: "The only people that made *any* money on this strange tour of America were the crew. Marillion themselves did not take pay checks from the shows. They paid the bills for travel, paid the crew, paid the expenses, but didn't get paid themselves. How many of YOU would work for six weeks, travelling nearly every day, without pay, just because someone 'called you a genius'?"

in the neck

Pete Trewavas was out for a spot of sightseeing one afternoon in Toronto, when he was mugged. This was no snatch-and-run, the villains beat Pete about the head with an implement. "I was a mess!" he says. Incredibly, despite the fact Pete went to hospital with concussion and horrendous bruising he still got up and played the next evening. "I felt I owed it to them," explains Pete.

"I'm not sure that Marillion really took us seriously at first," Jeff Woods was to say. "They gave us tacit approval to at least try, but in the beginning I don't think they expected us to pull it off!" Indeed. This was a one-off event, a combination of luck, bright ideas, circumstances, goodwill and hard work that consummated once and for all Marillion's relationship with its fans. For all these reasons as well, it could never happen again!" Explains Steve Hogarth, "It would be like getting a present, and then coming back and saying that was nice, can we have that again?"

And that was that - no more tour funds. But this wouldn't be the final demonstration of fan power, nor the greatest.

Excerpts From A Tour Fund Diary By Michelle Woods

Finally the Tour Fund CDs had arrived. My good friend Karin Breiter was coming to help Jeff and I assemble and ship the CDs to the Freaks that made the tour possible. I figured it would be a lot of fun and a great party. We soon realized a few hours into the assembly process that it was more complicated and time-consuming than any of us anticipated. We spent all of Friday night folding 1,400 letters (and getting many paper cuts), finishing late into the wee hours of Saturday morning with more than a few vodka and cranberries in our systems.

Saturday morning we awoke ready to get a fresh start. The CDs themselves did not come assembled, but rather on spindles. To make matters more complicated, they were not in numerical order. Jeff had ordered the CDs manufactured with serial numbers, and they were to be shipped by serial number in the order people contributed. Even the jewel cases were not put together. The following is a post submitted to the #Freaks mailing list that outlines all the steps.

1. Open jewel case
2. Fold back insert
3. Insert back insert
4. Insert disk one into foldout disk holder
5. Insert disk two into foldout disk holder
6. Insert fold out disk holder into jewel case
7. Insert liner notes (make sure they are signed, DON'T ask! - from Karin)
8. Match serial number (VERY difficult to read)
9. Fold 1,400 letters, make sure to bandage paper cuts as necessary! Sorry about the bloody ones!
10. Insert CD plus letter into jiffy mailer
11. Put address labels on mailer.
12. Double check label # vs. CD #
13. Determine correct postage and apply
14. Apply customs stickers if applicable
15. Drink some more
16. Apply small package/airmail sticker if applicable
17. Seal jiffy mailer
18. Sort into appropriate boxes for shipping - US, Europe, ROW
19. Drink some more
20. Rinse and repeat as necessary
21. Put on next Marillion CD to soothe ragged nerves

Just an update on how it is going. It took us about 2 hours to do 200 with 3 people. Only 1,100 to go. Happy Happy, Joy Joy.

We did hone the process down to an efficient assembly line if I do say so myself. Just when we were feeling really good, we found the biggest problem of all.

There had been an error with the artwork that was originally screened on the CDs. The name of the band was misspelled. The CDs were rescreened with the correct artwork, however, they didn't replace the serial numbers in order. So, about halfway through the assembly process we realized that we were not going to be able to ship them in the order we had intended. At this point Jeff had a minor (okay it was a MAJOR) meltdown. Most of it came from his feeling like he was letting down the Freaks, a group that he cared a lot about.

Finally we realized there was nothing we could do to rectify the situation, and we continued getting the CDs ready for shipment to the best of our ability (all the while drinking heavily!) Part of Jeff's post to Freaks about the incident follows:

All 25 boxes of signed, sealed and to-be-delivereds are headed to the post office on Monday. 1,353 CDs to 1,047 addresses. It's OVER. The bad news... when Nimbus remanufactured the CDs, they didn't restore the serial numbers -- they just kept going from the last highest. Thus, most of you will not be receiving the serial number you thought you were getting. Some of those numbers are as high as 2,750. There were NOT that many made, however!

That's it - I'm signing off. I'll replace your unplayable CDs or the ones that didn't reach you, but other than that, I'm out of the Tour Fund business, and back to being just another Freak (though we'll still be stupi^H^H^H^H^H[9] crazy enough to travel worldwide to see shows...).

It was a very good feeling when we finished and stuffed the last Jiffy mailer.

'Tales From The Engine Room'

Meanwhile, back across the Atlantic, other plans were afoot. Jersey-born Mark Daghorn, a Marillion fan of the first generation, had first approached John Arnison in April 1996 with the idea of producing a remixed version of *'Afraid Of Sunlight'*. "I had bought *'Market Square Heroes'* the day before playing my first gig," Mark D explains. "I regarded *'Afraid Of Sunlight'* as one of the best albums I had ever heard, and the idea of doing new versions of some of those songs excited me beyond anything I can possibly explain!" When requested to send some material, Mark posted a copy of his recently completed African Mission album, produced in collaboration with trance mixer Marc Mitchell, whom he also managed) under the moniker The Positive Light. The album ended up in Steve Hogarth's car without him having any idea who it was. "It's not the ordinary kind of trance, it's far deeper," explained Steve at the time. Eventually, in November 1996 and following a number of exchanges by telephone, Steve Rothery invited Mark Daghorn to the Racket Club. "I don't think I've ever been as nervous as I was on the day I was driving up to that meeting," wrote Mark. He needn't have worried - the band agreed to allow the pair to remix a track or two from *'This Strange Engine'*, which was virtually complete.

Mark Daghorn returned to the Channel Isle triumphant, with vocals and guitar parts from 'Estonia' and A' Man Of A Thousand Faces' in his back pocket. Being (in his own words), "a long time secret prog-head," Marc Mitchell was also suitably content. 'Estonia' was remixed in Marc's basement over the Christmas break: Marc's own recollections include thoughts of "vengeant Marillion fans wanting to hurt me, and that God somehow managed to get the duck-billed platypus together!" By January, the duo had completed their take on 'Estonia', and so Mark set off to the mainland to discover whether the effort had been worthwhile. "He appeared at my door and played me Positive Light's reconstruction... and I loved it," said Hogarth "We all loved it. And so the experiment was born." The band commissioned the rest of the album, and after "many management and record company meetings later" according to Mark, the pair got the thumbs up to continue the project. "I headed for Jersey, and we did 'Memory Of Water' next," remembers Mark. "H came over when we had finished it and were just starting 'Strange Engine'." Marc recalls how his first child Malachi was conceived during the recording of the track. "It took 6 weeks to complete - 120 tracks of mood-setting music evolving over 4 different sections." That's the track, not the child!

Back in the basement, Marc mixed and Mark produced what Marc himself refers to as "Some of my most diverse and best work." Comments Mark, "I think 'Strange Engine' and 'Estonia' are superb, mainly because H's lyrics were just so damn good and painted big pictures for us to work with." However, from this point onwards, professional and personal relations grew continuously worse between the pair. Delay compounded delay until finally they broke off relations, leaving Mark to finish the album with Tony Turrell. Tony was a partner in Mark Daghorn's other project, The Silent Buddhas, as well as a Marillion fan since the age of twelve. "The first fruit of my labours with Mark was 'Eighty Days'," recalls Tony. "We then went on to do other remixes of 'Memory Of Water' under our own project name." That'll be the Big Beat Mix, then!

did you know?

The dialect vocal in the break on 'One Fine Day' is from Richard Attenborough's film, 'Cry Freedom'.

Twisting To Tales

'Tales From The Engine Room' was mastered at Abbey Road Studios by Peter Mew, who was also busy with the Marillion remasters series. The album was eventually released on 22 June 1998, notably "the first time that a rock band had an entire album remixed by one remix team." The band loved the album: "It's very impressive - particularly sympathetic to the lyrical feelings" said Steve Hogarth in an Internet chat session.

To stir up the club scene, Mark Daghorn had 20 vinyl copies of 'Memory Of Water' pressed, which he distributed to trance DJs including Paul Oakenfold. Recalls Mark, "The idea of the acetates was to get grass roots interest in the track as a club single and then release it with the additional mixes as a 12 inch and CD single." According to Finnish fan Robin Lauren it became a personal favourite of club DJs, "who between them made it one of the anthems of both the Ibiza scene and New York's The Factory." Paul Oakenfold even called up Mark to say he was playing it! The additional releases didn't happen however - these were casualties of the quick-change label situation at the time.

The hardcore fans greeted the remix album with interest and scepticism in equal measure. A few were even "devoid of prejudice," as hoped for in H's liner notes! Robin Lauren surmises, "*'Tales From The Engine Room'* is a weird baby. It's not a prog album (at least not in the traditional sense), it's not a rock album. It's a dance album. I'm not into the dance scene, but I know what I like, and I like this album." "I thought it was superb, and a good way of alerting people to the new Marillion!" thinks fan Simon Hoban. "The only weak moments are 'Memory Of Water' and 'Man Of 1000 Faces' which are a bit too handbag dance for me. 'Estonia', and in particular 'One Fine Day' are better than the originals in my view, and almost prophetic of what Marillion came to do themselves with the dub influences on *'DotCom'* and *'Anorak'*." Ironically, as *'This Strange Engine'* had not been greeted with delight by all the fans, *'Tales From The Engine Room'* offered hope. As fan Joe Griffin relates, "To this day I'm actually more familiar with *'Tales'* than I am with *'This Strange Engine'*. I still prefer the *'Tales'* version of 'Memory Of Water'." Mark Donald concurs: "I was dubious before hearing it but I think they improved some of the tracks. I find it's great to put on and mellow out to. Trippy music from my fav band - what more could I ask for?" Says Rick Collins, "if I'd had to choose one album to remix, it would have to have been this one - the rest would have been ruined, they're too good!"

The remix was to experience no whitewash among the fans, however. "The only thing bearable to listen to on that album, in my opinion, is 'Estonia'," comments Marc Roy. "I can't stand any of the rest..." "The whole Positive Light album was something I feared for a long time," adds Bernard Koops. I listened to it twice, and now it's gathering dust." Recalls "quite polar" Liam Birch, "'Estonia' was a quick favourite, 'Eighty Days' also sat well with me, giving me a flavour of World Cup Soccer music. 'One Fine Day' and 'This Strange Engine' are okay, if not a bit thin and 'Memory Of Water' is kicking a dead cow when he's down. And don't get me started on 'Face 1004'!" The press were sceptical, seeing the album as a premeditated attempt at reinvention. Quoth the Dutch Progressive Rock Pages on the web, "Seemingly they thought that changing the music altogether and targeting the result at the club audiences is the way to ensure themselves of new fans... Who are they kidding?"

One track in particular would go on and on, namely Tony Turrell's Big Beat Mix version of 'Memory Of Water'. "I enjoy that," says Ian, "It's got a bit of energy. I like stuff that gets you between the eyes!" The fans do too: "Fantastic!" expounds Rick Collins. Bernard Koops (who was not too comfortable with the album version) comments, "With the integration of this track into the Radiat10n tour, my admiration for Marillion was renewed. To play this mix with original instruments as up-tempo as the mix is astounding. I don't believe Marillion has any other song which they play this fast!"

As with many experiments, *'Tales From The Engine Room'* hadn't quite turned out as anybody had expected. Meanwhile the handle of the sausage machine continued to turn: the band was already back at the Racket Club recording the next album, which would turn out to be an experiment as well. But first, it had been putting its own house in order.

tattoo you

"That thing on my head was a fake tattoo that I had done whilst on holiday in Turkey. I'm thinking about getting it done properly for real, but not just yet!"

Mark Kelly

'Radiat10n'

The creation of *'This Strange Engine'* had been the first opportunity for Marillion to stand on its own two feet without a major record label to act as either prop or shackle. Following the completion of the surprisingly extensive 1997 tour (including Marillion's reputedly one-thousandth gig, on 27 October at the Amsterdam Paradiso), the band took a month off before returning to The Racket Club in November. By this point, the approach was almost formulaic - using jamming sessions, recording them to DAT and building on the results. Perhaps a little too formulaic: following the departure from the norm that was

'This Strange Engine', the band no longer felt they had anything to prove - at least not musically. The last album had been a largely acoustic effort, so there was a strong desire to increase the tempo and have a bit more fun.

Alongside the continued development of its musical style, the band wanted to get in control of its own destiny. Between January and March 1998 changes were planned to both organisation and approach, each of which strengthened its independence still further.

Something Completely Different

On 22 January 1998 the band launched the online presence of the Racket Club. "Marillion's Racket Club Online is now officially live!" announced the email, with some aplomb. Barely concealed was a foray into e-commerce, as albums on the band's own Racket Records label as well as commercial releases were made available online for the first time. A month later, came Marillion's first eWeb missive, emailed to subscribers to the fan clubs and others who had registered on the web site. It announced the launch of a new-look "and tremendously improved" UK fan club, "with whom we're maintaining a cosy relationship to ensure we minimise the distance between you lot and us lot."

It was not just the fan club that was to change - the Marillos had also made the decision to part company with long-standing manager John Arnison. John had been managing the band for 16 years, but according to the aforementioned eWeb "things change and our vision and his were no longer one-and-the-same." John had been finding it increasingly difficult to devote the time Marillion needed - "He'd tried to get Tim Bricusse involved in the day-to-day management," says Rothers. The band had also been asking for a good while, for more visibility on the accounting side of the band. Continues Steve R, "John seemed to adopt a policy of 'deliberate vagueness'." Things came to a head when, a couple of months before the decision, John and the boys had met in a pub and he had quite rightly pointed out that the way things were going, the band should look for work to cover the shortfall in incomes. "I said that, the way the finances were looking, Marillion can take up six months of their time and they should find something else to do for the other six," recalls John. It was a wake-up call, indicating it was time to take matters into hand. "We don't want a manager who says that sort of thing," was Mark's response. Neither did John want to manage the band in that way. Explains Mark, "He said, 'what do you want me to do?' We all shrugged, he got the message!" As John drove away after sixteen years with the band, he felt like he had been through a divorce. "I'm not sure they did need me any more," John comments, ever the pragmatist. "Besides, it gave them a kick up the backside, it's probably what they needed at that point!" Management tasks were passed to Rod Smallwood at Sanctuary.[10] "He heard we were without a manager so he approached us," says Mark. "He looked after us for a year or so, then he got too busy with Iron Maiden, so we stopped using him!" Agrees H, "Rod struck me as a very moral and straight man (rare in artist management) but he was too busy managing Iron Maiden to focus on us. I remember him telling me he reserved one afternoon a week specifically for Marillion. It was supposed to impress us! I never managed to find out which afternoon it was."

The band could finally relax and get on with the album, but not before one last measure was taken to sate the hunger of the fans. A live compilation was planned, based on a number of shows from the Strange Engine tour, notably The Vooruit in Gent, Belgium, Paris' Bataclan and the Hanehof at Geleen in the Netherlands. In an eWeb Mark Kelly asked for suggestions for a name - "this live engine" or "these strange gents in Gent" or whatever suggestions you can come

shaker maker

The 'anorak' played on 'A Few Words For The Dead' in place of a shaker, was a crew jacket from the *'Brave'* tour, used with fingernails!

up with that are better!" Eventually, *'Piston Broke'* was released 1 June 1998, with a cover by Bill Smith Studios. Robert Lewis of AMZ wrote, "Buy it because it's a great taste of what I believe to be the best live band ever!" No bias there, then.

By the time *'Piston Broke'* was released, work on the new album was proceeding smoothly, with a number of "strong arrangements" already developed. According to Mark Kelly in an eWeb, "Some of the songs at work from 'trawling for olives': 'Answering Machine', 'Now She'll Never Know', 'These Chains', 'Tumble Down The Years', 'Under The Sun', 'Deserve', 'Or You Could Love', 'This House Aches', 'Upside Down', 'Swing Doors'. These songs may or may not appear on the album, and those that do may sound completely different than where we are now!" Eventually, the band divided the tracks into an A-list of songs ("that we felt suited each other, fitted together better," according to Pete) and a B-list that needed more work.

As the album progressed, there was "a desire for new sounds and a desire not to repeat ourselves and to fall into familiar patterns," according to Steve Rothery. Fair enough, but things didn't work out as well as they could have done as the desire was outweighed by the abilities of our fair fellows to operate well outside their comfort zone. "It was an effort to do something different - we'd made so many records," explains Steve. "I disagreed at first but went along with the challenge to do something different." Mark Kelly made extensive use of a new JP8000 keyboard, and deliberately avoided the generic strings sounds, which "are always a fall-back position when you can't think of anything else to do." Pete Trewavas reverted to his old Rickenbacker bass guitar, and Steve Hogarth used a recording Walkman in places to distort the vocals. Steve Rothery borrowed a few guitars from Dave Gregory. Explains Dave, "I think Steve H was anxious to tempt Rothers into experimenting with more retro, organic sounds. There was a Gretsch Country Club, a Gibson SG Junior (that actually sounds like a Gretsch), and I think my Charvel Surfcaster."

Once again the album was produced by the band, with Stewart Every receiving co-production credits for the first time. In a Web interview, Mark Kelly noted that using a co-producer was "more like having a sounding board than somebody steering the ship." Steve Hogarth agreed - "Using Stewart as a producer was a natural step. We've all got a lot of respect for his ears and his ability to mix so he was a natural choice." Erik Nielsen also gained a production credit for 'The Answering Machine'. Originally acoustic, the band were raising fears that it was, according to H, "a bit Jethro Tull." Explains Erik, "I said it was a bit Hey Nonny Nonny, you should speed it up a bit and give it a bit more guts!" And that's what they did - what you hear on the album was recorded in a single take!

The recording of the album lurched, rather than eased forward. 'On A Few Words For The Dead', there were a total of 96 tracks in the mix. Explains Mark, "We had a whole load of things going which we listened to during the mix. It was almost written in the studio. It could never have been written unless we recorded it." Adds H, "It has that tension that holds and breaks like a wire, if anyone else had done it, people would think it was amazing!"

For the first time since Steve Hogarth joined the band, there was no writing credit for John Helmer. The "decision" was more by chance, as 'Interior Lulu' and 'Tumble Down The Years' had already been recorded: trouble was, the band didn't feel comfortable with either. Explained H at the time, "At the last minute we decided not to master them due to musical reasons, nothing to do with the words and they may well reappear on the next album." And so

'Easter' blessings

The live chorus of 'Easter' on *'A Few Words for The Dead'* was a happy accident - the band were re-using an old tape for the mix, previously used to tape the band at Middlesbrough, and happened to find the chorus and a crowd roar. "They sounded great where they were so we left them in."

they would. H noted, "I'm a total coward and I haven't yet had the guts to tell him... If he believes me when I tell him it wasn't deliberate, I'm sure he'll understand. I always got on very well with John."

'Radiat1On'

The second album with Castle was created during a period when it became all too clear that the label weren't going to support the band and allow them to create music in the way they were used to. This doesn't however prevent the band from turning in an album that in hindsight showed the band well into their third 'era', (Fish being the first, and 'Seasons End' to 'Afraid Of Sunlight' being the second) ushering in the song-writing and sound experimentation that culminated in 2001's 'Anoraknophobia'. The album doesn't have a clear theme or concept, but is no less coherent for that. One thing that does crop up in the writing is the suggestion that all was not well chez Hogarth. To whatever extent this was borne out in reality, several songs appear to be about the disintegration of a relationship.

This album is particularly notable for Steve Rothery's changed guitar sounds; one moment funky wah-wah, the next Brit-poppy, then a Beatles pastiche and then a sheer blues tone, all the while conjuring magic in such a way that only the remarkable Rothery could have done. Again produced by the band, there's something a little muddy in some of the production. A crying shame, since it took live versions of the material to really showcase how strong it was.

Well, if you wanted a seriously different way to open an album, here it is! The whole album compressed in to a forty second slap in the face, followed by a Noel Coward-esque music hall number, 'Costa del Slough'. This sarky little nugget is the anti-*'Season's End'*! We then segue via a Hammond swirl into the scratchy funk of 'Under The Sun'. 'Under The Sun' continues the faux-naïve idea that global warming is a benefit to us, and that only a fool could think otherwise... Steve Rothery's guitar wah-wah's away over Pete's grooving bass and Ian's thumping drums, whilst Mark lays down slabs of Lesley-speakered Hammond organ that lift under us like a rolling wave against the shore.

'The Answering Machine' is another rocker, first previewed at the Walls restaurant show the year before. In that incarnation, it was an acoustic number with more than a hint of Jethro Tull about it. Now, it's a rollicking great juggernaut of a tune, powered by Ian's strangely off-kilter rhythms and Mark's arpeggiating keys. It's the first hint of the relationship theme which pokes its head up throughout the album, and whilst the music is fun, the lyric is anything but. Steve's metallicized voice phoned in from a distant continent trying to save his relationship, but being confronted with the eponymous answering machine.

'Three Minute Boy' is Marillion rising to a challenge. Okay, Oasis, you reckon you have a monopoly on the Beatles? Well, stitch this! H said the song is "Rock and Roll anthropology really. It's a cocktail of all my earliest memories of seeing John and Yoko in the registry office and Paul and Linda and Mick and Marianne Faithful, all those kinds of early bits of films I used to watch." And if that isn't Liam Gallagher and Patsy Kensit in the third verse, I'll eat my hat! Steve Rothery is in great form on the extended outro, with a two minute solo, during which the Beatles influence is acknowledged with a low rendition of the harmony from 'Hey Jude' thrown in!

After three big sounding songs, we settle into the impassioned 'Now She'll Never Know'. There's an intimacy here which makes it almost uncomfortable to listen to, a sense of 'Wooah! Hang on! I'm just a fan - this is too personal; you're not supposed to share this much with us!' With Pete playing acoustic, and faint keyboards from Mark, it's as though we're in the vocal booth with H as he sings, and the regret and introspection in his voice as he tries to make amends is almost that bit too much. Can you have too much heart?

'These Chains' finds H at the lowest ebb, desolate, alone and broken and with nowhere to go. Desperate for something, anything to break his black mood, he takes the car and drives out into the countryside, where he sees the first breaks of colour in the night, and as the dawn breaks, he takes inspiration from the sight. If he can just forget about what is expected of him, if he can ignore the strictures of convention and society, maybe he can find the hope and the strength to get over it. Another Beatles influence kicks in over the chorus, a first cousin to 'All You Need Is Love', with riffing strings, and a sixties sounding production, and a lovely solo by Rothery over the outro.

The bluesy 'Born To Run' is a simple and thoughtful tribute to the people of the North of England where H grew up. In many respects, it's a song about people who put their heads down, and get on with life, regardless of the many difficulties they might find. Having run with his dreams, H reflects on the fact that while he may live elsewhere, and he may have the trappings of success and a life that is so different from those he grew up amongst, he is still a product of that upbringing. Kudos goes to Steve Rothery, displaying yet another side to his mastery of the guitar, as he turns in a breathtaking performance of control and expression.

The band has described 'Cathedral Wall' as a James Bond villain's theme, and there's certainly something of John Barry's influence in the powerful string intro to the verses. The song finds an insomniac H finding solace from what we presume is again some troubles at home by lying against the imposing stones of the cathedral. Dark and terrifying, Mark Kelly's vast chords tower above us like the walls of the darkened church and H's double-tracked vocal certainly lends a creepy feel to the whole thing. As we reach the end, there is a reprise of 'These Chains', but with H alone on a piano. A song about hope reprising at the end of a song about despair...

...which brings us nicely into closing track 'A Few Words For The Dead', another song that starts off about despair. 'A Few Words' is Marillion at their atypical best. Beginning with the intoning voice of a Native American mystic saying that his music comes from the heart, and must be treated with respect, the song feeds into a mysterious mist of sound, through which we are vaguely aware of other sounds moving past. Hypnotic rhythms and motifs build and change against which, H spins a tale of machismo and blood feuds. Hate-filled and nihilistic, we're just at the point of wondering what has happened to the humane Marillion we know and love, when the song suddenly changes tack, and suggests, 'Or you could love...' And the song unfurls into an exquisite alternate universe of possibility and redemption, that shimmers and sparkles its way into the distance, tempting us to join it.

Bill Smith Studios were back on board for this album, the cover of which features a flame-spurting girl with a clutch of wildflowers in her hands standing on a beach, possibly that of the Costa del Slough. The flames that belch from the headless body resemble nothing so much as the terrible oil fires seen during the Gulf war in the early 1990s. Behind her, the beach is a lurid red, perhaps as a result of all that radiation. The album cover was distinctive and eye-catching. And as for the girl? Well, the tide's coming in...

A Candlelit Dinner

In June 1998 the band found themselves back at Phil Beaumont's Forge Studio at Oswestry, for the mixing of the new album. Says Ian, "We had a great time at the Forge, the World Cup was on, Nick Davis was there, we had great fun!" Following Steve Hogarth's successful one-nighter at The Walls restaurant the year before, with the first incarnation of the H-band, he suggested a repeat performance this time with Marillion as the main course. The plan was to hold a low-key, light-hearted event, with an acoustic set and a minimum of publicity - a "candlelit dinner with Marillion." With the go-ahead from the rest of the band, Steve approached Geoff Hughes (then restaurant manager of The Walls) with a deal: the band would be fed for the two weeks they were in Oswestry, in exchange for a one-night performance on Friday 26 June. Geoff readily agreed to the proposal and printed up a hundred tickets.

Low-key? Pah. The Walls mailed out its regulars, a couple of whom happened to be Marillion aficionados. Within days, the beacons on the worldwide network of Freaks were lit and air, hotel and restaurant bookings were being made from as far away as Mexico, Australia and Japan, so a second night was fixed to accommodate the demand. Said Steve Hogarth, "Before long we decided a couple of verses of 'Easter' simply wouldn't do... and we rehearsed for a week!" The band decided to make the gigs into something special, and planned an acoustic extravaganza of Marillion songs as well as a number of covers.

On the night, fans arrived to see a discreet set-up. Sitting on top of Mark's equipment, made up of a Hammond borrowed from Phil Beaumont and the restaurant's own grand piano, was Andrew Gent's Strange Engine. The set included songs that were destined to be acoustic, such as 'Runaway' and 'Now She'll Never Know', as well as a "some surprises" including 'Beyond You' and 'King'. 'The Answering Machine' was played in its original, "Tull" version. More surprises included a reggae take on 'The Lap Of Luxury' and a blues version of 'Hooks In You'. A number of covers followed: one of the most interesting was 'Fake Plastic Trees', a "conscious tip of the hat" to Radiohead, Marillion's stablemates during their EMI years. This made it to the B-side of the 'These Chains' single, in what Steve Hogarth terms "a throwing down

bishop's castle, Steven!

One local audience member at The Walls achieved a certain infamy due to his repeated, announcements of where he was from. Despite Stewart Every's best efforts to tone these down for the album, the calls could not be erased. The perpetrator finally turned up on the Opium Den mailing list in November 2001, and has since apologised!

cathedral wall

On 24 May 1998 the band played at Stewart Every's wedding, at the Hopcroft Hotel in Steeple Barton, Oxfordshire.

of a gauntlet and going, "Well there, what do you make of that then," to both press and sceptics alike. The Walls gigs were an inspiration to both fans and band, as an indication of how popular the band remained and how solid was the globally dispersed foundation that supported it. For one fan, Krys Boswell, it was the first occasion to see Marillion. "What a place to hear them live for the first time. "I was overwhelmed," Krys recalls. Another attendee was Simon Hanhart, who had engineered and mixed both *'Script For A Jester's Tear'* and *'Fugazi'*. "It was possibly the best gig I have ever been to," says Simon, "A wall of texture just washed over me!"

Overall, the band didn't feel that the quality of the Oswestry performances warranted a CD of their own. For a start, Mark had used the Restaurant's piano. "It was a standard piano, miked up so all the noise of the room was spilling into the piano mikes," explains Mark. "In particular, it was right next to the drums!" At one point, the intention was to take the acoustic arrangements back to the Racket Club and make a studio-grade acoustic album. In the end Mark re-recorded the piano parts, and the band released the 28 June performance in its entirety as the *'Unplugged At The Walls'* double CD.

Plugged at The Walls by Dave Rogers

What is fate? One of the most incredible fate experiences I had was one Friday night, after a long week at work. For some reason I decided to call the Web UK hotline - 'well, you never know…' I thought to myself. I found myself listening to a message advising of a 'very special event', planned to take place at a restaurant in Shropshire - The Walls. Thinking there was no chance of obtaining tickets, I made the call, and was delighted to learn my timing had been (unintentionally) perfect - I was now the proud owner of three reserved places. The plan was to take a very special lady and a good friend of mine who I knew would appreciate some fine musicians. Unfortunately for my friend, he had to drop out at the last minute, but it was a pleasure to help someone else enjoy an evening of such distinction.

The Walls - maybe I am getting old, but this was ideal for me, taking someone special to such a show was beyond my dreams. Fine food and drink, comfortable surroundings and like minded people from all four corners of the world, gathered to appreciate one of the finest live bands I have ever known. I remember standing outside in light rain, before the doors opened out of sympathy, and appreciating the contradictions at play - here I was amidst fans from many countries and, as we chatted and waited, Steve Rothery wandered through the car park, briefly acknowledging us all with an almost embarrassed smile. The whole experience was utterly magical, and the first time I really got to mix and meet up with folks that had the same music running in their veins. Yes, any gig has fans, but this gig was full of the most devoted, beautiful people. Everyone had time for everyone else, and it was so relaxed you could be forgiven for thinking it was a family celebration, it just happened that a few relatives could throw a tune together!

Learning where I was to sit for the performance I was overwhelmed - literally in front of the stage, about 15 feet away from H's mikestand - gulp. OK, I was just turned 38 ferchrissakes, but you can't help being starstruck when this is a new experience. The stripped down performances were absolutely sublime and if anyone ever needs proof as to the skill of the band, that album is the evidence. (Incidentally I have played that one to many a disbeliever and well, now they do believe!). Whenever I play *'Unplugged At The Walls'* it takes me right back there, and when I hear 'Blackbird' I smile a wry smile. Perfect in its simplicity and a wonderful homage to Lennon and McCartney, it turned into a personal moment as Pete came over to chat to me after he played it! He had obviously spent a lot of time rehearsing on an acoustic borrowed from Steve R, and I rather got the impression he had been quite nervous about the performance. It was a pleasure to tell him it was fantastic, and all his effort had been worthwhile! The Walls was also the first time I was able to meet a man I have admired for many, many years - the one and only Steve Rothery.

As far as I am concerned this man is a God. Although I had been hoping to meet him, I was overwhelmed when I got the chance - he is one of the nicest guys, and to shake his hand, the hand that has created such gorgeous sounds, was a genuine privilege. When I told him how long I had been waiting to thank him personally for all the wonderful music, he seemed genuinely taken aback. Obviously making and selling music is a job and income, but it's more than that due to the way it can turn people's lives. Finally I had the opportunity to really repay the man whose guitar skills always put a huge smile on my face - just look stage left at a gig and that's me with the grin when the 'guvnor' hits a sweet solo! Others may knock 'Kayleigh' and 'Easter' as 'past it', but my God, those solos are still sublime.

Radiating Out

Following a final mix by Stewart Every in Oswestry before assembly at Abbey Road, *'Radiat10n'* [11] was released on 21 September 1998. The cover was back with Bill Smith Studios, who had, "come back in through the side door," according to Bill Smith, referring to some work Carl had been doing on Marillion's own Racket Records releases. The front and back covers were graced by Carl's partner Christine Bone, from an afternoon session on Hayle Beach, near St Ives in Cornwall. "There were lots of holidaymakers staring at us as I was also in the sea covered in camera gear," says Carl. And no, her head doesn't normally look like that.

Prior to the European release date, Mark Kelly emailed his fellow Freaks, requesting "that anyone who was going to purchase *'Radiat10n'* to please do so the week of its release." The fans duly did, resulting in chart positions for the album across Europe. Despite the feeling that *'Radiat10n'* was a bit of a mistake, the reviews were as positive as any. On AMZ, Robert Lewis wrote: "*'Radiat10n'* is definitely something you don't want to miss. As a whole, this album steers Marillion in a whole different direction from which they were pointed with the last album." ITVNet remarked, "It demonstrates an impressive level of musical intervention while maintaining a playfully humanistic energy." Dale Jensen wrote in All Music Guide, "'Answering Machine', 'These Chains' and 'Under The Sun' are appealing tracks, while 'Three Minute Boy', yet another Marillion examination of the impact of fame, contains some of Steve Rothery's best guitar work in years." Oh, the irony!

Many fans were quite happy with the new sound. "Believe it or believe it not," writes Chris Brockwell, "*'Radiat10n'* is my favourite album, I return to it time and time again because of its raw edge and deeper-than-deep meanings!" Mark Donald writes, "'Cathedral Wall' is up there in my top five whilst 'A Few Words For The Dead' gets better every listen, and its had many I can assure you!" Mike Richichi wrote how, "*'Radiat10n'* is, quite simply, amazing. It's probably the most stylistically varied Marillion album, going from near-metal to quiet, haunting ballads." However, for some fans, the concern this time was the album's modern influences rather than their lack of them - in particular the issue of sounding like Radiohead, an accusation that was met with raised eyebrows by the band. As for the deliberate attempt to ditch the 'prog rock' image, Steve Hogarth noted "The whole progressive label is yours, not ours, in the first place!"

Certain fans criticised the production quality of the album, a criticism that was seen as a little unfair by the band. "The choice of sounds and arrangement of parts was deliberate and radical," remarks Pete. Steve Rothery is more dubious: "It was a half-baked attempt to sound younger than our years." "I haven't got a problem with that, I don't agree!" says H. Ian does, "I didn't enjoy that album," he says. "We tried to step outside ourselves, it sounds like a second rate version of who we were trying to copy! It backfired. I found it too harsh, not musical enough." All players agree that the sonic quality could be better, even for the US version which was mastered again by Simon Heyworth at Chop 'Em Out Studios (now owned by Sanctuary), before its release. "If we were going to remaster one album of recent years, it would be *'Radiat1On'*," says Pete. Agrees Rothers, "its more edgy than it needs to be. Steve Wilson thought it was good album but really wanted to remix it. If Sanctuary/Castle ever deleted it, that would be the moment." Concurs Steven, "I wanted to completely remix it. I think it's an album with good material, poorly mixed. Sonically it's a bit flat."

Money, or lack of it, was a deciding factor when the band came to decide the tour itinerary. Mark Kelly used Glasgow as an example: "On the Afraid Of Sunlight tour we played there, we didn't get that many people there and so on the following tour we weren't going to play there and we were hounded by people to play Glasgow so eventually we put a warm-up date in there and of course we didn't get that many people which was exactly what the promoter predicted and so on this tour we're not playing Glasgow because for the last two tours it has cost us money to go there." Follow that? The tour started on September 14, following warm-up fan club shows in Oxford, Utrecht and Cologne. The continental fan show dates were significant for their transport arrangements - both the Tivoli Theatre, Utrecht on 5 September 1998, and Alter Wartesaal, Cologne on the 12 September were performed with a cut-down rig that could be put through the check-in desk rather than going on as cargo. "We did get hammered a couple of times for the extra gear!" laughs Mark.

As with the album, after the more acoustic nature of This Strange Tour, this tour featured a faster set. "The last tour seemed like a slower paced set and I suppose we were compensating for that in a way as well," adds Mark Kelly. Ian Mosley agreed - "There's 'Gazpacho' and 'Cannibal [Surf Babe]' which we really get off on. That's why we do them!" For the first time ever on tour, there were no Fish-era songs. Again, pragmatism was claimed as the key - "We're playing our most recent material really which is six albums worth," claimed Mark at the time. Added H, "When you've got a two hour show it's natural to spend 40 minutes on the new album which leaves you 1 hour 20 minutes to cover the previous nine. So it's unlikely that the first two or three albums are going to get much of a look in."

Highs and Lows by Paul Rael

The Hogarth era has somewhat mysteriously mirrored the highs and lows of my life over the last eight years or so. The music really does get wrapped up in people's lives. For example around the *'This Strange Engine'* album era I was involved with this girl and she got into the band through me, I took her to see them on that tour and it was the first gig she'd seen and she was blown away.

I can remember seeing the band at the Oxford Zodiac just before *'Radiat10n'* during one of the blackest periods of my life. Somewhere along the line it went wrong and it was at the pre-*'Radiat10n'* gig in Oxford (it was a fan-club/convention type gig) where a Marillion gig first coincided with a SEVERE low point. The music hit home like a lightning bolt that night and 'King' in particular was like the band were talking directly to me. 1997 had been financially successful for me beyond my wildest dreams and then, a year on, it was turning very sour indeed. This wasn't a gig it was a revelation, it was time to change my life!!!

The music just got into my soul that night and after the gig I got to talk to Steve Hogarth for the first time and what started as a simple autograph request turned into a 15-minute chat whilst we were literally mobbed by fans, it was like talking in the middle of a rugby scrum but it was just enough to lift me out of my trough of depression as I'd really had a chance to talk to one of my 'Heroes' (I know that may sound a bit corny) and he was cool, did live up to my expectations and did give a shit!

I saw two shows on the Radiat10n tour which were excellent but they were somehow marred for me by the fact that this special girl wasn't there with me, she was a fellow fan and we weren't even in touch although, bizarrely, her sister came to the Forum gig with me!! Moving on to 1999 and my life was improving again and best of all I was friends with this girl again and we went up to Dudley to see the band play. I was emotional as hell and barely kept a lid on my emotions, life had gone full circle and had proved that things do sometimes work out OK and again this band was at the heart of it.

A few weeks later I was at the London gig with a group of friends including another girl who I was crazy about. She was a glamour model and left her mark on the band to this day by getting them to sign her tits (honest!) in the backstage bar afterwards! I was crazy about this girl and bought her *'Brave'* and *'Afraid Of Sunlight'* and I remember 'phoning her up more than once and hearing 'Beautiful' playing in the background...

So for me Marillion is always the band that somehow seems to be wrapped up in my cantankerous emotional life. It's like they bloody know!!

'Marillion.com'

The relentless pace of the band continued immediately after the final scream of the Radiat10n tour, on 18 November 1998 at the Elysée Montmartre. Under the terms of the deal, this was to be the third and final album distributed on the Castle label. After this the band would be looking for a new deal - or would they?

Meanwhile Marillion continued to develop its fine romance with its fans. Christmas 1998 saw the first fan club CD, brainchild of Simon Clarke and the first fruit of the brainstorming sessions between the new Web team and the band. "We thought it would make a nice change, instead of giving you a newsletter or a dodgy piece of A4 parading as such, to put out a CD this Christmas," announced H, with a background of laughter and heckling by the rest of the band. "We thought that'd be smashing! Please spend a thought for those less fortunate - people in the media, bankers, politicians..." The CD featured a selection of cuts from the new album, plus several karaoke tracks. "We've put down a few of the masters without my dulcet tones," explained Steve, "So make a tape, sing on the karaoke and send it to us!" The prize was a visit to the Racket Club to record the winning version professionally - "You'll be able to take a CD away with you to impress your chums - we'll also be providing a CD for the very worst!"

A staggering 132 entries were received, and the band painstakingly set to listening to the tapes to find the best - and worst - among them. On 1 May three winners were announced - Anne Bond and her primary school class, who spent a grand day out at the Racket Club on 8 October, plus Michelle De Luca (singing 'These Chains') and Bob van Ingen (singing 'Beautiful'), both of whom had the chance to perform with the band at the 1999 fan club convention.

As the writing sessions for the next album were kicked off, Marillion was still taking stock of experiences such as the Tour Fund and the karaoke competition. An imago strategy was emerging, the starting point for which was to get the band out of the labels and into... something else, what it was, nobody knew.

Cradley's Grand Day Out by Anne Bond

When the karaoke competition was announced I thought I might enter myself but then I had this crazy idea of entering the children. It wasn't easy teaching them the song, it was not really in their range and I did not think the end result was brilliant so I left it at home for a few weeks thinking that I was being stupid to enter it. But a friend told me I had to send it off.

I will never forget the day that Erik phoned me to say that they would love me to bring the kids to the Racket Club. It was in May and I never believed it would happen, especially as they kept putting me off and delaying until we finally fixed it up for October.

It was a brilliant, special day and I remember being really nervous, especially when I had to sing a line of 'Beautiful' in front of Steve Hogarth. Everyone was lovely and Stewart Every was very patient with the children. H played them all the instruments and they all crowded around him and asked questions. Some of the girls were totally smitten and asked him for a kiss. Steve sang 'Beautiful' especially for us, and the children spontaneously gave him a standing ovation. They certainly made the band feel like celebrities, asking for autographs and shaking their hands at the end. It had been rather a hectic day, with such a small studio filled with 10 and 11 year olds and I was worried they would regret inviting us. I asked Steve Hogarth about it several weeks later and he said it had been a lovely, special day for him too and it had meant a lot to him to hear the words he had written sung by children.

My mum and dad came too, they also enjoy Marillion and come to all the Wolverhampton concerts (even at the age of 68). My mum did a video and my dad stood and drank coffee and smoked with Ian. We were also recorded for Central News South and photographed and interviewed for a large article in the Aylesbury News.

As a result of all this, I was contacted by people over the internet from all over the world. Later, I was given a pass to see Marillion on the Dot com tour and I went four times. It never occurred to me that I could get to concerts all

> over the country (on a school night) and I was amazed to find a number of fans doing the same. Well, since then I have seen them at nearly every concert in Britain. The people at school think I am mad and don't know how I stay awake the next day at school.
>
> "Isn't it always the same?" they say. But I can't explain the compulsion I have to go.

Caught in the Net

Writing started at the end of November 1998 with the B-list of songs that hadn't made it to *'Radiat10n'*. There were a couple of Helmer-penned tracks already in the bank - 'Interior Lulu' and 'Tumble Down The Years' - but both were wanting for better arrangements. Other 'canned' *'Radiat10n'* ideas were also ready to roll, including 'Enlightened' and 'Go!'. Additional John Helmer lyrics were also brought in, including 'A Legacy' and 'Built-In Bastard Radar'. "John had delivered a few juicy lyrics right at the end of the *'Radiat10n'* sessions," remarked H. "It was too late to do anything with them then!"

Things took an unexpected turn on January 11, 1999, when Pete Trewavas was hit by a car when cycling home from The Racket Club. Pete suffered multiple injuries and spent a time in intensive care, not to mention undergoing surgery which included inserting an inches-long metal pin in his leg. Not only did Pete make quick progress by the end, he was raring to get back into the studio. As he explains, "The band were incredibly supportive of me while I was recovering. I felt obliged however to get back to writing and being part of the band as soon as possible, which was a huge struggle at times before I got sufficiently fit. I remember being in quite a lot of pain just from the exertion of getting around." Pete fought back hard enough to make not just a Marillion album but also, six months later, an album with his supergroup Transatlantic. What a trouper.

Meanwhile, the show went on. Rothers had been working at home on a completely new arrangement for 'Interior Lulu'; at the same time H was developing the ideas for 'House' and 'A Legacy'. The writing sessions now included one variation on the now-traditional process - recordings were made to Minidisc rather than DAT. By January, the songs were ready in arrangements that the band felt comfortable with, this time with harsh edges replaced with an altogether better-honed sound. Explains Pete, "We'd learned with *'Radiat10n'*, so we tried to choose warmer, nicer, more encouraging sounds!" The other lesson the band had learned was how to write songs in other ways than layering instruments on top of the bass section. Mark was particularly pleased with 'Go!' - "We wrote that for *'Radiat10n'*, but just couldn't get it to happen. It was a nice surprise how it turned out!"

Recording started in earnest at the beginning of April, and by June 1999 the band went off to The Forge at Oswestry, where Nick Davis mixed the more commercial oriented tracks, 'Deserve', 'Rich' and 'Tumble Down The Years'. "I spent a long weekend up there and boshed out the three tracks, two of them were very good!" says Nick. Stewart Every stayed behind at the Racket Club to work on the "marathon" 'Interior Lulu', using a new digital mixing desk. Unfortunately, on the band's return they decided they didn't like what the mixing desk was producing. "Unfairly to Stewart, we'd bought this brand new, digital desk, and expected Stewart to just get on with it," explains Mark. "Stewart didn't like the sound he was making, but didn't know why or how to make it better." The band didn't like it either, so with much relief it was agreed to can the desk. Time was running short, so Steve Hogarth proposed Trevor Vallis (who had worked with The

Steven Wilson and Porcupine Tree

Steven went to his first Marillion gig when he was 10 years old, at the Berkhamstead Civic Centre. Liking what he saw, in 1982 (while still at school) he set up his first band, Karma, to do the same. "When I was a teenager they were a big influence on me. Karma even covered some of their songs!" smiles Steven. Despite all the members still being at school, Karma still managed 40 gigs in its 3-year existence.

In 1987 Steven would start two projects, one serious and one satirical. The serious project was No-Man, a collaboration with singer Tim Bowness and violinist Ben Coleman. In parallel with this, Steven developed an entirely fictional history af a band called Porcupine Tree, "Complete with non-existent band members, an absurd discography," and several hours of music that Steve recorded to back up the story.

Eventually Steven signed No-Man to One Little Indian Records, and ironically Porcupine Tree was also starting to see some success, so Steven gave up his day job as a computer technician to work full-time on his musical projects. He has never looked back, with both No-Man and Porcupine Tree being consistently successful to this day.

Porcupine Tree were later to tour with Marillion, and Steven also produced one album - *'Sunsets On Empire'* - for Fish. Most recently, Porcupine Tree has signed with Atlantic Records, and has released a new album - In Absentia - in the US. Expect world domination any time soon.

Europeans) to mix the remaining tracks at the Racket Club on the old analogue desk. When they heard the results, however, the band didn't like what he was producing either! "He had this little box you plug everything into, it was supposed to make everything sound more dynamic," says Mark. "It was the sort of thing everyone used in the Eighties, until somebody said it was rubbish!"

There was a feeling of impending panic as the band had already booked the cut of the album. As H explained to journalist Rich Wilson, the mix had to be completed by 15 August for a 1999 release. "The press needs a three-month deadline, so for an interview to appear in the press in time for the release, you have to do it three months up front." Some fan club shows had been booked as well, so in July 1999 it was time to come out from under the rock. A couple of fan club shows had been planned at the Zodiac, back to back with the shooting of the video for 'Deserve'. The shows were recorded by the Boom Boom Boys Paul and Jayce, who had contacted the band on-spec for the privilege. "They sent us a showreel, it looked like they could hold a camera and edit," says Mark, "plus they said they'd do it for nothing - that clinched the deal! We were a bit nervous as we knew we'd be stuck with them for a week, but as soon as we met them we knew it would be alright." Another attendee at the Zodiac gigs happened to be Porcupine Tree front man and long-time Marillion fan Steven Wilson, who got into conversation with Steve Rothery. "He mentioned they were having a few problems with the mixing of the new album," explains Steven, "I said I would be happy to have a crack at it and so they sent me over the tapes to 'Interior Lulu' as an "audition". It took me a couple of days (well it's 15 minutes long!) and I took a few liberties with it, editing and moving thing around, but the audition mix is the one that's on the album." Says Mark, "He's a talented guy; we liked what he did. We had to persuade him to use a bit less of the megaphone voice though - he said, that's my trademark!"

With tangible relief, Marillion let Steven loose on the other tracks. "We kept saying, could you just mix one more?"

hold the mayo

Little did BBC Radio 1 DJ Simon Mayo know what he was getting himself into when, one Friday morning on 23 July 1999, in the dead or alive segment of his show, he asked the question, "Where are Marillion now? And who cares anyway!" Over the weekend that followed, Simon received 1600 emails from Marillion fans all over the world; these continued during the week. A month later, after Simon took a well-earned break, his first guest was Mark Kelly! Who cares indeed!

laughs Mark. "He mixed five tracks in a week!" "Steve Wilson was a saviour!" says Pete. Only 'House' remains from Trevor's ill-fated sessions with the analogue desk. "That was his best one,"says Mark. The final mix was completed on 16 August and the master completed the next day. The band were feeling decidedly up-to-date, with 'House' considered by Steve Rothery as "the most contemporary sounding track we've done in a long time." Even Country and Western influences were acknowledged in 'Deserve'. Laughed Steve at the time, "We've finally written a song you can line dance to!" Incidentally, the lyrics for 'Rich' were based on a number of quotations from female writers. Explains Mark, "A PR agency had produced a proposal for us, it used these quotes so Steve [H] took them away and made a song out of them!"

Following the completion of the album the band went their separate ways, working on projects of their own (such as Ben Castle's 'Postmankind' for Ian) or taking some well-earned time off before reuniting at the International Managers Forum awards at the Hyde Park Hilton in London on 22 September 1999, with ex-Kula Shaker drummer Paul Winter-Hart[12] standing in for Ian, who was on holiday in Maui. "My wife had bought a house there, so I felt I should go," smiles Ian. It's a good job he did - the gig was reputed as one of the worst in Marillion's career, kicked off by Mark reciting Chas and Roy's 'Manager's Song' which went down like a lead balloon. "The boys rang me up and told me I'd done the right thing!" says Ian.

'Marillion.com'

By the late '90s Marillion were one of the foremost innovators when it came to the Internet. With a website packed to the gills, the band had learnt to harness the power of the net, and to use it as a way to keep in touch with their fans, something that would become even more apparent with their next album. 'Marillion.com' *was named in recognition of this factor. It also finds the band expanding their musical palette once more, although it should be noted that 'Tumble Down The Years' and 'Interior Lulu' were originally produced during the sessions for the* 'Radiat1On' *album - 'Deserve', 'Rich', 'Go!', 'Enlightened' and 'Built-In Bastard Radar' came from ideas originating at the same time. Again produced by the band, the disc benefits from having the touch of Porcupine Tree main man Steven Wilson on five of the nine tracks, but even the self-produced tracks sound much better production-wise than* 'Radiat1On'.

'A Legacy' is a song of many parts - according to H, "Film-noir through funk, grunge and The Beatles, with an accidental Beach Boys moment." With lyrics written by long-term collaborator John Helmer, the song dissects a marriage on the edge of destruction and the notion that ending the relationship doesn't necessarily mean all slates are wiped clean, or that everything turns out for the best. Its dominant musical theme, courtesy of Mark Kelly has been likened to a Bond theme - the flip side to the previous album's Bond Baddie theme 'Cathedral Wall'. The heroic sound however, is very much at odds with the almost callous lyrical content. If there's a fault with the song, it's perhaps that it's a tad busy in the earlier stages, and perhaps it seems somewhat out of step with the rest of the album.

The upbeat 'Deserve', featuring saxophone by Ben Castle concerns thinking about making positive changes to your life - because you might actually succeed! More specifically, as H wrote on the band's website, "You create your own joy and your own misery. Unhappiness isn't really related to anything other than state of mind." The song ends with a stomping Motown sounding groove, and is guaranteed to get the feet tapping. It's great fun.

Coming down the gears, 'Go!' starts with a bass pulse, and processed feedback, before Steve Rothery comes in with a delicate picked verse. Its serene gentleness is evidenced by the amount of space in the music itself - listen to Ian's cymbals shimmer like lazy sunlight across a Caribbean sea... Wistful and dreamy, the song is lyrically not dissimilar to 'These Chains' but without the barbs of that track. Steve Rothery delivers a smooth solo that caresses gently over Pete's cool bass groove. The song plays out with a coda that sees H, Pete and Mark building a delightful theme over Mark's enticing keyboards. Lovely.

Rich threatens to giggle as H leads us in a do-wop, sing-a-long intro! This is a song that is happy without being twee, joyous without being at anyone's expense. All through, the listener is struck by its gently quirky rhythms and the melodies which lead us to a chorus that demands to be sung out loud, "No fears, no lies, no pain, no doubt, no darkness, no confusion, no loneliness, despair no more, no way, no how, it's all illusion" and its positive belief that thinking happy thoughts, and facing life head on can be its own reward. It includes an idea taken from the French writer Anaïs Nin, "We don't see things as they are, we see things as we are." If you're not smiling during this song, you have a heart of stone, and that, my friends, is a fact!

'Enlightened' is almost a sister song to 'Go!'; again a very gentle track. The lyric was conceived in a Sao Paolo café called 'Viva Vida' (literally 'Live Life'). It concerns a feeling of gentle euphoria which H says can occur in moments of extreme tiredness, and is bound up with feelings of love and lovemaking with that special person. The song has a languid feel to it, bound up with the many references to tiredness and sleep. Steve Rothery's guitar is almost scratchy on the early part of the solo, yet, as it glides into a smooth outro, there's no sense that the serenity has been breached. A perfect song for when you're relaxing with your head against the one you love. Beautiful.

'Built-In Bastard Radar' sees John Helmer kick sand in the faces of men who once stole women from under his nose. Kicking in with a heavy guitar riff, almost reminiscent of heavier Queen, and with a Deep Purple riff on the Mellotron, it quickly gives way to a gentler verse. The lyric details the way that some women seem attracted to blokes without an ounce of decency in their souls. After a Garbage-y fuzz bass solo from Pete, the song implies that the writer (and by extension, H as singer) is now outdoing them all, using his fame as a star as a lure for those self-same women. A case of 'once, I was but the learner, now I am the master...'! H has commented that he doesn't know whether Helmer was taking the piss by making him sing such words.

'Tumble Down The Years' calls to mind Crowded House, as H and Helmer look back across a couple's relationship and muse about how they managed to end up where they are. John Lennon once famously said 'Life's what happens when you're making plans' and that seems to be the key on one of the most melodic songs on the album. It's a bright summery song with a great lyric, married to what is, although good, one of the less distinctive tracks on the album.

'Interior Lulu' is a sprawling epic of a song. Opinions amongst the fans are almost equally divided amongst the fans as to whether this song or 'This Strange Engine' is the best long song by the Hogarth-era band. Personally, I tend slightly more towards 'Strange Engine', but nevertheless, this song contains some of the band's best moments, both lyrically and musically. The intro sees Pete lope a meandering bass over Ian's almost reggae percussion, while H sings about a girl who has transformed herself on the Internet into a bohemian, whilst being rather drab in real life. Mark then launches into a Keith Emerson-esque extravaganza/mess (delete as applicable) of a Moog solo, which becomes a *tour de force* of pent-up pain with Ian and Steve Rothery straining at the leash to emote. We then see her trying to catch her essence in emails, attempting to write her pain into ascii characters, before shifting focus to find H is able to understand exactly what is going on. Over an acoustic chord vamp, H reveals she's not telling him anything he doesn't already know; in one of his best lyrics, he describes how "by writing from personal experience, you empower your work only to cheapen the memory or the emotion which inspired it". He describes the process in an sub-textually ironic passage that rates as highly as he's ever achieved:

> If you can carry it out, you can take it away,
> If you can buy it, it can be bought,
> If you can buy it, it can be stolen,
> If you can break it, it's already broken...

The coda finds H standing on top of London's Primrose Hill, staring down at the city below him, musing on how the Internet can connect us, but we never touch. As the thought hits home, the band explode into a squall of biting, nihilistic fury; bass and drums going crazy, Steve Rothery pouring sweat and tears into every finely wrung note, Mark's keyboards writhing like a nightmare-tortured sleeper.... Genius! The thought always occurs: 'What must H think of people like me who pour over the lyric sheets trying to wring out every last nuance of meaning?' I don't think I want to know.

'House' is a real change for the band, being a laid-back, dub/trip hop type vibe, partly inspired by Massive Attack. This one split the fans right down the middle - there doesn't seem to be much middle ground with this one - but if anything, 'House' was the track which pointed to the direction the band would take with *'Anoraknophobia'*. The song is a study, in bluesy, smoky jazz, of the near disintegration of H's marriage - something that had informed the *'Radiat1On'* album to quite a large extent. H said, "The house seemed to somehow ooze the pain we were in, even when nobody was there. There wasn't a level to which I could turn up the hi-fi that drowned out the silence that was still there." With Ian and Pete laying down a soulful rhythm, Mark, Steve H and guest trumpeter Neil Yates conjure a moving picture of a dark house full of longing and loneliness. It's a real antidote to the aggression at the end of 'Lulu', and personally I love it, especially since, by the time it was released, H's home life appeared to be back on track and in a happier place. Sublime.

The cover features a young alternative-looking girl standing on a cold London street corner holding a glowing computer monitor - possibly Lulu. Around her, what at first glance seem like time-lapsed tail lights slash across the scene. On closer inspection, they appear to be too well defined. I like to imagine them as kind of electronic ley-lines, signifying the interconnectivity of the Internet. The girl also calls to mind the cover of the previous album, with its similarly stiffly-posed girl. Inside, there are 784 passport photos. Who are they? They're some of the band's fans, contacted via the Internet. Marillion.com? They really are connected...

Virtual Light

'Marillion.com' was released on 18 October 1999, with cover art by Bill Smith Studios. "We wanted a layered feel going further and further into the void. From the girl holding the laptop, thru the passport pictures and finally into the screenshots," explains Bill. "The combination held the whole thing together." Explains Carl, "I'd just bought a medium-format camera that could take sixteen-second exposures, it got me thinking." After a couple of hours in a London pub waiting for dusk, ("The nights were long at that time of the year," he grins) photographer Carl and photographee Justine Leyland[13] went (stumbled?) out to see what could be done. The cover was taken at the end of Longacre and the centrepiece outside the Palace Theatre at the end of Charing Cross Road, capturing light trails which would eventually be built up as a montage. "Buses kept stopping which was a bit of a problem!" laughs Carl. "The light trails symbolise the Internet and our relationship with it." Then it was back to the lab to mock up the concepts for the cover. As for the passport pictures, "We wanted to make the sleeve relevant to the website itself, which is obviously visited by fans," explains Bill. "I suggested the band ask their fans to send passport pictures, some 7-800 did so and we used them all."[14] Fan Martin Thorpe comments, "It was good to get on the cover... just a shame that the pic I sent made me look like a Lebanese pimp!"

The album was hailed by many as a return to form for the band, following the less than enthusiastic response for *'This Strange Engine'* and the tacit approval for *'Radiat10n'*. As Mark commented, "The thing about new albums is that you never know what to expect, it's nerveracking, you've been so close to it for so long that it's difficult to judge it. But it has been a good reaction so that's really good." H's experiences confirmed this - "the most common comment that I've had is that it's the best work since *'Afraid Of Sunlight'*."

With *'Marillion.com'* the band confirmed their new style, not in terms of its influences but its approach of trying new ideas, of never standing still. In particular, 'Interior Lulu' acted as a demonstration of all that was good about the band, past and present. Indeed, in the lists the album was talked about more in terms of the few tracks people didn't like, rather than the few tracks they did. For old faithful fans, still hoping for a return to the more traditional Marillion, *'Dot com'* was still not there, nor would it ever be. The band was finding a groove, and the majority were saying that it was good - that was all that mattered.

Mad Jack of Stars

In 2000, the band were approached to produce the music for a film called 'Jack Of Stars', by director Michael DiCerto. Tipped to star in the film were James Coburn and Louis Diamond Philips. Unfortunately, it never happened - according to Rothers, after a year or so of waiting, the finance fell through at the last minute. Mike had previously co-directed the award-winning 'No Exit' with his cousin, David DiCerto.

As far as the pundits were concerned, Marillion were on form. Q Magazine's Rob Beattie wrote, "After 'A Legacy' (typically and wilfully unpredictable) this settles swiftly down with some of their most memorable and direct songs since *'Afraid Of Sunlight'* - melodically sound with refreshingly unfussy arrangements. The 15-minute 'Interior Lulu' is a troubling but somehow inevitable stumble back into extravagance, but 'Tumble Down The Years', 'Deserve' and 'Go!' offer considerable compensations." Gary Hill wrote in All Music Guide, "It is a very entertaining album that really grows on you."

Echoing the views of many fans, Mike Richichi wrote, "This is an astounding album synthesizing the best of their sound, '90s British pop and psychedelia, with some '70s prog rock widdly-widdly thrown in for good measure. This is an album that will both grab you at first listen, and grow its way into your head, riffs, sounds, and details working your way in, Steve Hogarth and John Helmer's lyrics suddenly resonating like they hadn't before."

In the HMV Music poll of December 1999, Marillion were voted 82nd best band of the Millennium, one above stablemates Iron Maiden. The band was also voted best band, best live act and best album by Classic Rock magazine. Things were clearly looking good for the future. Furthermore, *'Marillion.com'* was the last album on the Castle label, freeing the band from any contractual obligation. There was no shortage of offers, not least from Rod Smallwood of Sanctuary. Recalls Mark, "Rod had us in his office, he wanted us to re-sign to Castle as Sanctuary had bought Castle." This led to a bit of a conflict of interest, as Rod had been managing the band since the separation with John Arnison. The negotiations were now between Rod (representing Marillion) and Rod (representing Sanctuary). So it was inevitable that things came to a head. "Rod put his hands up and said, 'We can't manage you,' so we parted company with both label and management," remembers Pete. "We felt a bit let down, maybe we'd been expecting more than they could give us." Whatever - it was not to be.

Ironically however, the fans themselves were making negotiations difficult. Explains Steve H, "Our fan base gave the labels a disincentive to market the product. Our experience was that they would be queuing up to sign us, but they would blow a lot of smoke up our arses about how excited they were about the music. And then come the time of the record release, we would be lucky to get a quarter page advert in a magazine."

The labels might have been queuing up, but Marillion knew they were unlikely to accept any offers. Unbeknown to Castle, Marillion had come up with a plan to develop a relationship with the fans that went way beyond what any record label could provide. Explains Pete, "We knew we were out of the Castle deal, we thought to safeguard our futures, the best thing was to build up our database. It was win-win-win, whether we resigned from Castle or not!" Aided and abetted by Carl Glover, the album cover included a mail-off card for a supplementary CD. The question was, would Castle include the form? At one time, it was missed off a draft of the artwork, a cause for near-panic within the band. Comments Mark, "It was all planned - it was really hairy for a time that they'd fuck it up!" But fuck up they didn't – the album went out with the mail-off card intact.

By the end of 1999 there had been over 15,000 applications for the CD - clearly there was still a huge demand for Marillion's music. What was more, the applications served to add fourteen thousand more email subscribers to the Marillion eWeb mailing list, swelling its numbers from the 2,000 starting point - this proved to be vital in the next stage of the game.

The Dot Com tour started for real on 13 October at the MCM Café in Paris, and ended on 5 December. And then, it was time for something completely different again.

...With The Date In The Corner by Paul S Rowlson

In one way it all seems so incredibly distant... But in another it's like it happened yesterday...

The 1999 fan convention at The Zodiac - four hot and sticky nites in an upstairs room with a postage stamp for a stage. The first four Marillion concerts we ever saw - all through the lens of a camera I'd only really figured out how to use a few days before!

With the benefit of hindsight it's easy to see how our timing, for once, was just perfect.

It all started when we logged onto marillion.com. Funnily enough, at the time, we weren't even trying to find a better way of life - just some videos! And what did we find? We found what EVERYONE found when they came in search of content for their cathode!

Nothing! Zilch! Sod all!

We stewed on this for a short time and then - being uniquely positioned to actually do something - we chose to DO SOMETHING!

We knocked up a story board, drafted a rather lengthy missive and fired it into the digital domain.

A week later - having received the e-mail equivalent of Marillion's 1999 on-line video offerings - we sent another little note. You know "just making sure you got the last message, hoping to hear from you soon, no pressure, whenever you get a moment" - and returned to frantically chewing our nails.

What we didn't know was that Los Marrillos were - at that very moment - in the process of trying to secure some video footage in anticipation of their imminent departure from Castle. In fact, The Aylesbury Five were more receptive to the idea of video than they had been in quite literally years.

Thus, when Erik wandered into the RC clutching our unsolicited proposal, it could not have been at a better time. (And while we're on the subject please let the record reflect that TBBB can never say enough about the role played by Mr. Nielsen - we are forever in his debt and the longstanding offer to bear his children stands!)

The problem, however, was to be one of dates.

Not the dates of the gigs, but the possibility of the date appearing in the bottom left corner of whatever we would shoot if the restraining order was lifted!

I'm sure that most reasonably successful bands attract at least a few people for whom fan is too short a word. But, in the case of this particular boy band the proportion of fanatics to casual fans seems almost the exact opposite to the norm!

I for one have yet to meet a half-hearted Marillion fan!

However, being a Marillion fan(atic) is one thing, being a fan(atic) who claims to be a professional filmmaker is quite another. And so - while that we got any answer at all was a huge, shit-eating grin of a surprise - we were not overly surprised that this first response was somewhat... guarded.

But this is where our self-confessed cockiness came into its own.

The truth is Jayce & I had never done ANYTHING quite like this. However, what we lacked in experience we made up for in testicular fortitude! Ultimately, we had two things going for us:

One - Our showreel could prove that we were not complete idiots.

Two - we were offering to pay for the whole bloody thing ourselves!

Then we hit the first speed bump. We wanted to DHL our reel post haste. But Erik didn't even want to give us an address for Racket in case we, I dunno, knew the words to 'Helter Skelter'!

Eventually, in blatant disregard for his own safety, Erik threw himself in front of the bullet by giving us HIS address and we dispatched a tape that very day.

Then we waited... and waited and... waited some more until the tape landed, the lads watched it, and we got an e-mail that started with three words we will never forget...

Let's do it!

From that moment Jayce & I worked ourselves into an ever increasing state of panic. Not only had we never done anything like this but we didn't even know if it COULD be done!

It's no small thing to shoot four nites and make them look like one. Especially when the lighting designer is creating a different lighting show for every night and the band in question has a rather erratic approach to tempo - they all play at a different tempo and defy the laws of physics by arriving at the end of each song at the same time, but never IN the same time!

Add to that the challenge of shooting ten THOUSAND kilometers from the nearest source of favors and the need to spend MONTHS in an edit suite that ordinarily bills out at about five hundred Quid a day, and you've still only got the vaguest idea of the enormity of what we were attempting.

But we planned, schemed, prayed (and only occasionally wept) and by the time we left we had a fairly good idea of what we were going to do AND the wherewithal to do it.

All of which is quite fun because, as he admitted later, Erik was still terrified that we were gonna show up, haul out a coupla handicams, stand in the corner grinning inanely and shoot miles and miles of video footage - all with the date stamped in the corner!

In truth, even after we had been and gone - without showing too many signs of derangement - no one at RC really had a clue just WHAT we'd been doing! It was only after we hammered some ruff kuts together that everyone finally realized that this Shot in the Dark might just work.

Almost since the first day that Jayce & I recognized in each other kindred spirits, one of the things we have shared (apart from the proclivity to find humor in the most inappropriate places) is Marillion.

Together we have eagerly awaited albums, scoured the music press for even the tiniest mention and generally done everything that we all still do to this day. Now that is a pretty weighty responsibility for anyone to live up to. The higher the pedestal, the greater the potential for a fall.

But NOT in this case.

Perhaps the single greatest thing about our whole still developing relationship with the band is the discovery that behind the music are five fantastic people. And behind them is a fantastic group of other wonderful people... The Marillion team...

And behind them, serried rank upon serried rank of still more wonderful people... All of you... The freaks, the fans, the fanatics, the faithful...

This is a marvelous family with, at it's core, five incredible people.

And, just as Marillion's most incredibly moving, emotional and complex music is often the combination of surprisingly simple musical patterns, so too is their incredible moving, emotional and complex relationship with us created by the combination of some surprisingly simple things.

They care about what they do.
They care about who they do it for.
They understand the true value of their fans.
They work exceptionally hard to maintain the relationship they have with us all.
They DO NOT assume we will always be there.
They DO NOT take our passion for granted.
Above all, they absolutely understand that it is the fans that make it possible for them to continue doing what they do so well.

It's the perfect symbiotic relationship - made possible because, each in their own unique way, the five members of the world's best band™ are some of the world's best people.

Jayce & I know that we're pretty much the luckiest 'vidiots' in the whole world. But we also understand that we're no more or less important to the Marillion story than each and everyone reading these words...

So... Here's to us... Long may we all continue...

NOTES: 1 The estimate at the time was twenty. **2** At least, as part of that deal. **3** The saxophone solo was performed by Phil Todd, who performed the solo on 'Berlin'; live, it was sequenced by H using his cricket bat. **4** The sleeve notes included the band's first 'official' email – dorianmusic@dorianmusic.co.uk **5** This is actually press release guff, supplied with the promo edition. **6** This took place on 28 April 1996, at a Marillion gig at The Forum, London. **7** Charles Gingras. **8** The night of the Pittsburgh gig was also the night Lady Diana was killed in Paris, following a high-speed car accident in a Parisian underpass. The band were informed by fan Karin Breiter after the gig. **9** These characters relate to backspaces in email-speak. **10** Sanctuary had bought Castle in March 2000, Joe Cockell stayed on as head. **11** The album was originally to be called *'Turn Of The Century'*. H had the idea to put '10' in *'Radiat10n'*. **12** Ex-Kula Shaker - he was told earlier that day that his band was breaking up! **13** Girlfriend of Jim Stoddard, who also worked at Bill Smith Studios at the time. **14** Not to mention pictures of the band - can you spot them?

chapter five a better way of life/1999-2002

"You should keep on playing rock for as long as you have an axe to grind, and if you haven't got an axe to grind, you should go into cabaret."

Pete Townshend

Things were going reasonably well. It might have taken five years of learning (for most people, that's a PhD), but Marillion now knew what it meant to manage themselves, produce records, not to mention go on tour and run an online record business in a way that satisfied both the appetites of the fans and the bank balances of the band and its staff. Marillion had found its feet, this time its own feet, without requiring the support of record labels or management companies.

Whatever. All that was nice, reasonable, fine, OK. But there was more. Barely visible beneath the routines, glinting under the surface of the now-flowing revenue streams, there lay something more than a mere bankroll. The overwhelming responses to both the tour fund and the CD mail-in were signposts in the sand, indicators of a rich vein that, as yet, lay untapped.

Steve Hogarth once said, "Happiness is when you find a locked door will open." Marillion knew it had found a key to riches it could not yet fathom. All it had to do was find the door.

finding the door

Writing started in January 2000, after the band returned from their respective Christmas breaks. "We weren't in a hurry to come back, to be honest," commented Mark in a Web interview. In parallel, however, Marillion was also planning its next move. Album sales had continued to fall since the band first adopted 'indie' status in 1997. A chance remark by H illustrated the perceived way forward, "If a band's new album consistently fails to outsell the album before then you reach a point were you just have to call it a day or change drastically the way the band's operating." The options were to throw in the towel, to renegotiate, to start looking for a new label, or do something so bizarre that even Monty Python would be proud.

Once again, they went for option four.

Quite Simply Knocked Out

In the writing sessions for *'This Strange Engine'*, *'Radiat10n'* and *'Marillion.com'*, the band had the luxury of having material left over from the album before, but not this time. Marillion were starting with a clean slate and, as Mark commented at the time, "That usually makes it interesting!" "And long!" added Pete. As the sessions began, self-confessed gadget-fanatic Steve Rothery had turned up with some electronic gizmos that set the scene for the whole album. "I brought down most of my studio equipment early in the writing sessions so I had the capability to play loops and sequences to jam over. It made for an interesting change in the writing process!" The immediate result was a much more groovy sound. Says Ian, "They were not standard drum loops, they were great to play along with!" "The bass riffs are the boss a lot of the time and then things are looping," remarks H. "I guess it was my album," smiles Pete. "It's good to experiment with that stuff!" Before long the boys settled into the familiar routine of jamming and planning the next album, capturing and logging the happy accidents just like so many albums before.

By March, in parallel with reviewing the materials to date and arranging it into songs, the ongoing efforts to find a new deal were starting to take their toll. Despite negotiations with a number of companies including Castle/Sanctuary and Eagle Rock, nothing seemed quite right. "The labels weren't doing anything we couldn't do ourselves," explains Pete. "We were able to create as much press coverage as the record labels, without them creaming what they could off our percentage. They even wanted to deduct packaging costs for mp3 downloads!" The first conclusion was, if the band had to come

Lucy Jordache, band rep, bookings, you name it...

up with communications ideas itself, why didn't they employ someone to do so rather than following the unprofitable convention of paying a record label to do it? And so it was that, on 27 March 2000, Lucy Jordache joined from EMI.

This was only the first in a rapidly accelerating train of activities. "We realised what a power source our fans could be," commented H in an interview. Things came to a head in May when Mark, the most Internet-active band member (at least as far as the fans were concerned) had a rather novel idea. "I know," suggested Mark. "Why don't we ask the fans to buy the album a year in advance, thus raising enough money to pay for the album production?" H recalls the response - "That's a good idea, let's ask the fans if they'd go for it." So, just before H and Pete went off gallivanting with their respective solo projects, out went the eWeb missive that would change music history.

The response was astonishing. Ninety five per cent of fans responded in the positive ("and some even said they would buy two copies," noted the press release.) By the time the number of responses had been added up, a staggering 80,000 pounds had, in effect, been pledged to support the production of Marillion's latest effort. After a little thought, the band decided to take the risk, kick off a pre-order campaign and run label-less. Officially launched 16 June 2000, Marillion asked their fans for sixteen pounds each with only the band's promise that an album would be made. Once again the response was overwhelming. By the end of June, the pre-orders had already crashed two servers! By the end of the campaign, a total of 12,674 copies had been sold in advance sales, raising a massive sum of 180,000 pounds. Publications as diverse as Christian Science Monitor, the FT, USA Today, BBC and Reuters called the Racket Club to find out what had happened, not to mention a number of bands including The Levellers and Toad The Wet Sprocket[1]. Commented Steve H to Rich Wilson, "We get emails from people saying 'I'd like to order a copy of your album' twelve months before it's out and here's two hundred quid. I only want one copy, but I want to be part of this thing. Then we get emails from people who say things like 'I've had a bit of a flutter and won a few hundred quid on the lottery, and I'd like to send £150 to you and where do you want it sending. I mean, that doesn't happen to Duran Duran! And that is more important to me than selling records or being on the radio."

It was a call to arms. "Earlier this month we decided to take the ultimate leap of faith in our fans," read a Web newsletter. "We're going to kick out as many of the cynics and the businessmen as we can, and replace them with our own team of accomplished professionals who are driven by as much faith as we are."

As the money rolled in, the band quickly realised that they could afford Dave Meegan as producer. Remarks Pete, "We'd been thinking about Dave ever since we hadn't used him." Dave's attention to detail (and determination to get the best sound possible) required time, and time meant money, here as anywhere else. Adds Pete, "We wanted to make an album that people believe in. Bringing Dave in at a relatively

manchineely fatal

When over in Barbados with Nick Van Eede, H took a bite from a small green apple that was lying in the sand. He became a little perturbed as locals ran towards him saying, "That's a Manchineel apple! Did you eat some of that? You gonna die boy!" Steve took the advice to drink seawater, then a bottle of Pepto Bismol and a can of condensed milk, while the island's doctor was asked questions on the radio. The doctor advised that the small bite Steve had taken wouldn't be fatal. Says Steve, "I felt dodgy for the next three weeks, but that could have been down to drinking seawater, condensed milk and too much rum punch!" Where was that one in the instructions?

early stage gave us a sense of belief, and the fans as well." The band did not get things all their own way, fan base or no fan base. In May 2000 there was an Internet poll where fans could vote their favourite band onto the Glastonbury shortlist. True to form, the Freaks list got wind of the event, and there followed a carefully orchestrated plan to vote for Marillion. "It was quite subtle hype and that was great," commented Mark at the time. Marillion reached the top three on the site, but despite this show of hands the application was rejected. "The management just said they couldn't take us or the poll seriously. As far as I could see, they were completely ignoring the results," said Mark. Can't win them all.

Meanwhile it was jamming, jamming, jamming. "We jammed forever!" says Ian.

The Recording

In early May 2000, Marillion were joined by Dave Meegan. Everything was very relaxed, with the band allowing time for each others' projects despite the feeling of the importance of getting it right. For example, three tracks were arranged with Pete still out of the country with Transatlantic. Once it started, recording proceeded at a brisk pace. "*'Anorak'* was one of those moments in time where we felt we had something to prove, we were very excited!" remarks Pete.

October 2000 saw Steve H take a break from the band, spending a week in Bath so he could finish off his lyrics. In an interview with Andy Fox on The Eagle FM, he commented, "I'm going to hole up in a little place there and get poetic for a bit!" One song in particular wasn't working - "I'd rewritten it about five times and every time I took it to Dave he'd say, 'Oh yeah, you know...' and I'd know it wasn't right, so I'd go away and write it again!" It wasn't until January 2001 that the track finally came together, helped by Nick Van Eede of Cutting Crew. For inspiration and support, Nick invited Steve out to where he was staying in Barbados; it would have been rude not to accept! Steve H recalled in an interview how, on one of his many sheets of paper Nick had written the words 'Map Of The World'. "I suggested we try this somehow as a chorus. On the fly he came up with the melody, and I moved it to coincide with a different part of the musical idea. This, at last, unlocked the song for me!" Despite the pain and anguish, H did without John Helmer's creative input once again. "I didn't actually get round to ringing John. I put it off and at one stage I thought I think I can do this myself and I suppose I more or less did..."

heart in the right place

Dave Meegan included some samples from 'Script', 'Brave' and 'Fugazi' in the middle section of 'If My Heart Were A Ball'. Can you spot them?

In January 2001 the album also picked up its name: *'Anoraknophobia'*. "What we are saying with the title," noted Rothers in an interview, "is that we have no fear of being known as a band with a devoted following." As H wrote on the fans-only cover, "We're anoraks too!" Dave Meegan took the role of chief fan. "I'm a big fan myself!" he laughs. "On *'Anorak'* there was an obligation to represent the fans. It makes a huge difference knowing that people really do care about the result. They spot the subtleties!" Echoing tracks like 'Out Of This World' on *'Afraid Of Sunlight'*, Dave used news clips in particular in 'When I Meet God'. These included reports varying from conflicts in Vietnam to the Middle East, from Sarah Payne and Damilola Taylor to Mohammed Jamal[2]. "If you have a tool like a song, you should take the opportunity to say something, says Dave. "It's a way to document history - you can smell it, feel it." True to form, Dave was left emotionally exhausted by the end of the production. "It's unavoidable when you're making records that do have emotions in them," he remarks. It was worth it: "It's probably the happiest I've ever been about anything I've worked on, 100%!" The band were also justly proud. "Dave's done a fantastic job, it's the band grooving, I mean really grooving for the first time ever!

The man is a God[3]!" laughed Steve H in a Web interview. "It's like having your own priest, engineering genius, philosopher, arbiter of taste, diplomat, best mate… rolled into one."

The pre-order deadline was extended from 31 December 2000 to early February 2001, by which time the mastering was complete. It was time to rock and roll.

'Anoraknophobia'

'Anoraknophobia', *then. Still, at the time of writing, "the new one"... As has been documented elsewhere,* 'Anoraknophobia' *was created under unique circumstances. Funded entirely by the fans, the band were conscious that there was an additional pressure to get it right, the band stating that they would need to pull something special from the bag to acknowledge the fans' contribution. As they would write in the fan-only edition of the album, "This is the 21st Century and everything is about hype - but not this. This is about passion."*

One of the key differences - as a result of the funding - was the ability to bring in the producer of choice - Dave Meegan, responsible for 'Brave' *and* 'Afraid Of Sunlight'. *One other thing happened before the release of the album, which hadn't happened for a while; the preview of material. The University tour saw 'Between You And Me', 'Quartz' and 'Map Of The World' all receive an airing, and those of us lucky enough to have seen the University tour knew we had something special waiting for us.*

'Anoraknophobia' then; a uniquely-funded, history-making, foot-tapping, gut-wrenching, heart-breaking, soul-shaking, brain-engaging, funk-tastic, soaring, grooving, glorious great beastie of an album.

From the opening notes of 'Between You And Me', the music is biting deeper, harder and more quickly than the last couple of albums. There's a freshness and an exuberance not heard for a while, and whilst 'BYAM' isn't seeking to be anything other than an anthemic rocker, it does it so, so well! Lyrically concerned with the magic that powers those special relationships, it is somewhat lightweight, save for the middle eight with its quiet insightful musing. If only someone would play this on the radio...

Barry-San not good man

It transpires that the artwork company had lifted the Barry character from a series of Nissan adverts in Japan, purportedly extolling the virtues of theft-proof cars.
You want to know what the coat hanger was really for? To break into the cars, of course!

'Quartz' is one of the most radical songs on the album. It's based around a monstrous walking bass line from Pete, and Steve Rothery's gonzo-funkoid wah-wah. Lyrically, the song details two people who are just that little bit too different to get along. The later part of the song uses images of two watches to contrast the two people - the clockwork person always half an hour late, easily wound up and susceptible to the elements, the digital watch immune to everything and always right. If there is a possible complaint to be made about the song, it is that (although it would mean losing a wonderful Rothery solo) it really should finish with the line, "One of these days... you're just gonna stop!"

Were 'Map Of The World' to come in contact with 'Holidays In Eden', they would explode! Where 'Holidays' was barbed and cynical about the idea of going travelling, 'Map' is joyous, looking at the journey as an escape from drudgery and greyness. There is something of Bruce Springsteen's 'Tunnel Of Love' to the main riff, and much of the spirit of Crowded House about the whole song (without rendering it a pastiche) and it is a song which revels in strong and simple songwriting.

The lush and expansive 'When I Meet God' certainly caused something of a stir with the fans when it came out. Powered by Mark Kelly's warmly textured keyboards, the song was recently described by H as saying, "Come down from that cloud and help us you uncaring, callous, bitch!" H is clearly being somewhat facetious there, but it gets to the core of the argument. What does not come through is that his frustration comes from a belief that such a beautiful galaxy seems to betray the hand of a guiding conscience... but how can such an entity not have the necessary compassion to help humanity rise above its failings? The sublime end section really does seem to suspend the listener in the vastness of space. "It's full of stars!" indeed...

'The Fruit Of The Wild Rose' comes in with a blues jazz riff from Steve Rothery then, with a clatter of snare from Ian, Pete joins with an insistent bass line. As H beings to sing, Mark comes in with a counterpoint melody. The lyric is a love song from the perspective of someone on tour missing his lover back in autumnal England, but there's something in the lyric which somehow calls to mind a 19th century sailor on the high seas. With a sudden burst of keyboards, the song picks up the tempo, whilst, almost buried in the background, Steve Rothery lays down a fuzzed solo. The traveller has turned and is heading for home and the music becomes full of a glorious pent-up eroticism, in anticipation of the two lovers meeting again. H spins a wonderful image of the woman's subconscious sexual writhing in her sleep - the pun "stir your hips" also referring to the red fruit that dots English hedgerows in the autumn.

'Separated Out' concerns feeling of unworthiness - "Am I enough of a freak to be worth paying to see?" There is a knowing wink to the Fish-era track 'Freaks' in the way the samples (from Todd Browning's 1932 movie 'Freaks') are used, by intimating that we're all freaks. The thumping track also has a resemblance to Julius Fucik's 'Entry of the Gladiators' (the clichéd choice of music used for film of clowns!). There is something of the feel of the *'Brave'*-era heavy tracks, but where those tracks weren't entirely convincing, 'Separated Out' and 'If My Heart Were A Ball' both fare much better. There's playfulness on show in the music that makes them far more convincing than if they had been played straight.

The centre piece of the album in many ways, 'This Is The 21st Century' sees Marillion incorporating a dancey drum loop, over which the band layer a moody classic. There are two main strands to the lyric; a discussion of science's debunking of the mysteries of life, and a couple finding their own magic in sensuality and love. H commented, "I personally refuse to accept that magic doesn't exist, and I think the day you accept that, you might as well throw yourself off a high building." As the song moves into an extended coda, the music becomes almost brutal, with Ian's drums smashing along with the beat, Pete's bass prowling malevolently, Mark's keyboards mechanized, with brutal bass chords throbbing underneath and Steve Rothery's guitar howling like a dangerous beast. Strangely, this section sounds simultaneously the most modern thing they have ever done but also recalls some of the more atmospheric parts of *'Misplaced Childhood'*. Sheer bloody genius!

'If My Heart Were A Ball, It Would Roll Uphill' is a strange hybrid beast of quasi-metal and film soundtrack stylings. H has said the lyric concerns, "Having a mad heart really. That simple. Having a heart that doesn't behave and can't and defies the laws of physics." Once more Pete's bass playing is really superb on this track, thrumming excitedly on the choruses and skulking along like the darkest funk you've ever heard on the verses. Ian sounds like he's having a ball too, battering around his kit like a mad thing. An echo of the past appears in the middle eight, with a sample of 'Chelsea Monday' from the debut album under it. The middle eight gives way to an 'Interior Lulu'-esque outro, with all the instruments gradually building and pushing the song home, whilst H strings together a collage lyric taken from all the songs on the album, until it gradually subsides into silence.

All the listener can do is sit back and contemplate. There's a feeling of having been somewhere amazing on this album - the very best of the band concentrated into 63 astonishing minutes - a huge amount of ground covered. It leaves the listener with one certainty - the magic certainly isn't dead. We can only wonder where this incredible band will take us next time.

The cover was a total departure from what had gone before. Featuring the iconic cartoon anorak Barry, the cover was brighter, simpler and fresher than anything in recent years. This clarity of cover reflected the music within. Barry has gone on to become something of an iconic figure for the band. Recently, a comment from Pete Trewavas hinted that the little fella still had gainful employment ahead of him...

the build-up

Coupled with a series of lucky coincidences, the considerable back-room effort from Lucy Jordache was starting to yield a number of high profile TV appearances. One appearance was on ITV's 'Airline'[4], triggered when the band had just flown in from Holland on EasyJet. "I was booking tickets for the fan club tour and I said I would be using cheap flights. When asked why, I said that's 450 quid but that's for 10 people!" On the Easyjet website there was a question - "If you are flying with EasyJet in the near future and have an interesting reason for your trip, why not let us know?" so Lucy did. The boys ended up playing an acoustic 'Eighty Days' to an impromptu audience in the middle of the arrival lounge, with a number of people (including Ian) throwing coins at them! Then, in December, a BBC team went to the Racket Club to film a documentary about how the Internet had changed people's lives. This time, the initiative came from the BBC. "An email was sent by a researcher who had read our website," explains Lucy. Called 'The Future Just Happened'[5], it was hosted by Michael Lewis, who even gave the band money for the pre-order! Together, the appearances served to generate a new perspective on the band - not as rock stars or prog revivalists, but as a band no more and no less.

Meanwhile, Marillion had a hungry audience to satisfy and the steps it took would not disappoint.

Steve H with the author, Oswestry

On the Stage

Marillion's emergence into the lights started in a gentlemanly fashion, with a number of one-off gigs and short tours starting in the middle of November 2000. The first stop was the Bass Museum in Burton On Trent, as Sam Hill, the bar manager had contacted the band to propose a couple of dates at his joint. As far as the Marillos were concerned, the venue was unusual, there was a gap in the schedules and so the go-ahead was given. "For us, it was the novelty factor," says Mark. Unfortunately, like Oswestry before it, Bass was not well-equipped to cope with the international onslaught of Marillion fans. Tickets for the dates on 16-17 November were made available through 'the Bass Museum telephone hotline', which was in fact a two-port switchboard. It was chaos: the lines jammed within minutes, and all tickets were sold out within a few hours of the switchboard opening. The Bass gigs may have been a cause of much wailing and gnashing of teeth amongst those who failed to get tickets, but were a stonking success for the fans who did. The gigs were recorded for a Web cast [6] by Matt Urban and his team from Möbius Media, who had come over from the US. "We love these guys," responded Matt. "It's just an excuse to cover the things we enjoy!" The band isn't likely to return to Bass, due to a Blues Brother-esque scene on the Thursday night. "We were offered free beer for a year if we performed," says Mark, "Trouble was, the first night we practically drank the bar dry, so they went back on their offer!"

Christmas 2000 saw a whirlwind fan club tour, with dates in Milan, Oslo, Rotterdam, Paris, Barcelona, London and Leeds. The Web Christmas convention was at La Scala, near Kings Cross in London, where Mark Kelly hosted an unforgettable 'Who Wants To Be A Marillionaire' trivia quiz, won by fan Paul Rose [7]. Then in early 2001, the band decided to "go back to its roots" and play to a new generation of fans. "We wanted a back to the floor approach," explains H. "We'd got into an impasse with our agent, we were a standing joke with the NME, we were not played on the radio, we thought if students could actually see the band it would cut through the prejudices! The agent said, 'There isn't a university circuit any more,' but what he really meant was that he wouldn't make any money! So Lucy got on the blower!" That she did, first by asking the mailing lists which universities might make suitable venues. Smiles Lucy, "People didn't believe it was *the* Marillion when I was phoning up! They wanted to know why we wanted to play in such small places, so I said we wanted to play to students as they had no preconceptions and would love the music if they got a chance to hear it." It wasn't an out-and-out success - no money was made on the University tour, but at least a new audience was made aware of the band. "It didn't quite achieve all we had hoped for," comments Mark Kelly. As such, it was illustrative of the try anything approach: not all shots were going to hit the target.

a wise man once wrote...

In Ridley Scott's 'Blade Runner', the line "If you could only see what I've seen with your eyes," was uttered by Rutger Hauer as replicant Roy Batty to Cho, the character who designed the eyes for replicants manufactured in the mirrored building of the Tyrell Corporation.

In February 2001, Steve Rothery played at the Royal Albert Hall with The Eddie Jordan All Stars for the Professor Sid Watkins[8] Brain and Spine Foundation. He managed to entice Tony Hadley and Nick Mason, as well as bringing along Ian and Pete for musical and moral support! Then, on 16 March came a 'Stranger By The Minute' performance at Oswestry, coinciding with the UK Comic Relief telethon. As well as Steve, Steve and Pete, the line-up included Phil Beaumont on drums, guitarist Matt Prior and Paul Sturman on vocals. "A very late addition," according to Pete, was Darren Wharton, keyboard player from Thin Lizzy and Dare. A highlight for Pete was to sing 'White Room' by Cream and Tom Petty's 'Freefalling'. "This was the first time I'd done any lead vocals since I was in my teens!" says Pete.

Out Of This World

The events of March 2001 were touching to all concerned. Bill Smith[9] was a Marillion fan and an established deep water diver who had been inspired by Hogarth's lyrics to look for Donald Campbell's Bluebird. "I was testing some underwater kit when I first heard 'Out Of This World'," recalls Bill. The footage that Dave Meegan had included in the middle section drew him in. "Donald Campbell was saying, 'Alpha to Base, Alpha to Base,' then I couldn't work out the next bit so I went and bought a video of the crash to see if I could figure it out." As Bill concentrated on deciphering Donald's words he knew he had no choice but to go and look for the ill-fated craft. "I was hooked on how it went from grace to violence in a split second... I thought, a couple of months up at Coniston, make a nice break..."

Finally, on 17 January 2001, after four years of weekends searching (during which nearly an entire team of divers had turned their backs on the skipper), Bill actually found it. With faithful sonar op. Al Douglas and a new chap called Graham Woodfield manning the surface vessel, Bill had dived with only one torch working. He was about to return when his flipper snagged on a piece of aluminium. "I knew immediately what it was," remarks Bill. "My blood turned to ice water as I realised." He swam back to what he discovered was the tail fin and wiped the silt and grime off a painted Union Jack, still preserved in the cold waters after 34 years. Bill had to spend several minutes decompressing just yards from the surface, before he could swim up and tell his remaining co-conspirators the good news. "I was buzzing when I came back up!" he laughs. In the days that followed, as well as informing Gina Campbell and the BBC, Bill got the two Steves' numbers from his old pal Fish and called them to tell them what had happened. "I asked, do you want to come to the lifting?" says Bill. Not only that, he asked Rothers to be his official photographer.

The raising of the Bluebird took place on 8 March 2001, attended by Messrs Rothery and Hogarth who had driven up the night before. As they arrived at Lake Coniston the next morning, they met a wet-suited and silly-hatted Bill Smith. He had a crocodile-tail hat that had been his 'searching hat' for ten years of diving. He marched them through the lines of police and "bemused officials" and out on to the jetty, where Rothers readied his cameras. Given that Bill had deliberately kept the massed ranks of media behind a barrier on the shore, journalists were visibly spitting when they saw the pair out on the jetty, cameras flashing and talking to whoever they pleased. Only one journalist, a lady from the Westmoreland Gazette, was allowed onto the jetty alongside H and Rothers. "I was asked, what about him with the cameras?" remembers Bill. "I said, He's a rock guitarist, name's Steve Rothery, you can ask him yourself if you like!" As for Rothers, he was honoured just to be there. "To have reported something that happened in history, and for that to be a catalyst to more history being made, it was amazing," says Steve.

Eventually, at 10.45, the Bluebird broke the surface. Remembers H, "I stood right next to the Bluebird as the tail fin broke the water. I was standing there thinking, My God, I've brought this about and nobody knows." The course of events unfolded as they should: with much skill and careful handling the craft was manoeuvred onto a trailer, towed up to the jetty and then into a boathouse on the shore. Steve H was photographed by Reuters man Jon Super, looking down the shore as he held the nose-cone. "To be handed the nose-cone, which was the first thing that hit the water..." H had his most disturbing moment in the boathouse when he spied a fragment of seat belt material still attached to a bent bolt. Despite the delight, there was an inordinate feeling of sorrow shared by onlooker and crew alike.

That evening, the boys checked into The Black Bull in Coniston, joining Bill and the divers at a celebration dinner before walking round the corner to The Sun Inn for a few jars. At 11.30, the boys went back to the Bull to find themselves locked out but eventually got to bed! Meanwhile, upset at being ostracised, the world's press were in no mood for celebration. They accused Bill Smith and his team of jubilant behaviour during and following the raising of the Bluebird. Bill wasn't helped by his penchant for silly hats, not to mention his thumbs-up sign from the back of the hull when it emerged from the water - a renowned symbol of irreverence. The final straw was undoubtedly his own and his crew's celebratory behaviour in the Sun Inn that evening. How very un-British and undignified to have a few jars at the end of a four-year journey to find a heroic craft, inspired by a song.

separating out

On the back of the pre-order, the band found itself in a unique negotiating position. It would have been so easy to cock a snoop at the big boys but instead, Marillion chose to woo the major labels with the promise of greater sales to come. Explains Lucy, "We told them we had already sold 12,000 albums, the projected sales were at least 100,000, the record was made and all they had to do was get it in the shops." This was a pragmatic decision - if there was one thing the majors could do, it was organise worldwide distribution. Adds Pete, "It costs money to put records in shops. Turnover is everything, and big record companies do have the bargaining power." They also had man-power, and the international presence necessary to arrange a globality of deals.

White Buffalo invade the stage at the end of the *'Anoraknophobia'* Tour

A number of labels bit the bait, including old, faithful EMI. In the end the album was released on the EMI label in UK and Europe, Sanctuary in the US and Canada, and EMI Liberty everywhere else.

Anorak and Roll

Prior to the launch of the album, in once-traditional style, a single was released - but, since this is the Internet age, it was no ordinary single. 'This Is The 21st Century' was made available for download from MP3.com, and was downloaded enough to achieve No.1 in the alternative charts (even the category was a credit), and No.2 overall on the entire MP3.com site.

Before the album went on general release, it was issued as a special edition to the fans which listed the first six thousand pre-ordering names. "This is your album" said H in

the sleeve notes. The official release date was accompanied by a press release, written in part by Rich Wilson, the rest dictated directly by the band. The first paragraph read, "You're all wrong about Marillion, just listen to it!" Unfortunately this served only to further entrench much of the music press. The response was one of, 'Who the hell do they think you are?' After all, Marillion were breaking the golden rule of never dictating to journalists. Even long-time allies Classic Rock were decidedly angry, as reflected by their album review. The Sun newspaper mentioned Marillion in its daily Bizarre column, with the words "I see rockers Marillion are as pretentious as ever…" It wasn't long before the fan emails started to fly. According to Lucy, "The Sun was overwhelmed with emails and said they had never seen a response like it!"

Far from the madding cries, Australian Guitar magazine awarded the album four stars out of five. "One of this years most interesting albums," went the review, with the "ponderous" 'If My Heart Were A Ball' more than made up for by "catchy summer song" 'Between You and Me', and the "slick grooves" of 'Quartz'. In the US, the Christian Science Monitor described the album as a "compelling series of long, intricate journeys, with unexpected tangents from rocking dub grooves to ambient moments."

With the release out of the way, it was back on tour again, with what was to be (according to the Web), "The most intensive bout of European touring in recent years." The first date was Dublin on 15 May 2001. The Manchester Academy gig four days later was attended by the Bluebird team including Bill Smith, who was chuffed to hear how 'Out Of This World' "got a fantastic reception from the fans." A second leg of the tour (with a set list largely decided by a poll of the fans) reached places that had long since been missed out, such as Poland (played last in 1994). One date was in the Azores, "The biggest gig the island had ever witnessed!" according to Colin Price. The event happened as a spin-off from the band's stop in Portugal, says Pete, "Our promoters got excited when they saw us play live in Portugal, they asked if we'd play the Azores as well! The show was amazing because we played to 10,000 people! It was weird because obviously they didn't really know anything about us." "We could have been anybody as far as they were concerned," agreed Steve Rothery. "Playing to that many people who don't know you from Adam, it's very hard work!" Surprisingly, 'Cannibal Surf Babe' wasn't in the set.

Alas, a US tour was still not a possibility. "We had been offered a 40 festival tour in September 2001, but the people organizing it dropped off the radar!" commented Steve Rothery.

An American Freak In London by Andy Saks

It's scary what can happen when you watch Marillion's 'Shot In The Dark' concert video, well, in the dark. All kinds of crazy thoughts can suddenly seem reasonable. Like how England isn't really that far away from Los Angeles. And how transcontinental plane tickets aren't really that expensive. And how intense, how driven, how passionate Steve Hogarth looks singing the ending section of 'Afraid Of Sunlight' in that video. And so it was that I found myself shoehorned into a window seat on a Virgin Atlantic red-eye to London, on my way to see my favourite band in the world, determined that if they couldn't cross the Pond to see us Americans, then I would cross it to see them. I had carved out just enough time for four shows over five days, in Hemel Hempstead, Manchester, Wolverhampton, and London, before reality called me Stateside again.

I landed at Heathrow and headed for the "flat" (note my use of the local lingo) of a freak named John Boye, who had graciously offered to put me up for the night. John met me with his wife and kids, and we spent the first couple of hours trading Marillion stories. After a long midday nap to recover my strength, we donned our concert t-shirts, and set out by car for the first show in Hemel Hempstead. We parked near the venue, and entered the pub next door, slated as the gathering spot of that evening's 'freak meet'. Suddenly I was surrounded by fans who were eager to discuss all things Marillion: favourite songs, best concerts, and stories of meeting the band. And in public, too! I was in heaven, and among friends.

It all passed in a heavenly blur. Four days later, I'd taken in the shows at the Dacorum Pavilion, the Manchester Academy and the Wolverhampton Civic, and now I was outside the Forum a couple of hours before showtime. I strolled next door to the Bull & Gate pub, where I discovered the usual cast of pre-show characters. Rumours were flying about Barry the Anorak. As he was born on May 22, 1980, this was his 21st birthday, and everyone suspected the band would do something special for the occasion. A birthday song? Perhaps the first live performance of 'This Is The 21st Century'? We'd have to wait and see. I drank a couple of pints and headed over to the Forum.

We got in, claimed our spots near the stage, and waited. Another great concert! Not quite on par with Manchester and Wolverhampton, but a solid, fun effort nonetheless. And we soon discovered how we'd celebrate Barry's 21st birthday: between 'Rich' and 'Man Of A Thousand Faces', Lucy brought a giant cake onstage, in the shape of Barry himself! We sang a sloppy version of 'Happy Birthday', and Lucy retreated backstage, promising to come back later and hand out the pieces. Sure enough, between encores, Mark came onstage with a box full of Barry cake, and started throwing pieces into the audience. He tossed one right to me, and I'm ashamed to say I bobbled it and dropped it! The "five second rule" was in effect, and I managed to quickly pick it up off the floor, and hand out a few scraps to the folks around me, who eagerly took their bites. As it turns out, Barry tastes a lot like cornbread!

Finally the show ended to thunderous applause, and I regrouped with John and new friends, Max and Fi at the back of the hall. Upstairs, we each grabbed a pint, and after a few minutes, the boys filtered into the room. I abandoned any pretence of maturity, and reverted to 'pathetic adoring fan' mode. Max and I set about getting me a picture with each of the boys. Max would tap each band member on the shoulder, and introduce me as "this bloke who came all the way from Los Angeles" and I would shake their hands, gush briefly, and grab a picture. We said a quick hello to H, Ian, Mark and Steve, and did manage a picture with each.

John and I drove back to his flat, I collapsed on his couch for a few hours, and suddenly it was morning. We walked together to the Tube station, John got off at his stop for work, and I continued all the way to Heathrow, and America. And then, just like that, it was over. I went straight from Dulles Airport in D.C. to a meeting at the Washington Convention Center with people who couldn't understand why I'd gone all the way to England to see a band they'd never heard of. I just smiled.

I came for the music, and I left with an adventure in my pocket, and the sounds of the best band in the world still ringing in my ears.

Case closed.

moving on

At the end of the summer 2001, with the band refreshed and ready for the tour's second leg, ideas started to form about what could happen next. Not everything went as planned, but nobody could have predicted the reasons why.

Taking Stock

Confidence was running high. On 10 September 2001, the band decided to release its first proper CD-based [10] single since 'These Chains' almost 3 years before. This was not done in the traditional way. Fans could buy the single from the Web site, and the offer was two-for-one, with the plan being that the second copy could be sent to radio stations, music mags, friends and family. Two days later, Steve Hogarth was down to sing at Donald Campbell's funeral, a poignant event which was almost inevitably going to reach the newspapers. But then came September 11, and all plans, thoughts and aspirations went out of the window. Steve's most personal of shows had to go on: he had "the honour" to cast a handful of earth onto Donald's coffin, once it had been lowered into the ground. "I said goodbye and wished him well as I did so. All this to a man I never knew." commented Steve in his diary. "And so, for me, a strange cycle was complete."

For Marillion as well, things had to continue. "We didn't contemplate cancelling the tour. Hard as it sounds, life had to go on or the terrorists would have won," remarks Lucy. The 15-date second leg of the tour was planned to start at the Palazzo Ducale in Lucca, Italy on 15 September, taking in the UK, France, Holland and Germany before finishing at Bydgoszcz, Poland on 26 October. H confided in Lucy that the Italy gig was the hardest gig he had ever done, because nothing seemed important any more. The line "There's a man up in a mirrored building, and he just bought the world," nearly brought everything to a halt as H could barely make it through the rest of the song. "Emotionally, logistically, everything was difficult," comments Lucy.

The band was supported by White Buffalo, who Marillion had met through Dave Meegan [11]. Initially a three piece with Matt Round on bass, Evan Jenkins on drums, and Phil Campbell on everything else, just before the tour Matt was replaced by Australian Rex Horan. "I was stoked, it was our first time as a group to play outside the UK." says Rex. "There was not much time for me to think about what was going on as I was called in without very much notice." Commented Phil in a Web interview, "We can't express enough gratitude toward Marillion. They've been so helpful. It gave us the opportunity to play in decent houses with appreciative audiences." The rapport between the two bands grew until, says Rex, "Our relationships had spilled over into our music and Steve R had asked to perform 'Stormtrooper' with us. He played with us at the Polish shows. He was communicative and considerate in his playing. The punters loved it!" Remarks H, "It was a privilege to have them there, just for the vibe!"

The band leaves the stage, Utrecht, November 2001

Meanwhile, the singles campaign was determined to keep on course. Aided by long-time fan (and New Yorker) Christine Cooper, Lucy Jordache set about the uphill struggle to gain the band some radio airplay. Comments Christine, "The politicians told us to try and live our lives as normal, so we felt the best thing to do was press ahead with the campaign." Soon, emails started flooding in from fans worldwide, saying where they had sent their singles, and confirmations of radio stations that had actually played it. The bulk may have been from well-established fanbases in the UK, France, Germany and the USA, but there were emails from far-flung corners of the world such as Australia, New Zealand, Mexico, Chile, Venezuela, the Czech Republic, Poland and even Brunei! The fans were in their element - one fan even manned the telephone lines of a charity telethon "so he could slip it on to the airwaves!" Another fan "hired someone to dress as a banana," who marched into the studio of his local radio station and handed the DJ a copy of the single! Remarks Christine, "These are by no means unusual examples!" The result was that the single was playlisted on some BBC local radio stations, and was played frequently by Whispering Bob Harris on BBC Radio 2.

Over 10,000 copies of the single were sold, easily enough to get chart status had the mail-order channel been seen as valid by the chart makers.

The last piece in the puzzle was the Front Row Club (FRC), announced shortly before Christmas 2001 in an eWeb. The FRC was initiated by Steve Hogarth: his plan was to make economically viable the release of audio material from Marillion's huge (and that's not understating it) archives. The eWeb described "live recordings - warts and all - for your listening pleasure!" Steve's first port of call was King Crimson, whose own initiative had inspired the FRC in the first place. "If you look at the description of the King Crimson Collectors Club, it's word for word the same as the Front Row Club," says Erik. "We decided we'd be happy as long as we hit 500 members, the number we'd need to break even," Erik continues. The numbers were more than triple the expectation.

Return Of The Sil

The idea for a convention formed as Lucy Jordache watched fans meeting up before gigs. "I had an idea that here was a chance to get two thousand people to meet up with each other, in a setting where it was acceptable to be a Marillion fan," says Lucy, who had worked with The Stranglers and their manager Sil Wilcox in her time at EMI. "I saw The Stranglers were having a convention at Pontins, so I called up Sil and it turned out he was setting up a company to manage conventions," says Lucy. So, she proposed it to the band. "They all said, 'but what if it doesn't work?' I said, 'Don't worry, it'll make a lot of money and the fans will love it!'" "Sil Wilcox had done it already, it had been a success spiritually and financially, and it sounded like a laugh!" enthuses H. "Nobody thought it was going to be as much of a success as it was!"

Following the tried-and-trusted formula of asking the fans, when sufficient 'Yes' votes arrived in Marillion's email, it was time to make it happen. Before long, however, it became clear what a huge challenge it was going to be: logistics were one thing, but there were also bands to invite, events to organise, set lists to decide. Then there came the big one: the band decided to play *'Brave'* in its entirety. Not only had this not been done since 1994, but all agreed to keep everything down to the last detail, with Michael Hunter's 'River' music, slide shows, men in balaclavas, even the re-emergence of Steve H's red Stratocaster. The rehearsals were less fraught than expected. "We all did a bit of homework," commented Ian, "It's burnt into the old memory banks somewhere because, when we actually start playing, I'll start doing fills and whatnot and it'll just happen." Ian had the idea of putting *'Brave'* on the Friday night, that way the band could relax for the rest of the weekend. "The whole weekend should be a party, but it's a bit difficult with *'Brave'* isn't it, to have a laugh..."

As the plans developed and information started leaking out, the excitement of the fans became palpable. "Wild horses couldn't keep me away from hearing *'Brave'* live at last!" says fan Krys Boswell. Adds fan John Boye, "Ironic indeed, considering the mixed reaction that *'Brave'* had received the first time around, that it would be the mainstay of the weekend seven years later." Before the weekend proper, the band organised a *'Brave'* warm-up gig. Steve H had been talking to old friend Billy Manning, who used to run Dingwalls, and who was now operating Jumping Jak's club in Cardiff. "He asked, would we fancy doing it," recalls H. The band was worried about spoiling the one-off nature of Pontins, but after all, commented Ian, "Every show in the West End has a dress rehearsal!"

Taking place between 5-7 April 2002, the convention itself was a ball. The international fans braved the hardships of the Pontins chalets and had a good time. No, an excellent time. Some of Marillion's favourite support acts were there, including Robin Boult, Aziz Ibrahim, White Buffalo and Cry No More. Says Aziz Ibrahim, "Pontins was one of those places I always wanted to go when I was a kid, I'd only ever seen it in the Beano and 'Carry On' films. When I got there it was quite a shock!" There was even an outing, of Steve Rothery's Wishing Tree Project with Hannah Stobart, Paul Craddick and Steve's wife Jo. A Marillion museum showed exhibits including Mark's original Mellotron, which had sat gathering dust in his parents' garage for many years, and a newly restored Strange Engine. "It was a task slightly bigger than I anticipated," explained James Fishwick of the Web UK, who was tasked with the restoration work. "Most of the parts I made had to be hand-finished from either wood or metal to look like the album photo."

As well as *'Brave'*, and the band's own performances, a highlight of the weekend was Swap The Band, in which competition-winning fans had the chance to take the place of their favourite band member. The band were on hand most of

from dusk till dot

Following the success of *'The Making Of 'Brave'*, a series of *'Making Of...'* albums was released. The titles were set by the winners of a competition. According to Pete, the "painstakingly slow trail" resulted in band members and staff each taking home tens of hours of DAT tapes to listen to. "Most of the time it was a lot of fun, but some of it was tedious to say the least!" Carl Glover designed the covers - "For the cover to *'Making Of Radiat1On'* I had my daughter in a carrier on my back, she started screaming 'cos it was so cold!"

Lucy Jordache

Lucy first got into Marillion when she saw a picture disc at her local record shop in St Albans. "I used to take pocket money and buy something because I liked the look of them," Lucy explains. "I saw *'Market Square Heroes'*, I really liked the cover for some bizarre reason!" Though Lucy found the music to be lacking, sibling rivalry took its effect. "My brother hated it so I pretended I liked it!" The first album pretty much passed Lucy by, but *'Fugazi'* did not. "I heard 'Assassing' and became an überfan overnight! But then, all my friends hated it, so maybe I was being stubborn again..." It was the live performances that hooked Lucy in the end, in particular, the nights spent at the Hammersmith Odeon. "I just kept going back to see them," she says.

Joining an advertising agency after leaving college, Lucy decided after two years that music was where her heart was. "I'd always had a passion for music," says Lucy, "I'd always spent my money on music and spent my time watching bands. I realised I should go and follow my heart." Taking a major pay cut, she joined EMI's sales department as a junior. Meanwhile, her passion for Marillion had continued to grow unabated. In 1994, Lucy offered her services to Bonnie and Wayne at The Web ("I was angry - I'd found out some tour dates from Kerrang! so I wrote to them and asked if I could assist.") and would go up at weekends to help.

Lucy's time at EMI was punctuated by first the *'Best Of Both Worlds'* album (which she helped with in her spare time while she was still working in the sales division) and the remasters series. Lucy's role as fan representative prompted Mark Kelly to call her up. "Come and talk, we want you to work for us," he said. The brief was to try and get Marillion's name back out there. From Lucy's perspective it was, "in a sad and sappy way, a dream come true. I was intrigued!"

Lucy's role has changed beyond recognition in the 18 months since she joined the band - within 6 months, the band had fired its agent/promoter and Lucy has been looking for record deals, fixing gigs as well as acting in the marketing role. "I'm a manager with a small m," explains Lucy. "When the PR went out with the album, it said 'Representation by Lucy Jordache,' I thought that's cool!" To quote H, "although we manage ourselves, to all intents and purposes you are our manager." "I don't know anyone else in the industry who does what I do," comments Lucy. "My job is different every day, I'm given free rein. 9 times out of 10 things will fail but the one that comes together is worth its weight in gold."

"And," Lucy concludes, "I'm still not bored of Marillion!"

the weekend, milling around, chatting and signing autographs with impunity. A signing session was organised, but the queue was so long that after several hours of diligent attention to their fans, the band members had to call it a day. After all, they had a gig to play! Even then, the boys organised another session the next day to deal with the fans who had gone away empty handed. Proof, if it were still necessary, of the commitment from both sides. What marked the event in particular was the lack of trouble. "I've never seen anything like it," remarked one of the security staff. "Not a single fight, everyone's been wonderful". To cap it all, a team of journalists from Q magazine attended the event, giving Marillion its first column inches in that particular magazine for several years.

An average bunch of fans at Pontins

When the weekend was over, as the fans left with their t-shirts, photos and happy memories, the band, its crew and staff were left to clear up, tie up loose ends and make their own ways back home. Wrote Steve Hogarth, "We've all become caught up in something that transcends any relationship a band has had with its fans in the past." What was clear was that the vein had been tapped, the door had been opened.

The Road To Pontins by Joe del Tufo, Studio M

We were listening to 'This Is The 21st Century' on the morning the World Trade Center was destroyed. It was hauntingly appropriate, especially in retrospect. It was a sad, strange, but somehow uplifting time. I was listening to '21st Century' on my iPod as we left the rain of Philadelphia for Heathrow - our first flight since the disaster. Sure, there were the ambitious security measures, and the ever-present Atlantic turbulence, but for the most part we were focused on getting to film Marillion for three days for a DVD and webcast release.

On arrival in England, the four-man Studio M team (Barry Crell, Matt Urban, Derek Perduta and myself) vaulted out of London and headed for Brean. The rolling hills and lush countryside were a welcome departure from the overdeveloped metamall that we call nature back home. As we approached however, a surreal, Stephen King-like carnival atmosphere rose over the horizon. I remember someone mouthing "I hope this isn't it." But it was, basically, it. We had arrived at Pontins.

Erik soon fetched us from the reception area, and we found ourselves listening to the band winding up their weeks of warm-ups for the gig. Somewhere inside a very inspired version of the 'This Town' suite, I suddenly felt all of the exhaustion just slip out of me. We were here. And it didn't matter where here was. Ian played effortlessly, the ubiquitous cigarette smoke spiralling up. H was hopping around, Mark seemed relaxed and ready to go, and Steve R. was just shredding the solo. There were maybe 15 people in the room.

We met the enigmatic and unforgettable Boom Boom Boys, Paul and Jayce, who produced the stellar 'Shot In The Dark' show. They seemed as energized and excited as us. The plan was that they would produce the *'Brave'* show, and utilize our hands to help with the nine camera shoot that would occur that night. We were to produce the Saturday Setlist Bingo show, and we were going to handle the Swap The Band, Acoustic Set and The Wishing Tree sets

The fans queue to meet their heroes at Pontins

separately. We had a few pints at the Queen Vic and discussed how we were going to pull off this rather complex shoot. A rough working plan in place, we grabbed a few monitors and headed back to the room, where we watched hours of archival footage shot by the Boys de Boom over the last few years. Barry and Derek returned with dinner, but even our lard-loving American bodies were not quite prepared for the full horror of Brean fish and chips.

Friday dawned. Paul and Jayce had matching bags full of chocolate and other caramel-based goodies they had deemed "Vitamin F," to keep everything moving smoothly through the morning. Sound check for the *'Brave'* set went well, with the piece sounding more like the album itself than ever before. We filmed Aziz and Robin Boult, who were both very diverse and exceptional in their own ways. Music was in the air. It had all begun.

It was worth the trip just to finally get to experience *'Brave'* in its full glory. I saw a lot of tears in the crowd, in and around 'Falling From The Moon'. As I stood on top of the riser with the camera, I saw a kid on his dad's shoulder, singing along; and a woman who must be pushing seventy, singing along. I don't think I'd really "gotten" the Marillion community until this weekend - just what one band can do. This is something very distinct from what Radiohead or Dave Matthews or even U2 fans have - on a different scale it kind of reminds me of the magic I see in the eyes of Beatles' fans, when they talk about way back when. Not just obsessed, not just emotionally invested, but also related. It's cool to be part of.

Saturday, and this was the big one for Studio M. On top of the main event we were filming the Swap The Band and Wishing Tree set as well. We were 'only' using six video cameras for this one with both DVD and webcast material in mind, and I would be shooting still photos in the pit. Barry and Jayce were set up on tripods and Paul had a roamer. We had pencil-cams fixed on Ian and Mark, and Matt was shooting from a riser by the soundboard.

Swap The Band was much, much cooler than I had imagined. Despite nerves, and in some cases having to play songs they had not practiced, everyone involved did a top-notch job. This was really the heart and soul of the weekend, and it was appropriate that it anchored the event as it did. Could there be a better story than a guy who sells his drum kit to fly from Australia to the event to play drums with his favorite band? If you thought that guy nailed the solo in 'Easter' you should have heard it during soundcheck. I was standing next to Rothers sidestage, he raised his eyebrow and grinned.

The Wishing Tree were glorious in their much-too-brief set. I'm happy to shoot photos of Hannah any time, please find me. Cry No More was amusing, and their one 'hit' song really was quite memorable. Setlist Bingo was finally upon us and, again I won't go into detail about the show itself, but it was as if the hand of God was actually selecting the songs. In actuality, it was Roy from Cry No More, who was funny in an intensely crass kind of way. The music itself, as well as the band's stage presence, stood in stark contrast to the 'Brave' set. The performance was rife with energy, and it was certainly a challenge tracking H across the stage.

For Sunday Brunch, we were treated to a brief acoustic thank you. It was really something of a long encore to a very long weekend. If anything is going to make this band it is the passion of the people involved in it. To a person, Marillion

Marillion Weekend at Pontins

surround themselves with people who not only love the music, but are also passionate about making sure you get the opportunity to love the music too (and in the coolest ways).

After that it was homeward bound, the Brean winds at our back. A real close call on the M3 on the way back to London notwithstanding. One second we were going 85, the next second we were stopped with five cars spinning off the road behind us. Back in the USA, where the line at customs was almost as long as the Marillion signing line. Back in the real world. Until next year, that is...

look on the bright side

As the doors closed on the Pontins Holiday Centre at Brean Sands, so did a chapter. The past five years have been a time of withdrawal, of discovery and learning, from experience, that there really is a better way of life than that proposed by the mainstream music industry. Like a mid-life company worker who leaves a steady job and sets off to follow a dream, Marillion chose to break with convention and trust its instincts. As a result it has toured a continent at the invitation of its fans, recorded an album without an advance, played its biggest tour in years and seen 1,800 people travel from all over the world to its convention. At each stage people said it couldn't be done, but it has, again and again and again. Extrapolate a few years more and all the dreams will come true: the hit single, the radio play, the household name across the globe. Or will they?

Not only are such thoughts trite and unrealistic. They may also be counter-productive, if they go against the spiritual core of what the band has become. Paradoxically central to the vision is a desire that Marillion will be re-adopted by the mainstream, that the name that has been a millstone for so many years can stand for something else in people's minds than a quirky Eighties rock band. The band's biggest challenge lies in the future, as it attempts to sustain its growing popularity and build its image, while keeping true to its ideals and avoiding the complacency that comes with having such a devoted following.

Rather than dwelling on such matters, it would be better to take a few leaves from Pete, Ian, Steve, Steve and Mark's own book. First and foremost, Marillion's focus is on the music, as they continue to play what they want to hear. This is coupled with an overwhelming desire to experiment, to try out new musical ideas and new ways to relate to the fans: nothing is ever rejected out of hand. Finally there is a determination in each and every person to succeed, to improve, to give the very best possible. Says Aziz Ibrahim, "Their perseverance, their will to survive, I've never seen it so strong in a band."

This isn't about master plans and strategies, or fears and dreams; this is about a passion for making the best music possible, and against a background of cynics and thieves, getting it out to those who care.

On 22 April 2002, twenty-five years after the partnership between Mick Pointer and Doug Irving was first cemented, Marillion released a live album. Titled *'Anorak In The UK'*, it's a great live album, recorded on an occasion when the rapport between band and audience has never been stronger. There will be more music, and, whether it is adopted by the mainstream or not, it will be great music. There will be more gigs, and they will be great gigs. There will be new ways for fans to participate in what is a truly unique relationship, forged over many years, with a band of fellows whose hearts are so absolutely in the right place that it hurts.

Never mind the hobbits, indeed.

NOTES: 1 The famous one, not the same band that gave advice to Pete, all those years ago! **2** All children who have been killed in acts of violence, in war or in peace. **3** His son was born on Christmas Day. **4** Shown in April 2001. **5** Shown in June 2001. **6** To be issued from Racket Records on DVD. **7** He won an exclusive recording of the Beatles' 'Let It Be', from the Bass soundcheck. **8** Chief Medial Advisor to Formula One motor racing. **9** Not the same as Bill Smith Studios. **10** As opposed to download. **11** The name comes from a song on *'Fresh New Life'*, Phil Campbell's solo album produced by Dave Meegan.

the anorak bit...

appendix one we're the band

Marillion is no ordinary bunch of fellows, and how could they be? Who in their right mind would choose a life that alternates time on the road away from family and friends, spent in cramped buses, airport lounges and hotel rooms, with time in and out of the studio spent under intense pressure to produce yet more creative output. In addition, players need to get on with each other. Forget the hiking treks and Outward Bound courses, there can be no more intense team building experience than working as a band. Every note, every chord, every key press and drum beat needs to be tightly bound with the outputs of the others. In writing and recording, the steps of a delicate dance are performed as one person's evolving ideas are accepted, rejected or built upon by the others.

For the outsider, there appears to be a strange magic involved in making and performing music, as if it comes from nowhere in an inspired, near-final form. From the inside, there may be magical moments but there is no magic formula. There is no fount of inspiration from which the band gaily drink before producing yet another spectacular number. If anything, exactly the opposite is true.

To do it for a month is one thing; to spend up to half of your life doing it beggars belief.

making music

Apart from two major injections of creative capital on the arrival of each vocalist, there was rarely an album in Marillion's twenty-year history that didn't start its life against an empty backdrop. *'Fugazi'* was a strain on the band, *'Misplaced Childhood'* needed a major rethink, and the writer's blocks at the start of the band's fourth album were a deciding factor in the break-up. *'Seasons End'* was smooth, but *'Holidays In Eden'* was another difficult conception. Following *'Holidays'* came a vow: never again to let creativity suffer under the pressure to produce a release. The fear gave way to a realisation that the lack of inspiration at the start of the process was, in fact, part of the process. *'Brave'* was the first album in which no artistic stones were left unturned, even if it meant falling out with EMI in the process.

After *'Brave'* the band made another vow, never to let an album consume them the way that it had! But the principle of creativity over schedules was to stay.

grains of inspiration

"I like to write words that
mean three things -
something obvious,
something metaphorical
and something hidden,
that you'd have to know me
to know what it is.
A name on a grain of rice
is to love someone;
in the modern world, rice
symbolises the simplest
form of sustenance,
and there were people
selling names on grains of
rice in Copacabana
last time I was there!"

Steve Hogarth

Happy Alchemy

The initial stage of any album is to try out some ideas and see what feels right. "It's about having a feel," says Pete. "We want to make music that makes people feel alive." No wonder that inspiration doesn't come easy, considering the constant push to move in new musical directions. "It's harder every time not to repeat ourselves," comments Rothers. "I always try to find a new starting point, rather than starting with doing the same because it's cool and it works." "Certain styles we could pretty much record in our sleep," agrees H, "but I'm always striving to say something more important than the songs I hear everywhere. The higher you aim the harder it is to hit the target."

Once initial ideas have been considered, it is time for the band to get together and jam.

If there is any magic, it is here that it happens. Put five musicians into a room, each with a parcel of ideas, and let them catalyse each other to change the basic ideas into fully-fledged Marillion songs. "We are all open for everything," comments H. "Every idea is welcome, we have no rules, everything is allowed." Adds Ian, "We're up for experimenting a lot more now, but because we're older, we're guilty of being a bit too careful sometimes. But you don't want to write the same album every time!" The band knows enough about each other to make jamming a valuable seam of material. Continues H, "We jam for weeks and record it all. Most of it is rubbish, but every now and then there will be a happy accident."

It was perhaps Dave Meegan's work on *'Brave'* and *'Afraid Of Sunlight'* that turned the habit into an art form. While *'Brave'* involved many individual sessions, *'Afraid Of Sunlight'* saw the whole band recording together, with Dave Meegan picking out the best takes of the different instruments. Recalls Steve Rothery, "Dave would take all his favourite moments, and not always the most technically perfect live parts either." The artistic, if not commercial, success of both albums was to firmly cement the approach for the future, helped by the use of digital technologies such as DAT and minidisc, the Petri dishes upon which happy accidents can grow. Says Pete, "At around about tape six or seven, the good ideas start to come. We take the best things and put them on compilations. We sometimes end up with compilations of compilations, or supercomps!" Adds H, "We take musical ideas and try to find the lyrics to correspond. The lyrics could be five years old, and the music could be new. What the songs have in common is still a certain craftsmanship, musicianship which is inevitable when you've got a band of musicians of this calibre."

Finally, the band decides what is good and what is not. As Pete mentioned in an Internet chat session, "We tend to write one song at a time, and we never even know how that's going to turn out until it's evolved on its own." Naturally, this is an occasionally contentious area that requires certain rules. "We work according to a certain pattern, in which each band member has his say in choosing the songs," says H. As they are chosen, the structure of the album starts to form. "We don't decide the theme of the album," H explains. "The results always surprise us." Words are also produced in parallel with the initial musical ideas, sometimes aided by John Helmer. As H notes, "He's not too precious about what I do with them. He just sends them down the fax line! We meet up a couple of times a year and get drunk and talk about the meaning of life and what have you. It's a very odd co-writing relationship!"

With jamming complete, demos are recorded that are then used as a reference to make the final recording. "It's not until you record something that it gets defined," says Pete. A producer helps considerably: he has many roles, from recording engineer to arranger and peacemaker. Explains Steve Rothery, "In a band like this, with so many

off the scales

"My knowledge of scales is a bit sketchy so I tend to work out parts and solos by ear. Some of the most interesting pieces of music we have come up with happen when we don't have a clue what the others are playing! If you use chord structures and scales to work out solos then nothing unexpected happens and things can sound predictable."

Mark Kelly

accidents will happen

Perhaps the first happy accident was 'The Slide' from *'Brave'*, which started with a bass riff from Pete, which the other band members jammed on top of. When played back it was generally agreed that the band should learn it for the record.

creative people, it is good to have another person involved who can make the best of what's there and who can get us to focus attention." In other words, explains Dave Meegan, "They get into such a state they can't physically enjoy making an album without a producer!" Chris Neil agrees, "Somebody has to drive the bus. The producer provides a musical shoulder to cry on, taking all their aspirations and helping to take them on to the goal."

Is it any wonder then that the band refuses to define its musical style? Not that it won't, but it can't. "You never know how something is going to come out until it's recorded, mixed and finished," says Ian. For band and fans alike, each release is made with baited breath. As French fan Ed Wood puts it, "I always buy a Marillion album without knowing what will be on it, and I buy it with confidence built up over the years." Fan and Web Holland activist Jeroen Schipper concurs: "The best element of Marillion's history is how they keep changing themselves in their musical style and don't hang on to something successful. Every new album is a surprise."

But Is It Prog?

The term 'progressive' has picked up something of a bad reputation recently. No, let's be realistic, it has always had a bad reputation. At the height of the seventies many jumped on the prog bandwagon, but they all very quickly jumped off when they thought the pomp and ceremony had had its day. It never went away, however. Notes Mark Kelly, "There were two dozen bands with pub status, several had their roots in the seventies like The Enid, Twelfth Night and Pendragon, but none had any success to speak of." Then along came Marillion and picked up a couple of hit singles, and suddenly there was a ready-made new wave of British prog. "All the bands were dragged into the limelight, Kerrang! started talking about it, but the reality was it was all total bollocks!" frowns Mark.

At the outset, Marillion was unashamedly a progressive rock band but even then it was uncomfortable with being associated with the genre, not least because it was an immediate turn-off to music journalists and public alike. Of course, the other bands were most definitely prog! "IQ, Solstice and so on, they all seemed too derivative. In hindsight we were too!" admits Mark. Even as late as 1986, band members would continue to confirm Marillion's prog status. "It's always been progressive rock," Steve Rothery would proclaim. Trouble is, Marillion was never just about prog. As Pete explains, "Marillion was borne out of several bands, many of which weren't prog bands - The Beatles, The Who, Led Zeppelin. We all have similar record collections, and less than half of the records are prog! Me and Steve Rothery share a liking for James Bond themes by John Barry!" Work that one out if you can!

When Steve Hogarth joined Marillion, given his mainstream background it appeared the band would lose the reference altogether. "He was much more anti-prog," remembers Mark. "He tried to get us to move in other directions, the technique he used was why-not-give-it-a-try?" Indeed, if *'Holidays In Eden'* succeeded at anything it was in remodelling the band as a straightforward rock band. It was almost inevitable that *'Brave'* was both a return to form and a return to type, this time with H in concurrence. He hated the genre label even more than his forebear, largely due to the fact it imposed unspoken limitations on what Marillion could do. As he remarked in an interview, "I'd love to think Marillion is progressive rock, in the sense that it's experimental, it doesn't work necessarily with a three-minute format, it's deeper than pop music, and it's not derivative. If progressive is derivative, it's a contradiction in terms."

With *'This Strange Engine'*, even H succumbed to the release of artistic tension (some would say indulgence) that progressive rock allows. Perhaps not coincidentally, this came at the same time that the rest of the band was feeding on influences from the outside.

At the end of the day, the term progressive is not harmful, it is how people use it that counts. H sums things up: "We're not on a mission to be re-categorised, it's just because we just drag this progressive rock label like a lot of chains. We don't really see music as falling into categories. What is commercial? It is something which sells. Did *'Brave'* sell? It sold more copies than *'Marillion.com'*, so it must have been more commercial, wouldn't you say." H doesn't so much have a problem with the prog label, as complacency. "The progressive thing within this band is to be fought against," says H. "It's the path of least resistance. If the five of us went into a room and did what comes easiest and simplest, we'd probably make... a prog album!"

Marillion fans have as much trouble with the label as anyone else, falling into one of three camps - Marillion is unashamedly prog and should be proud of it; Marillion's music is far too diverse to suffer a label such as prog; and, never quite understood what all the fuss was about in any case. Perhaps one would do well to follow Mark Kelly's lead. "I ask journos, what do you mean by prog? Answer me that and I'll tell you if we are or not!"

playing live

Following the stasis of the studio, the thought of hitting the road is a welcome one. "Once we've been in the studio for 6-7 months writing and then three months recording, I'm thinking, I'm going to be out on the road in a couple of weeks - great!" comments Mark. Trouble is, for each couple of hours in the limelight, there's weeks of preparation, rehearsal, travel, more preparation, sound checks, and waiting. Waiting. Waiting for trains and planes. Waiting to go places. Waiting to get there. Waiting to get back. Waiting in the wings for things to happen. From start to finish, every moment of glory is the product of weeks of graft and faffing.

Not that the live performance isn't worth all the effort. As Rothers noted, "The feeling of playing to an audience, large or small, there's nothing like it!" Ian Mosley agrees, "I think for this band the concerts are probably the most important thing. We've always been known as a live band and everybody still feels the same, we just want to get out there and tour."

Preparation

Everything starts with the set list. Explains Steve Hogarth, "We all have different agendas, for instance, Ian wants to play songs that have different drumming, not 4/4 all the time. I can imagine how tedious that must get!" Then the band needs to work things through. Says Ian, "If it's a new album, if there's a fade out we have to work out a proper ending or a segue." Adds Steve R, "We write it as it comes and worry about it later!" For some in the band, this means repetitive practicing and re-arranging, for others, hours of programming and sequencing. Singing is no easy ride, as emotions are difficult to fake, even in rehearsals. Explains H, "I sing the lyrics with a lot of passion, and if one of the band makes a mistake, I'm in the middle of all these emotions and then have to start all over again, it's very frustrating!"

Alongside rehearsals, the band has to get booked in at venues. When the band was at its pinnacle of popularity it used booking agents, but these days, as when it set out on the road to success, Marillion (that is, Lucy Jordache) prefers to handle the bookings themselves.

When everyone's done, it is probably time to get on the bus. To get on the bus, of course somebody must first book the bus. Two weeks before a tour is to start, the band contacts tour manager Tim Bricusse and the tour bookings are turned into actions.

"My job is transport, hotels, guest lists and general dogsbody!" laughs Tim, who has been tour-managing the band for the past eight years. "If anybody wants something, I'm the one to ask!" The band owns its own equipment, but everything else (such as PA's, sound and lighting rigs) is usually hired. Says previous tour manager Paul Lewis, "A month would be nice but all the arrangements could be turned around in a week if need be. The only restriction on this would be if any visas are required, which takes things out of our hands."

Leaving home to go on tour is not always a pleasant experience. "Missing your family, that's probably the most difficult thing," remarks Steve Rothery. Before leaving for Mexico, 31 August 1994, he wrote in his diary, "I climbed into the back of the car feeling I'm to blame for the misery of the people I love." Finally, the band unites with crew at an appropriate location, and it's time to climb aboard. Different members of the band have different experiences of the tour bus. Ian, for example, can never sleep, whereas H loves it. "I love lying on one of these little bunks late at night, drifting out of sleep and knowing that when I wake up I'll be in another city," he commented in an interview.

a line on his jeans

"For many years, we never felt we could leave 'Easter' out. Now it means just as much to me, but it's almost impossible not to go through the motions because it's so familiar. It's like a pair of jeans you put on every day. You stop looking at them after a while, but they're just as important to you. You wouldn't let your wife throw them in the bin, but you don't look at them and say what a great pair of jeans."

Steve Hogarth

Arrival at venues involves checking into a hotel, taking a shower, having a walk before going for the sound check. Then it is down to the tour manager to ensure that things slot into place in the run up to the gig. "Fortunately, Marillion is an easy band to manage, they don't want much pampering!" comments Tim Bricusse. "Some acts are more demanding, the types who want the blue M&M's taken out (or only the blue ones left in...) I mean honestly; they'll all go back home and eat any colour!"

Setting up for a gig has to happen in a certain order, explains Paul Lewis: "It starts with loading in the lights and getting them off the ground so that the other equipment can be loaded underneath. Then it would be the PA and monitors and finally the back line. While the back line is being set up we would normally do any interviews to get them out of the way before the soundcheck. Around 4.30 the soundcheck would start and that would take 15 minutes to an hour and a half, depending on whether there are any problems with the sound. Around 6 pm the band and crew would sit down to dinner, after which a few may go back to the bus to relax or watch a movie. 7.30 doors open and the opening act would normally go on about 7.45 - 8.30 giving us an hour to change over the equipment for Marillion to start at 9.00, usually playing for two hours including the encore after which the whole process is done in reverse with the truck doors closing at about 1.30am."

"I've done most venues before, so I know what to do in advance of the gig," remarks Tim. "I compile a book for the whole tour, covering each venue, transport details, hotels, rider arrangements (which are sent to the promoters so they know what

Evian the Bottle

On 30 September 1992, Tim Bricusse, John Arnison and Ian Mosley were hanging out at the hotel, waiting for a midnight flight after the show in Caracas. Ian was trying to open a two-litre bottle of Evian when he got fed up and threw it out of the window. Unfortunately it was several storeys up, so when the bottle hit a canopy below it exploded! It wasn't long before the perpetrators had been discovered and thrown out of the hotel!

to expect) and so on. Every venue is different." Before the main set comes the support act, which will either have bought on to, or have been invited to join, the tour. Laughs H, "We prefer solo support artists, they don't take up much space! Seriously, support bands are technically a pain in the arse, as they will always compromise your own sound. Most of all we like people who put out a good vibe - we just don't need it otherwise!"

The first few dates of a tour will inevitably be less polished than later ones. "The first two weeks for me is like playing squash for the first time after laying off for a year," says Ian, "I just feel like I've been run over a couple of times! It's quite a physical thing to play the drums!" For H, things can go the other way. "When you're in the middle of the tour the high notes become harder to sing," he remarks. "Certain songs are so hard to sing technically so it detracts just a little bit from the enjoyment because there's so much responsibility to come up with the intensity of the performance."

As the tour progresses, set lists will be changed round, swapping songs in and out to suit the audience, the mood, the timing. "Eventually you end up with a structure of songs that works, but even then we still swap songs in and out just as we feel," comments Mark. Adds H, "It's quite important that we vary the show from one night to the next, because so many of our fans come to many of our shows, and then complain."

The important part of a successful tour is to keep it fun. "It's got to be fun," comments Tim Bricusse. "It's a very close, claustrophobic experience, so if anyone isn't happy - the band, the management, the crew - it rubs off on everyone else. Everyone has off days, that's why it's important that everyone gets on." Eventually, the time out of time that is touring must come to a close. "Coming back and adapting to a normal life can be difficult," remarks Rothers. "It's reality - you know, you've got to cut the lawn and pay the bills!"

baby can I tow your car...

To get to a fan club show in Utrecht, Holland, the band shared two cars - Tim, Ian and Steve H in one, Rothers, Mark and Pete in the other. All ended well, as recalls Tim Bricusse: "Ian parked the car in a disabled space, threw his drumsticks on the dash and said 'There's a disabled sticker!' The other was parked up next to it, on some yellow lines... we came out of the gig to find that both cars had been towed! Fortunately we could get them out of the 24-hour pound in time to get on to Amsterdam, so it was OK!"

Atmosphere Friendly

Waiting to go up on stage at a gig is a bit like standing on the teleport deck of the Starship Enterprise. One minute, there's a small group of people in their own, protected environment, picking up signals from another planet. Seconds later, they are transported into the heart of the new world. The adrenaline rush is inevitable. Remembering a stadium gig in Sao Paolo, H recalls, "As we went on, I don't know whether they were camera flashes or people flashing their lighters or something, but there was a very bright light flickering right the way round the stadium and this enormous noise! It was like the greatest excitement and the greatest terror happening simultaneously!" Then it's into positions, and the mix of careful orchestration, intra-band chemistry and the artistic muse takes over.

Hand signals provide liaison with technicians and front of house engineers. Explains engineer Privet Hedge, "I try as much as possible to recreate the general mix of the album, but performances and arrangements change. Steve Rothery may play four different guitar parts on an album track but only one part live." The vocals are one of the hardest things to mix, due to the spillage of sound into the vocal mikes from the other instruments. Continues Priv, "If the singer has a weak voice, you're knackered. Steve H does not, thank heavens, 'cos they're loud up there!"

It's a very different experience to perform live compared to in the studio. Mark

Kelly: "When we play live, I concentrate on the music and make sure I get it right and in time. In the studio, it's a different thing, you tend to work with the overall music and lyrics and the meaning behind it." Mistakes are more acceptable live, as they will be hidden in the overall mix; hence why recording a live performance can be particularly dicey. "The band are usually worse live," remarks H. "On the one hand, you are thinking, "I better be good," and, "I better sing in tune," because it's being recorded. But on the other hand, you don't want it to inhibit you or constrain your performance."

There are many factors that determine a successful show, including the venue. Comments H, "I've often come off stage thoroughly depressed from a gig to find people coming back going, 'That was an amazing gig - didn't you feel the vibe?' and I'm like, what vibe?" Happily, such occasions are in the minority. "The atmosphere the crowd generates at each show is just not really like any other band you might see," says Mark. "It still makes my pulse race." Adds H, "I would give up touring only at the point of a gun. When a man is tired of touring, he is tired of life."

the sharp end

Perhaps the hardest thing for a label-independent band such as Marillion is to marry the need for creative output with the fact that it is a business, with cashflows, bank accounts, salaries, marketing budgets and all the horrible paperwork that goes with it. As Steve Hogarth says, "We're in business to make money, otherwise we're not here next year." But this is not at any cost.

One of the biggest decisions Marillion has had to make was whether to run its own affairs. Already, on Steve Hogarth's arrival, a number of initiatives were being considered that would give the band more independence. In particular, there was Racket Records and the Racket Club.

It's A Racket

Racket Records was originally set up by John Arnison as a direct response to the trend for bootleg CDs at exorbitant prices. "The bootlegs were expensive and of really crap quality," remarks John. First the band had to get the go-ahead from EMI to release the 'official bootlegs' - "We explained how we wanted to sell live recordings of a tour to the fan club only - they limited the figure to no more than a few thousand a year, and it kind of grew from there!" "They gave us the go-ahead to sell a small number of CDs," remembers Pete. The first Racket CD was Live at the Borderline, a recording made at the Web UK convention on 4 May 1992, at the Borderline Club in London

Racket was never set up to be a label in its own right, but opportunism led to signing artists such as John Wesley for his first album, *'Under A Red And White Sky'*. Recalls Wes, "John Arnison said to me, we're bringing you on tour, we'll sell some records!" It also helped that Mark, Ian and Steve R were all deeply involved in the album's production! Another early signing was Mike Hunter's ambient mix of Marillion samples, 'River'. "Arnison being ever one to spot an opportunity said, 'Let's knock up a thousand!'" says Mike. "Years later, people would come up to me and say, did you know, my missus used it to give birth to!"

When Erik Nielsen was recruited, first as Mark's keyboard technician and then as Web site manager, little did he realise what he was getting into. In 1997, Racket Records was still very much a cottage operation. "Stewart Every was packing a few CDs every day, and popping down to the village post office to stick the stamps on," says Erik. All was soon to change, when the tour fund gave the band an insight into the powder keg it was sitting on top of. A live CD (*'Rochester'*) was issued to each of the few thousand donors to the tour fund, but these were distributed mainly by fund organiser Jeff Woods (and friends) in the USA. Coupled with Marillion's increasing visibility through the Internet, it was the next two Racket releases that lit the touch paper. First, *'Tales From The Engine Room'* was initially sold only over the Web. Second, another live CD, *'Piston Broke'*, was released to capitalise on the demand for Marillion live performances. Back at Racket, the visible effect was that Stuart was spending all of his time packing CDs and taking them to the post office. This posed a bit of a problem, as he was supposed to be acting as engineer! So Erik was roped in to deal with the demand.

The past five years has seen much progress in Marillion's operation. Fortunate it was, that as the Internet took off so did the band's desire to operate more and more autonomously. A major source of ideas and inspiration was Mark, comments John Arnison, "Mark really stepped forward when Fish left the band." Steve H concurs, "We've got Mark to thank for a lot of the business side. It's his vision that has led us to the degree of self-sufficiency that we now have." As Erik got his head around the complexities of running a mail order service at the same time as managing a Web site, he started to add initiatives of his own. "I was pretty much left to my own devices," says Erik, who was the catalyst behind

Tim Bricusse

Tim Bricusse worked though a number of trades including car mechanic, before packing it all in late in the Eighties when a mate offered him a job as a roadie on a Gary Numan tour.

Starting on the backline ("I didn't have a clue what I was supposed to do, I just kept my head down and got on with it!"), he worked his way through the system until he took the post of guitar tech, which he performed for such acts as Robert Plant, Simple Minds and Duran Duran.

Through his contacts (he knew both Privet Hedge and John Callis, as they had worked together many times on the circuit), Tim became guitar tech for Steve Rothery. He kept this role until he replaced Paul Lewis as Production Manager in 1994, following which he handed over the guitar job to John Wesley. Tim has remained Marillion's tour manager to this day, as well as tour-managing other bands, such as The Pretenders, Roger Taylor and UB40.

"I'm just doing a job, nobody's my idol," remarks Tim. "Having said that, meeting Marlon Brando was a bit of a buzz!"

the band's increasing independence. "I said, why are we paying other companies to do things we could do ourselves? And thus the mood was set. When John Arnison and the band went their separate ways in 1998, management tasks were passed to Rod Smallwood at Sanctuary. "He heard we were without a manager so he approached us," says Mark. "He looked after us for a year or so, then he got too busy with Iron Maiden, so we stopped using him!" Meanwhile, the band started to take over the administration and what was a label became a business. "I'd been going once a year with John to see the bank manager," explains Ian. "When John left, I went in with Mark, and somehow at that meeting I ended up being the person who signed the cheques..." Ian was the logical choice as the money man. "I guess I'm quite good at moving money around, and making it last if there's not much of it!" he says. "He's very meticulous," comments Mark. "He's very tight!" laughs Erik.

Operating as a business has been (and continues to be) a major learning experience for everyone involved. "We've been flying by the seats of our pants," says Erik. For Steve Rothery, setting up Dorian Music was a major learning experience. "When I did

Wishing Tree, I got more experience on the business side of things," he comments. "For example, how record companies and radio stations are dominated by quick profit thinking, that all the bands who are marginal and who aren't mainstream are pushed to one side." Remarks Ian, "None of us are businessmen, but we're doing just as good a job as anyone ever did for us." In 2000, the work started to exceed the resource available once again, so Racket went hunting for recruits. First in was Lucy Jordache, who built up her initial role of promotional responsibilities to take on the job of agent and band management. "She's always been into the band and done great stuff with EMI, so we just offered her a job," says Mark. Adds Ian, "Lucy's been on a massive learning curve, she's coped brilliantly!" In August 2000 Colin Price was welcomed to the team. Colin was a long-time Marillion fan with the added advantage of having spent 15 years managing a warehouse for the Oxford University Press. The recruitment of a fan was deliberate, explains Erik, "We searched the fan database for postcodes in the local area, and e-mailed them about the job." Colin responded and was delighted to be accepted. Says Erik, "Colin had a trial by fire, almost as soon as he arrived, we went on tour and left him to it!" "Some days, I can't believe I'm here," laughs Colin, "but other days I can believe I'm here, it's a lot of hard work!" One of Colin's tasks was to make the packaging area more usable and efficient. "We've completely re-designed it," continues Colin. "The main area used to be above the studio in the loft and could only be accessed by a huge ramp. Sliding boxes of shirts and CDs up and down was hazardous to say the least, not to mention Mad Jack Kelly hurling downwards at a hundred miles per hour towards you!" Lucy, Colin and Erik handle most of the operational side of the business, explains Erik, "Lucy covers eighty to ninety percent of the marketing and bookings, Colin and I deal with eighty to ninety percent of the merchandising and the Web, and the band handles all of the music. The rest, we share!" To ensure that communications are functioning correctly, each staffer has a 'band buddy', a member of the band who meets for a chat every now and then. "They don't really know what we do!" grins Erik. "Besides, if anyone needs band buddies, it's probably the band!"

So, how does the band balance creativity with the need to make money? Fortunately, it doesn't have to. Explains H, "There's a big enough fan base out there to pay the rent and to get by and make the next record. To make records is a great privilege, because it's a chance to be immortal. You're a fool if you leave something behind which isn't a part of you and is just an experiment to make money. You might as well leave something behind that you felt strongly about." Indeed, and meanwhile the team is in place. "We plan further ahead now, we're shipping most orders in under two weeks and we continue to develop new ideas," concludes Erik, who is not likely to have a dull day any time soon.

Join The Club

It was Steve Rothery who first came up with the idea of The Racket Club. "I suggested to the band that we could save a fortune if we had our own storage and rehearsal facility," says Rothers. "Until that time we'd been storing our equipment at Nomis studios in London and going away to expensive residential studios to write." Instead, the band opted for a place he had found in Buckinghamshire, with Steve Hogarth and his family electing to move up from Windsor to be near.

When the Racket Club opened its doors for the writing sessions of *'Brave'* in November 1992, it quickly became obvious that to have a recording area would be a huge asset to the band. "We realised the biggest cost was recording," explains John Arnison. "We had to rent a writing studio, then go away and record, it all cost money!" Coupled with this, the band members were all settling down a bit and didn't want to spend so long away from home. "They were all having young kids, they wanted to make their lives more sensible. Only Steve Hogarth wasn't that keen as his kids were *very* young!" Commented Pete in the sleeve notes to the *'Brave'* remaster, "It was not a glamorous affair by any standard, but the freedom we had to go in at any time and work on ideas helped make it a good environment." Steve Rothery suggested EMI paid for some recording equipment that the band had acquired. "We'd used it to record various live B-sides around *'Holidays In Eden'* time," explains Rothers. "It still forms the basis for part of the Racket Club studio today." Mike Hunter, who had helped mix *'Brave'* in Liverpool, was brought in as engineer. "I kipped on the studio floor," says Mike. "I can play bass, drums and piano so, if they knocked it on the head at about 7.30, I would spend the evenings practicing on their instruments. I was happy as a pig in shit!" Ian remembers how the band clubbed together to raise some cash so Mike could buy a car. "It was an old Vauxhall, he had it for about an hour before it blew up!"

By 1994 the Racket Club studio had outgrown its original location, moving lodgings, and gaining some new equipment, for the recording of *'Afraid Of Sunlight'*. Of course, when the band left EMI after that album, the Racket Club changed from being something nice to have to being an essential facility. Mike Hunter moved back up to Liverpool, claiming it was too far to travel every Saturday to watch Everton play. "He really missed Liverpool," says Ian. After a few interviews the band found a replacement: Stewart Every, who used to work with Dave Meegan at Maison Rouge. Since this time the Club has been a second home to the band and a work place for all its employees, not to mention a place that has gained almost mythical status in the hearts and minds of the fans. Not bad for a money-saving idea.

Promoting The Band

Since the band started managing its own affairs in 1997, it has also been responsible for its own promotion. This has never been an easy ride - indeed, John Arnison was first selected due to his experience with non-mainstream acts. For a while in the Eighties, Marillion's popularity was on a steady rise, but Fish's departure put a spanner in the works. Today it is as it has been for many years, an uphill struggle. Not that the band are downhearted! "There's nothing like being in a band such as Marillion, it's the whole us-against-the-world thing!" said Ian in a Web interview. "We're all in it together."

With promotion comes the need to understand how the media perceives the band. Remembers Steve H at his first appearance, the 'Hooks In You' video shoot: "I remember seeing someone in an Iron Maiden shirt standing next to someone in a Sugarcubes shirt. No wonder the media can't understand us!" Marillion are particularly opposed to marketing the band to a particular audience. In an interview with Jon Epstein of Rock List, Steve H commented, "It's like going into a restaurant and seeing people eating tomatoes and identifying them as "the guys who eat tomatoes." So you get all their names and addresses and send them to the guys who grow tomatoes and we'll hook them up and make a lot of money." Responded Jon, "I once spent a week eating nothing but melons, and to this day I can't deal with them anymore. I was in the desert with no job near a melon farm. So that's what I ate." "Right!" answered Steve. "A record company would have identified you as a melon-oriented person and put you on the list. Melon-oriented rock!"

For several years, the band have tried to square the circle of growing its audience while being outside the mainstream, coupled with an absence of major label backing. Explains Steve Rothery, "People don't realise that in the US, you need at least a couple of hundred thousand dollars to get a song on the radio. That doesn't make it a hit. You pay the independent plugger to plug your record. And that's it. To be honest, we don't play that game." Why should they, and how could they? "To be fair to Radio," comments Steve H, "it does generally take us three minutes to get to the chorus!" The de facto rules are stacked against bands like Marillion, so they have wisely chosen to ignore the rules and make up their own.

With the Tour Fund tour as the wake up call, Marillion spent five years testing new ideas and the courage of their convictions. It has been a case of striking a careful balance between preaching to the converted and growing the fan base, ignoring the reviews and acting on feedback, going it alone and using the infrastructure of the major labels. "It's been a difficult trek, because we see ourselves as artists," remarked H in an interview. "By nature we don't like the idea of promoting ourselves." Of course, the *'Anoraknophobia'* pre-order campaign has changed this perspective. Continues H, "The thing about the Internet is that we can reach people one to one, and it feels more natural and real, rather than the usual promotional activities that bands get up to." The new rule book is a series of blank pages, and nobody, not the industry nor the band, really knows what it will contain. With the Internet, the confidence Marillion is developing, and the increasing reach it develops every time it runs a campaign, there really is hope for the future.

appendix two reaching out

"I don't want to achieve immortality through my work... I want to achieve it through not dying."

Woody Allen

Since the beginning Marillion has actively nurtured a relationship with its fans. Things started simple, with handwritten notes listing forthcoming gigs and contact phone numbers. As the band became more popular, photocopied newsletters gave way to a more professional format; in parallel, the fan club itself emerged, evolved and adapted to meet the needs of band and fans – providing a focus point but also inserting a fan-friendly comfort zone between the two parties.

Things were not always rosy. Ironically (but perhaps understandably), the low point of the fan club mirrored the peak in the band's career. It wasn't until 1997 that Marillion firmly grasped the nettle and managed to fully harness the relationship with its fans. Throughout its life, the club has used all possible channels of communication, from flyers and phone numbers in the beginning, to the global reach of today's internet.

a brief history of the web

In the beginning, there was Tim. In fact, there was Mick Pointer's girlfriend Stef Jeffries, but she was too busy at the time so she asked fan Tim Hollings to muck in and write a few newsletters. Early newsletters were no more than a handwritten, photocopied sheet with the occasional illustration provided by whoever wanted to draw it! Eventually Stef took over from Tim, continuing even after Mick left the band. "She carried on for about a year!" says Mick. "That made for a nice, healthy atmosphere!" A fan called Angie took over in 1983 and held the post until 1987… or so it seemed. "When the real Angie left, we kept the name for continuity!" 'Angie' was 'helped' by various people including John Arnison's assistant Ann Lawler and indeed John himself! At the time of 'Incommunicado' in 1987, Angie was actually a person called Patsy Smith. "Fan clubs weren't as much of a tool as they are now," comments John Arnison. Indeed – they were more a slow cooker than a pot boiler, keeping the relationship warm.

From Club To Community

By the summer of 1988, 'Bernie' was running the fan club. "Bernie was a girl from New Zealand who assisted Ann Lawler for a while," explains Steve Rothery. Eventually Bernie went back to the Antipodes; in keeping with tradition, the name remained and Jo Rothery, Steve's wife took over. Continues Steve, "It was such as shame - people wrote saying they wanted to meet him at gigs!" Jo managed to keep up the momentum for five years, before throwing in the towel.

In 1994 it was decided to hand over the reins to the fans themselves. Fans Bonnie Alberts and Wayne Kensett took the job, and before long accepted the offer of assistance from long-time fan (and current band employee) Lucy Jordache. Andy Rotherham was recruited in the same year, when he bumped into the pair at a record fair. James Fishwick met the team at the album launch party for *'Afraid Of Sunlight'*, at The Mean Fiddler on 18 June 1995, and he too was recruited into the fold. "I was conned!" he laughs. Rob Crossland also became involved, helping typeset the magazine for Bonnie and Wayne. And thus, the Web team came into existence.

"The Web then was very different to the setup we have now," explains Andy. "For a start, it was kept at some distance from the band. The idea was that if the fan club sank, then the band wouldn't be liable." Explains Pete Trewavas, "John Arnison used to have a problem with the fans, they always wanted much more than he wanted to give." These dubious dynamics had one result: the fans were not getting the club they were paying for. Personality clashes and breakdowns in communication culminated in an unforgivable error, that members of the Web were not informed about the tour fund in 1997. Not only did it mean that they couldn't donate, but also they were also denied access to the limited edition CD that was only available to donors!

In 1998, when Marillion started to take management matters into their own hands, one of the first things to change was the fan club. After some asking around, a team was drawn up to include Andy and James, Rob and Alexis Crossland, Simon Clarke and Vicki Harding. Out of the blue (for them), each person was invited to the Racket Club. "I answered the phone and it was Mark Kelly," recalls Andy Rotherham. Simon and Vicki were informed at a charity event on Oxford Street, for World Aids Day. "There was a whole bunch of artists at the Virgin Megastore, including Mark, H and Ian who were doing a signing session. Mark was outside with a collecting bucket, he said, 'I've a question for you two, would you like to help run the fan club?' We replied, 'Yeah - sounds great!'" Andy Rotherham recalls the meeting at the Racket Club a week or so later. "When we went, it was all very surreal," says Andy, "H sat down between myself and Vicki, asked who everyone was and we got down to business!'

In 1998, Rob and Alexis departed and replacements were found in the form of Lynn and Pete Wells, giving us the Web UK team that has remained the same to this day. There is also a team of helpers, such as fans Georgina Wistow, Dave Cooper and Mark Nelson, people who muck in for fun, solidarity, the opportunity to meet the band and the occasional after-gig party. Says Mark Nelson, "It's unpaid, eats into your spare time, consumes your holidays from work to go on tour and help out, but the rewards are great!" Today's Web UK is distinguished by its commitment to helping the band and its fans work in harmony. There is a regular, 64-page, packed fan club magazine, and the commitment is still right up there, as illustrated by April 2002's Pontins convention during which the Web UK team spent as much time manning merchandise stalls and stewarding fans through museums, as they did enjoying themselves. "It's completely taken over our lives!" says Vicki with a smile. Well, it was almost a smile!

Helping Out by Mark Nelson

For some long-forgotten reason I was ringing the (now-extinct) Web hotline. The recorded message ended with something like the words, "If you are interested in helping out at the fan club and live in the vicinity of Junction 15 of the M1, please give us a call." As this was only 15 miles up the road from where I lived, I thought I'd give it a go. I had got so much pleasure from the band in the prior 13 years that I felt I should give something back, and if I could help out with the fan club that was a way of giving something back.

I arrived and found Bonnie and Wayne handling the fan club at that time in their house in Northampton. I brought the fan club work force up to a grand total of five people! The division of labour between us fell broadly into four areas. The pinnacle was the production of the in-house magazine and dealing with the band directly over interviews, articles, reading reader submissions etc. The next trusted layer down was handling member enquiries regarding the band, i.e. when did the band play venue X, what's the meaning of song Y, what's Mark's dog called, etc. This job obviously had to be done by someone who knew a lot about the band and their history as answers sent back by The Web UK were treated by a lot of the members like tablets of stone passed down from on high. The next job was handling merchandise sales and the lowest rung on the ladder was membership applications renewals. This is where the new people started and "paid their dues" before being allowed to do the more interesting jobs outlined above.

In those days, all the membership records were held on index cards. All the address labels were handwritten, with the amount of labels remaining on file giving the indication of when your membership renewal was due. We asked people to submit their own labels with their application, but the majority never did. Vast quantities of time (and ink) were consumed writing out four address labels per member. If an address change happened mid-membership, it meant more labels. It was enough to make you weep tears of gratitude when some kind soul actually included their own pre-written labels. I'm glad to see that this task has been consigned to history and that the new Web UK is more up to date technology wise.

The only break from the monotony of that job was getting to use the membership card laminating machine. This was a valuable skill that has stood me in good stead in subsequent years! The other wrinkle was matching up overseas bank transfer notifications with applications as we usually got the notification from the bank way before the application ever arrived.

In December 1997 the band restructured the fan club into the fine body it is today. Most of the road-blocks that had hampered the running of the Web UK were resolved at a stroke by more frequent band involvement and the fact that Erik was now able to focus on the Web as a full time job. The band were good to their word and nearly everything promised has come to pass, and I believe that the Web UK is in better shape today than it probably ever has been.

An International Web

Marillion's desire to tour very quickly took the band abroad, and it treated its international fan base with as much respect as in the UK. Unsurprisingly, then, a number of fan clubs sprang up in many countries, including Blue Angel in France, Real to Read in Italy, and other organisations in Spain and Germany and Holland. Today these are largely subsumed into the Web. Web fan clubs worldwide work as a 'franchising operation', each running its own affairs (for example, accounts etc). It is up to individual countries to make their operations successful or otherwise. New clubs are being considered all the time; for example The Web Scandinavia is a recent development, run by Jan Henrik Ohme in Norway. Marillion Fan clubs in Europe have a wider remit than with many bands. "The clubs are involved in organizing gigs, particularly in Germany and Spain," explains Erik Nielsen of Racket Records. "They find the venues, they know them better than we do!"

Outside Europe the main fan centre was the USA. The Web North America started life as an informal structure, as organizer Dan Sherman explains. "During the 'Holidays In Eden' tour there was an apparent need to strengthen the communication between the band and American fans, as the fan base was growing due to a radio promotion from IRS records." With the benefit of a background in writing and editing, Dan and his wife Dana started the Web USA, which became formally adopted by the band during the Brave tour. Dan was held in great esteem by Marillion. In an interview with Jon Epstein, Steve H commented, "We're very pleased with the job that Dan does, and we're happy to remain close to him. He's easy to work with, and never gets in the way of our work. He's a gentleman. We think of him more as a friend than anything else." High praise indeed! The Web USA's publications were second to none, as anyone knows who has seen them – full glossy numbers that put the output of the Web UK to shame, "We had a great reputation for quality publications and accuracy of information," says Dan. Like all good things, it could not last forever - by 1997 Marillion was taking things more in-house and with the arrival of the Internet, membership was dwindling. "We were left with only a few hundred members, producing a magazine better than any of the European ones who had a few thousand members," says Dan. Finally, in Spring 1998 Dan and Dana decided to call it a day. "I feel we left amicably, I turned over the data base and every dollar we had left in the bank account after a talk with Mark and Steve H." A gent to the end.

Conventions

Marillion conventions started very much as an informal affair, involving fan clubs inviting members to a venue to share stories and watch videos. The band was not expected to turn up, though the Marillos were kept informed and sometimes made an appearance. Meanwhile Marillion also ran fan club-only gigs for the hardcore, the first of these was held 10 September 1985 at The Marquee. It is a compliment to the band that it continued to be so even at the height of its success.

The conventions were eventually to get more and more organised, including events like the Skoolhouse convention, held 2 June 1994 in Milton Keynes. 'Brave' the movie saw its first outing and Jump, John Wesley and Cry No More also played. "It was a very hot day – we got the gig because the people running the convention couldn't afford Pendragon!" recalls John Jones of Jump. Mark Kelly made an impromptu appearance on keyboards, and even helped roadie for the acts.

The whole band turned up the following year, on 18 June 1995 at the Mean Fiddler in London, to play an acoustic set, with Jadis and Jump in support. A full electric set wasn't possible, as Pete remarked, "We would have liked to, but we're in the middle of writing and recording." All the same, John Jones was impressed by what, to him, was the new singer. "I was struck by what a great voice he has. It isn't really my cup of tea, but that gig was fantastic!"

The 1996 convention was disappointing to say the least, as only Steve and Pete turned up. Things picked up in 1998, as the new, fan-friendly spirit pervaded everything that the band were involved in. "The band really made an effort," says Web UK team member Simon Clarke. Indeed they did, with a full electric performance at the Zodiac Club in Oxford. "The Zodiac's a lovely place, it's got a nice vibe to it," comments Pete. This was repeated in 1999, and by 2000, things came full circle as the conventions adopted the same pattern as the fans-only gigs of years before.

Karaoke Nights

The Grapes, just off the bottom of the Market Square in Aylesbury, was host to a Web UK Karaoke night on 14 December 1998. Four members of the band turned up, including Pete and H who both took the opportunity to sing! "That was a good night, karaoke's a funny thing," ruminates H... Incidentally, one of the singers, Mark Kilminster, was later selected to sing on the BBC's Saturday Show!

Afraid Of Sunlight - Web Preview Party 18 June 1995 by Helena Powell

It was our first Marillion convention and we didn't know what to expect, but the butterflies in my stomach had already started as we arrived. We made our way towards the stage and secured a place in the front row. First up were Jadis who were really good and got the audience warmed up nicely. Jump were next. I know a few people around us had already seen this band live and were really enthusing about the forthcoming performance. I thought Jump were excellent with their energetic tunes, which had the crowd jumping and cheering along. Next up was the video for 'Beautiful' (which is now my favourite Marillion video), shown on a screen over the stage. It was nicely shot and went well with the song. I loved the lovely close-ups of Steve Hogarth!

The first ever hearing of the *'Afraid Of Sunlight'* album was to follow. I always get excited about hearing new material and I loved looking around and seeing the crowd sitting quietly with their heads bowed, completely absorbed in the music. On first listen, you could tell it was something special, with 'King' being the stand-out track for me, at the time. I loved the contrasting moments of the heartfelt verses and the sheer power of the following instrumental. Fabulous.

During the album preview my husband, John, pointed out Steve Hogarth who was chatting with fans by the bar. I'd never met him before and this seemed the perfect opportunity. What would I say?! He was completely surrounded by fans, so I decided to stay where I was, rather than lose my place and still not be able to speak to him.

It seemed like we'd been standing there forever when Steve H appeared on the stage and sat at his piano for a stunning version of 'Cover My Eyes'. He was grinning away, meandering through the song and pointing his fingers to his head (as if to shoot!) when he couldn't remember the words.

I was rooted to the spot!, I had only seen the band live twice before and that was from way up in the balcony. I had (ahem) become increasingly fond of Steve H, watching 'From Stoke Row' and the 'Singles Collection' videos, and then suddenly there he was right in front of me! I couldn't believe it! The rest of the band gradually joined Steve on stage and performed a brilliant set. I particularly enjoyed 'Cannibal Surf Babe', 'Hide Your Love Away' and 'Made Again' which Steve H didn't want to end so he could shake his maracas a bit longer!

The band seemed relaxed and in high spirits throughout. I loved watching them enjoying playing. There was a moment when Mr Rothery was tuning his guitar directly in front of us and Steve H came over to talk to him, and he sat on the stage just in front of me! My first instinct was to reach out and touch him as he was only inches away from me, but that would have been a bit daft. I'd done that teenybopper thing back in 1986/7 and I wasn't about to do it again!

thank God for the Internet

Since its first creation in 1969, the Internet has evolved and had some dramatic impacts on all corners of the globe. It has been used for to-the-second news, electronic commerce, disparate families reuniting and virtual weddings; it has also served as a conduit for all kinds of diverse discussions including, for some, a favourite band. In the beginning there was email and news, then interactive communications such as chat. Finally, in the early '90s, the Internet found its 'killer app' in the form of the World Wide Web.

We all know that Marillion is unique, but it is with the Internet that it has managed to be truly groundbreaking.

Click to enter.

Getting The Message

There was life before the World Wide Web, and indeed there was life before the

Internet, when a loosely knit bunch of computers, spread around the globe, started to exchange messages with each other. The backbone, UUCP was used to pass a primal form of email communication between both individuals and groups, in a manner now synonymous with news and discussion boards. Here is the first recorded news item on the Web concerning Marillion: as you can see, it is typical of its era!

> Relay-Version: version B 2.10 5/3/83; site utzoo.UUCP
> From: messina@ihuxl.UUCP
> Newsgroups: net.music
> Subject: Another Genesis ??
> Posted: Fri Jul 1 18:49:21 1983
>
> GREAT! FANTASTIC! EXCELLENT!
>
> A new group just hit the US from England, and they are a great relief from the commercial blues.
>
> Who is it you ask????
>
> Its Marillion - Script for a jester`s tear
> They may be a genesis rip off but their damn good at it. In fact they are much better that the current genesis.
>
> The singer named Fish, has a voice some where between Gabriel and Collins. At times he sound almost like Gabriel.
>
> The band has an early genesis sound but with an 80`s twist.
>
> I would rate this album a 8 on the 1 - 10 scale. (only the WALL gets a ten because of its perfection).
>
> If you are into progressive rock and have been depressed because of all the commercial crap on the market you`ll find this album a great relief. It contains 6 songs (not your average 20) each song is about 8 mins long. This ablum was definately not produced for the commercial market. I think most of the genesis fans will love this album, but the real strong and serious Grabriel freaks will probably turn their nose up on this one. (sic)

Eventually Marillion achieved status of its own news feed: alt.music.marillion. This continues to this day, with a reputation of being not for the faint hearted!

Once email arrived, it yielded a different form of mailing list. According to the original Marillion FAQ, Graham Orndorff started a mailing list called Freaks, after the single. One early subscriber was Jeroen Schipper. He explains, “It was in 1990 I think. I subscribed when I saw the announcement in alt.music.marillion, which was then the only source of Marillion information on the Internet.”

Bizarrely, when Graham lost interest, nobody could leave: as Jeroen noted in the FAQ, “(Un)subscribing was no longer possible as it was not automated but done by Graham himself. This runaway list went on for quite a while, but died a slow death.” It might have died, but its spirit lived on. In September 1992, Ken Bibb started a new freaks list at bnf.com, moved in August 1994 to arastar.com. It was about this time that Mark Kelly was introduced to the list by a fan called Miranda Benson. "She phoned the studio at Parr Street while we were recording *'Brave'*," says Mark. "How she knew we were there, I don't know! She asked me if I knew about the Freaks list and offered to show me some printouts. A couple of months later I subscribed!"

In February 1996, Jeroen moved the list to ax.com, who were also responsible for the Marillion FAQ. Initially a slow starter, by the late 1990s the Freaks list had become one of the key resources for information and ongoing discussion about the band. In 1997, Freaks was moved to torchsong.com, where it can still be found today, run by Brian Vogelsang and old-timer Jeroen Schipper.

When Lucy Jordache discovered Freaks in 1997, she found it to be more than just a bunch of people exchanging emails. "People were meeting face to face too, – there was a bunch called CamFreaks in Cambridge, they'd chat on the Internet then meet up in a pub."

The band found Freaks a fascinating source. By 1998 Mark Kelly carried around a Psion 5 palmtop computer for email, onto which he could download the latest freaks messages. Laughs Mark, "The Freaks mailing list was interesting, and they didn't know that members were reading it!" Eventually the temptation to post a message became too much to resist. Mark became a regular contributor, with one of his posts prompting a response from Jeff Pelletier and catalysing the 1997 USA tour fund. Other active posters have been Steve Rothery, Fish, Mark Wilkinson and John Wesley. The fans, too, found it invaluable. Max Rael remarks, "In 1999 I happened to look up Marillion on the Internet... a quick look around the site led to me joining the freaks list just to see what it was like. Everyone was talking about the new album *'Marillion.com'* so I went out and got it!" For offshore fans, like John Stevens in Bermuda, Freaks has been a lifeline: "It's is a bit of a cultural backwater if your tastes run anything to the right or left of mainstream - in that way it has been very valuable!"

Freaks is no longer the only (nor the preferred) online community for fans of Marillion and Fish. Inevitably as the two sides have developed their own followings, separate lists now exist to support them. FishFans is exclusively for fans of Fish (makes sense) and The Opium Den exists for "the current line up of Marillion." Comments Jeroen Schipper, "There's so many other lists these days, many are more specialized. I think Freaks will go on for a while, but I am not sure for how long. There's still about 1700 subscribers." Freaks may never die, but whether it remains the up-to-date source of all things Marillion and Fish, or whether these roles will be subsumed into the newer lists (or the brand new, Marillion on-line forum), only time will tell.

Freaks by Mike Rengel

I started university in the fall of 1997. A few years earlier, in high school, a bass-playing friend had turned me to on to Rush. A helpful record store clerk also had alerted me to the existence of Dream Theater. I went through most of high school as the only person I knew who liked bands of that ilk (this was the alt-rock heyday, mind you). I got to Uni and for the first time, I had an email address and consistent web access. So, I discovered there were mailing lists where people could (gasp) discuss bands like Rush and DT. After a month or two hanging out on The National Midnight Star (the late Rush list), I was hearing repeated mentions of a band called Marillion. I'd never heard of them before, but their fans were frighteningly dedicated to pushing 'em on-list. So, home for Thanksgiving break in November '97, I went to the same record shop where I'd met the DT-recommending clerk. Purely by chance, I spied a copy of *'Brave'*. Now, Knowing absolutely nothing of the band, I plopped down my dollars and bought the album. I believe I spent most of the next three days listening to it.

The innate emotion and melodic nature of the band is what really sold me. The guitar solos, too, who was this guy? I also quickly recognized H as one of the most incredible singers I'd ever heard. "Why have I never heard of these guys before?" was my biggest question. Next couple of visits home, I discovered another record shop in town that had a relatively large stockpile of Marillion discs. I took a chance on something called *'Fugazi'*, took it home, pressed play, and heard the martial opening drums of 'Assassing'. That was the first time I heard Fish's voice. I didn't know the story of Fish leaving the band, I wasn't aware of the politics. I was just wowed by the fact that a band had at one point had two singers of such fantastic quality.

In the time that followed, I somehow stumbled across the Freaks list. (freaks@ax.net back in that day!) This was '97, so resources on the band were extremely limited. Freaks was incredible... people who not only knew the history of the band, all about each release, but who also had debates about lyrical interpretations and who behaved like a group of friends. I also found out that I'd just missed a US tour, and that something called a 'tour fund' was winding down. That was four years ago. I stayed on Freaks, I eventually tracked down all the F and H era albums, and I haven't looked back since.

IRC Chat

With the arrival of the Internet proper, came a number of new developments. One of these was Internet Relay Chat, (IRC) which enables multiple computer users to exchange messages or "chat" interactively. For those of you who think this is a sad way to spend an evening, answer this: Where (and how) else can you talk to people in over six countries from the comfort of your own home?

The first Freaks chat was initiated by Marillion fan Mark Bredius (a.k.a. Itchy) on 27 April 1996, and regular chat sessions have continued to this day. Every Friday night there is a chat session involving devoted fans from all over the world – it's the fact that people cannot be with each other easily, that makes it so useful!. In its history, Freaks has been graced with the presence of band members past and present.

IRC chat has proved a popular mechanism for the band to communicate with its fans while still keeping a distance. Commented Steve Hogarth, not ironically in a chat session, "Chat is great fun, extremely good for having direct conversations with strangers whilst being able to maintain a discreet distance. Because the net's so international, it's possible to broadcast to the world from your home and have the world listen and reply. It's like having a cross section of the globe in your house for a party, but you don't have to clean up the house afterwards." Indeed, he was so impressed he wrote about it in one of his songs. The lyrics to 'Interior Lulu' provide further insight to H's feelings.

Sexy MFP

At the height of Freaks, it was possible to 'win' a most frequent poster crown. One winner was Bruno Galli, who posted 93 messages in one month. "I got flamed a lot for that!" laughs Bruno.

From Web To Web

Perhaps one of the biggest disappointments in Marillion's online history is that nobody thought to register "Web.com" as a domain name, but then, who could have predicted the rise of the World Wide Web? Nonetheless, the band made up for this missed opportunity by using the Internet in ways that are both admired and copied by the rest of the industry.

Fans were quick to demonstrate how to use this new medium. According to Jeroen Schipper, "The first Marillion site was somewhere in France, it was a Gopher site, before the Web even existed. I forget who set it up but he moved it to the Web and he also put up the first HTML version of the FAQ list, with my permission. I started the first site which was dedicated to Marillion only, the French site was a combination of Fish / Marillion. The location was at www.let.uu.nl (where I still work)." There are today some 30 Web sites devoted to Marillion, and hundreds more that include Marillion pages. Why do fans do it? Paul Hughes gives as good an answer as any, "Sometimes, Marillion feels like an almost religious experience, and that's why I've decided to open another place of worship for anyone else who gets the shivers." Some of the best sites are long gone, such as the web site for AIR Marillion, "A Marillion tribute Air band. Air guitar, air drums, air vocals, airheads!"

It is difficult to believe that just five years ago the band did not have a web site at all. Jeroen Schipper registered the Marillion.com site on 19 December 1996. He recalls, "The first band member I talked to about the Internet was Mark Kelly. He already saw its importance and supported me in setting up the first Web Online website. He provided me with info and other stuff like sound samples from his keyboards. That helped a lot in making the site a success." The band's first official email address was printed on the cover of *'This Strange Engine'* (*'TSE'*) in 1997, (yes, that was five years ago now) - but even that was pointed to Dorian Music, Steve Rothery's own label. Not that the band were netophobes. Back in the '80s Mark was an avid Multi-User Dungeon player, as he notes

Erik Nielsen

Privet Hedge started it, just before the tour fund tour of the United States in 1997. When Priv took the gig to tour with Genesis, Stewart Every was offered the post of Front Of House engineer, leaving Mark Kelly without a keyboard technician. So, when Mark posted a request on Freaks for a replacement, Erik jumped at the chance. "Before joining the tour with Marillion, I was working at the campus IT help desk at Case Western Reserve University, in Cleveland, Ohio," explains Erik. "I was working in theatres and concert venues as a lighting designer, and I was helping out in a recording studio." Handily, he was also developing web sites on the side. Recalls Mark, "He applied, I enjoyed the tone of his email, he's been doing stuff with us ever since!"

Erik first met the band at the start of the tour in San Juan Capistrano, California. As it progressed, he and Mark discussed one of the hot topics at the time, the Web. "During the tour we began the crusade to use the Internet to its full potential," says Erik. The conversations led to Erik being asked to run both the Marillion site and to help out with Racket Records' operation. Continues Erik, "I initially ran the website from Cleveland whilst waiting for various work visas to get arranged." Eventually, on 30 March 1998, he came over to the UK.

There was only the occasional hiccup, notably one time when he was refused entry back into the UK following a few dates in Scandinavia. "It was 20 September 1998," says Erik, "I was allowed back in the country for a day to pick up my things, then they flew me to Philadelphia." Before long, a visa had been sourced and Erik was back, this time for good.

on the sleeve notes for the *'Clutching At Straws'* remaster, "It enables a bunch of sad individuals to hack each other to bits with virtual broadswords, without ever meeting, while running up extortionate phone bills."

Over the 18 months following *'TSE'*, as the band were building up to leaving Castle, the full potential of the Internet was being grasped. In an interview with El Mercurio in Chile on 28 October 1998, H commented that, "its potential as a global mass-communication medium-for-all is still to be fully realised." Marillion had every intention of achieving just this. Earlier in the same year, Erik Nielsen was recruited to build a "proper" Web site for Marillion. One of his first actions was to register Marillion.co.uk in December 1997, but Marillion needed to be represented as a global concern. "Marillion owned Marillion.co.uk as the official site, and the band wanted to call the next album *'Marillion.com'* when *'Radiat10n'* came out," explains Erik. "Jeroen Schipper at The Web Holland owned Marillion.com, so we asked Jeroen him if we could switch Marillion.com over to us and he said fine!" Jeroen was, and remains, delighted. "Erik's done an excellent job in maintaining it," he comments.

Today, Marillion's Web site is one of the best and most popular fan sites on the Web. In a review of the album *'Marillion.com'*, a journalist commented, "Marillion have embraced the Internet not as new technology, which it isn't, but as new culture, which it still is." The band believe its Web site is more than just "another channel" or a nice-to-have. Notes Mark Kelly, "Without the Internet, the future of the band is less sure." A sobering thought – thank God indeed.

Thank God For The Internet by Mike Stoor

In Spring 1989, I was finishing my freshman year at the University of Minnesota, Duluth and pledging to a fraternity. As a mere pledge I was required to be at the beck and call of the actives. One night I was summoned to the apartment of the president and his roommate who was the secretary. Tanqueray flowed freely and tongues were loosened. Discussions of supply and demand and libertarianism soon moved on to music. Those two guys had made a trip to Milwaukee for a Rush show and had been completely wowed by Marillion who were supporting. At some point *'Script For A Jester's Tear'* had been put on as backdrop to our conversation. I don't remember details but I do remember thinking that I had never heard anything like it. It was explained to me that this band had four albums which told the story of a man looking back on his life, and it went chronologically backwards. In other words, 'Album One' was old age and 'Album Four' was childhood. Not quite right, as you know. I'm not sure if their explanation, or my less than sober state, were to blame but it was enough to pique my interest. I had never heard of such a thing; a whole album dedicated to a theme. This was something I needed to know more about.

I asked for copies and shortly thereafter received *'Script For A Jester's Tear'* and *'Fugazi'*. I'm not sure what it was that struck a chord. It was not like I understood all the words - I didn't have lyric sheets and I'm not sure I would have understood the references if I had. Mark Kelly's atmospheric backdrop torn apart by flashes of guitar wizardry by Mr. Rothery, Fish's vocals - so much emotion I wondered how one voice could contain it all. 'Jigsaw' was a favourite.

"Stand straight, look me in the eye and say goodbye. Stand straight, we've drifted past the point of reasons why. Yesterday starts, tomorrow, tomorrow starts today. And the problem always seems to be we're picking up the pieces of the ricochet..."

Punk had emotion, AOR had hooks; here was a perfect blend of both.

A few months later I found a promotional cassette which contained 'Kayleigh' and 'Incommunicado'. That did it. I had to have more. In the fall I found a used copy of *'The Thieving Magpie'*. I borrowed a copy of *'Season's End'* and though I liked the music of 'King of Sunset Town', I couldn't get over the new voice and never bothered getting through the second track. I threw my allegiance to Fish and acquired *'Vigil'*. I also at some point laid hands on *'Real To Reel'* and *'Six of One'*... The latter exposed me to more H-Marillion, but I was still too bitter to listen with the open mind necessary, though that 'Easter' track was interesting. I got *'Internal Exile'* but never got into it, apart from 'Shadowplay and 'Credo'. That was the last I would know of either band for a long time.

By Fall 1997, there had not been a whole lot of Marillion or Fish in my life since graduating college. I was in my senior year of dental school in Omaha and was able to get on my school's computer and while surfing found The Web Online. So they were still kicking, eh? Not only that, but they had just been back in the US, in the Midwest, not too far from where I was sitting. The news of The Tour Fund amazed me and I thought, okay, I'll give it another try. I picked up 'Made Again' and was completely blown away. The Internet was the answer. I got a computer in the Spring of 1998 and first order of business was subscribing to Freaks and completing back catalogues for Fish and H-Marillion. I had Internet access and disposable income. Not only could I keep up with the news in both camps, I could order without relying on the pathetic music stores in Minnesota. I had rediscovered Fish as well and had even won autographed CDs (*'Kettle Of Fish'* and *'Raingods With Zippos'*). It was about this time I fired off a drunken thank-you to Freaks for the camaraderie signing off with "Thank God for the Internet", still waiting for the credit on that one!

appendix three enough of a freak

"It's not the size of the ship, it's the size of the waves."

Little Richard

Since its earliest days Marillion has had a fan base that most bands would die for. As some fans have dropped away, new ones have arrived to replace them and provide a consistent, continuous backbone of strength that has supported the band through thick and thin. Where do they come from, these fans? Why do they do it? Are these the happiest or the saddest people alive?

Being a fan isn't about endless debates on lyrical meanings, or devoted purchases of yet another item of memorabilia. Well okay, it is, but only in part - 'fan' is short for fanatic, after all. All fans must by nature be a little obsessive but most have day jobs, appearing to the outsider as perfectly ordinary people even once you get to know them. But they share one fundamental truth - they all get it, whatever it is, and are happy to go with it.

As commented Ian, "The magic and muscle behind Marillion's music is a mystery to many yet understood by masses." So - do you get it?

where do they come from?

Marillion's original fan base was no accident. Very early on, the band realized that their non-mainstream musical style would need more than a few gigs and a catchy tune to grow a following. Instead, the boys copied the traditional approach of the '60s and '70s - to grow by popular vote. Not that this was the easy option, but for a band as determined, dynamic and downright unusual as Marillion, it was the most logical. And for numerous reasons, it worked: even before Fish joined, the band was developing a local following, which grew exponentially when the big man arrived. It was a rare person who could resist the urge to clap when Fish said clap, or sing when he said sing. The music itself was also a major factor: it was good, it was tight, and it was unlike what everyone else was doing. Remarks Canadian fan Miles Macmillan, "They were playing a style of music at that time that no one else was playing anymore." Early fan Dave Rogers comments, "I liked these guys as players, and the songs themselves struck a chord with my male angst, borne of a society that did not seem to care about its youth. I guess I wasn't alone in those sentiments, and in the eyes of many, these really were the days of Market Square Heroes." Fan Marc Roy was struck by Steve Rothery's guitar playing: "Finally a guy playing the guitar the way I'd always been looking for. He's probably the reason why I make no particular distinction between the different eras of Marillion." Finally, many fans felt that they were discovering something new - notes Miles Macmillan, "It was cool to be into a band that not a whole lot of people knew about and watch them slowly gain popularity." Peter Gifford agrees - "It felt special and was very exciting to be involved at the start of something. I felt like I was getting in on the ground floor of something new with bands like Marillion." Adds Peter Gee, "It was perfect for that moment and how people were feeling at the time." And so the band were off towards the limelight. Not that they didn't work at it - here were people who lived for their music (and those who didn't, or couldn't, were quickly culled and replaced). The band was determined to prove something, to take on a battle against the odds and win. "It was us against the world," remarks John Arnison.

When the first album came out, it set in train a number of new factors. The combination of Fish's complex lyrics and Mark Wilkinson's detailed covers layered new qualities on top of the music and the live act. Recalls fan Miles Macmillan, "When I interviewed Fish in the early days, he talked about the album covers and hidden clues, and said that each successive album was going to have a theme and it would all make sense as they went along. It always sounded like they were putting a great deal of work into their concepts and not just slapping together a bunch of tunes." Indeed they were, and together

local band for local people

Marillion's base in Buckinghamshire is surrounded by pockets of fans, who emerge in the most surprising of ways. One, a local sandwich producer who'd drive around the businesses in the area with a loudspeaker announcing his presence, could hardly believe his luck when he stumbled on the Racket Club. "That's great," said Colin Price of Racket Records, "But unless you want your van appearing on every Marillion release from now on, I'm not being funny but is there anyway you can turn that bloody noise down!?"

with the live act they formed the something that people could really believe in. As word of mouth became something, well, bigger, fans developed a spread-the-word attitude that remains to this day. Writes Rick Collins, "In 1983, one thing that amazed me was the evangelical nature of the Marillion fan." Rick was among their number, as he recounts: "This strange desire I have to share the news that I've found something amazing and I'm concerned that no-one else seems to see it... seems so scary when you listen to born again Christians and hear that same strange excitement!" It wasn't long before Marillion spread its wings beyond the shores of Britain. Unless you count 11 April 1982, at Bathgate in Scotland as the first international gig, continental Europe was the first target, and Mannheim, Germany was the location on 21 May 1983. Largely due to this European push, the first couple of albums generated a reasonable following in Germany, Holland and the Nordic countries.

All in all, it was quite a package. For the fans, the stage was set for the first three albums, which bore out the principles that the band had allied itself with. Forays across the Atlantic had not been as successful as hoped, but *'Misplaced Childhood'* opened the door to a new fan base. Not that Marillion ever really broke America, but they certainly gave it a fair crack of the whip. The fourth album took a new direction - gone were the hidden depths, here was a more current, relevant album, but fans sought solace in the remaining, more contemporary imagery and the fact that the music was going from strength to strength. However it was not to last, as to many fans' despair the instigators would be brought to an apparent halt in late 1988. When Fish left the band, there was a split of the fan base as well, as its members felt forced to declare their allegiances to Fish or the rest of the band. This was in no small part down to the loyalty that the front man inspired: it would be folly not to recognise that many fans saw Marillion as Fish's band, however good their collective musical output was. Says Peter Gee, "many felt that Fish was Marillion, and without him they were as good as dead. The expectation was that Fish's solo career would flourish and be successful like Phil Collins's had, and that Marillion would stop."

Skyline Drifters by Rich Harding, July 2002

It all began when Andy 'Tosh' McIntosh sent a post to Freaks in early 1998 asking for other UK fans to contact him: he'd had a great idea to club together to pay Mark Wilkinson to create a bespoke piece of artwork, as a 40th birthday present for Fish. The 40-strong group who contributed set up a private mailing list to keep in touch and, later that year, we decided to throw a party for charity and invite the wider Freaky community to come along or buy raffle tickets (Fish, the band and others had contributed a very large number of prizes - we made £1500 for charity).

Close before the party, it was suggested that there should be some Marillion and Fish music to go with the band that had been booked, and so Tony Makos and Richard 'Tricky' Reeves volunteered to play guitar, with myself on vocals. We all trooped off to the local scout hut for a practice during the afternoon, continuing later in a tent (!), and Skyline Drifters were born. Backing vocals on some tracks were provided by Lucy Jordache (then still at EMI) and Vicki Harding (no relation) of the Web UK; 'Waiting To Happen' will never sound the same again! The set list also included, amongst others, 'After Me', 'Sugar Mice' and 'Kayleigh', to which I forgot the words!

The Skyline Drifters moniker was first used on the occasion of the second Just Good Friends (JGF) party, also in Nottingham, on 10 May 1999, where Adrian Holmes joined us on drums, with Tony Makos moving to bass duties, enabling us to cope with heavier tracks like 'Assassing'. We also threw some acoustic numbers into the mix, including 'The Great Escape' - my debut on guitar! This was also a charity do and again Gary and Val Grove deserve name checks.

For JGF3, the following year, Tosh had the bright idea of inviting Tony Turrell (of The Positive Light and Fish fame) to play keyboards. We also added a couple of non-M/F tracks into the mix, including Porcupine Tree's 'Signify' and Pink Floyd's 'Have A Cigar'. This event was held at The Mitre, in Ade's home town of Stourbridge, and was the first for which we properly practiced together beforehand (although still minus Tony T), following it up with the inaugural Drifters' Curry Evening! The gig was well attended and raised close to a thousand pounds for the local maternity unit.

Into 2001 and things got more ambitious: we decided to push the boat out and organise, with much help from Andy Westmoreland, Darren Newitt, Ian Avery, Tosh and others, Garden Party 2001, at Stourbridge Rock Cafe - a proper venue with a stage and lights! This would be a full, two-hour-plus set, supported by another tribute band, Made Again, and John Young, so we actually, shock horror, had two rehearsals! Tricky had left due to other commitments so we recruited Dave Woodward of the Genesis tribute band, Invisible Touch. Despite technical glitches at the start, this was an awesome gig to play and included a thirty-minute 'abridged' 'Brave' (segued between 'Standing In The Swing' and 'The Great Escape'), part of 'Plague Of Ghosts', 'Cinderella Search' and 'Beyond You', closing with 'Market Square Heroes'.

For Ade's 40th birthday, in January of this year, we reprised this performance at the same venue, adding 'Splintering Heart', 'Script', the 'Clutching At Straws' opening trilogy and 'Between You And Me' to the repertoire, and did a similar set a week later at Pete and Annette Goosey's wedding in Leicester. We're currently choosing non-M/F songs for two upcoming gigs, which will involve stand-ins for Tony's Turrell and Makos respectively because of other commitments; didn't I mention how amazing it is that we get this together at all? I live in Bristol, Ade in Stourbridge, Tony T in Ipswich, Dave in Sheffield and Tony M in Edinburgh!

It's a great privilege to play this wonderful music with a brilliant bunch of people for an appreciative audience. Thanks all.

Keeping The Faith

It was to the surprise of many that both parties managed to pick up where they had left off. The quality of the two albums that emerged was enough to ensure the continuity of the wider fan base (particularly the hardcore who found their favoured lyrical elements on one album, and musical elements on the other). The 'new guy' in Marillion would even manage to win over many die hard fans, who succeeded on the strength of his incredible voice and total devotion to the cause. "The power of his voice was a big bonus in his favour," says Peter Gee. Outside the hardcore, however, the public popularity of both sides waned despite the best efforts of all concerned (not to mention a number of legal cases on Fish's side, instigated by him, that had the unfortunate effect of his career being stopped in its tracks). It seemed that, whatever Marillion tried, the band continued its slide downhill. Things came to a head after *'Afraid Of Sunlight'*, the new Marillion's fourth album, which coincided with the band's departure from EMI. The next few albums were rightly referred to as the band's own wilderness years, before it departed from record labels altogether and sought to reach out to its fan base on its own terms once again. With *'Anoraknophobia'* in 2001, Marillion did far more than discover a new way to fund an album. They relit the fires under many thousands of hardcore fans. The message was that, whatever happened in the future, band and fans would be in it together.

Today's fans are the reward for twenty years of hard graft on the part of the band. Marillion has a truly international fan base, with its numbers boasting from as far afield as Brazil and Japan, as well as the more familiar haunts of the UK (naturally), France and Germany. For some reason that nobody has ever managed to fathom, none are as devoted as the Dutch: "The Netherlands has always been a very passionate following," says H. Not that the location matters that much - fans will come, where ever the band decides to play. "I'm amazed and moved by how far people are willing to travel to see us," remarked H in an interview. Mark Kelly agrees - "wherever we have fans, they're in it up to their necks!" And they will travel. When the first candlelit dinner was announced in Oswestry, the band wasn't amazed just because of the numbers of people who wanted to attend but the distances they were prepared to travel. The distance poses difficulties - particularly for the further out pockets of fans. "It's very difficult being a Marillion fan on this side of the world, especially South America or the Caribbean," comments Carmen Julia Quintero, "You practically miss all the concerts and special presentations, which you can not afford to go to every time, call it time or call it money."

Looking into the future, Marillion's support network is growing once again. Today's fan base is still in the hundreds of thousands, the mailing lists have never been bigger, the sales are growing, press coverage is increasing and new initiatives are being tried all the time. The band may or may not reach the soaraway scale that they achieved in the eighties, but in the meantime things are looking good in terms of the continuity of support and the foundation for its future success.

Marillion fans today include barristers and exotic dancers, DJs and schoolteachers, teenagers and grandparents and a whole spectrum of people in between, all of whom love the music, love the band and are often prepared to go that extra mile. What was that - exotic dancers? Indeed, one-time 'dancer' Heidi Huff became a fan when she was given a tape with Marillion songs by a suitor. "'Just For The Record' caught me," she says, "It reminded me of my father." Heidi had a wide repertoire of songs that she used in her act, from 'Lady Nina' to 'Three Minute Boy' (puts a new spin on that one). "That was my way to spread some Marillion joy to the world. It worked," comments Heidi.

You never know, things just might take off again for Marillion - big time. Whether they do or not, with fans like these you can be sure that the hardcore will remain as strongly devoted as ever.

Hit By A Bat For The Very First Time... by Carmen Julia Quintero

My first encounter with Marillion took place in 1989. When I first listened to them I felt like I was hit with an extra large bat. I still don't know which tornado passed over me. It was love at first listening, it was being captivated by a magic that still remains today…

Afterwards, I started building up my Marillion collection. In the beginning I had to rely entirely on tapes recorded by more resourceful friends, because I didn't have the money to buy CDs, I didn't even own a CD player. But, at that time, tapes were more than enough to catch the magic of Marillion.

As time passed, I became not only a fan but an obsessed freak with Marillion. The same friends who introduced me to them started to look at me strangely, and to tell me that I was on my way to become a real freak (well, that's the whole point, isn't it?). Finally, news came that Marillion was going to have a concert in Caracas on 30 September and 1 October 1991; we were ecstatic, in disbelief: Marillion right there, in our backyard!!! Quickly, we ran to get our tickets for any of them (some people even bought tickets for both concerts!) and to start learning the songs they might be playing those nights. For weeks prior to the concerts, nobody in USB could speak about anything else; everything was Marillion, Marillion and Marillion.

Finally the great day came. I couldn't pay attention in class, I was eager, anxious, and with a degree of expectancy I had never experienced before. From my group of friends, about 30 of them were going to the concert, so we organized ourselves for the rides to the place where the gig was going to be held: Poliedro de Caracas. As a matter of fact we were the very first to arrive and so early that a local music TV program interviewed us, giving us a nickname: Los Fiebruos (The Feverish Ones, which means 'the extremely fanatical ones'). After a long, long wait we got into the place and just hanged out while the support band were on stage (up to now I don't know what kind of music they played, a pastiche of genres, very influenced by Marillion, how strange!).

When the lights came out and the first notes of 'Splintering Heart' were heard, the crowd couldn't help themselves, we started to scream and chant and do whatever a lovesick fan would do. And then, they came on stage. You could have sworn that they were rehearsing in their house's backyard, they seemed to be playing so effortlessly, so at ease, but what was coming out the speakers was pure and raw magic.

I was in the front row at 5ft. from the stage and I was OK until Steve H and me looked each other in the eyes; well, at that moment I thought I met the father of my kids. Oh, my goodness! These were the bluest and most hypnotic eyes I have ever seen in my life! For the rest of the concert I couldn't help but keep looking at him, I was in love (platonic, but love anyway) as I am still today. There is nothing in this world that would take me apart from Marillion and their music.

I don't have to say that this was one of the best concerts, ever. The atmosphere was unique, ethereal, almost surreal. The boys played like never before and they actually had fun!! If you ever listened to the CD *'Live In Caracas'* you will be able to feel it too. Even though the place wasn't full to capacity, we made up for it 100 times (that's one of the good things about the Venezuelan crowd: energetic to the max, always giving themselves to the artist, warm and beautiful). The band couldn't believe they had such a fanatic audience in a place that most likely they never heard about before, so it also was a new and refreshing experience for them too.

what kind of a fan?

We are all equal, but some of us are more equal than others. So it is with Marillion fans, who are as regular a bunch of folks as could be imagined, but who revel in their status of a breed apart.

Fans express their appreciation in different ways. There are the tour followers, with some travelling around the country (or the world!) to see their band perform. Explains Simon Clarke, "You bump into people at gigs and get chatting, they say, 'Are you going to so-and-so-place?' and the whole thing snowballs big time!" An infamous fan called Rob the Vending Machine would, according to fan Bubba, "Hitchhike across the USA and follow Marillion. He smelled real bad, but he knew everything about Marillion and lived on the road in truck stops. He was wild! A lot of Marillion fans gave him a hard time, but I thought he was the most unique Marillion fan ever." Second, there are collectors, who will locate and purchase every obscure item of music and memorabilia that they can find. At the end of a gig, collectors ask for plectrums, drum sticks, set lists - "I've never understood the set lists!" laughs Colin Price, who is frequently on the giving end. "I think people get hyped, the atmosphere at the front gets so intense!" For every fan, there will always be another who is more obsessive, more anorakish, more of a collector. The top of the class are the lord high anoraks, those whom the masses consult for advice on all things Marillion. Finally, there is the category for those whom Marillion has become even more than a way of life. Confides Erik Nielsen of Racket Records, "There's a list of about ten true obsessives that we know, but they're harmless in their own way. If the band ever stopped we'd have serious problems!" Interestingly, these people are largely outside the UK. "Fans in general tend to be more obsessive in the UK, but the real nutters are outside the UK!"

There are fans that try to step over the line - or at least to determine whether there is a line at all. Occasionally, a fan will discover the location of the Racket Club, as Colin recalls. "We had a forces guy stationed nearby, well he just turned up! He said, 'Hello; just thought I'd pop in!' and then he was gone again! For every fan that turns up, there are a thousand fans that ask, 'I'm over for a holiday, could I just come over and say hello?' The answer is always a polite, yet firm, no." From his independent perspective (and having been in a successful band himself), John Helmer remarks, "There are people who want to touch the garment. As you don't experience the adoration yourself, it can be quite puzzling and bemusing!"

But most fans just aren't like that - it's more the sharing of a common purpose and the will to go the distance that separates out Marillion fans from the chaff. From the fan's perspective, it's a lot of fun: "It's an escape from the job, a chance to catch up

keeping the tradition

Fan garden parties have their roots in the traditional conventions of ten years ago. A date is planned, a few bands are booked and the stage is set for a fun night out.
The UK Garden Party 2001 was held at the Rock Café, Stourbridge, on Saturday 7 July 2001.
Fish's keyboard player at the time John Young, and tribute bands Skyline Drifters and Made Again. Profits were donated to Nordoff Robbins Music Therapy.

with people and enjoy the music," comments Judith Mitchell. "Plus, I need my fix!" But is it really any different from football supporters or listeners to 'The Archers'? The only identifiable difference is the personal level on which the relationship works. "I think the fact that the band members are so obviously genuine has a lot to do with the loyalty they engender," says fan John Deveraux. This loyalty has bred a structure that goes beyond such loose-knit structures than supporters or listeners. Explains Steve H, "What we've got going is that it's all real. The vibe is so rare and precious, it surprised us - it's a bigger deal than a bit of music, it's grown into something resembling a church. We have to be careful as artists, I can't put it into words without sounding pompous or hippy."

To come out and say it, Marillion is a cult band, with all that it entails. Perhaps the most surprising thing is how genuine and down to earth are the band members themselves. Remarks John Helmer, "Artists in general deserve respect for what they do, but are ordinary and even deficient in other ways. Marillion are extremely down to earth - I admire that about them."

In an interview with Jon Epstein of RockNet, Steve H commented, "We don't really understand it, but for some reason people either live for us or don't like us at all. There aren't many people who just think we're OK. It's nice, we're probably the biggest cult band in the world with the exception of the Grateful Dead!" Despite being unsure about exactly what it is that Marillion has, the band are keen to ensure that 'it' is distributed as widely. "We try to encourage fans to be as close as is humanly possible, but without hindering the performance," says Colin.

tribute

Tribute bands used to be rife. There remain a few, boasting names such as Jester Hoax in Italy, Seasons End in Germany and Skyline Drifters in the UK. Each has its preferred songs and styles - Jester Hoax specializes in Fish-era, whereas Skyline Drifters boast a balanced set from both eras, taking pride in playing many songs that have been shelved or forgotten by both Fish and Marillion camps.

One thing the band will not do is compromise the very source of its success, namely its music. Even decisions that may not have appeared to be the best ones have come from within the band, without seeking the opinion of the outside. Mark Kelly remarked in a Web interview, "Not to say we don't value our fans opinions, but we don't consider what they might think at all when we are writing." With reason, as Rothers explained succinctly in a chat session - "When you start writing music for your fans as such then you are severely limiting your possibilities. You've got to have the artistic freedom to go where you will, as opposed to worrying about what everybody will think about what you're trying to do." Added H, "The chances of us knowing what our fans want are almost zero. To try to imagine what you think they want is a terrible mistake because you are trying to pin down smoke!"

Again with Jon Epstein, H remarked, "It's something that they personally actually believe in. Something that they appreciate, and for all the work we put into creating these records and writing these songs, these people got it. They understand it."

With fans like Carmen Julia Quintero, the devotion looks set to continue: "I cannot conceive a day without listening to them or without learning something new about them, it is like a necessity, like the oxygen you need to breathe every day. It's a life that has been lived the past 13 years in the mysticism and magic of a group of people that you might think them common, but they are not. They are poets, they are lifesavers, inspirational speakers, a motivation to go on without minding the terrifying world around."

Putting The Sociology Into Marillion by Martin Johnes

Fandom is not just about supporting a team or liking a band. It is about developing a sense of identity and belonging; it's about possessing (or being assumed to possess) certain codes of behaviour, values and characteristics; it's about having fun; it's about something personal. What we like says something about who we are, both in our own eyes and the eyes of those who look upon us.

This can cause dilemmas for people who like the unfashionable. After all, self-esteem matters. It matters to Marillion and it matters to the fans. They want critical acclaim and we don't want people to think we like an out-of-date Scottish heavy metal band. Fan groups across the globe, whether we are talking football, Star Trek or Marillion, always try to ensure that their fandom is seen in a positive light. Thus, fans of lower division soccer teams who never win anything, turn supporting a useless team into a symbol of their personal perseverance, dedication and loyalty. Furthermore, they argue that they are proper/superior football fans when compared to the armchair-Sky-TV-Premiership bandwagon followers. Thus being a fan of something that fails actually becomes a matter of status and esteem.

It's the same with Marillion fans. No one likes our band so we make a joke and virtue out of being 'fashion unconscious' and claim that the band is only prevented from world domination (or at least critical appreciation) by media prejudice. The band, of course, have done the same with their embracing of the anorak.

As a lecturer in sports sociology, this is a parallel I use in classes about fan cultures. Unfortunately, it tends to be rather spoiled by the fact that none of the twenty-year-olds I teach have ever heard of Marillion. I think at one time I really did believe that being uncool was clever irony and that my favourite band would be number one if only the radio played their songs. But now I'm not so sure. I'd like to say it was my sociological training that encouraged me to question my dominant beliefs. Sociologists, after all, deconstruct myths and norms, but now I think it was actually harsh reality that made me face the truth (assuming there is such thing, another sociological argument…).

The week after I last gave my fandom lecture, someone in my class told me that he'd since heard Marillion on an old compilation CD. "No offence," he said, "But they were crap". This year, when wearing my "Uncool as f**k" T-shirt, my wife said to me "You do realise that that statement is fact. It's not ironic." I lamely argued that coolness was subjective. She replied, "Maybe, but whatever way you look at it, Marillion are crap." Given such dominant societal discourses, it's no wonder we retreat in search of alternative interpretations that maintain our dignity. We can argue all we want that if there was some objective measure of musical quality then Marillion would do okay but such a measure does not exist. All we have is subjective accounts of what makes good music and, whichever way you look at it, most people don't share our taste in Marillion.

There's nothing irrational about our irrational interpretations of the world. The music makes us feel good. My very bad and obscure football team makes me feel good. Okay, I am uncool and into a band that does nothing for most people, but it's not my fault the majority have no taste…

hope for the future

Apart from the tour fund, one of the fans' most coordinated efforts was the release of an entire album. This was started by Jon Epstein and his then-wife Cathleen in 1998. Explains Cathleen, "Several tribute albums had been released during late '96 through early '97. There was a lot of interest in the tour fund, the Marillion tour and then Fish's tour. I think the idea grew from there." Jon continues, "It occurred to us that there were quite a few musicians on freaks, and quite a few popular bands that were into Marillion," recalls Jon. "We spoke about it quite a bit with Fish and Mark before we did it, wanting to make sure they were all OK with it. As I recall Fish was fairly indifferent, H was, well, H! and Mark was into it in a big way."

As demos rolled in Cathleen and Jon set about putting together an album while Cathleen hunted for a suitable cause for the proceeds. "The response was pretty interesting," says Cathleen, "Some of the demos were amazingly good and some were eye-bulgingly appalling!" Meanwhile, the pair were faced with the age-old difficulty of finding a record deal. Recalls Jon, "We originally approached Magna Carta records, and when they expressed doubts about the project, we decided to try and do it ourselves." Jon invited Gina Achord, who was Marillionised by her husband Ray in 1997 on the This Strange Engine tour, to help out with the project. At the time Gina was working for Surgeland Records as product marketing manager, so she seemed an ideal fit. "Of course, I said yes!" remarks Gina. Jon also approached better-known artists to participate, but unfortunately they wanted payment, and this was to be a charity record.

When Jon and Cathleen found themselves unable to complete the project, they handed the reins over to Gina. "He sent over all the tapes and CD-Rs already contributed by the bands. Of course, I knew nothing about all the workings and legalities of pressing a CD. Just contacting publishers and waiting to hear back took several months!" Gina arranged that all profits (the band and Fish had waived their rights to royalties) were to go to children's charity Interplast. Marillion were not the only supporters of the project, recalls Gina, "Michael Gardiner was a great help with legal matters and offered to help free of charge; the wonderful Carl Glover at Bill Smith Studios agreed to do the artwork free of charge; and Scott Jones and Larry P. Sipes at Bernie Grundman Mastering mastered the CD at no cost. Steve Hogarth had said "Bernie Grundman is God's own engineer," so just hearing that made me happy!"

So far, everything had gone relatively smoothly, however Gina found the biggest problem had nothing to do with publishers or royalties. "Out of all the entries for the CD, I picked the best ones, and they were put on a website in mp3 format to be voted on. However, it became apparent that obvious stuffing

made again, again

When Irish fan Brandon O'Connell was 17, he made his first film - an eight minute flick including a few pieces from the feature-length 'Brave' as well as glimpses of Richard Stanley's 'White Elephant'. It was made in Brandon's bedroom, and the only equipment was a C-VHS camera and two VCR's. The film was entered into the Fresh Film Festival in Limerick coming third - most inspiring, as most other entries were made semi-professionally with financial backing! Brandon is planning a follow-up, focusing on the *'Afraid Of Sunlight'* album. This is at an early stage due to relocations, but Brandon is feeling positive for the future - "We have a treatment and we are starting a finalised Script," he says.

of the ballot box was weighing the votes in favor of certain bands," recalls Gina, who resolved to take matters into her own hands. "I cancelled the voting and called upon 10 longtime fans/friends of the band to complete the voting process." You can imagine how that went down on the lists, particularly by fans whose offerings were voted out - a cause for some consternation. Explains Gina, sadly, "I believe I lost a lot of friendships due to not choosing certain people's bands, or how I handled other aspects of the project. That's unfortunate as I can separate business from personal matters, but I guess for some this is not so easily done."

Not Alan Walker, who had heard about the project on the Marillion website and who had recommended Interplast as the charity, as well as submitting a number of songs including 'Out Of This World'. He commented, "Gina was an absolute joy to work with. She was very professional and persevered when others would have given up." The final result also included songs from John Wesley, Tracey La Barbera (who had sung backing vocals for Wes). Gina laboured on - "It would have been very easy to give up and say, 'I don't want to do this anymore,' but I felt there should be at least one tribute CD for the greatest band in the universe, by the fans for the fans!"

The project still required financial backing, which came in the form of a pre-order campaign. Gina contacted an old friend, Derek Sivers at CDBaby.com, who set up a pre-order page including a final list of who would appear on the CD. "I figured out how much money it would take to press 1,000 CDs, and announced that it was in the hands of the fans. If I received enough money for pre-orders, the CD would be able to be released. Luckily it did!" Ray Achord, a fan since *'Fugazi'*, contributed a history of the band to the liner notes, "Attempting to emulate the enthusiasm the original writers of Kerrang! magazine had for Marillion at one time."

Then it was just a case of sending the CD for manufacture, and awaiting the results. "I was very pleased with the outcome of the CD," remarks Gina. "It took 9 months or so in total from the time I started the project to its completion, and I definitely felt like I had given birth to this CD when the boxes arrived on my doorstep with the 1,000 discs within!" Over $5000 was raised for Interplast.

Unsurprisingly given that only 1000 copies were made, there was an absence of mainstream reviews. The Dutch Progressive Rock Pages paid tribute to Gina "for the wonderful work she has done." As for the songs, DPRP remarked, "Half of the music is good, the other half isn't, at least not if we keep in mind that this is supposed to be a tribute. If you're a big Marillion fan it's still worth checking out though!"

As with any feedback from Marillion fans, there was, of course, a lot of criticism about who was chosen for the CD, the songs on the CD, etc. Until one embarks on such a project, it may be difficult to understand just how much time and effort goes into it. But how did the band feel? "There's some interesting stuff on there," says Steve Rothery, non-commitally. In an interview, H commented, "Obviously it is flattering if someone wants to do it, that's a good feeling. The only way a tribute album could be interesting for me is if an artist I really admire was involved in it, but there aren't that many. If Joni Mitchell sat down and played 'Estonia', I really would like to hear it."

The fans' opinions: Marc Roy - "Well, for one, I really liked it. A good mix of totally reworked songs, some very faithful renditions and some new twists on familiar themes. Most artists are very little known, but it doesn't matter... lots of talented people out there. 'Beautiful' by Tracy La Barbera is simply breathtaking. Sounds like it was written for her. But if you can't stand H singing Fish, Mosley playing Pointer, Usher playing Rothery or Patterson playing Kelly, this is not for you. For everyone else, it provides really good entertainment (what this business is all about after all) for a good 50-60 minutes!"

Going Under by Joe Griffin

Well, my brother Pete actually was the one who got me doing it; he's Braintree, basically (at least, he was the only member of the band at that point). He really wanted to do a tune, and went through his Marillion collection and picked 'Going Under'. He wanted to make something as different from the original as possible, and had been listening to quite a lot of David Bowie's *'Earthling'* CD. So he was very into the drum and bass style, and very much into digitally cut-up guitars and vocals and such. We'd used these techniques on a couple of previous Braintree songs, but not as extensively as we did on 'Going Under'.

Anyway, when we were done with the track we submitted it - this I think was around the time Gina Achord took over the project - and found out the deadline had been extended. I emailed out, "Hey, is there time for me to submit a track of my own?" and the answer came back yes, so I dug through my own Marillion discs and started 'Just For the Record' (*'Clutching At Straws'* is my favourite Fish-era album, and Pete's too I think).

So oddly, I got almost all the way through the Braintree track without even considering doing one myself. Partly though, this was because Evil Genius were broken up at the time, so I had no band. I was able to use an old drum track of Pete's, lopping off the last eighth note to create a 7/8 drum loop (that's the time signature 'JFtR' is in - most of it anyway) and recruiting my ex-bass player to come in and jam a part out one afternoon.

When I decided to do the track, it was for a couple of reasons: I've always liked covering Marillion live - here was an opportunity to cover them on record. I wanted to take a tune and re-realize it and this was a good chance (I'm not so good at doing that with my own material; I guess I'm too close to it). I thought that inclusion on the CD might bring my band some attention from a fan base I knew to be open to new and different sounds, as well as loyal to music they liked. (This is what you do when you're an unsigned artist - you look for as many opportunities to expand your fan base as possible) The Braintree sessions were lots of fun, and I wanted to keep going. An interesting side note - Pete told me he heard (not sure from whom - we'd have to ask him) that when the CD was played for Marillion, Mark Kelly said the Braintree 'Going Under' was better than the original. Don't know whether that's true but it certainly is rewarding if it is.

appendix four solo in the game

"If you can walk you can dance.
If you can talk you can sing."

Zimbabwean Proverb

Marillion has achieved a great deal as a band, yet it always has and always will be a close-knit, yet disparate, set of personalities, each with his own strengths. Along with Fish's departure and the arrival of Steve Hogarth, it is also appropriate to explore the individual characters inextricably linked with the Marillion story.

Fish

Name: Derek William Dick
Born: 25 April 1958

The big man, the charismatic Scot, the poet, the hero, the assassin, the tyrant. Fish has been called many things in his lifetime. In 1984 Fish described himself as a hedonist, attracted to the fringe activities of life, "to experience and learn; the human magpie collecting things, collecting experiences," not confident and yet ready with his mouth. "Actually I'm a vicious bastard with my tongue!" Restless, never comfortable stuck in any one place, yet still hankering after the predictability of home comforts and family life, Fish's story was never going to be the path of least resistance.

Making it in the music business was Fish's ambition from an early age, but things did not start as well as they could have. Here was a gawky, shy lad whose musical prowess was overshadowed by his incapability to toe the line. The young Derek Dick's debut came at King's Park Primary School in Dalkeith near Edinburgh, the town where he was born. "I sang 'Ye Banks And Braes' and 'St. Lucia', at Donaldson's School for the Deaf," he recalled. "I was fired for not attending rehearsals. I still have the same problem today!" - as good an illustration as any of the turbulent relationship Fish has always had with music.

Like his lyrical ability, Fish's legendary charisma was not a given. When he was unable to swagger in the appropriate manner at Dalkeith High School, his peers ridiculed him for his size. Eventually he learned to deal with the verbal abuse through humour. "It's like the Les Dawson thing," he commented in an interview. "There were a lot of people laughing at me and I was really hurt, so I learnt that if you can turn that and make them laugh with you, you conquer them with a smile." Neither was school the seed bed for the poetry which would make him famous (among his fans; it was ironically coined "schoolboy poetry" by his detractors). "I always wanted to [write poetry], but I felt very self-conscious when I wrote anything down," he remarked later. "I felt as though I was betraying something."

At home, Derek was getting into music. He picked up The Kinks' 'Lola' at a jumble sale. "I immediately fell in love with the lyrics and the ability to tell a story through song," he would comment. When he wasn't off watching Hibs play ("They were a really happening club!" says Fish), his youth was peppered not only with the opuses of the prog giants. T Rex, Elton John, Deep Purple and Paul McCartney, all helped to broaden and deepen the pool of influences. Remarked Fish, "I never felt part of any tribe and I could get a kick out of Led Zeppelin as much as Carole King."

When he was 18, Fish turned his back on school altogether, trying a variety of jobs (most notably with the Forestry Commission), before admitting his path lay elsewhere. Four years later Fish started to indulge his passion for singing. "I never had the confidence, and I wasn't living in an environment that music was a part of," explains Fish, who was also considering acting. "I quickly found it was easier to get a singing job than an acting job!" While still a forestry worker, he failed an audition for Not Quite Red Fox, whose bassist/vocalist had been approached in March 1980 to replace a chap called Doug in some Aylesbury band. Finally, at the age of 22, he auditioned for a covers band called Blewitt and got the gig, moving down to Galashiels, much to the chagrin of his parents, who still hoped for some sensible life for their son.

Blewitt's set included material from Steely Dan and the Average White Band, a good mix for Fish's broad tastes. Fish's first night at the Golden Lion was below par. Stage nerves had led to desperate calming measures, resulting in Fish taking to the stage a bit the worse for wear. "I threw up over my all-white outfit of Indian cotton shirt and flared trousers as soon as the gig finished." Fish's perception that he nearly got the boot was true, but it wasn't for his behaviour. "We should have sacked him. He sung really bad that night," commented guitarist Frank Usher in an interview with Claus Nygaard. Ironically, it was Frank who really helped Fish to develop his vocal capabilities, "He kept on pushing," recalls Fish.

Before long, Fish started looking towards the more fruitful plains south of the border. He went for an audition with the Stone Dome Band in Retford, Nottinghamshire, where he met bassist Diz Minnitt. Fish gave up his day job and moved down, staying with Diz's parents. The pair quit shortly afterwards, moving to the more lucrative environment of Cambridge. They spent a few months living at a girls' hall of residence ("I remember thinking it strange that no-one minded" says Diz), going to unwelcoming parties, including a formal dinner party with both Fish and Diz in full face makeup ("To wind up the hoi polloi," according to Fish), and attempting to form a band before returning to stay with Fish's parents at Dalkeith in Scotland, where at least they knew they could get a gig.

The pair moved to Ettrick Bridge to sign on. They managed to blag a holiday cottage to stay in, convincing the owner that they were a band called Sirius who were seeking inspiration. "Fish said we needed somewhere to write over the winter," smiles Diz. Fish returned to Blewitt in November 1980 and played a total of 15 gigs; in the meantime, they got on with their isolated, hard up, depressing lives. "It was horrendously depressing, we felt completely isolated," says Diz. "Our lifestyle got so totally out of sync, we went to bed at 5am and got up at 5pm."

Eventually Fish and Diz had sunk so far, they'd reached the bottom. "Fish said, 'We have to do something', he went and bought Musicians Only and I went thorough it and found a couple of adverts." The second was for a vocalist/bassist, and included an Aylesbury phone number. "I was almost salesmanlike, it was one of those experiences where you meet someone or do something, it just felt absolutely right!"

A tape was sent, which included Fish singing in Blewitt and Diz playing with the Stone Dome Band. "He sang the 'Guards of Magog' section from [Genesis'] 'Supper's Ready', a couple of Yes tracks, something by Peter Gabriel [1] and a version of 'Garden Party'," recalls Diz. In the return post, Mick sent 'Lady Fantasy' and 'Close'. It was like coming home, Fish's first reaction to Steve Rothery's fretwork was, "Fuck, this guitarist is brilliant!" Unabashed, he set about working one of his existing lyrics around the piece, which he titled 'The Web'. Following a final gig with Blewitt, supporting Alexis Korner in Melrose on 13 December, Fish and Diz sold up, signed off and drove south once again. It was New Years Eve 1980. Notes Fish, "We decided, this is what we have to do. We burned our bridges behind us."

So Here I Am Once More

When Fish quit Marillion, many thought it was the end of

> ### counting time
>
> In the early '90s, an accountant called David arrived back in Edinburgh after a long spell abroad. He bumped into an old friend who suggested they meet up with a guy they were at school with, if he was around. David turned up in his best casual gear to find the pub was a heavy music haunt, full of bikers with long hair. Undaunted, he ordered a drink and waited for his old pal, who eventually turned up with a very tall chap called Derek Dick. David didn't notice anything unusual about how the crowd parted to let Derek through, nor the admirers who were pointing at him and staring. David's first words were along the lines of, "so what have you been doing since you left school then Derek?"
>
> **Chris Lewington**

The Stone Dome Band

There was nothing much to do in Laneham near Retford, on the Notts/Lincs border, so 18-year-old Diz Minnitt and a bunch of mates decided to make music. "Someone lied to me that after a couple of months I'd be quite good," says Diz, "it wasn't true, but by then we had a set already!" Calling themselves Plastic Surgeon, they played at the Stonehenge Free Festival in 1979 ("to get a gig, all you have to do is call,") with Diz making funny noise effects on a synthesiser, "it was sort of punk/experimental, some of it was even ambient!"

Whatever it was, it didn't last. Diz moved on to bass and with the drummer from the Surgeons, formed the Stone Dome Band. "The keyboard player was recruited via an advert, the rest were friends of friends," explains Diz. If the previous band was experimental, this crowd were somewhere else. "It was like a cross between King Crimson in its most experimental phase and Planet Gong," says Diz. "We'd set the tape off in my father's corn mill, and we used to go around banging things and shouting!" Techniques included the drummer playing the bass (with his sticks) while Diz was doing the fretwork. He admits, "It was complete and utter self-indulgent claptrap!"

Deciding a vocalist was in order, the band put an ad in Musicians Only. It was answered by Derek Dick. "He was just Derek back then, he answered the ad and moved down," says Diz. "His singing raised the hairs on the back of my neck, he was the first singer I'd heard who could do that!" The newly completed band developed music, including the original version of 'The Web' and a song called 'Eyes In Sand'. Before long, Fish was encouraging the others in the band to get organised, to develop a coherent set list and so on. The keyboard player announced he was not prepared to turn pro, so Fish and Diz left to try their luck in the more happening climes of Cambridge, and that spelt the end of the Stone Dome Band!

both his career and that of the band he left behind. Yet though Marillion had played such a major part in his life, Fish would prove that there was plenty more to the man than those seven years had encompassed. Just as Marillion wasted none of the musical ideas that had been developed in the final writing sessions, neither did he waste any of the words. Both felt the uphill struggle of filling gaps the other side had left. However, while Marillion simply had to find a singer, Fish had to source an entire band. He also decided to pursue his claim to more revenue, in Court. "It was like a divorce situation, like getting divorced with four women at the same time," says Fish.

First to arrive was Mickey Simmons, who Fish met through Mike Oldfield, another resident of Buckinghamshire. "Bringing an awareness of melody and hooklines, Mickey guided me down the first avenue of solo creations," commented Fish. Andy Field, another close friend, also stuck around in the difficult times. Finally, there was John Cavanaghan, a senior EMI executive, who agreed to become Fish's manager. Things were still reasonably open between Fish and Marillion - well, Steve and Ian at least - to the extent that he even asked the pair if they wanted to work on his new album. "Steve quite rightly turned my offer down, as did Ian, as they felt that for us to be working together so soon, would be detrimental to both our new careers," Fish commented later.

Almost immediately, Fish and his wife decided to relocate from Gerrards Cross to Scotland, a decision cemented when his parents found an old farmhouse in Haddington. Spittalrig Farm had a number of outbuildings suitable for use as a rehearsal rooms. Primarily it was cheap, freeing Fish of any debts and giving him enough to live on while he got his act together. One of the first songs to be written was 'A Gentleman's Excuse Me', composed as Mickey and Fish drove to a baptism. In November 1988, Fish went on the hunt for a producer. First

pick up a penguin

Fish and I had to take a PA system to Edinburgh. For some reason, we then had to pick up a load of unstuffed, cuddly toy penguins. We popped in on a mate on the way back and skinned up... later, there we were, trying to drive home in a weird state with a truck full of penguins!

Diz Minnitt

choice was Chris Kimsey, who had worked with Marillion on the previous two albums, but his Rolling Stones commitments (*'Steel Wheels'*) made things difficult. In the end Jon Kelly, who had worked with artists as diverse as The Damned and Kate Bush, was selected. According to fan and all-round knowledgeable source, Andy McIntosh, "What tipped the balance was his work with Deacon Blue on *'Raintown'*." Recording began in May 1989 at the Townhouse Studios in London. "In retrospect I don't think Chris would have been the right man," Fish commented later, "I needed to get away from the Marillion connection and I needed to learn from experience, a different environment and source."

By August 1989, the album was complete. Mark Wilkinson produced the cover, not least because he had already started it, as the artwork intended for Marillion's fifth studio album. Continues Mark, "I had dealt with Fish 99% of the time on the cover designs with Marillion. It seemed natural to carry on that relationship for his solo career." Although the album was ready, it could not be released, as Marillion's album had been finished first. "Both my and Marillion's albums were ready," explains Fish, "EMI didn't want to go head to head, they thought my profile was bigger so they asked myself and John Cavanagh to put the release back a few months."

This gave Fish and Mark Wilkinson a chance to see the cover for Marillion's new album. It was never the intention to insult Mark or his icons, according to Mark Kelly, "We merely wanted to show some continuity with the past, while, showing that we were moving on." From Mark Wilkinson's perspective however, his imagery was being trashed: there was a clown sinking in a pond and a jester vanishing in the sand, not to mention a solitary magpie feather floating down. It didn't take much persuasion to add some subtle enhancements to his own artwork. Lying scrapped next to the hill was a white Porsche (Steve Rothery drives one), while around the fire sat two tramps, with the faces of Mark Kelly and John Arnison. "It was a trifle mischievous... but then so was having my illustrated clown from *'Fugazi'* drowning in a muddy pool on *'Season's End'*!" says Mark, for whom the water is long under the bridge. Things were very different at the time, particularly for Mark Kelly. "I thought, bloody cheek!" he says. "I told EMI I wanted all the albums destroyed." Eventually a compromise was reached, the next batch had the tramps' faces painted out.

streets apart

There has been speculation whether Iain Banks' 'Espedair Street' was written about Fish. It remains one of Fish's favourite books, and he once tried to buy the film rights. Is it true? Steve Rothery thinks so: "Too many coincidences!" he smiles.

Fish was ready to go live and booked a series of dates in his homeland. "I hadn't been on the road for a while, I wanted to get out there and do a pub tour," he says. "Financially it was a fucking disaster, but in terms of confidence boosting it was immense!" He performed with Robin Boult and Frank Usher, both names from the past, with whom Fish still had a good relationship. "Playing the solo stuff was great," says Robin. "Playing the Marillion stuff was different, it felt like being in a covers band but not." Adds Fish, "The costumes were terrible! People said we looked like extras from 'Blake's Seven',[2] I came across it on satellite recently and cringed because they were right!" The tour was a boost for the fans, preparing the ground for the album, and giving the two singles a bit of a lift. Five days after it commenced, on 16 October 1989 'State Of Mind' was released and reached No.32 in the UK charts. It was followed up by 'Big Wedge', Fish's Christmas single, which despite not being particularly Christmassy, made it to No.25.

'Vigil In A Wilderness Of Mirrors', came out on 29 January 1990. It contained a mix of songs and styles, and was generally (and genuinely) well received. Steve Rothery described the album as, "Interesting, if a little poppy for my tastes!" The follow-up single,

Tara

Tara Rowena was born 1 January 1991, according to Fish, "weighing in 8lbs 6ozs and the most wonderous creation I've ever seen in my life."

released on 11 March 1990, 'A Gentleman's Excuse Me' achieved a reasonable 30 in the UK charts. The tour also started in March and despite its success, was expensive; all of his musicians were being paid session rates, and Fish was trying to build a recording studio at the same time. On July 9, Fish played to a packed audience at The Royal Albert Hall. He performed in the shadow of a high court injunction which prevented him from recording anything else, due to his legal battles with EMI, to resolve the contractual issues he was left with when he went solo. It was unrelated to the action he had already started against his former band members, for what he saw as a fair share of Marillion's royalties. Promoters typically were insensitive to what was going on behind the scenes, happily advertising Fish and Marillion on the same poster wherever their paths happened to cross.

Among the acknowledgements on the album cover was a thank you to Marillion, "for showing me the hill." But it was a false summit. The injunction prevented Fish from releasing albums for almost a year; he went AWOL for the duration of the case, which he eventually lost due to lack of funds. What had started as a bluff, intended to shock EMI into submission, ended in disaster. "I had to leave the table, tail between my legs and a huge legal bill to follow!" recalled Fish. He was also advised to settle with his former bandmates. Coupled with what was, self-admittedly, "an overambitious tour," and the prior decision to turn the farm's outhouses into a fully fledged studio, Fish was broke again, and broken.

Romantic Poetic Type Or So They Say... by Andy McIntosh

Other collectors have often asked me what the most prized item in my collection is and I'm happy to been able to have given the same answer every time I've been asked. Quite simply the best things I have are the memories, nobody can take them away and they stay with you forever.

One of my best memories dates back to the early days of Fish's solo career, I'd caught the last show of the State Of Mind tour at London's Town and Country club and was really looking forward to the full Vigil tour and the return of Fish to Nottingham after several years' absence. After making it to one of the warm-up shows at Newcastle Polytechnic, which incidentally was meant to be for students only, but after Fish asked for a show of hands proved to have fewer students than 'guests', I was really up for it.

The show in question was at the Royal Concert Hall on 31 March 1990 and it was rather special for me because it was the first time I'd managed to get my then fiancée, Lesley, to come to a gig with me. In actual fact it was her very first gig of any kind and I'd been lucky enough to get tickets on the second row. The show was just a couple of months before we were due to be married and, unbeknown to Lesley, I had written to Fish and asked if it would be possible to dedicate a song to us at the Nottingham gig.

The day of the gig came and off we went to Nottingham, had a beer, bought the T-shirts and took our seats. Lesley had picked up the words to many of the songs from my constant playing of them at home and did well to keep up with the new solo material as well as the older Marillion tracks. The set had a good mix of old and new and everyone was enjoying the show, but as the show went on further and further without the dedication I was beginning to get a little disappointed. The main set ended with 'Heart Of Lothian' and the band left the stage to thunderous applause.

After a few minutes the band returned and Fish had a bit of paper clutched in his hand. He began to introduce the first encore and checking with his bit of paper dedicated 'Cliché' to us. Fish had asked whereabouts in the hall we were and I'd sheepishly raised my hand only to find that we were instantly 'bathed in the spotlight's glare'. Apart from going beetroot red with embarrassment it was great to hear the best wishes for our coming wedding and the rest of the encores seemed to float by.

After the show had finished we were invited round to the stage door to come in and say 'Hi' along with getting a few photos from the album which were to be enlarged, signed and framed as a reminder of a truly awesome night.

You won't be surprised to hear that we travelled home on cloud nine that night. A great band, a great show and a fantastic memory.

Exile In The Wilderness

Fish's legendary confidence had suffered a major blow, still, despite the feelings of "defeat and betrayal" that accompanied the completion of the court cases, the only way was up and on to the next album. Productive talks with Polydor had still not resulted in that all-important signing and funds had all but run out, but Fish did have a recording studio.

Once again Chris Kimsey's name was in the frame as producer. He went to Haddington in October 1990 to talk tactics, however there was a slight complication, he was also tabbed to produce *'Holidays In Eden'*, Marillion's next album. Chris working on both projects was not an option: "To have the albums stamped with the same production, would destroy two years work, on both parts, establishing individual identities," Fish commented at the time. In the end, time was the decider. Chris had a live album to produce for the Stones in February 1991, Marillion had booked the slot before it, Fish's material was planned for late April. "Marillion still hadn't enough songs, in Chris's opinion, to start as they intended in January," recalls Fish. "This time the Stones schedule came in my favour, a neat coincidence!"

A signing with Polydor was in sight, involving David Munns who had been responsible for marketing Marillion at EMI during *'Misplaced Childhood'*. "His enthusiasm and drive is infectious and his belief in me as an artist is undeniable!" wrote Fish. Meanwhile, he had been playing a part in the BBC thriller, 'Jute City'. Partially recorded in Liverpool, it gave Fish an opportunity to meet up with old mates Dave Lloyd and Paul Lewis.

Chris's experiences on *'Internal Exile'* were, frankly, weird. He brought with him Thomas Stiehler, recreating the production team for *'Misplaced Childhood'* of five years before. "Fish had nearly finished his studio, there was a good feel there," says Thomas. Unfortunately for the team, the success of Berlin was still too fresh. "Chris tried to work like he did with *'Misplaced Childhood'*," explains Thomas. "Musically, I missed Marillion," says Chris. "In hindsight I was trying to make a Marillion album."

Despite the pleasure of signing a deal with Polydor in early summer 1991, the album didn't achieve the level of success it should have. Its single, 'Internal Exile', made 37 in the

get back

When we supported Fish on tour, we never wanted to overrun, so I had a clock on the monitors. When our time was up, we finished and came off… I was met in the corridor by this 6'5" apparition, I thought, oh God, what have we done wrong? But he said, "Get back on! They fucking love it! Get back on!"

John Jones, Jump

charts for one week. Fish was bitter, twisted and difficult to work with, the new studio was plagued with problems and the songs were a mixture of styles, which, according to Fish, "never got into a particular groove or locked into a direction." The Scottish nationalism previously rising during Fish's Marillion days, was now well and truly at the fore, resulting in an album that, while cementing his homecoming, failed to inspire a wider audience. Says Thomas Stiehler, "Some people said that Fish went too Scottish, the English companies didn't like it!" Neither did many fans. "It just didn't sell!" commented Fish. "Polydor had rushed the album out with my acquiescence, resulting in a fractured promotion campaign and disappointing sales."

The tour to accompany the album was to Fish "Disastrous. The UK promoter (Bandstand) went bankrupt just as it was about to kick off!" It was an inauspicious start for Yatta, who had joined Fish as Production Manager!

The final blow to Fish's confidence, credibility and fan base was the next album, a covers album following ideas Fish had during the *'Misplaced Childhood'* recordings in 1985. Financially and creatively broke, recording the songs of others seemed to be more accessible than a new set of material. "It was the worst decision I have ever made," admits Fish. "It was one of those moments, like when a coyote gets his leg caught in a trap, it was something I had to do." Somehow Fish managed to convince Polydor and the album was recorded in summer 1992. It was produced by Irishman James Cassidy, who had been engineer on Jeff Wayne's *'Spartacus'*, a project on which Fish had collaborated. Like *'Spartacus'*, on its release in January 1993, *'Songs From The Mirror'* bombed, leaving a crater most would not have attempted to crawl out of. The album included a cover of 'I Know What I Like'. The song which had lived alongside Fish's time with his old band, by now seemed almost a lament. The record deal was over and sadly during the recording, Andy Field had finally passed away. The funeral saw a brief reunion with old band members. "I was quite cut up, he was a great bloke and we'd had some fantastic times together." says Pete. Adds Ian, "Up until that point, I'd never been around death, he was my drum roadie, crew boss, it was my first funeral. Andy was very old school, he showed people respect. He'd always say, 'sorry to trouble you.'"

Mickey Simmonds had gone to work with Mike Oldfield, "He paid better than I could," says Fish, who also had to sack John Cavanagh because he could not afford to pay him. "It was a pretty bleak period," says Fish. All was not lost, however. The tour that accompanied the album made a profit, and Fish had been finding some creative acorns of his own, mainly rooted in his cynical feelings towards the music industry. Here was proof that the greatest adversity could yield something, maybe not triumphant flames, but certainly the sparks of hope. *'Songs From The Mirror'* had also enabled a catharsis. "The album was a turning point for me as an artist," Fish commented in an interview. "By delving into my past and the influences that had made me what I was, I rediscovered myself and the Magic that had brought me here in the first place."

present of two halves

My wife bought me a set of full size football goalposts for my 35th birthday, soon after my team, Hibernian FC won the League Cup. I opened the bedroom curtains and saw the two sets decorated in green and white rosettes and bunting!

Fish

Label Free

Onward and upward he went. A session with a spirit medium, led Fish to form a record company. "The medium passed on a message from my grandfather," Fish recalls. The company was called Dick Brothers, after his forebear's garage business.

As the company was being set up and plans for the next

radio star

For a period, Fish had a radio show every Sunday evening on Scotland's Radio Forth. "Jay Crawford was a good friend, he'd been after me to do a rock show for years!" says Fish, who was offered the job full time but had to turn it down.

ice of reason

9 April 1999, Steve
:hery turned up at a Fish
. It was only a matter
ime before he got up
olay with Fish. The song
s 'Sugar Mice'.
ys Steve, "I'd heard about
range problems, but
ouldn't just play it
a different key. He did
OK job though - at least
good as he was on the
utching' tour!"

album were being taking shape, five releases were made on the Battleside label, including *'Uncle Fish And The Cryptcreepers'* and *'Pigpen's Birthday'*. According to Fish, these were "official bootlegs," aimed at providing an income and, "A quality alternative to the illegal bootlegs that plagued my career."

For the new album the cynical subject matter remained, but its tone tempered, as the calming effects of time and a pinch of realism, took their course. The failure of the album, *'Suits'*, was not an option. "There was a lot of pressure because I was using the Dick Brothers name," says Fish. "I had to pull something from the bag after *'Songs'*!" Back on board was James Cassidy, who co-wrote many of the songs, as well as producing the album. *'War Of The Worlds'* was still a little too much of an influence, comments Fish, "I was finding a groove, but I didn't yet have the maturity to know when to stop. 'Jumpsuit City' goes on far too long!"

Two months before the release of *'Suits'* came *'Sushi'*, supported immediately by a tour, as Fish resorted to his skills as a promoter, to ensure his bills were being paid. As well as touring determinedly, including a 14-date HMV in-store promotion, "I did interviews with anyone who would listen!" The touring paid off, not only did it give Fish an opportunity to write and rehearse new material, it also led to his band working together as never before. "Touring led to a tightness in the band not often found in a session musician-based outfit," Fish recalls. Furthermore, the time on the road enabled Fish to develop his singing style, well beyond the limitations of '80s Marillion.

'Suits' was released 16 May 1994, followed by more dates, both electric and acoustic. "A by-product of endless in-store promotions and radio sessions to support the first single 'Lady Let It Lie'," says Fish. The stripped-down Fish, was able to reach out to new places and tour longer. With the release of two 'Best Of' albums in 1995, *'Yin'* and *'Yang'*, Fish was able to stay on the road for nearly two years. The albums were engineered

Andy Field RIP

The one thing that was always in the fore of his mind was the show. The gig never suffered and always went on and I watched him load in and out in thunderstorms, torrential downpours, snowdrifts and blistering sun. Nothing was ever a problem. A smoke and a brandy or a vodka and orange during the day took the edge off as he thought out the problems and set up the show. He became one of the top production managers in the world and was one of five to stage manage the Rock in Rio Festival in '89. He was approached many times by other bands but through thick and thin he stuck by Marillion and then myself. A more loyal person I could not hope to know.

I have stories, most hysterical and a few sad, as have many others and for years to come in tour buses, hotel bars and backstage areas these stories will be told of the wee man with the big heart. His name, his memory and his legacy will always be with us. I'll miss him.

Epitaph reprinted by kind permission of Fish

by Avril Mackintosh, now a close friend of Fish's sister Laura and a fully fledged engineer. She explains, "I was up at Laura's wedding, I went round to see Fish and he said, would you like to do some work for me?" A bonus for Avril was to spend a week in New York with mastering supremo Bob Ludwig, "to cut the album".

With experiences and emotions accumulating all the time, Fish was surprisingly uncreative as he toured. No words were written, no music was considered or rehearsed, apart from the back catalogue. It wasn't until 1996 Fish once again found the muse, following a tour of Bosnia playing to the UNIFOR troops. Everything Fish had ever written about the horrors of war, 'Forgotten Sons', 'Fugazi', 'White Russian', was brought to life in those few short weeks. "I had to get the experiences onto paper, or crack up through the intensity," Fish recalls. Soon after, he was back in the studio writing and recording what was to become *'Sunsets On Empire'*.

Fish had been introduced to Steve Wilson, lead singer of Porcupine Tree and a mixer and producer in his own right. Steve explains, "Fish contacted me through our mutual publishing company Hit And Run/Charisma. He had heard some of my albums and was actually more interested in what I was doing with No-Man (using breakbeats and trip hop rhythms but combining them with rock) than he was in Porcupine Tree." Despite what Fish described as a healthy friction between the pair, "as we fought for our identities in the material," a number of songs were written earning the label "progressive nouveau" as they brought Fish bang up to date.

band reunited

In late 1999, Marillion and Fish started to discuss the possibility of a reunion gig. There was to be a set from Fish, then Marillion playing *'Brave'*, then Fish and Marillion performing *'Misplaced Childhood'*. Unfortunately, the idea was shelved when neither side could agree on how the money should be split.

Mickey Simmonds was also back on keyboards. Fish was delighted with the overall result, widely lauded as a return to form. "A lot of people have been saying it's the best thing I have done so far," he remarked. Unfortunately there is more to making money in the music business than having a good album. Despite an 18-month, 115-date promotional tour of 22 countries including the USA, and a number of favourable reviews, it didn't make the money it was expected to make and the tour made a major loss. "It was an absolute fucking nightmare," Fish commented to interviewer Paul Rose.

Fish was determined to succeed one way or another. The breakthrough came in May 1997, when Miles Copeland invited Fish to participate in a songwriting retreat with 23 others, at Château Marouatte in France, ironically the same haunt where Marillion had recorded *'Brave'*. "I was at my lowest point and it gave me the incentive to get up and do it again." While there, Fish met a number of established songwriters, such as Sam Brown, Liz Antwi (who later sang the backing vocals on a version of 'Just Good Friends', as well as touring with Fish for a couple of years) and Charlotte Caffey of the Go-Go's. Songs that resulted included 'Incomplete', 'Tumbledown' and 'Chasing Miss Pretty'. "The whole Marouatte session gave me the chance to flex my muscles, it was like a songwriter's gym!" reflected Fish. With six songs and "a sackful of confidence," he returned to base.

class act

Fish' acting credits, include parts in 'The Bill' in April 1998, and 'The Young Persons Guide To Becoming A Rock Star' in June 1998.

Dick Bros was struggling, admits Fish, "It had no expertise whatsoever. We were just relying on luck and taking gambles." On his return from France, Fish closed down Dick Brothers, closed the residential studio as a commercial concern and signed a deal with Roadrunner for a new album, *'Raingods With Zippo's'*. The album was notable for its collaborations, "Collaboration is what I like best about being a solo artist," Fish remarked. With Mickey Simmonds, Steve Wilson and Robin Boult, not to mention '80s veterans Rick Astley and Paul Thorn, the album culminated in the 25-minute, epic highlight, 'Plague Of Ghosts', featuring Tony Turrell and Mark Daghorn. "They mentioned this 20-minute ambient piece, which became the foundation and outline for 'Plague Of Ghosts'." Claiming it to be the track he was most proud of in his entire career, Fish boasted, "Its as valid to a 14-year old dance music fan, as it would be to the fans of the old Marillion prog stuff."

John Wesley's first touring experience with Fish, came at the end of January 1999, at a pub in Chigwell. With the Roadrunner deal settled (the first release was the *'Kettle Of Fish'* compilation) the album was released in April 1999. "Easily the best thing I have ever done, the reviews were fantastic!" Fish remarked. Difficulties with Roadrunner led to Fish once again setting out on his own, but by now a pattern was emerging. Fish commented, "There's a change in me now. Before, I think my life revolved around our music. Now I think the music revolves around my life."

Also in 1999, Fish took on new staffer Kim Waring, who had first become a Fish (and Marillion) fan in 1982, on the 'Script' tour. She explains, "I was browsing around The Company (Fish's web site) message boards in my lunch hour, I saw one about a job, I got an interview, took a day off work to come to Haddington and that was that!"

So Fellini

With the creation of Chocolate Frog Records, it was once again up to Fish to take matters into his own hands. John Wesley, former support act for Marillion, was enticed by Mark Daghorn, who had produced Wes's second album *'The Emperor Falls'*. "Mark found out Fish was looking for a guitar player," remembers Wes. "Fish called up Mark Kelly and Steve Rothery to check up, they said, 'Go for it!', so Fish called me up and I was hired!" A worldwide tour followed in late 2001 that covered venues across Europe and South America (including Venezuela, Chile, Brazil and Argentina).

Today, Fish's stage show includes a fair amount of banter and, pointedly, a medley of early Marillion tracks, such as 'Market Square Heroes', 'Fugazi' and (of course) 'Kayleigh'; not because it was a hit, but because it was his song, his girlfriend and his angst which made the lyrics what they were. The newer fans stand nonplussed, enjoying the music but refraining to join the foray in front of centre stage. Meanwhile, to many of the old faithful, Fish has come home. He hasn't, of course. Home today is the recording studio in Haddington, incorporating living quarters, a kitchen fitted by the man himself ("They honestly didn't provide the right screws!") and an attitude that looks forward to what is to come.

Fifteen years ago, Fish predicted, "There's no point hiding away; you cannot get it from TV, you've got to go out and collide and spark with people." Today Fish is older, undoubtedly wiser and yet still treading the paradox.

Haddington 2001 by Andreas Dahl

I usually need some time before I'm able to reflect properly on what happened on any Fishian event, this time is no exception. My greatest fear is writing something that doesn't sufficiently capture the spirit of what has been an absolutely fantastic weekend. How can one describe a weekend like this, without resorting to old clichés?

Belhaven Brewery Trip

The first hellos to familiar faces and the first shakes of new hands, free beer, free conversations, the start of a great weekend. Monks Muir, the den of iniquity, the home of debauchery, Tikifour. There's no five star suite in the world can match this place. Andy's party tent, the pleasure dome, the scene of felonious karaoke, experienced drinking, uncountable cheers, perfumed cigarettes and lurkers in shadows. The beach party, a dream fulfilled, the vision I've had in my head for most of the year materialized and the result exceeded my wildest imaginations. The sight of beachclad people in torchlight, talking and laughing, superimposed over the stunning backdrop of Fidra lighthouse, will stay with me forever. The gigs, my first time at St Mary's, a magical venue, sends shivers down my spine. Chelsea Monday, thank you Fish, Frank, Robin and Wes, hunched over their axes, an awesome sight.

Sunday Electric Gig at the Exchange

Great warm-up at the pub next door, set us up for what was going to be the best Fish concert ever. Fish used less than ten seconds to let us know he wasn't going to let us out alive. Absolutely stunning, one of the best live performers in the world. I'm never going to forget 'Market Square Heroes', or a full 'Assassing'; The Wes gig with Andy the wine waiter, thanks mate all is forgiven. My fav is flyboy.

The Tyneside and Poldrate, where we ended up afterwards. A beer garden where conversations were easy, two bars within tiptoeing distance, the venue of the priceless 'who let the Wes out' singalong, and a 'Grendel'-singing Fish. The football tournament, our sporting alibi, great triumphs were to be experienced. Congrats to the Dutch-German team, a celebration of friendship and peace; Norway placed third.

The small and bizarre, but oh so important things...

The dancing beams of the Fidra lighthouse; I now know exactly what Fish means. Just enough mist at the lighthouse to see the beams clearly and the way they were sweeping over the beach, there's a song in there somewhere. Merlin leading the French delegation off into the darkness with a single torch, until they were just a flicker in the distance. Walking back to the Tyneside after the electric gig, hearing the Russian being sung up ahead, the low voices echoing between the stonework of Haddington. A torchlit and solitary Rolf, wearing a jesters hat, singing 'Warm Wet Circles', magical. A sombrero in silhouette on the top of the pleasure dome. Timo's penguin guarding his tent, the friendly security doing their job, confiscating bottles with a smile.

Watching a certain video EP in a certain singer's TV room, singing along and miraculously not being thrown out. The stop at a bakery 3.30am, on the way back from the beach, the smell of fresh pastry. Thanks Colin, we go nowhere in Hadders lest it is in your cab. The stars, can't forget the stars, the sky was magnificent, the veil of the Milky Way for all to see. Fish walking sombrely amongst the gravestones before the gig.

The 'Grendel' rendition, clad only in seaweed, holding torches. Telling blonde jokes, the party tent Sunday, with nobody even remotely interested in leaving, air guitars and endless singing.

The beautiful weather, the only thing we can't be sure of next year. Most importantly, the people. All four or five hundred of them, especially the debauched lot at Monks Muir. Can't wait for next year.

Mick Pointer

Mick Pointer, the man who dropped the 'Sil' from Silmarillion, went to the local secondary school, in the village of Long Crendon near Brill, Buckinghamshire. "We were all lining up to be cannon fodder at the local car factory," he says. "My brother

Name: Michael James Pointer
Born: 22 July 1956; Brill, Bucks

was a carpenter, some courses came up so I did an apprenticeship." Mick left school at 16 and went to college instead.

Three years into his course, Mick met up will old classmate Martin Butler, who had started a band called Stockade with his brother Clive. "The guy doing drums had a really crappy drum kit, I went and bought one, a week later I was the drummer 'cos I had a better kit!" laughs Mick. Things were fine for a while, but after 18 months things fizzled out. Clive left the band, and Martin started to have a new set of aspirations. "He decided he wanted to be a pop star, and sort of vanished!" says Mick, who was left to look for other people to play with. He also picked up the flute and took some lessons. "I'm no flute player, I just thought it might give me a better chance!" he explains. When a neighbour's daughter's boyfriend (a drummer), said he was leaving a band called Electric Gypsy, Mick auditioned for the job and got the gig. He remained on good terms with Martin, a factor that would prove important 15 years later.

The Long Road To Arena

Disillusioned following his departure from Marillion, it was Mick's intention to turn his back on the music business altogether. "I don't think I even listened to music," says Mick, who picked up his old trade and took a job as a kitchen designer and fitter. It was 12 years before an unsuspecting fan put Mick back on the road again. He explained in a Web interview, "This fan called Richard Jordan actually phoned up, he said, 'I've been trying to track you down, I'm a mad Marillion fan and I love all the early Marillion stuff. There are thousands of people around that would really love to hear this again, so why don't you do an album?'"

It so happened that Martin Butler, still a friend of Mick's, knew Pendragon keyboardist Clive Nolan and the pair were introduced. "That was really the catalyst for getting things moving," says Mick. "Clive was a proper musician, his take on music was totally refreshing for me!" The meeting led not only to discussions about Mick picking up his sticks once again, but also the creation of a new record label, a trick Clive had already learned through Pendragon's Toff Records.

Sil-Mar-Ril-Lion

When we split, I suggested to Doug that every time somebody leaves, we should get rid of a bit of the front of the name, that's why 'Sil' went. The first Arena album is called *'Songs From The Lion's Cage'*, because by the time I left, if we'd split everything off from Marillion, we'd have been left with 'Lion'. My little joke!

Mick Pointer

By November 1994, the pair were writing. "We wanted to get the album completely intact before we started introducing other people to it," recalls Mick. Arena was formed with singer John Carson from Asia, Cliff Orsi on bass, and session guitarist Keith More (Porcupine Tree and later Fish). When Steve Rothery found out about the project, he couldn't resist offering his support as well. "I did it as a favour," says Steve. "He was booted out of Marillion. It was a small recompense." Steve was sent a track with vocals, drums and keyboard, and the message, "As soon as the vocals finish, put the solo in." Steve recorded two solos for the band to choose from. "He made a brilliant job out of it," commented Mick.

Arena's debut album, *'Songs From The Lions Cage'*, was released in 1995 to no small amount of acclaim, Arena achieved Best New Band and Best New Album categories in the Classic Rock Society awards in 1996. In the first of many line-up changes, John Carson left just before the awards ceremony, so Arena quickly found Paul Wrightson as replacement singer. Several albums followed, including *'The Cry'* (again featuring Rothers, on 'Only Child'), *'The Visitor'* and *'Immortal'*. On April 2nd 2000, the band released its second live album, *'Breakfast In Biarritz'*, recorded on October 17, 1999 at the Amsterdam Paradiso. The most recent (and most stable) line-up of Arena, consists of John Mitchell on guitar, bassist Ian Salmon, vocalist Rob Sowden and the irrepressible Mick Pointer. A new album, *'Contagion'*, is being recorded and is due out at, or around, the end of 2002. Says Mick, "I want to do it for the enjoyment, that's why I got into it in the first place!"

Ian Mosley

Name: Ian Mosley
Born: 16 June 1953; Paddington, North London

Probably the least changed (grey hair apart) of all band members past and present, Ian has always been more musician than rock star.

Ian grew up in a musical household. His Dad used to play as a violin soloist, at one time playing in six orchestras in theatres in London's West End. Ian's teenage years were spent at Abbotsfield school in Ickenham, where in 1966 the music teacher (Mr Bean, no less!) set the seal on Ian's future career, inviting him to join the school's jazz orchestra. He recalls, "I was into Duke Ellington, Count Basie, Buddy Rich, then I went through the jazz/rock fusion thing. Those bands heavily influenced me."

Ian wanted to be a drummer.. "At seventeen, I was obsessed with technique, I just wanted to be able to play faster than anybody else! I used to practice with my eyes shut, one beat on every drum!" When he left school in 1968, Ian immediately went and joined a band called Walrus. The following year he found himself replacing Peter Wolf in the musical 'Hair' in the West End. The next four years were mainly session work (with a film appearance as a drummer in 'The Romantic English Woman', a film starring Michael Caine and Glenda Jackson), before landing a job in 1974 with Darryl Way's Wolf, with John Etheridge and (of course) Darryl Way. More session work (and a little bit of destitution) followed in Holland 1976, before joining the Gordon Giltrap Band in 1978. The following year he was offered a post with Manfred Mann, as regular drummer (and friend) Geoff Britton was off sick. He didn't take the job. "Geoff rang me up. He said if you take it I'll not get the gig back. Besides he was British champion at Judo at the time!" In 1980 Ian took up with Steve Hackett, a role he held for three years. Recalls Ian, "After gigs we used to do signings. At the time there was the comparison between Genesis and Marillion, so people were asking me and Steve Hackett what we thought. I'd never heard of Marillion but being a true professional I said, 'Yeah, they're great!'"

Roundbush City limits

The Roundbush Garage, opposite the Roundbush Pub in the hamlet of Roundbush, is where Ian washed cars for a few weeks after he came back from a tour when he was still in his teens.
The boss of the garage came out one day and said, "You don't give a toss about this, do you?" "Not really," replied the youthful Ian. "That's fine, carry on!"

At the end of his time with Steve Hackett, a chain of events began which led Ian to Marillion's door. He remembers, "At the end of the tour I thought I'd buy a Melody Maker, something I very rarely did but I just wanted to catch up a bit. I saw this advert, 'Marillion need drummer.' Well, I thought, this is too much of a coincidence!" Ian decided to see whether there

bloody Genesis

"Steve Hackett wasn't known for his sense of humour, so when he'd had enough of one number on a US tour and he started playing his guitar with his teeth, it was quite a surprise! He turned around and he had blood running down his chin and all over his shirt, turned out he'd gone out that afternoon and bought some blood capsules!"

Ian Mosley

was a place for him. "I thought, I must know someone in the Marillion camp. I found that Paul Crockford[3], who used to work with Steve Hackett, also knew John Arnison. I called him and said, 'Paul, recommend me, send flowers!'" Ian then set out on a drum clinic tour for Zildjian and Yamaha. "John phoned asking if I could come for an audition, there was no way I could, I was in the middle of this tour!" He returned two days later to be told the job had already been taken, by young American, Jonathan Mover. But that wasn't the end of the story. Says Ian, "A few weeks later, John called again. He said 'Ian, the boys are in Monmouth writing *'Fugazi'*, they've just sacked the drummer, could you go up and just help?' He asked me where I lived and I said Tring, near Aylesbury, he told me that was where the band was from, it was spooky!" Ian even lied about his age to get the gig. "I was 30 but I told them 29!"

As Mark and Fish were up in Monmouth already, Ian suggested he drive Pete and Steve up to Wales. Only then did he realise what he was getting into. "I went to Pete's house and when I came to the door I thought, he's so young! I thought the same about Steve!"

Crossing The Desert

It was Ian who first proposed a collaboration with French guitarist Sylvain Gouvernaire, who was, in early 1996, living in Ian's flat in Aylesbury. "Steve Rothery had invited him over. He approached me and said 'Sylvain needs somewhere to live.'" As Ian was living in Florida at the time, he agreed, only to find himself sharing with Sylvain a few weeks later, when his marriage to Wanda broke up and he returned to Britain. "Sylvain was working on it, I could hear it coming through the wall! That's when I thought, let's do something!" Much of the material was based on leftovers from Sylvain's Arrakeen days. "I wrote some pieces of it ('Memory Of Eagle', 'War', 'Ocean Song') during the Arrakeen time, other parts were written while I lived in England," says Sylvain. "The ideas were often generated by events in my life or moods I was in, or short impressions from a film, or a book, or a walk in the mountains, anything that impresses me, really..."

there's an albeumb

Ian has described the Iris sessions as, "A bit Clouseau." He noted in a Web interview, "Whenever I suggest a break for a cuppa, Sylvain will start a discussion on why it is not a good time for him to stop right now." The similarities were uncanny: as the mixing dragged on, Ian was said to gain a more than passing resemblance to Chief Inspector Dreyfus!

Sylvain had already worked with other members of the band, but it was Pete who expressed an interest in getting involved. In March 1996 Ian became free so he and Sylvain started jamming. "Racket Club was empty and we had all this equipment lying around, I said it was criminal if it wasn't being used effectively!" says Ian. Explains Sylvain, "The titles 'Train de Vie' and most of 'Crossing The Desert' (the title track) were inspired by jamming along with Ian; I used some of his amazing drum patterns as the starting point."

With Pete's input, the three were a sufficient starting point for the instrumental album. "I was amazed to have the luck of working with some of my very favourite musicians. They were both very excited by the project," says Sylvain. "Ian and Pete played extremely well, they're so used to playing together it's magic! Pete was like reading Ian's mind, guessing his fills in advance." Adds Pete, "I was enhancing what was already played, without knowing exactly what Sylvain wanted. In Iris there is none of the structure, no fitting around vocals, so I could let rip!"

Mixing took a little longer than anyone had expected. "Sylvain spent months, much to the dismay of Ian!" laughs Pete. It was worth it - "I am very proud of the result" says Sylvain. Finally, there remained what to call the project. "Ian wanted it to be called "Sylvain Gouvenaire," recalls Sylvain. "But I wanted to see the album with the name of the project.

President Mosley

"Ian Mosley for President!" has become a regular and familiar cry at gigs. "I've seen the guy who shouts it, he always wears a baseball cap," says Simon Clarke of the Web UK. On one occasion, at the Forum, the cry went out during the silence in the intro to 'King'. "H just cracked up," recounts Simon, "He said, 'You've got bloody good timing'!"

Finally I chose 'Iris', the name of the messenger between the ancient gods of Greek mythology. I liked the symbols attached to this name and its multiple interpretations." *'Crossing The Desert'* was released on April 22nd 1996, the same date as the start of the Made Again tour, on the Racket Records label. Science fiction artist Danny Flynn, who had bumped into H in an artists' materials shop, provided the artwork.

Postmankind

Returning to Ian's Jazz roots, Postmankind was a collaboration with saxophonist (and big band, The Big Blue, band leader) Ben Castle, son of UK music and TV celebrity, the late Roy Castle. Ben had first seen Marillion play at the Milton Keynes Bowl on 28 June 1985, he was 12. By coincidence, he used to live in the same village as Ian (and Fish). Remembered Ben in a Web interview, "At the time I used to play a lot of drums, when by sheer coincidence I met Ian at Nice airport. When we got back to England he gave me a lift home, and we kind of stayed in touch."

A few years later, Ben happened to be playing in Wolverhampton on the same night as Marillion[4]. Ben's gig finished early, so he made his way to the Marillion gig. "We met at the gig and I said to him, do you fancy doing something?" says Ian. Ben came to the Racket Club with his friend Mark, who was to play keyboards, and a head full of ideas. "Pete and I had done the backing tracks, then he came down and added the brass section. He had all these amazing arrangements, I thought, if I'd known he was going to do that, I would have tried harder!" Once the main structures were sorted, Ian made some calls. Answering in the affirmative were Steve Rothery and John Etheridge. Even Steve Hackett managed to squeeze in a solo! "Steve Hackett was a real inspiration," says Ian. "I'd played the track ['Someday In May'] to a couple of guitarists; he was the one who said, 'I'll have a go at this.' I loved what he did on it!"

In a Web interview Ian mentioned, "The thing I've noticed throughout the whole process of recording this album so far, is that it has been extremely enjoyable. Everybody is just having a bloody good time. Hopefully this will be reflected in the finished project, however trying to describe the music is like trying to glue down smoke, it is so diverse."

The project was finished in early 2001, with final mixes by Steve Wilson at his own studio, No Man's Land. The cover involved Racket Records' own Colin Price, packaged in brown paper and packing tape!

"It was really good fun," says Ian. "We might do something again at some time, I'd like it to have more guitars than brass next time, but if Ben could be involved then great!"

Mark Kelly

Name: Mark Colbert Kelly
Born: 9 April 1961; Dublin, Eire

Mark moved from Dublin to Essex in 1969, first to Hornchurch, then Romford. His moment of truth came when he heard Rick Wakeman's *'Journey To The Centre of The Earth'* when he was 15. "I thought, yes, that's the instrument for me!" Mark persuaded his Mum to buy a transistor Hammond Everett Organ for £185. "I paid her back five pounds per week from my Saturday job," he says. "It only had this tiny little keyboard, it didn't sound very good! It was this big thing, I took a saw to it and chopped it down, inside it was just an empty cabinet really!"

Mark spent the next four years working through Rick Wakeman's entire repertoire, first on his Hammond, then on a Farfisa. He also got his hands on a Kawai synthesizer ("I couldn't afford a Mini-Moog!"). He joined a band in his last year at school (which was when the Hammond-chopping took place, "It was too big to take to rehearsals!"). The following year he went to Art College in Bath, ostensibly to find other musicians. There were none, and he flunked the second year entry so he went home. "I re-applied and they refused me! I hadn't been to any History Of Art lectures… the lady who interviewed me was the History of Art lecturer. She said, 'I should have known you, why haven't we met?'"

Mark returned to Essex and started joining bands again, playing for Spilt Grass, before forming Chemical Alice with Jack Grigor on Bass and Dave Weston on guitar. The band got a regular slot at the Electric Stadium at Chadwell Heath, where he bumped into the band that had lost its Sil not long before.

Mark's first impressions of his new band were mixed. "I thought, 'Interesting music, pretty weird singer, wearing a priest's outfit, with big bare feet on stage,'" he says. "They all looked rather strange, but the music was good."

cottage talk

I remember a conversation with Mark in 1994, in which he was saying that the Internet was the way forward, and I was saying that Marillion as a cottage industry was the way forward. Funny how things turned out!

John Jones

Production Credits

At the end of 1991 Mark produced John Wesley's first album, *'Under A Red And White Sky'*. He also played keyboards on the album. "It was a case of having to!" he recalls.

Following *'Afraid Of Sunlight'*, Mark produced Jump's fourth album at The Racket Club. John Jones remembers, "We did a fan club show at the Skoolhouse in June 1994, it went down quite well and we had a chat afterwards about our next album." Mark recalls in a Web interview "I thought they were maybe a bit Prog, but they didn't fit into the typical '70s prog rock pigeon hole!" A few months later, says John, "The phone rang and a voice said, 'Hi, this is Mark Kelly from Marillion. That new album, how about me producing it?'" John invited Mark to see the band again in October at the Captain Cook in Acton. "We really hit it off," says John. At the time, Jump were running a rehearsal studio in High Wycombe, and Mark turned up a few times to help out on pre-production. "I'd listen in to the writing process and provide some thoughts on the arrangements, and they would listen, take some ideas up or think about it." After a few months the band had about 15 songs, and work moved to the Racket Club. "It was a novelty to us not to have to worry about recording costs," says John. Recording started on Good Friday 1995 and finished a few weeks later. As John would recall in a Web diary, "Marillion's flight cases, a candlestick on the piano and a good area for soccer outside. Yes, the studio's fine!" As most of the songs were complete, it was a case of "getting the parts down," arranging and mixing them. Mark selected songs to come up with a balanced album, even dropping one and requesting a new one with a better fit.

Unlike Wes's album, Mark was keen to keep his musical involvement to a minimum. "I didn't really want to try and muscle in on it," he explained. "I did do a little bit on 'Val Addiction'; only the one piece though."

Mark also played some gigs with Cry No More, who supported the band on the Seasons End tour.

The Solo Project

In 1996, Mark initiated a project based on Danté's 'Inferno'. The plan was for a mainly instrumental album, with John Helmer providing a few lyrics to be sung by John

Jones from Jump. "It's inspired by Dante's imaginary trip through Hell, so it's a bit dark. In fact I'm beginning to think I shouldn't devote the entire album to Inferno, as it might be a bit heavy going," wrote Mark at the time.

The project has gone through a number of incarnations. Explains Mark, "It's changed quite a lot, mainly because my musical tastes have changed." The actual whereabouts of Mark's solo project are today unknown.

Pete Trewavas

Name: Peter Trewavas
Born: 15 January 1959; Middlesbrough

For Pete it was the excitement of playing live that drew him into the music business. "I definitely wanted to be a musician because I wanted to play in front of people. I wanted to hear the roar of the crowd and feel the thrill of it all!"

Pete found himself distracted by music from an early age. "I always thought about music, nothing else really," he remarked in an interview. "I was quite a selfish person in that way." Pete was encouraged by his Dad: "He was a complete muso," comments Pete. "He would play me stuff like Glenn Miller, and say 'that's good, isn't it?', then he'd play me Artie Shaw and Benny Goodman and say 'now that's really good'…"

Having moved from Middlesbrough at an early age, Pete went to The Grange secondary school in Aylesbury, where he became mates with Robin Boult and the pair first formed a band. Says Pete, "There was Robin, Mark Marsh, John Hill and me, it was just a Hawkwind type band. We played the school assembly, it proved so popular we were asked to put on lunchtime shows for everyone." Pete won his first bass guitar in a raffle at the local music shop. "To this day I don't know if it was rigged!" says Pete. "It was a Fender Mustang bass, converted to fretless, not a brilliant idea really." Sadly, it vanished, never to be seen again. "I loaned it to a friend, who sold it!"

On leaving school, Pete and Robin joined a band called Manantus, followed by a prog band called Orthi. "Terrible songs, bad long solos," remembers Robin, "But we were playing proper gigs for the first time, especially Friars supports." Also in the band was Malcolm Allen. "Malcolm was the first musician I knew who went on to do quite big things, like getting a recording contract, I thought, if he can do it then so can I," says Pete. Orthi used to rehearse in Long Marston Village Hall, and was voted best local band, three years in a row, at Friars. "Doug Irvine was my roadie!" Pete laughs. Meanwhile, Pete found a job as an apprentice TV engineer, for the security. Eventually, Orthi was to fold, explains Robin, "We had some great times and a reasonable local following, but the band never had any proper sense of direction or concept and eventually it came to a halt."

Following Orthi, Pete and Robin worked through a number of bands, including The Robins, Heartbeat, Tamberlane ("I was playing bass and singing as well, it was a bit of a tall order!" says Pete), The Cameras (who played at the Marquee) and finally Red Stars. Robin left to work with a singer-songwriter called John Wilson. ("Mari Wilson's brother," says Robin, "Although at that point Mari hadn't had any hits.") On 1 January 1981, Pete joined a Haircut 100-style band The Metros: his stage name was Pete True. The Metros released an EP that proved so popular, it had to be re-pressed. Flushed with the success, they tried their luck in New York. It didn't work, but Pete did have the pleasure of supporting Duran Duran. "Because they looked good on 'Top Of The Pops' we all assumed they couldn't play," says Pete. "In fact it was a good gig with the songs coming across really well." Pete maintained his interest in Haircut 100 until June 1982, when he claimed he didn't like them anymore. "It's a good job our fans aren't as fickle," Tim wrote in The Web.

Transatlantic

Two years after Steve Rothery and Steve Hogarth's appearance with Dream Theater at Ronnie Scott's club in London, on 31 January 1995, Mike Portnoy emailed H to ask whether Pete would be interested in playing bass on a solo project he was planning. Explains Mike, "My love for Marillion and respect for Pete as a (very underrated) player put him on the top of my list. I also remembered when we played with them in 1989, at Marillion's soundcheck, Pete was fiddling with some bits of Yes' 'Close To The Edge' and that stuck with me. I remember thinking, seems this guy has some good taste!" "Mike and Steve were in discussion over the use of tapes from the Ronnie Scott's gig," says Pete. "Steve H passed a message on to me asking if I would like to join Mike in a fun thing involving people who Mike wanted to play with!" Pete was unsure, both from the perspective of leaving his own band for a while and his own competence. "I had various conversations with Mike about what he wanted and if I was right for the project. He assured me that he wanted me to do my thing as he liked my melodic approach, which was reassuring."

With the addition of Neil Morse from Spock's Beard and Roine Stolt from Nordic band The Flower Kings, the line-up was complete. Says Pete, "I liked the idea of two Americans and two Europeans working together. It adds to the music immensely and brings a charm to the whole thing." The biggest challenge was to get the different musicians in the same place at the same time. The "Portnoy Project" as it was known, was planned for June 1998, but it was put back to January 1999 due to various commitments. The whole thing (and nearly, Pete) was almost canned in January 1999, when he was hit by a car while on a bike. "I ended up in hospital," remembers Pete, who had a suspected fractured spine and required a pin through his leg. "I thought the project would probably go on without me. However, I got a message from Mike saying, 'Hope you get better soon' and the project would be put back till the summer for me to recover. I cannot tell you how much that meant to me at that particular time in my life. I was very depressed and wondering if I would ever walk properly again. That one thing really helped me keep my strength."

Eventually, with Pete recovered and diaries matching, the four managed to get together in the summer of 1999. Pete remarked, "It was a bit of a supergroup, I felt privileged to be in the same room as them!" In the end, the recording process was lightning quick. "We recorded the bass and drums in about a week," remembers Pete. "Mike is a scary bloke and he likes everything to be done as quickly as possible!" It helped that Neal and Roine already had some song ideas, "We decided to work on one of Neal's songs first, it ended up over 30 minutes long, which we really like!" Following the end of the recording sessions, everyone took away a copy of the tapes and added sounds and instruments, as they saw fit. "Some of them got used and some of them didn't, 'cos we were all recording blind after the moment we left the studio." The album was unashamedly Prog. "It's totally retro, I make no bones about it!" laughs Pete. "I think if you're going to be Progressive there's only two ways to do it really, one of which is to say, look, this is

Scott free

We had this idea to do a small fan-club show, doing cover songs. To be honest, our manager had originally contacted Fish to do 'Sugar Mice' and Pink Floyd's 'In The Flesh' with us and he was into it. A few weeks before the show, Fish had to cancel as another engagement came up that he couldn't get out of. Somebody at our label in the UK (East West) made some contact with the Marillion camp and invited the boys. No contact was made so I assumed it wasn't happening, then to my delight, the two Steves showed up at soundcheck! We ended up doing The Beatles' 'Happiness Is A Warm Gun' with H and then 'Easter' with both of them!

Mike Portnoy

what we really, really love about progressive music and we don't really care what anyone else thinks!" For Pete it was new freedom, "It's great! I'm allowed to play like whoever I want to be and no-one's looking down at me, saying, 'Don't you think that's a bit old'?" or 'Don't you think that's a bit derivative?' It was absolutely, very, very self indulgent!"

The final album was mixed by Rich Mouser (who had worked on a number of Spock's Beard albums), a second mix was also done by Roine. Explains Pete, "Roine had recorded some overdub guitar tracks that were left off Rich's version." In the end it was agreed to go with the Mouser mix.

With an album out, a tour was inevitable. In 2000, during the recording of *'Anoraknophobia'*, Pete played six shows in seven days, varying from the hordes of the Nearfest festival, to a handful of people in Boston. "It was a back-to-basics, spit and sawdust kind of Busman's holiday for me," says Pete. "I even set my own gear up and took it down again at Nearfest, which was dangerous, but not as frightening as doing your first show ever in front of a full house of prog fanatics, after rehearsing for two and a half days together."

By January 2001, the second album was underway, recorded in Nashville at a studio once used by Yes. At the time, Pete explained in the Web magazine, "I'm trying to get the band to play Europe, obviously Roine and I would like to, but the Americans are a bit reluctant. I think it's the weather!" The album, *'Bridge Across Forever'*, was released on 8 October, again with a cover by Per Nordin. "It's definitely more rounded and listenable than the first album," comments fan Adrian Holmes. The release was followed by the long-debated European tour, and the 'band' were determined to make the most of it, playing "as many dates as we could." Between 9-21 November 2001, 11 dates were played in England, France, Germany, Holland and Italy. Rehearsals took place at The Fruit Farm near Oxford, a converted apple barn Radiohead used for rehearsals and "allegedly where they wrote *'OK Computer'*."

So, would he do it "Yes, although it was incredibly stressful!" said Pete in a Web interview. And how did Pete's melodic approach pan out? Over to Mike Portnoy. "I love playing with the guy! Pete has got (hands down) the most melodic sensibilities of anybody I have ever played with."

Next Collaborations

Pete recently spent a couple of days at the Racket Club days playing bass with Dave Meegan's Pave project, which showcases singer/songwriter Mark Pavey. "He's really talented," says Pete. "Dave said, 'These are only demos', but they're the best sounding demos I've ever heard!"

Also in the pipeline, is a project with singer Ray Wilson (Stiltskin, Genesis), guitarist John Mitchell (Arena, The Urbane), drummer Steve Alexander (who has worked with Jeff Beck and Duran Duran) and John Beck (It Bites) on keyboards. The project started when Pete had a chat with Thomas Weber, who runs the German record label that signed Transatlantic. Pete suggested the collaboration with John Beck, and Thomas remarked how John was already planning to work with John Mitchell. Says Pete, "I think Thomas is hoping for some radio friendly hits, but the end result will probably be more of a muso thing." With a background like Pete's, how could it be anything else?

Steve Rothery

Steve Rothery is the consummate guitar player (how do people learn to play like that?). His determination is illustrated by the evolution of his guitar collection. His first guitar

Name: Stephen Rothery
Born: 25 November 1959; Brampton, South Yorkshire

was a dodgy acoustic at the age of 14; two years later he graduated to a clone Stratocaster, and six months after that, owned a Yamaha S.G 2000. Steve left school at 16 and picked up a job as a van driver, largely because anything else would have wasted valuable practice time. "When I went to see careers advisers, they'd ask me, 'What are you going to do with your life?'" and I'd answer, 'I'm going to be a guitarist in a rock band!' They'd fall about laughing!" With old school mate Edwin Hart, he joined a band called Purple Haze. "Jimi Hendrix was one of his biggest influences," confirms fan and chronicler Claus Nygaard. "My first gig was the Queen's 25th Jubilee in 1977," says Steve.

Steve was 19 when an opportunity arose, that that seemed too good to miss. "All the people I was in bands with had gone to Art College or University, while I did nothing but play guitar for a year." When Steve saw the ad in Melody Maker, it was like a dream yet to come true. "I sensed the possibility of something happening, to follow my dream and play this style of music, it was worth giving everything up for."

Wishing Well

Since the early days, Steve has frequently jumped at offers of guest appearances, contributing to (and playing with) Sylvain Gouvernaire's old band Arrakeen, as well as John Wesley and Jadis, "Friends whom I wanted to give a little push." In August 1993, in parallel with the completion and mixing of *'Brave'*, Steve produced and remixed the debut album for Enchant, *'Blueprint Of The World'*. Doug Ott and Paul Craddick of Enchant were both Marillion fans who had first seen the band play at The Cabaret in San Jose. When the opportunity came, they were delighted to ask and even more delighted when Steve accepted the opportunity to help out.

Enchant's album had been partially completed by Paul Schmidt, and now the band needed help to finish it. "They're good friends which makes it all the more fun to be working with them." Steve commented in a Web interview. Doug and Paul agreed, "He's been a real inspiration, an all round great guy!" Steve picked up the nickname 'The Compiler', due to his systematic approach to recording; capture each section a few times, select the best parts of each, assemble the resulting fragments into a completed section and move on. With five of the nine tracks produced by Steve, the CD was released in October 1993.

Also at the time of *'Brave'*, Steve had met Miles Copeland who told him about a largely instrumental label he had set up. "Miles asked me to make an instrumental album for his No Speak label. He offered me a considerable sum of money to do it!" This got Steve thinking how much money he could generate if he made such an album himself. Converting his garage and investing in studio equipment ("I was one of the first users of Digital Design ProTools in the country"), one of his first outputs was 'Winter Trees', the B-side of the 'Hollow Man' single.

still freaking!

'Carnival Of Souls' was named after "A dark, sinister American B-movie, about a travelling freak-show."

It wasn't long before enough momentum had built up to make a whole album, something Steve had wanted for many years. Keen to make more than an instrumental album, Steve had already approached John Helmer to produce some lyrics. Steve's original idea was to work with Julianne Regan from All About Eve. "John Arnison approached their management, but they weren't really interested," remembers Steve. The second try was for the singer in Hit And Run stable mates, The Escape Club. "Her voice reminded me of Annie Haslam [of Renaissance], but I didn't like her attitude. I thought, life's too short!" The big break came on 16 May 1994, when Hannah Stobart introduced herself at the Colston Hall, Bristol, following a 'Brave' gig. After a discussion, Hannah sent Steve a tape, which included covers of 'She Moved Through The Fair' (an Irish folk song previously covered by All About Eve) and 'Me And A Gun' by Tori Amos. Says Steve, "I finally found what I had been looking for for years: vocal purity!" By 1995, Steve and Hannah had taken the opportunity to produce a number of demos at his home. The first recording (which later turned up on the remastered album) was 'She Moved Through The Fair'.

The project was named 'The Wishing Tree', after a film by Russian director Tenghiz Abuladze, "about a community on the eve of revolution," according to Steve. Most of the material was to be written and recorded across a two-week period in the first months of 1996, but some were much earlier, such as the song 'Evergreen', which had its origins alongside the recording of *'Clutching At Straws'*. "The chorus part in 'Midnight Snow' dates from when we were writing *'Holidays In Eden'*, while 'Nightwater' is something we used to play when Steve Hogarth did his audition to join Marillion, although he found the lyrics too 'gothic'." Enchant's Paul Craddick played drums and Pete Trewavas contributed a bass line; Steve's wife Jo, also added some backing vocals. Steve knew only too well that the album that it would have to be squeezed in to fit with the demands of his day job. "At one given point I had decided that the album was finished and it had to be released," says Steve. One last push enabled Steve to finish the rough mix at 6am one Sunday morning. With perfect timing, 21 hours later, another series of pushes saw the arrival of Steve's son. "Every time the phone rang, we thought, This Is It!" recalled Stewart Every in a Web interview.

'Carnival Of Souls' was released in September 1996 on Steve's Dorian label. The Wishing Tree then made a couple of appearances on Italian TV, followed by an acoustic showcase organised by Marillion's Italian fan club, Real To Read. There is still plenty of potential for follow-up albums; a new Wishing Tree album is in the works, and Steve still fancies doing an instrumental album. "There's still tons of material I haven't used," says Steve, "There's three days of recording I did with Paul Craddick, some of that's pretty interesting!" As for the happy ending, Paul Craddick later married Hannah Stobart.

Riding With Rothery by Dan and Dana Sherman

In Cleveland one afternoon, having discovered that the Web editors were travelling between gigs in a nice, comfortable Buick Skylark, Steve Rothery had a brainstorm. "It's only a few hours between cities," he thought, "Why don't I ditch the bus, sleep in the hotel and have the Webitors drive me in!" As long as he's there for soundcheck by 5.00. "Besides, you can utilize my excellent navigational skills!" Steve proudly exclaimed as he hopped into the front passenger side. He snatched up the road atlas from the floor and proceeded to turn it around in different directions. "Okay Dan, where the hell are we and where are we going?"

Dan briefed him on the route from Pittsburgh to Columbus, and Steve popped in The Wishing Tree demos. "These are far from finished," he explained. If it gets better than this the final product will be stunning! Steve showed us pictures he had taken of Hannah. "She's beautiful," Dana exclaimed, "Keep your eyes on the road there, Dan!" Merrily we cruised along. As we passed one particularly scenic stretch of stunning landscape, we came around a hill and suddenly saw a majestic road sign that shouted "Welcome to WEST VIRGINIA."

"Ahhhhhhh!!!" The three of us screamed in unison as our fearless driver slammed on the brakes and skidded onto the shoulder. A quick check of the atlas revealed a thin finger of West Virginia protruding between Ohio and Pennsylvania. "That wasn't there when we left!" Dan noted. Three sighs of relief as we resumed our quest. "Are we there yet?" Dana asked. "I would say those very tall buildings on the horizon are a good indicator," Steve commented, "That we are approaching a city of some sort." "Hopefully it's Columbus," Dana said.

So it was. It would have been nice, we realized, if we at least had directions to the Newport Music Hall. "We'll just exit here and ask at a gas station." We exited at Fourth Street and drove for several blocks with no sign of a gas station. "I don't know what the petrol stations in your country look like," Steve admitted, "But if I see one I will surely let you know." We found a deserted BP with a dusty 'Sorry We're Closed' sign. Down another street we came upon a bus station. "That's not our bus," Steve said as Dan and Dana went in to get a map or address or anything to help while our poor English passenger remained deserted in the parking lot... in a No Parking zone... an alien in an alien land.

Got the address but no map, at least an idea of where to go. We went North on 71 and exited West... right into the Ohio State Fairgrounds! The street was blocked with police directing traffic every which way. At this point Dan was going insane, saying "Don't worry we'll have you to the gig by 4.00" as he weaved around and headed back to 71 to take another exit. "Wait! There's a hotel there!" he exclaimed, "I bet they have a map!" "However you seem to be halfway up the entrance ramp," Dana noticed. "No problem!" Riding the shoulder in reverse, our fearless driver took us back through the fairgrounds. There was a marching band leaving the fair, crossing the street to the hotel. "Well there's a band but it's not ours," Steve acknowledged.

Dan entered what he thought was the hotel parking lot, but was actually bus parking for the fairground. "Well there's another bus but it's not ours..." Steve acknowledged again "...and there's that band again..." he added as the car weaved in and out of the marching band, who were apparently trying to return to their bus. Finally, Dan stopped the car. "Don't worry I'll have you to the gig by five!" he shouted as he ran in to get a map. Turns out we were mere blocks away, but were going to have to go around the fair.

Back to the on ramp, driving forward this time and with the marching band safely out of the way, we headed South to the next exit, 11th Avenue. We came across more policemen directing traffic but at least the road wasn't blocked. Dan rolled down the window and in a rare moment of intelligence, asked the officer in the middle of the street for directions. We were only a few blocks away! "Don't worry I'll have you to the gig by six!" as he began to go forward. Unfortunately the officer decided to go to the other side of the street and Dan had to jam on the brakes. "He was very helpful, you don't have to kill him!" Steve pointed out.

Another few minutes of chaos, running circles down One Way streets "Don't worry, I'll have you to the gig by seven!" we finally found the Newport Music Hall. "Oh yeah, I remember this place, I know how to get here!" Steve cried in a belated moment of navigational assistance. Dan apologized to Steve for getting lost, etc. "Oh no problem, we get lost all the time on tour, particularly in Europe where we can't communicate with anyone," Steve said. We deposited him at the rear entrance... at 5.01!

We parked and went into the sweltering 100 degree heat of the Newport. Steve was alone on stage and like a scene from 'Back To The Future' he picked up his Squire, and at full volume cranked out the "Your mother sits..." riff from 'Forgotten Sons'. We waved goodbye and set out in search of an air conditioned restaurant while the band began their soundcheck. Steve waved back and we wondered if anyone would ride with us again after word of our trip got out to the others.

Dorian Music

Following the completion of *'Carnival Of Souls'*, Steve was looking for distribution channels, when he happened to be talking to Mick Pointer (through his collaborations with Arena) and his then-partner, Mandy. Mick and Mandy had set up Verglas records for Arena, and offered to 'sign' The Wishing Tree. Shortly afterwards, Mick split up with Mandy, all the same she offered to set up a similar operation for Steve, called Dorian Music. "She worked for me to set up distribution," says Steve.

An additional motivation behind Dorian Music was to give artists the opportunity to use recording studios such as Racket Club and Steve's own studio. "A lot of the very expensive studios have the atmosphere of a factory!" commented Steve to John Bollenberg of Progressive World. "A small, family type of studio sometimes is much more interesting than a studio bulging with all the latest technical developments." Dorian's focus was undeniably progressive. The Wishing Tree's *'Carnival Of Souls'* was the label's first release, followed in 1997 with *'Somersault'* by Jadis, as well as the third album from Mr So & So, *'The Overlap'*, which included a couple of solos by Rothery (including one keyboard solo!). Mr So & So had already played support for Marillion, on the 1996 This Strange tour. "Steve is a really knowledgeable musician and understood what we were trying to do," said Mr So & So's Dave in an interview. The feeling was mutual, "I really liked them, they were the best young band I'd seen in a long time," says Steve. "They had real chemistry!"

Dorian also handled the distribution of the Iris album, *'Crossing The Desert',* before, finally, things got too much for Mandy. "I'd already been paying her more than she'd earned, so most of the profits had gone to pay her wages," says Steve. "Then she turned around and said she didn't think she'd have time to do Mr So & So and I'd have to find someone else, to say that pissed me off would be an understatement!" Mr So & So had to be farmed out to Voiceprint ("I'm still down on what it cost me to make it!" says Steve), and another hot prospect, the *'Positive Light'* album, went to Eagle Rock; meanwhile, various bad payers made Steve think hard about the whole label thing. Today, while Dorian still exists as a company, it is largely inactive. "I thought, I'm a musician, I don't want to spend my whole time chasing money!" That leaves Steve to get on with what he is best at. Who would want it otherwise?

Steve Hogarth

Name: Steve Hogarth ("but it won't say that on my passport")
Born: 14 May 1959; Helme Chase, Kendal

Steve caught the music bug early. "Almost as soon as I could talk I started singing," he remembered in later interviews. "I was in a choir when I was a kid. I'd always loved to sing, especially on my own in echoey places. I'd stay behind after school sometimes and sing in the corridors of the empty school to myself for the sheer joy of hearing it." Steve's road to Astoria moment came in 1973, when he went to see his first gig, Deep Purple at Sheffield City Hall, on the Machine Head tour. "It was inspirational. I went from just really loving and enjoying the music, to actually

white strings

"When I was about 21, I had a gig on an ocean liner. One night about 3 o'clock in the morning, the bass player decided to murder the drummer and attacked him with a broken glass. The rest of the band tried to prevent the drummer's demise, and it turned out that I got very badly cut up. I nearly bled to death. There wasn't a doctor on the ship, so I was stitched up by a Swedish sailor. He saved my life. The glass severed the tendon in my thumb, it took two years of surgery, physiotherapy and pain to get it going again. My hands were constantly bandaged. Later, I kind of saw the funny side of it; I used to bandage my fingers on stage for nostalgia and from there it turned into a kind of good luck thing."

Steve Hogarth

wanting to be one of the people on the stage," remarked Steve in an interview with Mick Wall. "This is what I should do! What's the point of doing anything else?" A few weeks later, he had talked his parents into getting hold of a piano, and off he went.

Steve attended Danum Grammar School for boys ("Girls were admitted later when I was in the 6th form," says Steve, "I met my wife there."). "I always felt different to the other kids, not superior or anything, just not the same. I always wanted to have a job that was removed from everything, where I could live independently and different from society." Danum school was in Armthorpe, a stronghold of miners' leader Arthur Scargill. "Doncaster was an old, conservative town, conservative as in with old, entrenched views of how to fit in with the "normal" working class fashions and prejudices," says Steve. "I was being beaten up on a fairly regular basis, I used to wear a lot of pink even in those days." Steve's early musical tastes were diverse, but (contrary to public opinion) included a measure of prog. "The last progressive rock album that moved me was *'Close To The Edge'* by Yes. I was a big fan of Yes, I think Yes's best album was *'The Yes Album'*; it was my favourite because it was raw. I loved *'Nursery Cryme'* and *'Foxtrot'*... but, man, that was a long time ago!" While at school, Steve participated in his first band, The Last Call.

Steve left school and went to study Electrical Engineering at Trent Polytechnic (now Nottingham Trent University). In the third year, while working for a wire-drawing company based in Doncaster, Steve joined a band called Harlow which used to do the circuit of the local working men's clubs. "We steadfastly refused to play covers, it used to get us into all sorts of trouble." Steve said to Mick Wall, describing one time when the band played to an audience of fishermen. Says Steve, "I was in the toilets and this huge bloke came in and pulled a very large hunting knife at me, saying, 'Do 'Delilah'!' [5] He said if we didn't, we'd regret it!" Of course, the first song in the next set was 'Delilah', despite Steve only knowing the first verse. "Once we started, all these fishermen just took over and finished the song by themselves..."

Harlow folded in 1980, when the band's plans to go to London ground to a standstill, due to the guitarist whose girlfriend didn't want him to move. Steve had been offered a full-time job with the company in Doncaster, but instead he decided to go to London anyway. "I thought, if I take this job, that's it, you can nail the lid down on my coffin." So, he didn't.

On The Buses by John Deveraux

I was travelling home from work on the train one Friday night. Just over halfway through the journey from London, we were advised that the train was terminating due to engineering works, and we were being transferred to a coach for the remainder of the journey. Mightily peeved, I dragged myself off the train and thought I'd better let my beloved know I'd be even later. Whilst standing next to the coach, I was vaguely aware of a guy next to me going through the same humble apologies to his wife on his mobile. I looked down at his open toed sandals and checked trousers, and as I finished my call, realised that I recognised his voice. It was one of those "don't look now, but..." moments, but I couldn't resist, and a quick sideways glance confirmed that it was indeed Steve Hogarth.

I allowed him on to the coach, and on boarding, noticed the seat in front of Steve was free (actually most of them were free but that was the only one I was concentrating on!). As I walked towards him, I could see he looked really fed up and was probably knackered, so I decided to leave him alone. As we pulled away, the situation dawned on me. Here I was, sitting next to a man whose music and words had moved me for so many years, and had formed the soundtrack to so much of my adult life. Just a few days before, the Web UK magazine had arrived, with a picture of Steve, as a boy, wearing a red coat with a bulldog, on the front (as depicted in 'This Strange Engine'). I attempted to summon up courage, but while I was trying to formulate that all important opening line, Steve leaned across and spoke to me! He was only asking me how long the journey would take, but it sparked off a conversation that lasted for the whole hour or more before we disembarked. Steve signed the Web magazine for me (still a treasured item), and chatted happily about the Marillion world - the band had spent the day in London at meetings with various management companies, including Rod Smallwood at Sanctuary (who eventually got the job). I saw the famous H diary (though not its contents), and we discussed the forthcoming Oswestry gigs, the recently recorded, though unmixed, *'Radiat10n'*, and life in general. We had a long conversation about Brazil, where my mother was born, and which turned out to be the favourite country of us both. I can honestly say Steve was as interested in me as I was in him, and the journey flew by! We parted with a handshake and a heartfelt, "Pleased to have met you", and I ran home like I did when I was told I was in the junior school football team and couldn't wait to tell my mum. Needless to say, my wife's response was not as enthusiastic as I had hoped, but it was late, and, let's face it, as a Marillion fan, you get used to it.

I remember asking Steve H on that bus journey, if he found it hard making music that he truly believed to be the best he could, only to be greeted with apathy, ridicule and ignorance. He said it was incredibly difficult, and at times it gets him down terribly, but it's usually the reaction of the fans that gets him up and feeling good about his work again and restores his self-belief.

The Europeans

Meanwhile, in May 1980 a new wave band called Motion Pictures had travelled from Scotland for the same reason. "We just jumped in a van and came down," smiles guitarist, Colin Woore. As the keyboard player left after a few months, the band put an ad into Melody Maker. One of the people to respond was Steve Hogarth, who had moved into a flat in Shepperton (west of London) with his girlfriend. He got the gig, and the now-named Europeans set about getting their new name into the lights. The Europeans played "streamlined rock affected by punk", according to Carl Glover who saw them in Maidstone. They also gigged as John Otway's backing band for one album (*'All Balls And No Willy'*, referring to John's old partner Wild Willy Barrett) and one tour. Explains Colin, "We'd done some session work for them and they liked us enough to use us on the album, then they offered us to tour it!" Not wanting to become John Otway's band, the foursome (Steve on vocals and keyboards, Colin on Guitar, Ferg Harper on Bass and Geoff Dugmore on drums) proposed that they should play silhouetted behind a curtain with John in front. Not only that, but they also played a complete support set as The Europeans, loaned the PA and did a lot of the roadie work. "We were absolutely knackered," says Colin, who put a tea towel and top hat on his head to appear like Wild Willy Barrett, "Wild Willy would magically appear, it was hysterical!"

The Europeans signed with A&M Records in 1982, releasing their first album (*'Vocabulary'*, produced by Vic Coppersmith-Heaven and including additional vocals by Tony Childs and Kiki Dee) in October 1983. The recording started at the Townhouse studios in London, before moving to at The Manor studios in Oxfordshire ("Richard Branson was living there at the time," says Colin), before moving back to the Townhouse again. It was at the latter that Steve first met Dave Gregory of XTC. Says Dave, "I first met him in the canteen. In those days, he wore these little white bandages on his fingers, even at the breakfast table, which I thought a bit strange! But he was very chatty and friendly, and instantly likeable." The release of *'Vocabulary'*, with a sleeve by Daevid Western, was followed almost immediately by a live album, recorded at Dingwalls in London in December 1983. Explains Colin, "The band was playing really well live, we were really tight, the spirit never got captured on the studio album. Our management [Mark Thompson] realised this and so did A&M, so we said, let's do a live album!" Despite the NME being reputed to say the album sounded like a coal-scuttle full of vomit, the cut-price release still managed to sell 100,000 copies.

The next and final Europeans album was *'Recurring Dreams'*, recorded in 1984. It started on the back foot, with Ferg in hospital; arriving at a gig with "raging flu", he had imbibed a combination of aspirin, beer and Jack Daniels to get him through the gig. He managed the concert, but the cost was a ruptured stomach. "This led to me collapsing in Baker Street station a day later," remembered Ferg to fan and chronicler Tim Glasswell. "As I crawled home, little did I know I was actually bleeding to death inside." Bassist Steve Greetham was hastily pulled in to fill the gap. The producer was slated to be David Lord, fresh from working on *'Peter Gabriel 4'*. According to Steve, "The sax player, Barney Rachabane, turned up again later on Paul Simon's *'Graceland'*." *'Recurring Dreams'* was recorded at Rockfield Studios and Crescent Studios in Bath, where Steve bumped into Dave Gregory once again. Says Dave, "They bought a bass amp from us, I believe!" The album was mixed at Sarm East, Dave Meegan's old haunt. "We had a lot of mutual friends," remarks Dave, "I rented a flat from Geoff Dugmore's ex-girlfriend [Claudine Arenot]. Steve Hogarth was round there once when I was out and he broke my CD player!"

'Recurring Dreams' "really captured the essence of the band," says Colin Woore. Concurs Steve, "It was a much better album than *'Vocabulary'* on the whole." Sadly, the music is only one part of record sales. Little did the band know that Derek Green, head of A&M at the time and who was "right into it," was looking to leave the label. "He resigned the day before the release," says Colin. "There was no promotion, no single." Eventually the band did their own, offering a double A-side free giveaway to the shops. Such best endeavours failed to raise the profile of the band, and it never recovered: as it floundered trying to decide what to do next, offers came in but not for the unit as a whole. "Geoff [Dugmore] was being offered fantastic tour deals with big-name bands, and our manager came to us and said people were interested in a Hogarth/Woore collaboration," says Colin. Adds Steve, "No one

just *'So'*

"Colin and I went up to his old house one day and he had just finished mixing 'Red Rain' - a track from the *'So'* album. We were the first outsiders to hear it. Nobody could know how successful *'So'* was about to be."

Steve Hogarth

wanted to split the band but, the way I saw it, there was no viable alternative. Looking back, it still feels like I betrayed Geoff and Ferg, and maybe I should have stuck it out for a year longer. The irony is that the Europeans at that stage had never sounded better!" However well they sounded, the Europeans were no more. Geoff remarked in an interview with fan Tim Glasswell, "I was devastated. This band had been my life since the age of 10 and now it was taken away. You have to grow up fast in these situations."

day by day

"My Dad made me promise to keep a diary. I phoned him from Iceland a few years ago. He said, 'What are you doing?' and I said, 'I've just come down off the mountain.' I had been helicoptered on top of a glacier because we were making a video. And he said, 'You should keep a diary because this stuff just doesn't happen to people.' So I have been trying to keep it going ever since."

Steve Hogarth

How We Live

In between the Europeans and How We Live, both Steve and Colin took up singing lessons with Tona De Brett, who has taught everyone from All Saints to Ozzy Osbourne. Steve was told that he didn't really need the lessons, as explains Tona, "If a voice is really good, frankly I like to leave it alone!" But, Steve says, "I had three. To be honest, it was because I fell a little bit in love with the singing teacher, who appeared about 80."

Following some showcase performances, the pair eventually signed to CBS using the name Jump The Gun,[6] later changing it to How We Live. The new album, *'Dry Land'* was recorded back with David Lord in Bath in late 1986. Some of the songs, such as 'Lost At Sea', were leftovers from The Europeans, while other material was new. Various items of equipment were borrowed from local performers including Peter Gabriel and Dave Gregory. Recalls Dave, "David Lord called and asked if he could borrow our Mellotron for a project he was working on, How We Live. I said, sure, if you collect it, bring it back and do all the lifting and carrying! So the van pulls up at my house, out jumps the driver with Steve H!" As Dave wouldn't accept payment, Steve bought him a bottle of whisky. "We sort of became chums," says Steve.

Just as *'Dry Land'* was being released in January 1987, disaster stuck again. CBS was getting its house in order to sell up to Sony, and the axe fell for any new signings that had yet to make a profit for the label. How We Live carried on for a while but the pair eventually went their separate ways. Steve's disillusionment with the music business, together with the arrival of his first child, had made him ready to throw in the towel. "I planned to become a postman or something," said Steve in an interview. "We put the house on the market, we were going to move up North, live the quiet life and get out of it all." Just prior to Christmas 1988, a chance remark by Steve to his publisher Alan Jones at Rondor, would change the course of events. "I bounded into the place and said, 'Can anyone think of anything for me to do?' - I really meant like a bit of typing - and Alan said, 'Well, do you know Marillion are looking for a singer?'" Steve was aware of Marillion, but wouldn't have classed himself as a fan. "I had a copy of *'Misplaced Childhood'* somewhere, but it wasn't what I put on every day!" In any case, Steve and Alan sent off a tape which included 'Kingdom Come' from *'Recurring Dreams'*, and 'Games in Germany', *'Dry Land'*.

After the tape was sent, Steve and his wife went to Derbyshire to look for houses, fully intending to quit the industry. No wonder, that when the call came, Steve was initially reluctant! "I just thought they were a bunch of hippies who knitted their own shoes and stuff. The last thing I wanted was to be back on centre stage with the whole to-do. I'd also had a call from Matt Johnson about playing piano on his Mind Bomb tour. I quite fancied that, as I would have a lot less responsibility and I could just get back into enjoying playing again, which was just what I needed after a couple of years of being signed to CBS. So it took quite a few phone calls for them to even persuade me to turn up!" As it happened, a friend of Steve's, Darryl Way, set him on the right track.

Ice Cream Genius

A few years into Steve's time with Marillion, he felt the need for an alternative release of artistic ideas. He told Robert Lewis of AMZ magazine, "I had introduced a couple of lyrics and musical ideas that I was convinced were very strong, very interesting, but that the band didn't want to pursue for whatever reason. Those ideas get stuck in your creative tubes and they start to create a blockage and get in the way." "He saw it as an opportunity to do the things we wouldn't let him do!" laughs Mark Kelly. In addition, Steve was keen to be judged on his own merits. "In my mind, rightfully or wrongly, any success I've had with Marillion, to some extent I've inherited. I'm very conscious of that."

Steve spent much of the Christmas break 1995, putting the finishing touches to his compositions, before contacting friends and admired colleagues among his fellow musicians. The first call was to Dave Gregory. "I said, sure, and went to his house to listen to some demos and discuss tactics," says Dave. "He didn't have a producer, so I suggested Craig Leon, with whom I'd worked the previous year, and thought Steve would like." Craig's credits included everyone from The Ramones to The Bangles), and he in turn, introduced Steve to the Eurythmics' Clem Burke and Chucho Merchan. The final recruit was Richard Barbieri, a familiar face from The Porcupine Tree, who had supported Marillion at the London Forum.

house of the holy

The Sol Mill Studios had previously been owned by Jimmy Page of Led Zeppelin. "It was a spooky little room we were working in, and yet at the same time, very, very comfortable. A bit like working in an old gentlemen's club."

According to Dave Gregory, "Craig has a number of snappy phrases for any given situation, these often abbreviated to '(I scream) Genius!' for good stuff, or 'Torture' for the not-so good." As a joke, Steve wrote 'Ice Cream Genius' on the tape box for the album. 'Genius' seemed an appropriate term for the album as each person involved in the project seemed to have a long and proven musical heritage!

Recording commenced at The Racket Club, and the vocals were added at Chris Rea's Sol Mill studios in Cookham. Mixing took place at the Woolhall studios in Somerset, owned by Van Morrison. There was a break for the Made Again tour in April, and *'Ice Cream Genius'* was finally completed on 20 July 1996. Following a turbulent previous year, H described the album as, "A reflection of someone with an unsettled mind, trying to laugh at himself a little bit, and figuring out what makes him tick and what makes other people tick." This was the key to the variety of songs on the album, from the melodic 'Better Dreams', through more poppy tracks like 'Until You Fall', the downright weird 'Cage', to the straight rock 'n' roll of 'You Dinosaur Thing'. US fans were also treated to a sublime final track, 'The Last Thing', left off the UK release as Craig wasn't sure it fitted with the rest of the album! *'Ice Cream Genius'* was released in February 1997, through Castle in the UK and Europe, and on the Resurgence label in the USA. Douggie Dudgeon, who had originally brought the band to Castle, was tapped to do the A&R. But things did not work out as planned.

"Shortly before the album *'ICG'* was released, Douggie left Castle to form Snapper Music, effectively abandoning the whole project," explains Steve H. "I found out quite by accident during a conversation at Steely Dan's Wembley Arena show. I was devastated. He did the original deal and we worked together on it for months! He didn't even call me to say he was quitting. Once again the rug had been pulled from beneath me by record company politics, he's never spoken to me since. Nice people in the music business!"

let's play

Along with artists like Francis Dunnery, Ian Brown, Aziz Ibrahim, and Mike Peters of The Alarm, The Forge in Oswestry was also the recording location for the Tweenies' Christmas album!

The release of *'Ice Cream Genius'* was accompanied by a 4-date mini-tour starting 9 February and covering London, Paris, Amsterdam and Cologne. The H-band consisted of the same players as on the album, with the addition of guitarist Aziz Ibrahim, who was first introduced to Marillion through Steve Rothery. "I met Steve [Rothery] at Metropolis Studios when they were mixing," says Aziz. "He showed me his rig and gear, and the sounds he could get, it was inspiring. I hope it worked both ways!" Steve Hogarth made Aziz's acquaintance through Forge Studios owner Phil Beaumont, who explains, "We had a covers band called Total Chaos, Aziz was with us and we were going to play at the Boars Head in Oswestry. Steve [Hogarth] was up in Liverpool, they'd just finished recording, he gave me a call and I said why don't you come down?" Steve H was immediately impressed by Aziz's unique style and approach. "My music doesn't fit into a category," says Aziz. "I call it Asian Blues, no-one's created a shelf for that!" In an interview with Music Street Journal, Steve remarked, "Aziz can make a Les Paul sound like a sitar or a koto, and then a full-on Les Paul rock guitar, from moment to moment. He has this great chemistry with Richard Barbieri and I regret not meeting him until it was too late for him to be involved in the record."

Festival Of Hope by Judith Mitchell

Fish told my friend Steve Williams and I that if we got to the show, he'd meet up with us for a drink. Easyjet had only been flying out of Liverpool for two weeks to Geneva, it seemed destined. We arrived and met up, drinks turned into dinner, followed by lunch the next day with his family and a return trip on their coach to the venue and hotel. Fish had said over dinner that Steve Hogarth was going to be on the bill. Even the show's organiser turning up at the restaurant and stating the same thing, failed to convince me, until I arrived the next day at the venue and saw the line-up with his name on it.

Hogarth was first up, doing a short solo set with some local musicians for backing. 'Easter' was the opener, complete with huge grin on the Liverpool line, Fish was watching from the wings I noted. This was followed by 'No One Can', 'Waiting To Happen' and a remarkable version of 'Hope For The Future'. The latter was introduced by Hogarth as being a very appropriate song. Halfway through, he was joined by some familiar backing singers, Sue his wife, Wes and Fish. The song broke down in to a series of repeated choruses with everyone cheering at the end and huge hugs onstage. The audience, especially me, went crazy, I'd no idea about this and my obvious surprise was greeting with large grins from them all.

A French/Algerian act followed, The Pogues meets folk and punk, very fast, very fun and a very bouncy crowd! Fish followed all this fun, but his set was definitely the day's highlight for the majority of the audience. The reception he received was like a conquering hero returning, it was so loud! Half way through 'Tilted Cross', the electrics broke down, so Fish, Liz [Antwi] and Wes, on a true acoustic guitar, continued the set, singing over the quiet audience until the power came back up. The last sections of 'Plague Of Ghosts' saw them offstage and I screamed my head off for more, along with everyone else. The wait was only a few minutes, but seemed like a lifetime. Back came Fish to introduce the band and his new friend Steve Hogarth. 'Lavender' was the result, Fish singing the verses and Hogarth joining in the choruses and also singing the 'Blue Angel' section. The reception as they all left the stage was magnificent.

Afterwards we all met up backstage, I can truly say I was completely dumbstruck and exhausted emotionally by the whole series of events. I can't describe what I felt seeing Hogarth and Fish in the same place, I still can't. It remains one of the most emotive, if not the most, of the entire time I've spent watching both Marillion eras and Hogarth and Fish's solo shows.

The H Band

In 1999, Steve Hogarth was invited to perform at the Festival of Hope in Geneva. Interestingly, Fish was also on the guest list. "It was only at a late stage that I heard Fish was doing it," says H. "I thought Oh God, and I felt a bit, not nervous, but I didn't want to end up sitting at a table with him all night, with him bending my ear. And of course I did end up sitting at a table with him all night, but we had a great time. He wasn't bending my ear, we just had a laugh really." The meeting culminated in a joint performance, explains H, "Wes rounded up people to sing BV's on 'Hope For The Future', Fish says 'I'll sing on it, will you return the favour?', and I said, 'Well, if you're sure then yes I will.' I don't think it was premeditated, it just sort of happened."

The following year Steve was asked back, this time to perform a whole set and he decided to reform his band of geniuses. Unfortunately, Clem and Chucho had touring commitments elsewhere, so Mike Wilson (of Texas) stepped in on drums, and Derek "Jingles" Jhingoree (who has played with Howard Jones and Gabrielle) on bass. The gig on 27 May 2000, was a tremendous success. In his diary, Steve H wrote, "I still can't believe how much the musicians have put into this venture. Everyone involved is doing the show for expenses only. It's meant many hours of work, learning the songs at home, followed by three long rehearsal days, just to arrive at this point. It's a great feeling to have a band of this calibre entering into the spirit of it and playing purely for pleasure." Nick Eede, an "old chum" from Cutting Crew was there, as was Fish once again. "It was pretty cool," says Dave Gregory, "certainly our biggest crowd!" Agrees Jingles, who had played four years with BBMak in the United States, "I was earning great money [with BBMak], but I was not happy, I was feeling drained. This was like a holiday!"

H recalled in a Web interview, "After that, the boys said, 'Why don't we do another one?' So I called a chum [Billy Manning] who was running Dingwalls and he said we could come and play there." Dingwalls on 8 August 2000, was another great success. "It was terrific - everyone even got paid!" While he was there, fan and Web Holland staffer Natasja Gravendahl convinced him it would be worth playing again, this time in her country. "She sort of convinced me it could make sense, despite my initial reticence!" laughed H in a Web interview. The show took place in Utrecht on Hallowe'en night. This time it would be Mike Wilson who couldn't make it, but he put H in touch with Andy Gangadeen. "Andy defies all conventional wisdom, he looks, plays and is like no-one I have met. When I saw him on TV playing with Massive Attack I never imagined I'd someday have him in my band, I'd have done a back flip if I'd known!" The Utrecht show was "a real performing high," says Dave Gregory.

In the summer of 2001, H played two more gigs at

really like

The guitar Dave Gregory uses for the guitar solo on 'Really Like' is Steve H's old Rickenbacker, bought in San Jose. "It's on permanent loan to Dave, who gets a MUCH better sound out of it than I ever did," admits Steve.

whose name is it anyway?

Steve Hogarth is not Steve Hogarth's name, but it is what he's always been called. Let me explain. Steve's first name isn't exactly Steve, but it is what he's always been called. Neither is his surname exactly Hogarth, but it is what he's always been called. There - simple.

Dingwalls, on 8 and 9 August.[7] These were "two unmissable gigs" according to fan Heloise Brown, writing in The Web. "Anyone who came along expecting to hear all of *'Ice Cream Genius'*, or indeed much Marillion material, would have been disappointed." Instead, the audience were treated to a wide array of cover versions, including, 'I Don't Remember' (Peter Gabriel), 'Dream Brother' (Jeff Buckley) and 'Life On Mars' (David Bowie). A surprise guest was Colin Woore, H's partner in crime from The Europeans and How We Live, playing 'Working Town', from the just-re-released How We Live album, *'Dry Land'*. The set lists were drawn up by H "leafing through the old memory banks...I love psychedelia, I love anything with a spiritual depth and I'm a sucker for a bit of pathos." There were two complete sets to learn for the two days. Dave Gregory, who helped choose the set lists, commented, "I've never worked so hard! Steve does have a habit of giving us too much to learn in too short a space of time!" Agrees Jingles, "It was a nightmare!" Aziz is sanguine, "That's just graft, that is!" he says.

All the players have derived enormous pleasure from the H-band experience. "I've gained a wealth of musical knowledge," says Aziz. "Even though you think your tastes are diverse, it's a shock when you meet someone who really is!" For Dave Gregory, it has provided welcome opportunities to play live. "Having spent so much time away from it, I do get incredibly nervous nowadays, make that terrified!" says Dave. "But a friendly audience can make all the difference." Agrees Jingles, "Every gig is different. We never think about the money - the reason why I took this gig and stuck with it is the people. No band has ever given back what I get from this one."

The H-band continue to schedule dates. Roll on.

H-band: Andy Gangadeen, Dave Gregory, Richard Barbieri, H, Aziz Ibrahim, Pete Trewavas

NOTES: 1 According to Mark Kelly, "Karaoke style over the original recordings!" **2** A late-'70s TV science fiction series. **3** Later, manager of Tears For Fears. **4** probably 4 November '98, when Marillion were playing the Civic Hall. **5** A song popularised by Tom Jones. **6** The Stimulus Brothers was another name proposed by Steve. **7** These were recorded and have since been released as *'Live Spirit/Live Body'* double CD.

appendix five discography/bibliography

The following discography is entirely the work of Bert ter Steege's, taken with his generous permission from his website (for link, see Bibliography).

MARILLION with FISH:

First Demo (No Name) 1981
Demo Cassette UK: No label/number (sold at gigs during 81-82 tour)
Oxfordshire, Watlington, Roxon Studios, Recorded 18-19 Jul 81
He Knows, You Know / Garden Party / Charting The Single

Market Square Heroes 25 Oct 82
7" Single UK: EMI EMI 5351, yellow label
UK: EMI EMI 5351 black label re-release,
7" Test Press UK: EMI EMI 5351, red label
Market Square Heroes (Antichrist version) / Three Boats Down From The Candy (7" version)
7" Promo UK: EMI EMI 5351 ADJ, red label, 2 different mixes
Battlepriest version of MSH is only released as video clip, and on promo.
Market Square Heroes (Antichrist version) / Market Square Heroes (Battlepriest version)
12" Single UK: EMI 12 EMI 5351, yellow label
UK: EMI 12 EMI 5351, black label
UK: EMI 12 EMI 5351, purple label
Eur: EMI 052 0772 6
12" Promo UK: EMI 12 EMI 5351, white label
12" PD UK: EMI 12 EMIP 5351
Apr 83, 3000 copies
Market Square Heroes (Antichrist version) / Three Boats Down From The Candy (7" version) / Grendel (12" version)

He Knows, You Know 31 Jan 83
7" Single UK: EMI EMI 5362, yellow label, hard paper cover, push-out
UK: EMI EMI 5362, blue label, hard paper cover
NL: EMI 1A 006.07713, yellow label
D: EMI 1C 006 07713
CAN: Capitol ??
7" Promo E: EMI 006-07713
Title: El Sabe Tu Sabes
AUS: EMI EMI 1032
7" Test Press UK: EMI, white label
7" Acetate UK: Abbey Road, one sided
He Knows, You Know (edited 7" version) / Charting The Single (single version)
12" Single UK: EMI 12 EMI 5362, yellow label
UK: EMI 12 EMI 5362, black label re-rel.
UK: EMI 12 EMI 5362 violet label
NL: EMI 052 Z 07 713 hard cover with purple border
NL: EMI 052 Z 07 713 soft cover, yellow label
12" PD UK: EMI 12 EMI P 5362, unrel.
He Knows, You Know (12" version - edit of album version) / Charting The Single (single version)
12" Promo USA: Capitol SPRO-9930 / 9931, Apr 83, white label
He Knows, You Know (edited) / Chelsea Monday (edited)
with red and white sticker: 'Voted 'Best New Act' in Great Britain's Sounds Readers' Poll 1983'

Special Edits for AOR Radio from the forthcoming album SCRIPT FOR A JESTER'S TEAR ST 12269
He Knows, You Know SPRO 9930 / Chelsea Monday SPRO 9931
12" Promo USA: Capitol SPRO-9964
He Knows, You Know (edited version)

SCRIPT FOR A JESTER'S TEAR
14 Mar 83
LP UK: EMI EMC 3429, green letters on the spine of the album
LP UK: EMI EMC 3429, yellow letters on the spine of the album
UK: EMI/Fame FA 3235, May 90
D: EMI 1C 064 07 715
I: EMI 64 107715 1
E: EMI 6007715, fold out cover
F: EMI 064 07715, fold out cover
JAP: EMI EMS 81584, yellow label, insert
USA: Capitol ST-12269
CAN: Capitol ST-12269
ISR: Portrait EMS 3429
VEN: EMI EMI 4486
BRA: EMI 064 07715
RSA: EMI EMCJ L 5307, yellow label
TWN: Nova 73004
ARG: EMI EMI 8161, yellow label, non-g/fold, b/w back cover, Title: Partitura Para El Llanto De Un Bufon
GRI: EMI 064 - 107715 1
POR: EMI 107715 1
AUS: EMI EMC 3429 Code 32
12" PD UK: EMI EMCP 3429, Jun 84
UK: EMI EMCP 3429, same pic. on A+B
Promo LP ARG: EMI EMI 8161
USA: Capitol ST-12269
No g/fold, 2 different versions: one burgundy label, one black with rainbow border, both promo stamp on front.
JAP: EMI EMS 81584, white label, insert
AUS: EMI EMC 3429 Code 32
Test Pressing UK: EMI EMC 3429 red label, 250 signed copies
UK: green label
UK: white label
UK: 2 one-sided test pressings
MC UK: EMI TC EMC 3429
UK: Fame TC FA 3235, May 90
NL: EMI 1A 264 07 715
F: France EMI 50999 107715 4 PM410 5 099910 771549 1988
USA: Capitol 4XT-12269
CAN: Capitol 4XT-12269
VEN: EMI 4486
Chile: ?
Promo MC USA: ?
CD UK: EMI CDEMS-1517, 27 Dec 85
NL: EMI CDP 7 46237 2, 27 Dec 85
NL: EMI CDP 7 46237 2, reissue 95
UK: EMI CD-GOLD-1012 EMI Gold, 1985
UK: Fame CD FA 3235, May 90
I: EMI CDPM 7 46237 2
NL: Disky CD 867362, Oct 96
USA: Capitol DIDX 1298 / CDP 7 46237 2 / 07777-46237 2 8
CAN: Capitol C2 46232
JAP: EMI CDP 7 46237 2
JAP: EMI TOCP 8315, rerelease ?
2CD Remaster UK: EMI REMARIL 001
7243 8 57865 2 5, 29 Sep 97
USA: Sanctuary SANCTUARY 4506, 28 Dec 99
USA: Sanctuary ZAN84528CD, 11 Mar 01
Promo 2CD UK: EMI REMARIL 001
1CD Remaster UK: EMI CD 527 1152, 28 Aug 00
Script For A Jester's Tear / He Knows You Know / The Web / Garden Party / Chelsea Monday / Forgotten Sons
Bonus CD for European Remastered Ed.
Market Square Heroes (single version with Battlepriest edit) / Three Boats Down From The Candy (single version) / Grendel (Fair Deal Studios Demo) / Chelsea Monday (Manchester Square Demo) / He Knows, You Know (Manchester Square Demo) / Charting The Single (single version) / Market Square Heroes (re-recorded version)

Garden Party 'Great Cucumber Massacre' 6 Jun 83
7" Shaped PD UK: EMI EMI P 5393
Also very limited unshaped version
7" Single UK: EMI EMI 5393, limited with inscription 'A run' and 'Card Verkerke AC 9468', yellow label
UK: EMI EMI 5393, yellow label, with inscription 'A run'
NL: EMI 1A 006 10 7767 7, yellow label
D: EMI 1C 006 10 7767 7
AUS: EMI EMI 1122
7" Promo AUS: EMI EMI 1122
Garden Party (edited version) / Margaret (edited live: Edinburgh Playhouse, 7 April 83)
12" Single UK: EMI 12 EMI 5393, black label
UK: EMI 12 EMI 5393, yellow label, there are also copies with 12 EMI 5393 on Side A and 12 EMIS 5393 on Side B
UK: EMI 12 EMIS 5393, limited, poster
NL: EMI 1A 062 Z 10 7766 6, hard and soft cover versions
Garden Party (full version) / Charting

The Single (live 18 Apr 83, Hammersmith Odeon) / Margaret (live 07 Apr 83, Edinburgh Playhouse)

Punch And Judy 30 Jan 84
7" Single UK: EMI MARIL 1, silver label
UK: EMI MARIL 1, yellow label, push-out
NL: EMI 1A 016 200041 7, yellow label
E: EMI 006-200041 7, textured cover
USA: Capitol 4 track ep??
RSA: EMI J4464, yellow label
7" Promo E: EMI 006-200041 7, white label
Punch And Judy (7" version) / Market Square Heroes (edited re-recorded version) / Three Boats Down From The Candy (re-recorded version)
7" Promo UK: EMI One Side, green label
Punch And Judy (7" version)
7" JAP: EMI EMS 17438, generic cover with insert, yellow label
7" Promo JAP: EMI EMS 17438 generic cover, insert, white label
Punch And Judy (7" version) / Market Square Heroes (edited re-recorded version)
12" PD UK: EMI 12 MARILP 1
12" Single UK: EMI 12 MARIL 1, yellow label
UK: EMI 12 MARIL 1, black label, picture sleeve
UK: EMI 12 MARIL 1, black label, black sleeve re-release, also with print error
Eur: EMI 1C K0622001586, yellow label
D: EMI 1C K0622001586, tan label
12" Promo UK: EMI ???, white label
Punch And Judy (7" version) / Market Square Heroes (re-recorded version) / Three Boats Down From The Candy (re-recorded version)

FUGAZI 12 Mar 84
LP UK: EMI EMC 24 0085 1 MRL 1
UK: EMI/Fame FA 3196, re-release May 88
D: EMI 1C 064 24 0085 1
F: EMI 64 240085 1 FOC, fold out cover
I: EMI 64 240085 1 non-openable sleeve, no lyrics
E: EMI 006-240085 1, tan label
NL: EMI 064.240085 1
NL: EMI 064.240085 1, 'Direct Metal Mastering' on back cover
Eur: EMI/Fame 1C 0381577391, yellow label, FOC
POR: EMI 240085 1
GRI: EMI 064-240085 1
ARG: EMI EMI 8213, yellow label, g/fold
ARG: EMI EMI 8213, yellow label, g/fold
AUS: EMI EMC 219
USA: Capitol ST-12331
CAN: Capitol ST-12331
BRA: EMI 064 240085
MEX: EMI SLEM 1198 FOC
ISR: Portrait EMC 240085
RSA: EMI EMCJ L 240085 1, yellow label
JAP: EMI EMS 81647, yellow label, insert
TCH: EMI/Globus International 210094-1 311, re-release 91, in colours black / red / pink / multicolour
12" promo UK: EMI EMC 24 0085 1
Promo package: picture disc in a g/fold album cover, 8x10 b&w pic of band, 8x10 colour pic of Fish and 25 page 8x11 booklet with press clippings.
USA: Capitol ST-12331 black label, Promo stamp, OIS
JAP: EMI EMS 81647, white label, insert
TCH: EMI/Globus International 210094-1 311, re-release 91, black vinyl on label 'Promotional only' in English and Czech
AUS: EMI EMC 240085 FOC
ARG: EMI EMI 8213 White label, g/fold sleeve,'incluye ASESINANDO' printed on front cover
Test Pressing UK: EMI MRL 1, red label, 250 signed copies
UK: EMI MRL 1 Different track-order
UK: EMI, white label
D: EMI 1577391, plays Side A both sides
12" PD UK: EMI EMCP 240085 0 MRLP1
MC UK: EMI TC MRL 1
UK: EMI TC EMC 24 0085 4
UK: EMI TC FA 3196, re-release May 88
I: EMI 64 240084
D: EMI 1C 264-24 0085 4
E: EMI 266-240085 4
POL: Bager B032
USA: Capitol 4XT 12331
CAN: Capitol 4XT 12331
Promo MC USA: Capitol 4XT 12331
CD UK: EMI CDEMS-1516, released 86
UK: EMI/Fame CD FA 3196
D: EMI CDP 7 46027 2
CH: EMI CDP 7 46027 2
Eur: EMI CDP 746027 2 07777 4602723
NL: EMI 7 46027 2, re-release 95
USA: Capitol DIDX 910
JAP: EMI CDP 7 46027 2
JAP: EMI TOCP 8316, re-release
2CD Remaster EU: EMI 7243 4 93369 26 23 Feb 98
CAN: EMI 7243 4 93369 2 6, 21 Apr 98
USA: Sanctuary SANCTUARY 4507 28 Dec 99
USA: Sanctuary ZAN84529CD,11 Mar 02
Assassing / Punch And Judy / Jigsaw / Emerald Lies / She Chameleon / Incubus / Fugazi
Bonus Disc for remaster:
Cinderella Search (12" version) / Assassing (92 Alternative Mix) / Three Boats Down From The Candy ('84 re-recorded version) / Punch And Judy (demo, previously unreleased) / She Chameleon (demo, previously unreleased) / Emerald Lies (demo, previously unreleased) / Incubus (demo, previously unreleased)

Assassing 30 April 1984
7" Single UK: EMI MARIL 2, black label, push-out
NL: EMI 1A 006 20 0157 7
POR: EMI 2002977
CAN: Capitol 729454
Assassing (7" version) / Cinderella Search (7" version)
12" PD UK: EMI 12 MARILP 2
UK: EMI 12 MARILP 2 (misspressing with a green picture)
12" Promo UK: EMI 12 MARIL 2, white label
12" Single UK: EMI 12 MARIL 2, black label
UK: EMI 12 MARIL 2, purple label
I: EMI 50-240146-1
D: EMI 1C K 062 20 0158 6, yellow label with or without printed 'Hit Single'
D: EMI 1C K 062 20 0158 6, light brown border
Assassing (full version) / Cinderella Search (full version) / Assassing* (7" version) * Not on UK release
12" Promo USA: Capitol SPRO 9132
Fugazi Cover + stickers
Assassing (edited remix)
12" Promo CAN: Capitol SPRO 245
Assassing (edit) / Punch And Judy / Jigsaw (edit)

REAL TO REEL 5 Nov 84
LP UK: EMI JEST 1 EG 26 0303 1, yellow label
UK: EMI Gold
D: EMI 1C 038 26 0303 1, with German tour dates
NL: EMI Electrola 1 C 0382603031 5099926030319
E: EMI 066-260303 1
F: EMI 2603031 Yellow Label, OIS
ARG: EMI EMI 8375, yellow label, back-cover black/white
BRA: EMI 064 2603031
VEN: EMI EMI 25030
ISR: Portrait EG 260303
GRI: EMI 062-260303 1
I: EMI 54 2603031
Eur: EMI/Fame 1C 038 15 7623 1
UK: EMI/Fame FA 413142 1, re-release Nov 85, yellow label
JAP: EMI EMS 63038
CAN: Capitol SN 66174 green label
CAN: Capitol SQ 6516, black label
Promo LP ARG: EMI EMI 8375, yellow label, b/w back cover
JAP: EMI EMS 63038
12" PD UK: EMI JESTP 1 EG 26 0303 6 Jan 85
UK: EMI JESTP 1, with printing error
Test pressing UK: Townhouse 2603031 One-sided with label test pressing 'B'
UK: EMI lime labels, orange inserts f&b, with extra thick clear sleeve
Mispressing? Plays B-side on both
MC UK: EMI TC JEST 1 EG 26 0303 4
D: EMI 1C 238 15 5325 4
I: EMI 54 155325 4
UK: EMI/Fame TC FA 413142 4
E: EMI 256-260303 4
CAN: Capitol 4XQ-6516
VEN: EMI 25030
CD UK: EMI/Fame CD-FA 3142, Oct 87
D: EMI CDP 7 46027 2
D: EMI CD-FA-3142
JAP: EMI TOCP 8318
Eur: EMI CDM 752021 207777 5202120
2CD Remaster UK: EMI CDEM 1603 6 Jun 97
Eur: EMI 7243 8 56107 2 1, 4 Jun 97
CAN: EMI 7243 8 56107 2 1, 8 Jul 97
USA: Sanctuary ZAN84537CD, 11 Mar 02
Disc 1 In MCe of the Remastered 2CD
Live at 'The Spectrum', Montreal, Canada, 19-20 Jun 84:
Assassing / Incubus / Cinderella Search / Emerald Lies*
Live at 'De Montford Hall, Leicester, England, 5 Mar 84:
Forgotten Sons / Garden Party / Market Square Heroes *Not on Vinyl versions
Bonus CD for the Remastered Edition.
Lady Nina (extended version) / Freaks (7" version) / Kayleigh (live version) / Fugazi* (live version) / Script For A Jester's Tear* (live version)
*Credits say recorded Jan 86 London, but you can hear Fish say during Fugazi "Goodnight Leicester" so probably recorded during same concert as Real To Reel Side 2

Kayleigh 7 Apr 85
7" Single UK: EMI MARIL 3, black label
UK: EMI MARIL 3, silver label
UK: EMI MARIL 3, silver label, black cover, re-issue

NL: EMI 1A 006 20 0638 7
D: EMI 1C 006 20 0638 7
F: EMI 20 0638 7
POR: EMI 20 0638 7
E: EMI 006 20 0638 7
I: EMI 06 20 0638 7
AUS: EMI EMIJ 4489
NZ: EMI EMIJ 4489
RSA: EMI, yellow label
CAN: Capitol 72972
7" Mini-EP PER: 01212475, 33rpm
7" Promo E: EMI 006-200638 7
I: EMI 006-200638 7
AUS: EMI America EMI 1534, no picture sleeve
JAP: EMI PRP-1149
7" Flexi Disc UK: EMI
7" PD UK: EMI MARILP 3, 14 Apr 85
Kayleigh (single edit) / Lady Nina (single edit)
7" Single USA: Capitol B-5493, Rainbow Capitol label
Kayleigh (single edit) / Heart Of Lothian (single edit)
7" Promo USA: Capitol P-B-5493, white label (mentions Intro 00:27) / Kayleigh (single edit)
12" Single UK: EMI 12 MARIL 3, black label
UK: EMI 12 MARIL 3, yellow label
D: EMI 1C K 060 20 0639 6
NZ: EMI GOOD 71
E: EMI 2007026
E: EMI 2007026, printing error on cover
12" Promo E: white label
AUS: EMI
12" PD UK: EMI 12 MARILP 3
Kayleigh (alternative mix) / Kayleigh (extended version) / Lady Nina (extended version)
12" Promo USA: Capitol SPRO 9417-9418, black cover with red and yellow sticker: '12" Single Marillion Kayleigh Single Version b/w alternative mix spro 9417-9418 Promotional Copy/Not For Sale/33rpm/Stereo/Printed in the USA
Kayleigh (extended version) / Kayleigh (alternative mix)

MISPLACED CHILDHOOD 17 Jun 85
LP UK: EMI EJ 24 0340 1 MRL 2
UK: EMI EJ 24 0340 1, purple label
Eur: EMI 1C 064 24 0340 1
D: EMI 1C 064 24 0340 1
Eur: EMI 1C 064 24 0340 1, with Kayleigh print on cover
Eur: EMI 427039 FOC, club-edition
Eur: EMI FOC, different club-edition
I: EMI 64 240340 1
F: EMI 50999 24034012 FOC
USA: Capitol ST 12431
CAN: Capitol ST 12431
ARG: EMI EMI 56320, yellow label, non-g/fold sleeve, back-cover black/white
Title: Ninez Extraviada
AUS: EMI EMC 259
YUG: EMI LSEMI 11145
E: EMI 066-240340 1
GRI: EMI 064-240340 1
VEN: EMI 25044, different logo
COL: EMI 111027, different logo
BRA: EMI 064 240340 FOC
IRL: Portrait EJ 240340, with lyric-sheet
RSA: EMI EMCJ D 2403401 FOC, yellow label
ZBW:
JAP: EMI EMS 81728
UK: EMI EMI 100 CENT26, 180gr. vinyl, Nov 97
Promo LP USA: Capitol DJ-12431, banded on virgin vinyl
USA: Capitol ST-12431, promo stamp, insert
AUS: EMI EMC 240340 FOC
ARG: EMI EMI 56320
ARG: EMI EMI-8320, white label
E: EMI 066-240340 1, white label
JAP: EMI EMS 81728, white label
12" PD UK: EMI EJ 24 0340 0 MRLP 2
Test pressing UK: Townhouse one-sided acetate
UK: Townhouse 2 one-sided acetates, tape version
UK: Test pressing
USA: different cover
MC UK: EMI EJ 24 0340 4 TC MRL 2
D: EMI 1C 264 24 0340 4
E: EMI 266-240340 4
GRI: EMI 264-240340 4
TUR: EMI EJ 24 0340 4
POL: ? M-058
USA: Capitol 4XT 12431, also as promo with the same Number
F: France EMI Pathe Marconi 2403404 PM464 5099924034043
F: EMI 238-746160 4, re-release
IND: EMI EQ-105-9
RSA: EMI South Africa L 4 EMCJ N 2403404
CD UK: EMI CDP 7 46160 2
CH: EMI CDP 7 46160 207777 46160 27
NL: EMI CDP 7 46160 2 CDEMS 1518
CAN: Capitol Canada C2 46160
USA: Capitol DIDX 1251
JAP: EMI CDP 7 46160 2
NL: EMI 7 46160-2, re-release 1995
JAP: EMI TOCP 8317, re-release
2CD Remaster F: EMI 7243 4 97034 2 1 17 Oct 98
Can: EMI 7243 4 97034 2 1, 17 Nov 98
USA: Sanctuary 4508, 28 Dec 99
USA: Sanctuary ZAN84530CD,11 Mar 02
1CD Remaster UK: EMI CD 527 1162 28 Aug 00
Pseudo Silk Kimono / Kayleigh / Lavender / Bitter Suite / Heart Of Lothian / Waterhole Expresso Bongo / Lords Of The Backstage / Blind Curve / Childhoods End / White Feather
Remaster Bonus CD:
Lady Nina (extended 12" version) / Freaks (single version) / Kayleigh (alternative mix) / Lavender Blue (remix) / Heart Of Lothian (extended mix) / Psuedo Silk Kimono (Demo, Feb 85) / Kayleigh (Demo, Feb 85) / Lavender (Demo, Feb 85) / Bitter Suite (Demo, Feb 85) / Lords Of The Backstage (Demo, Feb 85) / Blue Angel (Demo, Feb 85) / Misplaced Rendezvous (Demo, Feb 85) / Heart Of Lothian (Demo, Feb 85) / Waterhole Expresso Bongo (Demo, Feb 85) / Passing Strangers (Demo, Feb 85) / Childhoods End? (Demo, Feb 85) / White Feather (Demo, Feb 85)

Lavender 27 Aug 85
7" Single UK: EMI MARIL 4, small and big hole versions
UK: EMI MARIL 4, silver label, small hole
D: EMI 1C 006 200777 7
NL: EMI 006.200777 7
E: EMI 6 200777 7
F: EMI
AUS: EMI EMI-1578
EIR: EMI MARIL 4, black label
NZ: EMI 4 EMI 922
RSA: EMI J 200777 7, yellow label
USA: Capitol B-5539, white label, label mentions Intro of 00:14
CAN: Capitol B-72990, different cover
7" Promo E: EMI 6 200777 7
AUS: EMI EMI 1578
NZ: EMI EMI 922, yellow label
Lavender / Freaks
12" Single UK: EMI 12 MARIL 4, black label
UK: EMI 12 MARIL 4, purple label
D: EMI 1C K 060 20 0778 6
E: EMI 052-200778 6
12" Promo AUS: EMI ED-134
NZ: EMI GOOD 82
USA: Capitol SPRO 9510-9511
12" PD UK: EMI 12 MARILP 4
UK: EMI 12 MARILP 4, mispressing: the A-side picture is printed on both sides.
Lavender Blue / Freaks / Lavender
7" Promo USA: Capitol P-B-5539
Lavender / Lavender

Heart Of Lothian 18 Nov 85
7" Single UK: EMI MARIL 5, black label
UK: EMI MARIL 5, silver label
NL: EMI 006.200958 7
D: EMI 1C 016 200958 7
RSA: EMI EMI J 200958 7, yellow label
CAN: Capitol B 72993
AUS: EMI EMI-1649, yellow label
7" Promo AUS: EMI EMI-1649, no picture sleeve
RSA: EMI EMI J 200958 7, yellow label with promo stamp
7" Test Press UK: EMI MARIL 5B, 1-sided disc with only the B-side
Heart Of Lothian / Chelsea Monday (live 15 Oct 85, Utrecht Vredenburg)
12" Single UK: EMI 12 MARIL 5, black label
D: EMI 1C K 060 200959 6
AUS: EMI ED 159
12" PD UK: EMI 12 MARILP 5
12" Promo AUS: EMI ED-159
Heart Of Lothian (full version) / Chelsea Monday (live 15 Oct 85, Utrecht)
Heart Of Lothian

THE STORY SO FAR 1985
Promo LP CAN: Capitol SPRO 281
Market Square Heroes / Real To Real (live version) / He Knows, You Know (12" version) / Garden Party (album version) / Punch And Judy (album version) / Kayleigh (alternative mix) / Lavender (7" version)

Lady Nina Apr 86
7" Single USA: Capitol B-5561
Lady Nina / Heart Of Lothian (special edit)
7" Promo USA: Capitol P-B-5561
Lady Nina / Lady Nina
12" Promo USA: Capitol SPRO-9593 / 9594
UK: ?, also as acetate
Lady Nina (extended version) / Lady Nina (7" version)

BRIEF ENCOUNTER Apr 86
LP USA: Capitol MLP-15023 0 7777-15023-1, with sticker: 'Recorded Live Marillion Brief Encounter Mini LP featuring Lady Nina - Freaks - Kayleigh - Fugazi - Script MLP-15023 Printed in USA'
LP Promo USA: Capitol MLP-15023
Test pressing USA: Capitol, different cover

MC USA: Capitol 4LP-15023
MC Promo USA: Capitol 4LP-15023
As bonus with the Real To Reel Remaster:
2CD Remaster UK: EMI CDEM 1603 06 Jun 97
Eur: EMI 7243 8 56107 2 1, 04 Jun 97
CAN: EMI 7243 8 56107 2 1, Jul 97
USA: Sanctuary ZAN84537CD, 11 Mar 02
Lady Nina / Freaks / Kayleigh (live Jan 86, Hammersmith Odeon)
Script for a Jester's Tear (live) / Fugazi (live) /
Credits say recorded Jan 86 in London, but you can hear Fish say during Fugazi "Goodnight Leicester" so probably recorded during same concert as Real to Reel Side 2, others think Fish said "Goodnight, last song!"

Interview Picture Disc 1986
12" PD NL: Baktabak BAK 2021, contains interview
12" PD NL: Baktabak BAK 2183, contains interview

Interview With Fish 1986
12" PD NL: Red Door RD PD 23, contains interview

Welcome To The 'Garden Party' Jul 86
7" Single D: EMI-Electrola 1C 006 20 1189 7 5 099920 118976, yellow label
Garden Party (edited version) / Market Square Heroes (edited re-recorded version)
12" Single D: EMI-Electrola 1C K 060 20 1190 6 5 099920 119065, yellow label, sleeve printed 'Maxi Single 45 rpm'
Garden Party (live 05 Mar 84, Leicester) / Kayleigh (live Jan 86, Hammersmith Odeon) / Script For A Jester's Tear (live Jan 86, Hammersmith Odeon)

Incommunicado 11 May 87
7" Single UK: EMI MARIL 6, small hole / soft cover, big hole / hardcover version & big hole / soft cover
UK: EMI MARIL 6, silver label, soft cover
D: EMI 1C 006 20 1817 7 5099920181772, black label
F: Same as above but with sticker with French tour dates
I: EMI 06 201817 7, yellow label
E: EMI 006 2018177, yellow label with textured cover
POR: EMI 2018177
EIR: EMI MARIL 6, black label
JAP: EMI EMS 17709, yellow label
AUS: EMI EMI 1953
NZ: EMI EMI 880, yellow label
RSA: EMI J 201817 7, yellow label
7" Promo E: EMI 006-201817 7, white label with textured cover
JAP: EMI EMS 17709, white label
Incommunicado / Going Under
12" Single UK: EMI 12 MARIL 6
D: EMI 1C K 060 20 1816 6 5 099920 181666, black label
F: EMI same number + sticker with French tour dates
I: EMI 14 201816 6
E:
NZ: EMI GOOD 182
AUS: EMI ED 268
12" Promo E: EMI, white label
12" Test Press UK: EMI 12 MARIL 6, blank white Label
12" PD UK: EMI 12 MARILP 6, also a mispressing with 2 A-sides
Incommunicado (album version) / Incommunicado (alternative mix) / Going Under
5" CD Single UK: EMI CD MARIL 6, has a g/fold cover.
F: EMI CDP 560 201 816 2
Incommunicado (album version) / Incommunicado (alternative mix) / Going Under

CLUTCHING AT 1987
5" CD Video UK: EMI EMCDV 1, never had a full official Release
Audio: Hotel Hobbies / Warm Wet Circles / That Time Of The Night
Video PAL: Incommunicado

CLUTCHING AT STRAWS 22 Jun 87
LP UK: EMI EMD 1002, has merchandise order-form
UK: EMI ATAK 135
D: EMI 064 24 0785 1, raised letters with Lorelei sticker
Eur: EMI 064 24 0785 1
Eur: EMI 064 24 0785 1, logo in relief
Eur: EMI 146720, club edition
I: EMI 64 - 240785 1
GRI: EMI 062-240785 1
2 versions: English and Greek print
USA: Capitol ST-12539
CAN: Capitol ST-12539
JAP: EMI EMS 91230
ARG: EMI EMI 10026, yellow label, OIS
Title: Pendiendo de Un Hilo
GUS: M94 RAT 30780
AUS: EMI EMC 240785 Black Label
YUG: EMI LSEMI 78049
MEX: EMI SLEM 1464
ISR: EMI 1002-1
NL: EMI 038 7468661 07777 46866 1 7, re-release
ARG Promo LP: EMI EMI 10026
JAP: EMI EMS 91230, white label
USA: Capitol ST-12539, promo stamp
E: EMI 006-240-785-1, white label
RSA: EMI ?, inner sleeve, promo stamp
12" PD UK: EMI EMDP 1002, has die-cut sleeve
12" PD Mispressing UK: EMI EMDP 1002 B-side contains Amnesty International interview (or something like that)
UK: EMI EMDP 1002 Michael Jackson's 'Bad' music on the disc
12" Testpress UK: EMI EMD-1002, autographed, message in run-off
MC UK: EMI TC EMD 1002, no bonus track
UK: EMI TC ATAK 135
Eur: EMI 1C 264.24 0785 4
USA: Capitol 4XT 12539
USA: Capitol 4XT 12539, label mentions 'Recorded in UK'
CAN: Capitol 4XT 12539
POR: EMI 2407851
TUR: EMI TCP 2213
GRI: EMI 262-240785 4
IND: EMI EQ 106-8
Promo MC D: EMI 264-240785 4
USA: Capitol 4XT 12539
CD UK: EMI CD EMD 1002
UK: EMI CZ 214
Eur: EMI CDP 7468662 07777 46866 24
USA: Capitol DIDX 1638
JAP: EMI CP 32-5449
Remastered 2CD UK: EMI 724349861121, 22 Mar 99
USA: Sanctuary 4511, 21 Mar 00
USA: Sanctuary ZAN84534CD, 11 Mar 02
1CD Remaster UK: EMI CD 527 1172, 28 Aug 00
Hotel Hobbies / Warm Wet Circles / That Time of The Night / The Short Straw / Going Under (only on CD / MC / Just For The Record / White Russian / Incommunicado / Torch Song / Slainte Mhath / Sugar Mice / The Last Straw
Enhanced Bonus CD for remastered edition:
Incommunicado (alternative version) / Tux On (single version) / Going Under (extended version) / Beaujolais Day (previously unreleased) / Story From A Thin Wall (previously unreleased) / Shadows On The Barley (previously unreleased) / Sunset Hill (previously unreleased) / Tic-Tac-Toe (previously unreleased) / Voice In The Crowd (previously unreleased) / Exile On Princes Street (previously unreleased) / White Russians (previously unreleased demo) / Sugar Mice In The Rain (previously unreleased) / Warm Wet Circles / Rock'n'Roll (hidden track)
* Enhanced Multimedia section with a hidden unreleased demo track, this part also contains a presentation of all released remasters and quicktime movie slide-show of some b/w photos

Sugar Mice 13 Jul 87
7" Single UK: EMI MARIL 7, black label, hard cover
UK: EMI MARIL 7, silver label, hard cover
D: EMI MARIL 7, yellow label
D: EMI 1C 016.201937 7, label states Sugar Mice is 4:59 but plays 5:47 album version
F: EMI 2019377 7, silver label
EIR: EMI MARIL 7, black label
POR: EMI 201937 7
CAN: Capitol B-44060, black label
USA: Capitol B-44060
Sugar Mice (album version) / Tux On
7" Promo UK: EMI MARIL DJ 7, has a plain die-cut black sleeve with white sticker bearing the release date, contains an edited version
F: EMI 201937 7, silver label
D: EMI 1C 016.201937 7
7" PD UK: EMI MARILP 7 5099920198701, contains a poster in foldout sleeve
Sugar Mice (radio edit) / Tux On
7" Promo USA: Capitol P-B-44060, yellow label, mentions Intro of 0.07
Sugar Mice (radio edit)
10" Acetate UK: Abbey Road Tracks?
12" Single UK: EMI 12 MARIL 7 5 099920 193669, black label
D: EMI K 060.201936 6
D: EMI 060 201936 6, tan label
12" PD UK: EMI 12 MARILP 7
12" Acetate UK: 2 sided with the same tracks as normal 12", the record is contained within a die-cut Abbey Road studio sleeve, Abbey Road labels with handwritten cat nos 12-MARIL-7-A / 12-MARIL-7-B, group and track names.
Sugar Mice (extended version) / Sugar Mice (album version) / Tux On
5" CD Single UK: EMI CD MARIL 7 056 20 1954 2
Sugar Mice (radio Edit) / Tux On /

Sugar Mice (extended version)

Warm Wet Circles Remix 26 Oct 87
7" Single UK: EMI MARIL 8, hard cover
UK: EMI MARIL 8, soft cover
NL: EMI 006 202158 7
D: EMI 1C 016 202 158 7
Eur: EMI 1C 006 202 158 7, yellow label with advert for Clutching on back cover
EIR: EMI MARIL 8, black label
7" Acetate UK: Abbey Road, one-sided Warm Wet Circles (7" remix) / White Russian (live 18 Jul 87, Lorelei)
12" Single UK: EMI 12 MARIL 8 509992019863, black label
Eur: EMI K 060 20 2168 6
NL: EMI K 060 20 2168 6, with different back cover
ARG: EMI EMI 6177, yellow label, b/w back cover, Title: Circulos Humedos Y Calidos, B-side: Ruso Blanco / Incomunicado
12" PD UK: EMI 12 MARILP 8
12" Acetate UK: Abbey Road, one-sided, Tape Mix 37
12" Acetate UK: Abbey Road A one-sided 12" but was the B-side of the 12" single with live versions of White Russians and Incommunicado (no mention of tape mix), die-cut Abbey Road studio sleeve with Abbey Road labels with handwritten group and track names.
5" CD Single UK: EMI CD MARIL 8
Warm Wet Circles (7" remix) / White Russians (live 18 Jul 87, Lorelei) / Incommunicado (live 18 Jul 87, Lorelei)
12" has the following warning sticker: 'WARNING THIS RECORD CONTAINS MATERIAL WHICH MAY CAUSE OFFENSE 12MARIL 8'

B'SIDES THEMSELVES 4 Jan 88
LP UK: EMI EMS 1295077774880718LP, Jun 88
UK: EMI CZ-39
UK: EMI ATAK 113
D: EMI/Fame 1C 038.1557734 1
I: EMI 74 8807 1
F: EMI 74 8807 1 PM254
POR: EMI 74 8807 1
BRA: EMI 0647488071
VEN: EMI 25159
ISR: EMI EMS 12951
CAN: Capitol Canada C1 48807
MC UK: EMI TC EMS 1295
UK: EMI TC ATAK 113
Eur: EMI 262.748807
I: EMI 74 8807 4
GRI: EMI 262-788074 4
POL: ? 0012
CD UK: EMI CDP 7 48807 2 / CZ 39 0777 7 48807 2 5
Grendel / Charting The Single / Market Square Heroes (re-recorded edit) / Three Boats Down From The Candy (re-recorded version) / Cinderella Search (edit on CD, full version on LP) / Lady Nina (7" edit) / Freaks / Tux On Margaret (live 7 Apr 83, Edinburgh Playhouse)

Freaks 21 Nov 88
7" Single UK: EMI MARIL 9, black label
Eur: EMI 006 20 3087 7
E: EMI 006 20 3087 7, tan label
7" Shaped PD UK: EMI MARIL P 9, with card insert
Uncut Shape PD UK: EMI MARIL P 9
Freaks (live - Thieving Magpie version) / Kayleigh (live - Thieving Magpie version)
7" Single NL: EMI 006 20 3087 7, re-release Jan 89
Kayleigh (live - Thieving Magpie version) / Freaks (live - Thieving Magpie version)
12" Single UK: EMI 12 MARIL 9, black label
NL: EMI 060 20 30886 Tan Label
Eur: EMI K 060 20 3188 6
I: EMI 14 20 3188 6
5" CD Single UK: EMI CD MARIL 9
Eur: EMI 560 20 3088 2
Freaks (live - Thieving Magpie version) Kayleigh (live - Thieving Magpie version) Childhoods End?* (live - Thieving Magpie version) / White Feather (live - Thieving Magpie version) * CD only

'THE THIEVING MAGPIE' - 'LA GAZZA LADRA' 29 Nov 88
2CD UK: EMI CD MARL 1
CH: EMI CDS 791463 2 07777 91463 21
USA: Capitol CDP 7 91463 2, 2 sep.CDs
JAP: EMI CP 25 5767/68
2CD Promo JAP: EMI CP 25-5767.68, sticker on back cover + words 'Sample not for sale' on disc in red.
Intro - La Gazza Ladra / Slainte Mhath / He Knows, You Know / Chelsea Monday / Freaks / Jigsaw / Punch And Judy / Sugar Mice / Fugazi / Script for A Jester's Tear / Incommunicado / White Russian
Pseudo Silk Kimono / Kayleigh / Lavender / Bitter Suite / Heart Of Lothian / Waterhole Expresso Bongo / Lords Of The Backstage / Blind Curve / Childhoods End? / White Feather
2LP UK: EMI MARL 1
Eur: EMI 164 791463 1
I: EMI 2 62 791463 1
F: Pathe Marconi 164-791463 1 0777 7 91463 1 4
USA: Capitol C1-91463 2
POR: EMI 7914631
BRA: EMI 164 7914631
VEN: EMI 25169 FOC
VEN: EMI 25169 No FOC
ISR: EMI MARL 1-1
MC UK: EMI 464 7 91463 4 TC MARL 1
Eur: EMI 464 7 91463 4
USA: Capitol C4-91463 4
TUR: EMI TCP 2331
IND: EMI EQ 104-9
GRI: EMI 264-91464 4
2LP Promo F: Pathe Marconi 164-791463 1 0777 7 91463 1 4 7914651 / Disc2: 7914641
Intro - La Gazza Ladra / Slainte Mhath / He Knows, You Know / Chelsea Monday / Pseudo Silk Kimono / Kayleigh / Lavender / Bitter Suite / Heart Of Lothian / Jigsaw / Punch And Judy / Sugar Mice / Fugazi / Freaks (not on 2LP) / Script For A Jester's Tear / Incommunicado / White Russian
12" Promo USA: Capitol SPRO 79521, 4 tracks - same on each side, black / grey sleeve, sticker: '4 Track Sampler from Thieving Magpie', 33 rpm
Promo MC USA: Capitol C4-91463-S 4
Kayleigh / Incommunicado / He Knows You Know / Sugar Mice

A SINGLES COLLECTION, 1982-1992 8 Jun 92
LP UK: EMI EMD 1033
EUR: EMI 064-799370 1
POL: MJM Music MJM 141
POR: EMI 7993701SPA, yellow label, OIS
MC UK: EMI TC EMD 1033
UK: Abbey Road Studios
EUR: EMI 264-799370 4
IND: EMI E0188
USA: IRS X4-13157, Rel. 13 Jul 92 as: **Six Of One, Half A Dozen Of The Other**
Promo MC UK: Abbey Road Studios 14 Apr 92
CD UK: EMI CD EMD 1033
NL: EMI 0 7777 99370 2
I: EMI 072 7993702
JAP: EMI TOCP 7262
USA: IRS X2-13157, Rel. 13 Jul 92 as: **Six Of One, Half A Dozen Of The Other**
Promo CD UK: EMI CD EMD 1033, with sticker: 'June 8th sees the release of A SINGLES COLLECTION '82-'92, a compilation album featuring some of MARILLION'S finest moments, to commemorate 10 years with EMI, Marillion play Wembley Arena on Sept. 5th, their only UK show this year.'
BRA: EMI 368 799370 2
JAP: EMI TOCP 7262, normal edition, with purple print on CD: 'Sample not for sale', sticker promo on back cover.
Cover My Eyes (Pain And Heaven) (album version) / Kayleigh (7" version) / Easter (album version) / Warm Wet Circles (7" version) / Uninvited Guest (7" version) / Assassing ('92 remix) / Hooks In You (album version) / Garden Party ('92 remix) / No One Can (album version) / Incommunicado (album version) / Dry Land (album version) / Lavender (7" Version) / I Will Walk On Water (album version) / Sympathy (single version)

MARILLION 3CD BOX 27 Nov 92
3CD Box UK: EMI 777 78 0634 2 1
SCRIPT FOR A JESTER'S TEAR / FUGAZI / MISPLACED CHILDHOOD

MUSIC COLLECTION 1993
CD I: EMI 0 777 78 9346 2 2
Grendel / Lady Nina / Freaks / Sugar Mice / She Chameleon / Hotel Hobbies / Forgotten Sons / La Gazza Ladra / Slainte Mhath / Chelsea Monday / Pseudo Silk Kimono 02:20

LIVE FROM LORELEI 06 Mar 95
CD UK: Sound & Vision / EMI 7243 8 3169 6 2 7
Box: SAV 4913723 7243 4 91372 3 3
MC IND: Golden Lion G 2700, all tracks incl. Incubus / White Russian, essentially the soundtrack of Video with the same name, only available in combination with Video as DoublePack
Slainte Mhath / Assassing / Script For A Jester's Tear / Sugar Mice / Hotel Hobbies / Warm Wet Circles / That Time of The Night / Kayleigh / Lavender Heart Of Lothian / The Last Straw / Incommunicado

3 CD BOX 29 May 95
3CD Box NL: EMI MACDBX 3
MISPLACED CHILDHOOD / CLUTCHING AT STRAWS / HOLIDAYS IN EDEN

THE ORIGINALS 25 Sep 95
3CD Box UK: EMI CDOMB 015 7243 8

35271 2 0
3 CD cardboard box with g/fold CD size covers of the original LPs
SCRIPT FOR A JESTER'S TEAR BC: 7243 8 35272 2 9
FUGAZI BC: 7243 8 35273 2 8
MISPLACED CHILDHOOD BC: 7243 8 35274 2 7

MARILLION BOX 1996
2CD Box F: EMI 8-53158-2 2 CD, in a slipcase containing **CLUTCHING AT STRAWS / SEASONS END**

KAYLEIGH 28 May 96 NL / **ESSENTIAL COLLECTION** 7 Oct 96 UK
These are identical releases with different covers and linernotes
CD NL: Disky DC 867182 0 724348 671820
CAN: Disky E2 86718 0 724348 671820
CD UK: EMI Gold CD-GOLD-1058 7243 8 53593 2 3
Grendel (single version) / He Knows You Know (album version) / Jigsaw (album version) / Punch And Judy (album version) / Cinderella Search (edited 7" version) / Kayleigh (edited 7" version) / Lavender (edited 7" version) / Lady Nina (edited 7" version) / Torch Song (album version)

THE BEST OF MARILLION 1996
CD Pol: ??? CDK-3356-41
Kayleigh (single version / Market Square Heroes (B-sides album version) / Freaks (single version) / Garden Party ('92 remix version) / Warm Wet Circles (album version) / Fugazi (album version) / Heart Of Lothian (album version) / Assassing (album version) / Incommunicado (album version) / Lavender (album version) / That Time Of The Night (album version) / Punch And Judy (album version) / Sugar Mice (album version) / Chelsea Monday (album version)

BEST OF BOTH WORLDS 24 Feb 97
2CD Promo UK: EMI CDADV 103
2CD UK: EMI CDEMC 3761
Eur: EMI 7243 8 55184 2 3
CAN: EMI 7243 8 55184 2 3, 18 Mar 97
USA: Sanctuary ZAN84538CD, 25 Feb 02
Script For A Jester's Tear (album version) / Market Square Heroes (edited re-recorded version) / He Knows, You Know (album version) / Forgotten Sons (album version) / Garden Party (album version) / Assassing (7" version) / Punch And Judy (7" version) / Kayleigh (7" version) / Lavender (7" version) / Heart Of Lothian (7" version) / Incommunicado (album version) / Warm Wet Circles (7" version) / That Time of the Night (album version) / Sugar Mice (album version) / The Uninvited Guest (album version) / Easter (7" version) / Hooks In You (Meaty Mix) / The Space (album version) / Cover My Eyes (Pain And) Heaven (album version) / No One Can (album version) / Dry Land (album version) / Waiting To Happen (album version) / The Great Escape (album version) / Alone Again In The Lap of Luxury (radio edit) / Made Again (album version) / King (album version) / Afraid Of Sunlight (album version) / Beautiful (radio edit) / Cannibal Surf Babe (album version)

BEST OF BOTH WORLDS, 1982-1988 24 Mar 97
Double PD UK: EMI EMCF 3761 7243 8 55187 1 3, the 2 discs are contained in a single die-cut sleeve.
NL: EMI EMCF 3761
2 PD Promo UK: EMI EMCF 3761, with sticker 'Promotional copy not for sale'
Script For A Jester's Tear (album version) / Market Square Heroes (edited re-recorded version) / He Knows You Know (album version) / Forgotten Sons (album version) / Garden Party (album version) / Assassing (7" version) / Punch And Judy (7" version) / Kayleigh (7" version) / Lavender (7" version) / Heart Of Lothian (7" version) / Incommunicado (album version) / Warm Wet Circles (7" version) / That Time Of The Night (album version) / Sugar Mice (album version)

KAYLEIGH - THE ESSENTIAL MARILLION COLLECTION 4 May 98
CD UK: EMI 7243 4 94564 2 6, only at Woolworth's (British store)
UK: EMI CD-MFPE-6420
MC UK: EMI TC-MFPE-6420
Kayleigh (single version) / Lavender (single version) / He Knows, You Know (album version) / Garden Party ('92 remix) / Punch And Judy (single version) / Market Square Heroes (re-recorded (edited version) / Cinderella Search (full version) / Cover My Eyes (album version) / No One Can (album version) / Freaks (album version) / Sympathy (single version) / Hooks In You (album version) / Dry Land (album version) / 100 nights (incl. a bit of The Rakes Progress and This Town Reprise / Cannibal Surf Babe (BoBW version) / Afraid of Sunlight (album version)

MARILLION THE CD SINGLES '82-'88 Jul 00
12 CD Box UK: EMI 7243 8 88 667 2 9 Box of all tracks released on CD singles, all tracks are remastered.
4 CDR UK: EMI no-number promo with 3 singles on each CDR.
CD 1: Market Square Heroes / Three Boats Down From The Candy / Grendel
CD 2: He Knows, You Know (7" version) / Charting The Single (edited studio version missing first seconds) / He Knows, You Know (12" version) Garden Party (edited version) / Margaret (edited live: Edinburgh Playhouse 7 April 83) / Garden Party (album version, not alt. 12" version) / Charting The Single (live: Hammersmith Odeon 18 April 83 / Margaret (live: Edinburgh Playhouse 7 April 83)
CD 4: Punch And Judy (7" version) / Market Square Heroes (7" re-recorded version) / Three Boats Down From The Candy (re-recorded version) / Market Square Heroes (re-recorded version)
CD 5: Assassing (7" version) / Cinderella Search (7" version) / Assassing (album version) / Cinderella Search (12" version)
CD 6: Kayleigh (7" version) / Lady Nina (7" version) / Kayleigh (alternative mix) / Kayleigh (extended version) / Lady Nina (12" version)
CD 7: Lavender (7" version) / Freaks Lavender Blue
CD 8: Heart Of Lothian (7" version) / Chelsea Monday (live: Utrecht Vredenburg, 15 Oct 85) / Heart Of Lothian (full version)
CD 9: Incommunicado (7" version) / Going Under / Incommunicado (album version) / Incommunicado (alternate version)
CD 10: Sugar Mice (album version) / Tux On / Sugar Mice (radio edit) / Sugar Mice (extended version)
CD 11: Warm Wet Circles (7" remix) / White Russians (live: Lorelei 18 July 87) / Incommunicado (live: Lorelei 18 July 87)
CD 12: Freaks (live, Thieving Magpie version) / Kayleigh (live, Thieving Magpie version) / Childhoods End? (live, Thieving Magpie version) / White Feather (live, Thieving Magpie version)

MARILLION with STEVE HOGARTH:

Hooks In You 24 Aug 89
7" single UK: EMI MARIL 10, white label, hard cover
?: EMI MARIL 10, silver label
?: EMI MARIL 10, re-release, black label
EUR: EMI 006 20 3495 7, yellow label, soft cover
F: EMI K006 20 3495 7
I: EMI 06-20 3495 7
AUS: EMI EMI 2322
Cassette Single UK: EMI TC MARIL 10
USA: Capitol 4 JM-44499
Hooks In You (7" mix) / After Me (album version)
7" promo Mex: EMI SEC 803, no picture sleeve
Hooks In You (7" mix)
7" promo USA: Capitol 7PRO-79890 / 79911, white label, factory sleeve
Hooks In You (7" mix) / Hooks In You (Meaty Mix)
5" Promo CD USA: Capitol DPRO-79751
Hooks In You (7" mix)
12" single UK: EMI 12 MARIL 10, black label
EUR: EMI 060 20 3495 6
F: EMI K060 20 3495 6, yellow label
12" posterbag UK: EMI 12 MARILP 10, black label, limited edition, only the cover has 12 MARILP10, the disc is the standard verson
12" 12 MARIL 10, includes inner black cover within the folded poster.
12" promo UK: EMI 12 MARIL 10, white label
3" CD single A: EMI 552 20 3495 3 5 099920 349530
5" CD single UK: EMI CD MARIL 10
EUR: EMI 552 20 3495 2
Hooks In You (Meaty Mix) / Hooks In You (7" mix) / After Me (album version

SEASONS END 25 Sep 89
LP UK: EMI EMD 1011
EUR: EMI 064-792877 1
EEC: EMI 250391 FOC, club-edition

I: EMI 7928771 OIS
E: EMI 006-792877 1
BRA: EMI 066 792877 1 FOC, yellow label
MEX: EMI 2001, title in Spanish
VEN: EMI
USA: Capitol C1-92877, burgundy label
RSA: EMI EMCJ L 7928771
ZBW:
KOR: EMI EKLP 0030
LP Promo UK: EMI, white label
USA: Capitol C1-92877 OIS, light violet label, sleeve with promo-info
12" PD UK: EMI EMDPD 1011 00777 7 92877 0 3, has card insert containing the full lyrics
UK: EMI EMDPD 1011, same pic. A+ B
EUR: EMI 064-792877 0
Test pressing UK: white vinyl for PD
MC UK: EMI TC EMD 1011
EUR: EMI 264-792877 4
USA: Capitol C4 - 92877
TUR: EMI TCP 2385
IND: EMI TC-EMD-1011
IND: EMI E0139 - 9
IND: PMT A-778, bootleg / pirate
Dub: Peacock 4358 Dub Dubai
Promo MC USA: Capitol C4 - 92877
CD UK: EMI CD EMD 1011
EUR: EMI CDP 7 92877 2 00777 7 92877 2 7
USA: Capitol CDP 7 92877 2
JAP: EMI TOCP-5929
Promo CD UK: EMI CD EMD 1011, in cardboard box with band photo
JAP: EMI TOCP-5929
2CD Remaster UK: EMI REMARIL 005 7243 8 57713 2 3, 29 Sep 97
CAN: EMI 7243 8 57713 2 3, 21 Apr 98
USA: Sanctuary 4510, 07 Mar 00
USA: Sanctuary ZAN84533CD, 11 Mar 02
1CD Remaster UK: EMI CD 527 1182, 28 Aug 00
In Case of the Remastered 2CD
The King Of Sunset Town / Easter / The Uninvited Guest / Seasons End / Holloway Girl / Berlin / After Me (bonus track on CD) / Hooks In You / The Space 06:15
Bonus CD for European Remastered Ed.
Uninvited Guest (extended 12" version) / The Bell In The Sea (single version) / The Release (single version) / The King Of Sunset Town (Mushroom Farm Demo, Mar 89) / Holloway Girl (Mushroom Farm Demo, Mar 89) / Seasons End (Mushroom Farm Demo, Mar 89) / The Uninvited Guest (Mushroom Farm Demo, Mar 89) / Berlin (Mushroom Farm Demo, Mar 89) / The Bell In The Sea (Mushroom Farm Demo, Mar 89)

Uninvited Guest 27 Nov 89
7" single UK: EMI MARIL 11, black label, hard cover
EUR: EMI 006 20 3582 7
7" Promo UK: EMI MARIL 11, with white promo sticker: 'With Compliments John Myers', 27 Nov 89
7" shaped PD UK: EMI MARIL PD 11 5 099920 358204, has a card insert. 2 versions: 1: logo has black background colour / 2: white
Uncut PD UK: EMI MARIL PD 11
Clear vinyl PD UK: EMI MARIL PD 11
Cassette Single UK: EMI TC MARIL 11
Uninvited Guest (7" version) / The Bell In The Sea
7" promo USA: Capitol ?
5" promo CD USA: Capitol DPRO-79922
Uninvited Guest (7" version)
12" single UK: EMI 12 MARIL 11
EUR: EMI K 060 20 3582 6
12" door-pack UK: EMI 12 MARILS 11, only the cover has 12 MARILS 11, the disk is 12MARIL 11.
Uninvited Guest (12" Version) / The Bell In The Sea / Uninvited Guest (7" version)
5" CD single UK: EMI CD MARIL 11
EUR: EMI 552 20 3582 2
3" CD single A: EMI 552 20 3582 3
Uninvited Guest (7" version) / Uninvited Guest (12" version) / The Bell In The Sea

Easter 19 Mar 90 Cassette, all other items 26 Mar 90
7" single UK: EMI MARIL 12, white label
UK: EMI MARIL 12, silver label
UK: EMI MARIL 12, black label, hard cover
I: EMI 2037607
EUR: EMI 006 20 3760 7, Released in Germany 29 Mar 90, France May 90
7" Promo UK: EMI MARIL 12, silver label, some promo info
F: EMI 2037607, silver label
7" PD UK: EMI MARIL PD 12 5 099920 376000
Cas UK: EMI TC MARIL 12
Easter (7" Edit) / The Release
12" single UK: EMI 12 MARIL 12, black label
EUR: EMI 060 20 3760 6
5" CD single UK: EMI CD MARIL 12
EUR: EMI 560 20 3760 2
NL: EMI 560 20 3760 2, re-released 24 Aug 92 with same number
Easter (12" edit) / The Release / Uninvited Guest (live, UK, Glasgow Barrowlands, 4 Dec 89)
12" single UK: EMI 12 MARILS 12, limited edition of 5000 Copies
Easter (12" edit / The Release / Warm Wet Circles (live) / That Time Of The Night (live)
12" G/fold UK: EMI 12 MARILG 12 5 0999 20 3760 8 6, numbered limited edition
Easter (7" edit) / Uninvited Guest (live, UK, Glasgow, Barrowlands, 4 Dec 89) Warm Wet Circles (live) / That Time Of The Night (live)

Cover My Eyes 28 May 91
7" single UK: EMI MARIL 13, silver label, hard cover
EUR: EMI 006 20 4348 7, yellow label, released Germany 23 May 91
7" Promo MEX: EMI 7001072, Title: Cubro Mis Ojos
Cassette Single UK: EMI TC MARIL 13
NL: EMI 300050 4
Cover My Eyes (Pain And Heaven) / How Can It Hurt
12" single UK: EMI 12 MARILP 13, black label, contains free poster, number on the label is 12MARIL13
EUR: EMI 060 20 4348 6
5" CD single UK: EMI CD MARIL 13, blue disc
UK: EMI CD MARIL 13, red disc
NL: EMI 20-4348-2, blue disc
NL: EMI 20-4348-2, red disc
EUR: EMI CDP 560 20 4348 2 5099920434823
5" CD box UK: EMI CD MARILS 13, contains a free poster.
Cover My Eyes (Pain And Heaven) / How Can It Hurt / The Party
5" promo CD USA: IRS DPRO 67084
Cover My Eyes (Pain And Heaven)

Holidays in Eden 10 Jun 91
Promo Cassette
Cover My Eyes / No One Can / Holidays in Eden / Dry Land

HOLIDAYS IN EDEN 24 Jun 91
LP UK: EMI EMD 1022
EUR: EMI 064 7 96822 1
CZ: Popron 50135-1, Paper OIS
BRA: EMI EMI 7698221
COL:
VEN: EMI 25191
LP Promo BRA: EMI EMI 7698221
Cas UK: EMI TC EMD 1022
EUR: EMI 264 7 96822 4
F: EMI PM 464 7 96822 4
I: EMI 64-7 96822 4
Pol: Ryth 196
IND: EMI E0172-2
CD UK: EMI CD EMD 1022
CAN: EMI/Capitol Canada C2 96822, track list and cover art same as UK
EUR: EMI CDP 7 96822 2 00777 7 96822 2 5
NL: EMI CDP 7 96822 2, first press in pink, 2nd press blue
JAP: EMI TOCD-6784
Promo CD JAP: EMI TOCD-6784
2CD Remaster Eur: EMI 7243 4 9337220
UK: EMI 493 3722
USA: Sanctuary 4509, 10 Feb 00
USA: Sanctuary ZAN84532CD, 11 Mar 02
Splintering Heart / Cover My Eyes (Pain And Heaven) / The Party / No One Can / Holidays In Eden / Dry Land / Waiting To Happen / This Town / The Rakes Progress / 100 Nights
Bonus CD for European Remastered Ed.
Sympathy (single version) / How Can it Hurt (single version) / A Collection (single version) / Cover My Eyes (Pain And Heaven) (acoustic single version) / Sympathy (acoustic single version) / I Will Walk on Water (alternative '98 remix) / Splintering Heart (live 11 Dec 90, Moles Club) / You Don't Need Anyone (Moles Club Demo, Dec 90) / No One Can (Moles Club Demo, Dec 90) / The Party (Moles Club Demo, Dec 90 / This Town (Moles Club Demo, Dec 90) / Waiting To Happen (Moles Club Demo, Dec 90) / Eric (Stanbridge Video Soundtrack) / The Epic Fairground (Mushroom Farm Demo, Mar 89)

No One Can 22 Jul 91
7" single UK: EMI MARIL 14, black label, hard cover
UK: EMI MARIL 14, silver label, hard cover
EUR: EMI 006 20 4409 7, soft cover
F: EMI 006 20 4409 7, with light border
7" Box UK: EMI MARILS 14, box contains a badge, 2 sleeves and 2 group photos, black cover or full colour cover, only the box has MARILS 14 the sleeve and label MARIL14
MC single UK: EMI TC MARIL 14
No One Can / A Collection
12" single EUR: EMI 060 20 4409 6, tan label

12" testpress D: EMI 20 4409 6, white label, no cover
5" CD single UK: EMI CD MARIL 14
EUR: EMI 560 20 4409 2
No One Can / A Collection / Splintering Heart (live, UK, Bath, The Moles Club, 11 Dec 90)
Promo box UK: EMI MARILS 14, box contains badge, 2 sleeves and 2 group photos, same as box above but with 7" and CD both with promo sticker
7" Single: No One Can / A Collection
CD Single: No One Can / A Collection Splintering Heart (live, UK, Bath, The Moles Club, 11 Dec 90)

Dry Land 23 Sep 91
7" single UK: EMI MARIL 15 5 0999 204517 7 6, silver label, hard cover
EUR: EMI 006-204542 7, tan label, soft cover
Dry Land (edit) / Holloway Girl (live) / After Me (live, only on UK release)
10" single UK: EMI 10 MARIL 15 5 0999 204517 8 3, numbered limited edition clear vinyl with wrap-around cover.
Dry Land (album version) / Waiting To Happen (live) / Easter (live) / Sugar Mice (live)
5" CD single UK: EMI CD MARIL 15 5 0999 204517 2 1
Dry Land (edit) / Holloway Girl (live) / Easter (live) / Dry Land (album version)
5" CD single NL: EMI 5 0999 204542 27, 1st pressing UK tracks and Dutch print
Dry Land (edit) / Holloway Girl (live) / Easter (live) / Sugar Mice (live)
12" PD UK: EMI 12 MARILPD 15 5 0999 204517 0 7, 30 Sep 91
Has a card cover with cut-out
12" EUR: EMI 060-204542 6, 30 Sep 91
Dry Land (album version) / Holloway Girl (live) / King Of Sunset Town (live) / Substitute (live)
All Dry Land live tracks UK, London, Borderline Club, 22 May 91

HOLIDAYS IN EDEN 25 Feb 92
Cassette USA: IRS X4-13138
CD USA: IRS X2-13138 02207-13138-2
Cover My Eyes (Pain And Heaven) / No One Can Take You Away From Me / Splintering Heart / The Party / A Collection / Holidays In Eden / How Can It Hurt / Dry Land / Waiting To Happen / This Town / The Rakes Progress / 100 Nights

Sympathy 14 Apr 92
MC UK: Abbey Road Studios ??
7" single UK: EMI MARIL 16, silver label, soft cover, 11 May 92
5" Promo CD F: EMI PM 110 880 6162
Sympathy / Kayleigh (live, Birmingham, Aston Villa Leisure Centre, 27 Sep 91)
12" PD UK: EMI 12 MARILPD 16 7243 8 80008 6 4, has a card insert.
Sympathy / Kayleigh (live, Birmingham, Aston Villa Leisure Centre, 27 Sep 91) / Dry Land (live, London, Hammersmith Odeon, 29 Sep 90)
12" Promo F: EMI SP 1596, one track, different sleeve
Sympathy
5" CD single UK: EMI CD MARILS 16 7243 8 80009 2 5, Digipack
Sympathy / Kayleigh (live, Argentina TV Studio, 30 Feb 92) / I Will Walk On Water (5" mix)
7" single EUR: EMI 006 880008 7, tan label, textured cover, 18 May 92
7" Promo Mex: EMI 700 1194
Sympathy / Kayleigh (live, Birmingham, Aston Villa Leisure Centre, 27 Sep 91)

5" CD single UK: EMI CD MARIL 16 7243 8 80008 2 6
EUR: EMI CDP 564 880008 2
5" Promo CD UK: EMI CD MARIL 16, CD + Cassette + Factsheet in white plastic box
Sympathy / Kayleigh (live, Birmingham, Aston Villa Leisure Centre, 27 Sep 91) / Dry Land (live, London, Hammersmith Odeon, 29 Sep 90)

A SINGLES COLLECTION, 1982-1992 8 Jun 92
LP UK: EMI EMD 1033
EUR: EMI 064-799370 1
POL: MJM Music MJM 141
POR: EMI 7993701 SPA, label yellow, OIS
MC UK: EMI TC EMD 1033
UK: Abbey Road Studios
EUR: EMI 264-799370 4
IND: EMI E0188
USA: IRS X4-13157 Rel. 13 Jul 92 as: **Six Of One, Half A Dozen Of The Other**
Promo MC UK: Abbey Road Studios, 14 Apr 92
CD UK: EMI CD EMD 1033
NL: EMI 0 7777 99370 2
I: EMI 072 7993702
JAP: EMI TOCP 7262
USA: IRS X2-13157 Rel.13 Jul 92 as: **Six Of One, Half A Dozen Of The Other**
Promo CD UK: EMI CD EMD 1033, with sticker
BRA: EMI 368 799370 2
JAP: EMI TOCP 7262 normal edition,with purple print on the hole of the CD: 'Sample not for sale', sticker promo on back cover
Cover My Eyes (Pain And Heaven) (album version) / Kayleigh (7" version) / Easter (album version) / Warm Wet Circles (7" version) / Uninvited Guest (7" version) / Assassing ('92 remix) / Hooks In You (album version) / Garden Party ('92 remix) / No One Can (album version) / Incommunicado (album version) / Dry Land (album version) / Lavender (7" version) / I Will Walk On Water (album version) / Sympathy (single version)

No One Can 13 Jul 92
7" Single UK: EMI MARIL 17, silver label, hard cover
7" Promo UK: EMI MARIL 17, with a white promo sticker: 'Manufacturers Property Not For Sale'
No One Can / Cover My Eyes (Pain And Heaven) (Mike Stone remix)
Cassette Single USA: IRS X4-13871
No One Can / I Will Walk On Water (single mix)
12" PD UK: EMI 12 MARIL PD 17 7243 8 80149 6 0, card insert.
No One Can / Cover My Eyes (Pain And Heaven)(Mike Stone remix) / Sympathy (Racket Club acoustic session, May 92)
5" CD Single UK: EMI CD MARILS 17, Digipack
No One Can / Cover My Eyes (Racket Club acoustic session) / Sugar Mice (Racket Club acoustic session)
5" CD Promo USA: IRS DPRO-67096, with US tourdates on the back
No One Can (radio edit album version)
5" CD Single UK: EMI CD MARIL 17
NL: EMI CDP 560 8 80149 22, 20 Jul 92
5" CD Promo UK: EMI CD MARIL 17
Sticker on the cover
No One Can / Cover My Eyes (Pain And Heaven) (Mike Stone remix) / Sympathy (Racket Club acoustic session)

Xth ANNIVERSARY, LIVE AT THE BORDERLINE 20 Aug 92
CD UK: Racket RACKET 1
limited edition of 2000 copies
UK: Racket RACKET 1, re-release Jan 98
UK: Front Row Club FRC-004, re-release Feb 02
Splintering Heart / Easter / King Of Sunset Town / Waiting To Happen / Sympathy / Kayleigh / Lavender / Heart of Lothian / Uninvited Guest / Slainte Mhath / The Release / Hooks in You Garden Party
Recorded live: London, The Borderline Club, 9 May 92.

LIVE IN CARACAS 8 Feb 93
CD UK: Racket RACKET 2, limited edition of 1000 copies
UK: Racket RACKET 2, re-release Jan 98
Splintering Heart / Holidays In Eden / Script For A Jester's Tear / Easter / Hotel Hobbies / Warm Wet Circles That Time of The Night / Kayleigh / Lavender / Heart Of Lothian / Cover My Eyes / Slainte Mhath / The Space... / Waiting To Happen / Hooks in You
Recorded live: Venezuela, Caracas, The Poliedro Arena, 30 Sep 92

LIVE AT GLASGOW BARROWLANDS 23 Nov 93
CD UK: Racket RACKET 3, limited edition of 1000 copies
UK: Racket RACKET 3, re-release Jan 98
UK: Front Row Club FRC-005, re-release Feb 02
King Of Sunset Town / Slainte Mhath / Uninvited Guest / Easter / Warm Wet Circles / That Time Of The Night / Holloway Girl / Seasons End / Berlin / The Space...
Tracks 1-8, UK, Glasgow, Barrowland Ballroom, 04 Dec 89; tracks 9-10, UK, Bradford, St. Georges Hall, 10 Dec 89

The Great Escape 10 Jan 94
CD single NL: EMI 243 8 81164 2
The Great Escape (alternative ending) / Made Again / Marouatte Jam
5" CD promo UK: EMI CDBRAVE 1 LC0542, Jan 94
The Great Escape (alternative ending) / Alone Again In The Lap of Luxury / Hard As Love / The Hollow Man

Brave: 3 Track Album Sampler Jan 94
5" CD promo UK: EMI CDEMDDJ1054
Brave: An Introduction (spoken biog during orchestral version of The Great Escape / The Hollow Man / Alone Again In The Lap of Luxury / The Great Escape

BRAVE 7 Feb 94
2LP UK: EMI EMD 1054 8280321, limited edition with double groove on

Side 4 with 2 versions of The Great Escape + 7 minutes of water sounds under the bridge at the end
CD UK: EMI CD EMD1054 72438 2803225
EUR: EMI 7243 8 28032 2 5
NL: EMI 7243 8 28032 2 5
I: EMI LC-0542
JAP: EMI TOCP 8186
JAP: EMI TOCP 3429, reprint 23 Jun 00
CAN: EMI Canada 7243 8 28032 2 5
USA: IRS 7243 82803225 ? X2-28032 ?
CD Promo USA: IRS DPRO-6729, Jan 94
JAP: EMI TOCP 8186, normal edition, with brown print on the hole of the CD 'Sample not for sale' and sticker
MC UK: EMI TC EMD 1054 7243 8 28032 4 9
EUR: EMI 1828032 4
NL: EMI 82803-24
USA: EMI X4-28032
Tur: EMI TCP 2693
IND: EMI TC 828032-4 E0388
Remastered 2CD UK: EMI 72434 97038 2 7, 17 Oct 98
USA: Sanctuary 4512, 10 Feb 00
USA: Sanctuary ZAN84535CD, 11 Mar 02
Bridge / Living With The Big Lie / Runaway / Goodbye To All That (Wave / Mad / The Opium Den) / The Slide / Standing In The Swing / Hard As Love / The Hollow Man / Alone Again In The Lap of Luxury / Now Wash Your Hands / Paper Lies / Brave / The Great Escape / The Last Of You / Falling From The Moon / Made Again
Second groove on Side 4 of 2LP has the following tracks: The Great Escape (alternative ending) / Water Sounds (no track name mentioned)
Bonus CD for European Remastered Ed: The Great Escape (orchestral version) / Marouette Jam (single version) / The Hollow Man (French acoustic version) / Winter Trees (single version) / Alone Again In The Lap of Luxury (French acoustic version) / Runaway (French acoustic version) / Hard As Love (instrumental) / Living With The Big Lie (demo, 23 Jan 93 at the Racket Club) / Alone Again In The Lap of Luxury (demo, 23 Jan 93 at the Racket Club) / Dream Sequence (demo, 23 Jan 93 at the Racket Club) / The Great Escape (Spiral remake)

Marillion Acoustic 7 Feb 94
5" CD Promo F: EMI SPCD 1714, very limited edition
Alone Again In The Lap of Luxury (acoustic version) / Runaway (acoustic version) / The Hollow Man (acoustic version)

The Hollow Man 14 Mar 94
7" UK: EMI EM 307 8812437
MC UK: EMI TCEM 307 8812434
10" Acetate UK: Abbey Road
The Hollow Man (album version) / Brave (album version)
CD single 1 UK: EMI CDEMS 307 7243 8 81243 2
The Hollow Man (album version) / Brave (album version) / Marouatte Jam
CD single 2 UK: EMI CDEM 307 7243 8 81244 2
CD single EUR: EMI 7243 8 81244 2, 21 Mar 94
NL: EMI 8-81244-2
The Hollow Man (album version) / The Great Escape (orchestral version) / Winter Trees (instrumental)

Alone Again In The Lap of Luxury
25 Apr 94
CD Promo UK: EMI CDEMDJ 318
Alone Again In The Lap of Luxury (radio edit)
CD Promo USA: IRS DPRO-10746
Alone Again In The Lap of Luxury (radio edit)
Cas UK: EMI TCEM 318 8 81353 4
Alone Again In The Lap of Luxury (radio edit) / Living With The Big Lie (album version)
12" PD UK: EMI 12 EMPD 318 7243 8 81353 0 6, card insert.
Alone Again In The Lap of Luxury (album version) / Living With The Big Lie (album version) / The Space... (live, Cambridge, Corn Exchange, 2 Mar 94)
CD single 1 UK: EMI CDEMS 318 7243 8 81353 2
Alone Again In The Lap of Luxury (radio edit) / River (instrumental, live) / Bridge 02:51 (live) / Living With The Big Lie 06:36 (live)
CD single 2 UK: EMI CDEM 318 7243 8 81354 2, 2 May 94
CD single D: EMI 7243 8 81354 2, 9 May 94
NL: EMI 8-81401-2
Cas Pol: Hiton 0820 Title: Alone Again + Greatest Hits
Alone Again In The Lap of Luxury (album version) / Cover My Eyes (live, UK, London, Forum, 5 Mar 94) / Slainte Mhath (live) / Uninvited Guest (live)

3 CD BOX 29 May 95
3CD Box NL: EMI MACDBX 3
MISPLACED CHILDHOOD / **CLUTCHING AT STRAWS** / **HOLIDAYS IN EDEN**

THE MAKING OF BRAVE 22 May 95
2CD UK: Racket RACKET 6
UK: Racket RACKET 6, re-release Jan 98, outtakes:
Jones, The Fog / Early Sketch for Bridge / You Get Used To It / Big Lie / Musical Theme Guitar / Musical String Theme / Guitar Solo / Tube Train / Musical String Theme 2 / Argument / Runaway / Goodbye To All That / Magma / Wave / Mad 1 / Mad 2 / Mad 3 / Mad 4 / Opium Den / The Slide / Standing In The Swing / Hard As Love / Hollow Man / Lap Of Luxury / Echo Jam / Now Wash Your Hands 1 / Now Wash Your Hands 2 / Paper Lies / The Great Escape / Falling From The Moon / Made Again / Cabin Fever
Brave demo version:
Bridge / Living With The Big Lie / Runaway / Goodbye To All That / Wave / Mad / The Opium Den / The Slide / Standing In The Swing / Hard As Love / The Hollow Man / Alone Again In The Lap of Luxury / Now Wash Your Hands / Paper Lies / Brave / The Great Escape / The Last Of You / Fallin' From The Moon / Made Again

Beautiful 29 May 95
Cassette UK: EMI TCMARIL 18, the cover mentions Icon as B-side!
Beautiful / Afraid Of Sunrise
5" CD single UK: EMI CDMARIL 18 7243 8 82174 2 2
Beautiful / Afraid Of Sunrise / Icon 5"
CD single UK: EMI CDMARILS 18, 3 colour prints included.
EUR: EMI 8 82183 2 7243 8 82183 2 0
NL: EMI 8-82183-2
Beautiful / Live Forever / The Great Escape (demo version) / Hard As Love (demo version)
5" CD single F: EMI 882182 2, 6 Jun 95
Beautiful / Icon 06:10
5" Promo CD UK: EMI CDMARILDJ 18
Beautiful (edit)
5" Promo CD NL: EMI-Electrola CDP-519482
Beautiful (edit)

Cannibal Surf Babe Jun 95
5" CD Promo USA: IRS DPRO 10769
Cannibal Surf Babe (radio edit) / Cannibal Surf Babe (album version)5"
CD single NL: EMI 882408 2, unreleased but test pressings were made, was planned for 2 Oct 95
Cannibal Surf Babe (Special Mix) / Beautiful (live) / Sugar Mice (live) / A Collection (live) / Easter (live)

AFRAID OF SUNLIGHT 24 Jun 95
LP UK: EMI EMD 1079 7243 833874 1 0
Cas UK: EMI TCEMD 1079
NL: EMI 8-33874-4
USA: EMI X4-33874
IND: EMI E0580 07243 8 33874 4 1
Cas Promo UK: EMI, track listings typed on EMI imprinted J-Card
CD UK: EMI CDEMD 10797243 83387427
EUR: EMI 7243 8 33874 2 7
NL: EMI 8-33874-2
CAN: EMI Canada 7243 8 33874 2 7
USA: IRS IRS-31722, 4 Jul 95, info listed on the promo
USA: IRS IRS-33874, 4 Jul 95, info on actual disc
JAP: EMI TOCP 8568
Promo CD USA: IRS/Eldorado DPRO10764
USA: IRS/Eldorado 8338742, 2 versions: one is promo with sticker on CD insert + silkscreened white 'promo' label on disc itself, other lacks those features and appears to be a regular release
UK: EMI CD-EMD-1079, autographed
JAP: EMI TOCP 8568, normal edition with purple print on the hole of the CD 'Sample not for sale' + sticker
Remastered 2CD UK: EMI 7243 4 98614 2 8, 22 Mar 99
USA: Sanctuary 4510, 21 Mar 00
USA: Sanctuary ZAN84536CD, 25 Feb 02
Gazpacho / Cannibal Surf Babe / Beautiful / Afraid Of Sunrise / Out Of This World / Afraid Of Sunlight / Beyond You (mono version) / King
Enhanced Bonus CD for Remastered ed: Icon (single version) / Live Forever (single version) / Second Chance a.k.a Beautiful (previously unreleased demo) / Beyond You (previously unreleased stereo demo) / Cannibal Surf Babe (previously unreleased demo) / Out Of This World (previously unreleased demo) / Bass Frenzy (previously unreleased demo) / Mirages (previously unreleased demo) / Afraid Of Sunlight (previously unreleased acoustic demo) / Sympathy For The Road Crew* (alternative version, hidden track)

* Enhanced multimedia section, contains a presentation of all released remasters and quicktime movie slide-show of some b/w photos

MADE AGAIN 25 Mar 96
2CD UK: EMI CDEMD 1094 7 243 8 37678 2 3
EUR: Castle Comm. PLC / Intact RAW DD111
USA: Castle Comm. PLC / Intact Castle 117-2 600234 011720
USA: Castle Music America No.570, 8 Feb 00
UK: Sanctuary/Castle CMDDD123, 19 Feb 01
2MC UK: EMI TCEMD 1094
Euro 2CD in a cardboard box with small poster, USA release 9 Apr 96, Holland release 22 Mar 96
Recorded UK, London, Hammersmith Odeon, 29 Sep 91:
Splintering Heart / Easter / No One Can / Waiting To Happen / Cover My Eyes / The Space...
Recorded: NL,Rotterdam Ahoy, 29 Sep 95
Hooks In You / Beautiful / Kayleigh / Lavender / Afraid Of Sunlight / King
Rec: F, Paris, La Cigale, 29 Apr 94
Living With The Big Lie / Runaway / Goodbye To All That / Wave / Mad / The Opium Den / The Slide / Standing In The Swing / Hard As Love / The Hollow Man / Alone Again In The Lap of Luxury / Now Wash Your Hands / Paper Lies / Brave / The Great Escape / The Last of You / Falling From The Moon / Made Again 05:25

Made Again 1996
Promo CD NL: Castle Comm. PLC / Intact RAWP 1019
No One Can (live) / Beautiful (live) / Made Again (live)

MARILLION BOX 1996
2CD Box F: EMI 8-53158-2 2, in slipcase
CLUTCHING AT STRAWS / SEASONS END

BEST OF BOTH WORLDS 24 Feb 97
2CD Promo UK: EMI CDADV 103
2CD UK: EMI CDEMC 3761
EUR: EMI 7243 8 55184 2 3
CAN: EMI 7243 8 55184 2 3, 18 Mar 97
USA: Sanctuary NR 4529
USA: Sanctuary ZAN84538CD, 25 Feb 02
Script Of A Jester's Tear (album version) / Market Square Heroes (edited re-recorded version) / He Knows, You Know (album version) / Forgotten Sons (album version) / Garden Party (album version) / Assassing (7" version) / Punch And Judy (album version) / Kayleigh (7" version) / Lavender (7" version) / Heart Of Lothian (7" version) / Incommunicado (album version) / Warm Wet Circles (7" version) / That Time Of The Night (album version) / Sugar Mice (album version) / The Uninvited Guest (album version) / Easter (7" version) / Hooks In You (Meaty Mix) / The Space... (album version) / Cover my Eyes (album version) / No One Can (album version) / Dry Land (album version) / Waiting To Happen (album version) / The Great Escape (album version) / Alone Again In The Lap of Luxury (radio edit) / Made Again (album version) / King (album version) / Afraid Of Sunlight (album version) / Beautiful (radio edit) / Cannibal Surf Babe (album version)

BEST OF BOTH WORLDS 1989-1995 24 Mar 97
Double Picture Disc UK: EMI EMCH 3761 7243 8 55190 1 7
NL: EMI EMCH 3761
The Uninvited Guest (album version) / Easter (7" version) / Hooks In You (Meaty Mix) / The Space... (album version) / Cover My Eyes (album version) / No One Can (album version) / Dry Land (album version) / Waiting To Happen (album version) / The Great Escape (album version) / Alone Again In The Lap of Luxury (radio edit) / Made Again (album version) / King (album version) / Afraid Of Sunlight (album version) / Beautiful (radio edit) Cannibal Surf Babe (album version)

THIS STRANGE ENGINE 21 Apr 97
CD Digipack UK: Castle Comm. PLC / Intact RAW DP 121
CD Jewel Case UK: Castle Comm. PLC / Intact RAW CD 121
JAP: Pony Canyon PCCY-01098, Mar 97
USA: Velvel VEL-79791, 07 Oct 97, no bonus tracks, matrix # at bottom of disc in reflective print
USA: Velvel VEL-79791-2, Dec 97, with sticker for bonus tracks & error on track 5, matrix # at bottom of disc in black print
USA: Velvel VEL-79791-2, Feb 98, sticker for bonus tracks, track 5 corrected
CAN: EMI-Can, 07 Oct 97
UK: Sanctuary/Castle CMRCD071, 19 Feb 01
CD Promo UK: Castle Comm. PLC/Intact RAW PR 121 No cover
JAP: Pony Canyon PCCY 01098, with stickered promo jap on obi+ word 'Sample' on the hole disc
MC JAP: Pony Canyon ACCY 01098 P1432, no bonus tracks
Man Of A Thousand Faces / One Fine Day / 80 Days / Estonia / Memory Of Water /An Accidental Man / Hope For The Future / This Strange Engine / Beautiful (unplugged Jap. bonus track) / Made Again (unplugged Jap. bonus track) / Estonia (Positive Light Mix - USA bonus track) / 80 Days (acoustic - USA bonus track)

This Strange Engine Edited Excerpts Apr 97
Promo CD UK: Castle Comm. PLC / Intact RAWP 1047
Man Of A Thousand Faces (excerpt) / This Strange Engine (excerpt) / One Fine Day (excerpt) / An Accidental Man (excerpt)

Man Of A Thousand Faces 15 May 97
CD Digipack Eur: Castle Comm. PLC / Intact RAWX 1044
UK: Castle Comm. PLC / Intact RAWX 1044, 2 Jun 97
Promo CD UK: Castle Comm. PLC / Intact RAWX 1044, no picture sleeve, with promo sticker
Man Of A Thousand Faces (radio edit) / Beautiful (unplugged) / Made Again unplugged) / Man Of A Thousand Faces (extended version)

Eighty Days 29 Sep 97
CD Eur: Castle Comm. PLC / Intact RAWX 1049 5 02638 414 905
UK: 13 Oct 97
Promo CD UK: Castle Comm. PLC / Intact RAWX 1049 5 02638 414 905, standard copy with white promo sticker reading 'Release date 6/10 Lisa Davies 0181-393-6298'
Eighty Days (album version) / This Strange Engine (live, Paris 20 May 97) / The Bell In The Sea (live, Paris 20 May 97)

Memory Of Water 1997
12" Acetate UK: no number, white label, A Whitfield Street recording.
Memory Of Water

TALES FROM THE ENGINE ROOM 21 Jan 98
CD UK: Racket RACKET 7
Estonia / The Memory Of Water / This Strange Engine / One Fine Day / Face 1004

MARILLION ROCHESTER 4 May 98
2 CD USA: Racket RACKET 8
First 1000 numbered and signed by the band, limited edition of 2000 copies, signed discs not all numbered under 1000, because of fault during manuf.
Emmanuel - Seasons End / Alone Again In The Lap of Luxury / Hard As Love / Eighty Days / Kayleigh / Lavender / Afraid Of Sunlight / Man Of 1000 Faces / Estonia... (combined due to an error) Easter / This Town / 100 Nights / Slainte Mhath / King / This Strange Engine / The Great Escape / Falling From The Moon / Garden Party

KAYLEIGH - THE ESSENTIAL MARILLION COLLECTION May 98
CD UK: EMI 7243 4 94564 2 6, only at Woolworth's, a British store
UK: EMI CD-MFPE-6420
MC UK: EMI TC-MFPE-6420
Kayleigh (single version) / Lavender (single version) / He Knows, You Know (album version) / Garden Party (92 remix) / Punch And Judy (single version) / Market Square Heroes (re-recorded edited version) / Cinderella Search (full version) / Cover My Eyes (album version) / No One Can (album version) / Freaks (single version) / Sympathy (single version) / Hooks In You (album version) / Dry Land (album version) / 100 Nights (incl. a bit of The Rakes Progress and This Town Reprise) / Cannibal Surf Babe (BoBW version) / Afraid Of Sunlight (album version)

TALES FROM THE ENGINE ROOM 1 Jun 98
CD UK: Eagle EAG CD 033
EC: Eagle EAGCD033
GAS 0000033 EAG - EDL EAG 085-2 5 034504 103320
Released France 30 Jun 98
USA: Cleopatra/ Purple Pyramid PURP 375, 29 Sep 98

USA: Big Eye 4042 Bar Code 66649640422, 17 Apr 01
AUS: Eagle Australia 857380476 2
MC EC: Eagle EAGMC033
CD-R acetate UK: Eagle CD-REF
tape to tape acetate, 27 May 98, same inscriptions on the gold disc
CD + 12" Promo UK: Eagle EAG CD 033 + 12033P
Estonia / The Memory of Water / This Strange Engine / One Fine Day / Face 1004 / 80 Days (not on first pressing, USA release corrected in Dec)
Cas PL: Eagle Records/BMG 74321601634
Estonia / This Strange Engine / The Memory of Water / One Fine Day / Face 1004 / 80 Days

Face 1004 1 Jun 98
12" Promo UK: Eagle 12033P, one-sided promo with 1500 copies of Tales From The Engine Room
Face 1004

PISTON BROKE - This Strange Engine Live in Europe 5 Jun 98
CD UK: Racket RACKET 9
Man of 1000 Faces (19 May 97 B, Gent 'Vooruit') / Hard As Love (19 May 97 B, Gent 'Vooruit') / Gazpacho (19 May 97 B, Gent 'Vooruit') / Afraid Of Sunlight (19 May 97 B, Gent 'Vooruit') / 80 Days (20 May 97 F, Paris 'Bataclan' / Estonia 08:49 (19 May 97 B, Gent 'Vooruit') / Alone Again In The Lap of Luxury (23 May 97 NL, Geleen 'Hanenhof') / The Space (19 May 97 B, Gent 'Vooruit') / Easter (May 97 NL, Geleen 'Hanenhof' / Brave (20 May 97 F, Paris 'Bataclan') / The Great Escape (23 May 97 NL, Geleen 'Hanenhof' / This Strange Engine (20 May 97 F, Paris 'Bataclan') / Sugar Mice (14 Oct 97 D, Hannover 'Capitol') / This Town (13 Oct 97 D, Hamburg 'Docks') / 100 Nights (13 Oct 97 D, Hamburg 'Docks' / The Bell In The Sea (23 May 97 NL, Geleen 'Hanenhof') / Hope For The Future (23 May 97 NL, Geleen 'Hanenhof') / King (23 May 97 NL, Geleen 'Hanenhof')

These Chains 14 Sep 98
CD Single UK: Castle Comm. PLC / Intact RAWX 1051
NL: Release 5 Oct 98
These Chains / Fake Plastic Trees (live: Oswestry 26 Jun 98) / Memory Of Water (Big Beat Mix)

RADIAT1ON 21 Sep 98
CD UK: Castle Comm. PLC / Raw Power RAWCD 126 GSA0000126RAW 5 026389 412628
F: 6 Oct
JAP: Pony Canyon / Canyon International PCCY-01281
USA: Eagle / Velvel 63467-79760-2, 27 Oct 98
UK: Sanctuary / Castle CMRCD113, 19 Feb 01
MC JAP: Pony Canyon / Canyon International PCTY-01281
Promo CD UK: Castle Comm. PLC / Raw Power RAW PR 126
JAP: Pony Canyon PCCY 01281, with sticker on obi + word 'Sample' on the hole disc
Press Pack UK: Promo copy and A4 advertisement plus an 8x10 b/w photo
MC PL: Metal Mind CAST 0034
Costa del Slough / Under The Sun / Answering Machine / Three Minute Boy / She'll Never Know / These Chains / Born To Run / Cathedral Wall / A Few Words For The Dead 10:31
Bonus track not on the MC:
The Space... (live, Oswestry)
Bonus tracks on Japanese CD:
Fake Plastic Trees (live, Oswestry) / Estonia (acoustic)
Bonus track on USA CD:
Memory Of Water (Big Beat Mix)

MARILLION & THE WEB CHRISTMAS 1998 Dec 98
Mini CD UK: Racket WEBFREE01
Free Fanclub CD
The Christmas Song / Tumble Down The Years (excerpt) / Interior Lulu (intro) / Interior Lulu (middle) / Karaoke intro / Cover My Eyes - Karaoke / No One Can - Karaoke / Beautiful (Dave Meegan mix) - Karaoke / These Chains - Karaoke / Spoken Conclusion

UNPLUGGED AT THE WALLS 23 Mar 99
2CD UK: Racket RACKET 10
'Unplugged' gig in a small restaurant: The Walls, Oswestry 25-26 June 98, setlist is of 26 Jun 98 with omission of Under The Sun, 3rd encore
Beautiful / Beyond You / Afraid Of Sunrise / Runaway / Now She'll Never Know / Lap Of Luxury / The Space... / Fake Plastic Trees / Holloway Girl / King / The Answering Machine / Gazpacho / Cannibal Surf Babe / First Encore: Blackbird / Abraham Martin & John / Second Encore: Hooks In You / 80 Days

Deserve Oct 99
Promo CD UK: Castle Comm. PLC rawp 2144, cardboard sleeve
Deserve / Rich / A Legacy

MARILLION.COM 18 Oct 99
CD UK: Castle Comm. PLC rawcd 144 5 026389 414424 Digipack
NL: Castle Comm. PLC rawcd 144 5 026389 414424 Digipack, 15 Oct 99
D: Castle Comm. PLC rawsd 144 5 026389 414424, jewel case
USA: Sanctuary 4505 6 0070-44505-2 3, 6 Nov 99
USA: Sanctuary ZAN84531CD,11 Mar 02
Pirate CD RUS: Castle Comm. PLC rawcd 144, with four bonus tracks, with Fish off Russian CD compilation: Kayleigh / Market Square Heroes / Freaks / Garden Party
Promo CD UK: Castle Comm. PLC rawpr 144 5 0 63 9 414424, card sleeve with 2 promo stickers, press-release contains promo photo
USA: Sanctuary NR 4505
A Legacy / Deserve / Go! / Rich / Enlightened / Built-in Bastard Radar / Tumble Down The Years / Interior Lulu / House

Beautiful Oct 1999
CDR UK: no cover - just Stuart Every's writing
Beautiful (Anne Bond & Cradley CE Primary School / Beautiful H + children / Beautiful (album version)

MARILLION.ZODIAC 18 Nov 99
CD UK: Racket RACKET 11
Live at The Web UK fanclub Convention 1999
Rich / Uninvited Guest / Goodbye To All That / Afraid Of Sunlight / Deserve / Sugar Mice / Answering Machine / Berlin / Cathedral Wall / Waiting To Happen / Garden Party

MARILLION.CHRISTMAS 1 Dec 99
CD UK: Racket WEBFREE 02
Free Fanclub CD
Gabriel's Message / The Answering Machine (single edit) / Interior Lulu (Radiat1On version) / Tumble Down The Years (Radiat1On version)
Memory Of Water (Technopox Remix) / Abraham Martin and John (Racket Club acoustic session / Runaway (Racket Club acoustic session) / Estonia (Racket Club acoustic session) / Beautiful (Anne Bond & Cradley CE Primary School) / Spoken Conclusion

MARILLION - STEVE HOGARTH - HEROES, VILLAINS, MILLENNIUM PREDICTIONS 22 Dec 99
Interview CD-R UK: Masterpiece, no number promo, silver and blue CD-R with letter from H.

MARILLION.CO.UK 10 Mar 00
CD UK: Racket RACKET 12
Bonus CD for **MARILLION.COM**
The Answering Machine (from Unplugged at The Walls) / Afraid Of Sunrise (from Unplugged at The Walls) / The Space... (from Live in Caracas) / The Great Escape (from The Making of Brave) / Afraid Of Sunlight (from Piston Broke) / Berlin (from Zodiac) / The Bell In The Sea (unreleased Zodiac outtake) / Band Interview (unreleased Zodiac outtake)
Enhanced with ideos of: Deserve (live) / The Bell In The Sea (live) / Interview / Biography / Hogy's Diary / photos

MARILLION CHRISTMAS 2000: A PISS-UP IN A BREWERY 22 Jan 01
Fan club CD UK: Racket WEBFREE 03
Go! / After Me / Lap of Luxury / Cinderella Search / The Space... / A Collection / Sympathy / Number One / Dry Land / Gazpacho / How Will You Go / Cannibal Surf Babe 05:52

CRASH COURSE - AN INTRODUCTION TO MARILLION 13 Feb 01
Promo CD UK: Racket Records RACKET 15
UK: Racket RACKET 15, re-release 10 Sep 01 with different back cover, no tourdates, only sold at the University Tour 2001, re-release was only sold with the single Between You and Me
This Is The 21st Century (Anoraknophobia version) / Rich (marillion.com version) / Afraid Of Sunlight (Afraid of Sunlight version) / A Legacy (marillion.com version) / Under The Sun (Radiat1On version)

This Is The 21st Century 23 Feb 01
MP3 USA: MP3.com
Internet single for free download
This Is The 21st Century (edit)

Between You And Me Apr 01
Promo CD UK: EMI CDLRL 049, cardboard Sleeve
Between You And Me (radio edit) / Map Of The World (radio edit)

ANORAKNOPHOBIA 7 May 01
CD UK: EMI / Liberty 0 7243 532321 2 2
US: Sanctuary ZAN 84506CD
Mex: EMI Ltd 7243 532321 2 2
Promo UK: EMI CDLRL046, Mar 01, 250 copies only, full album promo, white card sleeve
CDR UK: EMI / Liberty No Number
2CD UK: Intact 12674, pre-order special edition, hard-bound book package with 40 pages of band notes, bonus disc, only available with pre-orders
Between You And Me / Quartz / Map Of The World / When I Meet God / The Fruit Of The Wild Rose / Separated Out / This Is The 21st Century / If My Heart Were A Ball It Would Roll Uphill
Bonus Disc for Pre-Order Special Edition: Number One (non-album track) / The Fruit Of The Wild Rose (demo) / Separated Out (demo) / Between You And Me (Mark Kelly remix)
Video content: Number One (recording of) / Map Of The World (recording of)

REFRACTED! - FROM DUSK 'TIL DOT, Volume 1 May 01
2CD UK: Racket Racket 17
CD 1: Album Demo: Gazpacho / Cannibal Surf Babe / Beautiful / Afraid Of Sunrise / Out Of This World / Beyond You / Afraid Of Sunlight / King
CD 2: Writing Sessions: Gazpacho Mid-8 / Gazpacho Shuffle / Heavy Groove Gazpacho / Gazpacho Guitar / Gazpacho Chorus / Big Soul Surf Babe / X-Ray Surf Babe / Jangly Surf Babe / Beautiful Piano /AOS Cabaret / Out Of This World Original End / Out Of This World Actual End / Pulse Beyond You / Beyond You Piano Version / Beyond Blade Runner / Beyond The '80s / Beyond The Stones / Beautifully Disturbing / Latin AOS / Work On AOS / More AOS / The Electronix King / Heavy King / Hendrix King / Funkadelic King / Talking Kings / Hero King

Between You And Me 10 Sep 01
CD UK: Intact 011001, mail-order release
Between You And Me (Mark Kelly radio mix) / Map Of The World (radio edit) / Quartz (live in Manchester, 19 May 01) / If My Heart Were A Ball It Would Roll Uphill (Pete Trewavas edit)

ANOTHER DAT AT THE OFFICE - FROM DUSK 'TIL DOT, Volume 2 Sep 01
2CD UK: Racket Racket 18
CD1 - Album Demos: Man Of 1000 Faces / One Fine Day / Memory Of Water / Accidental Man / AOS Demo / This Strange Engine / Secret Track
CD2 - Writing Sessions: The Monkee Song / McCartney Faces / Tribal Faces / 1000 Faces Piano Intro / Man Of 1000 Crows / Voice Of Command / Beyond 80 Days / Acoustic Beyond 80 Days / 79 Days / Estonia Groove / Estonia Rock / Estonia Engine / Accidental Groove / Accidental Acoustic Man / Accidental Duke Of York / Accidental Guitar Riff / Accidental Chorus / Chord Workshop Man / New Accident / Chill for The Future / Hope for The Pretenders / Hope for Ry Cooder / Hope for Jeff Buckley / Hope for A Chorus / Strange Stones Engine / Acoustic Lamb Engine / This Strange Jam / This Strange Intro / Wax On Wood / Ever Since An Idea / The Lounge Navy Cloud of Bees Jam / Acoustic Mummy Daddy / Electric Mummy Daddy / Blue Pain Guitar Solo / Red Coat Ending / Run Like Hell Ending / Groove Ending / This Strange Ending

A VERRY BARRY CHRISTMAS 1 Dec 01
CD UK: Racket WebFree 04
I Saw Three Ships / This Is The 21st Century / Between You And Me / Map Of The World / Separated Out / Number One / House / Aspect of I Remix / Go! / Wide Awake Remix / This Is The 21st Century Instrumental

LUDWIGSHALLE, DIEBURG, GERMANY, 9 NOVEMBER 1998 17 Jan 02
2 CD UK: Front Row Club FRC-001
A Few Words for The Dead / Cathedral Wall / Under The Sun / First Encore: Man of A Thousand Faces / This Strange Engine / Mad / Second Encore: Three Minute Boy / Memory Of Water / Big Beat / 80 Days / King / Splintering Heart / These Chains / The Answering Machine / Cannibal Surf Babe / Gazpacho

ACADEMY, MANCHESTER, ENGLAND, 18 NOVEMBER 1999 9 Mar 02
2 CD UK: Front Row Club FRC-002
Go! (first 30 sec. missing) / The Great Escape / Under The Sun / Memory Of Water / Rich / King / The Uninvited Guest / First Encore: A Legacy / Interior Lulu / House / Second Encore: Goodbye To All That / Mad / Kayleigh / Afraid Of Sunlight / Lavender / Blue Angel / Deserve / Slainte Mhath / Easter / The Answering Machine

FALLOUT - FROM DUSK 'TIL DOT, Volume 3 11 Mar 02
2 CD UK: Racket RACKET 19
CD 1- Album Demos: Under The Sun / The Answering Machine / Three Minute Boy / Now She'll Never Know / These Chains / Born To Run / Cathedral Wall / A Few Words for The Dead
CD 2 - Writing Sessions: Under The Talking Heads / Under The Sun Jam / Under The Time Signature / Rock Machine / Tull Machine / Tull Outro / Blade Runner Boy / Three Minute Piano Sketch / Full Band Never Know / Chains Early Idea / Chains Development / These Few Words / Born To Jam / Born To End / Wobbly Walls / Failed Cathedral Chorus / Cathedral Chorus / Cathedral Chains / Cathedral Lyrics / Popadom Jam

2 Track Album Sampler Mar 2002
Promo CD UK: EMI CDLRL 058
Map Of The World (live version) / Between You And Me (live version)

Between You And Me Live Apr 02
MP3 USA: MP3com
Internet single for free download
Between You and Me (live)

ANORAK IN THE UK LIVE 8 April 01
Double Disc Mail-order version
2CD EU: Intact 080202
Intro / Separated Out / Rich / A Man Of A Thousand Faces / Quartz / Go! / Map Of The World / Out Of This World / Afraid Of Sunlight / Mad / Between You And Me / The Great Escape / If My Heart Were A Ball It Would Roll Uphill / Waiting To Happen / The Answering Machine / King / This Is The 21st Century / When I Meet God

ANORAK IN THE UK LIVE 22 Apr 01
Single Disc EMI version
CD EU: EMI / Liberty 7243 538727 2 4
Promo CDR UK: EMI, no catalogue number, released Mar 02, in colour paper sleeve, 'Promotion Use Only: Not for Resale'
Intro / Separated Out / Quartz / Map Of The World / Out Of This World / Between You And Me / The Great Escape / King / If My Heart Were A Ball It Would Roll Uphill / Waiting To Happen / Easter

LUXOR, ARNHEM, NETHERLANDS, 23 JUNE 1995 10 May 02
CD UK: Front Row Club FRC-003
Cover My Eyes (Pain And Heaven) / The Bell In The Sea / Sugar Mice / A Collection / Beautiful / Easter / The Uninvited Guest / King Of Sunset Town / First Encore: Bike / Made Again / You've Got to Hide Your Love Away

SOLO PROJECTS

FISH solo after Marillion:

State Of Mind 16 Oct 89
7" single UK: EM 109
EUR: 006 20 3562 7
7" Promo UK: EM 109, standard single with white sticker on reverse: 'Manufacturers property not for sale'
MEX: EMI SEC 830, yellow label, no p/s
Cassette Single UK: TCEM 109
State Of Mind (edited version) / The Voyeur I Like To Watch
12" single UK: EMI 12 EM 109
EUR: EMI 060 20 3562 6
I: EMI 14 20 3562 6
State Of Mind (Presidential Mix) / State Of Mind (edited version) / The Voyeur I Like To Watch
12" Picture Disc UK: EMI 12 EMPD 109, limited edition, card insert
12" Picture Disc UK: EMI 12 EMPD 109, mispressing, plays Madonna's Cherish
3" CD single EUR: CDP 552 20 3562 3
5" CD single UK: EMI CDEM 109
EUR: 056 20 3562 2
State Of Mind (album version) / The Voyeur I Like To Watch / State Of Mind (Presidential Mix)

Big Wedge 27 Dec 89
7" single UK: EM 125 5 099920 365578
EUR: 006 20 3655 7

7" Wallet Pack UK: EMS 125 5 099920 365585, numbered edition vinyl EM125
Cassette Single UK: TCEM 125
Big Wedge (7" version) / Jack And Jill
7" Promo Fr: SP 1455
Big Wedge / Big Wedge
MC Promo UK: Abbey Road Studio, no number, 1 track
12" Single UK: 12 EM 125
EUR: 060 20 3655 6
12" PD UK: 12EMPD 125, limited edition, card insert
Big Wedge (12" remix) Jack And Jill / Faith Healer (live 89)
5" CD Single UK: CDEM 125
EUR: CDP 560 20 3655 2
Big Wedge (album version) / Jack And Jill / Faith Healer (live 89)

VIGIL IN A WILDERNESS OF MIRRORS 29 Jan 90
LP UK: EMD 1015
EUR: 064-793634-1
12" PD UK: EMDPD 1015, with poster
Cassette UK: TCEMD 1015
EUR: 264-7 93634 4
CD UK: CDEMD 1015
EUR: CDP 7 93634 2 0 077779 363421
JAP: TOCP 6103
CD Promo JAP: TOCP 6103, normal edition, special wrapping with red print 'Sample not for sale' around the transparent hole of CD
CD Remaster UK: Dick Bros DDICK28CD 5 034349 000044, 18 Dec 97
Eur: Roadrunner RR 8687 2, 28 Oct 98
Vigil In A Wilderness Of Mirrors / Big Wedge / State Of Mind / The Company / A Gentleman's Excuse Me / The Voyeur I Like To Watch (not on LP) / Family Business / View From The Hill / Cliché
Bonus tracks on Remastered CD:
Jack And Jill / Internal Exile / The Company (demo) / A Gentleman's Excuse Me (demo) / Whiplash

A Gentleman's Excuse Me 5 Mar 90
7" Single UK: EM 135
EUR: 006 20 3755 7
7" Red vinyl UK: EMS135, limited edition, card insert
7" Shaped PD UK: EMPD 135 5 099920 376208, limited edition, card insert
7" Uncut shape UK: EMPD 135
Cassette Single UK: TCEM 135
A Gentleman's Excuse Me (album version) / Whiplash
12" Single UK: 12 EM 135
EUR: 060 20 3755 6
12" PD UK: 12 EMPD 135 limited edition
5" CD single UK: CDEM 135
EUR: 560 20 3755 2
A Gentleman's Excuse Me (album version) / Whiplash / A Gentleman's Excuse Me (demo version)

The Company 18 Jul 90
7" single EEC: 016 20 3946 7
The Company (album version) / Punch And Judy (live version)
12" Single EEC: 060 20 3946 6
The Company (album version) / Family Business (live version) / The Company (demo version) / Punch And Judy (live version)
5" CD Single EEC: CDP 560 20 3946 2
The Company (album version) / Family Business (live version) / Punch And Judy (live version) / The Company (demo version)

Internal Exile 9 Sep 91
7" Single UK: FISHY 1
EUR: 867 750-7
Cassette single UK: FISHC 1
EUR: 876 750-4
Internal Exile (7" edit) / Carnival Man
12" single NL: 867751-1
Internal Exile (7" edit) / Internal Exile (album version with intro) / Carnival Man
12" PD UK: FISHS 1, numbered edition
Internal Exile (album version) / Internal Exile (Karaoke Mix) / Carnival Man
12" Promo UK: FISHS 1 DJ, white label
Internal Exile (album version) / Internal Exile (Karaoke Mix) / Carnival Man
5" CD PD UK: FISCD 1
5" CDS NL: 867 887-2 VIS 1 Digipack
5" CDS EUR: 867 751-2
Internal Exile (7" edit) / Internal Exile (album version with intro) / Carnival Man / Internal Exile (Karaoke Mix)

INTERNAL EXILE 28 Oct 91
LP EUR: 314 511 049 1
Cas EUR: 314 511 049 4, 2 versions, same cat.no., minor changes to sleeve
USA: 314 513 765-4
Pol: Compact ST-730, Pirate?
CD UK: Polydor 511 049-2
EUR: 314 511 049 2 7 31451 10492 3
USA: 314 513 765-2
JAP: POCP 1162
RUS: CD Media N 2139
CZ: Popron 5051-2, Pirate?
Remastered CD Eur: Roadrunner RR 8687 2, 28 Oct 98
CD Promo JAP: POCP 1162
Shadowplay / Credo / Just Good Friends / Close / Favourite Stranger / Lucky / Dear friend / Tongues / Internal Exile
Bonus tracks on Remastered CD:
Poets Moon / Carnival Man
Bonus track on all CD / Cassette versions: Something In The Air

Credo 2 Dec 91
7" single UK: FISHY 2
EUR: 865 118-7
7" promo UK: FISH 2 DJ
Cover as standard 7" but with sticker with release date, silver label, Side A with cat.no. FISH 2 DJ, however B-side has standard cat.no. FISHY 2
Cassette Single UK: FISHC 2, exists?
Credo (7" edit) / Poet's Moon
12" Single UK: FISHX 2
Credo (album version) / Credo (7" edit) / Tongues (demo version)
12" Single Box UK: FISHS 2, limited edition numbered box + large poster
12" Promo UK: FISHS 2 DJ, red label
Credo (album version) / Credo (7" edit) / Poet's Moon
5" CD PD UK: FISCD 2, limited edition numbered Digipack
5" CD single EUR: 865 119-2, limited edition Digipack
5" CD promo USA: CDP 728
Credo (7" edit) / Credo (album version) / Poet's Moon

BBC TRANSCRIPTION CD May 92
CD UK: TCD 0291 Radio Show, less than 100 copies, 8 live tracks: Nottingham, Royal Concert Hall, 15 Nov 91
Vigil In A Wilderness Of Mirrors / Credo / Tongues / Incubus / The Company / Big Wedge / Internal Exile / Market Square Heroes / Heart Of Lothian

Something In The Air 22 Jun 92
7" Single UK: FISHY 3
EUR: 863 118-7
Cassette Single UK: FISHC 3, existence unsure?
Something In The Air (album mix) / Dear Friend (live, D, Hamburg 16 Dec 91)
12" Single UK: FISHX 3
12" Promo UK: FISHX 3 DJ, white label
Something In The Air (Teddy Bear Mix) / Something In The Air (album mix) / Dear Friend (live, D, Hamburg 16 Dec 91)
5" CD Single UK: FISHP 3, white long-pack + poster
5" CD EUR: 863 119-2, slim CD case
Something in the Air (radio edit)
Something In The Air (album mix) / Something In The Air (Teddy Bear Mix) / Dear Friend (live, D, Hamburg 16 Dec 91)
5" CD Single UK: FISHL 3, black long-pack + backstage pass
Something In The Air (album edit) / Something In The Air (Christopher Robin Mix) / Credo (live, NL, Enschede 19 Dec 91) / Shadowplay (live, D, Hamburg, 16 Dec 91)

Never Mind The Bullocks 12 Dec 92
7" Single UK: FISHY 4
EUR: 863 938-7
Promo 7" UK: FISHY 4, white promo sticker 'Promo Copy Not For Resale'
Cassette Single UK: FISCS 4
Hold Your Head Up (edited version) / Question (edited version)
5" CD single UK: FISCD 4, beige disc
EUR: 422 86 3939 2, orange disc
Hold Your Head Up (edited version) / Question (album version) / Hold Your Head Up (album version) / 5 Years (album version)

SONGS FROM THE MIRROR 20 Jan 93
LP UK: 517 499 1
CD UK: 7 314 517 499 2 6
CD Promo UK: 517 499 2, normal edition, sticker 'Promo only not for sale', same printed on CD
MC UK: 517 499 4, 2 versions, same cat.no., minor changes on sleeve
Question / Boston Tea Party / Fearless / Apeman / Hold Your Head Up / Solo / I Know What I Like / Jeepster (not the remaster) / Five Years
Remastered CD Eur: Roadrunner RR 8682 2, 28 Oct 98
Question / Boston Tea Party / Fearless Apeman / Hold Your Head Up / I Know What I Like / Solo / Bonus tracks: Time And A Word / The Seeker / Five Years

SONGS FROM THE MIRROR 20 Jan 93
MC UK: no number, 5-track sampler

Five Years 93
5" CD single D: LC 0309
Five Years (radio edit)

TOILING IN THE REEPERBAHN Jun 93

Battleside
2CD UK: FIS 001
UK: Voiceprint / Chocolate Frog CFVP001CD, 6 Nov 00
Credo / Something In The Air / Voyeur / Lady Nina / Punch And Judy / The Company / Just Good Friends / Lucky / Pipeline / Big Wedge / Out Of My Life / Kayleigh / Incubus / Lavender / Raw Meat / Heart Of Lothian / Internal Exile / Market Square Heroes / Roadhouse Blues
Live at D Hamburg, Grosse Freiheit, 23 Jun 92

PIGPEN'S BIRTHDAY Jun 93
Battleside
2CD UK: FIS 002
USA: Griffin GN 0831-2
Eur: Roadrunner RR 8684 2, 28 Oct 98
US: Renaissance RMED00159-2, 24 Sep 96
UK: Dick Bros Record Co. DDICK16CD
2CD in Box USA: Griffin FI103, 250 copies in a walnut wooden box
Voyeur / Punch And Judy / State Of Mind / Family Business / Assassing / Assassing continued / The Company / Script For A Jester's Tear piano intro Script For A Jester's Tear / A Gentleman's Excuse Me / Happy Birthday / Sugar Mice / Vigil In A Wilderness Of Mirrors / Kayleigh / Lavender / Heart Of Lothian / Cliché / Big Wedge / Internal Exile*
Live at UK London, Hammersmith Odeon, 2 Apr 90; * UK Edinburgh Playhouse, 27 Mar 90

DEREK DICK & HIS AMAZING ELECTRIC BEAR Jun 93
Battleside
2CD UK: FIS 003
USA: Griffin GN 1031-2
UK: Voiceprint/Chocolate Frog CFVP003CD, 19 Mar 01
Vigil / Dear Friend / Credo / Geezabun / State Of Mind / Lucky / Tongues / Big Wedge / Family Business / Fugazi / Incubus / Heart Of Lothian / Shadowplay / The Company / Forgotten Sons / Internal Exile / Market Square Heroes
Live at UK Haddington, Corn Exchange, 3 Nov 91, 1st Company Convention

UNCLE FISH & THE CRYPT CREEPERS Jun 93
2CD UK: Battleside FIS 004
USA: Griffin GN 1032-2
US: Renaissance RMED00160-2, 24 Sep 96
AU: Dick Bros Record Co. DDICK17CD, 96
Eur: Roadrunner RR 8685 2, 28 Oct 98
Vigil / The Company / Credo / Lucky Tongues / Big Wedge / Family Business / Windswept Thumb / Heart Of Lothian Incubus / Fugazi / Shadowplay / Internal Exile / Dear Friend / Market Square Heroes / Forgotten Sons *
Live at: D Dusseldorf, Philipshalle, 7 Dec 91; *F Paris, Olympia, 9 Dec 91

FOR WHOM THE BELLS TOLL! Jun 93
Battleside
2CD UK: FIS 005
2CD USA: Griffin GN 0832-2
2CD in Box USA: Griffin FI102, 250 copies in a walnut wooden box
UK: Voiceprint / Chocolate Frog CFVP002CD, 19 Mar 01
Vigil / Shadowplay / Credo / Dear Friend / Tongues / Auld Lang Syne / Family Business / Lucky / Incubus / Big Wedge / Geezabun / Heart Of Lothian / The Company / Forgotten Sons / Shadowplay / Internal Exile* / Market Square Heroes*
Live at: UK Edinburgh, Playhouse, 31 Dec 91; *F Paris, Olympia, 9 Dec 91

SUSHI 15 Mar 94
The Dick Bros Record Company
2CD UK: DDick2CD-UK
EUR: DDick2CD-GAS Made in Austria
D: IRS DoCD 991.051 + previous code
BEN: DDick2CD-BEN
JAP: Pony Canyon PCCY-01118
EUR: DDick2CD-Promo, normal edition, white area with 'Promo not for sale'
US: Renaissance RMED00135-2, 24 Sep 96
Eur: Roadrunner RR 8680 2, 28 Oct 98
2CD promo JAP: Pony Canyon PCCY 01118, sticker red on obi + word 'Sample' on the hole disc
2MC UK: DDick2Cass
Pol: Metal Minds PROG 0005/0006
2MC Promo UK: no number
Fearless / Just Good Friends / Big Wedge / Jeepster / Boston Tea Party / Hold Your Head Up / Credo / Lucky / Family Business / Internal Exile / View From A Hill / Cliché / He Knows You Know / The Last Straw / She Chameleon / Poets Moon / Kayleigh / 5 Years / White Russian / The Company
Live at: NL, Utrecht, Vredenburg, 18 Mar 93, complete concert

Lady Let It Lie 5 Apr 94
The Dick Bros Record Company
12" PD UK: DDick3PIC In a die-cut sleeve, numbered limited edition, contains a lyric sheet
Lady Let It Lie (album version) / Out Of My Life / Suits ('94 session) / Black Canal
Cassette Single UK: DDick3Cass
Lady Let It Lie (single version) / Out Of My Life / Suits ('94 session) / Black Canal
5" CD Single UK: DDick3CD1 5 020 66720035 8 Digipack
GER: DDick3CD2GAS, slim jewel case
Lady Let It Lie (single version) / Out Of My Life / Suits ('94 session) / Black Canal / Lady Let It Lie (live, Rheinberg 30 Oct 93)
5" CD Single UK: DDick3CD2 5 020 66720032 7, slim jewel case
5" CD Single GER: DDick3CD1GAS Digipack
Lady Let It Lie (album version) / Emperor's Song (live, Rheinberg 30 Oct 93) / Just Good Friends (live, Utrecht 18 Mar 93) / Out Of My Life (live, Rheinberg 30 Oct 93)

SUITS 16 May 94
The Dick Bros Record Company
CD UK: DDick4CD 5 020667 200426 PIAS 105.0004.20, first release with extra photobook + sticker 'Limited edition PD and 12 page photo booklet'
EUR: DDick4CDGAS
JAP: Pony Canyon PCCY-01117
US: Renaissance RMED00134,17 Sep 96
CD promo JAP: Pony Canyon PCCY 01117, sticker red on obi & word 'Sample' on the hole disc
Remastered CD Eur: Roadrunner RR 8686 2, 28 Oct 98
MC UK: DDick4MC
MC promo UK: no number
Mr 1470 / Lady Let It Lie / Emperor's Song / Fortunes Of War / Somebody Special / No Dummy / Pipeline / Jumpsuit City / Bandwagon / Raw Meat
Bonus tracks on Remaster: Black Canal / Out of My Life
2 x 12" UK: DDick4LP PIAS 105.0004.18
Mr 1470 / Lady Let It Lie / Emperor's Song / Fortunes Of War / Somebody Special / No Dummy / Pipeline / / Black Canal / Out Of My Life / Jumpsuit City / Bandwagon / Raw Meat
12" PD UK: DDick4PIC PIAS105.0004.12, die-cut sleeve, numbered limited edition, contains a lyric sheet
Mr 1470 / Lady Let It Lie / Emperor's Song / Fortunes Of War / Somebody Special / No Dummy / Jumpsuit City / Raw Meat (edit)

ACOUSTIC SESSION 94
The Dick Bros Record Company
CD AUS: DDick6CDFan, fanclub members only release
AUS: DDick6CDPromo, normal edition, white area with 'Promo not for sale'
AUS: DDick6CD IRS 991.054, mail-order only
Pol: Metal Mind PROG CD 0019
USA: Renaissance RMED00136,17 Sep 96
Recorded live at the Funny farm 1994
Lucky / Internal Exile / Kayleigh / Fortunes Of War / Dear Friend / Sugar Mice / Somebody Special / Jumpsuit City / Lady Let it Lie

Fortunes Of War 19 Sep 94
The Dick Bros Record Company
5" CD single EUR: DDick8CD1 5 020667 208125 PIAS NO 105:008:22, 4-tray Digipack with dummy discs detailing the other 3 discs
Fortunes Of War (single edit) / Somebody Special (live - Norwich) / State Of Mind (live - London) / Lucky (live - Newport)
5" CD Single EUR: DDick8CD2 5 020667 208124 PIAS NO 105:008:22, in a plastic sleeve with sticker
Fortunes Of War (live - London) / Warm Wet Circles (live - Newport) / Jumpsuit City (live - London) / The Company (live - London)
5" CD single EUR: DDick8CD3 5 020667 208123 PIAS NO 105:008:22, in a plastic sleeve with sticker
Fortunes Of War (acoustic session, July 94) / Kayleigh (live - London) / Internal Exile (live - London) / Just Good Friends (acoustic session, July 94)
5" CD single EUR: DDick8CD4 5 020667 208122 PIAS NO 105:008:22, in plastic sleeve with sticker
Fortunes Of War (acoustic session, July 94) / Sugar Mice (live - London) / Dear Friend (live - London) / Lady Let It Lie (acoustic session, July 94)
5" CD Promo UK: DDick8CDPromo, in Digipack
EUR: DDick8CDPromo, in jewel case,

12 Sep 94
Fortunes Of War (radio edit) / Fortunes Of War (single edit) / Fortunes Of War (live - London)

Emperors Song 94
The Dick Bros Record Company
Promo CD EUR: DDick9CDPromo
Emperors Song / Fortunes Of War

YIN & YANG RADIO EDITS Jun 95
The Dick Bros Record Company
CD UK: DDick13Promo
UK: DDick13Fan
Every song spoken introduction by Fish Introduction / Kayleigh / Introduction / Lucky / Introduction / Boston Tea Party / Introduction / Lavender / Introduction / Somebody Special / Introduction / Just Good Friends / Introduction / Lady Let It Lie / Introduction / Punch And Judy

Just Good Friends 14 Aug 95
The Dick Bros Record Company
CD1 UK: DDick14CD1
EUR: DDick14CD1 5 02066721454
D: DDick14CD1 IRS 977.045 7243 4 72397 2 4
Just Good Friends (single edit) / Somebody Special (radio edit) / State Of Mind (Yang album version)
CD2 UK: DDick14CD2
EUR: DDick14CD2 5 020667201492>
Just Good Friends (Yin album version) / Roadhouse Blues (live 09 Jun 95, Grenoble) / Raw Meat (live 10 Jun 95, Lyon)
Cassette Single UK: DDick14MC
Just Good Friends (single edit) / Somebody Special (radio edit)

YIN 4 Sep 95
The Dick Bros Record Company
CD UK: DDick11CD PIAS 105.0011.20
D: DDick11CD IRS 991.056
Pol: Metal Mind PROGCD0014
US: Renaissance RMED00127, 10 Sep 96
UK: Voiceprint / Chocolate Frog CFVP004CD, 26 Jun 00, simply the actual Dick Bros CD Dick Bros cat.no. etc. and booklet but with new back tray with new catalogue number
Cassette UK: DDick11MC
Promo CD UK: DDick11CDPROMO
JAP: Pony Canyon PCCY 00774, sticker red on obi + word 'Sample' on the hole disc
Promo Cassette UK: no number, Incommunicado (95 re-recording) / Family Business (original album version) / Just Good Friends (re-recording with Sam Brown) / Pipeline (original album version) / Institution Waltz ('95 recording) / Tongues (original album version) / Time And A Word (original album version) / The Company (original album version) / Incubus ('95 re-recording) / Solo (original album version) / Favourite Stranger ('95 re-recording) / Boston Tea Party ('95 re-recording with Sensational Alex Harvey Band) / Raw Meat (original album version)

YANG 4 Sep 95
The Dick Bros Record Company
CD UK: DDick12CD PIAS 105.0012.20
D: DDick12CD IRS 991.055
Pol: Metal Mind PROGCD0015
JAP: Dick Bros Record Company PCCY 00775, includes lyric sheet
US: Renaissance RMED00128,10 Sep 96
UK: Voiceprint / Chocolate Frog CFVP005CD, 26 Jun 00
Cassette UK: DDick12MC
Promo CD UK: DDick12CDPROMO
JAP: Dick Bros Record Company PCCY 00775
Promo Cassette UK: no number
Lucky ('95 re-recording) / Big Wedge ('95 remix) / Lady Let It Lie ('95 remix) / Lavender ('95 re-recording) / Credo ('95 re-recording) / A Gentleman's Excuse Me (original album version) / Kayleigh ('95 re-recording) / State Of Mind ('95 re-recording) / Somebody Special ('95 re-recording) / Sugar Mice ('95 re-recording) / Punch And Judy ('95 re-recording) / Fortunes Of War (original album version) / Internal Exile ('89 recording from Vigil sessions)

THE FUNNY FARM INTERVIEW - July 95 Aug 95
The Dick Bros Record Company
CD promo UK: DDick15CDPROMO, card sleeve with 17 Interview tracks
CD UK: DDick15CD, as above
Conversation with Fish on the subjects of the concept behind Ying & Yang / The artwork, the symbol, cover design / 'Institution Waltz', the early years, Redford '80, the mask, Cambridge, joining Marillion, LSD, Aylesbury '81 / Signing to EMI, '82, early influences, stage sets & costumes, first gigs, the how & why of becoming a singer / Derek to Fish, school, the nickname / The selection of tracks for Yin & Yang / The special guests, working with other musicians, Sensational Alex Harvey Band, Boston Tea Party, Sam Brown, 'Just Good Friends' - the recording session / Personal experience & lyrics, Family Business, Punch And Judy / Leaving Marillion, Clutching At Straws, 1988, the split / The litigations, Internal Exile album, Tongues, the Suits, Pipeline / Misplaced Childhood, Kayleigh, Berlin Lavender / Re-recordings / Progressive Rock '84, Incubus / Returning to Scotland '88, Internal Exile, the politics / The breaks, Lucky / The career curve, Erratic?, Songs From The Mirror, '93, the move to independence, the tour, the new album, the future / Dick Bros Record Company, Dream Disciples', the label, Tam White

FISH HEAD CURRY Jul 96
2CD UK: DDICK18CD, Mail order only, Live: Switzerland, Luzern 12 Nov 95, limited edition of 5,000 copies
Black Canal / Intro: Where's The Wine From? / Jumpsuit City / Kayleigh / Big Wedge / Pipeline / Emperor's Song / Incommunicado / Intro: See Rome And Die / Internal Exile / Lady Let It Lie / Lucky / Intro: The Observer / Lavender / Vigil In A Wilderness Of Mirrors / Shadowplay medley / Fugazi / Slainte Mhath / Credo

KRAKOW Aug 90
Live: Poland, Krakow, 24 Oct 95
2CD UK: DDICK19CD
US: Renaissance RMED00166-2, 10 Sep 96
Eur: Roadrunner RR 8681 2, 28 Oct 98
Black Canal / Jumpsuit City / Big Wedge / Emperor's Song / Lady Let It Lie / Vigil In A Wilderness Of Mirrors / Shadowplay medley / Fugazi / Slainte Mhath / Credo / Kayleigh / Pipeline / Incommunicado / Internal Exile / Lucky / Lavender / Boston Tea Party

KRAKOW - Radio Promo Aug 96
Live: Poland, Krakow, 11 Oct 95
Promo CD USA: DDick20CDPROMO
Big Wedge fade in / Big Wedge / Emperor's Song / Lady Let It Lie intro chat / Lady Let It Lie / Credo fade up / Credo / heckler / Kayleigh intro chat / Kayleigh / applause fade under / Lucky / Lavender applause fade / Lavender

Sunsets Promo CD Promo Pack Apr 97
Promo CD UK: DDICK24CDPROMO, in plastic bag with info sheet, 7x5 b/w photo of Fish, in colour card 9x6 folder with album cover on the front
Brother 52 (single edit) / Change Of Heart (album version) / What Colour Is God (edit) / Tara (edit) / Goldfish And Clowns (radio edit)

Brother 52 28 Apr 97
5" CD Single UK: Dick Bros DDICK24CD1, white cover
Brother 52 (single edit) / Brother 52 (Stateline Single edit) / Do Not Walk Outside This Area (non album track) / Brother 52 (album version)
5" CD Single UK: Dick Bros DDICK24CD2, black cover
Brother 52 (single edit) / Brother 52 (Stateline Mix) / Brother 52 (Dub Mix)
5" CD Promo USA: Viceroy / Lightyear PRCD 3037
Brother 52 (single edit)
12" Pic. Disc UK: Dick Bros DDICK24PIC
Brother 52 (Stateline Mix) / Brother 52 (album version) / Brother 52 (Dub Mix) / Brother 52 (Stateline single edit) / Brother 52 (single edit)
12" Promo UK: Dick Bros DDICK24 P, white label / sticker
Brother 52 (Stateline Mix) / Brother 52 (Dub Mix)

SUNSETS ON EMPIRE 19 May 97
CD UK: Dick Bros DDICK25CD
EEC: Dick Bros DDICK25CD 4844602
JAP: Pony Canyon PCCY-01110, 18 Apr 97, contains lyric sheet
Remastered CD Eur: Roadrunner RR 8679 2, 28 Oct 98
Promo CD UK: Dick Bros DDICK25CDPROMO, full CD with original artwork
UK: Dick Bros DDICK25CDPROMO, full CD with photographic slide of front cover but with Fish's face
JAP: Pony Canyon PCCY 01110, sticker red on obi+word 'Sample' on hole disc
Promo Pack UK: Dick Bros DDICK25CDPROMO, full CD with photo and biog
Enhanced CD US: Vinceroy / Lightyear 54197-2, 5 June, contains video-clip of Brother 52 as CDROM track.
2CD Digipack UK: Dick Bros DDICK26CD 6 04388 41542 7, with interview CD
EEC: Dick Bros DDICK26CD 4844632

MC UK: Dick Bros DDICK25MC
The Perception Of Johnny Punter / Goldfish And Clowns / Change Of Heart / What Colour Is God? / Tara / Jungle Ride / Worm In A Bottle / Brother 52 / Sunsets On Empire / Say It With Flowers / Do Not Walk Outside This Area (bonus track on Japanese and Remaster)
Bonus Interview CD with 15,000 Edition Digipack:
A conversation with Fish on the subjects of: The themes behind Sunsets On Empire, personal factors, the Yin & Yang world tour, global issues, characters on the album dawn to dusk / The concept running through the new album, comparison with Marillion and previous solo albums / The album title, inspiration from a dream, CNN, school maps, Hollywood history, Vietnam, the Net, Mark Wilkinson's artwork / Bosnia, Forgotten Sons and the Falklands War, phone calls from the front, Spike Milligan, Bosnia's scenic beauty / Writing the album, working with Steve Wilson, Porcupine Tree and No-Man, band problems / Musical styles, the fan base, 'movies for people's ears', dramatic vocals, Cinemascope production techniques / The recording progress, instruments used, working with Calum Malcolm and Avril Mackintosh, mastering the album / The Perception Of Johnny Punter, Lenny Bruce, influence of Bosnia v Croatia / Goldfish And Clowns, fairground images, 'the shows', marital problems / Change Of Heart, looking at relationships, glory in defeat, Scottish World Cup dreams, classic pop songs, Kayleigh, declaring love in black and white / What Colour is God?, Malcolm X, talking to Tara, St Lucia, racial stereotyping / Tara, Soweto and Brazil, growing up in the Sunsets world, fairy tale versus reality, another sunrise / Jungle Ride, beat poetry, the fastest ride in the fairground, the watering hole, the epitome of sex / Worm In A Bottle, the sad man's Happy Birthday song, drinking the dregs and crunching the Mezcal worm / Brother 52, grooves and loops, Doc's story, the video shoot, working with Duncan of Jordanstone College, Bim's Tattoo Studio, first live tattoo in a video / Sunsets On Empire, 'join the dots' lyrics, night of the big awakening / Say It With Flowers, sick lullabies, short red roses, problems during mixing

Change Of Heart 11 Aug 97
5" CD Single UK: Dick Bros DDICK27CD
5" Promo CD Single UK: Dick Bros DDICK27CDPROMO, 28 Jul 97
Change Of Heart (album version) / Goldfish And Clowns (radio edit) / The Perception Of Johnny Punter (US radio edit)

FORTUNES OF WAR May 98
The Dick Bros Record Company
CD UK: Dick Bros DDick30CD 5 034349 000068
Eur: Roadrunner RR 8689 2
Somebody Special (live - Norwich) / State Of Mind (live - London) / Fortunes Of War (live - London) / Warm Wet Circles (live - Newport) / Jumpsuit City (live - London) / The Company (live - London) / Kayleigh (live - London) / Internal Exile (live - London) / Just Good Friends (acoustic session, July '94) / Sugar Mice (live - London) / Dear Friend (live - London) / Lady Let It Lie (acoustic session, July '94 / Lucky (live - Newport)

TALES FROM THE BIG BUS Jul 98
2CD UK: Dick Bros DDICK29CD 5 034349 000051
Eur: Roadrunner RR 8688 2, 28 Oct 98
The Perception Of Johnny Punter / What Colour Is God? / Family Business MR 1470 / Conversation / Jungle Ride / Medley: Assassing / Credo / Tongues / Fugazi / White Feather / Conversation Cliché / Brother 52 / Lucky / Internal Exile / The Company

KETTLE OF FISH 28 Oct 98
Promo CD Eur: Roadrunner RR PROMO 365, printed on reverse of card sleeve is 'Not final version - for promotional use only'
CD Eur: Roadrunner RR 8678-8 0 16861 86788 1, the first 30,000 copies have extra CD-ROM with 3 videoclips and the back catalogue
Big Wedge ('90 original) / Just Good Friends ('95 version from Yin) / Brother 52 ('97 original) / Chasing Miss Pretty (new song) / Credo ('91 original) / Gentleman's Excuse Me ('90 original) / Goldfish And Clowns ('97 original) / Lady Let It Lie ('94 single edit) / Lucky ('95 version from Yang) / State Of Mind ('90 original) / Mr Buttons (new song) / Fortunes Of War ('94 original) / Internal Exile ('91 version)

Incomplete 22 Mar 99
5" CD Single Eur: Roadrunner RR 2185-3 0 16861 21853 9
Promo CD-R Eur: Roadrunner logo Fish & Roadrunner on white card & silver CD
Promo CD Eur: same as normal version but with large sticker: 'Release monday 5 April 1999' etc.
Incomplete (album version) / Wake Up Call (acoustic version) / Incomplete (demo version)

FISH @ HADDINGTON CORN EXCHANGE 1998 29 Mar 99
2CD UK: no label D3789/D3790, mail order, limited edition of 2000 copies, most are signed
Lucky / Mr 1470 / Family Business / Hotel Hobbies / Warm Wet Circles / That Time Of The Night Medley / What Colour Is God / Brother 52 / Assassing / Credo / Tongues Medley / Cliché / The Perception Of Johnny Punter / Kayleigh / Lavender / Heart Of Lothian Medley / GI's A Bun / Worm In A Bottle

RAINGODS WITH ZIPPOS 19 Apr 99
CD Eur: Roadrunner RR 8677-2 0 16861 86772 0
JAP: Pony Canyon PCCY 01389
CD Promo Eur: Roadrunner RR PROMO 386, card sleeve with text 'Not Final Version'
JAP: Pony Canyon PCCY 01389, normal edition, with word 'Sample' on hole of cd & red sticker promo jap on the OBI
MC Pol: Metal Mind PROG 0077
Tumbledown / Mission Statement / Incomplete / Tilted Cross / Faith Healer / Rites Of Passage / Plague Of Ghosts / Old Haunts / Digging Deep / Chocolate Frogs / Waving At Stars / Raingod's Dancing / The Wake Up Call / Make It Happen

FISH - THE COMPLETE BBC SESSIONS 11 Jun 99
2CD UK: Voiceprint / Blueprint BP297CD 6 04388 11392 7
JAP: Voiceprint Japan VPJ 109-110
Faithhealer / The Voyeur I Like To Watch / Punch And Judy / The Company / Script For A Jester's Tear / Family Business / Warm Wet Circles / Slainte Mhath / Vigil In A Wilderness Of Mirrors / Big Wedge / Fugazi / Kayleigh / Lavender / Heart Of Lothian / Vigil In A Wilderness Of Mirrors* / Credo* / Tongues* / Incubus* / The Company* / Big Wedge* / Internal Exile* / Market Square Heroes* / Heart Of Lothian*
Recorded at Town and Country Club, London, 11 Nov 89; *at Royal Concert Hall Nottingham, 15 Nov 91

ISSUE 30 CD May 00
CD UK: Chocolate Frog CFVP007CD
Only for subscribers of the Company, Mail Order, recorded live at Haddington Corn Exchange on 29 Aug 99
2nd Night of The Company Convention
Medley / Emperors Song / Credo / What Colour Is God? / Mr 1470 / Plague Of Ghosts / Medley / Cliché / Perception Of Johnny Punter / Incomplete / Sunsets On Empire / The Company

CANDLELIGHT IN FOG Jul 00
2CD UK: Chocolate Frog, no catalogue number, mail order only, numbered limited edition of 3000 copies
Recorded live in Philadelphia & New York City on USA mini-tour Jan 00
Faithhealer / Lucky / Intro - American Football and Jason's story / Just Good Friends / Intro - Happy Birthday and Doc's memorial / Brother 52 / Intro - Air conditioning and the Fog / Hotel Hobbies / Warm Wet Circles / That Time Of The Night / Tumbledown / Intro - Gas Cooker Rap / Plague Of Ghosts / Old Haunts / Digging Deep / Chocolate Frogs / Waving At Stars / Raingods Dancing / Wake-up Call / Make It Happen / Cliché / The Perception Of Johnny Punter / Intro - Company Address / The Company / The New York City Show / Hotel Hobbies / Warm Wet Circles / That Time Of The Night

ACOUSTIC SESSIONS 6 Nov 00
2CD UK: Voiceprint / Chocolate Frog CFVP006CD
CD1 straight remaster of DDick 6, CD2 is CD version of Krakow acoustic video set, recorded in Poland, Krakow, Bucklein Theater, 27 Oct 95
Lucky / Internal Exile / Kayleigh / Fortunes Of War / Dear Friend / Sugar Mice / Somebody Special / Jumpsuit City / Lady Let It Lie / Somebody Special / Jumpsuit City / Lady Let It Lie

/ Out Of My Life / State Of Mind / Kayleigh / Solo / The Company / Giz A Bun / Lavender

FELLINI DAYS RADIO EDITS 11 Apr 01
Promo CD UK: Chocolate Frog CFVP007CDPROMO, with small poster 16x11 of Edits cover i.e. Fellini Days cover on black background
So Fellini (radio edit album version) / Tiki 4 (radio edit) / Our Smile (radio edit) / Tiki 4 (album version) / Our Smile (album version) / What Are Fellini Days? (interview track) / Writing & Recording the album (interview track) / So Fellini intro (interview track) / Tiki 4 (interview track) / Our Smile (interview track) / The Tour (interview track) / The Band (interview track) / The Website / Internet (interview track) / Future Plans / Acting (interview track) / Album Release Schedule (interview track)

FELLINI DAYS 2 May 01
CD UK: Chocolate Frog CFVP007CD
CDR Promo UK: no number
3D / So Fellini / Tiki 4 / Our Smile / Long Cold Day / Dancing In The Fog / Obligatory Ballad / The Pilgrim's Address / Clock Moves Sideways

SASHIMI 3 May 01
2CD UK: Chocolate Frog CFVP008CD, mail order only, Recorded live at Zamek Centre of Culture, Poznan, Poland, 3 Oct 99
Faithhealer / Lucky / Just Good Friends / Brother 52 / Goldfish And Clowns / Hotel Hobbies / Warm Wet Circles / That Time Of The Night / Tumbledown / Intro: Riff Raff - the wine waiter! Plague Of Ghosts / Old Haunts / Digging Deep / Chocolate Frogs / Waving At Stars / Raingods Dancing / Wake-up Call / Make It Happen / Cliché / The Perception Of Johnny Punter / Sunsets On Empire / The Company

COMPANION CD Dec 01
CD UK: Chocolate Frog CFVP007CDB, released as 'thank you' to fans who bought as pre-order, now sold as a separate item
3D (live in Rotterdam, 10 May 01) / So Fellini (live in Poznan, 31 May 01) / Tiki 4 (live in Oslo, 18 May 01) / Pilgrim's Address (live in Oslo, 18 May 01) / Clock Moves Sideways (live in Oslo, 18 May 01) / Dancing In The Fog (History of Guns remix) / Obligatory Ballad (Spaced Out remix) / Clock Moves Sideways (Two Clocks in One Whole remix) / Our Smile (acoustic)

FISH sessions and appearances:

Tony Banks:
QUICKSILVER O.S.T. 86
Tony Banks with Fish on vocals:
LP USA: Atlantic 7-81631-1
UK: ?
JAP: ?
Promo LP Arg: Atlantic Argentinia 80003
Title: El Placer de Ganar
CD USA: Atlantic 7 81631-2
MC USA: Atlantic 7 81631-4-E
Shortcut To Somewhere

SOUNDTRACKS Jun 86
Tony Banks with Fish on vocals:
LP UK: Charisma CAS 1173
EUR: Charisma 207761
USA: Atlantic 7-81680-1
MC UK: Charisma CASTC 1173
CD UK: Charisma CASCD 1173
Shortcut To Somewhere

Shortcut To Somewhere 13 Oct 86
Tony Banks with Fish on vocals:
7" Single UK: Charisma CB 426
7" Test pressing UK:
Shortcut To Somewhere / Smiling Jack Casey
7" Promo USA: Atlantic ST-A-50303 SP, blue label
Shortcut To Somewhere / Shortcut To Somewhere
12" Single UK: Charisma CB 426-12
12" Promo UK: Charisma -
Shortcut To Somewhere / Smiling Jack Casey / K2

VARIOUS ARTISTS:
Live-In World Anti Heroin Project 24 Oct 86
7" single UK: EMI AHP 1, silver label
NL: EMI - 1A 006-201525 7, yellow label
12" Single UK: EMI 12 AHP 1
NL: EMI 1A K060-201524 6

IT'S A LIVE-IN WORLD Anti Heroin Project Nov 86
2 LP UK: EMI AHPLP 11
EUR: EMI 24.0669-3
One line by Fish: "... that a warm and loving hand touch your pain..." in the song Live-In World

Various Artists:
Spirit Of The Forest, Artists By Nature Autumn 89
7" single UK: Virgin VS 1191
12" single USA: 0-96551

EARTHRISE - THE RAINFOREST PROJECT Oct 92
LP EUR: Polydor 515 561-1
MC EUR: Polydor 515 561-4
CD EUR: Polydor 515 561-2
?: Polydor 515 587-2
One line by Fish: "I hear the cry of the Yanomani" in Spirit Of The Forest

Various Artists:
Sailing Rock Against Repatriation 16 Feb 90
7" Single UK: IRS EIRS 139
USA: IRS IRS 40
CD Single UK: IRS EIRSCD 139
USA: IRS IRSCD 40
Sailing / Sailing (instrumental)

Various Artists:
Say It With Pride - The Scottish World Cup Squad and Friends Jun 90
7" Single UK: RCA PB 43791 5012394379179
Say It With Pride / Rise Up
12" Single UK: RCA PT 43792
Say It With Pride / Rise Up / Say It With Pride (Tartan version)

THE TARTAN ARMY - SCOTTISH WORLD CUP ANTHEMS Jun 98
CD UK: Cherry Red CD GAFFER 26
Say It With Pride - Scotland World Cup Squad 1990

THE TARTAN ARMY Jun 98
CD UK: TVD Entertainment TV CD 2
Say It With Pride - The Scotland World Cup Squad 1990

Tony Banks:
STILL 1 May 91
LP UK: Virgin 211 638
MC UK: Virgin 411 638
CD UK: Virgin CDV 2658 5 012 981 2658 2 3
EUR: Virgin 261 638
Fish vocals on 2 tracks:
Angel Face / Another Murder of A Day

Jeff Wayne:
MUSICAL VERSION OF SPARTACUS Sep 92
2CD EUR: Columbia, Sony 472030 2
Fish portrays Crixus the Gaul in this Musical, with appearances:
The Eagle & The Hawk / Whispers / (spoken part by Fish) / The Parting Of The Ways

Various Artists:
Better World Sciennes Primary 6 Children Summer 1993
SCD UK: Bruces VOSTOK CD3
Better World / Better World (instrumental version)

Various Artists:
OUTPATIENTS '93
6 Nov 93, Official 19 November
CD UK: Fishy CD1, 7000 copies - 1000 numbered, 200 signed with The Company Holland print / 1000 numbered, all signed with The Company Scotland print Gold / 500 numbered 200 signed with The Company Germany print Gold
CD UK: Dick Bros DDick1CD, re-release
CD US: Renaissance RMED00158, 17 Sep 96
Contains 3 Fish Tracks: Time And A Word (Fish with Steve Howe) / The Seeker / Out Of My Life (acoustic)

Gomorrah:
REFLECTIONS OF INANIMATE MATTER Autumn 94
CD UK: Megapulse MAGAP1CD
D: Black Market BMCD 67 4 012743 006726
Fish speaks on track Human Trophies

Nostra:
Scotland By Our Side Scotia 1 Jun 98
CD-single UK: SNCD0015034349000075
Scotland By Our Side (vocals by Fish) / Lucky (95 Fish re-recorded version)

Ayreon:
INTO THE ELECTRIC CASTLE 5 Sep 98
2 CD NL: Transmission TM-014 8 712488 994659
Fish vocals + some lyrics for 3 tracks:
Isis And Osiris (vocals by Fish) / The Decision Tree - We're Alive (vocals by Fish) / Tunnel Of Light (vocals by Fish) / Across The Rainbow Bridge

SAS Band:
THE SHOW CD 200
CD UK: Voiceprint/Andy Briel Music ABMCD02
Just Good Friends (Fish)

T42:
THIS BIG WONDERFUL NIGHT

17 Dec 00
CD Lux: Kitty Music: T42-CD-08
The Company (T42, Kuffi & Fish) / Broomielaw (T42, Mario & Fish) / Roadhouse Blues (T42, Ezio, Booga & Fish) / Stay With Me (T42, Ezio, Booga, Fish & Tara)

STEVE HOGARTH history:

Harlow:
Harry de Mazzio Aug-Sep 78
7" Promo UK: Pepper Label UP 36457
Harry de Mazzio / Nothing To You

John Otway:
ALL BALLS AND NO WILLY 1982
LP UK: Empire Records, HAMLP 1
CD UK: The Music Corp. TMC9605, re-released in 1996 with Where Did I Go Right
In Dreams / Too Much Air Not Enough Oxygen / Telex / Montreal Baby, It's The Real Thing / Turn Off Your Dream / Don't Watch The Nightmare / Mass Communication / House Is Burning / Halloween / Nothing's Gone Except No.1 / Middle Of Winter Original Version 03:28
Bonus tracks on CD release: The LP / Where Did I Go Right / Makes Good Music / It's A Pain / Blue Eyes Of The Belle / Best Dream / What A Woman / Frightened And Scared / Waiting Waiting For You / Hurting Her More / The Highwayman
In Dreams 1982
7" Single UK: Empire HAM 3
In Dreams / You Ain't Seen Nothing Yet
Mass Communication 1983
7" Single UK: Empire HAM 6
Mass Communication / Baby, It's The Real Thing

Europeans:
Keyboards / Vocals: Steve Hogarth
COMPILATION LP
UK: Private RSB 1, limited edition 1000
Drink Pink Zinc! (demo)
The Animal Song Sep 82
7" Single UK: A&M AMS 8245
NL: A&M AMS 9239
7" Promo E: A&M AMS 9239, one side, picture sleeve
UK: A&M - AMS 8245, A-label demo, factory sleeve
The Animal Song / Someone's Changing
12" Single UK: A&M AMSX 8245
NL: A&M AMS 12.9239
The Animal Song (Cross Country version) / The Animal Song / Someone's Changing
A.E.I.O.U. Jul 83
7" Single UK: A&M AM 133
E: A&M AMS 9708
7" Promo UK: A&M AM 133
A.E.I.O.U. / Voice On The Telephone
12" single UK: A&M AMX 113
E: A&M AMS 12.9708
A.E.I.O.U. / Alphabet Soup / Voice On The Telephone / A.E.I.O.U. (LP version)
Recognition Aug 83
7" Single UK: A&M AM 138
NL: A&M AMS 9714
7" Promo UK: A&M AM 138
Recognition / New Industry
12" Single UK: A&M AMX 138
Recognition (New York Dance Mix) / Recognition (English Dance Mix)
12" Single NL: A&M 12-9714
Recognition / The Animal Song / A.E.I.O.U.
RECOGNITION 83
LP USA: A&M SP-12502
A.E.I.O.U. / Recognition / Innocence / Spirit Of Youth / American People / Kingdom Come (vocals by Steve)
VOCABULARY Oct 83
LP UK: A&M AMLX 68558
NL: A&M AMLX 68558
NZ: A&M L 38148
MC NZ: A&M AMLX 68558
The Animal Song / A.E.I.O.U. / Voice On The Telephone / American People / Falling / Recognition / Innocence / Spirit Of Youth / Modern Homes / Kingdom Come (vocals by Steve)
American People Nov 83
7" Single UK: A&M AMS 158
American People / Going To Work
12" Single UK: A&M AMX 158
American People / Going To Work (long version) / Someone's Changing / New Industry
LIVE 24 Jan 84
LP UK: A&M SCOT 1, limited edition
E: A&M - AMNP 193
LP Promo UK: A&M SCOT 1, limited edition, demo-sample
Typical / American People / Joining Dots (vocals by Steve) / Innocence / Spirit Of Youth / Going To Work (vocals by Steve) / A.E.I.O.U. / Animal Song / Tunnel Vision (vocals by Steve) / Falling
Typical 84
7" UK: A&M - AM 184
7" promo UK: A&M AM 184, A-label promo with picture sleeve
Typical (live) / Falling (live)
Listen 84
7" Single UK: A&M AM 201
Listen (vocals by Steve) / Climb The Wall
12" Clear Vinyl UK: A&M AMX 201
Listen (vocals by Steve) / Climb The Wall
RECURRING DREAMS 30 Oct 84
LP UK: A&M - AMA 5034
NL: A&M - AMA 5034
Test pressing UK: white label
Cassette UK: A&M AMC 5034
1001 Arguments / Home Town / Burning Inside You (vocals by Steve) / You Don't Want Me In Your Life (vocals by Steve) / Writing For Survival (vocals by Steve) / Love Has Let Me Down / Don't Give Your Heart To Anybody (vocals by Steve) / Acid Rain (vocals by Steve)
Acid Rain 84
7" Promo UK: A&M FREE 1
Acid Rain / Edits From Recurring Dreams / 1001 Arguments / Burning Inside You / Home Town
You Don't Want Me In Your Life
12" Promo UK: A&M SAMP 86
You Don't Want Me In Your Life (remixed) / Burning Inside You
HIT THAT PERFECT BEAT - Vol. 1
Compilation CD UK: Oglio Records / Warner OPCD-1689 including: Animal Song (Cross Country version)

Annabel Lamb:
ONCE BITTEN 1983
LP NL: A&M AMLH 64969
Dividing The Spoils Of Love (Steve on piano)

Do-Re-Mi:
Steve plays piano for this Australian band
DOMESTIC HARMONY Apr 85
LP UK: Virgin V 2367
D: Virgin 207 357-620
CD UK: Virgin CDV2367
Aus: Virgin 432070-2
Man Overboard 85
7" D: Virgin 107 609-100
12" D: Virgin 602 006-213

The The:
Steve Hogarth plays piano on:
Heartland Aug 86
7" UK: Epic / CBS TRUTH 2
12" UK: Some Bizarre EPCA12.6983
INFECTED Nov 86
LP UK: Epic EPC 26770
USA: Epic EK 40471, 9 Jan 87
CD NL: Epic CDCBS 26770 5 099702 677028
Steve plays piano on Heartland

Blue Yonder:
BLUE YONDER 1987
LP D: Atlantic 781 686-1
Steve does backing vocals on 2 tracks: The Long Haul / Secret Miracle

Julian Cope:
Steve does backing vocals on:
SAINT JULIAN 87
CD UK: Island IMCD 137 842 686-2
Eve's Volcano 87
12" D: Island - 609 003

Toni Childs:
UNION 88
LP D: A&M - 395175-1
UK: A&M - CD 5175/DX 3002
CD USA: A&M 395175-2 0 82839 517522
Steve plays some keyboard parts
Stop Your Fussin' 1988
12" D: A&M - 390 313-1
Steve plays some keyboard parts
Don't Walk Away 1988
12" D: A&M 390 351-1
Steve plays some keyboard parts

How We Live:
Working Town 7 Jul86
7" Single UK: Portrait A 7290
12" single UK: Portrait TA 7290
DRY LAND Jan 87
LP UK: Portrait PRT 450618 1
Promo LP UK: Portrait PRT 450618 1, with Golden promo stamp
Test pressing UK: white label
CD UK: Portrait PRT 450618 2
UK: Racket RACKET 13, 8 Aug 00
Cassette UK: Portrait PRT 450618 4
All The Time In The World original 1986 / re-release Apr 87
7" Single UK: Portrait PRT 650088 7
UK: Portrait PRT 650088 7, re-release,
12" Single UK: Portrait PRT 650088 6
UK: Portrait PRT 650088 6, re-release,
Promo Cass UK: Portrait XPC 650088 4
Working Girl Jul 87
7" Single UK: Portrait HWL1
12" single UK: Portrait HWLT1
Games In Germany 87

7" Single UK: Portrait PRT 650956 7
12" Single UK: Portrait PRT 650956 6

Various Artists:
ROCK POP IN CONCERT Summer 87
2LP compilatie D: Ariola Germany - 303101/2, g/fold cover
MC D: Ariola Germany 503103
CD D: Ariola Germany 303103
Steve plays on Games In Germany / All The Time In The World

Various Artists:
ROCK OVER LONDON # 426 28 Jun 87
Radioshow LP USA
Steve plays on All The Time In The World
ROCK OVER LONDON # 429 19 Jul 87
Radioshow LP USA
Introduction by Steve Hogarth / Dry Land

Various Artists:
ROCK AGAINST REPATRIATION - Sailing 16 Feb 90
For Details about this release see above in the Fish section

H:
Ice Cream Genius Jan 97
5" Promo CD UK: Castle Comm. PLC / When WEN P 1017, g/fold
You Dinosaur Thing / Cage / Nothing To Declare
ICE CREAM GENIUS 17 Feb 97
CD UK: Castle Comm. PLC / When WEN CD 016
Promo CD UK: Castle Comm. PLC / When WEN PR 016, no sleeve + promo sheet
CD-R acetate UK: Castle Comm. PLC, no number - Castle promo sleeve
CD + bonus track USA: Resurgence RES 134, 25 Aug 98 under the name Steve Hogarth
UK: Sanctuary / Castle CMRCD122, 19 Feb 01
The Evening Shadows / Really Like / You Dinosaur Thing / The Deep Water Cage / Until You Fall / Better Dreams Nothing To Declare / The Last Thing (bonus track)
You Dinosaur Thing 3 Mar 97
5" CD UK: Castle Comm. PLC / When WENX1021 CD
You Dinosaur Thing / The Deep Water / The Last Thing
Cage 3 Jan 02
5" CD UK: Poison Apple PACD057
Cage (live Dingwalls 8 Aug 01) / The Urban Spaceman (home demo) / Until You Fall (home demo) / See Emily Play (live Dingwalls 9 Aug 01)

Chucho Merchan:
OCEAN SONGS Autumn 1998
CD UK: United Nations Environment Programme OSCD 01
Steve H on vocals on tracks:
Ocean Blue / Save The Oceans For Life On Earth / Out In The Country

Ange:
GRANDS CRUS 98?
CD F:
Vocals by Steve Hogarth on:
Cantique - Hymne à la Vie

IAN MOSLEY history:

Ian plays drums on the following:

Darryl Way's Wolf:
CANIS LUPUS May 73
LP UK: Deram SDL 14
JAP: London Lax 1036
CD JAP: Deram P25L-25057, 89
SATURATION POINT Oct 73
LP ??: SHSP 1104
UK: Deram SML 1104
D: Deram SML 1104
JAP: London Lax 1037
DARRYL WAY'S WOLF 74
LP UK: London PS644 Compilation
NIGHT MUSIC Jun 74
LP UK: Deram SML 1116
JAP: London Lax 1116
D: Nova 6.22079, re-release 76
ONE AND TWO 75
2LP ??: 6-23113
D: Nova 8005/1-2
2LP release of Saturation / Canis Lupus
ANTHOLOGY 76
LP UK: King J 1008 Compilation

Darryl Way:
CONCERTO FOR ELECTRIC VIOLIN 78

Trace:
BIRDS Oct 75
LP NL /UK: Vertigo 6413 080
D: Philips 6413080
US: Sire SASD-7514
CD F: Musea FGBG 4176.AR, Apr 96

Gordon Giltrap Band:
THE PEACOCK PARTY 79
LP UK: PVK GIL1
D: Electric Intercord INT.161.543, re-release 82
UK: Prestige PRST 507, re-release 90
CD UK: Prestige CDPT 507, re-release 90
MC UK: Prestige ZPRST 507, re-release 1990
O Jerusalem 79
7" Single UK: Electric Label WOT42
Theme from The Waltons 80
7" Single UK: Cube Label BUG89
Heartsong
7" Single UK: Cube Label BUG95
Magpie Rag 80
7" Single UK: PVK PV101
Magpie Rag / Gypsy lane
GORDON GILTRAP LIVE 81
LP UK: Cube - ICS 1001
CD UK: La Cooka Ratcha Voiceprint - LCVP115CD, Mar 2000
Recorded Live at Oxford Polytechnic March 9 1979
LIVE AT THE BBC 95
CD UK: Windsong WHISC009
This compilation CD features cuts from 5 live concerts recorded by BBC mainly for the Old Grey Whistle Test programme.
Track 11 Fear of the Dark features Ian Mosley on Drums, and was recorded on 6 March 1979, i.e. 3 days before the live album above.
Fear of The Dark

Renaissance:
TIME LINE 83
LP NL: Illegal ILP 25532
UK: IRS SP 70033
CD UK: HTD HTD CD42
US: IRS 70033
DA CAPO
Contains 2 tracks recorded the around the same time as Time Line

Steve Hackett:
HIGHLY STRUNG Mar 83
LP UK: Charisma HACK1 / 811-209-1
US: Charisma BFE-38515
D: Charisma / Phonogram 811 209-1
JAP: Charisma, 25S-161
?: Epic 38515
UK: Virgin CHC40, re-release
MC UK: Charisma HAKMC 1
D: Charisma 811 209-4
UK: Virgin CHCMC40
CD UK: Virgin HACKCD 1, re-release 89
D: Virgin VIRG 7872442
JAP: VJCP 23035
NL: Virgin R64866
USA: Blue Plate, CAROL 1860-2
?: Plan 9 1860
TILL WE HAVE FACES Sep 84
LP UK: Lamborghini LMGLP4000
UK: Start STL11, re-release, 87
D: Lamborghini/Teldec 6.25987
?: Chrysalis FV 41571
MC UK: Lamborghini ZCLMG4000
UK: Start SMC11, re-release 87
?: Chrysalis FVT 41571
CD JAP: Lamborghini CDLMG4000, 85
JAP: Mercury Music PHCR 4302
UK: Start SCD11, 87
D: Castle Legends, re-release 90
D: SPV Record SPV 89132
F: Baillemont Productions, re-release 92
F: Musea FGBG4221AR
NL: Polygram R603423
NL: Rigu R66782
US: Herald Caroline HRL 10
CD UK: Kudos/Permanent PERMCDL20, re-release May 94
UK: Camino CAMCD9, re-release 97
A Doll That's Made In Japan 84
7" D: Lamborghini 6.14205
TIME LAPSE May 92
CD UK: Kudos/Permanent PERMLCD22
UK: Camino CAMCD11
USA: Blue Plate Caroline CAROL 1839-2
F: Baillemont Productions, 92
D: SPV Record SPV 89162
JAP: Mercury Music PHCR 4305
NL: Rigu R611764
NL: Polydor R52508
?: 500 001-2
?: Plan 9 1839
MC USA: Blue Plate CAROL 1839-4
FEEDBACK 86 8 Sep 00
CD UK: Camino CAMCD21, 9 Oct 00
Enhanced section with 20 bonus MP3s

Propaganda:
A SECRET WISH Sep 85
LP US: Island 90288
Por: Island/ZTT 10.207027.46
D: Island/ZTT 207.027
UK: Island/ZTT ZTTIQ 3
CD D: Island/ZTT/Ariola 610540, 86
D: Warner/ZTT 4509-94749-2 7 4509-94749-2 8
USA: Island CAD 90288-2, 86

Iris:
CROSSING THE DESERT 22 Apr 96
CD UK: IRIS CD1

Ian Mosley & Ben Castle:
POSTMANKIND 16 Apr 01
CD UK: RACKET Racket 16

PETE TREWAVAS history:

The Metros:
Driving Us Crazy
EP UK ?
I Don't Have Your Number (live) / Plastered In Paris (live) / I Saw Her Standing There (live) / Devil Rock Short Love Me Tomorrow / You Think Of Her / Devil Rock

Transatlantic:
Bass: Pete Trewavas
Guitar: Roine Stolt (Flower Kings)
Drums: Mike Portnoy (Dream Theater)
Keyboards: Neal Morse (Spock's Beard)
SMPTe 23 Mar 00
CD D: SPV 085-31992 CD
InsideOut: IOMCD057 4 001617 319722
USA: Metal Blade 3984-14290-2
2CD D: SPV 087-31970 DCD edition
InsideOut: IOMCD057 4 001617 319703
TRANSATLANTIC LIVE IN AMERICA 12 Mar 01
2CD USA: Radiant ??
D: SVP 089-41512 DCD
InsideOut: IOMCD057 4 001617 415122
BRIDGE ACROSS FOREVER 8 Oct 01
CD D: SPV 085-41702 CD
InsideOut: IOMCD086 4 001617 417022
USA: Radiant / Metal Blade 3984-143822
2CD D: SPV 088-41700 DCD edition
InsideOut: IOMLTDCD086 4 001617 417003

MARK KELLY history:

John Wesley:
UNDER THE RED AND WHITE SKY 94
Production and keyboards

WAITING FOR THE SUN TO SHINE IN PARIS
Keyboards on this live CD

Chemical Alice:
CURIOUSER AND CURIOUSER Aug 81
EP Acidic Gnome 1, 1000 copies

Jump:
THE MYTH OF INDEPENDENCE 95
CD UK: Cyclops CYCL 027
Production

STEVE ROTHERY history:

Jadis:
BABOON ENQUIRIES 84
Cassette UK: no label
OUT OF REACH 87
Cassette UK: DEM 1
DON'T KEEP ME WAITING 88
Cassette UK: DEM 2
JADIS LIVE 88
Cassette UK: DEM 3
LOST FOR WORDS 1989
Cassette UK: DEM 4
JADIS 89
LP UK: Backbeat 004/12

Various Artists:
ROCK AGAINST REPATRIATION
Sailing 16 Feb 90
For details see above in Fish section

Arrakeen:
PATCHWORK 90
CD F: 2C Production - 218753
Features Folle Marie Live with second guitar solo by Steve Rothery
Recorded in F, Paris, Le Zenith, 1990

Enchant:
BLUEPRINT OF THE WORLD 94
CD US: IRS CD 987.709
CD EUR: Dream Circle DCD 9310
CD JAP: with extra track
CD US: 1995 release with extra track
Steve plays guitar solo on Nighttime Sky and E-bow on The Thirst, Steve Rothery produced the following tracks: The Thirst / Catharsis / Acquaintance / East Of Eden / Nighttime Sky

Arena:
SONGS FROM THE LIONS CAGE 94
CD UK: Verglas Music VGCD001
Steve plays guitar solo on Crying For Help IV
THE CRY 97
CD UK: Verglas Music VGCD005
Steve plays guitar solo on Only Child

The Wishing Tree:
CARNIVAL OF SOULS Sep 96
CD UK: Dorian Music DM WT 001
Enhanced CD UK: Racket RACKET 14, Jan 01
Promo CD UK: Dorian Music DMWT 001, no picture sleeve, Steve produces and plays guitar (mostly acoustic) and on Bass guitar: Pete Trewavas

Mr. So & So:
THE OVERLAP 27 Jul 98
CD UK: Dorian Music DM SS 001 CD 6 04388 43532
Steve plays solo on Coup de Grâce and atmospheres on Spacewalk

bibliography

Thanks to all people and publications listed here, in particular Mark "Itchy" Bredius who has a superb list of links on his own site, www.markbredius.com. I'd also like to tip my hat to Mick Wall, who did such a superb job of documenting the early years that a major challenge was to find things out that he hadn't written, though might have known. This is not a complete list of everything out there. It is, however, everything I could lay my hands on and is all included, one way or another in the book. To save typing, Web links are reproduced at the site www.separatedout.com.

BOOKS
Market Square Heroes - Mick Wall, 1987, Sidgwick & Jackson
Marillion: The Script - Clive Gifford, 1987, Omnibus Press
Marillion In Words & Pictures - Carol Clerk, 1985, Bobcat Books
Masque, The Graphic World of Mark Wilkinson, Fish & Marillion - Mark Wilkinson and Derek W. Dick, 2000, Babel Books (available from www.the-company.com)
Directory of British Progressive Rock - David Robinson, 1995
Mother Tongue - John Helmer, 1999, Quartet Books (available from www.marillion.com)

MAGAZINES
Big Bang, 1997 - H Interview - http://www.markbredius.com/h/interv2.htm
BraveHearts Collection - Marillion Tribute, Allen Walker - http://www.andagain.com/interview.html
Christian Science Monitor, 18 May 2001 - Band Interview - http://www.csmonitor.com/cgi-bin/getasciiarchive?script/2001/05/18/p17s2.txt
El Mercurio, Chile - Oct 28, 1998
Gaudia, 19 May 1982 - The Venue gig review
H Interview - http://www.markbredius.com/h/interv14.htm
June 12 1985 - Fish Interview - http://www.the-webonline.com/archive/magazines/kerrang.95.p18.html
Kerrang, 158 - Oct 17, 1987 - Extract from Market Square Heroes
Kerrang, 257, Sept 23 1989 - H/Rothers Interview - http://www.btinternet.com/~europeans/Kerrang.htm
Kerrang, 257, Sept 23 1989 - Seasons End review - http://www.thewebonline.com/archive/magazines/kerrang.257.p18.html
Kerrang, 347 June 29, 1989 - Interview with Mark, h - http://www.the-webonline.com/archive/magazines/kerrang.347.p28.html
Kerrang, Feb 5 1994 - Brave article - http://www.the-webonline.com/archive/magazines/kerrang.940205.html
Kerrang, October 1982 - Reading report
Keyboard Magazine, July 1986 - Mark Kelly Interview - http://www.the-webonline.com/archive/magazines/keyboard.7.86.p19.html
Melody Maker, 26 June 1982 - Glasgow gig Review
Sound Barrier, November 1998 - John Wesley Interview - http://www.john-wesley.com/reviewcr3.htm
Sound Magazine, 1998 - John Wesley Interview -

http://www.john-wesley.com/reviewcr2.htm
Sounds, 15 Dec 1984 - Fish Interview
Sounds, 18 Feb 1984 - Fish Interview
Sounds, 19 Feb 1983 - Fish Interview
Sounds, 22 May 1982 - Glasgow Gig Review
Sounds, 23 Oct 1982 - Article
Sounds, 9 July 1983 - Mark/Fish Interview
Spiral Scratch - March 1990 - http://www.the-webonline.com/archive/magazines/spiral.scratch.14.p48.html

RADIO/TV INTERVIEWS
XFM, Copenhagen, 14 March 1997 - H Interview - http://www.markbredius.com/h/interv1.htm
WMMR, 14 Sept 1997 - H Interview - http://www.alabanza.com/lothian/h_interview_mmr.htm
NBC, 1 Sept 1996 - H Interview - http://www.the-webonline.com/archive/tv/selina.19960110.html
NBC, 23 April 1996 - H Interview - http://www.the-webonline.com/archive/tv/selina.19960423.html
TMF, May 1997 - Mark/H Interview - http://members.rott.chello.nl/whorssen/Transcript.html
Buzz, 17 Sept 1997 - Fish Interview - http://members.rott.chello.nl/whorssen/Transcript.html
BBC, September 2001 - Band Interview - http://www.bbc.co.uk/devon/entertainment/music/marillion1.shtml
ITV, Video Singles - http://www.itv.net/live/marillion/marillion.htm
MTV, 1988 - Fish Interview
Radio Forth, 14 March 1982 - Mick/Mark/Fish interview

FANZINES
The Web Magazine Issue 1 Feb 1982 / Issue 2 March 1982 / Issue 3 May 1982 / Issue 3 1-2 June 1982 / Issue 4 June 1982 / Issue 5 August 1982 / September 1982 / Issue 6 October 1982 / Flyer - Starting Gate - 75th gig / Flyer - Thanks/Geddy Lee T-shirt Nov 1986 / 1987 / Summer 1988 / Winter 89-90 / Spring 1991 / Autumn 91 / Winter 91-92 / Spring-ish 92 / Summer 92 / Issue 1 '93 (typo - 1/94 on cover) / Issue 2-93 / Issue 1-94 (the real one) / Issue 2-94 / Issue 3-94 / Issue 1-95 / Issue 2-95 / Issue 3-95 / Issue 1-96 / Issue 2/3-96 / Issue TSE cover 1997
Twisting Tales No.4 December 1999 / No.1 June 2000 / No.4 February 2001

FAQ
Part 1 - http://www.faqs.org/faqs/music/marillion-faq/part1/preamble.html
Part 2 - http://www.faqs.org/faqs/music/marillion-faq/part2/preamble.html

OFFICIAL INFORMATION
The Company Germany - http://www.raingods.de/links/cougalinks.cgi
The Company - http://www.the-company.com/
In particular, with thanks to Fish - Andy Field Obituary - http://www.the-company.com/usa/7pg1.html
Marillion.com - http://www.marillion.com/
Tour History - http://www.marillion.com/tour/tourhistory.html
The Web North America Staff - www.alabanza.com/lothian/web_staff.html
H Band - www.stevehogarth.com
The Web Online - http://www.the-webonline.com/

ALBUM SLEEVE NOTES
Script For A Jester's Tear / Fugazi / Clutching At Straws / Misplaced Childhood / Seasons End / Holidays In Eden / Brave

WEB SITES
RockNet, May 1996 - Mark Kelly Interview - http://www.rocknet.com/may96/mrillion.html
RAM.org, 11 April 1996 - Mark Kelly Interview - http://www.ram.org/music/articles/marillinterview.html
RAM.org, 26 Oct 1996, Steve Rothery Interview - http://www.ram.org/music/articles/rotheryinterview.html
Rivendell Progpage, Sept 19 1998 - H Interview - http://www.algonet.se/~polzer/interviews/interviews.htm
The Artist Shop, 7 Nov 1999 - Chat with H, Rothers - http://www.artist-shop.com/irc/marill2.htm
The Artist Shop, Sept 14 1997 - Chat with Mark, H, Rothers - http://www.artist-shop.com/irc/marilion.html
Rock Online, Nov 8 1999 - Chat with H, Mark, Pete - http://www.rockonline.com/liveinchat/marillion110899.html
The Musician's Olympus, Ian Mosley biography - http://www.geocities.com/SunsetStrip/Palladium/2214/imosl_b.htm
Ytsejam.com, Apr 27 2001 - Steve Rothery Interview - http://www.ytsejam.com/interviews/ints/42001/rothery42001.htm
DocRock, 29 November 1999 - Chat with Steve Rothery - http://www.infomusic.de/chat/archiv/1999/marillion/
Bubblegun, 1999 - Fish Interview - http://www.bubblegun.com/features/probefish.html
Progressive World, Review of Hope for the Future Tribute - http://www.progressiveworld.com/hope_future.html
Progressive World, 1997 - Steve Rothery Interview - http://www.progressiveworld.net/srotheryinterv.html
DIY Today, 31 August 2000 - Article
Blistering.com, 2000 - H Interview - http://www.blistering.com/interviewdet.php3?intid=29
Dutch Progressive Rock Pages, Live at the Walls - http://www.dprp.vuurwerk.ml/concrev/mar5.htm
Dutch Progressive Rock Pages, Marillion Tribute Review - http://www.dprp.vuurwerk.nl/reviews/9906.htm
Dutch Progressive Rock Pages, 12 Sep 1998 - German Web Convention Review - http://www.dprp.vuurwerk.nl/concrev/mar7.htm
Cymbiosis, Summer 1986 - Pete/Rothers Interview - http://www.tf.hut.fi/Nados/Interviews/cymbiosis.html
AMZ, Nov 1998 - Radiation Review - http://www.amzmusiczine.com/11_98/newrel15z.htm
AMZ, Sept 1998, Piston Broke Review - http://www.amzmusiczine.com/09_98/newrel13y.htm
Music Street Journal, 30 Sept 1998 - H Interview - http://www.markbredius.com/h/interv13.htm
Rock Notes Online, 8 Sept 1998 - H Interview - http://www.markbredius.com/h/interv12.htm
Oor, 1998 - H Interview - http://www.markbredius.com/h/interv9.htm
Zondagskrant, 9 March 1997 - H Interview - http://www.markbredius.com/h/interv7.htm
Mind Magazine, March 1997 - H Interview - http://www.markbredius.com/h/interv5.htm
RockStyle, March 1997 - H Interview - http://www.markbredius.com/h/interv6.htm
IO Pages, February 1997 - H Interview - http://www.markbredius.com/h/inerv8.htm
Music News Network, March 1996, H Interview - http://www.markbredius.com/h/interv11.htm
Progfreaks, Marillion Feature - http://www.progfreaks.com/Marillion/index.htm
Hard Radio, 1995 - Mark Kelly Interview - http://www.hardradio.com/metalmama/marillion.html
Furia, The Wall Of Silence - 1997 Reviews - http://www.furia.com/twas/twas0147.html

FAN SITES
Fraser Marshall's Explanations of Song Elements www.marillionlyric.co.uk <http://www.marillionlyric.co.uk/>
Paul Hughes, Rest Of Both Worlds - http://www.fortunecity.com/tinpan/rumba/309/index.htm
UK Garden Party - www.ukgardenparty.com
Michael Huang, A Fairly Detailed History of Marillion - http://www.geocities.com/Area51/Corridor/8409/bandbio.html
Cannibal Surf Boy, CSB's Marillion Page - http://www.csshack.co.uk/bands/marillio.htm
AD Jensen, The NeoProg Home Page - http://adjensen.aatrix.com/NeoProgHome.html
United Fish Fans - http://www.nijvnet.com/
Liam Birch, Corwyn's Lair - http://cfly.utm.utoronto.ca/birches/Webpages/marillion.htm
W Horssen, Marillion Page - http://members.rott.chello.nl/whorssen/homepage.html
Cameron Smith - http://www.extraneous.demon.co.uk/index-frame.html
Robin Lauren, Nados - http://www.tf.hut.fi/Nados
Bert Der Steege, Marillion Discography - http://members.tripod.com/~Marillion_disco
Mike Eldon, Saliva Tears - http://www.eldonm.freeserve.co.uk/index1.html

Bill Frech, Complete Tour History - http://www.billfrech.com/tourhistory/
JJEEE, Fish Dans L'Air - http://home.worldnet.fr/~jjeee
Andreas Erle, Freaks/Tribute CD - http://www.aerle.de/Freaks/CDs/Tribute/tribute.htm
Made Again, Tribute CD Review - http://www.madeagain.demon.co.uk/reviews.html
Hulme, Famous Encounters - http://www.eng.buffalo.edu/~hulme/famous.html
Ed Wood, A Fred of Sunlight - http://www.multimania.com/edwood/index.htm
Jonathan Mock, Yet Another Marillion Fan Site - http://web.ukonline.co.uk/jonathan.mock/marillion/content.html
Jan Hendrick Fennema, Waving at Stars - http://www.fennema-1.myweb.nl/thissite.html
Gord Beacock, The Mad Doctor's Marillion Page - http://www3.sympatico.ca/gord.beacock/music/marillion/marillion.html
Drew, Drew's Home Page - http://members.aol.com/DrewDGR/Personal.html
Lise, Berliner Girl - http://berlinergirl.statusbar.com/lisechains.html
9898, Pittsburgh Pages - http://www.geocities.com/SunsetStrip/Backstage/ 9898/Marillion1.html
Steinman, Tour Fund CD - http://www.iwc.net/~steinman/marillion.htm
RCOTEC, RCOTEC's Enchant Page - http://www.roltec.de/enchant/wishing.html
Rolef Hoekstra, Hoekie.net - http://www.geocities.com/roelof_hoekstra/index.htm
L Horbach - http://home-4.tiscali.nl/~t317175/

COLLABORATOR LINKS

John Helmer/The Piranhas - http://www.whodeenyproductions.com/punk/piranh.html
Steve Wilson/Mike Portnoy Interview - http://porcupinetree.free.fr/interview_sw_mp.htm
Steven Wilson Interview - http://www.porcupinetree.com/inter005.htm
Chat with Mike Portnoy, 20 July 1997- http://www.gabbo.net/dt/portnoy/chat.shtml
Chris Hedge - Privet Investigations - http://www.meyersound.com/news/press/psn_privet.htm
Mr So & So - Interview - Foreword by SR - http://white-elephant.homeip.soandso/general/competition.htm

OTHER RESOURCES

British Criminology, Blair Peach - http://www.lboro.ac.uk/departments/ss/bsc/bccsp/vol01/VOL01_05.HTM
Friars History - http://archnt2.tamu.edu/rburt/fun stuff/FRIARS/FRIARS_MAIN.htm